# The European Tour
# Yearbook 2007

OFFICIAL

PUBLICATION

# Introduction from The European Tour

The European Team's emphatic victory in The 2006 Ryder Cup at The K Club, echoing as it did a similar success at Oakland Hills two years earlier, exhibited once again the extraordinary transformation of our game on the world stage in addition to the brilliance of Captain Ian Woosnam and his twelve superb Team Members.

When The European Tour began in 1972, two years before I joined from a stockbroking career in the City of London, the calendar showed tournaments in nine countries with the majority of prize funds between £8,000 and £15,000.

When the first edition of The European Tour Yearbook was published in 1988 we had just completed a schedule in which 14 countries were visited with the vast majority of prize funds between £200,000 and £300,000.

Since then, European golf has travelled a considerable distance. The total prize fund for The European Tour, the European Seniors Tour and the European Challenge Tour in 2006 was in excess of £128,000,000. Now, as we review another riveting twelve months in the history of the Tour, we also look forward to 2007 when The European Tour International Schedule includes a minimum of 50 tournaments played in 26 countries. We are also particularly proud that, with the victories of Austria's Markus Brier and Singapore's Mardan Mamat in 2006, players from no fewer than 33 countries have now won on The European Tour.

It is exciting to be involved in the growth of the game and I make no apology for singling out the exploits of one country. In 1986, Ove Sellberg became the first Swedish player to win on The European Tour, capturing the Epson

Grand Prix of Europe Match Play Championship, and twelve months later he was succeeded by fellow countryman Mats Lanner. I recall that Tony Jacklin, on the back of captaining Europe in 1985 to a first Ryder Cup success since 1957, predicted that Sweden would play a hugely influential role in the growth of The European Tour and indeed in supplying Ryder Cup players. How right he was.

In total, 24 Swedish players have now won no fewer than 69 tournaments on The European Tour, and in 2006 at The K Club, Robert Karlsson and Henrik Stenson took to eight the number of Swedish players to have played in The Ryder Cup. There might have been more. Johan Edfors, who graduated from The 2005 European Tour Qualifying School, triumphed three times on The 2006 European Tour International Schedule, playing magnificent golf to win the TCL Classic in China, The Quinn Direct British Masters in England and The Barclays Scottish Open. In past years that would have been an instant passport to a place on Europe's Ryder Cup Team.

That this was not the case provides ample evidence, in tandem with Europe's pulsating 18½-9½ victory in Ireland, of the increasing strength in depth of European golf. We have, with the development of The European Tour International Schedule, established the opportunity for all players to compete

on the world stage, and our Members have responded with their outstanding individual achievements.

Johan Edfors was joined as a multiple winner on The 2006 European Tour International Schedule by Paul Casey (Volvo China Open; Johnnie Walker Championship at Gleneagles; HSBC World Match Play Championship), Simon Dyson (Enjoy Jakarta HSBC Indonesia Open; The KLM Open); David Howell (HSBC Champions tournament; BMW Championship – The Players' Flagship); Niclas Fasth (Andalucia Open de España Valle Romano; Mallorca Classic); Robert Karlsson (The Celtic Manor Wales Open; The Deutsche Bank Players' Championship of Europe); Geoff Ogilvy (WGC – Accenture Match Play; US Open Championship); Jeev Milkha Singh (Volvo China Open; Volvo Masters); Henrik Stenson (The Commercialbank Qatar Masters; BMW International Open) and Tiger Woods (Dubai Desert Classic; 135th Open Championship; US PGA Championship; WGC – Bridgestone Invitational; WGC – American Express Championship). Casey, Howell and Karlsson, alongside Padraig Harrington, also vied for Number One honours on The European Tour Order of Merit and we congratulate Padraig in claiming The Harry Vardon Trophy for the first time.

Simon Dyson, of England, Johan Edfors and Australian Geoff Ogilvy were also three of the 13 first time winners on The European Tour

– the others being Spain's Alejandro Cañizares, America's Chris DiMarco, Italy's Francesco Molinari, Argentina's Cesar Monasterio, America's Kevin Stadler, Scotland's Marc Warren, who finished Number One on the 2005 European Challenge Tour Rankings and whom we congratulate on becoming The Sir Henry Cotton Rookie of the Year, and Korea's Charlie Wi in addition to Markus Brier, Mardan Mamat and Jeev Milkha Singh. Quite something, that, to have 13 first time winners supplied by 12 different countries – another indication of the cosmopolitan influence generated by The European Tour's policy of growing the game in all corners of the globe.

We are proud of this policy and proud, too, of the part that The Ryder Cup plays to showcase the game, with pictures of the biennial contest now beamed into more than 750,000,000 homes around the world. We never underestimate the importance of The Ryder Cup. It is the backbone of the Tour. To win again, to win five times in six contests, provides us with immense confidence. The class of 2006, led by the inspirational Ian Woosnam, took us to a new level but it would be remiss of me if I did not acknowledge the significant roles played by Severiano Ballesteros and Tony Jacklin in the past in galvanising Europe's challenge for The Ryder Cup. They set the standards for others to follow and we were delighted that both were at The K Club to share with us the latest success. Now we wish Nick Faldo all the best on taking the stewardship of Captaincy from Ian Woosnam for the next match at Valhalla in Kentucky in 2008.

Both Tony and Seve won Open Championships at Royal Lytham and St Annes where I played in my formative years. I must admit it seems like only yesterday that Seve was winning his five Major Championships, yet in 2007, along with Ryder Cup colleagues Ken Brown, Bernhard Langer and Nick Faldo, not to mention other familiar faces like Wayne Grady, Mark O'Meara and Nick Price, he will become eligible for the European Seniors Tour. There he will find Sam Torrance eagerly seeking to finish Number One in the European Seniors Tour Order of Merit for a third successive time following his defence of

that position in 2006 when he finished ahead of Carl Mason, José Rivero, Gordon J Brand and Stewart Ginn.

Meanwhile Mark Pilkington of Wales will be seeking to emulate Marc Warren by following up his position as Number One on the 2006 European Challenge Tour Rankings and winning on The 2007 European Tour. Mark overhauled Sweden's Johan Axgren to lead the way as the leading 20 players for the 2006 Challenge Tour graduated to The European Tour.

Bill Elliott's incisive essay on how The 2006 Ryder Cup unfolded is one of the many splendid chapters written by the leading golf writers for this, the 19th edition of The European Tour Yearbook, which superbly chronicles tournaments and experiences that will live with us for ever. I hope you enjoy the book and the wonderful photography which brings to life our glorious game.

On behalf of The European Tour I thank you for your continued support.

*George O'Grady*

**George O'Grady**
*Executive Director*
*The European Tour*

# Acknowledgments

**Executive Editor**
Mitchell Platts

**Production Editor**
Vanessa O'Brien

**Editorial Consultants**
Scott Crockett
Chris Plumridge

**Picture Editors**
Andrew Redington
Rob Harborne

**Art Direction**
Tim Leney
Andrew Wright
TC Communications Plc

**Print Managed by**
London Print & Design Ltd.

The European Tour Yearbook 2007
is published by The PGA European Tour,
Wentworth Drive, Virginia Water,
Surrey GU25 4LX.
Distributed through Aurum Press Ltd.
25 Bedford Avenue
London WC1B 3AT.

© PGA European Tour.

26 COUNTRIES. 49 TOURNAMENTS.
24 TIME ZONES.
# ONE OFFICIAL STARTER.

For over 30 years, Ivor Robson has been the Official Starter of the European Tour. Ensuring that the golfers tee off on time with their scorecards is an important responsibility, but one made much easier for Ivor by his Rolex. If you ask any golfer on the Tour which three familiar words they associate with Ivor, they will answer: "On the tee." **ROLEX IS OFFICIAL TIMEKEEPER TO THE EUROPEAN TOUR.**

# Contents

| | |
|---|---|
| THE 2006 RYDER CUP | 6 |
| THE EUROPEAN TOUR ORDER OF MERIT WINNER | 38 |
| THE YEAR IN RETROSPECT | 44 |
| HSBC CHAMPIONS TOURNAMENT | 50 |
| VOLVO CHINA OPEN | 54 |
| UBS HONG KONG OPEN | 58 |
| DUNHILL CHAMPIONSHIP | 62 |
| SOUTH AFRICAN AIRWAYS OPEN | 66 |
| THE ROYAL TROPHY | 70 |
| ABU DHABI GOLF CHAMPIONSHIP | 74 |
| THE COMMERCIALBANK QATAR MASTERS | 78 |
| DUBAI DESERT CLASSIC | 82 |
| JOHNNIE WALKER CLASSIC | 86 |
| MAYBANK MALAYSIAN OPEN | 90 |
| WGC-ACCENTURE MATCH PLAY | 94 |
| ENJOY JAKARTA HSBC INDONESIA OPEN | 98 |
| OSIM SINGAPORE MASTERS | 102 |
| TCL CLASSIC | 106 |
| MADEIRA ISLAND OPEN CAIXA GERAL DE DEPOSITOS | 110 |
| ALGARVE OPEN DE PORTUGAL CAIXA GERAL DE DEPOSITOS | 114 |
| MASTERS TOURNAMENT | 118 |
| VOLVO CHINA OPEN | 124 |
| BMW ASIAN OPEN | 128 |
| ANDALUCIA OPEN DE ESPAÑA VALLE ROMANO | 132 |
| TELECOM ITALIA OPEN | 136 |
| THE QUINN DIRECT BRITISH MASTERS | 140 |
| NISSAN IRISH OPEN | 146 |
| BMW CHAMPIONSHIP - THE PLAYERS' FLAGSHIP | 150 |
| THE CELTIC MANOR WALES OPEN | 160 |
| BA-CA GOLF OPEN PRESENTED BY TELEKOM AUSTRIA | 166 |
| AA ST OMER OPEN | 170 |
| US OPEN CHAMPIONSHIP | 174 |
| JOHNNIE WALKER CHAMPIONSHIP AT GLENEAGLES | 180 |
| OPEN DE FRANCE ALSTOM | 184 |
| SMURFIT KAPPA EUROPEAN OPEN | 188 |
| THE BARCLAYS SCOTTISH OPEN | 192 |
| 135TH OPEN CHAMPIONSHIP | 198 |
| THE DEUTSCHE BANK PLAYERS' CHAMPIONSHIP OF EUROPE | 206 |
| ENTERCARD SCANDINAVIAN MASTERS | 212 |
| THE KLM OPEN | 216 |
| THE IMPERIAL COLLECTION RUSSIAN OPEN | 220 |
| US PGA CHAMPIONSHIP | 224 |
| WGC-BRIDGESTONE INVITATIONAL | 230 |
| BMW INTERNATIONAL OPEN | 234 |
| OMEGA EUROPEAN MASTERS | 240 |
| HSBC WORLD MATCH PLAY CHAMPIONSHIP | 244 |
| XXXII BANCO DE MADRID VALLE ROMANO OPEN DE MADRID GOLF MASTERS | 250 |
| WGC-AMERICAN EXPRESS CHAMPIONSHIP | 254 |
| ALFRED DUNHILL LINKS CHAMPIONSHIP | 258 |
| MALLORCA CLASSIC | 264 |
| VOLVO MASTERS | 268 |
| WGC-BARBADOS WORLD CUP | 274 |
| THE EUROPEAN TOUR QUALIFYING SCHOOL | 276 |
| WINS AROUND THE WORLD | 278 |
| THE EUROPEAN SENIORS TOUR | 284 |
| THE EUROPEAN CHALLENGE TOUR | 294 |
| THE EUROPEAN TOUR GOLFER OF THE MONTH AWARDS | 304 |
| RBS SHOT OF THE MONTH AWARDS | 305 |
| EUROPEAN TOUR STATISTICS | 306 |
| THE EUROPEAN TOUR ORDER OF MERIT | 308 |
| THE EUROPEAN INTERNATIONAL SCHEDULE 2006 | 310 |
| CREDITS | 312 |

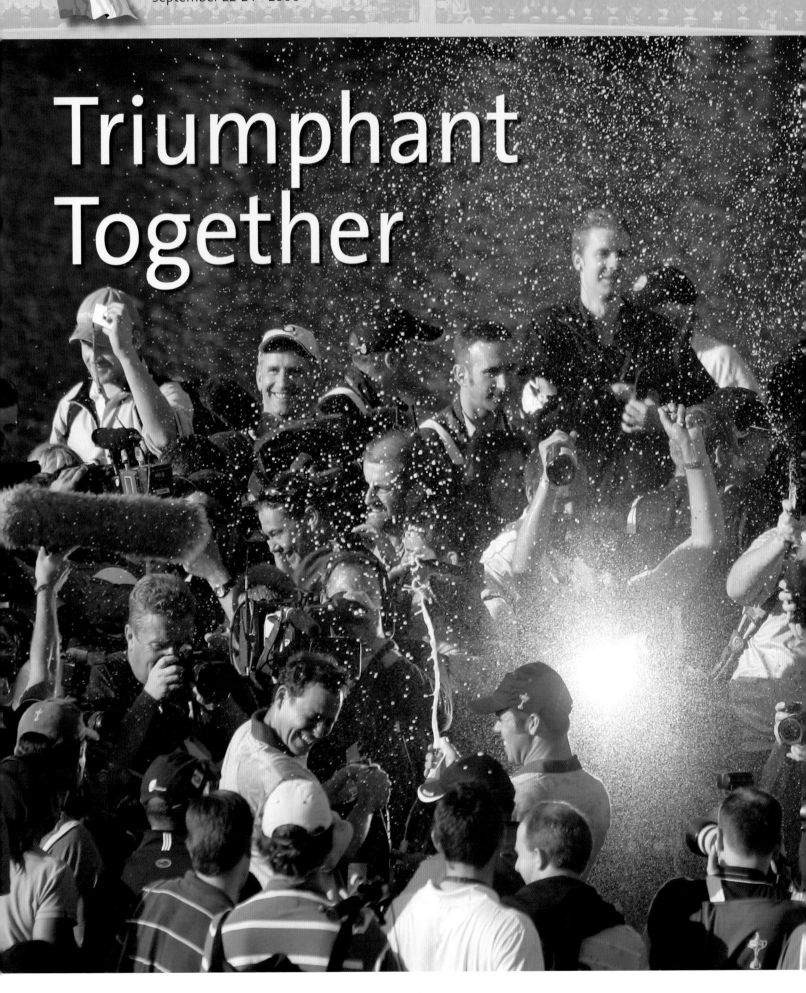

# Triumphant Together

# The 2006 Ryder Cup

**The K Club, Straffan, Co. Kildare, Ireland**
September 22-24 • 2006

Television, like the rest of us, loves contrasts. Black and white, rich and poor, and, of course, big and small. This, amidst the many reasons for its continuing success, is one of the core reasons The Ryder Cup remains such a vivid and satisfying contest.

Sergio Garcia

*"The Ryder Cup is The Ryder Cup – it is just a special event. If you add everything up that happens during the time here, and put it all together, it is just an unbelievable week"*
*– Sergio Garcia*

No image of the many millions transmitted to a global audience from The K Club in Ireland captured this thought better than the occasional friendly collision between Captain Tom Lehman of the United States and his European counterpart Ian Woosnam. When the tall American said something to his opposite number, Woosie had to tip back his cap just to look up to Lehman's face.

The contrast between the two men, Lehman, a man with the face of a Roman senator and the voice of a battlefield general; Woosnam, whose ruddy complexion and broad border tones underlined a youth spent labouring in his father's fields, was richly satisfying to those of us who treasure these things. It was, however, the only concession of any kind that the diminutive Welshman made all week.

Lehman may have been representing a nation that can boast almost half the estimated golfers on the planet but despite his attention to detail and close regard for what his players desired, he could do nothing to reverse the recently established tradition of the modern Ryder Cup which decrees that Europe's finest dozen golfers come, play and conquer.

Across three days of intense competition, the contest, set against wilful weather and played out to a sensational soundtrack supplied by the most committed crowd ever heard, raised the bar for Europe yet again. Two years earlier in Detroit, Bernhard Langer had inspired a record victory for the visitors, Europe winning 18½ - 9½, and the general consensus was that we would be lucky to see anything vaguely similar again in our lifetimes.

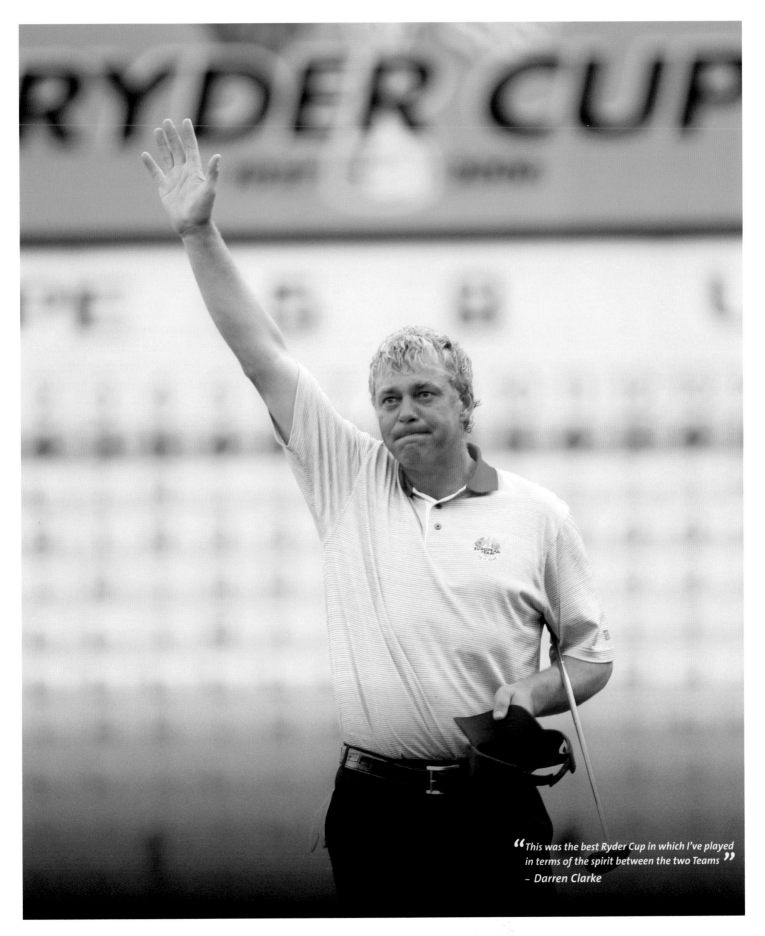

*This was the best Ryder Cup in which I've played in terms of the spirit between the two Teams* – Darren Clarke

For the last decade, the world's most prestigious golf
event has chosen to partner with Club Car. Now that's reliability.

Drive it once and you'll know.

*The European Team led by Captain Ian Woosnam with his wife, Glen, arrive at Dublin Airport*

# IRELAND

# Proud host of the
# RYDER CUP 2006

Ireland is a golfer's paradise with every shape, size and shade of green. It also boasts the friendliest 19th watering hole on the circuit. Ireland, for its size, has produced more than its share of Ryder Cup players and in 2006 proudly welcomed the world's top golfers to the Ryder Cup. Ireland, a perfect Ryder Cup venue and an ideal host.

www.ireland.ie

Flying high with the birdies and eagles. Priceless.

In the event, we had to wait just 24 months for a repeat. Had Paul McGinley not sportingly conceded a hugely missable putt to J.J. Henry after a clown in a wig and not much else spoiled the Irishman's personal campaign on the 18th green, then Europe surely would have established a fresh record with another half point. Does it matter? Not really.

McGinley, as decent and honest a man as you would wish to find, did the right thing in the circumstances. Woosnam, despite gently chastising the Dubliner afterwards, knew it, too. This Ryder Cup benefited from such presence of mind and clarity of vision, despite the elation and noise that swept around McGinley as his countrymen celebrated an overall victory already sweetly secured.

Minutes later the entire contest was over, anyway, a defiant Chris DiMarco finding the water twice as he searched for a killer blow against an exhausted and 'flu-affected' Lee Westwood, who had led by five holes at one stage but came to the final tee just one up. DiMarco's reluctant but inevitable concession highlighted not just his own competitive instinct, but reinforced the view that he and the rest of his team were, by then, in shock.

This, to be blunt, was partly at their own inadequacy to rise to the moment but it was also at the realisation that the European Team was undeniably superior in almost every way. This is no facile gloat at the demise of honourable opponents who eloquently acknowledged the better equipped side

Mary McAleese - President of Ireland at the Opening Ceremony

Captains Ian Woosnam and Tom Lehman lead their respective Teams at the Opening Ceremony

# The 2006 Ryder Cup

**The K Club, Straffan, Co. Kildare, Ireland**
September 22-24 • 2006

*The first tee at The K Club*

*José Maria Olazábal*

won, but a detached analysis of the way things were in Ireland. And, more to the point, of how they seem likely to remain for some time to come.

American golf has a problem. How can it dominate the sharp end of the Official World Golf Ranking and produce players of the sublime quality of Phil Mickelson and Tiger Woods, only to see them wither so dramatically in the face of a European Team that had only one player, José Maria Olazábal, who had won a Major Championship? Furthermore, what can they do about it?

While it is tempting to add - 'who cares?' - such temptation must be resisted. That Europe's traditional role as David to America's Goliath has been reversed is undeniable no matter how you look at things. What we on this side of the Atlantic must now look forward to is the revival of America as a truly

coherent force. It was never easy in Ireland but, in the end, it was much less demanding than many of us who fuss over this grand, old game could ever have imagined.

Yet while the PGA of America officials conducted a private postmortem on a colossal effort gone wrong, the powers that be in Europe retreated to their inner sanctums with a serious sense of a job well done. For this, of course, credit must be spread everywhere. The Ryder Cup is now a stupendous project, at least six years in the planning and two years in the execution. There is much that can go wrong at any one time but it says much for the imagination and work ethic of so many people that almost everything went absolutely right in this glorious corner of Co. Kildare.

What no-one could control, of course, was the weather. Ireland, at any time, is an

Luke Donald

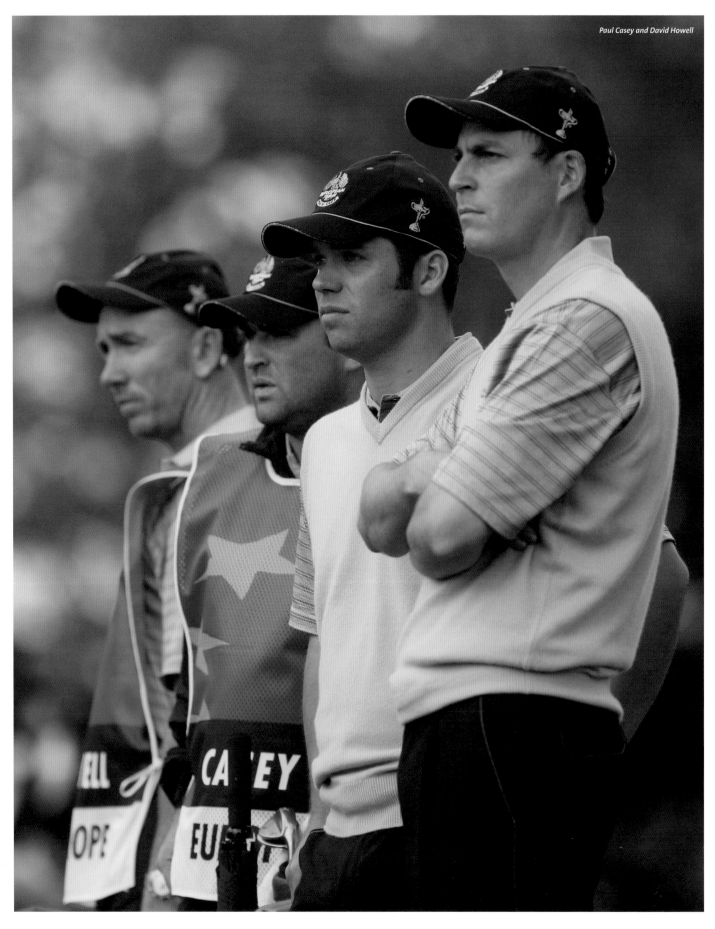

*Paul Casey and David Howell*

*Captain Ian Woosnam, his Team, and backroom staff at the Gala Dinner*

**"** *There was one reason only for our victory – talent. Nobody understands how strong this European Tour is. The standard is so good, the money is getting bigger and bigger. We might not be as big as the US Tour yet but we are getting there. At The K Club the Europeans raised their games two notches and just flat-out outplayed them. Because we raised our games, won the first series, got momentum going, they got demoralised. They lost because we played better and because we played better, we demoralised them* **"** *– Paul McGinley*

unpredictable beast. There are forty shades of green because there are forty types of rain to nourish them. This can vary from gently dismaying drizzle that soaks while pretending to caress to the violence of a full-on storm. For this week, the weather gods decided to put on a show.

Initially it was so shocking that fierce winds and rain closed the gates to the public before they even opened on Wednesday morning, Health and Safety officials rightly concerned about all aspects of safety. Understandably, some frustration abounded but it turned out to be merely a brief interruption to what turned out to be a wonderfully vibrant week for the Irish.

This was their moment and how they rose to the occasion. Mud, rain, car parks that had to be closed, roads that offered frustration rather than progress; none of these mattered. The locals were in buoyant mood and nothing was going to dismay them. They

*David Toms and Colin Montgomerie*

# The 2006 Ryder Cup

**The K Club, Straffan, Co. Kildare, Ireland**
September 22-24 • 2006

Paul McGinley

Christy O'Connor

never actually sang 'We Shall Overcome' but they damn near tried everything else. US President Bill Clinton, a celebrity American backer on a soulful Sunday, admitted he had never seen or heard anything like it. Stripped of the need for hyperbole or a resonant soundbite, the simplicity and sincerity of his reaction said it all.

The crowd, to their immense credit, never descended into tribalism, their forceful support for all things European tempered by a discerning appreciation for any decent American shot. A few days later, as he prepared at The Grove for the World Golf Championships - American Express Championship, Woods said it had been the best sports crowd he had ever performed for, their enthusiasm almost overwhelming.

Ah yes, Woods, the great American enigma. His dominance in every other golfing

Sir Terry Matthews (centre left), Chairman of The Celtic Manor Resort, with The European Junior Ryder Cup Team Captain Andy Ingram (centre right) and members of the team at The 2010 Ryder Cup Wales evening

Sergio Garcia

Paul Casey

arena is unparalleled but once again he did not quite bring this force of nature to, arguably, the greatest stage of them all. His involvement was the cornerstone of Captain Lehman's cunning plan and in the build-up he seemed to react positively to an intelligent leader's urgings.

He even interrupted his own carefully planned schedule to make the trip with his colleagues to The K Club for a practice get-together in August, and before that had dug into his own pocket to take America's four rookies out to dinner. Apparently, he proved an engaging host for that meal but once again he failed to bring the real thing to the bigger table.

Quite why this should be is for him to ponder, but there is no doubt that the one ingredient often lacking is a gambolling sense of fun. Woods, privately, has an engaging and sharp sense of humour but he is a truly serious

golfer, and while no-one suggests that The Ryder Cup is anything less than serious, it does present a chance for players to have fun during a week shorn of the need to make a cheque or notch another victory on the long march to posterity.

The Europeans grab such an opportunity with both hands and seem, on occasion, hard-wired to enjoy themselves above everything else. The scene used to be set by Severiano Ballesteros before Colin Montgomerie took on the role. Monty still clung on to the post in Ireland but only just. Fast approaching, indeed already there, is the hectic figure of Sergio Garcia, whose bustling golf and vibrant joie de vivre illuminated the tournament as never before.

Still only 26, Garcia is maturing but thankfully not that fast and retains an impish charm. He remains the favoured naughty child, a young man hell bent on enjoyment and the

*Enthusiastic spectators thronged the fairways at The K Club*

David Howell

*Both teams hung out with each other last night which is the way the spirit of The Ryder Cup is supposed to be. We were all having a great time and singing and dancing so I think it is a true celebration of golf* – Tiger Woods on the final night at The K Club

José Maria Olazábal and Sergio Garcia

sheer, delicious tasting of the moment. It is an attitude that is infectious to those with an eye for the big picture and one that the Spaniard will take into several Ryder Cups to come.

He may be slightly more subdued than in previous years and a tad more mature, but simmering under the surface is the same juvenile attitude that upsets some and inspires others. "The kid has what all greats need in any sport – passion," said Nick Faldo. "Sergio is Sergio," observed Lehman, sagely.

While Garcia was out there strutting his stuff on Saturday afternoon alongside the quieter Englishman Luke Donald, Swedish rookie Robert Karlsson called by the Media Centre for a chat. Karlsson is 11 years older

and eight inches taller than the Spaniard but in terms of experience it is Garcia who is the wrinkly one.

While Karlsson has swung between success and failure over the last decade, Garcia has won here, there and everywhere and banked millions. We are still waiting for the first Major but it is, surely, no more than a matter of time. Or maybe it is not, maybe he needs the charge of a Ryder Cup to pop his cork properly? At The Open this summer, for example, he played alongside Woods in the final round and may as well have stayed at home.

In Ireland, however, he was at the races every minute of every day while Woods struggled to book in properly. In the build-up, Garcia consistently said he hoped he would come

# The 2006 Ryder Cup

**The K Club, Straffan, Co. Kildare, Ireland**
September 22-24 • 2006

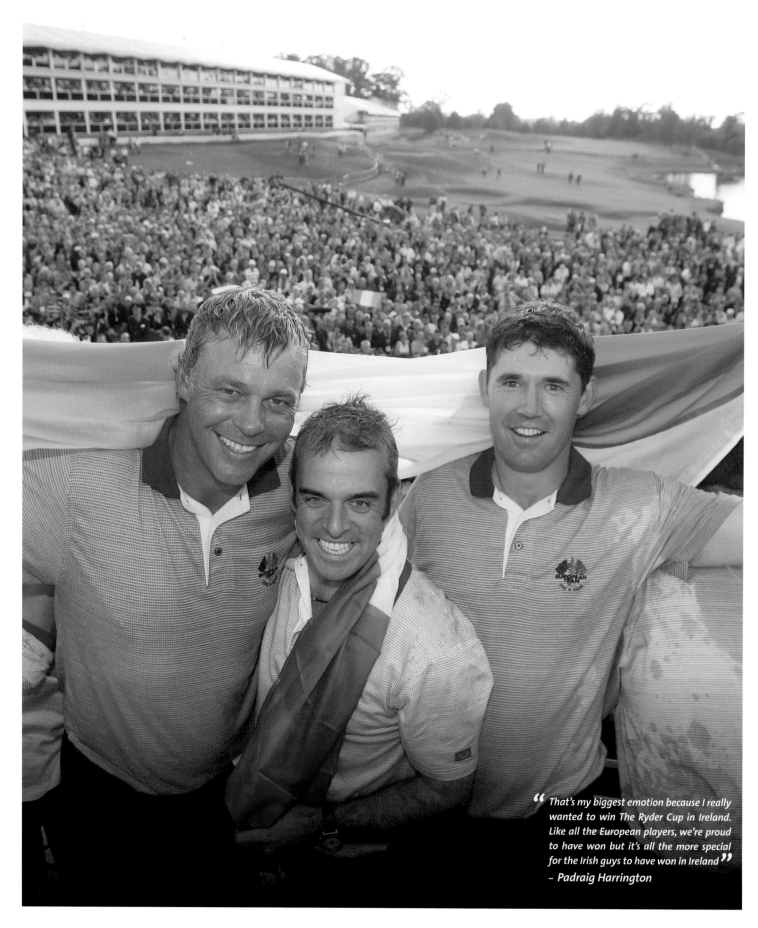

*"That's my biggest emotion because I really wanted to win The Ryder Cup in Ireland. Like all the European players, we're proud to have won but it's all the more special for the Irish guys to have won in Ireland"*
*– Padraig Harrington*

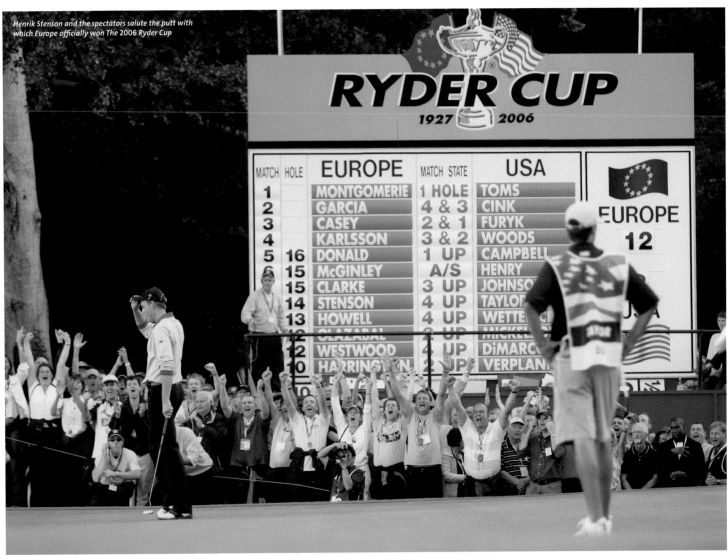

*Henrik Stenson and the spectators salute the putt with which Europe officially won The 2006 Ryder Cup*

| MATCH | HOLE | EUROPE | MATCH STATE | USA |
|-------|------|--------|-------------|-----|
| 1 | | MONTGOMERIE | 1 HOLE | TOMS |
| 2 | | GARCIA | 4 & 3 | CINK |
| 3 | | CASEY | 2 & 1 | FURYK |
| 4 | | KARLSSON | 3 & 2 | WOODS |
| 5 | 16 | DONALD | 1 UP | CAMPBELL |
| 6 | 15 | McGINLEY | A/S | HENRY |
| | 15 | CLARKE | 3 UP | JOHNSO |
| | 14 | STENSON | 4 UP | TAYLO |
| | 13 | HOWELL | 4 UP | WETTE |
| | | OLAZABAL | UP | MICKEL |
| | 12 | WESTWOOD | 4 UP | DiMARC |
| | 10 | HARRINGTON | 2 UP | VERPLAN |

EUROPE 12

up against Woods at some stage. On the first afternoon he did just that in the foursomes. It was not really a contest.

So I asked Karlsson who made the most noise back at the European HQ each morning and evening - he looked back at me and grinned. "Guess," he said. I declined. "Try Garcia," he responded. "Clarke, Westwood and Monty all talk but the most noise comes from Garcia. Yes, he is talking a lot."

But does anybody listen? And, more to the point, does it matter? Apparently not much. "We listen a bit but he is more the team entertainer. He's just a big heap of energy swirling around the room. He makes us smile."

Smiling is what set the Europeans apart from their American rivals. The visitors' idea of team bonding is a lot of high-fiving and gravely voiced 'heys' so that at any moment you expect one of them to lift a golf towel off a bag and start flicking backsides. The Europeans, on the other hand, bond in the way we always have on this side of the Pond...by taking the mickey out of each other. We only ever hurt the ones we love and the Americans simply don't get it.

It is why Lee Westwood deflates Montgomerie when the old warhorse threatens to disappear up his own sense of self-importance. He pulls his leg. And the Scot, to be fair, loves it. The next American to do this in a Ryder Cup may

*Robert Karlsson*

*Lee Westwood and Darren Clarke*

# The 2006 Ryder Cup

**The K Club, Straffan, Co. Kildare, Ireland**
September 22-24 • 2006

> **" I don't know in the history of The Ryder Cup any European Team that has played better than you guys. I tip my hat to them. They played incredibly well; they were inspired "**
> – Tom Lehman, United States Captain

*Padraig Harrington*

be the first. It is something they need to work on. Everyone, meanwhile, rips Garcia when he gets going but the affection is as obvious as the barbs are sharp and the baby of the Team responds with a big grin every time.

Woosnam astutely partnered him with Olazábal. The senior Spaniard had written his Ryder Cup curriculum vitae already thanks to a partnership alongside Ballesteros that is part of the contest's most revered folklore, but he responded to the younger man's presence brilliantly, feeding off his enthusiasm and slipping in a quiet word of caution when necessary. Together Garcia and Olazábal were an unstoppable fourball unit.

But then, each European contributed significantly to this victory. In an unpredictable week the most assured

Lee Westwood

> *There is no celebration quite like the one The European Team enjoy, well, just about every two years..... at Oak Hill in 1995, they were on the roof of the clubhouse. At Valderrama in 1997, they were singing in the rain. At The De Vere Belfry in 2002, they were awash in sunshine and champagne. At Oakland Hills in 2004, they wrapped themselves in flags and songs. And yesterday at The K Club, they were dancing on the soggy grass and celebrating once again* – Thomas Bonk, Los Angeles Times, writing in The Independent

event was the very first morning fourball match that pitched Padraig Harrington and Montgomerie against Jim Furyk and Woods. Here, the considered predictions suggested, was the match that would set the tone for both Teams. In a strange way, it did.

The American duo won but instead of inspiring the men behind them, it galvanised Europe. If this was indeed going to be tough then they would simply get tougher. So it proved. Europe won every segment of this Ryder Cup so that not once did Lehman's battered Team go into a hurried lunch or a subdued supper feeling anything other than dismay. Whatever they tried, they were bettered.

Paul Casey's hole in one on Saturday to close out his foursomes match alongside David Howell and against Stewart Cink and Zach Johnson may have been equalled by Scott Verplank's own ace at the same 14th hole against a momentarily dejected Harrington on Sunday, but by every other measurable statistic the Europeans were superior. By the time Woosnam attempted to hold the old trophy, a bottle of champagne and a pint of Guinness at the same time, almost every record was being amended.

The Captain's plan to confer with his senior Team members worked brilliantly and in the end, he played it by the heart as much as by the head. So often, as it had done before in his career, it all came off. Darren Clarke, on the other hand, tried very hard to play by the head and for all but the last few minutes of his personal campaign he managed superbly.

Woosnam and his lieutenants had inserted the big man in the middle of the singles order so that he had a chance of holing the winning putt. It nearly worked, too, but Henrik Stenson – an implacably impressive Swede – took the honour when he beat Vaughn Taylor on the 15th green as Clarke approached the 16th three up against Johnson.

It did not matter. Half of Ireland, and a few more besides, gathered beside the Liffey to watch Clarke win anyway. When Johnson quietly conceded, bedlam broke out. Clarke, meanwhile, dissolved into tears and so did everyone else. Following the tragic death of his wife Heather in August, Clarke was there

(l-r) Richard Hills, Ryder Cup Director; Phil Weaver, Chairman of The Professional Golfers' Association; An Taoiseach Bertie Ahern; George O'Grady, Executive Director of The European Tour, and Dr. Michael Smurfit, President of The K Club

*Darren Clarke with (l-r) Laurae Westwood, Jocelyn Hefner, Morgan Norman, Diane Antonopoulos, Alison McGinley, Caroline Harrington and Glen Woosnam before the Gala Dinner*

David J Russell, Des Smyth, Sandy Lyle, Ian Woosnam and Peter Baker with The Ryder Cup

*" The truth is that Ian Woosnam's Team won because they were, man for man, the better Team and on the three days that mattered they played better, especially on and around the green. But they won so crushingly, by a margin of 18 ½-9½, because they were not so much a Team as a gang " – Lawrence Donegan, The Guardian*

largely because of the urgings of friends – including Woods - and because Woosnam had the wit to pick him and his close friend Westwood. Each of those Captain's selections embroidered this Ryder Cup magnificently.

Half an hour after his tearful victory Clarke helped lead the celebrations from the clubhouse balcony, his laughter interrupted only by his inclination to swig from a pint of Guinness or a bottle of champagne; it was a picture of a man offered a short and happy break from a bleaker reality.

Tears followed by laughter. Another contrast from this wonderful Ryder Cup well worth remembering.

**Bill Elliott**

*The Observer*

Henrik Stenson and Robert Karlsson

# The 2006 Ryder Cup

**The K Club, Straffan, Co. Kildare, Ireland**
September 22-24 • 2006

# Final Results

| | Par | Yards | Metres |
|---|---|---|---|
| | 72 | 7335 | 6705 |

## EUROPE (Captain: Ian Woosnam)  |  UNITED STATES: (Captain: Tom Lehman)

**FRIDAY**
**Fourballs: Morning**

| EUROPE | | UNITED STATES | |
|---|---|---|---|
| P Harrington & C Montgomerie | 0 | T Woods & J Furyk (1 hole) | 1 |
| P Casey & R Karlsson (halved) | ½ | S Cink & J J Henry (halved) | ½ |
| S Garcia & J M Olazábal (3 and 2) | 1 | D Toms & B Wetterich | 0 |
| D Clarke & L Westwood (1 hole) | 1 | P Mickelson & C DiMarco | 0 |
| | **2½** | | **1½** |

**Foursomes: Afternoon**

| P Harrington & P McGinley (halved) | ½ | C Campbell & Z Johnson (halved) | ½ |
|---|---|---|---|
| D Howell & H Stenson (halved) | ½ | S Cink & D Toms (halved) | ½ |
| L Westwood & C Montgomerie (halved) | ½ | P Mickelson & C DiMarco (halved) | ½ |
| L Donald & S Garcia (2 holes) | 1 | T Woods & J Furyk | 0 |
| | **5** | | **3** |

**SATURDAY**
**Fourballs: Morning**

| P Casey & R Karlsson (halved) | ½ | S Cink & J J Henry (halved) | ½ |
|---|---|---|---|
| S Garcia & J M Olazábal (3 and 2) | 1 | P Mickelson & C DiMarco | 0 |
| D Clarke & L Westwood (3 and 2) | 1 | T Woods & J Furyk | 0 |
| H Stenson & P Harrington | 0 | S Verplank & Z Johnson (2 and 1) | 1 |
| | **7½** | | **4½** |

**Foursomes: Afternoon**

| S Garcia & L Donald (2 and 1) | 1 | P Mickelson & D Toms | 0 |
|---|---|---|---|
| C Montgomerie & L Westwood (halved) | ½ | C Campbell & V Taylor (halved) | ½ |
| P Casey & D Howell (5 and 4) | 1 | S Cink & Z Johnson | 0 |
| P Harrington & P McGinley | 0 | J Furyk & T Woods (3 and 2) | 1 |
| | **10** | | **6** |

**SUNDAY**
**Singles**

| C Montgomerie (1 hole) | 1 | D Toms | 0 |
|---|---|---|---|
| S Garcia | 0 | S Cink (4 and 3) | 1 |
| P Casey (2 and 1) | 1 | J Furyk | 0 |
| R Karlsson | 0 | T Woods (3 and 2) | 1 |
| L Donald (2 and 1) | 1 | C Campbell | 0 |
| P McGinley (halved) | ½ | J J Henry (halved) | ½ |
| D Clarke (3 and 2) | 1 | Z Johnson | 0 |
| H Stenson (4 and 3) | 1 | V Taylor | 0 |
| D Howell (5 and 4) | 1 | B Wetterich | 0 |
| J M Olazábal (2 and 1) | 1 | P Mickelson | 0 |
| L Westwood (2 holes) | 1 | C DiMarco | 0 |
| P Harrington | 0 | S Verplank (4 and 3) | 1 |
| | **8½** | | **3½** |
| **EUROPE** | **18½** | **UNITED STATES** | **9½** |

# Individual Player Performances

| EUROPE | PLAYED | WON | LOST | HALVED | POINTS | UNITED STATES | PLAYED | WON | LOST | HALVED | POINTS |
|---|---|---|---|---|---|---|---|---|---|---|---|
| Sergio Garcia | 5 | 4 | 1 | 0 | 4 | Tiger Woods | 5 | 3 | 2 | 0 | 3 |
| Lee Westwood | 5 | 3 | 0 | 2 | 4 | Stewart Cink | 5 | 1 | 1 | 3 | 2½ |
| Darren Clarke | 3 | 3 | 0 | 0 | 3 | Scott Verplank | 2 | 2 | 0 | 0 | 2 |
| Luke Donald | 3 | 3 | 0 | 0 | 3 | Jim Furyk | 5 | 2 | 3 | 0 | 2 |
| José Maria Olazábal | 3 | 3 | 0 | 0 | 3 | J.J.Henry | 3 | 0 | 0 | 3 | 1½ |
| Paul Casey | 4 | 2 | 0 | 2 | 3 | Zach Johnson | 4 | 1 | 2 | 1 | 1½ |
| David Howell | 3 | 2 | 0 | 1 | 2½ | Chad Campbell | 3 | 0 | 1 | 2 | 1 |
| Colin Montgomerie | 4 | 1 | 1 | 2 | 2 | Vaughn Taylor | 2 | 0 | 1 | 1 | ½ |
| Henrik Stenson | 3 | 1 | 1 | 1 | 1½ | Chris DiMarco | 4 | 0 | 3 | 1 | ½ |
| Robert Karlsson | 3 | 0 | 1 | 2 | 1 | David Toms | 4 | 0 | 3 | 1 | ½ |
| Paul McGinley | 3 | 0 | 1 | 2 | 1 | Phil Mickelson | 5 | 0 | 4 | 1 | ½ |
| Padraig Harrington | 5 | 0 | 4 | 1 | ½ | Brett Wetterich | 2 | 0 | 2 | 0 | 0 |

Ian Woosnam

Labour of Love

S ometimes, ironically, a golfer's best moments can be achieved while sitting down.

In the middle of January 2006 Padraig Harrington was doing just that. He was, in fact, reposing in a Dublin salon having his hair fussed over. Outside it was grey, bleak and cold. Inside it was warm and noisy. Harrington, however, was quiet and contemplative.

He was, at the time, towards the end of a nine week break from professional golf. He has always taken a significant breather from serious work at this time of year but even by his standards, this had been a longer holiday than usual. Now he was considering what lay ahead for him and, typically, nothing was being taken for granted.

By the end of the 2005 season he admitted he had been exhausted. Worse, his enthusiasm for the challenge of tournament golf had ebbed away. A combination of factors – not least, of course, the slow demise of his father – had combined to drain even this most equable of men.

Now he knew it was almost time to get back to work and he was wondering whether the old commitment to the cause would reignite? Would he enjoy the small slivers of good fortune all intelligent, successful men realise must fall their way? Would he, in short, still have what it takes to make an impact?

"After a break like that there is always the unknown to contemplate," he said. "Do I still have what it takes? You know, there is always a wee bit of doubt until you're back out there and it's all working fine again."

Ten months later Harrington was sitting down again. This time there were no

*Paul McGinley (left) and Padraig Harrington won for Ireland at the 1997 World Cup of Golf, Kiawah Island*

*(l-r) Padraig Harrington, Luke Donald, Sergio Garcia and Jeev Milkha Singh at the conclusion of the 2006 Volvo Masters*

# The European Tour Order of Merit Winner

**Padraig Harrington**

hairdryers screeching. Instead he was reclining in the middle of the relative calm that was the Players' Lounge at Club de Golf Valderrama while the final, nervy moments of a captivating Volvo Masters week were played out on the television screen in front of him.

Beside him his wife Caroline and young son Patrick watched closely, too. Behind him was a final round 69 that had lifted him towards the top of the leaderboard. He had the satisfaction of knowing he had given this final tournament his best shot. Now he was waiting for that sliver of luck.

Of course, one professional sportsman's decent fortune is another's heartbreak.

*The victorious 1995 Great Britain and Ireland Walker Cup team at Royal Porthcawl*

*A sparkling celebration at the Brazil Sao Paulo 500 Years Open at Sao Paulo Golf Club in the year 2000*

And so it proved. Paul Casey had entered the week as an outstanding favourite to end the season as Europe's top golfer but then suffered a desperately uncomfortable stomach virus that weakened him just when he needed more strength than ever.

Now, as he sat and watched, Harrington's accountancy-trained mind worked out he needed to finish no worse than in a share of second place if he was to achieve a cherished ambition. When Sergio Garcia failed to secure par at the last hole, the Irishman, alongside Luke Donald and Garcia, had done just that. The trio ended tied second, one shot adrift of winner Jeev Milkha Singh, and it was all over. An unlikely dice had fallen Harrington's way.

By finishing second for the 30th time in 11 years as a professional, Harrington had won the biggest prize of his life. When we spoke in that Dublin hairdresser's he was ranked 17th best player in the world. Now, several haircuts later, he was up to 11th

and, of course, The Harry Vardon Trophy for becoming Number One on The European Tour Order of Merit was cradled in his grasp.

Did Padraig Harrington still have what it takes in 2006? You bet your sweet life he did. But then he always has had it.

As an amateur he was outstanding, a phase of his life that, after embroidering it with several of Ireland's most prestigious titles, he capped as a member of the victorious 1995 Walker Cup team. When he looks back at those days, he smiles and admits he wishes he still had the short game he exhibited back then, convinced that this key element of his game was in some ways better when tinged with sepia.

This is typical of him. Harrington's worst days are the ones when he wakes up feeling absolutely tickety-boo, full of health, strength and tranquility. It is on these days that he worries most about what may go wrong.

This is not to say he is a hypochondriac but it is to edge towards the suggestion that he is never happier than when he feels there is something to worry about. He loves to fret and fidget and to work constantly on a game that most others would settle for in a heartbeat.

His need to improve is relentless. "Maybe I do fuss a bit too much but that's just

41

# The European Tour Order of Merit Winner

**Padraig Harrington**

*Following the Order of Merit triumph in Valderrama with wife Caroline and son Patrick*

me. It's the way I am and I can't change it. Technically, I'm not bad, so if I make a big leap forward it will be because I've improved between my ears I suppose," he admitted. "I know I get too broody at times and I have to be careful to avoid that because you have to be able to leave this game behind.

"The last thing you want is to be sitting in a cinema watching a film and find that you're thinking about golf. If that happens, you're in a bad place. A very bad place. You find this with the rookies on Tour. They can't leave the game alone and that's the way it stays until they start to feel comfortable with themselves and where they are."

Meanwhile, there is no harder working professional on the planet. Here, without doubt, is a man who subscribes to the simple theory that you only get out of something

what you put into it. In his case, this is many, many hours spent labouring over this shot and that.

His coach, Bob Torrance, loves him. Not just because his pupil is such a credit to his teaching, but because he knows the big effort that has gone into creating this latest European Number One. When Harrington telephones to say he is planning a trip to Torrance's base in Largs, the old maestro and his wife June sigh deeply, but affectionately, and prepare for a dislocated time.

"With a lot of players the problem can be to get them onto the practice ground to work really hard. With Padraig the big problem is getting him off it so we can all have some tea," grins Bob. "Without doubt he is a prodigious worker and a great talent. Plus he's a nice guy."

Not that the player would agree with all of this. He is forever wide-eyed at his own spectacular success, but it is this precise attitude that keeps him eternally grounded. Harrington does not think he is better than anyone else, and never has, for the simple reason he is not entirely convinced he is actually as good as he palpably is.

In a world filled with much that is self-obsessed to the point of rudeness, he represents something much more attractive. Affable and intelligent, he is a strong man with a clear sense of direction but little desire for self-importance. Back in Ireland, of course, he is a hero. Two years ago he put on a golf show in his home city to raise money for charity. Such was the demand by Dubliners to see one of their favourite sporting sons in the flesh

that an initial one-off performance swiftly became three sell-out productions.

"Ah well, you know, it was good fun," he said when asked if he had enjoyed the experience. Good fun, too, for the charities for whom in excess of €100,000 was raised.

Not, of course, that he is perfect. For a start, he does not drink although, to be fair, he will swiftly pour you one while he sips his ubiquitous Coca Cola. That apart, it is difficult to find anything negative to say about a man who is just basically a good bloke.

Now this good bloke is also the top European golfer for 2006. He is this not because he played a stellar final round in Spain in October and not because a respected rival contracted a virus at the wrong time, but because between leaving that hairdresser's

shop in January and arriving at Valderrama 40 weeks later, he played typically consistent golf, wringing the very best that he could out of himself in each tournament he played.

"I've been somewhere close to the top of the world rankings for quite a while now and I feel very comfortable with that. I feel I belong there. Getting up to where Tiger and Vijay, Phil and Ernie are, well now, that's a different thing," he said.

"But I tell you what I think about that...I think it requires a leap of faith rather than an improvement in ability to move up there. Can I do that? Yes, I think I can. I feel the best for me is yet to come."

**Bill Elliott**
*The Observer*

*Victory in the 2002 Alfred Dunhill Links Championship*

# A Golfing Odyssey Of Dreams

Ian Woosnam

Imagination is what lifts the human spirit. It is the catalyst to what we all are, as well as being the on-board fuel that promises an uncertain, although hopefully exciting, future.

Life, as John Lennon once mused, is what usually happens while we are making other plans and it is this core unpredictability that weaves colour into all our journeys. Few journeys, of course, are as unpredictable as a European Tour season. This remains a vibrant romp across and through much of the planet, a golfing odyssey that twists and turns, blows hot and cold, and features everything in between.

Nowhere in 2006, it should be stressed, was the action hotter than The K Club in Straffan, Co. Kildare, Ireland in September. As it happens, few places were as wet and windy either but when it is The Ryder Cup, the weather does not matter much, the occasion simply overwhelms everything else.

Of course, this was the stage for one of the most dominant displays by a European Team, one captained by Ian Woosnam and featuring a group of men taking their lead from the now established European tradition of enjoying themselves. The detail of this great occasion and of Europe's record-equalling victory can be found elsewhere in this publication, but the sheer joy of the occasion is illustrated by any one of a thousand laughing images of players and crowd gloriously joined together.

Ten months before this great celebration of game, three men set an early template for success that proved central to Europe's progress. Step forward please, David Howell, Paul Casey and Colin Montgomerie. It seems a long time ago now, but their individual victories in the Tour's opening three tournaments may now be set in a context that suggests here, actually, was the required kick-start to Woosnam's valedictory captaincy.

Howell's imagination, on top of some serious focus in the final round of the HSBC Champions tournament at Sheshan International Golf Club, Shanghai, China, allowed him to become one of the very few players to resist the challenge of Tiger Woods. Woods, to be fair, recognised this and led the applause for his final round opponent at the end of a thrilling week. Inspired by this success Howell endorsed his own curriculum vitae by winning the BMW Championship at Wentworth Club, Surrey, England, a supremely prestigious victory achieved in simply splendid style.

A fortnight after Howell's win in Shanghai, and still in China at the Shenzhen Golf Club for the Volvo China Open, another

David Howell

Paul Casey receives a framed image of the 14th at The K Club where he memorably holed in one during the Saturday afternoon foursomes session in The Ryder Cup. Casey was presented with the image by Tim Street, Chairman of The Golf Business Ltd, whose CourseGuide division compiled the yardage books for the Palmer Course. The image featured a personal message from course designer Arnold Palmer which read: 'Paul, what a time to play the ultimate shot! Well done!'

young Englishman began a sequence that would see him return to his best form and then get even better. Casey's win came after a difficult year during which his form reversed but we now know that all this muscular golfer needed was a serious confidence boost. What he took away with him from China was affirmation that his is indeed a special talent.

It was no surprise then that he built on this, lifting the Johnnie Walker Championship at Gleneagles in the shadow of The Gleneagles Hotel, Perthshire, Scotland, in June before a career-impacting victory in the HSBC World Match Play Championship staged, as ever, across the West Course of the Wentworth Club in Surrey, England. This, in a field that included the World Numbers One and Two in Tiger Woods and Jim Furyk, was some feat. The timing could hardly have been better either, coming as it did the week before The Ryder Cup.

But let us return to the beginning and our third man. This time, a Scot. No ordinary Scot,

however, for this was Colin Montgomerie who took the third tournament title available on The 2006 European Tour International Schedule when he won the UBS Hong Kong Open at the Hong Kong Golf Club, Fanling. What everyone, especially Woosnam, learned from this success was that the now middle-aged warhorse was still up for it, still heading forward, still hungry for success despite a career record that trumpets so much already achieved.

If The Ryder Cup will forever be the glittering cornerstone of the 2006 season, the four Major Championships remained elusive from a European Tour perspective. Phil Mickelson was an assured Champion in the Masters Tournament at Augusta National, Georgia, USA, and indeed could have added the US Open Championship at Winged Foot Golf Club, Mamaroneck, New York, USA, had he not suffered a breakdown on his final hole when all his previous careful consideration suddenly turned strangely panicky. It was a similar scenario for Montgomerie who had

his best ever opportunity to win a Major but whose stuttered seven iron approach to the 18th green left him frustrated again. Instead Australia's Geoff Ogilvy was the pleasantly surprised victor. Ogilvy had four months earlier won the WGC - Accenture Match Play at La Costa Resort & Spa, Carlsbad, California, USA, to establish his credentials.

Meanwhile, Woods was lurking. He was distracted at the Masters Tournament by his father's terminal illness and was still grieving Earl Woods' subsequent death when he played in the US Open Championship three months later, understandably missing his first cut in a Major as a professional. It was, of course, a different story when he competed in the 135th Open Championship when the great week returned to Royal Liverpool Golf Club, Hoylake, Cheshire, England, for the first time since 1967.

This was a glorious return both by the Championship and by Woods who was back to his dominant best, the field

*Masters Champion - Phil Mickelson*

*US Open Champion - Geoff Ogilvy*

*Open Champion - Tiger Woods*

*US PGA Champion - Tiger Woods*

ultimately kneeling before him, the local crowds unstinting in their admiration for a supremely gifted performer whose dismissal of such worthy foes as Ernie Els and Sergio Garcia when he partnered them on Saturday and Sunday respectively had to be seen to be believed.

Woods went on to win his 12th Major, the US PGA Championship at Medinah Golf Club, Medinah, Illinois, USA, before continuing a remarkable run of stroke play successes that included the WGC-Bridgestone Invitational at Firestone Country Club in Akron, Ohio, USA, and the WGC-American Express Championship at The Grove, Chandlers Cross, Hertfordshire, England. Back in March, of course, he had also won the Dubai Desert Classic staged once again at the Emirates Golf Club, Dubai, the man he pushed into second place after a play-off being Els.

This remained a commendable effort by Els, however, who suffered a career-threatening injury to his knee in the summer of 2005 and who had prematurely suggested he was fully recovered when he won the fourth tournament on the 2006 schedule, the dunhill championship at Leopard Creek, Mpumalanga, in his native South Africa.

A week after Els' victory the home fans were cheering again when their other favourite son, Retief Goosen, won the South African Airways Open at Fancourt Golf Club in George, South Africa. Like his fellow countryman, however, Goosen never quite managed to stride the high plateaux of achievement each of these gifted competitors more usually strolls. His win at least assured him of the title of the man currently with most consecutive winning seasons on The European Tour – eight, since 1999.

Normal play was then interrupted in January for the staging of The Royal Trophy at the Amata Spring Country Club in Bangkok,

(l-r) José Maria Olazábal, José Manuel Lara, Gonzalo Fernandez-Castaño, Miguel Angel Jiménez and Sergio Garcia

Thailand, a relaxed but compelling match between Europe and the best of Asia. In a portent of things to come, the Europeans won 9-7.

This was followed by the Abu Dhabi Golf Championship at the Abu Dhabi Golf Club and the year's opening first-time winner on The European Tour, Chris DiMarco, a New Yorker who is, arguably, his country's most obvious and committed competitor. This seemed to set a trend but first, Sweden's Henrik Stenson confirmed that he is one of the best golfers to emerge from that prolific golfing country in recent years, when he won The Commercialbank Qatar Masters at Doha Golf Club, Qatar. Six months later Stenson added the BMW International Open at Golfclub München-Nord, Eichenried, Munich, Germany, before segueing significantly into The Ryder Cup.

For a time in February and March, however, it seemed that if you were not winning on the Tour for the first time then you were not winning at all. Kevin Stadler, son of 'The Walrus', Craig, began this sequence with a sensational success in the Johnnie Walker Classic at The Vines Resort & Country Club, Perth, Australia.

He was followed by: Charlie Wi of Korea in the Maybank Malaysian Open at Kuala Lumpur Golf & Country Club, Malaysia; England's Simon Dyson in the Enjoy Jakarta HSBC Indonesia Open at the Emeralda Golf & Country Club, Indonesia; Singapore's Mardan Mamat in the OSIM Singapore Masters at Laguna National Golf & Country Club, Singapore; and then Sweden's Johan Edfors in the TCL Classic at Yalong Bay Golf Club, Sanya, Hainan Island, China. At this point, a name from the past made a welcome return.

*The European Tour's on-going policy of supporting charity was further enhanced in 2006. Firstly, €800,000 was raised by the auction of special Ryder Cup tickets and packages which Ryder Cup Europe LLP and the Dublin-based registered charity, the Links Golfing Society, put towards the purchase of 20 minibuses which were presented to 20 remarkable causes across the length and breadth of Ireland. Secondly, Ryder Cup Europe LLP donated €30,878 to both the Links Golfing Society and the Darren Clarke Foundation which will help breast cancer awareness and research, through the sale of Ryder Cup programmes. Picture shows An Taoiseach Bertie Ahern (left) with representatives of the Links Golfing Society and Ryder Cup Europe LLP, including Ryder Cup Director Richard Hills (second right) and Ian Woosnam's Vice Captain Des Smyth (right)*

(l-r) Johan Edfors, Robert Karlsson, Niclas Fasth and Henrik Stenson

Marc Warren

fruits again. Not once, but twice – firstly in The Quinn Direct British Masters at The De Vere Belfry, Sutton Coldfield, Warwickshire, England, in May and then in The Barclays Scottish Open at Loch Lomond, Glasgow, Scotland, in July. As follow-up victories go, this brace is almost as good as it gets. Dyson, meanwhile, also battered his way through the same door twice when he added The KLM Open at Kennemer Golf & Country Club in Zandvoort, The Netherlands, to his maiden win in Indonesia.

Praise, too, for Spain's Gonzalo Fernandez-Castaño, whose maiden victory came in 2005 and who was that year's Sir Henry Cotton Rookie of the Year. It was a good choice, for the Spaniard, who turned professional in 2004, won again in 2006, this time in the BMW Asian Open at Tomson Shanghai Pudong Golf Club, Shanghai, China, after a play-off that lasted just one hole against Stenson.

The following week, in April, saw another play-off, and on this occasion Niclas Fasth triumphed over John Bickerton at the fourth hole to seal the Andalucia Open de España Valle Romano at the San Roque Club, Cadiz, Spain. Bickerton's consolation, however, came in June with victory at the Open de France ALSTOM at Le Golf National, Paris, France.

Jean Van de Velde may have some critics but he has far more supporters in the game and everyone was pleased when he won again after a 13 year hiatus, this time in the Madeira Island Open Caixa Geral de Depositos at Santo de Serra, Madeira, Portugal.

Other first time winners in 2006 were India's Jeev Milkha Singh in the Volvo China Open at the Honghua International Golf Club, Beijing, China; Italy's Francesco Molinari in the Telecom Italia Open at Castello di Tolcinasco Golf & Country Club, Milan, Italy; Austria's Markus Brier in the BA-CA Golf Open presented by Telekom Austria at the Fontana Golf Club, Vienna, Austria; Argentina's Cesar Monasterio in the Aa St

Omer Open at Aa Saint Omer Golf Club, Lumbres, France; Scotland's Marc Warren, who won the EnterCard Scandinavian Masters at Barsebäck Golf & Country Club, Malmö, Sweden, a victory which helped him win The Sir Henry Cotton Rookie of the Year Award, and, finally, Alejandro Cañizares of Spain who took the honours in The Imperial Collection Russian Open at Le Meridien Moscow Country Club, Moscow, Russia.

While the majority now anxiously await their second, consolidating victory, Edfors has no such worry. The Swede was so pleased at the taste of his first victory that he quickly bit into this most delicious of

Elsewhere, Paul Broadhurst underlined his continuing class with the sixth title of a career that now spans 18 years when he lifted the Algarve Open de Portugal Caixa Geral de Depositos at Le Meridien Penina Golf & Resort on Portugal's Algarve.

Furthermore, a classy win came for Thomas Björn when the Dane won the Nissan Irish Open across the demanding acres of Carton House Golf Club, Maynooth, Co. Kildare. It was a gritty performance, for Björn had trailed the lead by nine shots after the first round but eventually produced a birdie-birdie finish to pass everyone on the line.

Bradley Dredge, winner in 2005 of the WGC-Algarve World Cup in Portugal with Stephen Dodd for Wales, struck individual gold again when he won the Omega European Masters at Crans-sur-Sierre, Crans Montana, Switzerland, the most dramatically beautiful venue of the season. His eight shot winning margin was matched only by Woods in the WGC-American Express Championship three weeks later.

Dodd was also triumphant, winning the Smurfit Kappa European Open at The K Club, Straffan, Co. Kildare, Ireland. The ever-modest, ever-quiet Dodd took this latest success as modestly and quietly as you would expect and thus offered a subdued contrast to the happily chaotic and noisy scenes that were to follow at this same venue in September.

Robert Karlsson, a big and genial Swede, and Padraig Harrington were two men at the heart of those Ryder Cup celebrations. Karlsson set up his debut thanks to two victories, the first in The Celtic Manor Wales Open at The Celtic Manor Resort, Newport, South Wales, where he was a stunning 14 under par after 36 holes and then in The Deutsche Bank Players' Championship of Europe at Gut Kaden, Hamburg, Germany

Ian Poulter

Harrington, meanwhile, found himself inspired by The Ryder Cup when after, for him, a rather subdued campaign, he struck top form a fortnight later when he triumphed in the Alfred Dunhill Links Championship across the hugely varied acres of the Old Course, St Andrews, Carnoustie and Kingsbarns, Scotland.

The timing of his return to form was perfect indeed for, three weeks after his victory in Scotland, he finished in a share of second place in the season ending Volvo Masters at Club de Golf Valderrama. This performance secured for him Number One position in The European Tour Order of Merit for the first time.

There was no Ryder Cup place in 2006 for Ian Poulter, but the flamboyant player chanelled his frustrations into a late season victory in the XXXII Banco de Madrid Valle Romano Open de Madrid Golf Masters played at La Moreleja II, Madrid.

Spain, as usual, also provided the setting for the final two events of the season, Fasth becoming the ninth multiple winner of 2006 with his victory in the Mallorca Classic at Pula Golf Club,

Mallorca, Spain, while Jeev Milkha Singh took that tally into double figures with his superb victory in the Volvo Masters a week later, completing a successful Volvo double after his win in the Volvo China Open in April. "This is the biggest victory of my career and is going to stay with me for the rest of my life," said Singh. "I think this is going to be big for Indian golf. I feel more sponsors will come out and more kids will try to make a career from the sport."

No sooner, however, was all the above put to bed than everyone was up and getting dressed again for a new season and packing, along with all the other necessary stuff, their imaginations. They leave behind on the 2006 shelf an astonishing 38 holes in one and an improbable six albatrosses. For the record, 35 records were either set or equalled along the way.

In 2007, of course, everyone will do even better. You may say I'm a dreamer.....but I'm not the only one...

**Bill Elliott**
*The Observer*

# Truth Dawns
# The Morning After

Paul Lawrie

Nick O'Hern

**Sheshan International Golf Club**

| Par | Yards | Metres |
| --- | --- | --- |
| 72 | 7143 | 6531 |

| | | | | |
| --- | --- | --- | --- | --- |
| 1 | **David HOWELL** | 268 | -20 | |
| 2 | Tiger WOODS | 271 | -17 | |
| 3 | Nick DOUGHERTY | 274 | -14 | |
| | Nick O'HERN | 274 | -14 | |
| 5 | Thomas BJÖRN | 275 | -13 | |
| | Vijay SINGH | 275 | -13 | |
| 7 | Paul CASEY | 276 | -12 | |
| 8 | Jean-Francois REMESY | 277 | -11 | |
| | Thaworn WIRATCHANT | 277 | -11 | |
| 10 | Michael CAMPBELL | 278 | -10 | |

# WEATHER REPORT

| Round One | Round Two | Round Three | Round Four |
| --- | --- | --- | --- |

# EUROPEAN TOUR ORDER OF MERIT
(After one tournament)

| Pos | | € | |
| --- | --- | --- | --- |
| 1 | **David HOWELL** | 704,516.80 | |
| 2 | Nick DOUGHERTY | 237,995.30 | |
| | Nick O'HERN | 237,995.30 | |
| 4 | Thomas BJÖRN | 164,018.10 | |
| | Vijay SINGH | 164,018.10 | |
| 6 | Paul CASEY | 126,818.10 | |
| 7 | Jean-Francois REMESY | 100,186.30 | |
| | Thaworn WIRATCHANT | 100,186.30 | |
| 9 | Michael CAMPBELL | 84,545.40 | |
| 10 | Paul LAWRIE | 77,950.86 | |

David Howell tasted what life at golf's next level offers even before he awoke on the morning of the final day of the HSBC Champions where he brilliantly turned a one shot lead into a three shot victory over the mighty Tiger Woods.

The night before, having forged his way ahead of Nick O'Hern and Woods, Howell found himself besieged by locals who wanted an autograph from this smiling Englishman who was somehow beating the World Number One.

"In the last five minutes," said the 30 year old once he had been safely extricated from the melee, "I've experienced what Tiger must experience every day of his life with the autographs and the chaos that surrounds him all the time. I was getting frustrated after a few minutes, so that brings home how well he handles himself and has done so for many years. He really is a class act."

The inaugural HSBC Champions came alive from the start. Nick Dougherty, Paul Lawrie and Peter O'Malley each returned 64s to finish the opening day at the top of the leaderboard. Yet by no means did all of the first day buzz come from the golf. The organisers were always going to face a challenge in separating the spectators from their phones-cum-cameras for, apart from anything else, the Chinese are among the most prolific picture takers in the world.

Woods was the amateur snappers' main victim but, to his credit, on what was his first official tournament participation in China, he did not see himself as that. He appreciated that golf is still a relatively new sport in this part of the world and that the spectators could not be expected to pick up everything about our Royal and Ancient game all at once.

Asked how he had become so adept at pulling out of a swing once he had been interrupted, Woods likened it to baseball or cricket. "When the ball is thrown and the player has his concentration artificially disturbed, he stops. It's the same thing," he said.

Kenneth Ferrie

the first place. "What I have at last learned to appreciate is that lots of people at home who tune into the golf at the end of a day in the office would give anything to be playing in this event with Tiger Woods in the field," said the 23 year old former Walker Cup player.

The conditions cheered up for a third round in which Howell provided everyone with something to talk about on the Saturday night when he handed in the 68 which gave him his one shot lead over O'Hern, who had compiled three successive 67s, and Woods.

The second day was grey and grim overhead but Kenneth Ferrie pierced the gloom with a hole in one at the sixth with a four iron, while the difficult conditions brought out the best in his fellow Englishmen Dougherty and Howell who moved into a share of the lead. Howell simply refused to let a good score get away, ultimately adding a 67 to his opening 65, while Dougherty's tactics, as he attached a 68 to his first round 64, were all about seeing beyond the conditions to how lucky he was to be playing golf for a living in

Everyone had an opinion on how the last day would go. Most of the golfing fraternity in Shanghai favoured Woods. In their eyes, he was well nigh invincible. Indeed, when, on the eve of the tournament, he had been called upon to hit balls over the barges on the Huang Po River, there were at least 20 calls to see if the missiles had actually reached the far bank – even though such a carry would have been over 580 yards.

*"Nothing says more about what a great job they have made of the course at Sheshan than the fact it is only a year old. It is an American-style course and in fantastic condition" – Nick Dougherty*

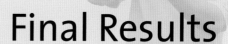

# Final Results

| Pos | Name | | Rd1 | Rd2 | Rd3 | Rd4 | Total | | € | £ |
|---|---|---|---|---|---|---|---|---|---|---|
| 1 | David HOWELL | Eng | 65 | 67 | 68 | 68 | 268 | -20 | 704,516.80 | 475,899.46 |
| 2 | Tiger WOODS | USA | 65 | 69 | 67 | 70 | 271 | -17 | 469,692.00 | 317,275.85 |
| 3 | Nick O'HERN | Aus | 67 | 67 | 67 | 73 | 274 | -14 | 237,995.30 | 160,765.27 |
| | Nick DOUGHERTY | Eng | 64 | 68 | 73 | 69 | 274 | -14 | 237,995.30 | 160,765.27 |
| 5 | Vijay SINGH | Fiji | 67 | 69 | 70 | 69 | 275 | -13 | 164,018.10 | 110,793.84 |
| | Thomas BJÖRN | Den | 67 | 69 | 69 | 70 | 275 | -13 | 164,018.10 | 110,793.84 |
| 7 | Paul CASEY | Eng | 67 | 68 | 73 | 68 | 276 | -12 | 126,818.10 | 85,665.33 |
| 8 | Thaworn WIRATCHANT | Thai | 67 | 68 | 69 | 73 | 277 | -11 | 100,186.30 | 67,675.61 |
| | Jean-Francois REMESY | Fr | 70 | 67 | 70 | 70 | 277 | -11 | 100,186.30 | 67,675.61 |
| 10 | Michael CAMPBELL | NZ | 66 | 70 | 69 | 73 | 278 | -10 | 84,545.40 | 57,110.22 |
| 11 | Paul LAWRIE | Scot | 64 | 75 | 70 | 70 | 279 | -9 | 77,950.86 | 52,655.62 |
| 12 | K J CHOI | Kor | 65 | 71 | 74 | 70 | 280 | -8 | 68,932.68 | 46,563.86 |
| | Arjun ATWAL | Ind | 69 | 70 | 73 | 68 | 280 | -8 | 68,932.68 | 46,563.86 |
| | Lee WESTWOOD | Eng | 70 | 69 | 74 | 67 | 280 | -8 | 68,932.68 | 46,563.86 |
| 15 | Thongchai JAIDEE | Thai | 67 | 73 | 71 | 70 | 281 | -7 | 59,076.10 | 39,905.77 |
| | Steve WEBSTER | Eng | 70 | 70 | 71 | 68 | 281 | -7 | 59,076.10 | 39,905.77 |
| | Padraig HARRINGTON | Ire | 69 | 72 | 72 | 68 | 281 | -7 | 59,076.10 | 39,905.77 |
| | Peter O'MALLEY | Aus | 64 | 72 | 73 | 72 | 281 | -7 | 59,076.10 | 39,905.77 |
| 19 | Ian POULTER | Eng | 67 | 69 | 73 | 73 | 282 | -6 | 49,515.42 | 33,447.55 |
| | Paul BROADHURST | Eng | 76 | 69 | 69 | 68 | 282 | -6 | 49,515.42 | 33,447.55 |
| | Robert-Jan DERKSEN | NL | 65 | 70 | 74 | 73 | 282 | -6 | 49,515.42 | 33,447.55 |
| | Peter HANSON | Swe | 69 | 70 | 70 | 73 | 282 | -6 | 49,515.42 | 33,447.55 |
| | John BICKERTON | Eng | 68 | 72 | 72 | 70 | 282 | -6 | 49,515.42 | 33,447.55 |
| | Steven BOWDITCH | Aus | 71 | 69 | 71 | 71 | 282 | -6 | 49,515.42 | 33,447.55 |
| 25 | Thomas AIKEN | SA | 72 | 72 | 69 | 70 | 283 | -5 | 40,666.34 | 27,470.02 |
| | Niclas FASTH | Swe | 70 | 74 | 69 | 70 | 283 | -5 | 40,666.34 | 27,470.02 |
| | Prayad MARKSAENG | Thai | 70 | 70 | 75 | 68 | 283 | -5 | 40,666.34 | 27,470.02 |
| | Richard STERNE | SA | 73 | 70 | 73 | 67 | 283 | -5 | 40,666.34 | 27,470.02 |
| | Kenneth FERRIE | Eng | 66 | 69 | 74 | 74 | 283 | -5 | 40,666.34 | 27,470.02 |
| | Lian-Wei ZHANG | PRC | 67 | 68 | 73 | 75 | 283 | -5 | 40,666.34 | 27,470.02 |
| | Raphaël JACQUELIN | Fr | 74 | 71 | 67 | 71 | 283 | -5 | 40,666.34 | 27,470.02 |
| 32 | Henrik STENSON | Swe | 74 | 74 | 72 | 69 | 284 | -4 | 33,691.34 | 22,758.42 |
| | Bradley DREDGE | Wal | 77 | 68 | 73 | 66 | 284 | -4 | 33,691.34 | 22,758.42 |
| | Gonzalo FERNANDEZ-CASTANO | Sp | 70 | 70 | 74 | 70 | 284 | -4 | 33,691.34 | 22,758.42 |
| | Charl SCHWARTZEL | SA | 68 | 70 | 76 | 70 | 284 | -4 | 33,691.34 | 22,758.42 |
| 36 | Maarten LAFEBER | NL | 72 | 71 | 74 | 68 | 285 | -3 | 29,619.07 | 20,007.61 |
| | Richard GREEN | Aus | 71 | 73 | 72 | 69 | 285 | -3 | 29,619.07 | 20,007.61 |
| | Titch MOORE | SA | 69 | 71 | 73 | 72 | 285 | -3 | 29,619.07 | 20,007.61 |
| 39 | Graeme MCDOWELL | N.Ire | 72 | 67 | 75 | 74 | 286 | -2 | 27,899.98 | 18,846.37 |
| 40 | Craig PARRY | Aus | 71 | 72 | 71 | 73 | 287 | -1 | 26,631.80 | 17,989.72 |
| | Colin MONTGOMERIE | Scot | 74 | 71 | 68 | 74 | 287 | -1 | 26,631.80 | 17,989.72 |
| 42 | Simon WAKEFIELD | Eng | 68 | 72 | 77 | 71 | 288 | 0 | 24,518.17 | 16,561.97 |
| | Stephen DODD | Wal | 73 | 75 | 71 | 69 | 288 | 0 | 24,518.17 | 16,561.97 |
| | Terry PILKADARIS | Aus | 69 | 72 | 76 | 71 | 288 | 0 | 24,518.17 | 16,561.97 |
| 45 | Ter-Chang WANG | TPE | 71 | 70 | 72 | 76 | 289 | 1 | 21,559.08 | 14,563.11 |
| | Emanuele CANONICA | It | 70 | 75 | 77 | 67 | 289 | 1 | 21,559.08 | 14,563.11 |
| | Jyoti RANDHAWA | Ind | 73 | 69 | 75 | 72 | 289 | 1 | 21,559.08 | 14,563.11 |
| | Barry LANE | Eng | 73 | 70 | 70 | 76 | 289 | 1 | 21,559.08 | 14,563.11 |
| 49 | Thomas LEVET | Fr | 70 | 73 | 73 | 74 | 290 | 2 | 18,177.26 | 12,278.70 |
| | Wen Teh LU | TPE | 72 | 75 | 72 | 71 | 290 | 2 | 18,177.26 | 12,278.70 |
| | Euan WALTERS | Aus | 70 | 72 | 75 | 73 | 290 | 2 | 18,177.26 | 12,278.70 |
| | Wen-Chong LIANG | PRC | 72 | 70 | 71 | 77 | 290 | 2 | 18,177.26 | 12,278.70 |
| 53 | Paul MCGINLEY | Ire | 73 | 70 | 71 | 78 | 292 | 4 | 16,063.63 | 10,850.94 |
| 54 | Miguel Angel JIMÉNEZ | Sp | 70 | 72 | 76 | 76 | 294 | 6 | 14,372.72 | 9,708.74 |
| | Adam LE VESCONTE | Aus | 72 | 70 | 80 | 72 | 294 | 6 | 14,372.72 | 9,708.74 |
| | Scott STRANGE | Aus | 69 | 76 | 76 | 73 | 294 | 6 | 14,372.72 | 9,708.74 |
| 57 | Chinarat PHADUNGSIL | Thai | 72 | 75 | 74 | 74 | 295 | 7 | 12,259.08 | 8,280.98 |
| | Neil CHEETHAM | Eng | 75 | 72 | 77 | 71 | 295 | 7 | 12,259.08 | 8,280.98 |
| 59 | Joakim BÄCKSTRÖM | Swe | 74 | 73 | 75 | 74 | 296 | 8 | 10,568.17 | 7,138.77 |
| | Richard LEE | NZ | 68 | 77 | 78 | 73 | 296 | 8 | 10,568.17 | 7,138.77 |
| 61 | Mu HU (Am) | PRC | 78 | 70 | 81 | 68 | 297 | 9 | | |
| 62 | Wei Chih LU | TPE | 71 | 75 | 77 | 76 | 299 | 11 | 8,877.27 | 5,996.57 |
| | Marc WARREN | Scot | 76 | 72 | 71 | 80 | 299 | 11 | 8,877.27 | 5,996.57 |
| | Sandy LYLE | Scot | 73 | 76 | 74 | 76 | 299 | 11 | 8,877.27 | 5,996.57 |
| 65 | Wu WEIHUANG | PRC | 73 | 75 | 79 | 73 | 300 | 12 | 7,820.45 | 5,282.70 |
| | Brett RUMFORD | Aus | 79 | 72 | 73 | 76 | 300 | 12 | 7,820.45 | 5,282.70 |
| 67 | Huang YONGHUAN | PRC | 77 | 76 | 76 | 72 | 301 | 13 | 6,975.00 | 4,711.59 |
| | Marc CAYEUX | Zim | 74 | 74 | 74 | 79 | 301 | 13 | 6,975.00 | 4,711.59 |
| 69 | Lei SHANG | PRC | 78 | 74 | 81 | 71 | 304 | 16 | 6,552.27 | 4,426.04 |
| 70 | Chao LI | PRC | 73 | 82 | 72 | 78 | 305 | 17 | 6,340.91 | 4,283.27 |
| 71 | Mikael LUNDBERG | Swe | 78 | 73 | 79 | 77 | 307 | 19 | 6,129.54 | 4,140.49 |
| 72 | Zhi-Feng QIU | PRC | 79 | 74 | 80 | 77 | 310 | 22 | 5,918.18 | 3,997.72 |
| 73 | Hao YUAN | PRC | 75 | 77 | 86 | 73 | 311 | 23 | 5,706.81 | 3,854.94 |
| 74 | Kim FELTON | Aus | RETD | | | | | | 5,495.45 | 3,712.16 |

The atmosphere on the Sunday had not a little in common with a Ryder Cup, what with spectators lining each of the first two holes. Some, looking for a bit of breathing space, headed off to watch Mu Hu, the richly gifted 16 year old rising Chinese star who is learning his trade at David Leadbetter's Champions Gate Academy in Florida. Most of the rest, as you would expect, attached themselves to the final three-ball of Howell, O'Hern and Woods.

At the outset, Howell had taken the precaution of giving himself a quiet talking to. "I reminded myself that Tiger can't punch me like in a boxing match and he can't hit the ball at me like in a tennis match," he said. "He can only shoot a score and I can only shoot a score."

On a day when O'Hern failed to ignite, Howell wasted no time in putting the pressure on Woods. After six holes of glorious iron play, he was as many as four ahead. Woods looked to be back in business when he pitched to within two feet of the flag at the seventh, only for Howell to foil his recovery by holing from 25 feet for a matching birdie three.

The tournament was more or less resolved at the 288 yard 16th where Woods, still three behind and with no option but to be aggressive, hit into the lakeside scrub and lost his ball. At that, Howell was four clear with two to play and the truth was beginning to dawn on him - he was about to defeat the world's best.

Having played his heart out, Howell spoke earnestly as he shook Woods by the hand on the home green. "I told him," said Howell, who is one of the few who could say what he did without sounding sycophantic, "that we were all honoured as golfers to have the chance to beat him - and that we were privileged to be playing in his era."

**Lewine Mair**

*Daily Telegraph*

# Total Prize Fund
€4,227,270  £2,855,511

# Volvo China Open

**Shenzhen, Guangdong Province, China**
November 24-27 • 2005

# Mysteries of The Orient

*Shiv Kapur*

| | | | | |
|---|---|---|---|---|
| 1 | **Paul CASEY** | 275 | -13 |  |
| 2 | Oliver WILSON | 275 | -13 | |
| 3 | Barry LANE | 276 | -12 | |
| 4 | Ross FISHER | 277 | -11 | |
| | Chawalit PLAPHOL | 277 | -11 | |
| 6 | Peter LAWRIE | 278 | -10 | |
| 7 | Thongchai JAIDEE | 279 | -9 | |
| | Jyoti RANDHAWA | 279 | -9 | |
| | Miles TUNNICLIFF | 279 | -9 | |
| | Lian-Wei ZHANG | 279 | -9 | |

**WEATHER REPORT**

| Round One | Round Two | Round Three | Round Four |
|-----------|-----------|-------------|------------|

**EUROPEAN TOUR ORDER OF MERIT**
(After two tournaments)

| Pos | | € | |
|-----|---|---|---|
| 1 | **David HOWELL** | 704,516.80 | |
| 2 | Paul CASEY | 311,351.22 | |
| 3 | Nick DOUGHERTY | 242,534.95 | |
| 4 | Nick O'HERN | 237,995.30 | |
| 5 | Thomas BJÖRN | 164,018.10 | |
| | Vijay SINGH | 164,018.10 | |
| 7 | Oliver WILSON | 123,022.10 | |
| 8 | Thaworn WIRATCHANT | 111,535.44 | |
| 9 | Jean-Francois REMESY | 100,186.30 | |
| 10 | Barry LANE | 90,871.85 | |

China's late paramount leader, Deng Xiaoping, will be remembered for many things, especially his economic miracle in the southernmost province of Guangdong, on the border with Hong Kong. In 1984, as part of China's reform and opening up programme, he created the special economic zone of Shenzhen, which now has one of the highest population densities of major cities in the country - more than ten million people crammed into 2,000 square kilometres.

In the heart of this concrete jungle is another miracle - namely the Shenzhen Golf Club, home for the first time to the co-sanctioned Volvo China Open, the second stop on The 2006 European Tour International Schedule and third last event on the 2005 Asian Tour.

"An oasis," said Paul Casey, on the eve of his final round 65 that set up his victory over fellow countryman Oliver Wilson in a play-off. "Amazing," said Nick Dougherty. "Awesome," said rookie Ross Fisher. Before the week, few players had heard of Shenzhen Golf Club and fewer still knew where it was. 'Somewhere close to Hong Kong,' was the general consensus, but once they laid eyes on this 'lung' of the city, they were hooked.

"The backdrop is spectacular," third round leader Fisher said of the skyscrapers that line nearly every hole. "You hit a tee shot and all you see is a white dot travelling straight towards a building. It's kind of strange but a pretty incredible atmosphere. The course is fantastic."

Casey played five tournaments in China in 2005, but Shenzhen was still pretty much a mystery. "I knew where it was because I looked on the map. But that's pretty much it," said the Englishman who firstly came from four shots behind Fisher on the final day before beating Wilson in a play-off down the 18th hole.

Dougherty, who, earlier in the week was in hospital and on a drip because of

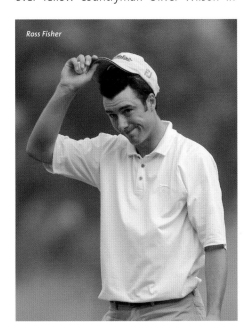
*Ross Fisher*

# Volvo China Open

*Barry Lane*

food poisoning, admitted he was a little shocked when he first laid eyes on the course, which was built in 1985 by Japan's Isao Aoki and remodelled by Canadian Neil Haworth in 1997.

"It's amazing how close it is to the city," he said. "I had never heard of Shenzhen and didn't realise how close it was to the border with Hong Kong. It reminds me of a city golf club. But the course is a tough test and can be very severe. When we play in China the courses are all pretty good. It's a credit to them."

Guangdong, the birthplace of golf in modern China, boasts the greatest concentration of courses - around 60 - in the country. The most famous is the Mission Hills Golf Club, the largest golf facility in the world with its ten courses, but in many ways the pioneer was Shenzhen, helped by its most celebrated member, the trail-blazing Lian-Wei Zhang. China's greatest golf export gave his fans plenty to shout about when charging into contention with a third round six under par 66, but the 40 year old admitted the expectation got to him in the final round as he could do no better than level par 72 to finish in a share of seventh place.

Zhang, the only Chinese player to make the cut from a record entry of 23, called on his country's young guns to start firing. "It's

*"I have played a lot in China this year, from Hainan Island to Beijing. I've seen a few places but this place is cool. This course is a cracker and it's in immaculate condition. It just shows you what wonderful facilities there are in China and they really are grasping the game and are very enthusiastic about it" - Paul Casey*

Oliver Wilson

# Final Results

| Pos | Name | | Rd1 | Rd2 | Rd3 | Rd4 | Total | | € | £ |
|---|---|---|---|---|---|---|---|---|---|---|
| 1 | Paul CASEY | ENG | 71 | 69 | 70 | 65 | 275 | -13 | 184,533.12 | 126,354.47 |
| 2 | Oliver WILSON | ENG | 68 | 67 | 71 | 69 | 275 | -13 | 123,022.08 | 84,236.31 |
| 3 | Barry LANE | ENG | 67 | 74 | 67 | 68 | 276 | -12 | 69,312.77 | 47,460.20 |
| 4 | Chawalit PLAPHOL | THA | 65 | 67 | 74 | 71 | 277 | -11 | 51,154.16 | 35,026.54 |
| | Ross FISHER | ENG | 69 | 68 | 68 | 72 | 277 | -11 | 51,154.16 | 35,026.54 |
| 6 | Peter LAWRIE | IRL | 69 | 72 | 68 | 69 | 278 | -10 | 38,753.15 | 26,535.26 |
| 7 | Lian-Wei ZHANG | CHN | 70 | 71 | 66 | 72 | 279 | -9 | 26,961.12 | 18,460.96 |
| | Jyoti RANDHAWA | IND | 71 | 67 | 71 | 70 | 279 | -9 | 26,961.12 | 18,460.96 |
| | Miles TUNNICLIFF | ENG | 68 | 70 | 70 | 71 | 279 | -9 | 26,961.12 | 18,460.96 |
| | Thongchai JAIDEE | THA | 72 | 70 | 70 | 67 | 279 | -9 | 26,961.12 | 18,460.96 |
| 11 | Scott STRANGE | AUS | 73 | 67 | 70 | 70 | 280 | -8 | 20,373.08 | 13,949.96 |
| 12 | Fredrik WIDMARK | SWE | 75 | 65 | 69 | 72 | 281 | -7 | 16,418.68 | 11,242.28 |
| | Francois DELAMONTAGNE | FRA | 65 | 70 | 74 | 72 | 281 | -7 | 16,418.68 | 11,242.28 |
| | Simon YATES | SCO | 68 | 68 | 74 | 71 | 281 | -7 | 16,418.68 | 11,242.28 |
| | Keith HORNE | RSA | 74 | 68 | 68 | 71 | 281 | -7 | 16,418.68 | 11,242.28 |
| | Anders HANSEN | DEN | 70 | 70 | 69 | 72 | 281 | -7 | 16,418.68 | 11,242.28 |
| | Kenneth FERRIE | ENG | 70 | 70 | 70 | 71 | 281 | -7 | 16,418.68 | 11,242.28 |
| | Gaurav GHEI | IND | 72 | 70 | 67 | 72 | 281 | -7 | 16,418.68 | 11,242.28 |
| 19 | Søren HANSEN | DEN | 70 | 72 | 70 | 70 | 282 | -6 | 12,910.33 | 8,840.03 |
| | Anthony WALL | ENG | 71 | 71 | 71 | 69 | 282 | -6 | 12,910.33 | 8,840.03 |
| | Søren KJELDSEN | DEN | 74 | 67 | 67 | 74 | 282 | -6 | 12,910.33 | 8,840.03 |
| | Johan SKÖLD | SWE | 68 | 75 | 69 | 70 | 282 | -6 | 12,910.33 | 8,840.03 |
| | Gregory BOURDY | FRA | 73 | 69 | 70 | 70 | 282 | -6 | 12,910.33 | 8,840.03 |
| 24 | Daniel VANCSIK | ARG | 73 | 70 | 68 | 72 | 283 | -5 | 11,349.14 | 7,771.04 |
| | David PARK | WAL | 69 | 73 | 71 | 70 | 283 | -5 | 11,349.14 | 7,771.04 |
| | Boonchu RUANGKIT | THA | 67 | 73 | 71 | 72 | 283 | -5 | 11,349.14 | 7,771.04 |
| | Thaworn WIRATCHANT | THA | 72 | 68 | 72 | 71 | 283 | -5 | 11,349.14 | 7,771.04 |
| 28 | Joakim HAEGGMAN | SWE | 74 | 69 | 70 | 71 | 284 | -4 | 10,020.46 | 6,861.26 |
| | José Manuel LARA | ESP | 69 | 75 | 70 | 70 | 284 | -4 | 10,020.46 | 6,861.26 |
| | Jean VAN DE VELDE | FRA | 73 | 70 | 69 | 72 | 284 | -4 | 10,020.46 | 6,861.26 |
| | Rahil GIANGJEE | IND | 72 | 71 | 71 | 70 | 284 | -4 | 10,020.46 | 6,861.26 |
| 32 | Shiv KAPUR | IND | 69 | 70 | 70 | 76 | 285 | -3 | 8,592.13 | 5,883.25 |
| | Brad KENNEDY | AUS | 72 | 70 | 70 | 73 | 285 | -3 | 8,592.13 | 5,883.25 |
| | Terry PILKADARIS | AUS | 68 | 71 | 76 | 70 | 285 | -3 | 8,592.13 | 5,883.25 |
| | Scott DRUMMOND | SCO | 73 | 70 | 70 | 72 | 285 | -3 | 8,592.13 | 5,883.25 |
| | Nicolas COLSAERTS | BEL | 73 | 69 | 74 | 69 | 285 | -3 | 8,592.13 | 5,883.25 |
| 37 | Robert KARLSSON | SWE | 73 | 71 | 69 | 73 | 286 | -2 | 7,197.01 | 4,927.98 |
| | Wen Teh LU | TPE | 73 | 69 | 76 | 68 | 286 | -2 | 7,197.01 | 4,927.98 |
| | Ter-Chang WANG | TPE | 71 | 72 | 73 | 70 | 286 | -2 | 7,197.01 | 4,927.98 |
| | Hendrik BUHRMANN | RSA | 76 | 68 | 70 | 72 | 286 | -2 | 7,197.01 | 4,927.98 |
| | Ariel CANETE | ARG | 73 | 70 | 71 | 72 | 286 | -2 | 7,197.01 | 4,927.98 |
| | Adam BLYTH | RSA | 70 | 72 | 73 | 71 | 286 | -2 | 7,197.01 | 4,927.98 |
| | Chapchai NIRAT | JPN | 72 | 71 | 73 | 70 | 286 | -2 | 7,197.01 | 4,927.98 |
| 44 | Ron WON | USA | 74 | 68 | 71 | 74 | 287 | -1 | 5,757.61 | 3,942.38 |
| | Steven JEPPESEN | SWE | 72 | 69 | 71 | 75 | 287 | -1 | 5,757.61 | 3,942.38 |
| | Adam GROOM | AUS | 70 | 71 | 74 | 72 | 287 | -1 | 5,757.61 | 3,942.38 |
| | Peter GUSTAFSSON | SWE | 72 | 72 | 74 | 69 | 287 | -1 | 5,757.61 | 3,942.38 |
| | Clay DEVERS | USA | 71 | 72 | 70 | 74 | 287 | -1 | 5,757.61 | 3,942.38 |
| | Leif WESTERBERG | SWE | 73 | 70 | 74 | 70 | 287 | -1 | 5,757.61 | 3,942.38 |
| 50 | Anthony KANG | USA | 69 | 72 | 73 | 74 | 288 | 0 | 4,539.65 | 3,108.42 |
| | Nick DOUGHERTY | ENG | 73 | 70 | 76 | 69 | 288 | 0 | 4,539.65 | 3,108.42 |
| | Gary RUSNAK | USA | 72 | 72 | 71 | 73 | 288 | 0 | 4,539.65 | 3,108.42 |
| | Marc WARREN | SCO | 71 | 73 | 71 | 73 | 288 | 0 | 4,539.65 | 3,108.42 |
| | Sung-Man LEE | KOR | 70 | 73 | 74 | 71 | 288 | 0 | 4,539.65 | 3,108.42 |
| 55 | Carl SUNESON | ESP | 71 | 73 | 71 | 74 | 289 | 1 | 3,653.87 | 2,501.90 |
| | Stephen DODD | WAL | 71 | 71 | 74 | 73 | 289 | 1 | 3,653.87 | 2,501.90 |
| | Joong Kyung MO | KOR | 71 | 73 | 74 | 71 | 289 | 1 | 3,653.87 | 2,501.90 |
| 58 | Tse-Peng CHANG | TPE | 69 | 73 | 74 | 74 | 290 | 2 | 3,100.25 | 2,122.82 |
| | Mårten OLANDER | SWE | 72 | 72 | 73 | 73 | 290 | 2 | 3,100.25 | 2,122.82 |
| | Gary MURPHY | IRL | 71 | 72 | 77 | 70 | 290 | 2 | 3,100.25 | 2,122.82 |
| | Andrew BUTTERFIELD | ENG | 68 | 72 | 75 | 75 | 290 | 2 | 3,100.25 | 2,122.82 |
| | Wei-Lan LU | TPE | 74 | 70 | 75 | 71 | 290 | 2 | 3,100.25 | 2,122.82 |
| 63 | Danny CHIA | MAS | 70 | 72 | 72 | 77 | 291 | 3 | 2,657.36 | 1,819.56 |
| | Gary EMERSON | ENG | 74 | 70 | 75 | 72 | 291 | 3 | 2,657.36 | 1,819.56 |
| | Alistair PRESNELL | AUS | 74 | 70 | 74 | 73 | 291 | 3 | 2,657.36 | 1,819.56 |
| 66 | Keng-Chi LIN | TPE | 70 | 74 | 71 | 77 | 292 | 4 | 2,435.91 | 1,667.69 |
| 67 | Joakim BÄCKSTRÖM | SWE | 69 | 73 | 74 | 77 | 293 | 5 | 2,325.19 | 1,592.12 |

# Total Prize Fund
€1,100,890  £753,805

time for them to stand up," he said. "I don't want to be the only player out there. I felt the extra pressure. It's difficult to have the flag on your shoulders all the time."

On the eve of the final round, Casey said he would have to shoot 65 to have a chance and, in the end, he accomplished exactly that. He then had to wait for over an hour as Wilson came back to him over the testing final few holes, before landing the first prize of €184,553 (£126,354) and his fifth European Tour title with a birdie four on the 18th hole at the first time of asking.

It was, therefore, a suitably fitting end to the first Volvo China Open at Shenzhen Golf Club, a tournament which Mel Pyatt, President and CEO of Volvo Event Management, promised would continue to travel the length and breadth of China in the future.

"It is the national Open after all," said Pyatt, who lived up to his words by announcing that the next staging of the event would be at the Honghua International Golf Club in Beijing.

**Noel Prentice**

*South China Morning Post*

Miles Tunnicliff

# Secret of Waxing Lyrical

Thongchai Jaidee

<A>nyone fortunate enough to have avoided the winter chill in Europe to attend the UBS Hong Kong Open would have learned many fascinating facts about Colin Montgomerie, some of which had previously escaped attention.

Firstly, when moving house the week before the event, it became apparent he did not own a kettle, a fact which did not go down too well with the removal company's finest who were eager for a brew to slake their rampaging thirst.

Secondly, one of the reasons for his move back to the countryside, and a house which afforded him his own front door, was that he could not hand wash his car in the basement of his exclusive London apartment complex. This happens to be a relaxing and rewarding activity which Montgomerie particularly enjoys.

Thirdly, the man knows how to make a gracious acceptance speech after seeing the fickle gods of golf frown upon the fine efforts of James Kingston and smile down on him instead in his ultimately successful bid for a 30th victory on The European Tour International Schedule.

One thing which has never been a secret, however, is the Scot's desire for success and it was that fact which ensured he was in a position to make the most of Kingston's misfortunes over the closing stretch on a nerve-wracking final day in Fanling.

Thomas Björn

Even getting to the Hong Kong Golf Club had been a victory for mind over matter for Montgomerie after an exhausting season which began much earlier than usual for the 42 year old as he battled to get back amongst the world's elite.

In the hunt for world ranking points, Montgomerie had played 27 events around the globe before arriving in the former British colony, and was scheduled to fly straight from the Far East to California at

## Hong Kong Golf Club

| Par | Yards | Metres |
| --- | --- | --- |
| 70 | 6703 | 6129 |

| | | | | |
| --- | --- | --- | --- | --- |
| 1 | Colin MONTGOMERIE | 271 | -9 | |
| 2 | K J CHOI | 272 | -8 | |
| | James KINGSTON | 272 | -8 | |
| | Keng-Chi LIN | 272 | -8 | |
| | Edward LOAR | 272 | -8 | |
| | Thammanoon SRIROT | 272 | -8 | |
| 7 | Thongchai JAIDEE | 273 | -7 | |
| | Wook-Soon KANG | 273 | -7 | |
| | Damien McGRANE | 273 | -7 | |
| 10 | Simon YATES | 274 | -6 | |

### WEATHER REPORT

| Round One | Round Two | Round Three | Round Four |

### EUROPEAN TOUR ORDER OF MERIT
(After three tournaments)

| Pos | | € | |
| --- | --- | --- | --- |
| 1 | David HOWELL | 704,516.80 | |
| 2 | Paul CASEY | 311,351.22 | |
| 3 | Nick DOUGHERTY | 246,424.42 | |
| 4 | Nick O'HERN | 237,995.30 | |
| 5 | Colin MONTGOMERIE | 197,222.30 | |
| 6 | Thomas BJÖRN | 175,277.07 | |
| 7 | Vijay SINGH | 164,018.10 | |
| 8 | Oliver WILSON | 133,052.82 | |
| 9 | Thaworn WIRATCHANT | 116,243.74 | |
| 10 | Thongchai JAIDEE | 112,444.63 | |

the invitation of Tiger Woods to take part in his Target World Challenge. During his seven years as European Number One from 1993-99, an average of 19 events a season had been enough to secure the Order of Merit title.

So, after squeezing in the trifling matter of a trip to Buckingham Palace to collect his OBE after events in Shanghai and Japan, it was no great surprise when Montgomerie could only manage an opening one under par 69.

A second round 66 was flawless in execution but left Montgomerie a little dissatisfied in that it had not moved him closer than four shots adrift of the leader, Canada's Rick Gibson, who had added a 66 to his opening 65.

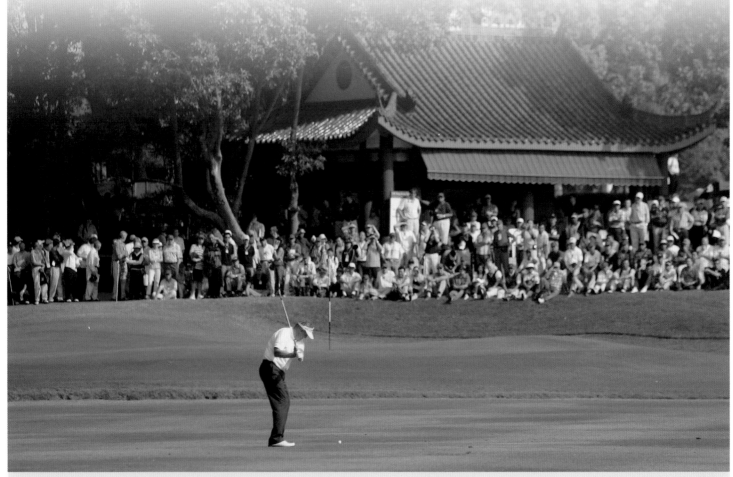

*It is one of the shortest courses on Tour but the tree-lined fairways and firm, fast greens place a premium on accuracy. It is a good old design, narrow off the tee and quite a test. There are numerous dog-legs and it does neutralise the long hitters* **– Colin Montgomerie**

*James Kingston*

| Pos | Name | | Rd1 | Rd2 | Rd3 | Rd4 | Total | | € | £ |
|---|---|---|---|---|---|---|---|---|---|---|
| 1 | Colin MONTGOMERIE | SCO | 69 | 66 | 66 | 70 | 271 | -9 | 170,590.50 | 116,584.09 |
| 2 | James KINGSTON | RSA | 68 | 69 | 64 | 71 | 272 | -8 | 61,639.46 | 42,125.32 |
| | Thammanoon SRIROT | THA | 71 | 67 | 66 | 68 | 272 | -8 | 61,639.46 | 42,125.32 |
| | K J CHOI | KOR | 67 | 72 | 64 | 69 | 272 | -8 | 61,639.46 | 42,125.32 |
| | Keng-Chi LIN | TPE | 68 | 69 | 66 | 69 | 272 | -8 | 61,639.46 | 42,125.32 |
| | Edward LOAR | USA | 68 | 64 | 71 | 69 | 272 | -8 | 61,639.46 | 42,125.32 |
| 7 | Thongchai JAIDEE | THA | 68 | 68 | 67 | 70 | 273 | -7 | 26,407.41 | 18,047.22 |
| | Wook-Soon KANG | KOR | 64 | 70 | 68 | 71 | 273 | -7 | 26,407.41 | 18,047.22 |
| | Damien MCGRANE | IRL | 68 | 71 | 63 | 71 | 273 | -7 | 26,407.41 | 18,047.22 |
| 10 | Simon YATES | SCO | 69 | 69 | 61 | 75 | 274 | -6 | 20,470.86 | 13,990.09 |
| 11 | Rick GIBSON | CAN | 65 | 66 | 71 | 73 | 275 | -5 | 17,639.06 | 12,054.80 |
| | Martin ERLANDSSON | SWE | 65 | 68 | 68 | 74 | 275 | -5 | 17,639.06 | 12,054.80 |
| | Peter GUSTAFSSON | SWE | 69 | 69 | 67 | 70 | 275 | -5 | 17,639.06 | 12,054.80 |
| 14 | Ted OH | KOR | 72 | 67 | 67 | 70 | 276 | -4 | 14,739.02 | 10,072.87 |
| | Maarten LAFEBER | NED | 72 | 68 | 63 | 73 | 276 | -4 | 14,739.02 | 10,072.87 |
| | Richard BLAND | ENG | 70 | 68 | 67 | 71 | 276 | -4 | 14,739.02 | 10,072.87 |
| | Andrew BUTTERFIELD | ENG | 69 | 65 | 69 | 73 | 276 | -4 | 14,739.02 | 10,072.87 |
| 18 | José Manuel LARA | ESP | 67 | 70 | 69 | 71 | 277 | -3 | 12,512.81 | 8,551.44 |
| | Jeev Milkha SINGH | IND | 69 | 69 | 66 | 73 | 277 | -3 | 12,512.81 | 8,551.44 |
| | Søren KJELDSEN | DEN | 66 | 69 | 70 | 72 | 277 | -3 | 12,512.81 | 8,551.44 |
| | Scott BARR | AUS | 67 | 72 | 67 | 71 | 277 | -3 | 12,512.81 | 8,551.44 |
| 22 | Wen-Chong LIANG | CHN | 72 | 69 | 66 | 71 | 278 | -2 | 11,258.97 | 7,694.55 |
| | Thomas BJÖRN | DEN | 70 | 68 | 72 | 68 | 278 | -2 | 11,258.97 | 7,694.55 |
| | Sam LITTLE | ENG | 69 | 72 | 65 | 72 | 278 | -2 | 11,258.97 | 7,694.55 |
| 25 | Marc CAYEUX | ZWE | 68 | 68 | 68 | 75 | 279 | -1 | 10,030.72 | 6,855.14 |
| | Joakim HAEGGMAN | SWE | 71 | 68 | 67 | 73 | 279 | -1 | 10,030.72 | 6,855.14 |
| | Gaurav GHEI | IND | 68 | 72 | 67 | 72 | 279 | -1 | 10,030.72 | 6,855.14 |
| | Simon DYSON | ENG | 71 | 67 | 71 | 70 | 279 | -1 | 10,030.72 | 6,855.14 |
| | Oliver WILSON | ENG | 75 | 64 | 64 | 76 | 279 | -1 | 10,030.72 | 6,855.14 |
| 30 | Marcus BOTH | AUS | 67 | 68 | 71 | 74 | 280 | 0 | 8,111.58 | 5,543.57 |
| | Shiv KAPUR | HKG | 69 | 70 | 68 | 73 | 280 | 0 | 8,111.58 | 5,543.57 |
| | Brad KENNEDY | AUS | 70 | 69 | 70 | 71 | 280 | 0 | 8,111.58 | 5,543.57 |
| | Adam LE VESCONTE | AUS | 68 | 70 | 69 | 73 | 280 | 0 | 8,111.58 | 5,543.57 |
| | Gary MURPHY | IRL | 68 | 73 | 67 | 72 | 280 | 0 | 8,111.58 | 5,543.57 |
| | Chawalit PLAPHOL | THA | 72 | 67 | 68 | 73 | 280 | 0 | 8,111.58 | 5,543.57 |
| | Anders HANSEN | DEN | 73 | 67 | 69 | 71 | 280 | 0 | 8,111.58 | 5,543.57 |
| | Gregory HAVRET | FRA | 71 | 70 | 68 | 71 | 280 | 0 | 8,111.58 | 5,543.57 |
| 38 | Miguel Angel JIMÉNEZ | ESP | 69 | 67 | 71 | 74 | 281 | 1 | 6,243.61 | 4,266.98 |
| | Jean VAN DE VELDE | FRA | 70 | 70 | 69 | 72 | 281 | 1 | 6,243.61 | 4,266.98 |
| | Miles TUNNICLIFF | ENG | 68 | 70 | 67 | 76 | 281 | 1 | 6,243.61 | 4,266.98 |
| | Robert-Jan DERKSEN | NED | 69 | 69 | 68 | 75 | 281 | 1 | 6,243.61 | 4,266.98 |
| | Pablo DEL OLMO | MEX | 68 | 70 | 70 | 73 | 281 | 1 | 6,243.61 | 4,266.98 |
| | Francois DELAMONTAGNE | FRA | 66 | 69 | 72 | 74 | 281 | 1 | 6,243.61 | 4,266.98 |
| | Ter-Chang WANG | TPE | 72 | 68 | 66 | 75 | 281 | 1 | 6,243.61 | 4,266.98 |
| | Prayad MARKSAENG | THA | 68 | 71 | 72 | 70 | 281 | 1 | 6,243.61 | 4,266.98 |
| | Angelo QUE | PHL | 74 | 65 | 70 | 72 | 281 | 1 | 6,243.61 | 4,266.98 |
| 47 | Philip GOLDING | ENG | 70 | 70 | 65 | 77 | 282 | 2 | 5,220.07 | 3,567.47 |
| 48 | Jyoti RANDHAWA | IND | 65 | 71 | 72 | 75 | 283 | 3 | 4,708.30 | 3,217.72 |
| | Thaworn WIRATCHANT | THA | 69 | 68 | 69 | 77 | 283 | 3 | 4,708.30 | 3,217.72 |
| | Kenneth FERRIE | ENG | 68 | 72 | 69 | 74 | 283 | 3 | 4,708.30 | 3,217.72 |
| | Adam GROOM | AUS | 70 | 70 | 70 | 73 | 283 | 3 | 4,708.30 | 3,217.72 |
| 52 | Scott STRANGE | AUS | 71 | 64 | 74 | 75 | 284 | 4 | 3,889.46 | 2,658.12 |
| | Nick DOUGHERTY | ENG | 71 | 70 | 69 | 74 | 284 | 4 | 3,889.46 | 2,658.12 |
| | Christian CÉVAËR | FRA | 72 | 68 | 70 | 74 | 284 | 4 | 3,889.46 | 2,658.12 |
| | Gary EMERSON | ENG | 69 | 69 | 72 | 73 | 284 | 4 | 3,889.46 | 2,658.12 |
| 56 | Peter LAWRIE | IRL | 72 | 69 | 71 | 74 | 286 | 6 | 3,036.51 | 2,075.20 |
| | Nicolas COLSAERTS | BEL | 69 | 69 | 71 | 77 | 286 | 6 | 3,036.51 | 2,075.20 |
| | Ian GARBUTT | ENG | 67 | 74 | 73 | 72 | 286 | 6 | 3,036.51 | 2,075.20 |
| | David PARK | WAL | 72 | 64 | 71 | 75 | 286 | 6 | 3,036.51 | 2,075.20 |
| | Gary RUSNAK | USA | 71 | 69 | 72 | 74 | 286 | 6 | 3,036.51 | 2,075.20 |
| | Prom MEESAWAT | THA | 71 | 69 | 72 | 74 | 286 | 6 | 3,036.51 | 2,075.20 |
| 62 | Terry PILKADARIS | AUS | 69 | 68 | 73 | 77 | 287 | 7 | 2,558.86 | 1,748.76 |
| | Amandeep JOHL | IND | 72 | 69 | 71 | 75 | 287 | 7 | 2,558.86 | 1,748.76 |
| | Tse-Peng CHANG | TPE | 67 | 73 | 72 | 75 | 287 | 7 | 2,558.86 | 1,748.76 |
| 65 | Joong Kyung MO | KOR | 70 | 68 | 75 | 76 | 289 | 9 | 2,149.44 | 1,468.96 |
| | Barry LANE | ENG | 70 | 70 | 73 | 78 | 289 | 9 | 2,149.44 | 1,468.96 |
| | Simon WAKEFIELD | ENG | 73 | 68 | 70 | 78 | 289 | 9 | 2,149.44 | 1,468.96 |
| | Richard MCEVOY | ENG | 66 | 73 | 69 | 81 | 289 | 9 | 2,149.44 | 1,468.96 |
| | Sung-Man LEE | KOR | 73 | 68 | 71 | 77 | 289 | 9 | 2,149.44 | 1,468.96 |

## Total Prize Fund
### €1,021,675 £702,953

Whatever they put in the water handed to the players on the course in the third round should be bottled and sold as Saturday's play produced a flood of low scores which turned the leaderboard into a sea of red figures. Cards of 63 and 64 abounded but were put in the shade by Simon Yates, the Thai-based Scot, who scorched round in 61 to lead.

However, it was hard to ignore the looming presence of Montgomerie in a share of second place, particularly as his name is so long it did not fit fully on many of the leaderboards around the course. How the hard-working scoreboard staff must long for a final group of Wi, Oh and Na!

Allied to the firm and fast greens, Sunday's windy conditions meant there would be no repeat of the previous day's low scoring, one birdie and a string of pars over the first 14 holes enough for Kingston to assume control of the tournament.

With his nearest rivals treading water - and a double bogey and triple bogey ending the chances of Yates - Kingston was two clear after a birdie on the 15th and arrived on the final tee in the classic situation, needing a par four for victory.

Twelve months earlier he had stood on the same spot sharing the lead with Miguel Angel Jiménez, only to pull his tee shot into the trees, make bogey, and lose to the Spaniard. Determined not to make the same mistake, he took an iron for safety, but this time found more timber to the right of the fairway. The South African's approach to the green came up short, and when his bogey putt slid past the hole, Montgomerie had secured the most unlikely victory of his career.

"Our hearts go out to James Kingston," said Montgomerie in his courteous winner's speech. "He played the better golf this week and should be standing here, not me. Golf is a cruel game sometimes."

**Phil Casey**
*Press Association*

# On
# Another
# Planet

Phillip Archer

## Leopard Creek

| Par | Yards | Metres |
| --- | --- | --- |
| 72 | 7250 | 6631 |

| | | | | |
| --- | --- | --- | --- | --- |
| 1 | Ernie ELS | 274 | -14 |  |
| 2 | Louis OOSTHUIZEN | 277 | -11 | |
| | Charl SCHWARTZEL | 277 | -11 | |
| 4 | Trevor IMMELMAN | 280 | -8 | |
| | Bobby LINCOLN | 280 | -8 | |
| | David LYNN | 280 | -8 | |
| | Ulrich VAN DEN BERG | 280 | -8 | |
| 8 | Sean FARRELL | 281 | -7 | |
| | Joakim HAEGGMAN | 281 | -7 | |
| | Alan MICHELL | 281 | -7 | |
| | Jaco VAN ZYL | 281 | -7 | |

"Having recovered from such a bad injury, it almost seems that 2006 is going to be the start of the second half of my professional career. I'm ready." Those were the words of Ernie Els on the eve of the dunhill championship in mid December 2005.

While the South African would go on to be proved prophetically correct, the only thing he got wrong was his timing. For a mere four days later, at the end of the fourth event on The 2006 European Tour International Schedule, Els proved conclusively that he was back already.

As hard to imagine as it may seem, before he incurred the anterior cruciate ligament damage to his left knee that required corrective surgery in July 2005, Els was far from 'ready' for the next chapter of his professional career.

Such is the aura which surrounds him both on and off the golf course, it is difficult for any observer to detect that his career is anything less than perfect. In this sense, he is a true sporting idol and watching Els play golf can lead mere mortals to assume he is indeed of superhuman stock.

The combination of awesome power, accuracy and a deadly short game, coupled with the fact he makes it all look so easy and enjoyable, is what makes Els one of the most watchable players on the planet. Away from the golf course, too, he is widely regarded as one of the game's gentlemen, someone who speaks with intelligence and a candidness that makes anyone listening think of him as a friend, as someone they know and trust.

So to hear that, before the injury, he was disillusioned and depressed by the game will come as something of a surprise. These

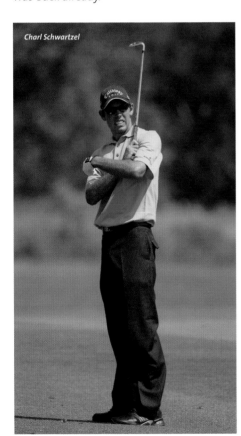

Charl Schwartzel

### WEATHER REPORT

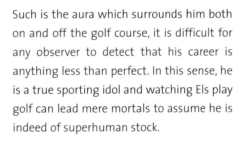

Round One    Round Two    Round Three    Round Four

### EUROPEAN TOUR ORDER OF MERIT
(After four tournaments)

| Pos | | € | |
| --- | --- | --- | --- |
| 1 | David HOWELL | 704,516.80 | |
| 2 | Paul CASEY | 311,351.22 | |
| 3 | Nick DOUGHERTY | 246,424.42 | |
| 4 | Nick O'HERN | 237,995.30 | |
| 5 | Colin MONTGOMERIE | 197,222.30 | |
| 6 | Thomas BJÖRN | 175,277.07 | |
| 7 | Vijay SINGH | 164,018.10 | |
| 8 | Ernie ELS | 158,579.29 | |
| 9 | Oliver WILSON | 133,052.82 | |
| 10 | Charl SCHWARTZEL | 125,787.39 | |

# dunhill championship

**Mpumalanga, South Africa**
December 8-11 • 2005

Mattias Eliasson

are not emotions commonly associated with a man who, when he revealed such thoughts, had won three Major Championships, 18 further European Tour titles and 35 other tournaments around the world – not to mention the riches he had garnered as a result of being among the elite golfers of the modern era.

Speaking before his victorious comeback, however, Els admitted: "I felt out of whack for most of the 2005 season. I felt flat, wasn't quite myself and just couldn't get out of it. It was both a mental and physical thing. But the mental aspect came first.

"It's a funny feeling. I've had it a couple of times in my career. It's a bit like a mild depression. I never felt like I was where I should be. I lost a bit of direction with my game. I was never sure about what I should be working on. I lost myself, in a way."

Els later reflected that the injury actually proved a blessing in disguise, as it afforded him the time to reflect and refocus his mind on getting back to full fitness and improving upon what is an already exemplary career. The result of his enforced period of reflection was there for all to see at the 2006 dunhill championship, where he recorded a three stroke victory to take the €158,579 (£107,213) first prize.

The manner of Els's victory was a testament to all of the aforementioned factors that make the man the sporting idol he is. Such is the power of his presence, he is one of only a handful of players in the world who can plant dangerous seeds of doubt in the

*"As scenery goes, Leopard Creek is one of the most outstanding golf courses we play all year. The course itself is in top condition, the layout rewards good shots, and it is one of the best in South Africa. It is a place I will always go back and play"* – Joakim Haeggman

Louis Oosthuizen

minds of his fellow professionals by simply moving up the leaderboard.

That phenomenon was very much in evidence over the last nine holes of the majestic Leopard Creek in Mpumalanga as Els began to chip away at the lead held by his fellow South African Ulrich van den Berg. Playing alongside Els, the 30 year old four time winner on the Sunshine Tour started his final round in blistering fashion with four birdies in the first six holes to move four strokes clear.

But as soon as Els began to make his move on the back nine, van den Berg felt his presence, a factor which manifested itself with a triple bogey on the 11th hole and a double bogey

on the 16th - paving the way for Els to mark his return in winning fashion with a closing 68 for a 14 under par total of 274.

Els's own prophetic words best summed up his dream return to The European Tour. The second half of his professional career was underway, and he was more than ready to conquer the world of golf once again.

Marcel Siem

**Michael Gibbons**

# Final Results

| Pos | Name | | Rd1 | Rd2 | Rd3 | Rd4 | Total | | € | £ |
|---|---|---|---|---|---|---|---|---|---|---|
| 1 | Ernie ELS | RSA | 71 | 67 | 68 | 68 | 274 | -14 | 158,579.29 | 107,213.37 |
| 2 | Charl SCHWARTZEL | RSA | 70 | 67 | 70 | 70 | 277 | -11 | 92,096.05 | 62,264.92 |
| | Louis OOSTHUIZEN | RSA | 69 | 67 | 71 | 70 | 277 | -11 | 92,096.05 | 62,264.92 |
| 4 | Bobby LINCOLN | RSA | 72 | 70 | 73 | 65 | 280 | -8 | 38,619.31 | 26,110.01 |
| | David LYNN | ENG | 73 | 68 | 71 | 68 | 280 | -8 | 38,619.31 | 26,110.01 |
| | Ulrich VAN DEN BERG | RSA | 70 | 69 | 65 | 76 | 280 | -8 | 38,619.31 | 26,110.01 |
| | Trevor IMMELMAN | RSA | 69 | 69 | 74 | 68 | 280 | -8 | 38,619.31 | 26,110.01 |
| 8 | Sean FARRELL | ZWE | 69 | 68 | 73 | 71 | 281 | -7 | 20,485.24 | 13,849.80 |
| | Joakim HAEGGMAN | SWE | 70 | 70 | 73 | 68 | 281 | -7 | 20,485.24 | 13,849.80 |
| | Alan MICHELL | RSA | 70 | 68 | 71 | 72 | 281 | -7 | 20,485.24 | 13,849.80 |
| | Jaco VAN ZYL | RSA | 68 | 71 | 69 | 73 | 281 | -7 | 20,485.24 | 13,849.80 |
| 12 | Thomas AIKEN | RSA | 69 | 71 | 73 | 69 | 282 | -6 | 15,607.80 | 10,552.23 |
| | Titch MOORE | RSA | 68 | 68 | 73 | 73 | 282 | -6 | 15,607.80 | 10,552.23 |
| | Phillip ARCHER | ENG | 66 | 70 | 74 | 72 | 282 | -6 | 15,607.80 | 10,552.23 |
| 15 | Johan EDFORS | SWE | 68 | 73 | 72 | 70 | 283 | -5 | 13,606.80 | 9,199.38 |
| | Gregory BOURDY | FRA | 74 | 69 | 69 | 71 | 283 | -5 | 13,606.80 | 9,199.38 |
| | Richard FINCH | ENG | 73 | 68 | 71 | 71 | 283 | -5 | 13,606.80 | 9,199.38 |
| 18 | Ross WELLINGTON | RSA | 72 | 68 | 76 | 68 | 284 | -4 | 11,572.45 | 7,823.98 |
| | Doug McGUIGAN | SCO | 68 | 69 | 72 | 75 | 284 | -4 | 11,572.45 | 7,823.98 |
| | Ariel CANETE | ARG | 72 | 69 | 71 | 72 | 284 | -4 | 11,572.45 | 7,823.98 |
| | Keith HORNE | RSA | 73 | 71 | 65 | 75 | 284 | -4 | 11,572.45 | 7,823.98 |
| | Mattias ELIASSON | SWE | 73 | 72 | 65 | 74 | 284 | -4 | 11,572.45 | 7,823.98 |
| | Pelle EDBERG | SWE | 71 | 71 | 71 | 71 | 284 | -4 | 11,572.45 | 7,823.98 |
| 24 | Gary MURPHY | IRL | 71 | 69 | 77 | 68 | 285 | -3 | 10,105.05 | 6,831.89 |
| | Gary CLARK | ENG | 69 | 73 | 74 | 69 | 285 | -3 | 10,105.05 | 6,831.89 |
| | Miguel CARBALLO | ARG | 70 | 75 | 69 | 71 | 285 | -3 | 10,105.05 | 6,831.89 |
| 27 | James KINGSTON | RSA | 70 | 67 | 73 | 76 | 286 | -2 | 8,470.90 | 5,727.06 |
| | Jarmo SANDELIN | SWE | 67 | 73 | 73 | 73 | 286 | -2 | 8,470.90 | 5,727.06 |
| | Jonathan LOMAS | ENG | 72 | 67 | 72 | 75 | 286 | -2 | 8,470.90 | 5,727.06 |
| | Damien MCGRANE | IRL | 70 | 70 | 76 | 70 | 286 | -2 | 8,470.90 | 5,727.06 |
| | Brandon PIETERS | RSA | 70 | 74 | 73 | 69 | 286 | -2 | 8,470.90 | 5,727.06 |
| | Matthew MILLAR | AUS | 73 | 67 | 73 | 73 | 286 | -2 | 8,470.90 | 5,727.06 |
| | Richard STERNE | RSA | 72 | 71 | 70 | 73 | 286 | -2 | 8,470.90 | 5,727.06 |
| | Michiel BOTHMA | RSA | 64 | 71 | 78 | 73 | 286 | -2 | 8,470.90 | 5,727.06 |
| | Martin MARITZ | RSA | 71 | 73 | 69 | 73 | 286 | -2 | 8,470.90 | 5,727.06 |
| 36 | Leif WESTERBERG | SWE | 70 | 73 | 71 | 73 | 287 | -1 | 6,603.30 | 4,464.40 |
| | David CARTER | ENG | 69 | 73 | 74 | 71 | 287 | -1 | 6,603.30 | 4,464.40 |
| | Steve VAN VUUREN | RSA | 72 | 72 | 73 | 70 | 287 | -1 | 6,603.30 | 4,464.40 |
| | Grant VEENSTRA | RSA | 69 | 68 | 74 | 76 | 287 | -1 | 6,603.30 | 4,464.40 |
| | Michael LAMB | ZWE | 73 | 72 | 67 | 75 | 287 | -1 | 6,603.30 | 4,464.40 |
| | Tjaart VAN DER WALT | RSA | 72 | 70 | 73 | 72 | 287 | -1 | 6,603.30 | 4,464.40 |
| | Jean-François REMESY | FRA | 71 | 71 | 74 | 71 | 287 | -1 | 6,603.30 | 4,464.40 |
| | Marcel SIEM | GER | 72 | 71 | 73 | 71 | 287 | -1 | 6,603.30 | 4,464.40 |
| | Stephen SCAHILL | NZL | 72 | 66 | 73 | 76 | 287 | -1 | 6,603.30 | 4,464.40 |
| 45 | Francesco MOLINARI | ITA | 71 | 71 | 76 | 70 | 288 | 0 | 5,102.55 | 3,449.77 |
| | Christian L NILSSON | SWE | 68 | 71 | 70 | 79 | 288 | 0 | 5,102.55 | 3,449.77 |
| | Garry HOUSTON | WAL | 74 | 69 | 70 | 75 | 288 | 0 | 5,102.55 | 3,449.77 |
| | Felipe AGUILAR | CHL | 71 | 70 | 71 | 76 | 288 | 0 | 5,102.55 | 3,449.77 |
| | Nic HENNING | RSA | 70 | 67 | 80 | 71 | 288 | 0 | 5,102.55 | 3,449.77 |
| | Tyrone VAN ASWEGEN | RSA | 70 | 75 | 70 | 73 | 288 | 0 | 5,102.55 | 3,449.77 |
| 51 | Tuomas TUOVINEN | FIN | 68 | 74 | 72 | 75 | 289 | 1 | 4,402.20 | 2,976.27 |
| 52 | Oliver WHITELEY | ENG | 73 | 69 | 71 | 77 | 290 | 2 | 4,002.00 | 2,705.70 |
| | Magnus P. ATLEVI | SWE | 70 | 73 | 73 | 74 | 290 | 2 | 4,002.00 | 2,705.70 |
| | Matthew RICHARDSON | ENG | 74 | 68 | 75 | 73 | 290 | 2 | 4,002.00 | 2,705.70 |
| 55 | Patrick O'BRIEN | RSA | 70 | 70 | 75 | 76 | 291 | 3 | 3,501.75 | 2,367.49 |
| | Ross FISHER | ENG | 68 | 72 | 71 | 80 | 291 | 3 | 3,501.75 | 2,367.49 |
| 57 | Ben WILLMAN | ENG | 71 | 71 | 74 | 76 | 292 | 4 | 3,101.55 | 2,096.92 |
| | Sam WALKER | ENG | 71 | 74 | 74 | 73 | 292 | 4 | 3,101.55 | 2,096.92 |
| | Gregory HAVRET | FRA | 71 | 70 | 70 | 81 | 292 | 4 | 3,101.55 | 2,096.92 |
| 60 | Hennie OTTO | RSA | 76 | 68 | 72 | 78 | 294 | 6 | 2,651.33 | 1,792.53 |
| | Andrew BUTTERFIELD | ENG | 72 | 73 | 73 | 76 | 294 | 6 | 2,651.33 | 1,792.53 |
| | Brett LIDDLE | RSA | 78 | 67 | 73 | 76 | 294 | 6 | 2,651.33 | 1,792.53 |
| | Mike MICHELL | RSA | 71 | 72 | 76 | 75 | 294 | 6 | 2,651.33 | 1,792.53 |
| | Justin WALTERS | ENG | 71 | 69 | 75 | 79 | 294 | 6 | 2,651.33 | 1,792.53 |
| | Jason KELLY | NOR | 73 | 70 | 79 | 72 | 294 | 6 | 2,651.33 | 1,792.53 |
| 66 | Johan KOK | USA | 69 | 74 | 73 | 79 | 295 | 7 | 2,251.13 | 1,521.96 |
| | Adilson DA SILVA | BRA | 73 | 71 | 72 | 79 | 295 | 7 | 2,251.13 | 1,521.96 |
| 68 | Jean HUGO | RSA | 67 | 74 | 74 | 81 | 296 | 8 | 1,900.95 | 1,285.21 |
| | Anders SJÖSTRAND | SWE | 75 | 67 | 73 | 81 | 296 | 8 | 1,900.95 | 1,285.21 |
| | Thabang SIMON | RSA | 71 | 72 | 75 | 78 | 296 | 8 | 1,900.95 | 1,285.21 |
| | Nico VAN RENSBURG | RSA | 72 | 72 | 76 | 76 | 296 | 8 | 1,900.95 | 1,285.21 |
| | Toni KARJALAINEN | FIN | 69 | 72 | 81 | 74 | 296 | 8 | 1,900.95 | 1,285.21 |
| 73 | Anton HAIG | RSA | 79 | 66 | 80 | 72 | 297 | 9 | 1,500.75 | 1,014.64 |
| | Darren FICHARDT | RSA | 71 | 73 | 76 | 77 | 297 | 9 | 1,500.75 | 1,014.64 |
| | Francisco VALERA | ESP | 72 | 71 | 76 | 78 | 297 | 9 | 1,500.75 | 1,014.64 |
| 76 | Phil WORTHINGTON | ENG | 73 | 71 | 77 | 81 | 302 | 14 | 1,398.00 | 945.17 |
| 77 | Neil CHEETHAM | ENG | 73 | 70 | 80 | 80 | 303 | 15 | 1,395.00 | 943.14 |

## Total Prize Fund
€1,002,793  £677,974

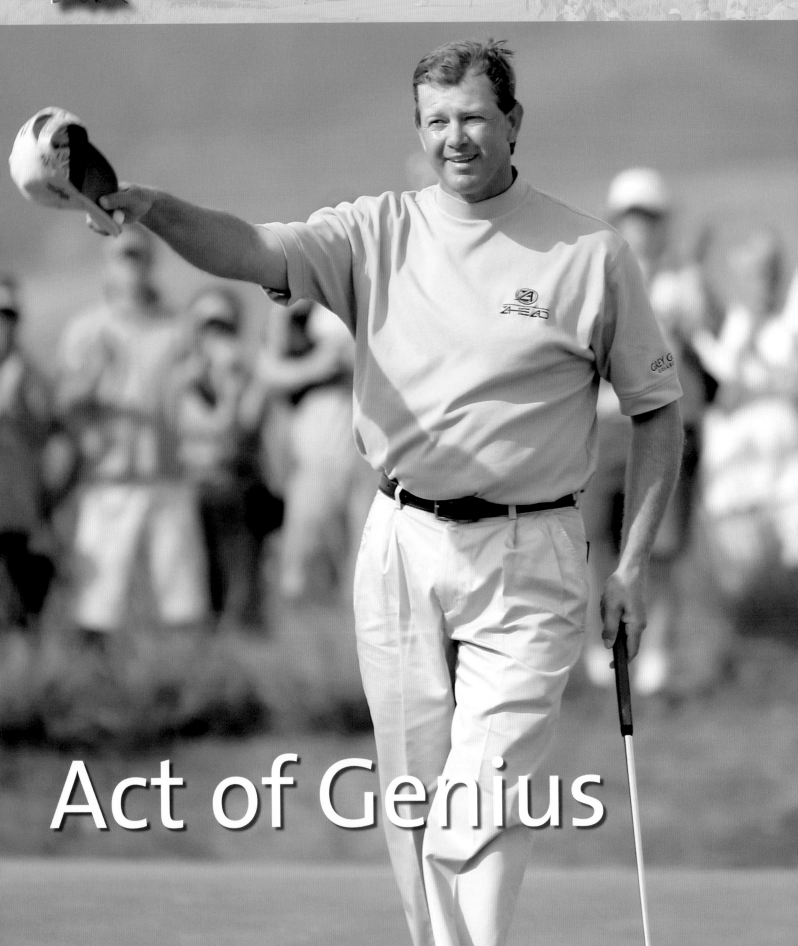

# Act of Genius

*Ernie Els*

## SOUTH AFRICAN AIRWAYS

### Fancourt Golf Club

| Par | Yards | Metres |
|---|---|---|
| 73 | 7435 | 6799 |

| | | | | |
|---|---|---|---|---|
| 1 | **Retief GOOSEN** | **282** | **-10** |  |
| 2 | Ernie ELS | 283 | -9 | |
| 3 | Gregory BOURDY | 290 | -2 | |
| | Darren FICHARDT | 290 | -2 | |
| 5 | Mattias ELIASSON | 292 | 0 | |
| | Gregory HAVRET | 292 | 0 | |
| | Keith HORNE | 292 | 0 | |
| 8 | Francesco MOLINARI | 293 | 1 | |
| 9 | Tim CLARK | 294 | 2 | |
| | Ross FISHER | 294 | 2 | |

In the end it boiled down to an act of genius, a shot so sublime that it was difficult not to conclude that the gods were having some sport of their own.

The scene was the final round of the South African Airways Open at Fancourt Golf Club in George, a four hour drive east of Cape Town, and the protagonists were two of the truly great players of the modern era: Ernie Els and Retief Goosen. This time it was Goosen on whom the gods were smiling; Els with whom they were having fun.

It is fair to say that The Links at Fancourt is not a place for the faint hearted. A beautiful but brutal course, it offers no let up over the 7,435 yards. The Gary Player-designed par 73 layout is a match for anybody - a true test of golf that only the best can subdue, but none can expect to tame. Yet the quality of play of the two South Africans that day, in what effectively turned into a head-to-head contest, simply took the breath away.

Goosen, on seven under par, began the day with a three shot lead over Els and a four shot advantage over another South African, Darren Fichardt, and Ross Fisher of England.

After eight holes, Els had made up all those shots. By the 12th, he had given them back but with three birdies in succession from the 14th he moved alongside Goosen once more. It was stunning play on a course that

*Darren Fichardt*

### WEATHER REPORT

Round One | Round Two | Round Three | Round Four

### EUROPEAN TOUR ORDER OF MERIT
(After five tournaments)

| Pos | | € | |
|---|---|---|---|
| 1 | **David HOWELL** | **704,516.80** | |
| 2 | Paul CASEY | 311,351.22 | |
| 3 | Ernie ELS | 273,636.82 | |
| 4 | Nick DOUGHERTY | 246,424.42 | |
| 5 | Nick O'HERN | 237,995.30 | |
| 6 | Colin MONTGOMERIE | 197,222.30 | |
| 7 | Thomas BJÖRN | 175,277.07 | |
| 8 | Vijay SINGH | 164,018.10 | |
| 9 | Retief GOOSEN | 158,579.29 | |
| 10 | Charl SCHWARTZEL | 141,395.19 | |

# South African Airways Open

**George, South Africa**
December 15-18 • 2005

Gregory Havret

had grudgingly surrendered its birdies all week and suggested that the momentum had shifted unerringly Els's way.

Now, however, Goosen, unfazed by all that had gone before, landed the decisive blow at the par three 17th with a stunning chip from eight feet below the back of the green that pitched delicately onto the putting surface, bounced a couple of times, and rolled into the hole for a birdie two.

For mere mortals, it would have been difficult to have got the ball close to the hole, let alone in it, and considering that the greens, hard and with steep run-offs, had been difficult to hold even with short irons, it must have been particularly galling for Els. He had been in the ascendancy all day but

now, waiting to play a chip of his own, he had seen his rival pull ahead once more.

Els, of course, did not concede defeat. Indeed he gave himself the chance of a play-off by setting up a five foot putt for eagle at the 18th. It missed and Goosen sank his birdie putt before raising his arms to salute his 13th win on The European Tour International Schedule.

Some say that Goosen has ice in his veins. Others that he has no veins at all, just levers and wires. In golfing terms, he resembles Arnold Schwarzenegger's Terminator, the indestructible cyborg that refuses to be beaten. It does not matter what is thrown at him, he continues unflinchingly towards his goal. His face betrays not a touch of emotion.

**"**The course is fantastic but very demanding. One bad shot and you can make any number. This golf course is going to get you, somewhere. It's just a question of how bad. You have to be able to limit the damage as best you can**"** – Ernie Els

David Lynn

# Final Results

It is impossible to tell from Goosen's body language whether he is five under or five over par for a round. His pace alters not a jot, his rhythm – smooth as maple syrup - remains in place, unaffected by what is going on around him. So it was at Fancourt.

It is a maxim of golf that you play your own game, closing your mind to what anybody else is doing. You cannot affect them, and they cannot affect you. While that is all very well in theory, when the likes of Phil Mickelson, as he did in the 2004 US Open Championship at Shinnecock Hills, and Els at Fancourt, are on the charge, it is easier said than done. Goosen, however, hardly seems to notice they are there.

The tougher it gets, the more he likes it. In some ways, the situation that unfolded at Fancourt was similar to what happened in New York State. On each occasion, Goosen found himself in a virtual shoot-out against another of the world's best players - and each time, he was the one left standing at the end.

Seasoned observers thought that Goosen's hopes had gone at Shinnecock when he lost his lead with four holes to go to an inspired and charging Mickelson. Yet he seemed oblivious to all the hoopla and, if anything, stepped his game up a gear, single putting five of the last six treacherously fast greens to seal a famous victory.

Goosen did not reach quite such heights in the final round at Fancourt. Indeed, Els put on the show of a master at work as he set about chasing down his friend and rival. It was Goosen, however, who produced the statistics which counted. He was the only player from a field of 156 who managed four rounds of par or better and it was he who came up with the shot of the tournament when it mattered most.

**Peter Dixon**
*The Times*

Ross Fisher

# Total Prize Fund
€1,006,955  £678,262

# Captain
# Fantastic

Graeme McDowell

THE ROYAL TROPHY

**EUROPE 9**          **ASIA 7**

**INDIVIDUAL PLAYER PERFORMANCES**

**EUROPE - Captain Seve Ballesteros**

| | | PLD | WON | LOST | HVD | PTS |
|---|---|-----|-----|------|-----|-----|
| Thomas Björn | | 3 | 2 | 1 | 0 | 2 |
| Nick Faldo | | 3 | 1 | 2 | 0 | 1 |
| Kenneth Ferrie | | 3 | 1 | 2 | 0 | 1 |
| David Howell | | 3 | 1 | 2 | 0 | 1 |
| Graeme McDowell | | 3 | 3 | 0 | 0 | 3 |
| Paul McGinley | | 3 | 3 | 0 | 0 | 3 |
| Henrik Stenson | | 3 | 3 | 0 | 0 | 3 |
| Ian Woosnam | | 3 | 1 | 2 | 0 | 1 |

**ASIA - Captain Masahiro Kuramoto**

| | | PLD | WON | LOST | HVD | PTS |
|---|---|-----|-----|------|-----|-----|
| Arjun Atwal | | 3 | 2 | 1 | 0 | 2 |
| Kelichiro Fukabori | | 3 | 1 | 2 | 0 | 1 |
| S K Ho | | 3 | 1 | 2 | 0 | 1 |
| Yasuharu Imano | | 3 | 1 | 2 | 0 | 1 |
| Thongchai Jaidee | | 3 | 1 | 2 | 0 | 1 |
| Jyoti Randhawa | | 3 | 1 | 2 | 0 | 1 |
| Thaworn Wiratchant | | 3 | 2 | 1 | 0 | 2 |
| Zhang Lian-Wei | | 3 | 0 | 3 | 0 | 0 |

**WEATHER REPORT**

Day One    Day Two

Okay, so he may not be quite the player he once was, but boy, is he a leader of men. When Seve Ballesteros walked up to receive the trophy on behalf of his team in the inaugural Royal Trophy in Thailand in January, he completed a treble that is likely to remain unique.

It meant that the Spanish maestro had now achieved what many might dream of but, thus far, has been granted to a club with just one member. He had captained teams that had won The Ryder Cup, The Seve Trophy and now this, the latest team event on the world stage.

But, even if he is no longer in his physical prime, that is to scratch the surface of the tale of this most complex of individuals. No matter that the back problems from which he has suffered for most of his career have reduced him to a shadow of the wondrous performer he was in his salad days. He is still a man who walks with the giants of the game from any era.

Five Major Championships, 82 victories in tournaments all round the world and a wonderful record in The Ryder Cup would make anybody one to be looked up to. Throw in a charisma that is still unmatched, even as he edges ever closer to his 50th birthday, and the cocktail becomes even more intoxicating.

He was, and still is, the inspiration who led millions of young players to take up the game, and not just in the country and the continent of his birth. He is a talismanic figure whose role in the early days of the modern European Tour was a pivotal one. He is its founding father and nobody would deny it.

We saw it on the first day of the match at the sumptuous Amata Spring Country Club on the outskirts of Bangkok. He watched as his men put a 6-2 lead on the board

Yasuharu Imano

and even weathered with equanimity what must have been the disappointment of seeing his senior partnership of Nick Faldo and Ian Woosnam beaten 6 and 5 by Thongchai Jaidee and Thaworn Wiratchant, pride of the host nation, in the opening foursomes.

This was Seve at his schoolmasterly best but it was the only setback for El Gran Señor on a grand opening day for Europe.

But that is to bring the now up to date before we have established the glorious past. The first demonstration of the aura that surrounds him came in 1997, when he captained Europe in the first home Ryder Cup to be played outside the British Isles. Club de Golfe Valderrama, on the south-west coast of Spain, was his feifdom on that rainy and storm-tossed week.

His captaincy style was not to everybody's taste. To describe him as energetic would be akin to suggesting that Sinatra was a decent crooner - true but a gross understatement.

Seve was like an ant on speed that week as he hurtled around the course on his buggy, busy almost to the point of being demented. He regularly awakened Miguel Angel Jiménez, his Vice-Captain, before dawn broke. 'The Mechanic' must have wondered what he'd let himself in for.

But - and this is the nub of the whole thing - it worked, as it did when he was in charge of the Continental Europe Team who played Great Britain and Ireland in the inaugural Seve Trophy, the competition that was named in honour of him, in 2000. He played in that match and defied all the odds by beating Colin Montgomerie, his opposing

*It's a great layout, especially over the closing holes which are tough in a close match. The last four holes in particular are a good test for any player. And the floating green on the eighth hole is pretty unusual as well* – **Graeme McDowell**

David Howell

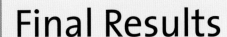

captain, in the last day singles. Seve's men won 13 ½ - 12 ½ and his was the victory that swung it - of course it was.

Imagine it - an old master against a much younger one. It should not have happened - Montgomerie won the official sterling equivalent of around £1 million that year, Ballesteros just over £16,000. Not the first time, somebody had been in thrall of the magic exuded by this guy and had paid a heavy price.

And now this. When it came to selecting a captain for this first match between Europe and Asia, there was only one name on the list. Seve it had to be. It was tight, especially on the last day, but Ballesteros's presence swung it vitally Europe's way.

The sorcerer's touch was seen at its best on a second and final day of singles. Things did not go entirely Europe's way after the triumph of the first eight matches but Seve stayed calm in the face of a determined assault by Asia.

Europe needed only 2 ½ points to win the trophy but at one point Asia were up in six of the eight matches, level in one and down in only one. But with the captain's hand firmly on the tiller, the visitors surged back, led by victories for Graeme McDowell and Paul McGinley.

It was a quiet word by Seve with McDowell on the ninth tee that did the trick and it was not long before things eventually turned

Europe's way. It was something of a surprise, Asia having seemed to be coasting to victory at one point, but in truth nobody should have really been shocked. This man has a record for being the heart and soul of any team with which he is involved.

Masahiro Kuramoto, the captain of the Asian team, is a distinguished presence himself. The one thing he isn't, however, is Seve and everything that goes with those four little letters. Nobody could even go close.

**Mel Webb**

Thaworn Wiratchant and Thongchai Jaidee

**Saturday Morning: Foursomes (Asian team names first)**

SK Ho (Kor) & Keiichiro Fukabori (Jpn) lost to
**David Howell (Eng) & Kenneth Ferrie (Eng)** 2 holes;

Arjun Atwal (Ind) & Jyoti Randhawa (Ind) lost to
**Paul McGinley (Ire) & Graeme McDowell (Nir)** 4 and 3;

Yasuharu Imano (Jpn) & Zhang Lian-wei (Prc) lost to
**Thomas Björn (Den) & Henrik Stenson (Swe)** 1 hole;

**Thaworn Wiratchant (Tha) & Thongchai Jaidee (Tha) beat**
Nick Faldo (Eng) & Ian Woosnam (Wal) 6 and 5

**Session Score: Asia 1 : 3 Europe**

**Saturday Afternoon: Fourballs**
**Atwal & Randhawa** beat Howell & Ferrie 1 hole;
Ho & Zhang lost to **McDowell & McGinley** 2 and 1;
Wiratchant & Jaidee lost to **Björn & Woosnam** 3 and 2;
Fukabori & Imano lost to **Faldo & Stenson** 1 hole

**Session score: Asia 1 : 3 Europe**
**Match Position: Asia 2 : 6 Europe**

**Sunday: Singles**
**Imano** beat Howell 2 holes;
Zhang lost to **McGinley** 2 and 1;
Randhawa lost to **McDowell** 3 and 2;
**Atwal** beat Faldo 3 and 2;
**Wiratchant** beat Woosnam 2 and 1;
**Ho** beat Ferrie 2 and 1;
**Fukabori** beat Björn 4 and 3;
Jaidee lost to **Stenson** 5 and 4;

**Session score: Asia 5 : 3 Europe**
**Final Match Score: Asia 7 : 9 Europe**

## Total Prize Fund
€1,266,674  £864,826

**Winners each received**  € 105,556  (£72,725)
**Losers each received**  € 52,778  (£36,362)

# Mature Beginning

George O'Grady, Executive Director of The European Tour, and H.H. Sheikh Sultan bin Tahnoun Al Nahyan

**I**t would be perfectly understandable for the promoters of any new golf tournament to dip their toes gently into the water and to treat their inaugural event as the first tentative steps on the road to a grand new adventure.

This, however, was clearly not the thought process that went into the staging of the Abu Dhabi Golf Championship as The 2006 European Tour International Schedule arrived on the shores of the Arabian Gulf, the tournament's sumptuous style setting a wonderful standard for the months ahead.

The setting was truly grand from the layout of the National Course, which barely a decade earlier had been desert scrubland, to the clubhouse fashioned in the shape of a giant falcon with its eyes scrutinising the players as they made their way towards the 18th green.

The style did not end at the course either, as the entire field of 120 were accommodated in the marbled expanse of The Emirates Palace, a hotel which gave a new meaning to the word deluxe. For example, the best brandy in the house – admittedly matured in oak casks for 140 years – cost a mere £1942 per measure.

Yet there were those present who could easily have afforded a tipple, for the cast assembled was surely one of the strongest ever for a European Tour event in January. The draw for the first two days, for example,

saw Vijay Singh, ranked second in the world, playing alongside Sergio Garcia, ranked sixth, and Colin Montgomerie, tenth.

Another threeball featured American Chris DiMarco, runner up to Tiger Woods in the 2005 Masters Tournament, playing alongside the current leader of The 2006 European Tour Order of Merit, England's David Howell, and the eight time European Tour winner Thomas Björn of Denmark.

Sergio Garcia and Vijay Singh

**Abu Dhabi Golf Club**

| Par | Yards | Metres |
|-----|-------|--------|
| 72 | 7348 | 6717 |

| | | | | |
|----|------------------------|-----|-----|---|
| 1 | **Chris DiMARCO** | 268 | -20 | |
| 2 | Henrik STENSON | 269 | -19 | |
| 3 | Sergio GARCIA | 270 | -18 | |
| 4 | Ricardo GONZALEZ | 271 | -17 | |
| 5 | Miguel Angel JIMÉNEZ | 273 | -15 | |
| 6 | Colin MONTGOMERIE | 275 | -13 | |
| | Jyoti RANDHAWA | 275 | -13 | |
| 8 | Charl SCHWARTZEL | 277 | -11 | |
| | Vijay SINGH | 277 | -11 | |
| 10 | David LYNN | 278 | -10 | |
| | Ian POULTER | 278 | -10 | |

**WEATHER REPORT**

| Round One | Round Two | Round Three | Round Four |
|-----------|-----------|-------------|------------|

**EUROPEAN TOUR ORDER OF MERIT**
(After six tournaments)

| Pos | | € | |
|-----|------------------|------------|---|
| 1 | **David HOWELL** | 704,516.80 | |
| 2 | Paul CASEY | 319,778.90 | |
| 3 | Ernie ELS | 273,636.82 | |
| 4 | Nick DOUGHERTY | 254,852.10 | |
| 5 | Colin MONTGOMERIE | 250,928.12 | |
| 6 | Nick O'HERN | 237,995.30 | |
| 7 | Henrik STENSON | 217,299.14 | |
| 8 | Vijay SINGH | 203,182.03 | |
| 9 | Thomas BJÖRN | 191,719.31 | |
| 10 | Charl SCHWARTZEL | 180,559.12 | |

Robert Karlsson

Yet putting the whole show together had not been without its headaches. The deaths of the rulers of both Dubai and Kuwait in the weeks leading up to the Championship and the subsequent periods of national mourning, created logistical difficulties in assembling the many components that go into building the grandstands, office complexes and tented village that form an integral part of modern golf tournaments.

There was sadness, too, inside the Tour camp. Three days before the first ball was hit, as the golfers began to arrive in the Emirate from all over the globe, a shadow was cast by the death of Harry Pithouse.

For 25 years Harry had been one of the unsung heroes of tournaments around the globe, being responsible for erecting the course ropes and stakes so vital for maintaining orderly galleries. Paying tribute to him, Peter German of promoters IMG, said: "Harry will be sadly missed. He was an artist and a perfectionist. He took tremendous pride in doing what for many was a straightforward and almost mundane role and turned it into an art form."

Harry would have been a stranger, though, to Keith Horne, whose name made a surprise appearance at the top of the first day leaderboard after shooting a course record 66.

The 34 year old South African, a late entry to the professional ranks after initially training as an industrial lawyer, only qualified for the

**❝** *The National Course is a great test of golf with a good mixture of holes, some which require length and others where shot making is the priority. The character of the course changes when the wind gets up* **❞** *– Phillip Price*

Andrew McLardy

| Pos | Name | | Rd1 | Rd2 | Rd3 | Rd4 | Total | | € | £ |
|---|---|---|---|---|---|---|---|---|---|---|
| 1 | Chris DIMARCO | USA | 71 | 67 | 63 | 67 | 268 | -20 | 275,411.69 | 188,162.59 |
| 2 | Henrik STENSON | SWE | 69 | 69 | 62 | 69 | 269 | -19 | 183,607.79 | 125,441.73 |
| 3 | Sergio GARCIA | ESP | 70 | 69 | 65 | 66 | 270 | -18 | 103,445.66 | 70,674.60 |
| 4 | Ricardo GONZALEZ | ARG | 68 | 68 | 67 | 68 | 271 | -17 | 82,624.34 | 56,449.34 |
| 5 | Miguel Angel JIMÉNEZ | ESP | 70 | 68 | 64 | 71 | 273 | -15 | 70,065.44 | 47,869.04 |
| 6 | Colin MONTGOMERIE | SCO | 72 | 68 | 65 | 70 | 275 | -13 | 53,705.82 | 36,692.07 |
|  | Jyoti RANDHAWA | IND | 71 | 70 | 69 | 65 | 275 | -13 | 53,705.82 | 36,692.07 |
| 8 | Vijay SINGH | FIJ | 68 | 70 | 69 | 70 | 277 | -11 | 39,163.93 | 26,756.98 |
|  | Charl SCHWARTZEL | RSA | 69 | 66 | 68 | 74 | 277 | -11 | 39,163.93 | 26,756.98 |
| 10 | David LYNN | ENG | 69 | 69 | 70 | 70 | 278 | -10 | 31,727.74 | 21,676.54 |
|  | Ian POULTER | ENG | 72 | 69 | 68 | 69 | 278 | -10 | 31,727.74 | 21,676.54 |
| 12 | Andrew MCLARDY | RSA | 71 | 70 | 69 | 69 | 279 | -9 | 25,580.49 | 17,476.71 |
|  | Mark FOSTER | ENG | 71 | 70 | 69 | 69 | 279 | -9 | 25,580.49 | 17,476.71 |
|  | Lian-Wei ZHANG | CHN | 74 | 69 | 68 | 68 | 279 | -9 | 25,580.49 | 17,476.71 |
|  | Francois DELAMONTAGNE | FRA | 71 | 69 | 69 | 70 | 279 | -9 | 25,580.49 | 17,476.71 |
|  | Thongchai JAIDEE | THA | 68 | 69 | 73 | 69 | 279 | -9 | 25,580.49 | 17,476.71 |
| 17 | Damien MCGRANE | IRL | 70 | 69 | 71 | 70 | 280 | -8 | 21,372.16 | 14,601.56 |
|  | Darren FICHARDT | RSA | 72 | 70 | 69 | 69 | 280 | -8 | 21,372.16 | 14,601.56 |
|  | Paul BROADHURST | ENG | 73 | 71 | 68 | 68 | 280 | -8 | 21,372.16 | 14,601.56 |
| 20 | Keith HORNE | RSA | 66 | 74 | 71 | 70 | 281 | -7 | 18,962.29 | 12,955.13 |
|  | Ignacio GARRIDO | ESP | 70 | 69 | 71 | 71 | 281 | -7 | 18,962.29 | 12,955.13 |
|  | Phillip PRICE | WAL | 73 | 70 | 67 | 71 | 281 | -7 | 18,962.29 | 12,955.13 |
|  | Richard GREEN | AUS | 70 | 70 | 70 | 71 | 281 | -7 | 18,962.29 | 12,955.13 |
| 24 | Raphaël JACQUELIN | FRA | 74 | 69 | 67 | 72 | 282 | -6 | 16,442.24 | 11,233.42 |
|  | Søren KJELDSEN | DEN | 72 | 70 | 68 | 72 | 282 | -6 | 16,442.24 | 11,233.42 |
|  | Stephen DODD | WAL | 73 | 71 | 70 | 68 | 282 | -6 | 16,442.24 | 11,233.42 |
|  | John BICKERTON | ENG | 72 | 70 | 68 | 72 | 282 | -6 | 16,442.24 | 11,233.42 |
|  | Thomas BJÖRN | DEN | 73 | 68 | 71 | 70 | 282 | -6 | 16,442.24 | 11,233.42 |
|  | José-Filipe LIMA | POR | 70 | 68 | 73 | 71 | 282 | -6 | 16,442.24 | 11,233.42 |
| 30 | Marcus FRASER | AUS | 73 | 69 | 68 | 73 | 283 | -5 | 13,715.64 | 9,370.59 |
|  | Robert KARLSSON | SWE | 73 | 69 | 67 | 74 | 283 | -5 | 13,715.64 | 9,370.59 |
|  | Gregory HAVRET | FRA | 70 | 68 | 74 | 71 | 283 | -5 | 13,715.64 | 9,370.59 |
|  | Steve WEBSTER | ENG | 73 | 66 | 72 | 72 | 283 | -5 | 13,715.64 | 9,370.59 |
|  | Anders HANSEN | DEN | 73 | 70 | 72 | 68 | 283 | -5 | 13,715.64 | 9,370.59 |
| 35 | Gordon BRAND JNR | SCO | 72 | 69 | 73 | 70 | 284 | -4 | 12,063.15 | 8,241.60 |
|  | Jamie SPENCE | ENG | 71 | 69 | 73 | 71 | 284 | -4 | 12,063.15 | 8,241.60 |
|  | Oliver WILSON | ENG | 72 | 72 | 71 | 69 | 284 | -4 | 12,063.15 | 8,241.60 |
| 38 | Wade ORMSBY | AUS | 74 | 70 | 70 | 71 | 285 | -3 | 10,410.67 | 7,112.62 |
|  | Simon WAKEFIELD | ENG | 75 | 68 | 68 | 74 | 285 | -3 | 10,410.67 | 7,112.62 |
|  | David PARK | WAL | 73 | 66 | 75 | 71 | 285 | -3 | 10,410.67 | 7,112.62 |
|  | Peter GUSTAFSSON | SWE | 69 | 73 | 73 | 70 | 285 | -3 | 10,410.67 | 7,112.62 |
|  | Gary EMERSON | ENG | 73 | 69 | 73 | 70 | 285 | -3 | 10,410.67 | 7,112.62 |
|  | Francesco MOLINARI | ITA | 73 | 70 | 71 | 71 | 285 | -3 | 10,410.67 | 7,112.62 |
|  | Jean-Francois REMESY | FRA | 73 | 70 | 73 | 69 | 285 | -3 | 10,410.67 | 7,112.62 |
| 45 | Anthony WALL | ENG | 73 | 70 | 74 | 69 | 286 | -2 | 8,427.68 | 5,757.83 |
|  | Marc CAYEUX | ZWE | 71 | 71 | 72 | 72 | 286 | -2 | 8,427.68 | 5,757.83 |
|  | Nick DOUGHERTY | ENG | 74 | 70 | 72 | 70 | 286 | -2 | 8,427.68 | 5,757.83 |
|  | Paul CASEY | ENG | 72 | 72 | 70 | 72 | 286 | -2 | 8,427.68 | 5,757.83 |
|  | Shiv KAPUR | IND | 75 | 66 | 73 | 72 | 286 | -2 | 8,427.68 | 5,757.83 |
| 50 | Graeme STORM | ENG | 72 | 72 | 73 | 70 | 287 | -1 | 5,873.84 | 4,013.03 |
|  | Alastair FORSYTH | SCO | 70 | 74 | 70 | 73 | 287 | -1 | 5,873.84 | 4,013.03 |
|  | Fredrik WIDMARK | SWE | 72 | 72 | 71 | 72 | 287 | -1 | 5,873.84 | 4,013.03 |
|  | Gary ORR | SCO | 74 | 70 | 69 | 74 | 287 | -1 | 5,873.84 | 4,013.03 |
|  | Peter HEDBLOM | SWE | 73 | 70 | 73 | 71 | 287 | -1 | 5,873.84 | 4,013.03 |
|  | Richard BLAND | ENG | 72 | 70 | 74 | 71 | 287 | -1 | 5,873.84 | 4,013.03 |
|  | Søren HANSEN | DEN | 70 | 66 | 74 | 77 | 287 | -1 | 5,873.84 | 4,013.03 |
|  | Barry LANE | ENG | 73 | 71 | 70 | 73 | 287 | -1 | 5,873.84 | 4,013.03 |
|  | Miguel Angel MARTIN | ESP | 74 | 69 | 71 | 73 | 287 | -1 | 5,873.84 | 4,013.03 |
|  | Costantino ROCCA | ITA | 71 | 73 | 71 | 72 | 287 | -1 | 5,873.84 | 4,013.03 |
|  | Ross BAIN | SCO | 69 | 73 | 74 | 71 | 287 | -1 | 5,873.84 | 4,013.03 |
| 61 | José Manuel LARA | ESP | 71 | 71 | 69 | 77 | 288 | 0 | 4,296.47 | 2,935.37 |
|  | Peter HANSON | SWE | 73 | 69 | 71 | 75 | 288 | 0 | 4,296.47 | 2,935.37 |
|  | Ian GARBUTT | ENG | 73 | 71 | 71 | 73 | 288 | 0 | 4,296.47 | 2,935.37 |
| 64 | Richard STERNE | RSA | 75 | 69 | 72 | 73 | 289 | 1 | 3,883.34 | 2,653.12 |
|  | Gonzalo FERNANDEZ-CASTANO | ESP | 70 | 74 | 71 | 74 | 289 | 1 | 3,883.34 | 2,653.12 |
| 66 | Mikael LUNDBERG | SWE | 72 | 72 | 73 | 73 | 290 | 2 | 3,387.60 | 2,314.42 |
|  | Stuart LITTLE | ENG | 72 | 72 | 71 | 75 | 290 | 2 | 3,387.60 | 2,314.42 |
|  | Mattias ELIASSON | SWE | 73 | 68 | 76 | 73 | 290 | 2 | 3,387.60 | 2,314.42 |
|  | Maarten LAFEBER | NED | 71 | 70 | 72 | 77 | 290 | 2 | 3,387.60 | 2,314.42 |
| 70 | Jean-Francois LUCQUIN | FRA | 71 | 72 | 74 | 76 | 293 | 5 | 3,015.79 | 2,060.40 |

tournament after a joint fifth place finish in the South African Airways Open before Christmas, but made the most of his early tee time to shoot six birdies before a wind gusting at up to 30 miles an hour blew in from the Gulf to make scoring difficult later in the day.

However, neither his record nor his pole position lasted long. By the third round, when the wind did not appear, the big names in the field began to shoot low numbers. Montgomerie moved into contention with a

Steve Webster

65 but held a share of the new course record with Garcia for just 63 minutes before Henrik Stenson signed off a 62.

Sandwiched between the trio with a 63 was DiMarco, clearly relishing his first appearance on The European Tour outside the Major Championships and the World Golf Championship events, even though, with his wife Amy carrying his bag, he had to work out all his own yardages and choose his own clubs.

In the end, it was DiMarco who went on to win the Championship. Setting off in the final round a shot behind Stenson, he birdied the first hole, sank a 35 foot eagle putt at the par five second and from the moment he picked up another shot at the fourth, he was at the top of the leaderboard and never to be caught.

As Montgomerie said: "He stayed in the Emirates Palace, which is second to none, the best hotel anywhere. It's nice that we can show the US PGA Tour that we have special events worldwide and I hope that when he gets home he can encourage more Americans to come and play over here."

**Graham Otway**

## Total Prize Fund
€1,652,450 £1,128,986

# Making Light of
# The Elements

Paul Broadhurst

### Doha Golf Club

| Par | Yards | Metres |
|-----|-------|--------|
| 72 | 7373 | 6742 |

| | | | | |
|---|---|---|---|---|
| 1 | Henrik STENSON | 273 | -15 | |
| 2 | Paul BROADHURST | 276 | -12 | |
| 3 | Darren FICHARDT | 277 | -11 | |
| 4 | Nick DOUGHERTY | 279 | -9 | |
| | Niclas FASTH | 279 | -9 | |
| | Richard FINCH | 279 | -9 | |
| | Ricardo GONZALEZ | 279 | -9 | |
| 8 | Graeme STORM | 280 | -8 | |
| 9 | Thomas BJÖRN | 282 | -6 | |
| | Maarten LAFEBER | 282 | -6 | |
| | David LYNN | 282 | -6 | |
| | Paul McGINLEY | 282 | -6 | |

W hen The European Tour left Abu Dhabi, few players could have been looking forward to the next event as much as Henrik Stenson. Even though the field for The Commercialbank Qatar Masters contained Ernie Els, the defending champion who was making his first appearance in 2006, as well as David Howell and Vijay Singh – together representing three of the top 14 players in the Official World Golf Ranking - the Swede had every reason to feel he was more in form than anyone. By the end of the week, he had proved that point conclusively with victory.

Ask around about the 29 year old Stenson and his fellow players talk of his length and his accuracy. To have one or the other of these attributes is not unusual but few people in Europe hit the ball so far as Stenson and no-one hits it so far and so straight. When this is coupled with good iron play and credible putting, as increasingly it is, then it becomes clear why Stenson's career has moved to

a new level and why he might be, as Paul Broadhurst, the man he edged into second place at Doha Golf Club put it, the "next special one in Europe."

Stenson turned professional in 1999, topped the Challenge Tour Rankings in 2000 and won the Benson and Hedges International Open in 2001. For a while after this he laboured in relative anonymity, even his victory in The Heritage in 2004 not removing entirely the feeling that he was one of many promising Scandinavian players with a victory or two to his name, who was either not ready or able to take the next step forward.

That changed in 2005. Solid performances throughout the year were underlined by the way he won three and halved two of his five matches at The Seve Trophy in September 2005. He followed that with an outstanding display at The Royal Trophy in Bangkok four

### WEATHER REPORT

| Round One | Round Two | Round Three | Round Four |
|-----------|-----------|-------------|------------|

### EUROPEAN TOUR ORDER OF MERIT
(After seven tournaments)

| Pos | | € | |
|-----|---|---|---|
| 1 | David HOWELL | 720,217.97 | |
| 2 | Henrik STENSON | 492,755.45 | |
| 3 | Nick DOUGHERTY | 319,887.99 | |
| 4 | Paul CASEY | 319,778.90 | |
| 5 | Ernie ELS | 299,585.06 | |
| 6 | Nick O'HERN | 257,266.42 | |
| 7 | Paul BROADHURST | 254,525.08 | |
| 8 | Colin MONTGOMERIE | 250,928.12 | |
| 9 | Thomas BJÖRN | 223,948.02 | |
| 10 | Vijay SINGH | 218,883.20 | |

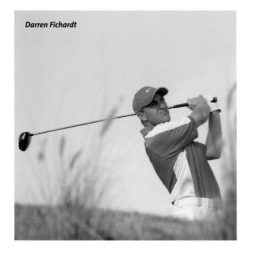

Darren Fichardt

Maarten Lafeber

Anthony Wall

months later where he won on all three of his outings. Then in Abu Dhabi, the first stroke play event of the 2006 calendar year, he finished runner-up to Chris DiMarco.

Qatar is not far from Sharjah where Stenson lives and all week he looked completely at home on the course where he finished second in 2005. The course is one that is as distinctive and testing in its own way as the Majlis Course in Dubai. Palm trees and rocky outcrops remind you it is laid out in a desert and raised tees create the impression that it

has more rise and fall to it than it actually has. Being in form and on such a course, Stenson was always going to be the man to beat.

This impression was heightened on the first day when he managed not to be outshone by 20 year old Englishman Danny Denison, who had won the Qatar Open, an amateur competition, before Christmas and gained entry to the professional event that way. When Denison went round in 67, four strokes fewer than Els and six less than Singh,

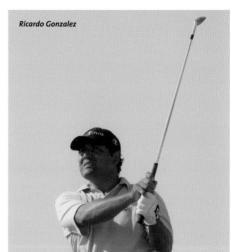

Ricardo Gonzalez

*This is a great test of golf. Length is a factor here which is good for me, especially this year as the fairways are a little softer and we are not getting so much run on the ball. The greens are in excellent condition, I think the best they have ever been* — Henrik Stenson

Richard Finch

# Final Results

| Pos | Name | | Rd1 | Rd2 | Rd3 | Rd4 | Total | | € | £ |
|---|---|---|---|---|---|---|---|---|---|---|
| 1 | Henrik STENSON | SWE | 66 | 68 | 71 | 68 | 273 | -15 | 275,456.31 | 188,716.53 |
| 2 | Paul BROADHURST | ENG | 72 | 67 | 67 | 70 | 276 | -12 | 183,637.54 | 125,811.02 |
| 3 | Darren FICHARDT | RSA | 67 | 72 | 70 | 68 | 277 | -11 | 103,462.43 | 70,882.64 |
| 4 | Ricardo GONZALEZ | ARG | 66 | 69 | 72 | 72 | 279 | -9 | 65,035.89 | 44,556.42 |
| | Niclas FASTH | SWE | 68 | 70 | 68 | 73 | 279 | -9 | 65,035.89 | 44,556.42 |
| | Nick DOUGHERTY | ENG | 69 | 67 | 73 | 70 | 279 | -9 | 65,035.89 | 44,556.42 |
| | Richard FINCH | ENG | 68 | 68 | 71 | 72 | 279 | -9 | 65,035.89 | 44,556.42 |
| 8 | Graeme STORM | ENG | 68 | 71 | 70 | 71 | 280 | -8 | 41,318.86 | 28,307.76 |
| 9 | Paul MCGINLEY | IRL | 69 | 70 | 70 | 73 | 282 | -6 | 32,228.71 | 22,080.05 |
| | Thomas BJÖRN | DEN | 71 | 68 | 71 | 72 | 282 | -6 | 32,228.71 | 22,080.05 |
| | David LYNN | ENG | 70 | 70 | 71 | 71 | 282 | -6 | 32,228.71 | 22,080.05 |
| | Maarten LAFEBER | NED | 71 | 68 | 72 | 71 | 282 | -6 | 32,228.71 | 22,080.05 |
| 13 | Ernie ELS | RSA | 71 | 71 | 69 | 72 | 283 | -5 | 25,948.24 | 17,777.27 |
| | Jarrod LYLE | AUS | 72 | 71 | 71 | 69 | 283 | -5 | 25,948.24 | 17,777.27 |
| 15 | Andrew BUCKLE | AUS | 71 | 72 | 70 | 71 | 284 | -4 | 22,808.01 | 15,625.88 |
| | Robert KARLSSON | SWE | 71 | 69 | 69 | 75 | 284 | -4 | 22,808.01 | 15,625.88 |
| | Thammanoon SRIROT | THA | 71 | 69 | 71 | 73 | 284 | -4 | 22,808.01 | 15,625.88 |
| | Anthony WALL | ENG | 74 | 71 | 68 | 71 | 284 | -4 | 22,808.01 | 15,625.88 |
| 19 | Steve WEBSTER | ENG | 72 | 71 | 71 | 71 | 285 | -3 | 19,271.12 | 13,202.74 |
| | Nick O'HERN | AUS | 71 | 74 | 71 | 69 | 285 | -3 | 19,271.12 | 13,202.74 |
| | Darren CLARKE | NIR | 71 | 74 | 72 | 68 | 285 | -3 | 19,271.12 | 13,202.74 |
| | Andrew COLTART | SCO | 69 | 72 | 73 | 71 | 285 | -3 | 19,271.12 | 13,202.74 |
| | Unho PARK | AUS | 71 | 70 | 70 | 74 | 285 | -3 | 19,271.12 | 13,202.74 |
| 24 | Charl SCHWARTZEL | RSA | 68 | 72 | 73 | 73 | 286 | -2 | 15,701.17 | 10,756.95 |
| | Thongchai JAIDEE | THA | 70 | 69 | 73 | 74 | 286 | -2 | 15,701.17 | 10,756.95 |
| | Bradley DREDGE | WAL | 69 | 72 | 74 | 71 | 286 | -2 | 15,701.17 | 10,756.95 |
| | Thaworn WIRATCHANT | THA | 73 | 69 | 71 | 73 | 286 | -2 | 15,701.17 | 10,756.95 |
| | Vijay SINGH | FIJ | 73 | 71 | 73 | 69 | 286 | -2 | 15,701.17 | 10,756.95 |
| | Joakim HAEGGMAN | SWE | 70 | 71 | 75 | 70 | 286 | -2 | 15,701.17 | 10,756.95 |
| | Jeev Milkha SINGH | IND | 72 | 71 | 70 | 73 | 286 | -2 | 15,701.17 | 10,756.95 |
| | David HOWELL | ENG | 73 | 71 | 69 | 73 | 286 | -2 | 15,701.17 | 10,756.95 |
| | José Manuel LARA | ESP | 72 | 72 | 71 | 71 | 286 | -2 | 15,701.17 | 10,756.95 |
| 33 | Miles TUNNICLIFF | ENG | 71 | 74 | 72 | 70 | 287 | -1 | 12,781.30 | 8,756.53 |
| | Richard STERNE | RSA | 72 | 68 | 71 | 76 | 287 | -1 | 12,781.30 | 8,756.53 |
| | Shiv KAPUR | IND | 75 | 67 | 77 | 68 | 287 | -1 | 12,781.30 | 8,756.53 |
| | Danny DENISON (AM) | ENG | 67 | 78 | 71 | 71 | 287 | -1 | | |
| 37 | Gonzalo FERNANDEZ-CASTANO | ESP | 77 | 68 | 73 | 70 | 288 | 0 | 11,238.73 | 7,699.71 |
| | Simon DYSON | ENG | 74 | 71 | 70 | 73 | 288 | 0 | 11,238.73 | 7,699.71 |
| | Prayad MARKSAENG | THA | 70 | 67 | 75 | 76 | 288 | 0 | 11,238.73 | 7,699.71 |
| | Angelo QUE | PHL | 71 | 72 | 72 | 73 | 288 | 0 | 11,238.73 | 7,699.71 |
| | Damien MCGRANE | IRL | 72 | 72 | 68 | 76 | 288 | 0 | 11,238.73 | 7,699.71 |
| | Anders HANSEN | DEN | 71 | 72 | 74 | 71 | 288 | 0 | 11,238.73 | 7,699.71 |
| 43 | Jean VAN DE VELDE | FRA | 69 | 71 | 75 | 74 | 289 | 1 | 9,090.15 | 6,227.71 |
| | Ian POULTER | ENG | 72 | 72 | 75 | 70 | 289 | 1 | 9,090.15 | 6,227.71 |
| | Marcel SIEM | GER | 69 | 71 | 74 | 75 | 289 | 1 | 9,090.15 | 6,227.71 |
| | James KINGSTON | RSA | 77 | 68 | 73 | 71 | 289 | 1 | 9,090.15 | 6,227.71 |
| | Chris RODGERS | ENG | 73 | 71 | 72 | 73 | 289 | 1 | 9,090.15 | 6,227.71 |
| | Christopher HANELL | SWE | 71 | 72 | 71 | 75 | 289 | 1 | 9,090.15 | 6,227.71 |
| | Peter GUSTAFSSON | SWE | 70 | 72 | 70 | 77 | 289 | 1 | 9,090.15 | 6,227.71 |
| 50 | Miguel Angel JIMÉNEZ | ESP | 71 | 73 | 70 | 76 | 290 | 2 | 7,602.67 | 5,208.63 |
| | Andrew OLDCORN | SCO | 71 | 74 | 72 | 73 | 290 | 2 | 7,602.67 | 5,208.63 |
| 52 | Joakim BÄCKSTRÖM | SWE | 71 | 69 | 75 | 76 | 291 | 3 | 6,776.29 | 4,642.47 |
| | Peter LAWRIE | IRL | 72 | 71 | 72 | 76 | 291 | 3 | 6,776.29 | 4,642.47 |
| | John BICKERTON | ENG | 72 | 72 | 68 | 78 | 291 | 3 | 6,776.29 | 4,642.47 |
| 55 | Rahil GANGJEE | IND | 75 | 68 | 70 | 79 | 292 | 4 | 5,619.37 | 3,849.86 |
| | Gaurav GHEI | IND | 72 | 73 | 74 | 73 | 292 | 4 | 5,619.37 | 3,849.86 |
| | Ignacio GARRIDO | ESP | 72 | 73 | 74 | 73 | 292 | 4 | 5,619.37 | 3,849.86 |
| | Emanuele CANONICA | ITA | 75 | 68 | 73 | 76 | 292 | 4 | 5,619.37 | 3,849.86 |
| 59 | Adam FRASER | AUS | 72 | 69 | 78 | 74 | 293 | 5 | 4,792.99 | 3,283.70 |
| | Scott STRANGE | AUS | 75 | 70 | 73 | 75 | 293 | 5 | 4,792.99 | 3,283.70 |
| | Terry PILKADARIS | AUS | 71 | 72 | 75 | 75 | 293 | 5 | 4,792.99 | 3,283.70 |
| 62 | Louis OOSTHUIZEN | RSA | 73 | 72 | 73 | 76 | 294 | 6 | 4,297.16 | 2,944.01 |
| | Simon YATES | SCO | 69 | 73 | 74 | 78 | 294 | 6 | 4,297.16 | 2,944.01 |
| | Chawalit PLAPHOL | THA | 67 | 74 | 71 | 82 | 294 | 6 | 4,297.16 | 2,944.01 |
| 65 | Kenneth FERRIE | ENG | 75 | 70 | 71 | 79 | 295 | 7 | 3,966.61 | 2,717.55 |
| 66 | Jyoti RANDHAWA | IND | 71 | 72 | 75 | RETD | 218 | 2 | 3,801.34 | 2,604.32 |

## Total Prize Fund
€1,636,185  £1,120,959

and left six European 2004 Ryder Cup Team Members in action – Darren Clarke, Miguel Angel Jiménez, Paul McGinley, Ian Poulter, Lee Westwood and Howell - at least two strokes behind him, Stenson had a 66 and shared the lead with Ricardo Gonzalez.

A 68 in the second round gave Stenson a one stroke lead, which he maintained after 54 holes. Sunday dawned unusually overcast and with a wind that was even stronger than Saturday's. However, with accurate ball striking and big-hitting, Stenson made light of the elements. At the tenth, he hit his drive 295 yards and followed that with a 260 yard three wood, both shots into a 20mph wind. On the downwind 11th, he hit his drive a conservative 360 yards.

Broadhurst twice got to within one stroke but each time he did so Stenson rallied and pulled away. On the 15th, Stenson flirted with a pond that guards the green to emerge with a birdie and on the 17th, after Broadhurst had once more drawn to within one stroke, he holed a 30 foot putt from the fringe of the green for a telling birdie two. A further birdie on the 72nd hole widened his lead and his margin of victory to three strokes.

This was an impressive performance by a young man who was three months short of his 30th birthday and it virtually assured his place in Ian Woosnam's European Team for The 2006 Ryder Cup. What is more, it probably had a few potential team-mates trembling with excitement at the thought of having such a big-hitting, accurate player with whom to play in the foursomes or fourballs at The K Club in September 2006.

**John Hopkins**
*The Times*

Niclas Fasth

# Fast Track
# To Glory

*Richard Green*

**Emirates Golf Club**

| Par | Yards | Metres |
|-----|-------|--------|
| 72  | 7264  | 6643   |

| | | | | |
|---|---|---|---|---|
| 1 | Tiger WOODS | 269 | -19 | |
| 2 | Ernie ELS | 269 | -19 | |
| 3 | Richard GREEN | 270 | -18 | |
| 4 | Anders HANSEN | 271 | -17 | |
| | Miguel Angel JIMÉNEZ | 271 | -17 | |
| 6 | Retief GOOSEN | 272 | -16 | |
| 7 | Darren CLARKE | 273 | -15 | |
| | Henrik STENSON | 273 | -15 | |
| 9 | Emanuele CANONICA | 274 | -14 | |
| | Nick DOUGHERTY | 274 | -14 | |

**WEATHER REPORT**

| Round One | Round Two | Round Three | Round Four |
|-----------|-----------|-------------|------------|

There was once a time when, to find the Emirates Golf Club, you would simply drive out of Dubai city on the main Abu Dhabi road until you found a lone building standing in the desert. It was the Hard Rock Cafe and it signalled the moment to turn left. That establishment still stands, but now amid a forest of skyscrapers all at various stages of construction. In fact, some locals now jokingly refer to it as the Hard Hat Cafe.

Dubai is currently home to a plethora of cranes and its skyline is ever changing. Stand on the 18th tee on the Majlis Course and you can count nearly fifty high-rise buildings. Office blocks, apartments, hotels and showrooms are springing up at an extraordinary rate. But some things never change, like the Dubai Desert Classic's unerring ability to attract fields of the highest quality and tournament finishes that constitute sporting drama of the highest order.

The staging of the 2006 event came a month or so earlier than usual but the field was as strong as ever, and the thrilling climax will live long in the memory. Not even the congested traffic on that Abu Dhabi road – a ten lane straight line equivalent of the M25 - could deter the likes of Ernie Els, Retief Goosen, Richard Green, Anders Hansen, Miguel Angel Jiménez and Tiger Woods from putting on a show to remember.

In many respects the traffic experience was the ideal preparation – or at least it offered a parallel - for the four days of action. To win the 2006 Dubai Desert Classic, the champion needed to be able to negotiate his way through a congested leaderboard. It was a case of ducking and diving, bobbing and weaving to find the right lane that would send you on the fast track to glory.

**EUROPEAN TOUR ORDER OF MERIT**
(After eight tournaments)

| Pos | | € | |
|-----|---|---|---|
| 1 | David HOWELL | 737,233.60 | |
| 2 | Henrik STENSON | 547,165.89 | |
| 3 | Ernie ELS | 519,419.78 | |
| 4 | Nick DOUGHERTY | 361,833.50 | |
| 5 | Paul CASEY | 346,489.49 | |
| 6 | Nick O'HERN | 281,009.16 | |
| 7 | Paul BROADHURST | 275,398.91 | |
| 8 | Colin MONTGOMERIE | 250,928.12 | |
| 9 | Thomas BJÖRN | 232,653.69 | |
| 10 | Retief GOOSEN | 227,828.96 | |

# Dubai Desert Classic

## Dubai, United Arab Emirates
### February 2-5 • 2006

Jyoti Randhawa

Woods was to prevail, but not before hitting several apparent roadblocks on the way. As he approached the halfway stage of his second round, the World Number One would have been oblivious to a mass of red brake lights that lay ahead. He was motoring on cruise control without a care in the world. Then he faltered and from that moment the tournament was anything but straightforward.

Going into the final round Woods, the reigning Masters Tournament and Open Champion, was sharing the lead with Hansen; Goosen, the World Number Three, was a shot back; and Els, the title holder bidding for a fourth Desert victory, lay in a group just two off the pace. We always dare to hope for such superstar scenarios, but given the depth of talent in world golf they do not always materialise.

The leaderboard remained as busy as the surrounding roads throughout that glorious final afternoon. Els was making serene progress and was soon leading. Goosen

faltered, while Woods was all over the place. Drives were going left and right, never - it seemed - down the middle, yet with the most extraordinary powers of recovery he was able to stay in touch.

But so, too, did Green. The left-handed

Australian had beaten Greg Norman and Ian Woosnam in a play-off to take this very title in 1997. It looked as though he had timed his run to perfection – overtaking playing partner Els with a burst of late birdies to take a one stroke lead to the 18th.

Miguel Angel Jiménez

*" The golf course is in good shape again and the greens are so smooth. As always it was a different test in the wind which made play in the afternoon a bit trickier. But overall the course played really nicely, the greens were holding and they were really good to putt out on. It was a pleasure to play "*
*- Søren Hansen*

Barry Lane

| Pos | Name | | Rd1 | Rd2 | Rd3 | Rd4 | Total | | € | £ |
|---|---|---|---|---|---|---|---|---|---|---|
| 1 | Tiger WOODS | USA | 67 | 66 | 67 | 69 | 269 | -19 | 329,760.33 | 225,568.14 |
| 2 | Ernie ELS | RSA | 68 | 66 | 68 | 67 | 269 | -19 | 219,834.72 | 150,375.00 |
| 3 | Richard GREEN | AUS | 64 | 69 | 69 | 68 | 270 | -18 | 123,857.98 | 84,723.39 |
| 4 | Anders HANSEN | DEN | 68 | 63 | 69 | 71 | 271 | -17 | 91,409.56 | 62,527.49 |
| | Miguel Angel JIMÉNEZ | ESP | 69 | 67 | 66 | 69 | 271 | -17 | 91,409.56 | 62,527.49 |
| 6 | Retief GOOSEN | RSA | 64 | 67 | 70 | 71 | 272 | -16 | 69,249.67 | 47,369.31 |
| 7 | Darren CLARKE | NIR | 68 | 68 | 70 | 67 | 273 | -15 | 54,410.45 | 37,218.74 |
| | Henrik STENSON | SWE | 6. | 70 | 68 | 68 | 273 | -15 | 54,410.45 | 37,218.74 |
| 9 | Emanuele CANONICA | ITA | 69 | 68 | 71 | 66 | 274 | -14 | 41,945.51 | 28,692.27 |
| | Nick DOUGHERTY | ENG | 67 | 66 | 70 | 71 | 274 | -14 | 41,945.51 | 28,692.27 |
| 11 | Niclas FASTH | SWE | 67 | 68 | 73 | 67 | 275 | -13 | 35,218.40 | 24,090.68 |
| | Raphaël JACQUELIN | FRA | 68 | 71 | 68 | 68 | 275 | -13 | 35,218.40 | 24,090.68 |
| 13 | Johan EDFORS | SWE | 69 | 67 | 72 | 68 | 276 | -12 | 30,403.90 | 20,797.38 |
| | Jyoti RANDHAWA | IND | 71 | 68 | 66 | 71 | 276 | -12 | 30,403.90 | 20,797.38 |
| | Bradley DREDGE | WAL | 70 | 66 | 68 | 72 | 276 | -12 | 30,403.90 | 20,797.38 |
| 16 | Christopher HANELL | SWE | 71 | 71 | 67 | 68 | 277 | -11 | 26,710.59 | 18,271.02 |
| | Richard STERNE | RSA | 69 | 69 | 70 | 69 | 277 | -11 | 26,710.59 | 18,271.02 |
| | Paul CASEY | ENG | 67 | 69 | 71 | 70 | 277 | -11 | 26,710.59 | 18,271.02 |
| 19 | Simon DYSON | ENG | 70 | 71 | 66 | 71 | 278 | -10 | 23,742.74 | 16,240.90 |
| | David LYNN | ENG | 66 | 74 | 71 | 67 | 278 | -10 | 23,742.74 | 16,240.90 |
| | Nick O'HERN | AUS | 67 | 72 | 73 | 66 | 278 | -10 | 23,742.74 | 16,240.90 |
| 22 | Paul BROADHURST | ENG | 69 | 69 | 67 | 74 | 279 | -9 | 20,873.83 | 14,278.46 |
| | Damien MCGRANE | IRL | 68 | 68 | 73 | 70 | 279 | -9 | 20,873.83 | 14,278.46 |
| | Peter LAWRIE | IRL | 69 | 66 | 69 | 75 | 279 | -9 | 20,873.83 | 14,278.46 |
| | Paul LAWRIE | SCO | 71 | 70 | 70 | 68 | 279 | -9 | 20,873.83 | 14,278.46 |
| | Stephen GALLACHER | SCO | 70 | 69 | 68 | 72 | 279 | -9 | 20,873.83 | 14,278.46 |
| | Thongchai JAIDEE | THA | 70 | 71 | 69 | 69 | 279 | -9 | 20,873.83 | 14,278.46 |
| 28 | Lee WESTWOOD | ENG | 68 | 71 | 69 | 72 | 280 | -8 | 17,015.63 | 11,639.31 |
| | Andrew COLTART | SCO | 71 | 70 | 67 | 72 | 280 | -8 | 17,015.63 | 11,639.31 |
| | Simon KHAN | ENG | 72 | 70 | 70 | 68 | 280 | -8 | 17,015.63 | 11,639.31 |
| | Ricardo GONZALEZ | ARG | 69 | 68 | 70 | 73 | 280 | -8 | 17,015.63 | 11,639.31 |
| | Alessandro TADINI | ITA | 69 | 74 | 67 | 70 | 280 | -8 | 17,015.63 | 11,639.31 |
| | David HOWELL | ENG | 70 | 69 | 70 | 71 | 280 | -8 | 17,015.63 | 11,639.31 |
| | Robert KARLSSON | SWE | 71 | 67 | 72 | 70 | 280 | -8 | 17,015.63 | 11,639.31 |
| 35 | Stuart LITTLE | ENG | 69 | 69 | 71 | 72 | 281 | -7 | 14,641.36 | 10,015.23 |
| | Jamie DONALDSON | WAL | 64 | 70 | 74 | 73 | 281 | -7 | 14,641.36 | 10,015.23 |
| 37 | Richard FINCH | ENG | 71 | 71 | 69 | 71 | 282 | -6 | 13,454.22 | 9,203.18 |
| | Ignacio GARRIDO | ESP | 70 | 70 | 75 | 67 | 282 | -6 | 13,454.22 | 9,203.18 |
| | David PARK | WAL | 70 | 71 | 72 | 69 | 282 | -6 | 13,454.22 | 9,203.18 |
| | Costantino ROCCA | ITA | 68 | 73 | 70 | 71 | 282 | -6 | 13,454.22 | 9,203.18 |
| 41 | Steve WEBSTER | ENG | 70 | 70 | 69 | 74 | 283 | -5 | 11,475.66 | 7,849.77 |
| | Søren HANSEN | DEN | 70 | 65 | 75 | 73 | 283 | -5 | 11,475.66 | 7,849.77 |
| | Jamie SPENCE | ENG | 70 | 71 | 71 | 71 | 283 | -5 | 11,475.66 | 7,849.77 |
| | Marc CAYEUX | ZWE | 69 | 66 | 74 | 74 | 283 | -5 | 11,475.66 | 7,849.77 |
| | Markus BRIER | AUT | 70 | 73 | 71 | 69 | 283 | -5 | 11,475.66 | 7,849.77 |
| | Phillip PRICE | WAL | 69 | 70 | 73 | 71 | 283 | -5 | 11,475.66 | 7,849.77 |
| 47 | Thomas BJÖRN | DEN | 69 | 70 | 74 | 71 | 284 | -4 | 8,705.67 | 5,955.00 |
| | Simon WAKEFIELD | ENG | 70 | 70 | 74 | 70 | 284 | -4 | 8,705.67 | 5,955.00 |
| | David CARTER | ENG | 72 | 71 | 69 | 72 | 284 | -4 | 8,705.67 | 5,955.00 |
| | Oliver WILSON | ENG | 68 | 75 | 70 | 71 | 284 | -4 | 8,705.67 | 5,955.00 |
| | Ian POULTER | ENG | 72 | 67 | 72 | 73 | 284 | -4 | 8,705.67 | 5,955.00 |
| | Ross BAIN | SCO | 66 | 71 | 78 | 69 | 284 | -4 | 8,705.67 | 5,955.00 |
| | Robert-Jan DERKSEN | NED | 71 | 72 | 69 | 72 | 284 | -4 | 8,705.67 | 5,955.00 |
| | Mark FOSTER | ENG | 68 | 68 | 74 | 74 | 284 | -4 | 8,705.67 | 5,955.00 |
| 55 | Barry LANE | ENG | 68 | 71 | 70 | 76 | 285 | -3 | 5,910.95 | 4,043.31 |
| | Garry HOUSTON | WAL | 73 | 68 | 70 | 74 | 285 | -3 | 5,910.95 | 4,043.31 |
| | Phillip ARCHER | ENG | 70 | 70 | 72 | 73 | 285 | -3 | 5,910.95 | 4,043.31 |
| | Joakim BÄCKSTRÖM | SWE | 68 | 73 | 71 | 73 | 285 | -3 | 5,910.95 | 4,043.31 |
| | Joakim HAEGGMAN | SWE | 72 | 71 | 71 | 71 | 285 | -3 | 5,910.95 | 4,043.31 |
| | Paul SHEEHAN | AUS | 73 | 68 | 72 | 72 | 285 | -3 | 5,910.95 | 4,043.31 |
| | Alastair FORSYTH | SCO | 70 | 71 | 72 | 72 | 285 | -3 | 5,910.95 | 4,043.31 |
| | Christian CÉVAËR | FRA | 72 | 71 | 72 | 70 | 285 | -3 | 5,910.95 | 4,043.31 |
| 63 | Gary ORR | SCO | 69 | 74 | 70 | 73 | 286 | -2 | 4,748.55 | 3,248.18 |
| | Peter O'MALLEY | AUS | 70 | 72 | 73 | 71 | 286 | -2 | 4,748.55 | 3,248.18 |
| | Mark O'MEARA | USA | 71 | 71 | 73 | 71 | 286 | -2 | 4,748.55 | 3,248.18 |
| 66 | Andrew OLDCORN | SCO | 71 | 67 | 70 | 79 | 287 | -1 | 4,154.98 | 2,842.16 |
| | Jonathan LOMAS | ENG | 72 | 71 | 72 | 72 | 287 | -1 | 4,154.98 | 2,842.16 |
| | Marcel SIEM | GER | 71 | 72 | 71 | 73 | 287 | -1 | 4,154.98 | 2,842.16 |
| 69 | Stephen DODD | WAL | 72 | 71 | 75 | 70 | 288 | 0 | 3,446.05 | 2,357.22 |
| | Scott DRUMMOND | SCO | 73 | 70 | 72 | 73 | 288 | 0 | 3,446.05 | 2,357.22 |
| | Marcus FRASER | AUS | 71 | 71 | 72 | 74 | 288 | 0 | 3,446.05 | 2,357.22 |
| 72 | John BICKERTON | ENG | 72 | 71 | 70 | 76 | 289 | 1 | 2,963.50 | 2,027.14 |
| | Peter HANSON | SWE | 71 | 70 | 74 | 74 | 289 | 1 | 2,963.50 | 2,027.14 |
| 74 | Martin ERLANDSSON | SWE | 68 | 75 | 71 | 77 | 291 | 3 | 2,959.00 | 2,024.06 |
| 75 | Wade ORMSBY | AUS | 70 | 73 | 79 | 70 | 292 | 4 | 2,956.00 | 2,022.01 |
| 76 | Gary EMERSON | ENG | 73 | 69 | 74 | 78 | 294 | 6 | 2,953.00 | 2,019.96 |

His challenge, however, was to prove nothing more than a mirage – at first he found sand and then real water to run up a costly bogey six. Els birdied to take the clubhouse lead before Woods, at last, found clear road to hit the accelerator pedal. He drove the 359 yard 17th to birdie before getting up and down from the back of the final green to pick up another shot and force a play-off with the South African.

On their return to the 18th, Els followed the same route as Green had earlier and a costly bogey enabled Woods to triumph with a routine par. It meant the American had won his first two tournaments of the year, following his Buick Invitational play-off victory over Nathan Green and José Maria Olazábal on the US PGA Tour the previous week.

His golfing life surely could not be any better? "It can always be better," said Woods, adding: "But that's golf." Like Dubai itself, Woods's golf game, apparently, is a construction job that will never end.

**Iain Carter**

*BBC Radio Five Live*

David Lynn

## Total Prize Fund
€1,996,320 £1,365,559

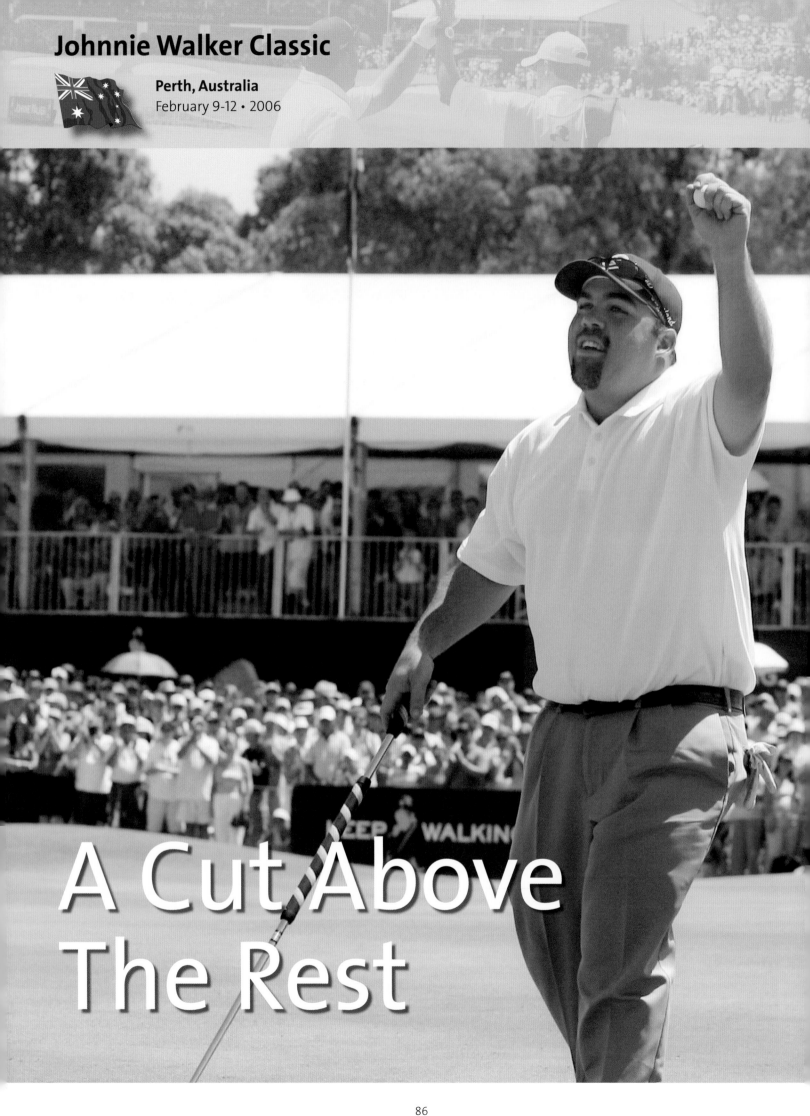

# A Cut Above
# The Rest

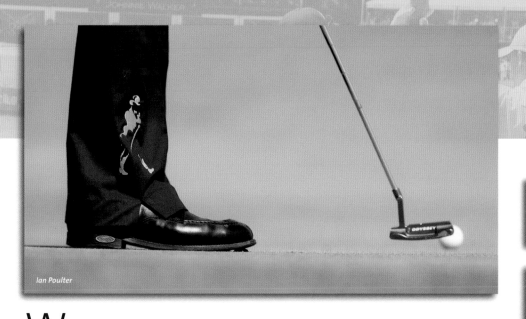
Ian Poulter

| Pos | Name | Score | To Par | |
|-----|------|-------|--------|---|
| 1 | Kevin STADLER | 268 | -20 | |
| 2 | Nick O'HERN | 270 | -18 | |
| 3 | Robert ALLENBY | 272 | -16 | |
| | Richard GREEN | 272 | -16 | |
| 5 | K J CHOI | 273 | -15 | |
| 6 | Francesco MOLINARI | 274 | -14 | |
| | Ian POULTER | 274 | -14 | |
| | Adam SCOTT | 274 | -14 | |
| 9 | Fred COUPLES | 275 | -13 | |
| | David DIAZ | 275 | -13 | |
| | Gavin FLINT | 275 | -13 | |

W hat price a pair of trousers? With a shirt thrown in? The answer, depending on the colour of the said garments, was: AU$3,250 for the red ensemble; AU$3,000 for the blue; AU$6,500 for the gold and AU$6,750 for those in black - Johnnie Walker Black, of course.

Ian Poulter, the man with the gathering of garments, may not have made his hoped for golfing impact in the Johnnie Walker Classic at The Vines Resort and Country Club in Perth, but golf's own fashionista nevertheless used his individual flair in the clothing department to raise AU$26,000 for environmental charities in Australia.

Poulter was to finish tied for sixth, behind Craig Stadler's not so little lad, Kevin, but he made full use of a brilliant marketing ploy to draw attention to himself and the sponsor before raising the equivalent of £11,555. The clothing colours equated to the various Johnnie Walker brand names - Red Label, Blue Label, Black Label and Gold Label - and the custom-tailored trousers and shirts were auctioned at a swish dinner in a Perth casino.

Top money was paid by Robert Allenby in buying the Black outfit, before immediately giving it back and inviting the under bidder to repeat his offer of AU$6,500, hence making up the AU$26,000 total.

It was a wonderful gesture by the Australian golfer, who was attempting to make history in his home country by winning four events in succession, following earlier successes in the MFS Australian Open, the Cadbury Schweppes Australian PGA Championship and the MasterCard Masters. He did not quite succeed, although a final round 66 to take him to joint third with Richard Green, meant a pay day of €103,188 (£70,375).

Stadler was a surprise winner not only because he does not currently possess a card for the US PGA Tour, but also because he nearly did not play in the first place. Having decided he would compete in the Nationwide Tour co-sanctioned Jacobs Creek event the following week, he realised it would make sense to play in Perth as well, and pleaded for an invitation. Fred Couples put a word in, and he was accepted.

Shiv Kapur

### WEATHER REPORT

| Round One | Round Two | Round Three | Round Four |
|-----------|-----------|-------------|------------|

### EUROPEAN TOUR ORDER OF MERIT
(After nine tournaments)

| Pos | | € | |
|-----|---|---|---|
| 1 | David HOWELL | 737,233.60 | |
| 2 | Henrik STENSON | 547,165.89 | |
| 3 | Ernie ELS | 519,419.78 | |
| 4 | Nick O'HERN | 484,644.76 | |
| 5 | Paul CASEY | 372,332.50 | |
| 6 | Nick DOUGHERTY | 361,833.50 | |
| 7 | Richard GREEN | 275,628.16 | |
| 8 | Paul BROADHURST | 275,398.91 | |
| 9 | Colin MONTGOMERIE | 250,928.12 | |
| 10 | Thomas BJÖRN | 232,653.69 | |

*"I think the last nine holes here at The Vines is the finest nine hole stretch in Australian golf and the last three holes are some of the toughest we face too. I love coming here and it is great to be back in Western Australia"* – **Michael Campbell**

Francesco Molinari

Those who have watched father Craig play would have no problem in identifying Kevin as his son. The word burly might have been coined for both of them and the ball is dispatched with a minimum of fuss. Thankfully however, Kevin, at least on the basis of this week, does not seem to possess dad's ability to leave a club quivering in the ground with all of the head and half the shaft buried. Admittedly he was playing well, but he still demonstrated a temperament that knows how to win.

One shot in particular will remain with all who saw it, and it was played when the pressure was at its height and the need for a good swing was paramount. Stadler, who had eagled the 514 yard 18th in the two previous rounds, came to the 72nd hole tied, at 18 under par, with Nick O'Hern.

# Final Results

| Pos | Name | | Rd1 | Rd2 | Rd3 | Rd4 | Total | | € | £ |
|---|---|---|---|---|---|---|---|---|---|---|
| 1 | Kevin STADLER | USA | 64 | 69 | 66 | 69 | 268 | -20 | 305,468.02 | 208,330.00 |
| 2 | Nick O'HERN | AUS | 67 | 71 | 64 | 68 | 270 | -18 | 203,635.57 | 138,880.00 |
| 3 | Richard GREEN | AUS | 66 | 69 | 66 | 71 | 272 | -16 | 103,188.75 | 70,375.00 |
| | Robert ALLENBY | AUS | 69 | 68 | 69 | 66 | 272 | -16 | 103,188.75 | 70,375.00 |
| 5 | K J CHOI | KOR | 65 | 66 | 70 | 72 | 273 | -15 | 77,712.31 | 53,000.00 |
| 6 | Francesco MOLINARI | ITA | 71 | 65 | 66 | 72 | 274 | -14 | 54,985.12 | 37,500.00 |
| | Ian POULTER | ENG | 70 | 66 | 69 | 69 | 274 | -14 | 54,985.12 | 37,500.00 |
| | Adam SCOTT | AUS | 64 | 71 | 70 | 69 | 274 | -14 | 54,985.12 | 37,500.00 |
| 9 | David DIAZ | AUS | 69 | 72 | 64 | 70 | 275 | -13 | 37,145.51 | 25,333.33 |
| | Gavin FLINT | AUS | 72 | 64 | 66 | 73 | 275 | -13 | 37,145.51 | 25,333.33 |
| | Fred COUPLES | USA | 71 | 67 | 65 | 72 | 275 | -13 | 37,145.51 | 25,333.33 |
| 12 | Chris CAMPBELL | AUS | 71 | 67 | 67 | 71 | 276 | -12 | 29,691.97 | 20,250.00 |
| | Ross FISHER | ENG | 69 | 67 | 68 | 72 | 276 | -12 | 29,691.97 | 20,250.00 |
| | Shiv KAPUR | IND | 68 | 71 | 67 | 70 | 276 | -12 | 29,691.97 | 20,250.00 |
| 15 | Andrew BUCKLE | AUS | 73 | 69 | 67 | 68 | 277 | -11 | 25,843.01 | 17,625.00 |
| | Paul CASEY | ENG | 68 | 69 | 67 | 73 | 277 | -11 | 25,843.01 | 17,625.00 |
| | Prayad MARKSAENG | THA | 72 | 66 | 70 | 69 | 277 | -11 | 25,843.01 | 17,625.00 |
| 18 | Stephen ALLAN | AUS | 72 | 69 | 67 | 70 | 278 | -10 | 22,788.28 | 15,541.67 |
| | Craig PARRY | AUS | 68 | 70 | 65 | 75 | 278 | -10 | 22,788.28 | 15,541.67 |
| | Sung-Man LEE | KOR | 71 | 71 | 64 | 72 | 278 | -10 | 22,788.28 | 15,541.67 |
| 21 | Peter O'MALLEY | AUS | 69 | 70 | 67 | 73 | 279 | -9 | 19,061.51 | 13,000.00 |
| | Steve WEBSTER | ENG | 71 | 68 | 68 | 72 | 279 | -9 | 19,061.51 | 13,000.00 |
| | Stephen LEANEY | AUS | 70 | 66 | 69 | 74 | 279 | -9 | 19,061.51 | 13,000.00 |
| | Søren KJELDSEN | DEN | 70 | 71 | 67 | 71 | 279 | -9 | 19,061.51 | 13,000.00 |
| | Peter SENIOR | AUS | 68 | 68 | 72 | 71 | 279 | -9 | 19,061.51 | 13,000.00 |
| | Kim FELTON | AUS | 71 | 68 | 67 | 73 | 279 | -9 | 19,061.51 | 13,000.00 |
| | Scott GARDINER | AUS | 70 | 66 | 74 | 69 | 279 | -9 | 19,061.51 | 13,000.00 |
| | Leigh MCKECHNIE | AUS | 73 | 66 | 70 | 70 | 279 | -9 | 19,061.51 | 13,000.00 |
| | Nick FLANAGAN | AUS | 72 | 68 | 66 | 73 | 279 | -9 | 19,061.51 | 13,000.00 |
| 30 | Ian GARBUTT | ENG | 71 | 69 | 70 | 70 | 280 | -8 | 15,762.40 | 10,750.00 |
| | Angel CABRERA | ARG | 73 | 68 | 71 | 68 | 280 | -8 | 15,762.40 | 10,750.00 |
| | Tony CAROLAN | AUS | 66 | 69 | 75 | 70 | 280 | -8 | 15,762.40 | 10,750.00 |
| 33 | Simon YATES | SCO | 72 | 70 | 73 | 66 | 281 | -7 | 13,593.54 | 9,270.83 |
| | Sam LITTLE | ENG | 70 | 71 | 70 | 70 | 281 | -7 | 13,593.54 | 9,270.83 |
| | Gary EMERSON | ENG | 70 | 70 | 71 | 70 | 281 | -7 | 13,593.54 | 9,270.83 |
| | Mark FOSTER | ENG | 70 | 69 | 69 | 73 | 281 | -7 | 13,593.54 | 9,270.83 |
| | Oliver WILSON | ENG | 72 | 68 | 66 | 75 | 281 | -7 | 13,593.54 | 9,270.83 |
| | Gary SIMPSON | AUS | 75 | 63 | 67 | 76 | 281 | -7 | 13,593.54 | 9,270.83 |
| 39 | Terry PILKADARIS | AUS | 68 | 72 | 72 | 70 | 282 | -6 | 11,913.44 | 8,125.00 |
| | Jarrod MOSELEY | AUS | 71 | 70 | 73 | 68 | 282 | -6 | 11,913.44 | 8,125.00 |
| | Bradley ILES | NZL | 68 | 74 | 67 | 73 | 282 | -6 | 11,913.44 | 8,125.00 |
| 42 | Raphaël JACQUELIN | FRA | 70 | 69 | 67 | 77 | 283 | -5 | 10,447.17 | 7,125.00 |
| | Marcus FRASER | AUS | 67 | 71 | 73 | 72 | 283 | -5 | 10,447.17 | 7,125.00 |
| | Paul SHEEHAN | AUS | 69 | 70 | 74 | 70 | 283 | -5 | 10,447.17 | 7,125.00 |
| | Richard FINCH | ENG | 72 | 67 | 71 | 73 | 283 | -5 | 10,447.17 | 7,125.00 |
| | Stephen GALLACHER | SCO | 71 | 66 | 70 | 76 | 283 | -5 | 10,447.17 | 7,125.00 |
| 47 | Lucas PARSONS | AUS | 69 | 73 | 71 | 71 | 284 | -4 | 8,614.34 | 5,875.00 |
| | Cameron PERCY | AUS | 71 | 70 | 72 | 71 | 284 | -4 | 8,614.34 | 5,875.00 |
| | Peter HANSON | SWE | 73 | 69 | 70 | 72 | 284 | -4 | 8,614.34 | 5,875.00 |
| | Robert KARLSSON | SWE | 72 | 69 | 69 | 74 | 284 | -4 | 8,614.34 | 5,875.00 |
| | Jean VAN DE VELDE | FRA | 66 | 76 | 71 | 71 | 284 | -4 | 8,614.34 | 5,875.00 |
| 52 | Joakim HAEGGMAN | SWE | 70 | 71 | 73 | 71 | 285 | -3 | 7,148.07 | 4,875.00 |
| | Graeme STORM | ENG | 74 | 68 | 71 | 72 | 285 | -3 | 7,148.07 | 4,875.00 |
| | John BICKERTON | ENG | 72 | 69 | 70 | 74 | 285 | -3 | 7,148.07 | 4,875.00 |
| 55 | Brett RUMFORD | AUS | 67 | 71 | 69 | 79 | 286 | -2 | 6,231.65 | 4,250.00 |
| | Ewan PORTER | AUS | 67 | 74 | 69 | 76 | 286 | -2 | 6,231.65 | 4,250.00 |
| 57 | Phillip ARCHER | ENG | 72 | 70 | 70 | 75 | 287 | -1 | 5,681.80 | 3,875.00 |
| 58 | Michael LONG | NZL | 73 | 69 | 73 | 73 | 288 | 0 | 5,406.87 | 3,687.50 |
| | Simon WAKEFIELD | ENG | 70 | 72 | 72 | 74 | 288 | 0 | 5,406.87 | 3,687.50 |
| 60 | Ter-Chang WANG | TPE | 73 | 66 | 72 | 78 | 289 | 1 | 4,857.02 | 3,312.50 |
| | Mardan MAMAT | SIN | 72 | 70 | 71 | 76 | 289 | 1 | 4,857.02 | 3,312.50 |
| | Anthony WALL | ENG | 72 | 67 | 71 | 79 | 289 | 1 | 4,857.02 | 3,312.50 |
| | Maarten LAFEBER | NED | 73 | 67 | 75 | 72 | 289 | 1 | 4,857.02 | 3,312.50 |
| 64 | Andrew MARSHALL | ENG | 70 | 69 | 76 | 75 | 290 | 2 | 4,398.81 | 3,000.00 |
| 65 | Ryan HALLER | AUS | 72 | 69 | 77 | 73 | 291 | 3 | 4,215.53 | 2,875.00 |

## Total Prize Fund
€1,814,450 £1,237,460

Nick O'Hern

"I knew I needed at least a birdie," he said afterwards, and he hit a good drive some 294 yards down the middle. That left 220 yards which the American admitted was, "the perfect distance for my three-iron." He then proceeded to hit an exquisite shot right on line, the ideal pitch leaving the ball rolling inexorably towards the hole. Indeed, for a few moments it looked like it might go in for an albatross two, but it pulled up a foot short. A tournament winning stroke if ever there was one.

It was an impressive denouement, the more so since Stadler is not really built to withstand temperatures in the mid-thirties that had even the locals gasping. Allenby, for instance, began with four successive birdies, but played the next five in figures of two over par. "It was mighty hot out there and I lost my focus and momentum," he said. Adam Scott suffered more than most, but his problem was partly self-inflicted. If large percentages of body heat escapes through the head, Scott was well insulated in that department.

Hair cascaded from under his cap, not having had it cut since September as the result of a bet between himself, Tim Clark and Sergio Garcia. Whoever succumbs to the barber's chair first has to pay the others US$1,000 each and as all three are pretty determined characters, long locks look inevitable for a while yet. The only way out of the bet is hardly an attractive proposition either. Take 80 or more and the perpetrator has to have his head shaved.

Stadler, however, suffered from none of these problems and had what was comfortably the best week of his golfing life.

**David Davies**

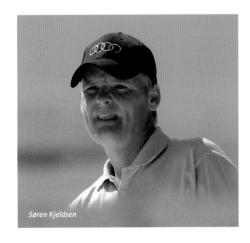

Søren Kjeldsen

# International Roll of Honour

Thongchai Jaidee

W hen The European Tour blazed the trail in the field of co-sanctioning events with other Tours, one of the first to feature was the Malaysian Open in 1999, a tournament which had been a regular feature on the Asian Tour since 1962. It is testament to its enduring appeal that, seven years later, the 2006 edition was as enthralling as ever.

Joint ventures between Europe and Asia are important on two counts. Not only do they offer The European Tour players an opportunity to compete throughout the winter months, they also provide much tougher competition on a regular basis for the golfers competing regularly in Asia. In general, the prize money on offer too is also considerably higher.

Everyone benefits, and the friendly rivalry provides spectators not only with great golf but also, on occasions, a nail-biting finish

David Park

as was exemplified by the 2006 Maybank Malaysian Open.

Persistent thunder and lightning storms compelled officials to reduce the tournament to three rounds for only the second time in its 44 year history but this did not detract from the quality of the golf at the Kuala Lumpur Golf & Country Club.

Los Angeles-based Korean golfer Charlie Wi eventually triumphed, ending the attempt by Thailand's Thongchai Jaidee to become the first Asian golfer to win the same tournament three years in a row – a feat only achieved on The European Tour by the select grouping of Ernie Els, Nick Faldo, Colin Montgomerie, Tiger Woods and Ian Woosnam.

Wi birdied the last hole on the tight and undulating Neil Haworth-designed course to deny Jaidee a play-off. Elegant Frenchman Raphaël Jacquelin, whose closing 62 would have been a record but for the preferred lies in operation, finished third ahead of Englishmen John Bickerton and Mark Foster. Indeed with an Australian, an Italian, a Swede and a Welshman also in the top ten there was a truly international look to the Malaysian Open for which Maybank were the title sponsors for the first time.

## Kuala Lumpur Golf & Country Club

| Par | Yards | Metres |
|-----|-------|--------|
| 72 | 6936 | 6340 |

| | | | |
|---|---|---|---|
| 1 | **Charlie WI** | **197** | **-19** |
| 2 | Thongchai JAIDEE | 198 | -18 |
| 3 | Raphaël JACQUELIN | 199 | -17 |
| 4 | John BICKERTON | 200 | -16 |
| | Mark FOSTER | 200 | -16 |
| 6 | Chinarat PHADUNGSIL | 202 | -14 |
| | Gary SIMPSON | 202 | -14 |
| 8 | Mattias ELIASSON | 203 | -13 |
| | Francesco MOLINARI | 203 | -13 |
| | David PARK | 203 | -13 |
| | Graeme STORM | 203 | -13 |

### WEATHER REPORT

| Round One | Round Two | Round Three | Round Four |

### EUROPEAN TOUR ORDER OF MERIT
(After ten tournaments)

| Pos | | € |
|-----|---|---|
| 1 | **David HOWELL** | **737,233.60** |
| 2 | Henrik STENSON | 547,165.89 |
| 3 | Ernie ELS | 519,419.76 |
| 4 | Nick O'HERN | 484,644.76 |
| 5 | Paul CASEY | 372,332.50 |
| 6 | Nick DOUGHERTY | 361,833.50 |
| 7 | Thongchai JAIDEE | 291,110.05 |
| 8 | Richard GREEN | 275,628.16 |
| 9 | Paul BROADHURST | 275,398.91 |
| 10 | Colin MONTGOMERIE | 250,928.12 |

# Maybank Malaysian Open

**Kuala Lumpur, Malaysia**
February 16-19 • 2006

*Mark Foster*

Naturally, the Asian players had an advantage in the searing heat and humidity. They have an innate understanding of the small, grainy greens. Nevertheless the players who compete on The European Tour International Schedule do so in the knowledge that their appreciation of contrasting conditions and courses improves their golfing education year on year.

Jacquelin is a case in point. He demonstrated his ability to raise his game in Asia when he was runner-up in the 2005 Enjoy Jakarta Standard Chartered Indonesian Open and his 62, including ten birdies, further emphasised the point.

In his heart of hearts, Jacquelin probably realised his finishing total was not quite

good enough as the spotlight turned on Wi and Jaidee, having their own battle royal behind. Could one, or indeed both of them improve on Jacquelin's clubhouse total?

Tensions built, but in the end it was Wi who stood tall to add his name to an international Roll of Honour which, since 1999, has an American, a Taiwanese, a Fijian, a Scot, an Indian, a Thai, and now a Korean imprinted upon it.

Wi became the second Korean to win on The European Tour following KJ Choi's success in the 2004 Linde German Masters and, naturally, was all smiles at the end. So too, however, and to his immense credit, was Jaidee, who praised the winner for his brave bogey-free final round. The former

*"Malaysia is a special place and this is a special course. There are a great many water hazards and the rough is challenging. The greens are small and narrow and if you miss them, then it is easy to make a bogey"* – **Zhang Lian-Wei**

John Bickerton

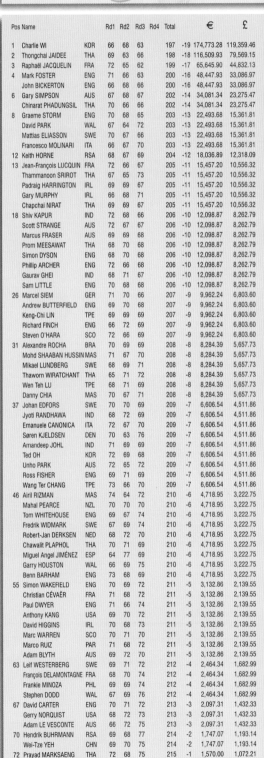

# Final Results

| Pos | Name | | Rd1 | Rd2 | Rd3 | Rd4 | Total | | € | £ |
|---|---|---|---|---|---|---|---|---|---|---|
| 1 | Charlie WI | KOR | 66 | 68 | 63 | | 197 | -19 | 174,773.28 | 119,359.46 |
| 2 | Thongchai JAIDEE | THA | 69 | 63 | 66 | | 198 | -18 | 116,509.93 | 79,569.15 |
| 3 | Raphaël JACQUELIN | FRA | 72 | 65 | 62 | | 199 | -17 | 65,645.90 | 44,832.13 |
| 4 | Mark FOSTER | ENG | 71 | 66 | 63 | | 200 | -16 | 48,447.93 | 33,086.97 |
| | John BICKERTON | ENG | 66 | 68 | 66 | | 200 | -16 | 48,447.93 | 33,086.97 |
| 6 | Gary SIMPSON | AUS | 67 | 68 | 67 | | 202 | -14 | 34,081.34 | 23,275.47 |
| | Chinarat PHADUNGSIL | THA | 70 | 66 | 66 | | 202 | -14 | 34,081.34 | 23,275.47 |
| 8 | Graeme STORM | ENG | 70 | 68 | 65 | | 203 | -13 | 22,493.68 | 15,361.81 |
| | David PARK | WAL | 67 | 64 | 72 | | 203 | -13 | 22,493.68 | 15,361.81 |
| | Mattias ELIASSON | SWE | 70 | 67 | 66 | | 203 | -13 | 22,493.68 | 15,361.81 |
| | Francesco MOLINARI | ITA | 66 | 67 | 70 | | 203 | -13 | 22,493.68 | 15,361.81 |
| 12 | Keith HORNE | RSA | 68 | 67 | 69 | | 204 | -12 | 18,036.89 | 12,318.09 |
| 13 | Jean-François LUCQUIN | FRA | 72 | 66 | 67 | | 205 | -11 | 15,457.20 | 10,556.32 |
| | Thammanoon SRIROT | THA | 67 | 65 | 73 | | 205 | -11 | 15,457.20 | 10,556.32 |
| | Padraig HARRINGTON | IRL | 69 | 69 | 67 | | 205 | -11 | 15,457.20 | 10,556.32 |
| | Gary MURPHY | IRL | 66 | 68 | 71 | | 205 | -11 | 15,457.20 | 10,556.32 |
| | Chapchai NIRAT | THA | 69 | 69 | 67 | | 205 | -11 | 15,457.20 | 10,556.32 |
| 18 | Shiv KAPUR | IND | 72 | 68 | 66 | | 206 | -10 | 12,098.87 | 8,262.79 |
| | Scott STRANGE | AUS | 72 | 67 | 67 | | 206 | -10 | 12,098.87 | 8,262.79 |
| | Marcus FRASER | AUS | 69 | 69 | 68 | | 206 | -10 | 12,098.87 | 8,262.79 |
| | Prom MEESAWAT | THA | 68 | 70 | 68 | | 206 | -10 | 12,098.87 | 8,262.79 |
| | Simon DYSON | ENG | 68 | 70 | 68 | | 206 | -10 | 12,098.87 | 8,262.79 |
| | Phillip ARCHER | ENG | 72 | 66 | 68 | | 206 | -10 | 12,098.87 | 8,262.79 |
| | Gaurav GHEI | IND | 68 | 71 | 67 | | 206 | -10 | 12,098.87 | 8,262.79 |
| | Sam LITTLE | ENG | 70 | 68 | 68 | | 206 | -10 | 12,098.87 | 8,262.79 |
| 26 | Marcel SIEM | GER | 71 | 70 | 66 | | 207 | -9 | 9,962.24 | 6,803.60 |
| | Andrew BUTTERFIELD | ENG | 69 | 70 | 68 | | 207 | -9 | 9,962.24 | 6,803.60 |
| | Keng-Chi LIN | TPE | 69 | 69 | 69 | | 207 | -9 | 9,962.24 | 6,803.60 |
| | Richard FINCH | ENG | 66 | 72 | 69 | | 207 | -9 | 9,962.24 | 6,803.60 |
| | Steven O'HARA | SCO | 72 | 66 | 69 | | 207 | -9 | 9,962.24 | 6,803.60 |
| 31 | Alexandre ROCHA | BRA | 70 | 69 | 69 | | 208 | -8 | 8,284.39 | 5,657.73 |
| | Mohd SHAABAN HUSSIN | MAS | 71 | 67 | 70 | | 208 | -8 | 8,284.39 | 5,657.73 |
| | Mikael LUNDBERG | SWE | 68 | 69 | 71 | | 208 | -8 | 8,284.39 | 5,657.73 |
| | Thaworn WIRATCHANT | THA | 65 | 71 | 72 | | 208 | -8 | 8,284.39 | 5,657.73 |
| | Wen Teh LU | TPE | 68 | 71 | 69 | | 208 | -8 | 8,284.39 | 5,657.73 |
| | Danny CHIA | MAS | 70 | 67 | 71 | | 208 | -8 | 8,284.39 | 5,657.73 |
| 37 | Johan EDFORS | SWE | 70 | 70 | 69 | | 209 | -7 | 6,606.54 | 4,511.86 |
| | Jyoti RANDHAWA | IND | 68 | 72 | 69 | | 209 | -7 | 6,606.54 | 4,511.86 |
| | Emanuele CANONICA | ITA | 72 | 67 | 70 | | 209 | -7 | 6,606.54 | 4,511.86 |
| | Søren KJELDSEN | DEN | 70 | 63 | 76 | | 209 | -7 | 6,606.54 | 4,511.86 |
| | Amandeep JOHL | IND | 71 | 69 | 69 | | 209 | -7 | 6,606.54 | 4,511.86 |
| | Ted OH | KOR | 72 | 69 | 68 | | 209 | -7 | 6,606.54 | 4,511.86 |
| | Unho PARK | AUS | 72 | 65 | 72 | | 209 | -7 | 6,606.54 | 4,511.86 |
| | Ross FISHER | ENG | 69 | 71 | 69 | | 209 | -7 | 6,606.54 | 4,511.86 |
| | Wang Ter CHANG | TPE | 73 | 66 | 70 | | 209 | -7 | 6,606.54 | 4,511.86 |
| 46 | Airil RIZMAN | MAS | 74 | 64 | 72 | | 210 | -6 | 4,718.95 | 3,222.75 |
| | Mahal PEARCE | NZL | 70 | 70 | 70 | | 210 | -6 | 4,718.95 | 3,222.75 |
| | Tom WHITEHOUSE | ENG | 69 | 67 | 74 | | 210 | -6 | 4,718.95 | 3,222.75 |
| | Fredrik WIDMARK | SWE | 67 | 69 | 74 | | 210 | -6 | 4,718.95 | 3,222.75 |
| | Robert-Jan DERKSEN | NED | 68 | 72 | 70 | | 210 | -6 | 4,718.95 | 3,222.75 |
| | Chawalit PLAPHOL | THA | 70 | 71 | 69 | | 210 | -6 | 4,718.95 | 3,222.75 |
| | Miguel Angel JIMÉNEZ | ESP | 64 | 77 | 69 | | 210 | -6 | 4,718.95 | 3,222.75 |
| | Garry HOUSTON | WAL | 66 | 69 | 75 | | 210 | -6 | 4,718.95 | 3,222.75 |
| | Benn BARHAM | ENG | 73 | 68 | 69 | | 210 | -6 | 4,718.95 | 3,222.75 |
| 55 | Simon WAKEFIELD | ENG | 70 | 69 | 72 | | 211 | -5 | 3,132.86 | 2,139.55 |
| | Christian CÉVAËR | FRA | 71 | 68 | 72 | | 211 | -5 | 3,132.86 | 2,139.55 |
| | Paul DWYER | ENG | 71 | 66 | 74 | | 211 | -5 | 3,132.86 | 2,139.55 |
| | Anthony KANG | USA | 69 | 70 | 72 | | 211 | -5 | 3,132.86 | 2,139.55 |
| | David HIGGINS | IRL | 70 | 68 | 73 | | 211 | -5 | 3,132.86 | 2,139.55 |
| | Marc WARREN | SCO | 70 | 71 | 70 | | 211 | -5 | 3,132.86 | 2,139.55 |
| | Marco RUIZ | PAR | 71 | 68 | 72 | | 211 | -5 | 3,132.86 | 2,139.55 |
| | Adam BLYTH | AUS | 69 | 72 | 70 | | 211 | -5 | 3,132.86 | 2,139.55 |
| 63 | Leif WESTERBERG | SWE | 69 | 71 | 72 | | 212 | -4 | 2,464.34 | 1,682.90 |
| | François DELAMONTAGNE | FRA | 68 | 70 | 74 | | 212 | -4 | 2,464.34 | 1,682.90 |
| | Frankie MINOZA | PHL | 69 | 69 | 74 | | 212 | -4 | 2,464.34 | 1,682.90 |
| | Stephen DODD | WAL | 67 | 69 | 76 | | 212 | -4 | 2,464.34 | 1,682.90 |
| 67 | David CARTER | ENG | 70 | 71 | 72 | | 213 | -3 | 2,097.31 | 1,432.33 |
| | Gerry NORQUIST | USA | 68 | 72 | 73 | | 213 | -3 | 2,097.31 | 1,432.33 |
| | Adam LE VESCONTE | AUS | 67 | 69 | 77 | | 213 | -3 | 2,097.31 | 1,432.33 |
| 70 | Hendrik BUHRMANN | RSA | 69 | 68 | 77 | | 214 | -2 | 1,747.07 | 1,193.14 |
| | Wei-Tze YEH | CHN | 69 | 70 | 75 | | 214 | -2 | 1,747.07 | 1,193.14 |
| 72 | Prayad MARKSAENG | THA | 72 | 68 | 75 | | 215 | -1 | 1,570.00 | 1,072.21 |

paratrooper dropped one shot to par – at the short eighth - and that, in the end, proved to be the difference between the two.

At a time when, of necessity, other Tours must work together to provide an effective alternative to the US PGA Tour, the Maybank Malaysian Open was a perfect example of how close co-operation provides, not only wonderfully entertaining golf, but also a showcase to millions on television, helping attract future sponsors and encouraging existing ones to invest more.

The members of the Kuala Lumpur Golf & Country Club had allowed their West Course to be closed for five weeks to enable green staff to prepare it properly. Their selflessness was rewarded with an exciting and engrossing tournament which even the weather could not spoil.

**Renton Laidlaw**

# Total Prize Fund
€1,051,799 £718,314

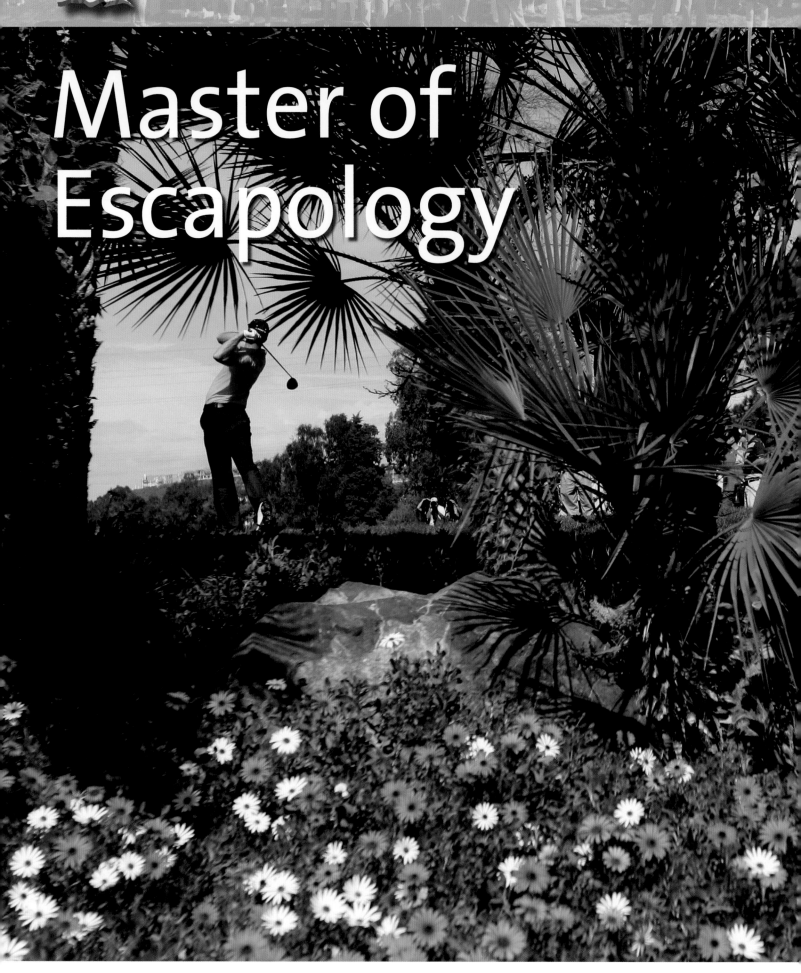

# Master of Escapology

*Padraig Harrington and Vijay Singh*

## La Costa Resort & Spa

| Par | Yards | Metres |
| --- | --- | --- |
| 72 | 7247 | 6628 |

**Champion - Geoff OGILVY**

Runner-Up - Davis LOVE III

Third - Zach JOHNSON

Fourth - Tom LEHMAN

**G**eoff Ogilvy was just 17 years old when he led going into the final round of the Victorian Open, an event with every famous Australian golfing name on the trophy. He did not win, but it was the day discerning Antipodean golf fans took note of another immense talent and awaited the day that it would be realised.

To be fair, it has probably been a longer journey than they anticipated; one fraught with growing pains and learning difficulties as Ogilvy attempted to grapple with a game that, for a while, defied all attempts to be mastered.

But with a nod in the direction of two legends in Peter Thomson and Colin Montgomerie, Ogilvy duly got there 11 years later, winning the World Golf Championships - Accenture Match Play at La Costa Resort & Spa, Carlsbad, California, that was graced from the first day by a series of spectacular matches and played under unbroken blue skies.

Ogilvy contributed more than anyone to the sense of drama the week's theatre provided. Four times in four successive matches leading up to the semi-finals he was taken to extra holes; four times he won.

"I just got lucky," he said when it was all over, and while anyone who wins via that route will definitely have had their share of fortune, he was, of course, being unduly modest. As the gracious runner-up Davis Love III noted before their final: "When someone wins four matches in a row in sudden death, it tells me they have loads of determination and they never give up."

Those natural skills were honed at the beautiful Victoria Golf Club in the sandbelt region of Melbourne, a place that Thomson also happens to call home. They were then refined in Europe at the end of the last decade as Ogilvy admired from afar the domination of Montgomerie.

He never asked the Scot personally for advice but then he never felt the need. It was all there in the Scot's control of every challenge The European Tour had to offer. "He was

### WEATHER REPORT

| Round One | Round Two | Round Three | Round Four |

### EUROPEAN TOUR ORDER OF MERIT
(After 11 tournaments)

| Pos | | € | |
| --- | --- | --- | --- |
| 1 | David HOWELL | 938,812.64 | |
| 2 | Henrik STENSON | 618,558.47 | |
| 3 | Nick O'HERN | 556,037.34 | |
| 4 | Ernie ELS | 548,816.70 | |
| 5 | Retief GOOSEN | 429,408.00 | |
| 6 | Paul CASEY | 401,729.44 | |
| 7 | Nick DOUGHERTY | 361,833.50 | |
| 8 | Vijay SINGH | 323,872.28 | |
| 9 | Colin MONTGOMERIE | 322,320.70 | |
| 10 | Richard GREEN | 305,025.10 | |

# World Golf Championships – Accenture Match Play

**Carlsbad, California**
February 22-26 • 2006

David Howell

awesome, the best player over there, and he showed me a lot without telling me anything," Ogilvy recalled.

Ogilvy's route to the semi-finals could be parcelled up and released as golf's own version of The Great Escape. He birdied the 18th hole in his opening match against US Open Champion Michael Campbell, and then chipped in to win at the first extra hole. After dispatching Nick O'Hern at the 21st in round two, another Major winner, former Masters Champion Mike Weir, was beaten in even more amazing fashion the following day as Ogilvy came back from four down with four to play, again birdieing the final hole before winning with an eagle three at the third extra hole.

Surely he couldn't survive against David Howell in the quarter-finals, who had underlined his rapid rise in golfing stature by

beating Phil Mickelson in his own backyard in Friday's third round? But survive he did and yes, you guessed it, he birdied the 18th to stay alive and the 19th to win.

Ogilvy was not the only one entertaining the crowd. Tiger Woods started out by winning the first nine holes of his first round match against Stephen Ames, a feat that has probably been done before in top-class professional golf but you might have to go back the best part of a century to find when. The World Number One won in the minimum amount of time, shaking hands on the tenth green for a tournament record 9 and 8 victory.

But Woods himself was beaten in a third round full of shocks, as Vijay Singh and Mickelson both went out at the same stage. Interesting how the quintet who defeated the top five players in the world – Chad

*" I love the golf course and I'm very sad that we're not playing here anymore. It brings back so many memories, not only my wins in the Tournament of Champions, but the experience of spending the day here with my dad and my friends, of coming here as a kid and watching from outside the ropes looking in "*
*- Phil Mickelson*

Retief Goosen and Luke Donald

# Final Results

## Total Prize Fund
€7,500,000  £5,146,201

Campbell (Woods), Padraig Harrington (Singh), Zach Johnson (Retief Goosen), Bernhard Langer (Ernie Els) and Howell (Mickelson) - also lost themselves in their next round, as if mentally exhausted by the feat. Or else proving the old adage that anyone can beat anyone else when the format is 18 hole match play and 64 of the world's top players are in attendance.

No-one could beat Ogilvy, however. Having survived for so long by the skin of his teeth, he showed a cool head to comfortably beat Tom Lehman in the semi-finals and Love in the 36 hole final, winning by margins of 4 and 3, and 3 and 2 respectively.

It signalled the end of elite golf at La Costa Resort & Spa too, with news that the WGC – Accenture Match Play will, next year, move to The Gallery Golf Club in Tucson, Arizona. The event had been held at La Costa for seven of the eight years since its inception in 1999 while, prior to that, it had staged the Tournament of Champions on the US PGA Tour from 1969 to 1998.

Like the Victorian Open, the winners at the fabled California venue read like a golfing Who's Who. The difference in the case of Ogilvy, now man not boy, is that in this instance, he did not blink once when it came to adding his name to the list.

**Derek Lawrenson**
*Daily Mail*

## Tournament Bracket

1. Tiger Woods
9 and 8 — Woods
64. Stephen Ames
1 hole — Woods
32. Robert Allenby
3 and 2 — Allenby
33. K J Choi
1 hole — Campbell
16. Henrik Stenson
1 hole — Stenson
49. Paul Casey
1 hole — Campbell
17. Chad Campbell
4 and 2 — Campbell
48. Tim Herron
21st hole — Lehman
8. David Toms
19th hole — Toms
57. Ian Poulter
2 and 1 — Toms
25. José Maria Olazábal
3 and 2 — Olazábal
40. Brandt Jobe
4 and 3 — Lehman
9. Adam Scott
2 and 1 — Scott
56. Lucas Glover
1 hole — Lehman
24. Stuart Appleby
3 and 2 — Lehman
41. Tom Lehman
4 and 3 — Ogilvy

4. Ernie Els
1 hole — Langer
61. Bernhard Langer
20th hole — Weir
29. Stewart Cink
4 and 3 — Weir
36. Mike Weir
21st hole — Ogilvy
13. Michael Campbell
19th hole — Ogilvy
52. Geoff Ogilvy
21st hole — Ogilvy
20. Nick O'Hern
4 and 3 — O'Hern
45. Fred Funk
19th hole — Ogilvy
5. Phil Mickelson
2 holes — Mickelson
60. Charles Howell III
2 and 1 — Mickelson
28. Bart Bryant
4 and 2 — Daly
37. John Daly
3 and 1 — Howell
12. David Howell
22nd hole — Howell
53. Steve Elkington
3 and 2 — Howell
21. Scott Verplank
26th — Verplank
44. Lee Westwood

Campbell / Lehman 21st hole
Ogilvy / Ogilvy 19th hole
Lehman / Ogilvy 4 and 3
Ogilvy / Love III 4 and 2
Ogilvy 3 and 2

2. Vijay Singh
5 and 4 — Singh
63. Graeme McDowell
2 and 1 — Singh
31. Rory Sabbatini
2 and 1 — Jiménez
34. Miguel Angel Jiménez
19th hole — Harrington
15. Angel Cabrera
1 hole — Cabrera
50. Peter Lonard
19th hole — Harrington
18. Padraig Harrington
4 and 2 — Harrington
1 hole — Love III
7. Chris DiMarco
2 and 1 — DiMarco
58. Mark Calcavecchia
6 and 5 — DiMarco
26. Tim Clark
21st hole — Oberholser
39. Aaron Oberholser
3 and 2 — Love III
10. Kenny Perry
1 hole — Petterson
55. Carl Pettersson
1 hole — Love III
23. Davis Love III
2 and 1 — Love III
42. Mark Hensby

Harrington / Love III 1 hole

3. Retief Goosen
5 and 4 — Goosen
62. Paul Broadhurst
2 and 1 — Goosen
30. Justin Leonard
4 and 3 — Crane
35. Ben Crane
1 hole — Goosen
14. Luke Donald
2 and 1 — Donald
51. Richard Green
4 and 3 — Donald
19. Darren Clarke
4 and 3 — Maruyama
46. Shigeki Maruyama
3 and 2 — Johnson
6. Jim Furyk
1 hole — Johnson
59. Zach Johnson
1 hole — Johnson
27. Fred Couples
19th hole — O'Hair
38. Sean O'Hair
4 and 3 — Johnson
11. Colin Montgomerie
23rd hole — Montgomerie
54. Niclas Fasth
3 and 2 — Katayama
22. Paul McGinley
2 and 1 — Katayama
43. Shingo Katayama

Goosen / Johnson 3 and 2

**CONSOLATION MATCH**
Zach Johnson bt Tom Lehman by 1 hole

| | € |
|---|---|
| Champion | 1,091886 |
| Runner-up | 639,934 |
| Third Place | 470,351 |
| Fourth Place | 377,960 |
| Quarter Finalists | 201,579 |
| Third Round | 104,989 |
| Second Round | 71,392 |
| First Round | 29,396 |

*NB: Players in bold denote European Tour Members*

# High Quality Duel

_Matthew Millar_

Indonesia Open 2006

## Emeralda Golf & Country Club

| Par | Yards | Metres |
| --- | --- | --- |
| 72 | 7082 | 6475 |

| Pos | | Score | | |
| --- | --- | --- | --- | --- |
| 1 | Simon DYSON | 268 | -20 | |
| 2 | Andrew BUCKLE | 270 | -18 | |
| 3 | Thongchai JAIDEE | 274 | -14 | |
| | Ter-Chang WANG | 274 | -14 | |
| 5 | Matthew MILLAR | 275 | -13 | |
| | Scott STRANGE | 275 | -13 | |
| 7 | David HIGGINS | 277 | -11 | |
| | Shiv KAPUR | 277 | -11 | |
| 9 | Peter GUSTAFSSON | 278 | -10 | |
| | Anders HANSEN | 278 | -10 | |
| | Brad KENNEDY | 278 | -10 | |
| | José Manuel LARA | 278 | -10 | |
| | Wei Chih LU | 278 | -10 | |
| | Steven O'HARA | 278 | -10 | |
| | Terry PILKADARIS | 278 | -10 | |

## WEATHER REPORT

| Day One | Day Two | Day Three | Day Four |
| --- | --- | --- | --- |

## EUROPEAN TOUR ORDER OF MERIT
(After 12 tournaments)

| Pos | | € | |
| --- | --- | --- | --- |
| 1 | David HOWELL | 938,812.64 | |
| 2 | Henrik STENSON | 618,558.47 | |
| 3 | Nick O'HERN | 556,037.34 | |
| 4 | Ernie ELS | 548,816.70 | |
| 5 | Retief GOOSEN | 429,408.00 | |
| 6 | Paul CASEY | 401,729.44 | |
| 7 | Nick DOUGHERTY | 361,833.50 | |
| 8 | Thongchai JAIDEE | 338,492.55 | |
| 9 | Vijay SINGH | 323,872.28 | |
| 10 | Colin MONTGOMERIE | 322,320.70 | |

It was fitting, in many ways, that Simon Dyson landed his first European Tour title in a co-sanctioned event in Asia. Appropriate, because he learned how to win in the Far East – as he showed when he topped the Asian Tour Order of Merit in 2000 – and because he loved the heat and humidity that can be so debilitating to others.

At a tournament where shirts clung to the bodies of the golfers as if they had been washed and put on dripping wet, Dyson coped brilliantly with the disruptive last day thunder and lightning. Sessions with sports psychologist Jamil Qureshi helped him contend with the mental demands of the delay while work with coach Pete Cowen helped give him the toughness and resilience to hold off the strong challenge from talented Australian Andrew Buckle.

Make no mistake, Buckle, a former World Junior champion and Australian Amateur title-holder, is good, but on the week, Dyson was better. Their high quality duel on the final day of the Enjoy Jakarta HSBC Indonesia Open was always engrossing and came right down to the wire.

An agency report indicated that Dyson - who comes from a sporting family and whose uncle Terry was a member of the famous Tottenham Hotspur League and Cup double winning side in 1961 - had cruised to victory, but that could not have been further from the truth. He won, but it was no cakewalk.

# Enjoy Jakarta HSBC Indonesia Open

## Jakarta, Indonesia
March 2-5 • 2006

Steven Jeppesen

Dyson, a three-time winner in Asia during his all-conquering 2000 season, had to work hard for his all-important first European Tour triumph. When it was over he knew he had been in a fight against a dogged opponent in Buckle who was resilient enough to recover after running up a quadruple bogey eight at the sixth when one ahead. When Dyson then eagled the seventh to Buckle's birdie, it meant a five shot swing in the Englishman's favour in just two holes, but he was wise enough to realise that the title had not yet been won.

That eventuality arrived when he holed a treacherous and sloping 15 foot birdie putt at the 17th to ensure he came down the last with a comfortable two shot advantage.

On a course with treacherous rough, his winning total was an impressive 20 under par 268, and such was the quality of Dyson's golf that he only dropped two shots to par all week. Understandably, he felt justifiably proud that he had won a European Tour title at last and in such commendable fashion.

"I thought it would never come and now that it has I cannot put into words how wonderful it feels," he said. "My rhythm was good until the rain came but, although I did not strike the ball as well nor hole as many putts after the restart, I kept getting pars."
Even that was almost not enough against Buckle whom the Englishman described as one of the best up and coming golfers he had played against. Dyson said: "He hits the

*"Emeralda is a great course. It coped with the heavy rain well, the greens were good and the rough was penal. You had to hit the fairways or you could easily drop a shot and that is the way a course should be"* – Simon Dyson

*European Tour winners Stephen Dodd (second from right), Thongchai Jaidee (third from right) and Thaworn Wiratchant (right) presented a cheque for $100,000 from The European Tour's International Relief Golf Fund to assist with the continuing relief efforts in Indonesia following the Tsunami disaster in December 2004. Accepting the cheque was Richard McHowat, Chief Executive Officer of HSBC Indonesia (third from left), Mike Gray, Regional Director Indonesia Rolls Royce (left), and Dr Eric Audras Guité, Medical Director Global Assistance and Healthcare (second from left). The money raised will go towards the Aceh Primary Healthcare Programme, a project with which HSBC and Rolls Royce have been heavily involved since the disaster*

ball like a top ten player, is a good putter and his mental strength is obvious. Not many players would have managed to cope with an eight as well as he did."

Often there are a number of golfers challenging for a title but on this occasion it was always going to be Dyson or Buckle who were going to triumph. Chinese Taipei's experienced Ter-Chang Wang was never a serious threat although, playing alongside the duellists, the 43 year old also earned winner Dyson's admiration. "I hope I'm playing as well as that when I'm his age," he said.

Initially, and typical of the sporting Dyson, he admitted that standing on the seventh tee he had felt sorry for Buckle. It was a natural reaction but one he knew he could not afford to have for long. "I remembered when I threw away a six shot advantage and lost to Miguel Angel Jiménez in the 2004 BMW Asian Open that nobody felt sorry for me then. So instead I pressed home my advantage with an eagle at the seventh to move further ahead. That was one of the best shots I have ever hit."

So, early in the season, Dyson had achieved his long-held goal. Just how badly he wanted to win the Enjoy Jakarta HSBC Indonesia Open you could see in his eyes as he played the last few holes and once the winning putt had dropped, nobody took the title of the event more literally than the genial Englishman.

Now all he wants do is win again. If he plays like this, do not count against that occurrence being sooner rather than later.

Stephen Dodd

**Renton Laidlaw**
*The Golf Channel*

# Final Results

| Pos | Name | | Rd1 | Rd2 | Rd3 | Rd4 | Total | | € | £ |
|---|---|---|---|---|---|---|---|---|---|---|
| 1 | Simon DYSON | ENG | 66 | 68 | 67 | 67 | 268 | -20 | 140,261.71 | 95,517.49 |
| 2 | Andrew BUCKLE | AUS | 67 | 69 | 65 | 69 | 270 | -18 | 93,510.90 | 63,680.43 |
| 3 | Thongchai JAIDEE | THA | 66 | 68 | 72 | 68 | 274 | -14 | 47,382.50 | 32,267.24 |
| | Ter-Chang WANG | TPE | 66 | 68 | 70 | 70 | 274 | -14 | 47,382.50 | 32,267.24 |
| 5 | Matthew MILLAR | AUS | 71 | 66 | 70 | 68 | 275 | -13 | 32,569.62 | 22,179.74 |
| | Scott STRANGE | AUS | 71 | 67 | 70 | 67 | 275 | -13 | 32,569.62 | 22,179.74 |
| 7 | Shiv KAPUR | IND | 72 | 68 | 66 | 71 | 277 | -11 | 23,143.69 | 15,760.73 |
| | David HIGGINS | IRL | 66 | 71 | 69 | 71 | 277 | -11 | 23,143.69 | 15,760.73 |
| 9 | Peter GUSTAFSSON | SWE | 72 | 65 | 70 | 71 | 278 | -10 | 14,920.11 | 10,160.52 |
| | Steven O'HARA | SCO | 71 | 71 | 70 | 66 | 278 | -10 | 14,920.11 | 10,160.52 |
| | Wei Chih LU | TPE | 71 | 70 | 66 | 71 | 278 | -10 | 14,920.11 | 10,160.52 |
| | Brad KENNEDY | AUS | 67 | 72 | 73 | 66 | 278 | -10 | 14,920.11 | 10,160.52 |
| | Terry PILKADARIS | AUS | 72 | 68 | 68 | 70 | 278 | -10 | 14,920.11 | 10,160.52 |
| | José Manuel LARA | ESP | 70 | 72 | 69 | 67 | 278 | -10 | 14,920.11 | 10,160.52 |
| | Anders HANSEN | DEN | 69 | 69 | 70 | 70 | 278 | -10 | 14,920.11 | 10,160.52 |
| 16 | Thammanoon SRIROT | THA | 68 | 69 | 72 | 70 | 279 | -9 | 11,361.28 | 7,736.98 |
| | Andrew MARSHALL | ENG | 73 | 67 | 71 | 68 | 279 | -9 | 11,361.28 | 7,736.98 |
| | Stephen DODD | WAL | 69 | 69 | 72 | 69 | 279 | -9 | 11,361.28 | 7,736.98 |
| 19 | Thaworn WIRATCHANT | THA | 72 | 67 | 71 | 70 | 280 | -8 | 9,414.60 | 6,411.29 |
| | Anthony KANG | USA | 67 | 70 | 71 | 72 | 280 | -8 | 9,414.60 | 6,411.29 |
| | Sam LITTLE | ENG | 70 | 69 | 72 | 69 | 280 | -8 | 9,414.60 | 6,411.29 |
| | Garry HOUSTON | WAL | 72 | 69 | 71 | 68 | 280 | -8 | 9,414.60 | 6,411.29 |
| | Steven JEPPESEN | SWE | 67 | 72 | 69 | 72 | 280 | -8 | 9,414.60 | 6,411.29 |
| | Wen-Chong LIANG | CHN | 68 | 73 | 72 | 67 | 280 | -8 | 9,414.60 | 6,411.29 |
| | Leif WESTERBERG | SWE | 70 | 67 | 76 | 67 | 280 | -8 | 9,414.60 | 6,411.29 |
| | Rahil GANGJEE | IND | 69 | 67 | 71 | 73 | 280 | -8 | 9,414.60 | 6,411.29 |
| 27 | David GRIFFITHS | ENG | 69 | 69 | 71 | 72 | 281 | -7 | 7,616.50 | 5,186.80 |
| | Iain STEEL | MAS | 72 | 68 | 71 | 70 | 281 | -7 | 7,616.50 | 5,186.80 |
| | David BRANSDON | AUS | 73 | 66 | 71 | 71 | 281 | -7 | 7,616.50 | 5,186.80 |
| | Boonchu RUANGKIT | THA | 73 | 70 | 69 | 69 | 281 | -7 | 7,616.50 | 5,186.80 |
| | Charlie WI | KOR | 72 | 70 | 70 | 69 | 281 | -7 | 7,616.50 | 5,186.80 |
| | Benn BARHAM | ENG | 70 | 67 | 74 | 70 | 281 | -7 | 7,616.50 | 5,186.80 |
| 33 | Prayad MARKSAENG | THA | 71 | 70 | 72 | 69 | 282 | -6 | 6,155.38 | 4,191.78 |
| | Peter LAWRIE | IRL | 73 | 69 | 73 | 67 | 282 | -6 | 6,155.38 | 4,191.78 |
| | Jamie DONALDSON | WAL | 72 | 66 | 74 | 70 | 282 | -6 | 6,155.38 | 4,191.78 |
| | Mahal PEARCE | NZL | 71 | 69 | 70 | 72 | 282 | -6 | 6,155.38 | 4,191.78 |
| | Adam GROOM | AUS | 72 | 70 | 71 | 69 | 282 | -6 | 6,155.38 | 4,191.78 |
| | Sung-Man LEE | KOR | 72 | 67 | 72 | 71 | 282 | -6 | 6,155.38 | 4,191.78 |
| | Scott BARR | AUS | 70 | 73 | 72 | 67 | 282 | -6 | 6,155.38 | 4,191.78 |
| 40 | Richard MOIR | AUS | 72 | 71 | 70 | 70 | 283 | -5 | 4,796.59 | 3,266.45 |
| | Gary RUSNAK | USA | 70 | 73 | 69 | 71 | 283 | -5 | 4,796.59 | 3,266.45 |
| | Unho PARK | AUS | 68 | 71 | 69 | 75 | 283 | -5 | 4,796.59 | 3,266.45 |
| | Felipe AGUILAR | CHI | 74 | 68 | 70 | 71 | 283 | -5 | 4,796.59 | 3,266.45 |
| | Jeev Milkha SINGH | IND | 72 | 71 | 73 | 67 | 283 | -5 | 4,796.59 | 3,266.45 |
| | Andrew BUTTERFIELD | ENG | 72 | 70 | 70 | 71 | 283 | -5 | 4,796.59 | 3,266.45 |
| | Keith HORNE | RSA | 70 | 70 | 72 | 71 | 283 | -5 | 4,796.59 | 3,266.45 |
| | Robert KARLSSON | SWE | 72 | 70 | 70 | 71 | 283 | -5 | 4,796.59 | 3,266.45 |
| | Miles TUNNICLIFF | ENG | 71 | 71 | 70 | 71 | 283 | -5 | 4,796.59 | 3,266.45 |
| 49 | Simon YATES | SCO | 71 | 69 | 71 | 73 | 284 | -4 | 3,534.22 | 2,406.79 |
| | Philip GOLDING | ENG | 69 | 74 | 73 | 68 | 284 | -4 | 3,534.22 | 2,406.79 |
| | David CARTER | ENG | 69 | 73 | 71 | 71 | 284 | -4 | 3,534.22 | 2,406.79 |
| | Joong Kyung MO | KOR | 71 | 68 | 75 | 70 | 284 | -4 | 3,534.22 | 2,406.79 |
| | Alexandre ROCHA | BRA | 70 | 72 | 67 | 75 | 284 | -4 | 3,534.22 | 2,406.79 |
| | Wilhelm SCHAUMAN | SWE | 68 | 68 | 74 | 74 | 284 | -4 | 3,534.22 | 2,406.79 |
| 55 | Wade ORMSBY | AUS | 69 | 74 | 73 | 69 | 285 | -3 | 2,776.60 | 1,890.85 |
| | Rick GIBSON | CAN | 72 | 71 | 72 | 70 | 285 | -3 | 2,776.60 | 1,890.85 |
| | Lian-Wei ZHANG | CHN | 72 | 71 | 69 | 73 | 285 | -3 | 2,776.60 | 1,890.85 |
| 58 | Henrik NYSTROM | SWE | 72 | 71 | 75 | 68 | 286 | -2 | 2,440.11 | 1,661.70 |
| | Jason DAWES | AUS | 71 | 72 | 76 | 67 | 286 | -2 | 2,440.11 | 1,661.70 |
| | David DIXON | ENG | 70 | 71 | 74 | 71 | 286 | -2 | 2,440.11 | 1,661.70 |
| 61 | Marcus FRASER | AUS | 77 | 66 | 78 | 66 | 287 | -1 | 2,103.61 | 1,432.55 |
| | Prom MEESAWAT | THA | 72 | 67 | 76 | 72 | 287 | -1 | 2,103.61 | 1,432.55 |
| | Jyoti RANDHAWA | IND | 71 | 71 | 72 | 73 | 287 | -1 | 2,103.61 | 1,432.55 |
| | Carl SUNESON | ESP | 72 | 71 | 71 | 73 | 287 | -1 | 2,103.61 | 1,432.55 |
| | Damien MCGRANE | IRL | 69 | 71 | 72 | 75 | 287 | -1 | 2,103.61 | 1,432.55 |
| 66 | Robert ROCK | ENG | 70 | 73 | 73 | 72 | 288 | 0 | 1,850.74 | 1,260.34 |
| 67 | Fredrik WIDMARK | SWE | 72 | 71 | 72 | 76 | 291 | 3 | 1,647.37 | 1,121.85 |
| | Jarmo SANDELIN | SWE | 70 | 69 | 78 | 74 | 291 | 3 | 1,647.37 | 1,121.85 |
| | Chinarat PHADUNGSIL | THA | 73 | 69 | 77 | 72 | 291 | 3 | 1,647.37 | 1,121.85 |
| | Chapchai NIRAT | THA | 73 | 68 | 76 | 74 | 291 | 3 | 1,647.37 | 1,121.85 |
| 71 | Mårten OLANDER | SWE | 72 | 68 | 77 | 75 | 292 | 4 | 1,260.50 | 858.39 |
| | Ron WON | USA | 72 | 69 | 76 | 75 | 292 | 4 | 1,260.50 | 858.39 |
| 73 | Andrew PITTS | USA | 73 | 70 | 74 | 76 | 293 | 5 | 1,253.50 | 853.63 |
| | Anthony BROWN | AUS | 69 | 74 | 77 | 73 | 293 | 5 | 1,253.50 | 853.63 |
| 75 | Angelo QUE | PHI | 70 | 71 | 74 | 80 | 294 | 6 | 1,249.00 | 850.56 |
| 76 | Paul DWYER | ENG | 73 | 70 | 76 | 76 | 295 | 7 | 1,246.00 | 848.52 |
| 77 | Anthony WALL | ENG | 74 | 68 | RETD | | | | | |

# Total Prize Fund
**€850,000  £578,231**

# Count On Me, Singapore

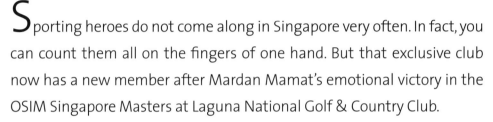

Peter Gustafsson

## Laguna National Golf & Country Club

| Par | Yards | Metres |
| --- | --- | --- |
| 72 | 7207 | 6589 |

| | | | | |
| --- | --- | --- | --- | --- |
| 1 | Mardan MAMAT | 276 | -12 | |
| 2 | Nick DOUGHERTY | 277 | -11 | |
| 3 | Ross FISHER | 278 | -10 | |
| | Charlie WI | 278 | -10 | |
| 5 | Jonathan LOMAS | 279 | -9 | |
| | Chapchai NIRAT | 279 | -9 | |
| 7 | Andrew BUTTERFIELD | 281 | -7 | |
| | Jyoti RANDHAWA | 281 | -7 | |
| 9 | Marcus BOTH | 282 | -6 | |
| | Marcus FRASER | 282 | -6 | |
| | Anders HANSEN | 282 | -6 | |
| | Prayad MARKSAENG | 282 | -6 | |

### WEATHER REPORT

Round One    Round Two    Round Three    Round Four

### EUROPEAN TOUR ORDER OF MERIT
(After 13 tournaments)

| Pos | | € | |
| --- | --- | --- | --- |
| 1 | David HOWELL | 938,812.64 | |
| 2 | Henrik STENSON | 618,558.47 | |
| 3 | Nick O'HERN | 556,037.34 | |
| 4 | Ernie ELS | 548,816.70 | |
| 5 | Nick DOUGHERTY | 454,209.89 | |
| 6 | Retief GOOSEN | 429,408.00 | |
| 7 | Paul CASEY | 401,729.44 | |
| 8 | Thongchai JAIDEE | 338,492.55 | |
| 9 | Vijay SINGH | 323,872.28 | |
| 10 | Colin MONTGOMERIE | 322,320.70 | |

S porting heroes do not come along in Singapore very often. In fact, you can count them all on the fingers of one hand. But that exclusive club now has a new member after Mardan Mamat's emotional victory in the OSIM Singapore Masters at Laguna National Golf & Country Club.

A trawl through the history books reveals the rarity of sporting milestones for this small nation – Tan Howe Liang's weightlifting silver medal at the 1960 Rome Olympics, Ang Peng Siong becoming the world's fastest swimmer over 50 metres in 1982, Fandi Ahmed becoming the first footballer to play in Europe and table tennis star Li Jiawai reaching the last four of the Athens Olympics in 2004 – the names of those who had thrilled the country over the past five decades.

Marcus Fraser

But now enter Mardan Mamat who, in front of his home crowd, made history as the first Singaporean to win on The European Tour International Schedule. It was not just the fact that he won either, the way he did it was hugely impressive.

For four days the 38 year old held the lead in the event jointly sanctioned by The European Tour and the Asian Tour and, try as they might, no-one could catch him. Many thought he would stumble, the pressure of leading such a huge event on home soil being too much to bear, but he stood firm.

Even with Nick Dougherty, the defending champion, snapping at his heels, and another young Englishman, Ross Fisher, playing so impressively in his rookie season, mounting a charge, Mamat did not waver. Korea's Charlie Wi, who won the Maybank Malaysian Open only three weeks previously, also hovered but Mamat was not to be denied. This was his moment.

Mamat's is a classic rags to riches tale. Having left school at the age of 13, he worked as a caddie at the Jurong Golf Club in Singapore, earning barely enough to finance his growing love of the sport. It

# OSIM Singapore Masters

**Singapore**
March 9-12 • 2006

*"If you miss the fairways, especially on the par fives, you cannot go for the green. The rough is so penal, especially around the putting surfaces. It is a fantastic course, great layout and in superb condition. The greens run really true"* – **Ross Fisher**

Simon Khan

was not long before his talent was noticed and he was given free use of the facilities and time to practise. Soon he was on the national team and showed promise as an amateur by winning the individual title in the 1993 Putra Cup as Singapore landed the team prize.

When he turned professional in 1994 he made an instant impact, holing-in-one in his first event to win a luxury car. In 1997 he shot to prominence as the first Singaporean to qualify for The Open Championship at Royal Troon and in 2004, a week after finishing joint eighth in the Singapore Masters after leading going into the final round, he won the Royal Challenge Indian Open on the Asian Tour.

Indeed it was the memory of that fortnight two years earlier that carried him through

to this historic victory while, in practical terms, the fact the club gave the local professionals free rein to practise on the Laguna National Course further helped him in his preparations.

An opening 65, seven under par, gave Mamat a share of the lead with Australian Marcus Fraser and after a second round 70, he was one clear of the field. The pressure was building although Mamat pulled further ahead, moving four clear at one stage in the third round, before being pegged back to being one ahead going into the final 18 holes.

Dawn arrived with a hot sun and a light breeze. Mamat had known many such mornings, but this was to be like no other day in his life. Dougherty, one shot off the

*Nick Dougherty*

# Final Results

| Pos | Name | | Rd1 | Rd2 | Rd3 | Rd4 | Total | | € | £ |
|---|---|---|---|---|---|---|---|---|---|---|
| 1 | Mardan MAMAT | SIN | 65 | 70 | 70 | 71 | 276 | -12 | 138,560.42 | 95,065.88 |
| 2 | Nick DOUGHERTY | ENG | 69 | 70 | 67 | 71 | 277 | -11 | 92,376.39 | 63,379.16 |
| 3 | Ross FISHER | ENG | 71 | 68 | 68 | 71 | 278 | -10 | 46,807.58 | 32,114.54 |
| | Charlie WI | KOR | 69 | 73 | 65 | 71 | 278 | -10 | 46,807.58 | 32,114.54 |
| 5 | Jonathan LOMAS | ENG | 71 | 74 | 68 | 66 | 279 | -9 | 32,175.02 | 22,075.18 |
| | Chapchai NIRAT | THA | 73 | 69 | 66 | 71 | 279 | -9 | 32,175.02 | 22,075.18 |
| 7 | Jyoti RANDHAWA | IND | 74 | 68 | 71 | 68 | 281 | -7 | 22,863.38 | 15,686.50 |
| | Andrew BUTTERFIELD | ENG | 74 | 69 | 66 | 72 | 281 | -7 | 22,863.38 | 15,686.50 |
| 9 | Prayad MARKSAENG | THA | 67 | 69 | 74 | 72 | 282 | -6 | 16,212.22 | 11,123.15 |
| | Marcus FRASER | AUS | 65 | 76 | 70 | 71 | 282 | -6 | 16,212.22 | 11,123.15 |
| | Anders HANSEN | DEN | 69 | 74 | 72 | 67 | 282 | -6 | 16,212.22 | 11,123.15 |
| | Marcus BOTH | AUS | 68 | 68 | 77 | 69 | 282 | -6 | 16,212.22 | 11,123.15 |
| 13 | Wei Chih LU | TPE | 69 | 72 | 71 | 71 | 283 | -5 | 11,535.62 | 7,914.55 |
| | Peter HANSON | SWE | 70 | 69 | 72 | 72 | 283 | -5 | 11,535.62 | 7,914.55 |
| | Joakim HAEGGMAN | SWE | 72 | 70 | 69 | 72 | 283 | -5 | 11,535.62 | 7,914.55 |
| | Thaworn WIRATCHANT | THA | 76 | 68 | 72 | 67 | 283 | -5 | 11,535.62 | 7,914.55 |
| | Wade ORMSBY | AUS | 67 | 71 | 72 | 73 | 283 | -5 | 11,535.62 | 7,914.55 |
| | Ahmad Dan BATEMAN | CAN | 70 | 69 | 74 | 70 | 283 | -5 | 11,535.62 | 7,914.55 |
| | Ter-Chang WANG | TPE | 72 | 70 | 71 | 70 | 283 | -5 | 11,535.62 | 7,914.55 |
| | François DELAMONTAGNE | FRA | 71 | 70 | 72 | 70 | 283 | -5 | 11,535.62 | 7,914.55 |
| 21 | Prom MEESAWAT | THA | 73 | 71 | 67 | 73 | 284 | -4 | 9,270.06 | 6,360.16 |
| | Simon YATES | SCO | 72 | 71 | 69 | 72 | 284 | -4 | 9,270.06 | 6,360.16 |
| | Stuart LITTLE | ENG | 71 | 69 | 72 | 72 | 284 | -4 | 9,270.06 | 6,360.16 |
| | Keith HORNE | RSA | 72 | 72 | 71 | 69 | 284 | -4 | 9,270.06 | 6,360.16 |
| 25 | Danny CHIA | MAS | 75 | 68 | 68 | 74 | 285 | -3 | 8,272.39 | 5,675.66 |
| | Anthony KANG | USA | 75 | 70 | 67 | 73 | 285 | -3 | 8,272.39 | 5,675.66 |
| | Wen-Chong LIANG | CHN | 73 | 72 | 70 | 70 | 285 | -3 | 8,272.39 | 5,675.66 |
| | Chris RODGERS | ENG | 72 | 70 | 71 | 72 | 285 | -3 | 8,272.39 | 5,675.66 |
| 29 | Søren HANSEN | DEN | 71 | 74 | 70 | 71 | 286 | -2 | 7,274.71 | 4,991.16 |
| | Andrew MARSHALL | ENG | 73 | 70 | 69 | 74 | 286 | -2 | 7,274.71 | 4,991.16 |
| | Thammanoon SIROT | THA | 73 | 72 | 67 | 74 | 286 | -2 | 7,274.71 | 4,991.16 |
| | José Manuel LARA | ESP | 70 | 74 | 72 | 70 | 286 | -2 | 7,274.71 | 4,991.16 |
| 33 | Peter HEDBLOM | SWE | 71 | 70 | 73 | 73 | 287 | -1 | 6,339.39 | 4,349.44 |
| | Wen Teh LU | TPE | 71 | 70 | 72 | 74 | 287 | -1 | 6,339.39 | 4,349.44 |
| | Gary RUSNAK | USA | 72 | 73 | 72 | 70 | 287 | -1 | 6,339.39 | 4,349.44 |
| | Matthew MILLAR | AUS | 73 | 69 | 70 | 75 | 287 | -1 | 6,339.39 | 4,349.44 |
| 37 | Robert KARLSSON | SWE | 72 | 73 | 70 | 73 | 288 | 0 | 5,736.63 | 3,935.88 |
| | Boonchu RUANGKIT | THA | 67 | 73 | 76 | 72 | 288 | 0 | 5,736.63 | 3,935.88 |
| | Søren KJELDSEN | DEN | 72 | 71 | 72 | 73 | 288 | 0 | 5,736.63 | 3,935.88 |
| 40 | Gary EVANS | ENG | 68 | 72 | 77 | 72 | 289 | 1 | 4,905.24 | 3,365.47 |
| | Jean VAN DE VELDE | FRA | 70 | 72 | 77 | 70 | 289 | 1 | 4,905.24 | 3,365.47 |
| | Steven O'HARA | SCO | 72 | 73 | 76 | 68 | 289 | 1 | 4,905.24 | 3,365.47 |
| | Unho PARK | AUS | 67 | 72 | 74 | 76 | 289 | 1 | 4,905.24 | 3,365.47 |
| | Charl SCHWARTZEL | RSA | 71 | 69 | 73 | 76 | 289 | 1 | 4,905.24 | 3,365.47 |
| | Simon DYSON | ENG | 73 | 67 | 78 | 71 | 289 | 1 | 4,905.24 | 3,365.47 |
| | Sung-Man LEE | KOR | 72 | 71 | 75 | 71 | 289 | 1 | 4,905.24 | 3,365.47 |
| 47 | Chinarat PHADUNGSIL | THA | 70 | 73 | 73 | 74 | 290 | 2 | 3,907.56 | 2,680.97 |
| | Ignacio GARRIDO | ESP | 74 | 70 | 75 | 71 | 290 | 2 | 3,907.56 | 2,680.97 |
| | Edward LOAR | USA | 74 | 68 | 75 | 73 | 290 | 2 | 3,907.56 | 2,680.97 |
| | Fredrik WIDMARK | SWE | 69 | 74 | 70 | 77 | 290 | 2 | 3,907.56 | 2,680.97 |
| | Gaurav GHEI | IND | 71 | 72 | 69 | 76 | 290 | 2 | 3,907.56 | 2,680.97 |
| 52 | Barry LANE | ENG | 71 | 69 | 78 | 73 | 291 | 3 | 2,921.76 | 2,004.61 |
| | Miguel Angel MARTIN | ESP | 69 | 73 | 73 | 76 | 291 | 3 | 2,921.76 | 2,004.61 |
| | Michael HOEY | NIR | 75 | 65 | 74 | 77 | 291 | 3 | 2,921.76 | 2,004.61 |
| | Jason KNUTZON | USA | 73 | 72 | 74 | 72 | 291 | 3 | 2,921.76 | 2,004.61 |
| | Simon KHAN | ENG | 73 | 71 | 74 | 73 | 291 | 3 | 2,921.76 | 2,004.61 |
| | Brett RUMFORD | AUS | 73 | 69 | 77 | 72 | 291 | 3 | 2,921.76 | 2,004.61 |
| | David HIGGINS | IRL | 71 | 72 | 76 | 72 | 291 | 3 | 2,921.76 | 2,004.61 |
| 59 | Simon WAKEFIELD | ENG | 72 | 71 | 76 | 73 | 292 | 4 | 2,327.91 | 1,597.17 |
| | Raymond RUSSELL | SCO | 70 | 72 | 74 | 76 | 292 | 4 | 2,327.91 | 1,597.17 |
| | Jean-François LUCQUIN | FRA | 74 | 71 | 77 | 70 | 292 | 4 | 2,327.91 | 1,597.17 |
| 62 | Peter LAWRIE | IRL | 72 | 69 | 76 | 76 | 293 | 5 | 2,036.92 | 1,397.52 |
| | Robert ROCK | ENG | 70 | 73 | 76 | 74 | 293 | 5 | 2,036.92 | 1,397.52 |
| | Daniel VANCSIK | ARG | 73 | 71 | 76 | 73 | 293 | 5 | 2,036.92 | 1,397.52 |
| | Scott STRANGE | AUS | 70 | 74 | 76 | 73 | 293 | 5 | 2,036.92 | 1,397.52 |
| 66 | Jason DAWES | AUS | 74 | 71 | 73 | 76 | 294 | 6 | 1,745.93 | 1,197.88 |
| | Peter GUSTAFSSON | SWE | 71 | 74 | 75 | 74 | 294 | 6 | 1,745.93 | 1,197.88 |
| | Amandeep JOHL | IND | 72 | 73 | 74 | 75 | 294 | 6 | 1,745.93 | 1,197.88 |
| 69 | Mike CUNNING | USA | 75 | 70 | 77 | 73 | 295 | 7 | 1,449.37 | 994.41 |
| | Marc CAYEUX | ZIM | 73 | 72 | 75 | 75 | 295 | 7 | 1,449.37 | 994.41 |
| | Rahil GANGJEE | IND | 77 | 68 | 75 | 75 | 295 | 7 | 1,449.37 | 994.41 |
| 72 | Christopher HANELL | SWE | 73 | 72 | 77 | 74 | 296 | 8 | 1,244.00 | 853.50 |
| 73 | Miles TUNNICLIFF | ENG | 73 | 72 | 77 | 75 | 297 | 9 | 1,241.00 | 851.45 |
| 74 | Bill FUNG | SIN | 72 | 72 | 75 | 79 | 298 | 10 | 1,238.00 | 849.39 |
| 75 | Bryan SALTUS | USA | 72 | 73 | 77 | 77 | 299 | 11 | 1,235.00 | 847.33 |
| 76 | Shiv KAPUR | IND | 71 | 73 | 80 | 76 | 300 | 12 | 1,232.00 | 845.27 |
| 77 | Martin ERLANDSSON | SWE | 70 | 74 | 76 | 81 | 301 | 13 | 1,229.00 | 843.21 |
| 78 | Kyi Hla HAN | MYA | 72 | 73 | 79 | 81 | 305 | 17 | 1,226.00 | 841.15 |
| 79 | Jarmo SANDELIN | SWE | 70 | 72 | RETD | | | | | |

## Total Prize Fund
€841,290 £577,204

lead going into the final round, was the favourite for the title. Fisher and Wi were to be feared. Mamat, however, struck the first blow. He birdied the first two holes to give himself breathing space. The chasing pack faltered. Dougherty dropped three shots on the front nine. Fisher was twice in the water over the same stretch. All the while, Mamat held his ground.

*Peter Hanson*

The two young Englishman rallied. Dougherty, in particular, putting up a proud defence of his title with four birdies on the back nine. The golfing gods were smiling on Mamat and when he pitched and putted for the par he needed on the final hole, his raw emotion was understandable.

Tears streamed down his face as he was embraced by his family, and the crowd erupted. As he accepted the €138,560 (£95,065) cheque, and with the knowledge he had also gained a two year exemption to The European Tour, Mamat began singing the words to 'Count On Me, Singapore', a popular national song "....There was a time when people said, that Singapore won't make it. But we did."

Mamat had certainly made it, too, and no-one would deny that he had deserved it.

**Roddy Williams**

# Riding The Crest Of a Wave

Charl Schwartzel

## Yalong Bay Golf Club

| Par | Yards | Metres |
| --- | --- | --- |
| 72 | 7172 | 6558 |

| | | | | |
| --- | --- | --- | --- | --- |
| 1 | Johan EDFORS | 263 | -25 |  |
| 2 | Andrew BUCKLE | 264 | -24 | |
| 3 | Prayad MARKSAENG | 265 | -23 | |
| 4 | Nick DOUGHERTY | 266 | -22 | |
| 5 | Gaurav GHEI | 267 | -21 | |
| | Wen Teh LU | 267 | -21 | |
| 7 | Warren ABERY | 268 | -20 | |
| | David HOWELL | 268 | -20 | |
| | Jeev Milkha SINGH | 268 | -20 | |
| 10 | Paul CASEY | 269 | -19 | |
| | Edward LOAR | 269 | -19 | |

**F**or a man who would not look out of place on any of the world's surfing beaches, it was fitting that Johan Edfors won his maiden European Tour title on the Chinese holiday island of Hainan, known as the 'Hawaii of the East.'

With his flowing locks, golden tan and colourful attire, the Swede's image is more in keeping with those who hang ten rather than those who hang around practice ranges, but on a glorious final day at Yalong Bay Golf Club in Sanya, Edfors rode the crest of a wave for a one stroke victory in the TCL Classic.

Hainan Island is fast developing as China's most popular tourist destination. It is not only the fact that it is on the same latitude as Hawaii that gives it a similar tropical feel to the US state, but also the abundance of tranquil sands, coconut palms and year round sunshine. It is undoubtedly one of the most relaxing of the many destinations on The European Tour International Schedule and, therefore, appropriate that one of the Tour's most laid-back professionals emerged victorious.

Although the week ended well for Edfors, it did not begin that way. Hainan Island also goes by the nickname 'The End of the World,' stemming from ancient Chinese folklore when poets and artists were exiled from Beijing and found their homes on the island. After the Swede missed his connecting flight in Shanghai on the way there and then discovered his travel agents had directed him to the wrong airport on the island, some four hours away, he could have been forgiven for thinking that was exactly where he was heading.

It was not the ideal preparation as he eventually arrived at his destination 12 hours late in the early hours of Tuesday morning nursing a sore back. However, he was soon in his stride.

Paul McGinley

### WEATHER REPORT

| Round One | Round Two | Round Three | Round Four |
| --- | --- | --- | --- |

### EUROPEAN TOUR ORDER OF MERIT
(After 14 tournaments)

| Pos | | € | |
| --- | --- | --- | --- |
| 1 | David HOWELL | 960,518.82 | |
| 2 | Henrik STENSON | 618,558.47 | |
| 3 | Nick O'HERN | 556,037.34 | |
| 4 | Ernie ELS | 548,816.70 | |
| 5 | Nick DOUGHERTY | 496,276.12 | |
| 6 | Retief GOOSEN | 429,408.00 | |
| 7 | Paul CASEY | 417,882.88 | |
| 8 | Thongchai JAIDEE | 341,052.58 | |
| 9 | Vijay SINGH | 323,872.28 | |
| 10 | Colin MONTGOMERIE | 322,320.70 | |

**Sanya, Hainan Island, China**
March 16-19 • 2006

David Howell

With barely a breath of wind, Yalong Bay became defenceless and the scores immediately reflected the ease in which the course was playing. On perfectly manicured fairways and greens, a birdie barrage began and records started tumbling. On the first day the course record was broken when, to the delight of the home crowd, Liang Wen-Chong of China equalled American Edward Loar's earlier ten under par 62 to take a share of the first round lead.

Tournament favourite David Howell, the leader of The European Tour Order of Merit entering the event, equalled his lowest round as a professional with an opening 64 before bettering it with a 63 the following

*"It is a very good course but, with no rough because of the time of year and the lack of wind, it played relatively easy. The greens are fantastic and the whole course is conditioned exceptionally well"* – *David Howell*

Paul Casey

| Pos | Name | | Rd1 | Rd2 | Rd3 | Rd4 | Total | | € | £ |
|---|---|---|---|---|---|---|---|---|---|---|
| 1 | Johan EDFORS | SWE | 66 | 66 | 63 | 68 | 263 | -25 | 140,215.18 | 96,580.90 |
| 2 | Andrew BUCKLE | AUS | 63 | 66 | 65 | 70 | 264 | -24 | 93,479.59 | 64,389.20 |
| 3 | Prayad MARKSAENG | THA | 66 | 66 | 68 | 65 | 265 | -23 | 52,666.93 | 36,277.24 |
| 4 | Nick DOUGHERTY | ENG | 66 | 67 | 64 | 69 | 266 | -22 | 42,066.24 | 28,975.43 |
| 5 | Wen Teh LU | TPE | 69 | 68 | 64 | 66 | 267 | -21 | 32,559.27 | 22,426.98 |
| | Gaurav GHEI | IND | 67 | 69 | 65 | 66 | 267 | -21 | 32,559.27 | 22,426.98 |
| 7 | Jeev Milkha SINGH | IND | 69 | 63 | 66 | 70 | 268 | -20 | 21,706.18 | 14,951.32 |
| | David HOWELL | ENG | 64 | 63 | 66 | 75 | 268 | -20 | 21,706.18 | 14,951.32 |
| | Warren ABERY | RSA | 63 | 68 | 71 | 66 | 268 | -20 | 21,706.18 | 14,951.32 |
| 10 | Paul CASEY | ENG | 65 | 68 | 68 | 68 | 269 | -19 | 16,153.44 | 11,126.56 |
| | Edward LOAR | USA | 62 | 69 | 68 | 70 | 269 | -19 | 16,153.44 | 11,126.56 |
| 12 | Ariel CANETE | ARG | 65 | 66 | 70 | 69 | 270 | -18 | 14,470.79 | 9,967.55 |
| 13 | Charl SCHWARTZEL | RSA | 65 | 67 | 69 | 70 | 271 | -17 | 12,928.36 | 8,905.11 |
| | Ter-Chang WANG | TPE | 66 | 67 | 69 | 69 | 271 | -17 | 12,928.36 | 8,905.11 |
| | Matthew MILLAR | AUS | 68 | 67 | 68 | 68 | 271 | -17 | 12,928.36 | 8,905.11 |
| 16 | Prom MEESAWAT | THA | 68 | 70 | 68 | 66 | 272 | -16 | 11,126.52 | 7,664.00 |
| | Anthony KANG | USA | 68 | 71 | 69 | 64 | 272 | -16 | 11,126.52 | 7,664.00 |
| | Paul MCGINLEY | IRL | 69 | 65 | 68 | 70 | 272 | -16 | 11,126.52 | 7,664.00 |
| | Keng-Chi LIN | TPE | 67 | 67 | 67 | 71 | 272 | -16 | 11,126.52 | 7,664.00 |
| 20 | Scott STRANGE | AUS | 68 | 64 | 71 | 70 | 273 | -15 | 10,095.90 | 6,954.10 |
| 21 | Amandeep JOHL | IND | 70 | 63 | 69 | 72 | 274 | -14 | 9,380.77 | 6,461.52 |
| | Daniel VANCSIK | ARG | 66 | 65 | 70 | 73 | 274 | -14 | 9,380.77 | 6,461.52 |
| | Alexandre ROCHA | BRA | 72 | 69 | 66 | 69 | 274 | -14 | 9,380.77 | 6,461.52 |
| | Joakim HAEGGMAN | SWE | 63 | 69 | 68 | 74 | 274 | -14 | 9,380.77 | 6,461.52 |
| 25 | Thaworn WIRATCHANT | THA | 69 | 70 | 65 | 71 | 275 | -13 | 7,866.39 | 5,418.41 |
| | Simon YATES | SCO | 67 | 72 | 71 | 65 | 275 | -13 | 7,866.39 | 5,418.41 |
| | Christopher HANELL | SWE | 66 | 68 | 68 | 72 | 275 | -13 | 7,866.39 | 5,418.41 |
| | Simon HURD | ENG | 69 | 68 | 68 | 70 | 275 | -13 | 7,866.39 | 5,418.41 |
| | David BRANSDON | AUS | 70 | 68 | 68 | 69 | 275 | -13 | 7,866.39 | 5,418.41 |
| | Brad KENNEDY | AUS | 68 | 66 | 73 | 68 | 275 | -13 | 7,866.39 | 5,418.41 |
| | Unho PARK | AUS | 71 | 64 | 73 | 67 | 275 | -13 | 7,866.39 | 5,418.41 |
| | Chao LI | CHN | 70 | 67 | 71 | 67 | 275 | -13 | 7,866.39 | 5,418.41 |
| 33 | Mahal PEARCE | NZL | 68 | 68 | 69 | 71 | 276 | -12 | 6,068.05 | 4,179.71 |
| | Jamie DONALDSON | WAL | 68 | 68 | 69 | 71 | 276 | -12 | 6,068.05 | 4,179.71 |
| | Rafael GOMEZ | ARG | 71 | 68 | 69 | 68 | 276 | -12 | 6,068.05 | 4,179.71 |
| | David GRIFFITHS | ENG | 68 | 67 | 69 | 72 | 276 | -12 | 6,068.05 | 4,179.71 |
| | Phillip ARCHER | ENG | 66 | 72 | 70 | 68 | 276 | -12 | 6,068.05 | 4,179.71 |
| | Gregory HAVRET | FRA | 67 | 66 | 72 | 71 | 276 | -12 | 6,068.05 | 4,179.71 |
| | Chris RODGERS | ENG | 67 | 72 | 69 | 68 | 276 | -12 | 6,068.05 | 4,179.71 |
| | Søren HANSEN | DEN | 66 | 69 | 67 | 74 | 276 | -12 | 6,068.05 | 4,179.71 |
| 41 | Hendrik BUHRMANN | RSA | 71 | 68 | 67 | 71 | 277 | -11 | 4,795.55 | 3,303.20 |
| | Marco RUIZ | PAR | 67 | 70 | 70 | 70 | 277 | -11 | 4,795.55 | 3,303.20 |
| | Wilhelm SCHAUMAN | SWE | 66 | 69 | 73 | 69 | 277 | -11 | 4,795.55 | 3,303.20 |
| | Richard MCEVOY | ENG | 68 | 71 | 70 | 68 | 277 | -11 | 4,795.55 | 3,303.20 |
| | Sung-Man LEE | KOR | 68 | 69 | 72 | 68 | 277 | -11 | 4,795.55 | 3,303.20 |
| | Shiv KAPUR | IND | 71 | 68 | 67 | 71 | 277 | -11 | 4,795.55 | 3,303.20 |
| | Rahil GANGJEE | IND | 66 | 69 | 69 | 73 | 277 | -11 | 4,795.55 | 3,303.20 |
| 48 | Jarrod LYLE | AUS | 68 | 65 | 75 | 70 | 278 | -10 | 3,870.09 | 2,665.74 |
| | Hennie OTTO | RSA | 69 | 68 | 68 | 73 | 278 | -10 | 3,870.09 | 2,665.74 |
| | Thammanoon SRIROT | THA | 68 | 74 | 65 | 71 | 278 | -10 | 3,870.09 | 2,665.74 |
| | Ignacio GARRIDO | ESP | 66 | 73 | 66 | 73 | 278 | -10 | 3,870.09 | 2,665.74 |
| 52 | Iain PYMAN | ENG | 69 | 70 | 70 | 70 | 279 | -9 | 3,281.17 | 2,260.08 |
| | Jason DAWES | AUS | 68 | 67 | 71 | 73 | 279 | -9 | 3,281.17 | 2,260.08 |
| | Wen-Chong LIANG | CHN | 62 | 74 | 71 | 72 | 279 | -9 | 3,281.17 | 2,260.08 |
| 55 | Thongchai JAIDEE | THA | 68 | 68 | 72 | 70 | 280 | -8 | 2,560.03 | 1,763.36 |
| | Ari SAVOLAINEN | FIN | 66 | 69 | 67 | 78 | 280 | -8 | 2,560.03 | 1,763.36 |
| | Angelo QUE | PHI | 71 | 67 | 71 | 71 | 280 | -8 | 2,560.03 | 1,763.36 |
| | Adam BLYTH | AUS | 66 | 66 | 73 | 74 | 280 | -8 | 2,560.03 | 1,763.36 |
| | Gary CLARK | ENG | 70 | 69 | 69 | 72 | 280 | -8 | 2,560.03 | 1,763.36 |
| | Keith HORNE | RSA | 72 | 67 | 69 | 72 | 280 | -8 | 2,560.03 | 1,763.36 |
| | Ross BAIN | SCO | 70 | 67 | 72 | 71 | 280 | -8 | 2,560.03 | 1,763.36 |
| 62 | Terry PILKADARIS | AUS | 69 | 68 | 69 | 75 | 281 | -7 | 2,187.44 | 1,506.72 |
| 63 | Brian AKSTRUP | DEN | 69 | 69 | 73 | 71 | 282 | -6 | 2,061.25 | 1,419.80 |
| | Stephen SCAHILL | NZL | 71 | 66 | 70 | 75 | 282 | -6 | 2,061.25 | 1,419.80 |
| 65 | Raymond RUSSELL | SCO | 70 | 67 | 72 | 75 | 284 | -4 | 1,850.91 | 1,274.92 |
| | Johan SKÖLD | SWE | 70 | 68 | 72 | 74 | 284 | -4 | 1,850.91 | 1,274.92 |
| | Richard MOIR | AUS | 69 | 66 | 81 | 76 | 284 | -4 | 1,850.91 | 1,274.92 |
| 68 | Marcel SIEM | GER | 70 | 68 | 71 | 78 | 287 | -1 | 1,682.65 | 1,159.02 |
| 69 | James KINGSTON | RSA | 67 | 70 | W/D | | | | | |

day. When he added a third round 66, he equalled The European Tour record for 54 holes with a 23 under par total of 193. The Englishman looked unstoppable, the only apparent question remaining being whether he could become the first player to shoot 30 under par for four rounds.

Amidst the fireworks, Edfors was quietly going about his business with two opening 66s before making a significant move with a third round 63 to lie two behind Howell going into the final round. Few gave him much chance of overhauling the leader even when the Swede pointed out that the last time they played together, some 13 years earlier in a boys' tournament in Switzerland, it was Edfors who emerged the victor.

His chances looked even slimmer when he dropped shots on the second and third holes of his final round but, to his surprise, with nine holes to play, he discovered his name at the top of the leaderboard. The reason for his elevation was because, in the final match behind, everything that could go wrong for Howell did so. A three over par outward half seriously dented his title hopes, along with any record pretentions, and he eventually shared seventh place after a final round 75.

It left the stage clear for Edfors, his playing partner Nick Dougherty of England, Australian Andrew Buckle and Thailand's Prayad Marksaeng, who made a late charge with a final round of 65 to contest the title.

Edfors was in pole position but three times in the last ten holes eagle putts slipped by, and when he dropped a shot on the 14th the challengers began to close in. However, he raised his game for one final push to the line. He birdied the 16th before playing an exquisite approach to eight feet at the last to set up a closing birdie for a final round of 68 and a 25 under par total of 263.

Dougherty was unable to catch him and bogeyed the last for fourth place behind Marksaeng, which left Buckle needing a birdie to force a play-off. The young Australian, who came close to winning the Enjoy Jakarta HSBC Indonesia Open two weeks earlier, gave himself a chance on the last but his birdie putt stayed above ground and once again he had to settle for second.

For Edfors, victory was the realisation of a childhood dream. His win was also another triumph for the Challenge Tour which he had dominated in 2003 on his way to topping the Rankings. After a couple of seasons of hard work, the 30 year old finally fulfilled the promise he showed in those earlier years. Now he was ready to make more waves on the biggest stage of all.

**Roddy Williams**

## Total Prize Fund
€839,785  £578,448

# Voyage of Discovery

*Bradley Dredge*

## Santo da Serra

| Par | Yards | Metres |
|---|---|---|
| 72 | 6826 | 6241 |

| | | | | |
|---|---|---|---|---|
| 1 | Jean VAN DE VELDE | 273 | -15 |  |
| 2 | Lee SLATTERY | 274 | -14 | |
| 3 | Pedro LINHART | 275 | -13 | |
| 4 | Simon WAKEFIELD | 276 | -12 | |
| 5 | Mattias ELIASSON | 278 | -10 | |
| | Richard FINCH | 278 | -10 | |
| 7 | David GRIFFITHS | 279 | -9 | |
| | Jarmo SANDELIN | 279 | -9 | |
| | Tom WHITEHOUSE | 279 | -9 | |
| 10 | Damien MCGRANE | 280 | -8 |   |

A compatriot of Jean Van de Velde – the 19th Century poet and philosopher Charles Baudelaire - might well have summed up the Frenchman's 18 year odyssey on The European Tour in his book 'Petits Poemes', and in particular in the ode entitled 'Le Voyage'. It features details of a rather tormented trip which, to quote the writer, is: "A search for some impossible satisfaction that forever eludes the traveller."

While Van de Velde was no ancient mariner, he did, before boarding the flight to the Madeira Island Open Caixa Geral de Depositos, seem doomed to roam the fairways of the world with no really happy horizon in sight.

At Santo da Serra, however, his ship finally came in, but Baudelaire was replaced by Robbie Burns to mark the moment. In Scotland's national bard's poem 'Robert The Bruce's March to Bannockburn' is the line: "Now's the day and now's the hour". For Van de Velde, the day was Sunday, March 26, 2006; the hour was four pm.

That was when it all came right for the amiable man from Mont de Marsan and it was appropriate that Burns had heralded the occasion. For Van de Velde knew all about Burns, well, one Burn in particular; the Barry Burn at Carnoustie. His experience there at the denouement of The 1999 Open Championship had given him legendary status, if, perhaps, for the wrong reasons. His triple-bogey seven at the 72nd hole, before losing out in the play-off to Paul Lawrie, was a story of misfortune and misjudgement, a true reflection of 'Le Voyage'.

So was his career-threatening spill while skiing. That particular excursion on the slopes cost him a badly injured knee, surgery in 2002, and three years wandering in the wilderness, watching others play golf while he hobbled.

Three comeback attempts failed but like the selfsame Robert The Bruce about which Burns had written, Van de Velde tried again.

### WEATHER REPORT

| Round One | Round Two | Round Three | Round Four |
|---|---|---|---|

*Jarmo Sandelin*

### EUROPEAN TOUR ORDER OF MERIT
(After 15 tournaments)

| Pos | | € | |
|---|---|---|---|
| 1 | David HOWELL | 960,518.82 | |
| 2 | Henrik STENSON | 618,558.47 | |
| 3 | Nick O'HERN | 556,037.34 | |
| 4 | Ernie ELS | 548,816.70 | |
| 5 | Nick DOUGHERTY | 496,276.12 | |
| 6 | Retief GOOSEN | 429,408.00 | |
| 7 | Paul CASEY | 417,882.88 | |
| 8 | Thongchai JAIDEE | 341,052.58 | |
| 9 | Vijay SINGH | 323,872.28 | |
| 10 | Colin MONTGOMERIE | 322,320.70 | |

# Madeira Island Open Caixa Geral de Depositos

**Madeira, Portugal**
March 23-26 • 2006

Ian Garbutt

Damien McGrane

*"I think the course has improved dramatically. You have to think your way around and you can have plenty of opportunities to pick up shots, but you have to play well to do so"* – Jean Van de Velde

His second place after a play-off with fellow-countryman Jean-Francois Remesy at Le Golf National in the 2005 Open de France began the rehabilitation in earnest and the 1999 Ryder Cup player regained his card in one fell swoop. His victory in Madeira completed it. Unlike his ball at Carnoustie, Van de Velde proved unsinkable.

There were many up the mountain that overlooks the Atlantic, in similar circumstances to the Frenchman, namely attempting to rebuild a career. Jarmo Sandelin for one. The extrovert Swede, renowned for his garish clothes and spectacular Italian belt-buckles, had hit hard times in 2005.

The man who had chalked up five European Tour titles, starting with his memorable maiden win in the 1995 Turespaña Open Canarias where he overcame Seve Ballesteros down the closing stretch, lost his card for the first time in over a decade.

He regained it, however, at the Qualifying School in November, 2005, and when he opened with a 66 to lead, there was encouragement that the turbulent part of what he called "a roller-coaster ride", was coming to an end. After two rounds, Sandelin still hoped he had turned the corner. He

Robert-Jan Derksen

# Final Results

| Pos | Name | | Rd1 | Rd2 | Rd3 | Rd4 | Total | | € | £ |
|---|---|---|---|---|---|---|---|---|---|---|
| 1 | Jean VAN DE VELDE | FRA | 69 | 65 | 71 | 68 | 273 | -15 | 116,660.00 | 80,998.70 |
| 2 | Lee SLATTERY | ENG | 74 | 68 | 66 | 66 | 274 | -14 | 77,770.00 | 53,996.82 |
| 3 | Pedro LINHART | ESP | 71 | 67 | 69 | 68 | 275 | -13 | 43,820.00 | 30,424.85 |
| 4 | Simon WAKEFIELD | ENG | 72 | 68 | 68 | 68 | 276 | -12 | 35,000.00 | 24,301.00 |
| 5 | Richard FINCH | ENG | 70 | 69 | 72 | 67 | 278 | -10 | 27,090.00 | 18,808.97 |
| | Mattias ELIASSON | SWE | 74 | 69 | 71 | 64 | 278 | -10 | 27,090.00 | 18,808.97 |
| 7 | David GRIFFITHS | ENG | 72 | 69 | 71 | 67 | 279 | -9 | 18,060.00 | 12,539.32 |
| | Tom WHITEHOUSE | ENG | 73 | 65 | 71 | 70 | 279 | -9 | 18,060.00 | 12,539.32 |
| | Jarmo SANDELIN | SWE | 66 | 68 | 74 | 71 | 279 | -9 | 18,060.00 | 12,539.32 |
| 10 | Damien MCGRANE | IRL | 68 | 69 | 71 | 72 | 280 | -8 | 14,000.00 | 9,720.40 |
| 11 | Garry HOUSTON | WAL | 68 | 69 | 72 | 72 | 281 | -7 | 11,725.00 | 8,140.83 |
| | Christian CÉVAËR | FRA | 74 | 69 | 68 | 70 | 281 | -7 | 11,725.00 | 8,140.83 |
| | Warren ABERY | RSA | 69 | 70 | 74 | 68 | 281 | -7 | 11,725.00 | 8,140.83 |
| | Ian GARBUTT | ENG | 72 | 69 | 70 | 70 | 281 | -7 | 11,725.00 | 8,140.83 |
| 15 | Francesco MOLINARI | ITA | 70 | 73 | 69 | 70 | 282 | -6 | 10,080.00 | 6,998.69 |
| | Marcus HIGLEY | ENG | 72 | 69 | 71 | 70 | 282 | -6 | 10,080.00 | 6,998.69 |
| 17 | Martin ERLANDSSON | SWE | 70 | 73 | 69 | 71 | 283 | -5 | 8,890.00 | 6,172.45 |
| | Mark ROE | ENG | 74 | 68 | 73 | 68 | 283 | -5 | 8,890.00 | 6,172.45 |
| | Fredrik ANDERSSON HED | SWE | 76 | 67 | 74 | 66 | 283 | -5 | 8,890.00 | 6,172.45 |
| | Niclas FASTH | SWE | 70 | 73 | 67 | 73 | 283 | -5 | 8,890.00 | 6,172.45 |
| 21 | Iain PYMAN | ENG | 71 | 69 | 74 | 70 | 284 | -4 | 7,490.00 | 5,200.41 |
| | David LYNN | ENG | 72 | 72 | 70 | 70 | 284 | -4 | 7,490.00 | 5,200.41 |
| | Fredrik HENGE | SWE | 68 | 75 | 75 | 66 | 284 | -4 | 7,490.00 | 5,200.41 |
| | Gary ORR | SCO | 74 | 68 | 69 | 73 | 284 | -4 | 7,490.00 | 5,200.41 |
| | Magnus PERSSON | SWE | 73 | 69 | 67 | 75 | 284 | -4 | 7,490.00 | 5,200.41 |
| | Oliver WILSON | ENG | 71 | 71 | 68 | 74 | 284 | -4 | 7,490.00 | 5,200.41 |
| | Alessandro TADINI | ITA | 73 | 68 | 72 | 71 | 284 | -4 | 7,490.00 | 5,200.41 |
| 28 | Mark FOSTER | ENG | 69 | 73 | 73 | 70 | 285 | -3 | 5,923.75 | 4,112.94 |
| | Louis OOSTHUIZEN | RSA | 74 | 68 | 73 | 70 | 285 | -3 | 5,923.75 | 4,112.94 |
| | Steven O'HARA | SCO | 72 | 71 | 76 | 66 | 285 | -3 | 5,923.75 | 4,112.94 |
| | Paul LAWRIE | SCO | 68 | 69 | 77 | 71 | 285 | -3 | 5,923.75 | 4,112.94 |
| | Bradley DREDGE | WAL | 72 | 65 | 77 | 71 | 285 | -3 | 5,923.75 | 4,112.94 |
| | Andrew COLTART | SCO | 75 | 66 | 75 | 69 | 285 | -3 | 5,923.75 | 4,112.94 |
| | Tiago CRUZ | POR | 71 | 71 | 69 | 74 | 285 | -3 | 5,923.75 | 4,112.94 |
| | Alastair FORSYTH | SCO | 72 | 70 | 69 | 74 | 285 | -3 | 5,923.75 | 4,112.94 |
| 36 | John BICKERTON | ENG | 74 | 70 | 75 | 67 | 286 | -2 | 4,830.00 | 3,353.54 |
| | Ben MASON | ENG | 69 | 73 | 71 | 73 | 286 | -2 | 4,830.00 | 3,353.54 |
| | Ariel CANETE | ARG | 71 | 69 | 72 | 74 | 286 | -2 | 4,830.00 | 3,353.54 |
| | Felipe AGUILAR | CHI | 72 | 72 | 73 | 69 | 286 | -2 | 4,830.00 | 3,353.54 |
| | Oliver WHITELEY | ENG | 70 | 73 | 68 | 75 | 286 | -2 | 4,830.00 | 3,353.54 |
| 41 | Johan AXGREN | SWE | 70 | 70 | 71 | 76 | 287 | -1 | 4,200.00 | 2,916.12 |
| | Stephen GALLACHER | SCO | 69 | 70 | 71 | 77 | 287 | -1 | 4,200.00 | 2,916.12 |
| | Gordon BRAND JNR | SCO | 71 | 72 | 72 | 72 | 287 | -1 | 4,200.00 | 2,916.12 |
| | Santiago LUNA | ESP | 73 | 71 | 72 | 71 | 287 | -1 | 4,200.00 | 2,916.12 |
| 45 | Christian L NILSSON | SWE | 75 | 67 | 74 | 72 | 288 | 0 | 3,500.00 | 2,430.10 |
| | Peter BAKER | ENG | 71 | 73 | 74 | 70 | 288 | 0 | 3,500.00 | 2,430.10 |
| | Sam LITTLE | ENG | 75 | 69 | 75 | 69 | 288 | 0 | 3,500.00 | 2,430.10 |
| | Robert-Jan DERKSEN | NED | 71 | 71 | 74 | 72 | 288 | 0 | 3,500.00 | 2,430.10 |
| | Hennie OTTO | RSA | 70 | 74 | 72 | 72 | 288 | 0 | 3,500.00 | 2,430.10 |
| | Ross FISHER | ENG | 70 | 74 | 76 | 68 | 288 | 0 | 3,500.00 | 2,430.10 |
| 51 | Wilhelm SCHAUMAN | SWE | 73 | 68 | 71 | 77 | 289 | 1 | 2,870.00 | 1,992.68 |
| | Sam WALKER | ENG | 69 | 69 | 76 | 75 | 289 | 1 | 2,870.00 | 1,992.68 |
| | Francisco VALERA | ESP | 73 | 68 | 77 | 71 | 289 | 1 | 2,870.00 | 1,992.68 |
| 54 | Gary EMERSON | ENG | 68 | 75 | 76 | 71 | 290 | 2 | 2,324.00 | 1,613.59 |
| | José-Filipe LIMA | POR | 72 | 72 | 75 | 71 | 290 | 2 | 2,324.00 | 1,613.59 |
| | Gregory BOURDY | FRA | 72 | 69 | 78 | 71 | 290 | 2 | 2,324.00 | 1,613.59 |
| | Gareth DAVIES | ENG | 73 | 71 | 71 | 75 | 290 | 2 | 2,324.00 | 1,613.59 |
| | David PATRICK | SCO | 73 | 71 | 78 | 68 | 290 | 2 | 2,324.00 | 1,613.59 |
| 59 | David DIXON | ENG | 72 | 72 | 75 | 72 | 291 | 3 | 1,995.00 | 1,385.16 |
| | Simon KHAN | ENG | 76 | 68 | 76 | 71 | 291 | 3 | 1,995.00 | 1,385.16 |
| 61 | Raymond RUSSELL | SCO | 76 | 67 | 76 | 73 | 292 | 4 | 1,855.00 | 1,287.95 |
| | Gary MURPHY | IRL | 69 | 75 | 74 | 74 | 292 | 4 | 1,855.00 | 1,287.95 |
| 63 | Anders Schmidt HANSEN | DEN | 71 | 73 | 71 | 79 | 294 | 6 | 1,750.00 | 1,215.05 |
| 64 | Stuart LITTLE | ENG | 74 | 70 | 74 | 77 | 295 | 7 | 1,645.00 | 1,142.15 |
| | Nicolas COLSAERTS | BEL | 70 | 67 | 81 | 77 | 295 | 7 | 1,645.00 | 1,142.15 |
| 66 | Ricardo SANTOS | POR | 72 | 71 | 77 | 76 | 296 | 8 | 1,540.00 | 1,069.24 |
| 67 | Fredrik WIDMARK | SWE | 70 | 72 | 76 | DISQ | 218 | 2 | 1,470.00 | 1,020.64 |

## Total Prize Fund
€695,980   £483,228

had been joined, however, on top of the leaderboard by Van de Velde, the pair three shots ahead of the field.

Van de Velde's second round 65, almost a year to the day he had made the decision to give the game one final try, gave him the belief that he was no longer "running after something I could not catch."

When the third round - affected first of all by low cloud that caused a four hour suspension of play and then bedevilled by capricious winds - ended, Van de Velde had taken a firmer hold of the tournament. Sandelin's quest for glory, however, at least

Simon Wakefield

for this week, appeared over as he slid into the pack.

In a week of attempted career revivals, it was a Spaniard who came through to challenge. Pedro Linhart, the winner in Madeira in Van de Velde's pivotal year of 1999, made a bid to return to The European Tour, becoming the Frenchman's nearest pursuer going into the final round.

Thankfully for Van de Velde, there was to be no disappointing déjà-vu this time. His journey over the first ten holes on Sunday was a satisfying one as a barrage of birdies took him towards a promised land he had not visited since 1993, with his victory in the Roma Masters. Not even Englishman Lee Slattery's second 66 of the weekend on his way to a 14 under par total of 274 and second place, one clear of Linhart on 275, could deny Van de Velde.

His finish was not exactly poetry in motion, as Van de Velde found what he called "the nastiest piece of grass on the whole course," using up all but one of the three strokes he had in hand over Slattery at the final hole. But it was no longer hard lines for Jean. His arduous voyage was over.

**Norman Dabell**

# Man on a Mission

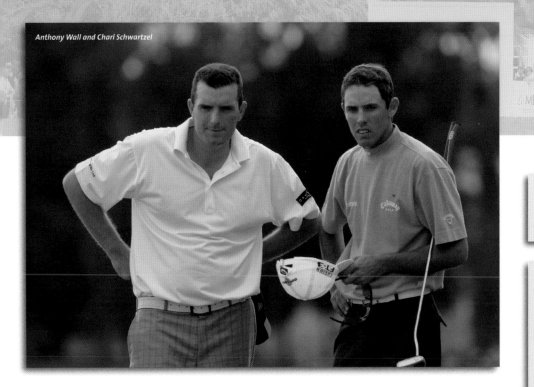

Anthony Wall and Charl Schwartzel

### Le Meridien Penina Golf & Resort

| Par | Yards | Metres |
|---|---|---|
| 72 | 6798 | 6217 |

| Pos | Name | Score | To Par | |
|---|---|---|---|---|
| 1 | **Paul BROADHURST** | 271 | -17 | |
| 2 | Anthony WALL | 272 | -16 | |
| 3 | Andres ROMERO | 273 | -15 | |
| 4 | Ricardo GONZALEZ | 274 | -14 | |
| | Charl SCHWARTZEL | 274 | -14 | |
| 6 | José Manuel LARA | 275 | -13 | |
| 7 | Markus BRIER | 277 | -11 | |
| | Mattias ELIASSON | 277 | -11 | |
| 9 | Jarmo SANDELIN | 278 | -10 | |
| 10 | Brian DAVIS | 279 | -9 | |
| | Niclas FASTH | 279 | -9 | |

There is an old story, well worth retelling, of a little lad who was asked by a stranger in the freezer aisle of a local supermarket what his dad did for a living. He replied, unhesitatingly: "He used to be a famous golfer." The dad in question, Paul Broadhurst, then a four time European Tour champion and a winner of two matches on his Ryder Cup debut at Kiawah Island in 1991, was suitably chastened when he heard of the exchange.

To be fair his twins Alex (the youngster in the aisle) and Sophie were barely 12 months old when their dad recorded that fourth success in the 1995 Peugeot Open de France. Subsequent sons Sam (1997) and Aaron (2004) had not even set foot on the planet. It was a shock to the system though, and made Broadhurst determined to show them he could still cut the mustard.

In 2005, a frustrating decade after his French title coup and a few months after that episode in the supermarket, he finally did the trick in the Estoril Open de Portugal Caixa Geral de Depositos. He felt, however, that his comeback at Oitavos Golfe had been a somewhat hollow affair. Leader Barry Lane had capitulated with a nine on the final hole and the 1999 Open Champion Paul Lawrie had triple-bogeyed the 71st before missing from ten feet at the last to force a play-off.

Broadhurst's growing family, he reckoned, were entitled to something a bit more convincing. Just five months before his 41st birthday, he duly obliged by successfully defending his Portuguese crown at Le Meridien Penina Golf & Resort.

Broadhurst opened with a course record equalling 64 to whet the appetite and was two clear following a second round 69. Ricardo Gonzalez inched a stroke ahead by eagling the last for a third day 64 of his own, but the big hitting Argentine's lead lasted only one hole as he began with a bogey five on day four. Broadhurst re-established his supremacy with four birdies on the trot from the second to be out in 30. When he chipped in to birdie the 12th, he was three strokes clear.

With the eyes of family and friends back home firmly glued to the television screens, Broadhurst, now a man on a mission, knew he still had to finish the job off. He explained: "After going in the water for a double bogey at the 13th, I hit it stone dead to birdie the next and I thought I was three clear standing on the 16th tee. But Anthony Wall up ahead had birdied there and I knew he

### WEATHER REPORT

| Round One | Round Two | Round Three | Round Four |

### EUROPEAN TOUR ORDER OF MERIT
(After 16 tournaments)

| Pos | Name | € | |
|---|---|---|---|
| 1 | **David HOWELL** | 960,518.82 | |
| 2 | Henrik STENSON | 618,558.47 | |
| 3 | Nick O'HERN | 556,037.34 | |
| 4 | Ernie ELS | 548,816.70 | |
| 5 | Paul BROADHURST | 513,125.85 | |
| 6 | Nick DOUGHERTY | 510,851.12 | |
| 7 | Retief GOOSEN | 429,408.00 | |
| 8 | Paul CASEY | 417,882.88 | |
| 9 | Thongchai JAIDEE | 341,052.58 | |
| 10 | Vijay SINGH | 323,872.28 | |

# Algarve Open de Portugal Caixa Geral de Depositos

**Portimao, Portugal**
March 30-April 2 • 2006

*Ricardo Gonzalez*

would make four at the long 18th. So when I bogeyed the 17th I knew I needed a birdie to win."

Alex, Sophie, Sam and Aaron must have been glowing with pride as they watched their dad courageously conjour the deftist of downhill chips from behind the green to two feet beyond the pin for that precise birdie four, a 67, a 17 under par total of 271, and a one stroke victory over Wall worth €208,330 (£143,859).

Broadhurst became the fourth man, and the first since Sam Torrance in 1982–83, to secure consecutive wins in this event which was celebrating its 50th anniversary on a masterpiece of a course carved from 360 acres of rice paddies some 40 years earlier by Sir Henry Cotton.

*"It is a tough but fair Championship test. Overall it is not particularly long but you have to hit the fairways, which are narrowed by masses of trees and pretty thick rough. It favours the guys who drive it straight" – Alastair Forsyth*

A skydiver lands on the fifth fairway

# Final Results

| Pos | Name | | Rd1 | Rd2 | Rd3 | Rd4 | Total | | € | £ |
|---|---|---|---|---|---|---|---|---|---|---|
| 1 | Paul BROADHURST | ENG | 64 | 69 | 71 | 67 | 271 | -17 | 208,330.00 | 143,859.41 |
| 2 | Anthony WALL | ENG | 71 | 67 | 67 | 67 | 272 | -16 | 138,880.00 | 95,901.67 |
| 3 | Andres ROMERO | ARG | 69 | 70 | 68 | 66 | 273 | -15 | 78,250.00 | 54,034.46 |
| 4 | Charl SCHWARTZEL | RSA | 69 | 70 | 67 | 68 | 274 | -14 | 57,750.00 | 39,878.47 |
| | Ricardo GONZALEZ | ARG | 73 | 66 | 64 | 71 | 274 | -14 | 57,750.00 | 39,878.47 |
| 6 | José Manuel LARA | ESP | 71 | 70 | 68 | 66 | 275 | -13 | 43,750.00 | 30,210.96 |
| 7 | Mattias ELIASSON | SWE | 70 | 67 | 71 | 69 | 277 | -11 | 34,375.00 | 23,737.18 |
| | Markus BRIER | AUT | 72 | 70 | 66 | 69 | 277 | -11 | 34,375.00 | 23,737.18 |
| 9 | Jarmo SANDELIN | SWE | 67 | 70 | 68 | 73 | 278 | -10 | 28,000.00 | 19,335.01 |
| 10 | Niclas FASTH | SWE | 71 | 68 | 67 | 73 | 279 | -9 | 24,000.00 | 16,572.87 |
| | Brian DAVIS | ENG | 70 | 71 | 67 | 71 | 279 | -9 | 24,000.00 | 16,572.87 |
| 12 | Christian L NILSSON | SWE | 65 | 71 | 71 | 73 | 280 | -8 | 19,781.25 | 13,659.67 |
| | Carl SUNESON | ESP | 67 | 72 | 66 | 75 | 280 | -8 | 19,781.25 | 13,659.67 |
| | Alastair FORSYTH | SCO | 73 | 71 | 65 | 71 | 280 | -8 | 19,781.25 | 13,659.67 |
| | Tom WHITEHOUSE | ENG | 72 | 72 | 68 | 68 | 280 | -8 | 19,781.25 | 13,659.67 |
| 16 | Daniel VANCSIK | ARG | 70 | 72 | 73 | 66 | 281 | -7 | 16,875.00 | 11,652.80 |
| | Richard BLAND | ENG | 74 | 70 | 69 | 68 | 281 | -7 | 16,875.00 | 11,652.80 |
| | Christian CÉVAËR | FRA | 66 | 69 | 72 | 74 | 281 | -7 | 16,875.00 | 11,652.80 |
| 19 | Søren HANSEN | DEN | 69 | 71 | 67 | 75 | 282 | -6 | 14,575.00 | 10,064.57 |
| | Alessandro TADINI | ITA | 69 | 73 | 69 | 71 | 282 | -6 | 14,575.00 | 10,064.57 |
| | Ian WOOSNAM | WAL | 70 | 74 | 69 | 69 | 282 | -6 | 14,575.00 | 10,064.57 |
| | Nick DOUGHERTY | ENG | 69 | 74 | 70 | 69 | 282 | -6 | 14,575.00 | 10,064.57 |
| | Paul LAWRIE | SCO | 68 | 70 | 76 | 68 | 282 | -6 | 14,575.00 | 10,064.57 |
| 24 | Simon WAKEFIELD | ENG | 70 | 71 | 72 | 70 | 283 | -5 | 12,062.50 | 8,329.59 |
| | Ross FISHER | ENG | 70 | 71 | 72 | 70 | 283 | -5 | 12,062.50 | 8,329.59 |
| | Gary MURPHY | IRL | 72 | 72 | 69 | 70 | 283 | -5 | 12,062.50 | 8,329.59 |
| | Kenneth FERRIE | ENG | 75 | 67 | 72 | 69 | 283 | -5 | 12,062.50 | 8,329.59 |
| | Steve WEBSTER | ENG | 70 | 73 | 70 | 70 | 283 | -5 | 12,062.50 | 8,329.59 |
| | Peter LAWRIE | IRL | 73 | 68 | 67 | 75 | 283 | -5 | 12,062.50 | 8,329.59 |
| | Peter BAKER | ENG | 72 | 72 | 71 | 68 | 283 | -5 | 12,062.50 | 8,329.59 |
| | Stuart LITTLE | ENG | 68 | 73 | 72 | 70 | 283 | -5 | 12,062.50 | 8,329.59 |
| 32 | Warren ABERY | RSA | 72 | 66 | 75 | 71 | 284 | -4 | 9,843.75 | 6,797.47 |
| | Robert KARLSSON | SWE | 69 | 73 | 70 | 72 | 284 | -4 | 9,843.75 | 6,797.47 |
| | Louis OOSTHUIZEN | RSA | 71 | 71 | 72 | 70 | 284 | -4 | 9,843.75 | 6,797.47 |
| | Gary CLARK | ENG | 71 | 67 | 75 | 71 | 284 | -4 | 9,843.75 | 6,797.47 |
| 36 | David LYNN | ENG | 71 | 72 | 69 | 73 | 285 | -3 | 8,375.00 | 5,783.24 |
| | Fredrik WIDMARK | SWE | 75 | 69 | 72 | 69 | 285 | -3 | 8,375.00 | 5,783.24 |
| | Steven JEPPESEN | SWE | 70 | 71 | 69 | 75 | 285 | -3 | 8,375.00 | 5,783.24 |
| | Nicolas COLSAERTS | BEL | 68 | 71 | 69 | 77 | 285 | -3 | 8,375.00 | 5,783.24 |
| | Joakim BÄCKSTRÖM | SWE | 70 | 71 | 71 | 73 | 285 | -3 | 8,375.00 | 5,783.24 |
| | Miguel Angel MARTIN | ESP | 72 | 72 | 69 | 72 | 285 | -3 | 8,375.00 | 5,783.24 |
| | Matthew MILLAR | AUS | 73 | 68 | 72 | 72 | 285 | -3 | 8,375.00 | 5,783.24 |
| 43 | Miguel CARBALLO | ARG | 69 | 71 | 70 | 76 | 286 | -2 | 6,250.00 | 4,315.85 |
| | Søren KJELDSEN | DEN | 74 | 65 | 73 | 74 | 286 | -2 | 6,250.00 | 4,315.85 |
| | Mark FOSTER | ENG | 74 | 70 | 70 | 72 | 286 | -2 | 6,250.00 | 4,315.85 |
| | Michael HOEY | NIR | 73 | 67 | 70 | 76 | 286 | -2 | 6,250.00 | 4,315.85 |
| | Jonathan LOMAS | ENG | 72 | 69 | 73 | 72 | 286 | -2 | 6,250.00 | 4,315.85 |
| | David GRIFFITHS | ENG | 69 | 73 | 75 | 69 | 286 | -2 | 6,250.00 | 4,315.85 |
| | Lee SLATTERY | ENG | 70 | 71 | 73 | 72 | 286 | -2 | 6,250.00 | 4,315.85 |
| | Rafael GOMEZ | ARG | 68 | 72 | 72 | 74 | 286 | -2 | 6,250.00 | 4,315.85 |
| | Steven O'HARA | SCO | 71 | 67 | 75 | 73 | 286 | -2 | 6,250.00 | 4,315.85 |
| | Toni KARJALAINEN | FIN | 72 | 70 | 70 | 74 | 286 | -2 | 6,250.00 | 4,315.85 |
| 53 | Simon KHAN | ENG | 69 | 73 | 73 | 72 | 287 | -1 | 4,178.57 | 2,885.45 |
| | Gonzalo FERNANDEZ-CASTAÑO | ESP | 71 | 70 | 75 | 71 | 287 | -1 | 4,178.57 | 2,885.45 |
| | André BOSSERT | SUI | 70 | 73 | 68 | 76 | 287 | -1 | 4,178.57 | 2,885.45 |
| | Paul DWYER | ENG | 70 | 72 | 73 | 72 | 287 | -1 | 4,178.57 | 2,885.45 |
| | Peter HEDBLOM | SWE | 69 | 72 | 73 | 73 | 287 | -1 | 4,178.57 | 2,885.45 |
| | Sam LITTLE | ENG | 70 | 71 | 71 | 75 | 287 | -1 | 4,178.57 | 2,885.45 |
| | Phillip ARCHER | ENG | 72 | 71 | 73 | 71 | 287 | -1 | 4,178.57 | 2,885.45 |
| 60 | Gary EMERSON | ENG | 70 | 73 | 74 | 71 | 288 | 0 | 3,375.00 | 2,330.56 |
| | Peter HANSON | SWE | 70 | 73 | 71 | 74 | 288 | 0 | 3,375.00 | 2,330.56 |
| | John BICKERTON | ENG | 70 | 73 | 71 | 74 | 288 | 0 | 3,375.00 | 2,330.56 |
| 63 | Andrew BUTTERFIELD | ENG | 73 | 71 | 71 | 74 | 289 | 1 | 2,937.50 | 2,028.45 |
| | Richard FINCH | ENG | 73 | 73 | 73 | 70 | 289 | 1 | 2,937.50 | 2,028.45 |
| | Scott DRUMMOND | SCO | 73 | 71 | 73 | 72 | 289 | 1 | 2,937.50 | 2,028.45 |
| | Andrew MARSHALL | ENG | 69 | 72 | 78 | 70 | 289 | 1 | 2,937.50 | 2,028.45 |
| 67 | Robert COLES | ENG | 73 | 71 | 68 | 78 | 290 | 2 | 2,447.50 | 1,690.09 |
| | Francisco VALERA | ESP | 70 | 71 | 74 | 75 | 290 | 2 | 2,447.50 | 1,690.09 |
| | Tiago CRUZ | POR | 72 | 72 | 76 | 70 | 290 | 2 | 2,447.50 | 1,690.09 |
| | Michael JONZON | SWE | 73 | 71 | 75 | 71 | 290 | 2 | 2,447.50 | 1,690.09 |
| 71 | Stuart MANLEY | WAL | 72 | 69 | 76 | 74 | 291 | 3 | 1,872.00 | 1,292.68 |
| | Raul BALLESTEROS | ESP | 76 | 68 | 73 | 74 | 291 | 3 | 1,872.00 | 1,292.68 |
| | Anders HANSEN | DEN | 71 | 70 | 77 | 73 | 291 | 3 | 1,872.00 | 1,292.68 |
| 74 | Michael KIRK | RSA | 71 | 73 | 73 | 76 | 293 | 5 | 1,866.00 | 1,288.54 |
| 75 | Martin ERLANDSSON | SWE | 70 | 74 | 76 | 74 | 294 | 6 | 1,863.00 | 1,286.47 |
| 76 | David DRYSDALE | SCO | 72 | 71 | 75 | 79 | 297 | 9 | 1,860.00 | 1,284.40 |

## Total Prize Fund
**€1,261,205 £870,907**

"It was a bit of a knee-jerker on the last but I've been playing those shots all my life," he said. "I knew, if my short game proved to be as good as it has been for the rest of my career, I could get it up and down. It was a case of déjà-vu. Just like last year, I wasn't playing well coming into the event. The key was missing the tournament in Madeira the week before and driving to Ayrshire from my home in the West Midlands for a day's intensive coaching from Bob Torrance."

As his son, Sam, was the last man to win successive Portuguese Opens, Bob must have been absolutely chuffed. "I put him through the mill a bit sometimes and this is the reward for all the work we've done together. I wanted to test myself when I was under the cosh and I proved I can still handle the pressure. I took the wrong club at the 13th but, apart from that, I didn't really hit a bad shot."

European Ryder Cup Captain Ian Woosnam, already on his way to Augusta National for the Masters Tournament after finishing in a share of 19th place, was swiftly on his mobile phone congratulating his old friend whom he had partnered to fourball glory over Paul Azinger and Hale Irwin in The 1991 Ryder Cup.

Then it was back home to a hero's welcome from his family, thoroughly deserved for the golfer now, no longer, a 'used-to-be' champion.

**Gordon Richardson**

# In Good Company

## Augusta National

| Par | Yards | Metres |
|-----|-------|--------|
| 72 | 7445 | 6807 |

| | | | | |
|----|------------------|-----|----|---|
| 1 | **Phil MICKELSON** | **281** | **-7** |  |
| 2 | Tim CLARK | 283 | -5 | |
| 3 | Chad CAMPBELL | 284 | -4 | |
| | Fred COUPLES | 284 | -4 | |
| | Retief GOOSEN | 284 | -4 | |
| | José Maria OLAZÁBAL | 284 | -4 | |
| | Tiger WOODS | 284 | -4 | |
| 8 | Angel CABRERA | 285 | -3 | |
| | Vijay SINGH | 285 | -3 | |
| 10 | Stewart CINK | 286 | -2 | |

## WEATHER REPORT

| Round One | Round Two | Round Three | Round Four |
|-----------|-----------|-------------|------------|

## EUROPEAN TOUR ORDER OF MERIT
(After 17 tournaments)

| Pos | | € | |
|-----|------------------|----------------|---|
| 1 | **David HOWELL** | **1,035,483.81** | |
| 2 | Retief GOOSEN | 689,478.87 | |
| 3 | Tim CLARK | 672,293.10 | |
| 4 | Nick O'HERN | 631,002.33 | |
| 5 | Henrik STENSON | 622,677.43 | |
| 6 | Ernie ELS | 589,759.12 | |
| 7 | Paul BROADHURST | 513,125.85 | |
| 8 | Nick DOUGHERTY | 510,851.12 | |
| 9 | Vijay SINGH | 496,868.42 | |
| 10 | Paul CASEY | 417,882.88 | |

# Masters Tournament

**Augusta, Georgia, USA**

April 6-9 • 2006

They say you can judge a man by the company he keeps, in which regard Phil Mickelson scores highly indeed. The left hander's triumph at the 70th Masters Tournament was his third Major Championship win in successive seasons and since 1960 only four other players have managed that. They just happen to go by the names of Jack Nicklaus, Arnold Palmer, Tom Watson and Tiger Woods.

Miguel Angel Jiménez

No-one who watched Mickelson as an amateur ever had any doubt that he would go on to become another American legend, but in the interim years he certainly had us worried.

Would he ever learn that winning Major Championships was not merely a Boy's Own adventure but required a flair player to occasionally rein in his natural instincts? How many times would we have to sit with our heads in our hands as he got drawn in by a sucker pin placement, and ran up a costly double bogey?

What a delight, then, to listen to him in the aftermath of this second Masters Tournament victory, and his second consecutive Major success following his US PGA Championship victory last August. "It took me years to realise that a par five was not a bad score on the 15th," he said. "I always assumed that anytime I took five there it meant I had dropped a shot to the rest of the field, with the result that I would become too aggressive, and run up sixes and sevens that would eventually cost me the tournament."

❝ *I was one of those players who was highly critical of the changes to the course in the build-up to this year's tournament. Having now had a chance to play four rounds under tournament conditions, I realise my criticism was premature* ❞ *– Stewart Cink*

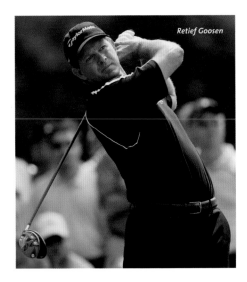

*Retief Goosen*

*José Maria Olazábal and Sergio Garcia*

Perhaps the ultimate wake-up call came before the tournament in 2003, when he was asked who he thought would become the first leftie to end a Major Championship drought that had lasted since Bob Charles won The Open Championship at Royal Lytham & St Annes in 1963. "I think we all know the answer to that one," he replied, only for the game to deliver a hard slapping four days later as Canadian southpaw Mike Weir put his arms into the Green Jacket.

Mickelson, by his own admission, worked a lot harder after that. He started visiting the sites of Majors the week before, learning the shots he would need in advance of the big event.

The breakthrough came at Augusta National the following year, when he and Ernie Els traded birdies during a memorable tussle over the back nine. This time, however, he won playing golf the Nick Faldo way. He was ahead and never gave any of the peloton that gathered in his slipstream an ounce of encouragement. His only bogey of the final round came at the 18th, but by then it was all over.

By then, the opposition had been broken trying to make birdies and eagles, and there is no scarier place than Augusta National when you have to force the issue.

Mickelson played the final round in the company of Fred Couples, an American dream pairing if ever there was. What pleasure they brought, congratulating each other on their birdies and departing several holes with arms around shoulders. This was golf doing what it does best, setting an example when it comes to sportsmanship.

There were other performances of note. Runner-up Tim Clark was outdriven by 50 yards on every hole by playing partner Woods but showed the sort of fighter he is by hanging in and beating the World Number One by a stroke. At the death, he reinforced the reputation of South Africans for sand play by holing from a greenside bunker.

The story in the build-up to the Masters Tournament was how a number of changes had destroyed the character of the course and the event, leaving only the

Over the course of 18 holes, you can
see how far you've come, and how far
the game can still take you.

United is proud to support the European Tour.

It's time to fly.® **UNITED**

A STAR ALLIANCE MEMBER

www.unitedairlines.co.uk

# Final Results

*Darren Clarke*

| Pos | Name | | Rd1 | Rd2 | Rd3 | Rd4 | Total | | € | £ |
|---|---|---|---|---|---|---|---|---|---|---|
| 1 | Phil MICKELSON | USA | 70 | 72 | 70 | 69 | 281 | -7 | 1,037,976.85 | 724,429.34 |
| 2 | Tim CLARK | RSA | 70 | 72 | 72 | 69 | 283 | -5 | 622,786.11 | 434,657.61 |
| 3 | Retief GOOSEN | RSA | 70 | 73 | 72 | 69 | 284 | -4 | 260,070.87 | 181,509.80 |
| | Chad CAMPBELL | USA | 71 | 67 | 75 | 71 | 284 | -4 | 260,070.87 | 181,509.80 |
| | Tiger WOODS | USA | 72 | 71 | 71 | 70 | 284 | -4 | 260,070.87 | 181,509.80 |
| | José Maria OLAZÁBAL | ESP | 76 | 71 | 71 | 66 | 284 | -4 | 260,070.87 | 181,509.80 |
| | Fred COUPLES | USA | 71 | 70 | 72 | 71 | 284 | -4 | 260,070.87 | 181,509.80 |
| 8 | Angel CABRERA | ARG | 73 | 74 | 70 | 68 | 285 | -3 | 172,996.14 | 120,738.22 |
| | Vijay SINGH | FIJ | 67 | 74 | 73 | 71 | 285 | -3 | 172,996.14 | 120,738.22 |
| 10 | Stewart CINK | USA | 72 | 73 | 71 | 70 | 286 | -2 | 155,696.53 | 108,664.40 |
| 11 | Mike WEIR | CAN | 71 | 73 | 73 | 70 | 287 | -1 | 132,630.38 | 92,565.97 |
| | Miguel Angel JIMÉNEZ | ESP | 72 | 74 | 69 | 72 | 287 | -1 | 132,630.38 | 92,565.97 |
| | Stephen AMES | CAN | 74 | 70 | 70 | 73 | 287 | -1 | 132,630.38 | 92,565.97 |
| 14 | Billy MAYFAIR | USA | 71 | 72 | 73 | 72 | 288 | 0 | 106,680.95 | 74,455.24 |
| | Arron OBERHOLSER | USA | 69 | 75 | 73 | 71 | 288 | 0 | 106,680.95 | 74,455.24 |
| 16 | Geoff OGILVY | AUS | 70 | 75 | 73 | 71 | 289 | 1 | 92,264.61 | 64,393.72 |
| | Scott VERPLANK | USA | 74 | 70 | 74 | 71 | 289 | 1 | 92,264.61 | 64,393.72 |
| | Rodney PAMPLING | AUS | 72 | 73 | 72 | 72 | 289 | 1 | 92,264.61 | 64,393.72 |
| 19 | Stuart APPLEBY | AUS | 71 | 75 | 73 | 71 | 290 | 2 | 74,964.99 | 52,319.89 |
| | Nick O'HERN | AUS | 71 | 72 | 76 | 71 | 290 | 2 | 74,964.99 | 52,319.89 |
| | David HOWELL | ENG | 71 | 71 | 76 | 72 | 290 | 2 | 74,964.99 | 52,319.89 |
| 22 | Jim FURYK | USA | 73 | 75 | 68 | 75 | 291 | 3 | 55,358.77 | 38,636.23 |
| | Davis LOVE III | USA | 74 | 71 | 74 | 72 | 291 | 3 | 55,358.77 | 38,636.23 |
| | Darren CLARKE | NIR | 72 | 70 | 72 | 77 | 291 | 3 | 55,358.77 | 38,636.23 |
| | Robert ALLENBY | AUS | 73 | 73 | 74 | 71 | 291 | 3 | 55,358.77 | 38,636.23 |
| | Mark HENSBY | AUS | 80 | 67 | 70 | 74 | 291 | 3 | 55,358.77 | 38,636.23 |
| 27 | Shingo KATAYAMA | JPN | 75 | 70 | 73 | 74 | 292 | 4 | 40,942.42 | 28,574.71 |
| | Carl PETTERSSON | SWE | 72 | 74 | 73 | 73 | 292 | 4 | 40,942.42 | 28,574.71 |
| | Adam SCOTT | AUS | 72 | 74 | 75 | 71 | 292 | 4 | 40,942.42 | 28,574.71 |
| | Ernie ELS | RSA | 71 | 71 | 74 | 76 | 292 | 4 | 40,942.42 | 28,574.71 |
| | Padraig HARRINGTON | IRL | 73 | 70 | 75 | 74 | 292 | 4 | 40,942.42 | 28,574.71 |
| 32 | Thomas BJÖRN | DEN | 73 | 75 | 76 | 69 | 293 | 5 | 33,373.43 | 23,292.13 |
| | Ted PURDY | USA | 72 | 76 | 74 | 71 | 293 | 5 | 33,373.43 | 23,292.13 |
| | Brandt JOBE | USA | 72 | 76 | 77 | 68 | 293 | 5 | 33,373.43 | 23,292.13 |
| | Zach JOHNSON | USA | 74 | 72 | 77 | 70 | 293 | 5 | 33,373.43 | 23,292.13 |
| 36 | Rory SABBATINI | RSA | 76 | 70 | 74 | 74 | 294 | 6 | 28,351.60 | 19,787.27 |
| | Rocco MEDIATE | USA | 68 | 73 | 73 | 80 | 294 | 6 | 28,351.60 | 19,787.27 |
| | Tim HERRON | USA | 76 | 71 | 71 | 76 | 294 | 6 | 28,351.60 | 19,787.27 |
| 39 | Justin LEONARD | USA | 75 | 70 | 79 | 71 | 295 | 7 | 24,796.11 | 17,305.81 |
| | Ben CURTIS | USA | 71 | 74 | 77 | 73 | 295 | 7 | 24,796.11 | 17,305.81 |
| | Jason BOHN | USA | 73 | 71 | 77 | 74 | 295 | 7 | 24,796.11 | 17,305.81 |
| 42 | Larry MIZE | USA | 75 | 72 | 77 | 72 | 296 | 8 | 21,336.19 | 14,891.05 |
| | Luke DONALD | ENG | 74 | 72 | 76 | 74 | 296 | 8 | 21,336.19 | 14,891.05 |
| | Rich BEEM | USA | 71 | 73 | 73 | 79 | 296 | 8 | 21,336.19 | 14,891.05 |
| 45 | Olin BROWNE | USA | 74 | 69 | 80 | 74 | 297 | 9 | 19,029.58 | 13,281.21 |
| 46 | Sergio GARCIA | ESP | 72 | 74 | 79 | 73 | 298 | 10 | 17,876.27 | 12,476.28 |
| 47 | Ben CRENSHAW | USA | 71 | 72 | 78 | 79 | 300 | 12 | 16,722.96 | 11,671.36 |

## Total Prize Fund
€5,624,350 £3,925,369

big hitters with a chance to win. All that criticism was negated, not only by the quality of the leaderboard, but the fact it was adorned by a wonderful array of different types of players.

It was not only Clark who spoke up for the medium hitters, but joint third-placed José Maria Olazábal as well. If truth be told he was worried that his days at Augusta National, a

*Angel Cabrera*

place that had seen him claim two Green Jackets, were numbered, and maybe that had something to do with his first round 76. But thereafter he played better than anyone, finishing with a final round 66, the highlight of which was a perfectly struck five wood from 245 yards to the 15th green for a tap-in eagle three, a shot later voted RBS Shot of the Month for April.

At the end, though, it was Woods who slipped the Green Jacket on to the shoulders of Mickelson in a reverse ceremony of the year before. Augusta National chairman Hootie Johnson, explaining the changes, said he hoped to recreate the course the players played in the 1960s. Now we have two players dominating as they did then, when Nicklaus and Palmer took turns to wear green.

Mickelson and Woods have won six of the last ten Masters Tournaments. Who would bet against them emulating Jack and Arnie before they are through, and have ten green jackets hanging on the wall?

**Derek Lawrenson**
*Daily Mail*

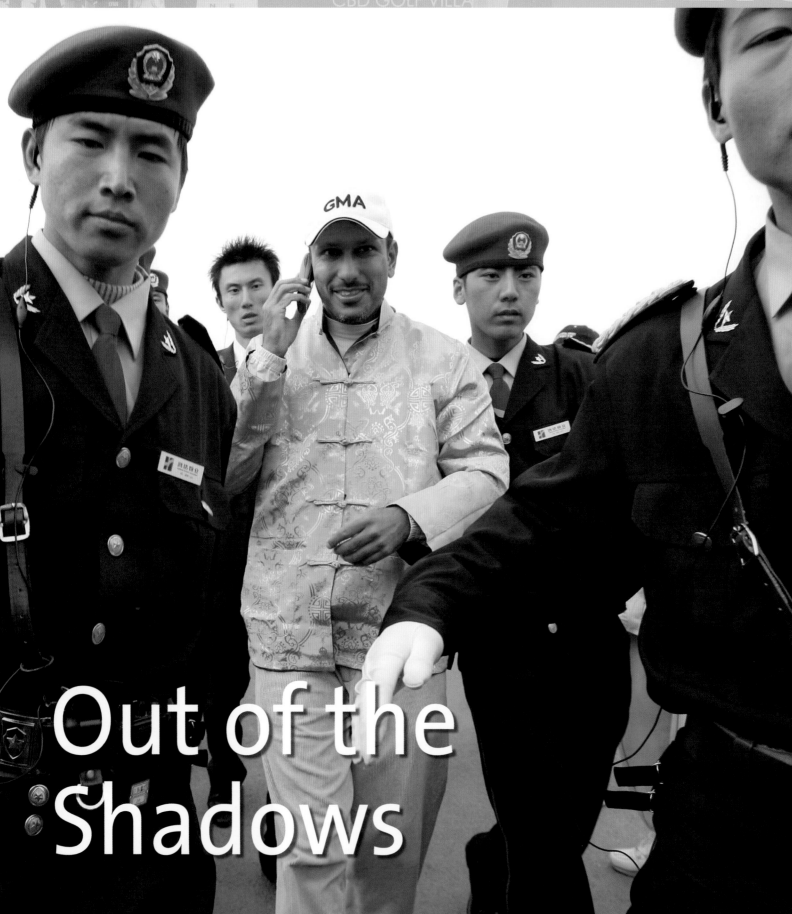

# Out of the Shadows

David Lynn

| Honghua International Golf Club | | |
|---|---|---|
| **Par** | **Yards** | **Metres** |
| 72 | 7203 | 6586 |

| | | | | |
|---|---|---|---|---|
| 1 | **Jeev Milkha SINGH** | **278** | **-10** |  |
| 2 | Gonzalo FERNANDEZ-CASTAÑO | 279 | -9 | |
| 3 | David LYNN | 280 | -8 | |
| 4 | Paul CASEY | 281 | -7 | |
| | Peter FOWLER | 281 | -7 | |
| | Jarrod LYLE | 281 | -7 | |
| | Simon WAKEFIELD | 281 | -7 | |
| 8 | Peter O'MALLEY | 282 | -6 | |
| | Ter-Chang WANG | 282 | -6 | |
| 10 | Simon DYSON | 283 | -5 | |
| | Peter HANSON | 283 | -5 | |
| | Paul LAWRIE | 283 | -5 | |
| | Prayad MARKSAENG | 283 | -5 | |

**WEATHER REPORT**

Round One  Round Two  Round Three  Round Four

It had been a long time coming. Then again, when the 34 year old Jeev Milkha Singh kept his nerve to win the Volvo China Open at the Honghua International Golf Club in Beijing, he knew that, finally, he had stepped out of the considerable shadow cast by his famous father, Milkha. Affectionately known back home in India as the Flying Sikh, in honour of his exploits on the athletics track, Singh Snr won a gold medal over 440 yards at the Empire Games in Cardiff in 1958 before going on to represent his country at the Rome Olympics two years later. He has been feted in India ever since, but in China it was Singh Jnr, the first Indian golfer to qualify for The European Tour in 1997, who claimed the spotlight.

Victory for Singh meant he had become only the second Indian to win on The European Tour International Schedule, following in the footsteps of Arjun Atwal, and, suddenly, he knew that there was a new road ahead with fresh challenges.

Prior to the event, Singh had not won for seven years, his last victory coming in the Lexus International, in Thailand, in 1999. Even so, the way he conducted and controlled himself on the final day, provided ample evidence of a player at home with his game and his nerves. Using reverse psychology, he had told himself not to worry if he did not win, but just to enjoy the thrill of being in contention. It was a ploy that worked to perfection.

Nothing, it seemed, could faze him. In the third round, for example, he was on the Nick Faldo-designed course when a mini-

José-Filipe Lima

**EUROPEAN TOUR ORDER OF MERIT**
(After 18 tournaments)

| Pos | | € | |
|---|---|---|---|
| 1 | **David HOWELL** | 1,035,483.81 | |
| 2 | Retief GOOSEN | 689,478.87 | |
| 3 | Tim CLARK | 672,293.10 | |
| 4 | Henrik STENSON | 638,824.45 | |
| 5 | Nick O'HERN | 631,002.33 | |
| 6 | Ernie ELS | 589,759.12 | |
| 7 | Nick DOUGHERTY | 522,424.52 | |
| 8 | Paul BROADHURST | 513,125.85 | |
| 9 | Vijay SINGH | 496,868.42 | |
| 10 | Paul CASEY | 476,376.32 | |

# Volvo China Open

**Beijing, China**
April 13-16 • 2006

*Paul Casey*

tornado twisted its way across the fairways, forcing some players to dive for cover as parts of a television tower came tumbling to the ground. Then, during the final round, he kept calm amid the ensuing storm after a spectator pocketed his ball in the trees at the 11th hole. It was eventually replaced and no harm was done.

Singh had rounds of 72–69–67–70 for a ten under par total of 278 that gave him victory by one stroke over Gonzalo Fernandez-Castaño, of Spain, and two over David Lynn, of England. The first prize of €247,748 (£172,344) was also by far and away the biggest cheque of his 13 year professional career.

Among those pushing for the title on an intriguing final day were a trio of Englishmen. There was Paul Casey, who, by a quirk of the

*" I like the layout. Nick Faldo is big on his course management so you have to think your way around here. There are a lot of bunkers out there which means shot making is at a premium and you have to be able to work the ball both ways " - Paul Casey*

Simon Wakefield

# Final Results

| Pos | Name | | Rd1 | Rd2 | Rd3 | Rd4 | Total | | € | £ |
|---|---|---|---|---|---|---|---|---|---|---|
| 1 | Jeev Milkha SINGH | IND | 72 | 69 | 67 | 70 | 278 | -10 | 247,748.61 | 172,344.46 |
| 2 | Gonzalo FERNANDEZ-CASTAÑO | ESP | 67 | 74 | 68 | 70 | 279 | -9 | 165,165.74 | 114,896.31 |
| 3 | David LYNN | ENG | 68 | 67 | 72 | 73 | 280 | -8 | 93,054.38 | 64,732.58 |
| 4 | Simon WAKEFIELD | ENG | 67 | 73 | 70 | 71 | 281 | -7 | 58,493.45 | 40,690.53 |
| | Peter FOWLER | AUS | 71 | 70 | 69 | 71 | 281 | -7 | 58,493.45 | 40,690.53 |
| | Paul CASEY | ENG | 71 | 68 | 70 | 72 | 281 | -7 | 58,493.45 | 40,690.53 |
| | Jarrod LYLE | AUS | 68 | 71 | 72 | 70 | 281 | -7 | 58,493.45 | 40,690.53 |
| 8 | Ter-Chang WANG | TPE | 69 | 72 | 71 | 70 | 282 | -6 | 35,229.85 | 24,507.38 |
| | Peter O'MALLEY | AUS | 72 | 72 | 70 | 68 | 282 | -6 | 35,229.85 | 24,507.38 |
| 10 | Paul LAWRIE | SCO | 73 | 70 | 73 | 67 | 283 | -5 | 26,645.36 | 18,535.65 |
| | Peter HANSON | SWE | 67 | 72 | 73 | 71 | 283 | -5 | 26,645.36 | 18,535.65 |
| | Prayad MARKSAENG | THA | 69 | 67 | 72 | 75 | 283 | -5 | 26,645.36 | 18,535.65 |
| | Simon DYSON | ENG | 67 | 72 | 73 | 71 | 283 | -5 | 26,645.36 | 18,535.65 |
| 14 | Brett RUMFORD | AUS | 69 | 75 | 71 | 69 | 284 | -4 | 22,743.32 | 15,821.22 |
| 15 | Richard STERNE | RSA | 72 | 72 | 70 | 71 | 285 | -3 | 20,097.37 | 13,980.58 |
| | José-Filipe LIMA | POR | 67 | 69 | 77 | 72 | 285 | -3 | 20,097.37 | 13,980.58 |
| | Marcus FRASER | AUS | 70 | 71 | 69 | 75 | 285 | -3 | 20,097.37 | 13,980.58 |
| | Prom MEESAWAT | THA | 71 | 72 | 71 | 71 | 285 | -3 | 20,097.37 | 13,980.58 |
| | Peter LAWRIE | IRL | 71 | 70 | 72 | 72 | 285 | -3 | 20,097.37 | 13,980.58 |
| 20 | Henrik STENSON | SWE | 73 | 68 | 74 | 71 | 286 | -2 | 16,147.02 | 11,232.55 |
| | Chawalit PLAPHOL | THA | 72 | 70 | 72 | 72 | 286 | -2 | 16,147.02 | 11,232.55 |
| | Damien MCGRANE | IRL | 72 | 70 | 73 | 71 | 286 | -2 | 16,147.02 | 11,232.55 |
| | Christian CÉVAËR | FRA | 66 | 72 | 79 | 69 | 286 | -2 | 16,147.02 | 11,232.55 |
| | Jean VAN DE VELDE | FRA | 74 | 68 | 73 | 71 | 286 | -2 | 16,147.02 | 11,232.55 |
| | Hendrik BUHRMANN | RSA | 72 | 68 | 71 | 75 | 286 | -2 | 16,147.02 | 11,232.55 |
| | Marc CAYEUX | ZIM | 71 | 65 | 80 | 70 | 286 | -2 | 16,147.02 | 11,232.55 |
| | Amandeep JOHL | IND | 75 | 70 | 72 | 69 | 286 | -2 | 16,147.02 | 11,232.55 |
| 28 | Søren HANSEN | DEN | 72 | 70 | 70 | 75 | 287 | -1 | 13,675.72 | 9,513.41 |
| | Miles TUNNICLIFF | ENG | 68 | 74 | 70 | 75 | 287 | -1 | 13,675.72 | 9,513.41 |
| | Søren KJELDSEN | DEN | 71 | 70 | 71 | 75 | 287 | -1 | 13,675.72 | 9,513.41 |
| 31 | Barry LANE | ENG | 72 | 68 | 75 | 73 | 288 | 0 | 11,573.40 | 8,050.95 |
| | Jamie SPENCE | ENG | 70 | 71 | 74 | 73 | 288 | 0 | 11,573.40 | 8,050.95 |
| | Gregory HAVRET | FRA | 71 | 72 | 72 | 73 | 288 | 0 | 11,573.40 | 8,050.95 |
| | Nick DOUGHERTY | ENG | 72 | 70 | 72 | 74 | 288 | 0 | 11,573.40 | 8,050.95 |
| | Stephen GALLACHER | SCO | 73 | 70 | 69 | 76 | 288 | 0 | 11,573.40 | 8,050.95 |
| | Wen-Tang LIN | TPE | 71 | 73 | 73 | 71 | 288 | 0 | 11,573.40 | 8,050.95 |
| | Jason KNUTZON | USA | 70 | 71 | 74 | 73 | 288 | 0 | 11,573.40 | 8,050.95 |
| 38 | Ross FISHER | ENG | 67 | 73 | 74 | 75 | 289 | 1 | 9,810.85 | 6,824.84 |
| | Terry PILKADARIS | AUS | 72 | 67 | 76 | 74 | 289 | 1 | 9,810.85 | 6,824.84 |
| | Stuart LITTLE | ENG | 71 | 73 | 76 | 69 | 289 | 1 | 9,810.85 | 6,824.84 |
| | Raphaël JACQUELIN | FRA | 72 | 70 | 73 | 74 | 289 | 1 | 9,810.85 | 6,824.84 |
| 42 | Scott DRUMMOND | SCO | 71 | 67 | 78 | 74 | 290 | 2 | 8,324.35 | 5,790.77 |
| | Joakim BÄCKSTRÖM | SWE | 69 | 72 | 77 | 72 | 290 | 2 | 8,324.35 | 5,790.77 |
| | Simon YATES | SCO | 69 | 70 | 77 | 74 | 290 | 2 | 8,324.35 | 5,790.77 |
| | Thaworn WIRATCHANT | THA | 72 | 71 | 75 | 72 | 290 | 2 | 8,324.35 | 5,790.77 |
| | Robert COLES | ENG | 70 | 69 | 77 | 74 | 290 | 2 | 8,324.35 | 5,790.77 |
| | Nico VAN RENSBURG | RSA | 75 | 64 | 76 | 75 | 290 | 2 | 8,324.35 | 5,790.77 |
| 48 | Fredrik WIDMARK | SWE | 73 | 68 | 77 | 73 | 291 | 3 | 7,283.81 | 5,066.93 |
| 49 | Adam GROOM | AUS | 75 | 70 | 74 | 73 | 292 | 4 | 6,837.86 | 4,756.71 |
| | Johan EDFORS | SWE | 72 | 71 | 75 | 74 | 292 | 4 | 6,837.86 | 4,756.71 |
| 51 | Gary EMERSON | ENG | 71 | 70 | 73 | 79 | 293 | 5 | 6,094.62 | 4,239.67 |
| | Charlie WI | KOR | 72 | 69 | 81 | 71 | 293 | 5 | 6,094.62 | 4,239.67 |
| | Wen Teh LU | TPE | 71 | 70 | 77 | 75 | 293 | 5 | 6,094.62 | 4,239.67 |
| 54 | Kahlon HARMEET | IND | 76 | 67 | 75 | 76 | 294 | 6 | 4,831.10 | 3,360.72 |
| | Alistair PRESNELL | AUS | 72 | 72 | 73 | 77 | 294 | 6 | 4,831.10 | 3,360.72 |
| | Chao LI | CHN | 72 | 72 | 72 | 78 | 294 | 6 | 4,831.10 | 3,360.72 |
| | José Manuel LARA | ESP | 71 | 69 | 80 | 74 | 294 | 6 | 4,831.10 | 3,360.72 |
| | Alessandro TADINI | ITA | 76 | 67 | 75 | 76 | 294 | 6 | 4,831.10 | 3,360.72 |
| | Robert-Jan DERKSEN | NED | 70 | 75 | 71 | 78 | 294 | 6 | 4,831.10 | 3,360.72 |
| 60 | Rick GIBSON | CAN | 72 | 72 | 77 | 74 | 295 | 7 | 3,864.88 | 2,688.57 |
| | Frankie MINOZA | PHI | 71 | 72 | 76 | 76 | 295 | 7 | 3,864.88 | 2,688.57 |
| | Rahil GANGJEE | IND | 68 | 70 | 82 | 75 | 295 | 7 | 3,864.88 | 2,688.57 |
| | Mahal PEARCE | NZL | 71 | 71 | 76 | 77 | 295 | 7 | 3,864.88 | 2,688.57 |
| | Jason DAWES | AUS | 71 | 70 | 78 | 76 | 295 | 7 | 3,864.88 | 2,688.57 |
| 65 | Scott STRANGE | AUS | 74 | 71 | 74 | 77 | 296 | 8 | 3,270.28 | 2,274.95 |
| | Richard BLAND | ENG | 70 | 72 | 76 | 78 | 296 | 8 | 3,270.28 | 2,274.95 |
| | Kenneth FERRIE | ENG | 74 | 69 | 75 | 78 | 296 | 8 | 3,270.28 | 2,274.95 |
| 68 | Angelo QUE | PHI | 71 | 73 | 79 | 75 | 298 | 10 | 2,972.98 | 2,068.13 |
| 69 | Paul DWYER | ENG | 70 | 75 | 76 | 79 | 300 | 12 | 2,824.33 | 1,964.73 |

## Total Prize Fund
€1,483,780  £1,032,182

calendar, found himself defending a title he had won barely five months earlier. There was Simon Wakefield, who moved quietly through the field to get himself to within a shot of the lead with six holes to play. And there was Lynn, the overnight leader, coming back to form following a potential life-threatening incident.

Lynn's story was one of bites, stings and three putts. In South Africa four months earlier, the 32 year old had feared for his life when he was stung by a scorpion while in his hotel room at the dunhill championship at Leopard Creek. The scorpion eventually came off worse in the encounter under a training shoe and, luckily for Lynn, it turned out not to be poisonous.

Then, in Beijing, Lynn brought water to the eyes of his audience with a tale of an insect bite on his groin that had turned into a festering boil. Not only was it painful, it affected his backswing and also prevented him from bending down properly to line up his putts. With antibiotics taking too long to kick in, he went under the knife.

"After I played my first round I went to see the doctor and he turned round and said that he needed to cut it out," said Lynn. "So he got out his scalpel and started to cut away! No anaesthetic or anything and I'm watching this whole thing take place! It left quite a big hole but he patched it up and did a great job."

As if to prove the time-honoured cliché that an injured golfer is a dangerous golfer, Lynn had rounds of 68–67–72 to move to the top of the leaderboard, but was let down in the final round by the one area of his game that had earlier seemed supreme - his putting.

With six holes to play, he shared the lead on ten under par. He had taken just 14 putts in his first ten holes but in the space of three holes from the 13th, the blade died in his hands as did his hopes of winning for the first time since The KLM Open in 2004. After taking three putts on each of the 13th, 14th and 15th greens, he fell back to eight under par and effectively out of the running.

Into the mix, however, came Fernandez-Castaño, who arrived at the 18th tee on ten under par and trailing Singh by a single shot. There, the 2005 Sir Henry Cotton Rookie of the Year hooked his drive and was unlucky to find the ball against a tree. He was forced to chip out one handed behind his legs to get the ball back on to the fairway and proceeded to drop a shot. It meant that Singh, playing in the group behind, could afford to bogey the hole and still win. Which is what he duly did.

**Peter Dixon**

*The Times*

# A Marriage Made in Heaven

*Christian Cévaër*

**Tomson Shanghai Pudong Golf Club**

| Par | Yards | Metres |
|-----|-------|--------|
| 72 | 7300 | 6674 |

| | | | | |
|---|---|---|---|---|
| 1 | **G FERNANDEZ-CASTAÑO** | **281** | **-7** |  |
| 2 | Henrik STENSON | 281 | -7 | |
| 3 | José-Filipe LIMA | 282 | -6 | |
| | Colin MONTGOMERIE | 282 | -6 | |
| 5 | Paul CASEY | 283 | -5 | |
| | Simon DYSON | 283 | -5 | |
| | Mahal PEARCE | 283 | -5 | |
| 8 | David BRANSDON | 285 | -3 | |
| | Paul LAWRIE | 285 | -3 | |
| | Peter O'MALLEY | 285 | -3 | |
| | Terry PILKADARIS | 285 | -3 | |

**WEATHER REPORT**

| Round One | Round Two | Round Three | Round Four |

Gonzalo Fernandez-Castaño let the cat out of the bag and, as hard as he tried, he could not stuff it back in. "I think I'm going to get married," he said after beating Henrik Stenson in a play-off to win the BMW Asian Open at the Tomson Shanghai Pudong Golf Club. With that, he buried himself in a bunker he could not play his way out of – not even with his silky Seve-like skills.

"Don't write it yet because I haven't asked her!" was his plea to the assembled media. "At least let me get back to Spain first. I need to buy a ring and then ask her. So you cannot write anything until Tuesday please, otherwise I won't be giving any more interviews! But in China you can write it!"

There may have been no paparazzi or tabloid press on the early season Asian swing of The European Tour International Schedule but Fernandez-Castaño should have known better. China is connected to the world and half an hour later the international news wires were proclaiming: "Marry Me, Alicia."

His favourite jeweller was probably waiting at the airport, rubbing his hands in glee, as the 25 year old's golf bag was bulging with the €412,975 (£286,226) he had collected from a rewarding two week sojourn in China. The winner of The Sir Henry Cotton Rookie of the Year on The European Tour in 2005 had finished second in Beijing the week before in the Volvo China Open before going one better in Shanghai.

There may be only one Seve Ballesteros, but Fernandez-Castaño did a pretty good

impression in China. In the final round in Beijing he played an outrageous backhand shot out of the trees and was all over the course again in Shanghai – in the trees, in the water and in the rough.

But à la Ballesteros, Fernandez-Castaño played two miracle chip shots in the final

*Henrik Stenson*

**EUROPEAN TOUR ORDER OF MERIT**
(After 19 tournaments)

| Pos | | € |
|-----|---|---|
| 1 | **David HOWELL** | **1,035,483.81** |
| 2 | Henrik STENSON | 804,031.76 |
| 3 | Retief GOOSEN | 689,478.87 |
| 4 | Tim CLARK | 672,293.10 |
| 5 | Nick O'HERN | 631,002.33 |
| 6 | Ernie ELS | 589,759.12 |
| 7 | Nick DOUGHERTY | 535,880.66 |
| 8 | Paul CASEY | 529,606.12 |
| 9 | Paul BROADHURST | 513,125.85 |
| 10 | Vijay SINGH | 496,868.42 |

BMW
Hole in One Award
一杆进洞奖

BMW Golfsport

BMW
Sheer Driving Pleasure

Par 3
195 m
213 yards
17

Official Car of
the Ryder Cup.

TOMSON GOLF CLUB

UBS

ROLEX

Colin Montgomerie

*" This course here is always windy but it is in fantastic condition. The greens are in great shape and the fairways are good. I love this golf course because I always seem to play well here "* – Jeev Milkha Singh

Peter O'Malley

# Final Results

| Pos | Name | | Rd1 | Rd2 | Rd3 | Rd4 | Total | | € | £ |
|---|---|---|---|---|---|---|---|---|---|---|
| 1 | Gonzalo FERNANDEZ-CASTAÑO | ESP | 71 | 71 | 69 | 70 | 281 | -7 | 247,810.96 | 171,330.66 |
| 2 | Henrik STENSON | SWE | 67 | 72 | 71 | 71 | 281 | -7 | 165,207.31 | 114,220.45 |
| 3 | Colin MONTGOMERIE | SCO | 69 | 74 | 71 | 68 | 282 | -6 | 83,710.54 | 57,875.50 |
| | José-Filipe LIMA | POR | 71 | 70 | 73 | 68 | 282 | -6 | 83,710.54 | 57,875.50 |
| 5 | Mahal PEARCE | NZL | 72 | 72 | 68 | 71 | 283 | -5 | 53,229.80 | 36,801.83 |
| | Paul CASEY | ENG | 72 | 71 | 69 | 71 | 283 | -5 | 53,229.80 | 36,801.83 |
| | Simon DYSON | ENG | 72 | 72 | 68 | 71 | 283 | -5 | 53,229.80 | 36,801.83 |
| 8 | Paul LAWRIE | SCO | 70 | 70 | 73 | 72 | 285 | -3 | 31,893.27 | 22,050.26 |
| | Terry PILKADARIS | AUS | 73 | 73 | 74 | 65 | 285 | -3 | 31,893.27 | 22,050.26 |
| | Peter O'MALLEY | AUS | 73 | 70 | 69 | 73 | 285 | -3 | 31,893.27 | 22,050.26 |
| | David BRANSON | AUS | 72 | 74 | 73 | 66 | 285 | -3 | 31,893.27 | 22,050.26 |
| 12 | Barry LANE | ENG | 74 | 71 | 72 | 69 | 286 | -2 | 25,574.09 | 17,681.32 |
| 13 | Peter LAWRIE | IRL | 69 | 72 | 75 | 71 | 287 | -1 | 20,630.26 | 14,263.28 |
| | Thaworn WIRATCHANT | THA | 70 | 73 | 73 | 71 | 287 | -1 | 20,630.26 | 14,263.28 |
| | Ignacio GARRIDO | ESP | 75 | 71 | 71 | 70 | 287 | -1 | 20,630.26 | 14,263.28 |
| | Christian CÉVAËR | FRA | 73 | 72 | 73 | 69 | 287 | -1 | 20,630.26 | 14,263.28 |
| | Charlie WI | KOR | 69 | 73 | 74 | 71 | 287 | -1 | 20,630.26 | 14,263.28 |
| | Steven JEPPESEN | SWE | 73 | 73 | 72 | 69 | 287 | -1 | 20,630.26 | 14,263.28 |
| | Graeme STORM | ENG | 74 | 69 | 72 | 72 | 287 | -1 | 20,630.26 | 14,263.28 |
| | Brett RUMFORD | AUS | 75 | 70 | 75 | 67 | 287 | -1 | 20,630.26 | 14,263.28 |
| 21 | François DELAMONTAGNE | FRA | 70 | 73 | 76 | 69 | 288 | 0 | 16,355.52 | 11,307.82 |
| | Simon WAKEFIELD | ENG | 73 | 70 | 73 | 72 | 288 | 0 | 16,355.52 | 11,307.82 |
| | Frankie MINOZA | PHI | 69 | 72 | 76 | 71 | 288 | 0 | 16,355.52 | 11,307.82 |
| | Andrew MARSHALL | ENG | 71 | 73 | 73 | 71 | 288 | 0 | 16,355.52 | 11,307.82 |
| | Jean VAN DE VELDE | FRA | 68 | 78 | 71 | 71 | 288 | 0 | 16,355.52 | 11,307.82 |
| 26 | Richard BLAND | ENG | 71 | 72 | 74 | 72 | 289 | 1 | 13,456.14 | 9,303.26 |
| | Alex CEJKA | GER | 71 | 74 | 74 | 70 | 289 | 1 | 13,456.14 | 9,303.26 |
| | Chawalit PLAPHOL | THA | 73 | 71 | 75 | 70 | 289 | 1 | 13,456.14 | 9,303.26 |
| | Jeev Milkha SINGH | IND | 72 | 75 | 72 | 70 | 289 | 1 | 13,456.14 | 9,303.26 |
| | Thomas BJÖRN | DEN | 69 | 78 | 71 | 71 | 289 | 1 | 13,456.14 | 9,303.26 |
| | Nick DOUGHERTY | ENG | 73 | 73 | 74 | 69 | 289 | 1 | 13,456.14 | 9,303.26 |
| | Shiv KAPUR | IND | 71 | 74 | 76 | 68 | 289 | 1 | 13,456.14 | 9,303.26 |
| | Chapchai NIRAT | THA | 70 | 75 | 72 | 72 | 289 | 1 | 13,456.14 | 9,303.26 |
| 34 | Jarrod LYLE | AUS | 71 | 71 | 74 | 74 | 290 | 2 | 10,556.75 | 7,298.69 |
| | Chris RODGERS | ENG | 72 | 72 | 73 | 73 | 290 | 2 | 10,556.75 | 7,298.69 |
| | Markus BRIER | AUT | 72 | 71 | 70 | 77 | 290 | 2 | 10,556.75 | 7,298.69 |
| | David HIGGINS | IRL | 73 | 70 | 73 | 74 | 290 | 2 | 10,556.75 | 7,298.69 |
| | Marcus FRASER | AUS | 69 | 76 | 73 | 72 | 290 | 2 | 10,556.75 | 7,298.69 |
| | Ted OH | KOR | 70 | 77 | 73 | 70 | 290 | 2 | 10,556.75 | 7,298.69 |
| | Miles TUNNICLIFF | ENG | 72 | 70 | 76 | 72 | 290 | 2 | 10,556.75 | 7,298.69 |
| 41 | Danny CHIA | MAS | 71 | 70 | 76 | 74 | 291 | 3 | 8,623.82 | 5,962.31 |
| | José Manuel LARA | ESP | 74 | 69 | 72 | 76 | 291 | 3 | 8,623.82 | 5,962.31 |
| | Sven STRÜVER | GER | 77 | 69 | 73 | 72 | 291 | 3 | 8,623.82 | 5,962.31 |
| | Scott DRUMMOND | SCO | 70 | 75 | 75 | 71 | 291 | 3 | 8,623.82 | 5,962.31 |
| | Garry HOUSTON | WAL | 71 | 71 | 76 | 73 | 291 | 3 | 8,623.82 | 5,962.31 |
| | Damien MCGRANE | IRL | 72 | 74 | 72 | 73 | 291 | 3 | 8,623.82 | 5,962.31 |
| 47 | Robert-Jan DERKSEN | NED | 71 | 78 | 68 | 292 | | 4 | 7,434.33 | 5,139.92 |
| | Shaun P WEBSTER | ENG | 73 | 71 | 77 | 71 | 292 | 4 | 7,434.33 | 5,139.92 |
| 49 | Miguel Angel JIMÉNEZ | ESP | 71 | 75 | 76 | 71 | 293 | 5 | 6,096.15 | 4,214.73 |
| | Raphaël JACQUELIN | FRA | 72 | 72 | 78 | 71 | 293 | 5 | 6,096.15 | 4,214.73 |
| | Jason KNUTZON | USA | 71 | 73 | 76 | 73 | 293 | 5 | 6,096.15 | 4,214.73 |
| | Christopher HANELL | SWE | 72 | 74 | 74 | 73 | 293 | 5 | 6,096.15 | 4,214.73 |
| | Jarmo SANDELIN | SWE | 73 | 71 | 75 | 74 | 293 | 5 | 6,096.15 | 4,214.73 |
| | Wen Teh LU | TPE | 75 | 70 | 75 | 73 | 293 | 5 | 6,096.15 | 4,214.73 |
| | Wen-Chong LIANG | CHN | 70 | 74 | 76 | 73 | 293 | 5 | 6,096.15 | 4,214.73 |
| 56 | Stephen GALLACHER | SCO | 68 | 77 | 76 | 73 | 294 | 6 | 4,490.33 | 3,104.51 |
| | Prom MEESAWAT | THA | 73 | 74 | 75 | 72 | 294 | 6 | 4,490.33 | 3,104.51 |
| | Sung-Man LEE | KOR | 75 | 72 | 74 | 73 | 294 | 6 | 4,490.33 | 3,104.51 |
| | Johan EDFORS | SWE | 71 | 74 | 78 | 71 | 294 | 6 | 4,490.33 | 3,104.51 |
| | Simon YATES | SCO | 73 | 74 | 72 | 75 | 294 | 6 | 4,490.33 | 3,104.51 |
| 61 | Jean-François LUCQUIN | FRA | 71 | 76 | 75 | 73 | 295 | 7 | 3,791.51 | 2,621.36 |
| | Oliver WILSON | ENG | 74 | 73 | 78 | 70 | 295 | 7 | 3,791.51 | 2,621.36 |
| | David DIXON | ENG | 71 | 76 | 76 | 72 | 295 | 7 | 3,791.51 | 2,621.36 |
| | Richard STERNE | RSA | 73 | 74 | 75 | 73 | 295 | 7 | 3,791.51 | 2,621.36 |
| 65 | Bryan SALTUS | USA | 71 | 73 | 75 | 77 | 296 | 8 | 3,419.79 | 2,364.36 |
| 66 | Boonchu RUANGKIT | THA | 70 | 76 | 78 | 73 | 297 | 9 | 3,122.42 | 2,158.77 |
| | Marc CAYEUX | ZIM | 75 | 74 | 75 | 73 | 297 | 9 | 3,122.42 | 2,158.77 |
| | Kenneth FERRIE | ENG | 72 | 75 | 77 | 73 | 297 | 9 | 3,122.42 | 2,158.77 |
| 69 | Jamie SPENCE | ENG | 73 | 72 | 80 | 73 | 298 | 10 | 2,825.05 | 1,953.17 |
| 70 | Adam GROOM | AUS | 71 | 75 | 78 | 76 | 300 | 12 | 2,709.40 | 1,873.22 |
| 71 | Stuart LITTLE | ENG | 73 | 71 | 81 | 76 | 301 | 13 | 2,230.00 | 1,541.77 |
| 72 | Alistair PRESNELL | AUS | 74 | 73 | 80 | 76 | 303 | 15 | 2,227.00 | 1,539.70 |
| 73 | Alessandro TADINI | ITA | 70 | 77 | 77 | 80 | 304 | 16 | 2,224.00 | 1,537.62 |

## Total Prize Fund

€1,493,545  £1,032,603

---

round in Shanghai, holing from 50 yards on the 16th hole, which propelled him to the outright lead for the first time, and produced another sensational pitch at the first hole of the play-off to set up a birdie and clinch the title, after both he and Stenson had ended their regulation 72 holes on seven under par 281.

"Seve was my idol," he said. "Everyone knows he was the best and what he has done for golf in Spain is amazing. I followed him when I was young and I've learned a few tricks from him, including playing out of the rough, which is typical of Spanish golfers. We are all a bit wild off the tee."

Fernandez-Castaño confessed to being exhausted after a wild ride through the Middle Kingdom, which had him diving for cover the week before as a mini tornado brought havoc to the Saturday of the Volvo China Open.

Paul Lawrie

In Shanghai however, when it came to the crunch against Stenson, the Spaniard steered himself through the storm of the challenge and proved equal to the task.

The Swede looked to be cruising to victory with a three shot lead coming to the ninth, but the gods conspired against him and a ricochet off a tree into a lake saw his lead evaporate. In the end, he did well to hold it together to force a play-off.

"That hole pretty much did me in," admitted Stenson. "A lot of bad things happened at the same time. If I had made a par or birdie that would have taken care of business. But that's the way it goes sometimes."

Colin Montgomerie, who finished in a tie for third with Portugal's José-Filipe Lima, was happy to be back in Asia and also back on the sports pages and he failed by only one stroke to join Fernandez-Castaño and Stenson in a play-off.

Although he is just starting out on his professional career, Fernandez-Castaño might have to get used to such dichotomies in the reporting of his achievements if he continues to make any more such pronouncements as he did during his winner's press conference! However, at least for the likeable Spaniard the outcome was the one he wanted. When he got home, Alicia said yes.

**Noel Prentice**
*South China Morning Post*

# Andalucia Open de España Valle Romano

**Cadiz, Spain**
April 27-30 · 2006

# Uninhibited Joy

José Manuel Lara

**San Roque Club, New Course**

| Par | Yards | Metres |
|-----|-------|--------|
| 72  | 7105  | 6497   |

| Pos | Name | Score | To Par | |
|-----|------|-------|--------|---|
| 1 | **Niclas FASTH** | 270 | -18 | |
| 2 | John BICKERTON | 270 | -18 | |
| 3 | Phillip ARCHER | 271 | -17 | |
| | Thomas BJÖRN | 271 | -17 | |
| | Mattias ELIASSON | 271 | -17 | |
| | David GRIFFITHS | 271 | -17 | |
| | José Manuel LARA | 271 | -17 | |
| | Gary ORR | 271 | -17 | |
| 9 | Carl SUNESON | 272 | -16 | |
| 10 | Robert KARLSSON | 273 | -15 | |

$S$eve Ballesteros would have definitely approved. The man with the most famous victory salute in golf could have been watching a protégé as Niclas Fasth celebrated in his own, very un-Swedish-like way.

Fasth thrives on the buzz of battle, or, as he calls it "high energy", and my how he shows it: fists knifing heavenwards, eyes ablaze, lips grimacing. It could almost have been Seve at St Andrews in 1984. And that was just to celebrate his first birdie putt of the week in Thursday's opening round on the New Course at the San Roque Club!

By the time he had given himself a belated birthday gift – he turned 34 on the Saturday of the tournament - with a notable sudden-death play-off success against England's John Bickerton, Fasth had thumped in as many uppercuts in four days as Mike Tyson did in 12 rounds in his heyday.

The Swede's extrovert fist-pumping displays, a rarity for a nation that considers a standing ovation tantamount to minor hooliganism, began in earnest in 2001 as he came through the field to take second place in The Open Championship at Royal Lytham & St Annes. They further endeared him to the galleries at The De Vere Belfry a year later when he was denied being Europe's Ryder Cup winner by Paul Azinger's chip-in from the 18th green bunker. And they also worked overtime when he won twice on The European Tour International Schedule in 2005.

At San Roque he was at it again, flexing his muscles on the course and then marking his efforts with typical uninhibited joy. His five under par 67 in the first round was merely

Seve Ballesteros

**WEATHER REPORT**

| Round One | Round Two | Round Three | Round Four |
|-----------|-----------|-------------|------------|

**EUROPEAN TOUR ORDER OF MERIT**
(After 20 tournaments)

| Pos | | € | |
|-----|---|---|---|
| 1 | **David HOWELL** | 1,035,483.81 | |
| 2 | Henrik STENSON | 804,031.76 | |
| 3 | Retief GOOSEN | 689,478.87 | |
| 4 | Tim CLARK | 672,293.10 | |
| 5 | Nick O'HERN | 631,002.33 | |
| 6 | Ernie ELS | 589,759.12 | |
| 7 | Nick DOUGHERTY | 535,880.66 | |
| 8 | Paul CASEY | 529,606.12 | |
| 9 | Paul BROADHURST | 513,125.85 | |
| 10 | Vijay SINGH | 496,868.42 | |

# Andalucia Open de España Valle Romano

**Cadiz, Spain**
April 27-30 • 2006

David Griffiths

sizing up the course and his opponents. Fasth was winding up, boxing clever to lie a mere two strokes off the pace.

Ironically, the name Ballesteros had sat briefly on top of the leaderboard that day - not Seve, but his nephew Raul. With Seve having to step aside because he felt he was not fully prepared, brother Baldomero's son put the family name to the fore. He was making a bid to win a Tour card in one fell swoop, playing on an invitation. Raul surged to nine under par after 16 holes with the field scattered. However, he then took a bogey, double-bogey finish on the chin and gave way to early pacemakers José-Filipe Lima and Graeme Storm, who both finished the day on 65.

Storm led going into the weekend, too, although Robert Karlsson and Carl Suneson following excellent rounds of 63 and 64 respectively, joined five players one back and Thomas Björn, who also shot 64, was only another shot adrift.

While the above named players excelled on Friday, Saturday was moving day for David Griffiths. The player who had fashioned his career on the American Nationwide and Hooters Tours while basing himself at Sea Island, was looking for his maiden title in only his second year on The European Tour. Griffiths, who had finished third in The European Tour Qualifying School played at the Cadiz venue the previous November, made course knowledge count and did

❝ It can catch you out if you don't fully concentrate. There are a lot of trees and some water. It is tight and tricky, but, obviously, if you get it on the fairway you will have some short clubs in ❞ – Niclas Fasth

George O'Grady, Executive Director of The European Tour (centre), presents Luis Alvarez De Bohorques, Secretary General of the Spanish Golf Federation, with a Silver Salver to mark his retirement after 40 years service with the Spanish Golf Federation. Left to right: Angel De La Riva, President of the Andalucian Golf Federation, Jorge Young, Amen Corner, Angel Gallardo, Vice Chairman of the PGA European Tour Board of Directors, Ivan Ballesteros, CEO of Amen Corner, O'Grady, Richard Hills, Ryder Cup Director, De Bohorques, Keith Waters, Director of International Policy at The European Tour and Emma Villacieros, President of the Spanish Golf Federation

# Final Results

| Pos | Name | | Rd1 | Rd2 | Rd3 | Rd4 | Total | | € | £ |
|---|---|---|---|---|---|---|---|---|---|---|
| 1 | Niclas FASTH | SWE | 67 | 68 | 66 | 69 | 270 | -18 | 275,000.00 | 190,464.32 |
| 2 | John BICKERTON | ENG | 68 | 65 | 74 | 63 | 270 | -18 | 183,330.00 | 126,973.90 |
| 3 | David GRIFFITHS | ENG | 68 | 65 | 66 | 72 | 271 | -17 | 67,375.00 | 46,663.76 |
| | José Manuel LARA | ESP | 68 | 66 | 69 | 68 | 271 | -17 | 67,375.00 | 46,663.76 |
| | Mattias ELIASSON | SWE | 68 | 68 | 68 | 67 | 271 | -17 | 67,375.00 | 46,663.76 |
| | Phillip ARCHER | ENG | 67 | 69 | 68 | 67 | 271 | -17 | 67,375.00 | 46,663.76 |
| | Thomas BJÖRN | DEN | 70 | 64 | 68 | 69 | 271 | -17 | 67,375.00 | 46,663.76 |
| | Gary ORR | SCO | 72 | 64 | 68 | 67 | 271 | -17 | 67,375.00 | 46,663.76 |
| 9 | Carl SUNESON | ESP | 69 | 64 | 70 | 69 | 272 | -16 | 36,960.00 | 25,598.40 |
| 10 | Robert KARLSSON | SWE | 70 | 63 | 68 | 72 | 273 | -15 | 33,000.00 | 22,855.72 |
| 11 | Miles TUNNICLIFF | ENG | 66 | 71 | 69 | 68 | 274 | -14 | 28,435.00 | 19,694.01 |
| | Peter HANSON | SWE | 67 | 69 | 68 | 70 | 274 | -14 | 28,435.00 | 19,694.01 |
| | Juan PARRON | ESP | 66 | 72 | 70 | 66 | 274 | -14 | 28,435.00 | 19,694.01 |
| 14 | Charl SCHWARTZEL | RSA | 68 | 70 | 71 | 66 | 275 | -13 | 24,750.00 | 17,141.79 |
| | Louis OOSTHUIZEN | RSA | 70 | 65 | 69 | 71 | 275 | -13 | 24,750.00 | 17,141.79 |
| 16 | José-Filipe LIMA | POR | 65 | 73 | 69 | 69 | 276 | -12 | 21,417.00 | 14,833.36 |
| | David DIXON | ENG | 67 | 70 | 72 | 67 | 276 | -12 | 21,417.00 | 14,833.36 |
| | Graeme STORM | ENG | 65 | 67 | 70 | 74 | 276 | -12 | 21,417.00 | 14,833.36 |
| | David BRANSDON | AUS | 71 | 65 | 69 | 71 | 276 | -12 | 21,417.00 | 14,833.36 |
| | Francesco MOLINARI | ITA | 67 | 71 | 70 | 68 | 276 | -12 | 21,417.00 | 14,833.36 |
| 21 | Santiago LUNA | ESP | 71 | 70 | 69 | 67 | 277 | -11 | 18,645.00 | 12,913.48 |
| | Fredrik WIDMARK | SWE | 69 | 65 | 73 | 70 | 277 | -11 | 18,645.00 | 12,913.48 |
| | Stephen BROWNE | IRL | 67 | 70 | 71 | 69 | 277 | -11 | 18,645.00 | 12,913.48 |
| 24 | Lee SLATTERY | ENG | 67 | 71 | 70 | 70 | 278 | -10 | 17,160.00 | 11,884.97 |
| | James HEPWORTH | ENG | 68 | 68 | 69 | 73 | 278 | -10 | 17,160.00 | 11,884.97 |
| | Jarmo SANDELIN | SWE | 68 | 71 | 74 | 65 | 278 | -10 | 17,160.00 | 11,884.97 |
| | Jordi GARCIA DEL MORAL (AM) | ESP | 68 | 68 | 70 | 72 | 278 | -10 | | |
| 28 | Rafael GOMEZ | ARG | 74 | 65 | 73 | 67 | 279 | -9 | 15,427.50 | 10,685.05 |
| | Kieran STAUNTON | ENG | 69 | 71 | 68 | 71 | 279 | -9 | 15,427.50 | 10,685.05 |
| | Mark ROE | ENG | 71 | 69 | 72 | 67 | 279 | -9 | 15,427.50 | 10,685.05 |
| | Colin MONTGOMERIE | SCO | 68 | 68 | 72 | 71 | 279 | -9 | 15,427.50 | 10,685.05 |
| 32 | Søren KJELDSEN | DEN | 69 | 71 | 68 | 72 | 280 | -8 | 12,846.43 | 8,897.40 |
| | Peter LAWRIE | IRL | 67 | 71 | 70 | 72 | 280 | -8 | 12,846.43 | 8,897.40 |
| | Titch MOORE | RSA | 66 | 67 | 75 | 72 | 280 | -8 | 12,846.43 | 8,897.40 |
| | Alexandre ROCHA | BRA | 70 | 68 | 73 | 69 | 280 | -8 | 12,846.43 | 8,897.40 |
| | Raymond RUSSELL | SCO | 70 | 69 | 70 | 71 | 280 | -8 | 12,846.43 | 8,897.40 |
| | Leif WESTERBERG | SWE | 69 | 72 | 68 | 71 | 280 | -8 | 12,846.43 | 8,897.40 |
| | Ross FISHER | ENG | 68 | 73 | 67 | 72 | 280 | -8 | 12,846.43 | 8,897.40 |
| 39 | Oliver WILSON | ENG | 71 | 69 | 72 | 69 | 281 | -7 | 10,560.00 | 7,313.83 |
| | David CARTER | ENG | 68 | 69 | 75 | 69 | 281 | -7 | 10,560.00 | 7,313.83 |
| | Alvaro QUIROS | ESP | 68 | 70 | 71 | 72 | 281 | -7 | 10,560.00 | 7,313.83 |
| | Darren FICHARDT | RSA | 71 | 68 | 71 | 71 | 281 | -7 | 10,560.00 | 7,313.83 |
| | Magnus PERSSON | SWE | 70 | 69 | 72 | 70 | 281 | -7 | 10,560.00 | 7,313.83 |
| | Miguel Angel JIMÉNEZ | ESP | 66 | 74 | 72 | 69 | 281 | -7 | 10,560.00 | 7,313.83 |
| 45 | Peter HEDBLOM | SWE | 68 | 70 | 70 | 74 | 282 | -6 | 8,580.00 | 5,942.49 |
| | Johan EDFORS | SWE | 72 | 69 | 68 | 73 | 282 | -6 | 8,580.00 | 5,942.49 |
| | Ricardo GONZALEZ | ARG | 72 | 68 | 71 | 71 | 282 | -6 | 8,580.00 | 5,942.49 |
| | Maarten LAFEBER | NED | 70 | 71 | 72 | 69 | 282 | -6 | 8,580.00 | 5,942.49 |
| | Robert-Jan DERKSEN | NED | 68 | 71 | 71 | 72 | 282 | -6 | 8,580.00 | 5,942.49 |
| | David HIGGINS | IRL | 70 | 68 | 72 | 72 | 282 | -6 | 8,580.00 | 5,942.49 |
| 51 | Ivo GINER | ESP | 72 | 69 | 74 | 68 | 283 | -5 | 6,765.00 | 4,685.42 |
| | Michael KIRK | RSA | 72 | 67 | 71 | 73 | 283 | -5 | 6,765.00 | 4,685.42 |
| | Marco RUIZ | PAR | 71 | 69 | 71 | 72 | 283 | -5 | 6,765.00 | 4,685.42 |
| | Jean VAN DE VELDE | FRA | 68 | 71 | 75 | 69 | 283 | -5 | 6,765.00 | 4,685.42 |
| | Raul BALLESTEROS | ESP | 66 | 71 | 71 | 75 | 283 | -5 | 6,765.00 | 4,685.42 |
| 56 | Fernando ROCA | ESP | 67 | 72 | 74 | 71 | 284 | -4 | 5,115.00 | 3,542.64 |
| | Ignacio GARRIDO | ESP | 70 | 71 | 72 | 71 | 284 | -4 | 5,115.00 | 3,542.64 |
| | Gary EMERSON | ENG | 72 | 67 | 70 | 75 | 284 | -4 | 5,115.00 | 3,542.64 |
| | Hennie OTTO | RSA | 68 | 73 | 74 | 69 | 284 | -4 | 5,115.00 | 3,542.64 |
| | Gonzalo FDEZ-CASTAÑO | ESP | 71 | 69 | 71 | 73 | 284 | -4 | 5,115.00 | 3,542.64 |
| | Sebastian FERNANDEZ | ARG | 73 | 68 | 70 | 73 | 284 | -4 | 5,115.00 | 3,542.64 |
| 62 | Francisco VALERA | ESP | 69 | 69 | 73 | 74 | 285 | -3 | 4,207.50 | 2,914.10 |
| | Pedro LINHART | ESP | 70 | 68 | 70 | 77 | 285 | -3 | 4,207.50 | 2,914.10 |
| | Barry LANE | ENG | 68 | 68 | 77 | 72 | 285 | -3 | 4,207.50 | 2,914.10 |
| | Steve WEBSTER | ENG | 67 | 71 | 72 | 75 | 285 | -3 | 4,207.50 | 2,914.10 |
| 66 | Robert ROCK | ENG | 71 | 68 | 72 | 75 | 286 | -2 | 3,795.00 | 2,628.41 |
| 67 | Sam WALKER | ENG | 69 | 71 | 74 | 73 | 287 | -1 | 3,382.50 | 2,342.71 |
| | Andrew OLDCORN | SCO | 72 | 68 | 73 | 74 | 287 | -1 | 3,382.50 | 2,342.71 |
| | Christian L NILSSON | SWE | 70 | 71 | 73 | 73 | 287 | -1 | 3,382.50 | 2,342.71 |
| | Fredrik HENGE | SWE | 70 | 70 | 74 | 73 | 287 | -1 | 3,382.50 | 2,342.71 |
| 71 | Klas ERIKSSON | SWE | 71 | 68 | 72 | 78 | 289 | 1 | 2,652.33 | 1,837.00 |
| | Ian GARBUTT | ENG | 70 | 71 | 69 | 79 | 289 | 1 | 2,652.33 | 1,837.00 |
| | Benn BARHAM | ENG | 70 | 71 | 73 | 75 | 289 | 1 | 2,652.33 | 1,837.00 |
| 74 | Andrew BUTTERFIELD | ENG | 70 | 69 | 76 | 75 | 290 | 2 | 2,469.00 | 1,710.02 |
| 75 | Ariel CANETE | ARG | 69 | 70 | W/D | | 139 | -5 | | |

not drop a shot until the 53rd hole. His third round 66 swept him to 17 under, but could the English youngster hold off the experienced Swedes two strokes behind him - the tall and ice-cool Karlsson and, in many ways, Karlsson's alter-ego, Fasth?

The answer came quickly. On the final day, the rest of the field looked out for the count when Fasth birdied five of the first six holes to establish a three shot advantage. Griffiths could not quite maintain his accuracy, Karlsson slipped back and late mistakes by Björn ruled him out. It appeared that Fasth had everyone on the ropes but then, suddenly, he failed to find the killer blow.

A couple of unexpected bogeys to finish his final round set up the shoot-out with Bickerton, who had produced a magnificent course record-equalling nine under par 63 to set the target of 18 under par 270.

Bickerton, who had only secured his playing rights the previous year at the eleventh hour when he won the Abama Open de Canarias, proved a worthy adversary. In fact, if it had been a boxing match, the referee might have stepped in and raised both men's arms aloft for a draw.

The play-off pair parred the awkward 18th three times. Even then, the Fasth right arm worked overtime as the adrenalin pumped as much as the fist. But then he produced the knockout blow. A stunning nine-iron approach to five feet for birdie separated the battling duo. Fasth had finally delivered the punchline to his latest winning story.

**Norman Dabell**

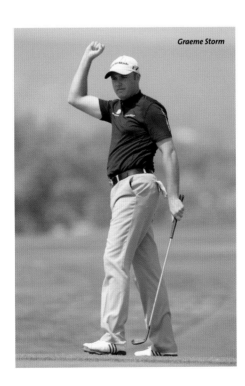

Graeme Storm

# Total Prize Fund
€1,657,420 £1,147,922

# Brothers in Arms

Anders Hansen

**Castello di Tolcinasco Golf & Country Club**

| Par | Yards | Metres |
|---|---|---|
| 72 | 7225 | 6610 |

| | | | | |
|---|---|---|---|---|
| 1 | Francesco MOLINARI | 265 | -23 | |
| 2 | Anders HANSEN | 269 | -19 | |
| | Jarmo SANDELIN | 269 | -19 | |
| 4 | Søren KJELDSEN | 270 | -18 | |
| 5 | Benoit TEILLERIA | 271 | -17 | |
| 6 | Phillip ARCHER | 272 | -16 | |
| | Bradley DREDGE | 272 | -16 | |
| 8 | Peter FOWLER | 273 | -15 | |
| | Garry HOUSTON | 273 | -15 | |
| | Alessandro TADINI | 273 | -15 | |
| | Marc WARREN | 273 | -15 | |

O n the outskirts of Milan on a hot May afternoon, the Molinari story turned into a double act the likes of which Continental European golf has not witnessed since Manuel Ballesteros was joined by his little brother Severiano on the campaign trail some 30 years before.

'Manolo', already a star turn, told the golfing world that young Severiano was going to be a great champion and in 1976, at the Dutch Open in Kennemer, he swiftly claimed the first of his 50 European Tour victories. The rest, as they say, is history.

With his surprise triumph in the 2005 United States Amateur Championship (he was the first European winner since England's Harold Hilton in 1911), Italy's Edoardo Molinari hinted that he could be the next young lion to grace the European game.

But he, too, alerted the world to watch out for his younger brother, Francesco, who caught the eye with his sixth place finish in the 2005 Johnnie Walker Championship at Gleneagles after having taken the fourth card in the previous year's Qualifying School at San Roque, where he followed an opening 79 with five fighting sub par returns.

The former Italian Stroke Play and Match Play Champion, twice an Eisenhower Trophy international, made his bow in the Masters Tournament at Augusta National in April 2006 – as brother Edoardo's caddie! A month later at the picturesque Castello di Tolcinasco Golf & Country Club, 25 year old Edoardo missed the halfway cut in the Telecom Italia Open and it was left to 23 year old Francesco to take up the baton. He did not disappoint.

Five behind leader Søren Kjeldsen after an opening 68, he not only went on to record

**WEATHER REPORT**

| Round One | Round Two | Round Three | Round Four |
|---|---|---|---|

Jarmo Sandelin

**EUROPEAN TOUR ORDER OF MERIT**
(After 21 tournaments)

| Pos | | € | |
|---|---|---|---|
| 1 | David HOWELL | 1,035,483.81 | |
| 2 | Henrik STENSON | 804,031.76 | |
| 3 | Retief GOOSEN | 689,478.87 | |
| 4 | Tim CLARK | 672,293.10 | |
| 5 | Nick O'HERN | 631,002.33 | |
| 6 | Ernie ELS | 589,759.12 | |
| 7 | Nick DOUGHERTY | 535,880.66 | |
| 8 | Paul CASEY | 529,606.12 | |
| 9 | Paul BROADHURST | 513,125.85 | |
| 10 | Vijay SINGH | 496,868.42 | |

# Telecom Italia Open

## Milan, Italy
May 4-7 • 2006

Benn Barham

his first Tour victory, he did so in spectacular fashion with follow-up rounds of 65-67-65 to finish four strokes clear of experienced champions Anders Hansen of Denmark and Sweden's Jarmo Sandelin and, in the process, rewrite Italian golf history.

Not since Massimo Mannelli did the trick in his native Rome 26 years earlier had there been a home grown Italian Open champion, and Molinari's winning score of 23 under par 265 was a Championship record. The son of a Turin dentist only dropped one stroke over the 72 holes, and that by three-putting the 13th on the opening day. A new star had surely appeared in the golfing firmament.

For one family to produce two champions in such quick succession is astonishing. Italy, of course, has had many fine players since the breakthrough by Mannelli,– none greater than Costantino Rocca. The former factory worker from Bergamo, who went close to winning The Open Championship at St Andrews in 1995 before losing a play-off to John Daly, went on to play in The Ryder Cup and did his country proud. But with Rocca 50 in December 2006, Italy is crying out for a

*" As one of the smaller guys, this is a favourite course of mine. The big hitters don't have too much of an advantage. It's a very pure layout with rough not too severe. You face lots of wedge shots and there is plenty of water to negotiate. The greens are perfect "* – **Søren Kjeldsen**

Ian Woosnam

| Pos | Name | | Rd1 | Rd2 | Rd3 | Rd4 | Total | | € | £ |
|---|---|---|---|---|---|---|---|---|---|---|
| 1 | Francesco MOLINARI | ITA | 68 | 65 | 67 | 65 | 265 | -23 | 233,330.00 | 161,666.48 |
| 2 | Anders HANSEN | DEN | 70 | 67 | 66 | 66 | 269 | -19 | 121,595.00 | 84,249.07 |
| | Jarmo SANDELIN | SWE | 69 | 68 | 67 | 65 | 269 | -19 | 121,595.00 | 84,249.07 |
| 4 | Søren KJELDSEN | DEN | 63 | 70 | 69 | 68 | 270 | -18 | 70,000.00 | 48,500.64 |
| 5 | Benoit TEILLERIA | FRA | 69 | 68 | 65 | 69 | 271 | -17 | 59,360.00 | 41,128.54 |
| 6 | Bradley DREDGE | WAL | 67 | 69 | 68 | 68 | 272 | -16 | 45,500.00 | 31,525.41 |
| | Phillip ARCHER | ENG | 66 | 67 | 68 | 71 | 272 | -16 | 45,500.00 | 31,525.41 |
| 8 | Alessandro TADINI | ITA | 66 | 72 | 67 | 68 | 273 | -15 | 30,030.00 | 20,806.77 |
| | Garry HOUSTON | WAL | 70 | 70 | 65 | 68 | 273 | -15 | 30,030.00 | 20,806.77 |
| | Peter FOWLER | AUS | 68 | 67 | 68 | 70 | 273 | -15 | 30,030.00 | 20,806.77 |
| | Marc WARREN | SCO | 69 | 68 | 70 | 66 | 273 | -15 | 30,030.00 | 20,806.77 |
| 12 | Steven JEPPESEN | SWE | 67 | 71 | 67 | 69 | 274 | -14 | 22,155.00 | 15,350.45 |
| | David DRYSDALE | SCO | 67 | 64 | 73 | 70 | 274 | -14 | 22,155.00 | 15,350.45 |
| | Andrew MCLARDY | RSA | 67 | 68 | 67 | 72 | 274 | -14 | 22,155.00 | 15,350.45 |
| | Nicolas COLSAERTS | BEL | 70 | 68 | 64 | 72 | 274 | -14 | 22,155.00 | 15,350.45 |
| 16 | Jonathan LOMAS | ENG | 67 | 68 | 71 | 69 | 275 | -13 | 17,290.00 | 11,979.66 |
| | Gregory HAVRET | FRA | 66 | 68 | 73 | 68 | 275 | -13 | 17,290.00 | 11,979.66 |
| | Titch MOORE | RSA | 71 | 67 | 67 | 70 | 275 | -13 | 17,290.00 | 11,979.66 |
| | Raphaël JACQUELIN | FRA | 70 | 67 | 68 | 70 | 275 | -13 | 17,290.00 | 11,979.66 |
| | Benn BARHAM | ENG | 65 | 68 | 67 | 75 | 275 | -13 | 17,290.00 | 11,979.66 |
| | John BICKERTON | ENG | 69 | 69 | 71 | 66 | 275 | -13 | 17,290.00 | 11,979.66 |
| | David GRIFFITHS | ENG | 70 | 68 | 69 | 68 | 275 | -13 | 17,290.00 | 11,979.66 |
| | Brad SUTTERFIELD | USA | 71 | 67 | 71 | 66 | 275 | -13 | 17,290.00 | 11,979.66 |
| 24 | Alessio BRUSCHI | ITA | 68 | 70 | 69 | 69 | 276 | -12 | 14,140.00 | 9,797.13 |
| | Steven O'HARA | SCO | 72 | 68 | 67 | 69 | 276 | -12 | 14,140.00 | 9,797.13 |
| | Andrew BUTTERFIELD | ENG | 66 | 68 | 74 | 68 | 276 | -12 | 14,140.00 | 9,797.13 |
| | Mark ROE | ENG | 69 | 66 | 71 | 70 | 276 | -12 | 14,140.00 | 9,797.13 |
| | Richard GREEN | AUS | 67 | 69 | 68 | 72 | 276 | -12 | 14,140.00 | 9,797.13 |
| 29 | Francisco VALERA | ESP | 69 | 70 | 70 | 68 | 277 | -11 | 12,250.00 | 8,487.61 |
| | Richard MCEVOY | ENG | 71 | 69 | 66 | 71 | 277 | -11 | 12,250.00 | 8,487.61 |
| | Alexandre ROCHA | BRA | 68 | 72 | 71 | 66 | 277 | -11 | 12,250.00 | 8,487.61 |
| | Peter GUSTAFSSON | SWE | 70 | 67 | 68 | 72 | 277 | -11 | 12,250.00 | 8,487.61 |
| 33 | Gregory BOURDY | FRA | 66 | 70 | 69 | 73 | 278 | -10 | 10,240.00 | 7,094.95 |
| | Lee SLATTERY | ENG | 69 | 71 | 69 | 69 | 278 | -10 | 10,240.00 | 7,094.95 |
| | Hennie OTTO | RSA | 69 | 68 | 67 | 74 | 278 | -10 | 10,240.00 | 7,094.95 |
| | David BRANSDON | AUS | 69 | 69 | 69 | 71 | 278 | -10 | 10,240.00 | 7,094.95 |
| | Emanuele CANONICA | ITA | 69 | 69 | 70 | 70 | 278 | -10 | 10,240.00 | 7,094.95 |
| | Marco CRESPI | ITA | 71 | 67 | 68 | 72 | 278 | -10 | 10,240.00 | 7,094.95 |
| | Miguel CARBALLO | ARG | 67 | 70 | 66 | 75 | 278 | -10 | 10,240.00 | 7,094.95 |
| 40 | Shaun P WEBSTER | ENG | 70 | 69 | 72 | 68 | 279 | -9 | 7,980.00 | 5,529.07 |
| | Anthony WALL | ENG | 70 | 65 | 73 | 71 | 279 | -9 | 7,980.00 | 5,529.07 |
| | Santiago LUNA | ESP | 72 | 68 | 67 | 72 | 279 | -9 | 7,980.00 | 5,529.07 |
| | Sven STRÜVER | GER | 70 | 65 | 73 | 71 | 279 | -9 | 7,980.00 | 5,529.07 |
| | Ian WOOSNAM | WAL | 70 | 66 | 73 | 70 | 279 | -9 | 7,980.00 | 5,529.07 |
| | Mark FOSTER | ENG | 69 | 67 | 74 | 69 | 279 | -9 | 7,980.00 | 5,529.07 |
| | Marcus FRASER | AUS | 71 | 66 | 70 | 72 | 279 | -9 | 7,980.00 | 5,529.07 |
| | Leif WESTERBERG | SWE | 69 | 69 | 71 | 70 | 279 | -9 | 7,980.00 | 5,529.07 |
| | David LYNN | ENG | 71 | 69 | 68 | 71 | 279 | -9 | 7,980.00 | 5,529.07 |
| 49 | Ricardo GONZALEZ | ARG | 74 | 65 | 70 | 71 | 280 | -8 | 6,440.00 | 4,462.06 |
| | Magnus PERSSON | SWE | 69 | 71 | 70 | 70 | 280 | -8 | 6,440.00 | 4,462.06 |
| 51 | Christian L NILSSON | SWE | 70 | 69 | 71 | 71 | 281 | -7 | 5,460.00 | 3,783.05 |
| | Paul DWYER | ENG | 73 | 67 | 67 | 74 | 281 | -7 | 5,460.00 | 3,783.05 |
| | James HEPWORTH | ENG | 66 | 71 | 74 | 70 | 281 | -7 | 5,460.00 | 3,783.05 |
| | Sebastian FERNANDEZ | ARG | 68 | 67 | 75 | 71 | 281 | -7 | 5,460.00 | 3,783.05 |
| | Michael KIRK | RSA | 66 | 72 | 70 | 73 | 281 | -7 | 5,460.00 | 3,783.05 |
| | Matteo DELPODIO (AM) | ITA | 67 | 69 | 70 | 75 | 281 | -7 | | |
| 57 | Fredrik HENGE | SWE | 72 | 67 | 71 | 72 | 282 | -6 | 4,620.00 | 3,201.04 |
| 58 | Stephen SCAHILL | NZL | 70 | 67 | 71 | 75 | 283 | -5 | 4,270.00 | 2,958.54 |
| | Gary ORR | SCO | 73 | 67 | 71 | 72 | 283 | -5 | 4,270.00 | 2,958.54 |
| 60 | Rafael GOMEZ | ARG | 67 | 70 | 73 | 74 | 284 | -4 | 3,990.00 | 2,764.54 |
| | Tom WHITEHOUSE | ENG | 70 | 68 | 72 | 74 | 284 | -4 | 3,990.00 | 2,764.54 |
| 62 | Louis OOSTHUIZEN | RSA | 67 | 68 | 75 | 76 | 286 | -2 | 3,780.00 | 2,619.03 |
| 63 | Andrea MAESTRONI | ITA | 72 | 67 | 74 | 75 | 288 | 0 | 3,570.00 | 2,473.53 |
| | Stephen DODD | WAL | 69 | 67 | 73 | 79 | 288 | 0 | 3,570.00 | 2,473.53 |
| 65 | Richard BLAND | ENG | 71 | 67 | 77 | 74 | 289 | 1 | 3,360.00 | 2,328.03 |
| 66 | Christopher HANELL | SWE | 67 | 70 | 75 | RETD 212 | | -4 | 3,220.00 | 2,231.03 |

new hero. The Molinari brothers have risen to the challenge.

Avid Inter Milan fan Francesco emerged from a last green champagne soaking from his brother and an army of friends to admit: "It's a dream come true – I wanted to bring joy to the Italian people by winning this Championship but I never thought it would happen so early in my career.

"It was incredible to have so many people cheering for me – it was like being in a football stadium. My brother and I are equal now. I had to win something to catch him. It's 1-1 now and we've got to go out and score some more goals.

"I hope winning the way I did will be used by the Italian Federation and the media to demonstrate that golf is a great sport. I think it should be more popular but the problem in Italy is that football is THE sport and all the others are in the shadows.

"Edoardo and I are young. We have a lot of work to do but we have a lot of chances ahead. There is a lot of competition between us but being able to practise every day with a person who is as good as you or even better helps to improve your game. Every time one of us gets a step ahead there is a short period only before the other gets a good result. So it is good competition.

"It was important I made a good start to the year. This was the third or fourth time I

have been in contention in the last round. I had a lot of pressure because I was playing in Italy but I proved to myself that I can play at a high level. I am very proud and happy about that."

Molinari's European Tour Media Guide entry appeared in 2006 on the facing page to Colin Montgomerie's – his Milan breakthrough dramatically boosts his chances of going face-to-face with the famous Scot, and Europe's other great golfing stars, more often than not in the coming years.

**Gordon Richardson**

Søren Kjeldsen

# Total Prize Fund
€1,385,960  £960,284

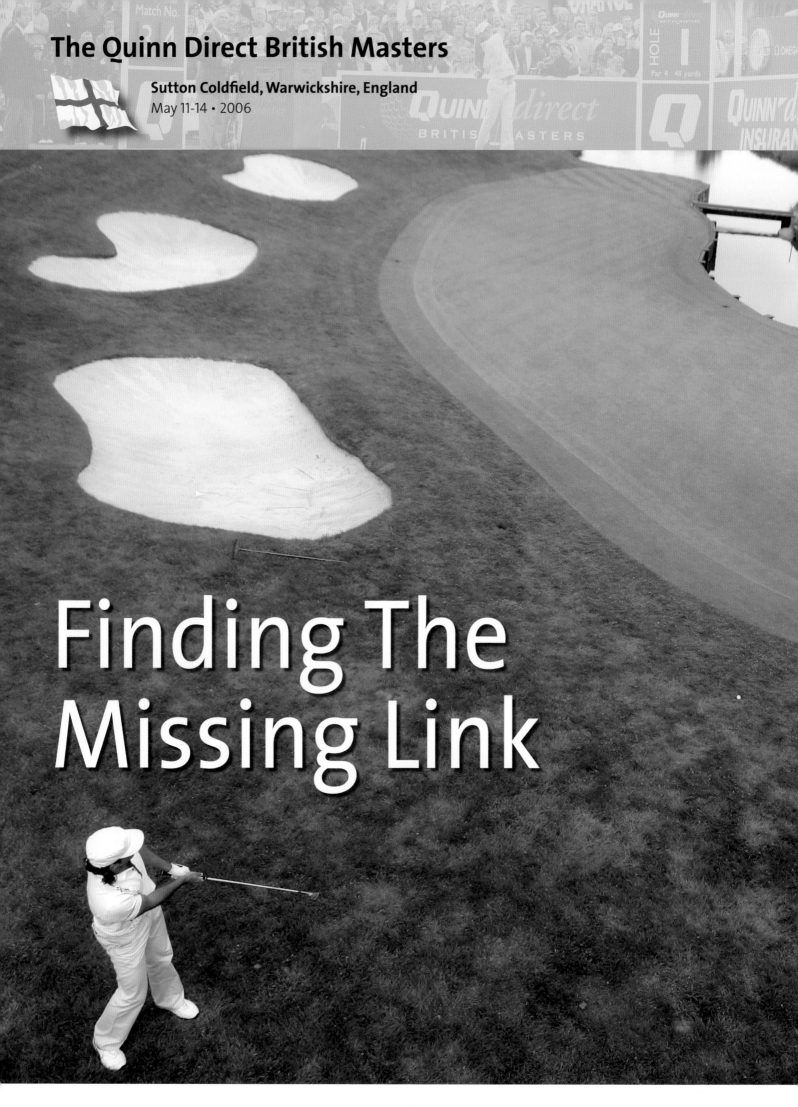

# Finding The Missing Link

THE
**QUINN** *direct*
BRITISH MASTERS

### The De Vere Belfry

| Par | Yards | Metres |
|-----|-------|--------|
| 72 | 7163 | 6551 |

| | | | | |
|---|---|---|---|---|
| 1 | **Johan EDFORS** | **277** | **-11** | |
| 2 | Gary EMERSON | 278 | -10 | |
| | Stephen GALLACHER | 278 | -10 | |
| | Jarmo SANDELIN | 278 | -10 | |
| 5 | Michael CAMPBELL | 279 | -9 | |
| | Paul CASEY | 279 | -9 | |
| 7 | Paul BROADHURST | 280 | -8 | |
| 8 | Jonathan LOMAS | 281 | -7 | |
| | Graeme McDOWELL | 281 | -7 | |
| | Tom WHITEHOUSE | 281 | -7 | |

### WEATHER REPORT

Round One  Round Two  Round Three  Round Four

### EUROPEAN TOUR ORDER OF MERIT
(After 22 tournaments)

| Pos | | € | |
|-----|---|---|---|
| 1 | **David HOWELL** | 1,080,767.74 | |
| 2 | Henrik STENSON | 804,031.76 | |
| 3 | Retief GOOSEN | 689,478.87 | |
| 4 | Tim CLARK | 672,293.10 | |
| 5 | Johan EDFORS | 660,620.58 | |
| 6 | Paul CASEY | 631,297.89 | |
| 7 | Nick O'HERN | 631,002.33 | |
| 8 | Paul BROADHURST | 591,956.67 | |
| 9 | Ernie ELS | 589,759.12 | |
| 10 | Nick DOUGHERTY | 535,880.66 | |

# The Quinn Direct British Masters

**Sutton Coldfield, Warwickshire, England**
May 11-14 • 2006

The talk was of the FA Cup Final and private helicopters; debut sponsors and a new venue, albeit one already dripping in golfing history. Indeed, the talk at The De Vere Belfry was of everything else apart from Johan Edfors. Until Sunday evening that was....

The Swede, who until 2006 was better known for once employing Sven Goran Eriksson's son as his caddie, came round the blind side at The Quinn Direct British Masters and ambushed several of the world's best in spectacular style.

It was his finest hour at that time and one worth not only €437,949 (£300,000) in prize money, but also inestimable amounts in self esteem and its immediate bi-product – confidence. If this was the peak of his career to date then Edfors had every right to enjoy the moment. Because for every peak, he has known a hundred troughs.

Prime example of that came when he emerged as principal graduate from the Challenge Tour in 2003. Two wins and nine top ten finishes convinced him that he had the game to hack it with the big boys. He suddenly realised when he did rub shoulders with them, that he did not. "I just wasn't good enough," he readily admitted. "I pretty soon realised that I didn't have the game necessary to compete at that level."

However, rather than accepting the option of selling tee pegs and half hour lessons to club members, Edfors wanted to discover if there was a player of substance waiting to emerge from an all-too-fragile shell. He came to the conclusion that if he was going to go a long way, he could only do it by taking golf's short route.

*" The De Vere Belfry is simply one of the great venues in golf and rightly known around the world. It has matured into a superb golf course and will get even better. There isn't a weak hole out there and it is a wonderful place for players and spectators alike "* – David Howell

Stephen Gallacher

Michael Campbell

Tom Whitehouse

Edfors embraced the answer Darren Clarke always gives when players ask him which areas of their game they should practise most to improve, namely: Tip One – Short Game; Tip Two – Short Game; Tip Three – Short Game.

Together with coaches Richard Fors and Lawrence Evertsson, Edfors worked hard to find the missing links but the results were far from instantaneous. Indeed, by the end of the 2004 season, he had lost his card and headed back to the Challenge Tour where, unlike in 2003, he failed to collect his playing privileges for the big league.

The Qualifying School, six days of the biggest test of patience and perseverance, nerve and skill, followed and saw Edfors emerge with the 13th card. It proved a lucky one because his efforts were repaid when he won the TCL Classic in China in March. It made him hungrier for more.

That craving was satisfied in the short term when the Tour arrived in the United Kingdom for the first time in 2006. "I think I proved myself in a really great field this week," said

Edfors when he finally acknowledged the enormity of his performance.

"I loved playing in front of the big crowds that came. I loved the feeling of adrenalin pumping through your system when you are going down the stretch and there is a chance of winning. That's the best feeling you can have."

Edfors could not be sure that he would experience that feeling when he entered the weekend action. Those who are sent to chronicle golf events for the world's media did not waste their ink or footage on him.

To them, the winner would come from one of the three big fish in the pond: US Open Champion Michael Campbell, Ryder Cup star Paul Casey, or crowd favourite Darren Clarke, who was so uncertain about his form at the start of the week that he was sure he would be on a helicopter on the way to the FA Cup Final in Cardiff on Saturday – a trip he hastily cancelled.

Edfors was mentioned only in small type amongst the names on the leaderboard.

To improve your performance we take a supporting role.

It's your success that matters.
We never forget that. That's why we provide print and
document management solutions tailored to your needs.
So you can always be fabulous.
Bravo.

**putting you first** | www.ricoh.co.uk/pyf

**RICOH**

Richard Green

By the end of a chill, but thankfully dry Sunday he would not only make a name for himself, but also be in a position to be asked about the prospect of making The Ryder Cup Team. Ryder Cup? Edfors had never even thought of it. He had been too busy winning his own Cup Finals to get that far ahead. Now his goals would change and with two wins already behind him, the idea was not as absurd as it may have sounded when he finally picked up his graduation papers from Qualifying School just six months previously.

Edfors had emerged from that examination with his sanity intact and his confidence high. This time he knew he was ready for the big boys.... even if at The De Vere Belfry they never saw him coming. They would the next time.

**Martin Hardy**

*Geoff Cousins, UK Managing Director for Jaguar, presents Ross Fisher the keys to a Jaguar XJ for winning the nearest the pin contest at the par 3 12th*

# Final Results

| Pos | Name | | Rd1 | Rd2 | Rd3 | Rd4 | Total | | € | £ |
|-----|------|---|-----|-----|-----|-----|-------|---|---|---|
| 1 | Johan EDFORS | SWE | 68 | 69 | 70 | 70 | 277 | -11 | 437,949.01 | 300,000.00 |
| 2 | Gary EMERSON | ENG | 68 | 70 | 73 | 67 | 278 | -10 | 195,948.12 | 134,226.67 |
| | Jarmo SANDELIN | SWE | 67 | 71 | 70 | 70 | 278 | -10 | 195,948.12 | 134,226.67 |
| | Stephen GALLACHER | SCO | 71 | 66 | 70 | 71 | 278 | -10 | 195,948.12 | 134,226.67 |
| 5 | Michael CAMPBELL | NZL | 67 | 70 | 68 | 74 | 279 | -9 | 101,691.76 | 69,660.00 |
| | Paul CASEY | ENG | 67 | 66 | 70 | 76 | 279 | -9 | 101,691.76 | 69,660.00 |
| 7 | Paul BROADHURST | ENG | 70 | 72 | 70 | 68 | 280 | -8 | 78,830.82 | 54,000.00 |
| 8 | Tom WHITEHOUSE | ENG | 70 | 71 | 69 | 71 | 281 | -7 | 59,035.53 | 40,440.00 |
| | Graeme MCDOWELL | NIR | 70 | 68 | 73 | 70 | 281 | -7 | 59,035.53 | 40,440.00 |
| | Jonathan LOMAS | ENG | 70 | 73 | 68 | 70 | 281 | -7 | 59,035.53 | 40,440.00 |
| 11 | Darren CLARKE | NIR | 66 | 70 | 70 | 76 | 282 | -6 | 45,283.93 | 31,020.00 |
| | David HOWELL | ENG | 70 | 72 | 72 | 68 | 282 | -6 | 45,283.93 | 31,020.00 |
| | Oliver WILSON | ENG | 68 | 74 | 68 | 72 | 282 | -6 | 45,283.93 | 31,020.00 |
| 14 | Padraig HARRINGTON | IRL | 75 | 66 | 74 | 68 | 283 | -5 | 34,981.18 | 23,962.50 |
| | Anders HANSEN | DEN | 73 | 69 | 69 | 72 | 283 | -5 | 34,981.18 | 23,962.50 |
| | Søren KJELDSEN | DEN | 68 | 74 | 73 | 68 | 283 | -5 | 34,981.18 | 23,962.50 |
| | Richard GREEN | AUS | 70 | 69 | 73 | 71 | 283 | -5 | 34,981.18 | 23,962.50 |
| | Ian POULTER | ENG | 68 | 69 | 74 | 72 | 283 | -5 | 34,981.18 | 23,962.50 |
| | Joakim BÄCKSTRÖM | SWE | 71 | 73 | 68 | 71 | 283 | -5 | 34,981.18 | 23,962.50 |
| | Emanuele CANONICA | ITA | 72 | 72 | 74 | 65 | 283 | -5 | 34,981.18 | 23,962.50 |
| | Gonzalo FDEZ-CASTAÑO | ESP | 71 | 71 | 72 | 69 | 283 | -5 | 34,981.18 | 23,962.50 |
| 22 | Peter O'MALLEY | AUS | 71 | 66 | 74 | 73 | 284 | -4 | 28,116.33 | 19,260.00 |
| | Miguel Angel JIMÉNEZ | ESP | 70 | 70 | 73 | 71 | 284 | -4 | 28,116.33 | 19,260.00 |
| | David BRANSDON | AUS | 69 | 72 | 74 | 69 | 284 | -4 | 28,116.33 | 19,260.00 |
| | Ross FISHER | ENG | 73 | 70 | 73 | 68 | 284 | -4 | 28,116.33 | 19,260.00 |
| | Steven JEPPESEN | SWE | 72 | 70 | 71 | 71 | 284 | -4 | 28,116.33 | 19,260.00 |
| 27 | Charl SCHWARTZEL | RSA | 71 | 69 | 72 | 73 | 285 | -3 | 23,780.63 | 16,290.00 |
| | Wade ORMSBY | AUS | 73 | 71 | 70 | 71 | 285 | -3 | 23,780.63 | 16,290.00 |
| | Jean VAN DE VELDE | FRA | 72 | 72 | 73 | 68 | 285 | -3 | 23,780.63 | 16,290.00 |
| | Robert KARLSSON | SWE | 71 | 73 | 69 | 72 | 285 | -3 | 23,780.63 | 16,290.00 |
| | Stephen DODD | WAL | 74 | 70 | 71 | 70 | 285 | -3 | 23,780.63 | 16,290.00 |
| | Simon WAKEFIELD | ENG | 71 | 73 | 70 | 71 | 285 | -3 | 23,780.63 | 16,290.00 |
| 33 | Bradley DREDGE | WAL | 71 | 71 | 71 | 73 | 286 | -2 | 19,219.71 | 13,165.71 |
| | David LYNN | ENG | 70 | 72 | 72 | 72 | 286 | -2 | 19,219.71 | 13,165.71 |
| | Graeme STORM | ENG | 74 | 64 | 74 | 74 | 286 | -2 | 19,219.71 | 13,165.71 |
| | Simon DYSON | ENG | 71 | 73 | 71 | 71 | 286 | -2 | 19,219.71 | 13,165.71 |
| | Andrew MARSHALL | ENG | 71 | 72 | 72 | 71 | 286 | -2 | 19,219.71 | 13,165.71 |
| | Anthony WALL | ENG | 75 | 68 | 72 | 71 | 286 | -2 | 19,219.71 | 13,165.71 |
| | Robert-Jan DERKSEN | NED | 72 | 72 | 70 | 72 | 286 | -2 | 19,219.71 | 13,165.71 |
| 40 | Christian L NILSSON | SWE | 69 | 72 | 74 | 72 | 287 | -1 | 16,291.70 | 11,160.00 |
| | Peter HEDBLOM | SWE | 70 | 71 | 73 | 73 | 287 | -1 | 16,291.70 | 11,160.00 |
| | David CARTER | ENG | 71 | 73 | 72 | 71 | 287 | -1 | 16,291.70 | 11,160.00 |
| | José-Filipe LIMA | POR | 70 | 74 | 70 | 73 | 287 | -1 | 16,291.70 | 11,160.00 |
| 44 | David HIGGINS | IRL | 68 | 75 | 71 | 74 | 288 | 0 | 14,452.32 | 9,900.00 |
| | Gary ORR | SCO | 70 | 73 | 71 | 74 | 288 | 0 | 14,452.32 | 9,900.00 |
| | Marcus FRASER | AUS | 69 | 74 | 72 | 73 | 288 | 0 | 14,452.32 | 9,900.00 |
| 47 | Simon KHAN | ENG | 74 | 68 | 75 | 72 | 289 | 1 | 11,824.62 | 8,100.00 |
| | Daniel VANCSIK | ARG | 74 | 65 | 75 | 75 | 289 | 1 | 11,824.62 | 8,100.00 |
| | Warren ABERY | RSA | 71 | 68 | 73 | 77 | 289 | 1 | 11,824.62 | 8,100.00 |
| | Jean-François LUCQUIN | FRA | 69 | 72 | 76 | 72 | 289 | 1 | 11,824.62 | 8,100.00 |
| | Gregory HAVRET | FRA | 72 | 70 | 75 | 72 | 289 | 1 | 11,824.62 | 8,100.00 |
| | Carlos RODILES | ESP | 74 | 70 | 72 | 73 | 289 | 1 | 11,824.62 | 8,100.00 |
| | Kenneth FERRIE | ENG | 70 | 73 | 74 | 72 | 289 | 1 | 11,824.62 | 8,100.00 |
| 54 | Ian WOOSNAM | WAL | 69 | 71 | 73 | 77 | 290 | 2 | 9,196.93 | 6,300.00 |
| | Peter HANSON | SWE | 66 | 72 | 72 | 80 | 290 | 2 | 9,196.93 | 6,300.00 |
| | Jyoti RANDHAWA | IND | 70 | 72 | 72 | 76 | 290 | 2 | 9,196.93 | 6,300.00 |
| 57 | Barry LANE | ENG | 75 | 67 | 74 | 75 | 291 | 3 | 7,883.08 | 5,400.00 |
| | Jamie DONALDSON | WAL | 72 | 71 | 77 | 71 | 291 | 3 | 7,883.08 | 5,400.00 |
| | Leif WESTERBERG | SWE | 69 | 73 | 75 | 74 | 291 | 3 | 7,883.08 | 5,400.00 |
| 60 | Niclas FASTH | SWE | 73 | 71 | 73 | 75 | 292 | 4 | 7,094.77 | 4,860.00 |
| | Ricardo GONZALEZ | ARG | 74 | 70 | 73 | 75 | 292 | 4 | 7,094.77 | 4,860.00 |
| | Miguel CARBALLO | ARG | 71 | 73 | 75 | 73 | 292 | 4 | 7,094.77 | 4,860.00 |
| 63 | Lloyd SALTMAN (Am) | SCO | 69 | 75 | 76 | 73 | 293 | 5 | | |
| | Thomas BJÖRN | DEN | 75 | 69 | 79 | 70 | 293 | 5 | 6,437.85 | 4,410.00 |
| | Richard MCEVOY | ENG | 76 | 68 | 78 | 71 | 293 | 5 | 6,437.85 | 4,410.00 |
| 66 | Steven O'HARA | SCO | 70 | 74 | 77 | 74 | 295 | 7 | 5,912.31 | 4,050.00 |
| | Gary EVANS | ENG | 69 | 75 | 77 | 74 | 295 | 7 | 5,912.31 | 4,050.00 |
| 68 | Phillip PRICE | WAL | 70 | 73 | 77 | 77 | 297 | 9 | 5,386.77 | 3,690.00 |
| | Fredrik WIDMARK | SWE | 69 | 74 | 80 | 74 | 297 | 9 | 5,386.77 | 3,690.00 |
| 70 | Shiv KAPUR | IND | 70 | 74 | 80 | 75 | 299 | 11 | 4,992.62 | 3,420.00 |

# Total Prize Fund
€2,622,910  £1,796,720

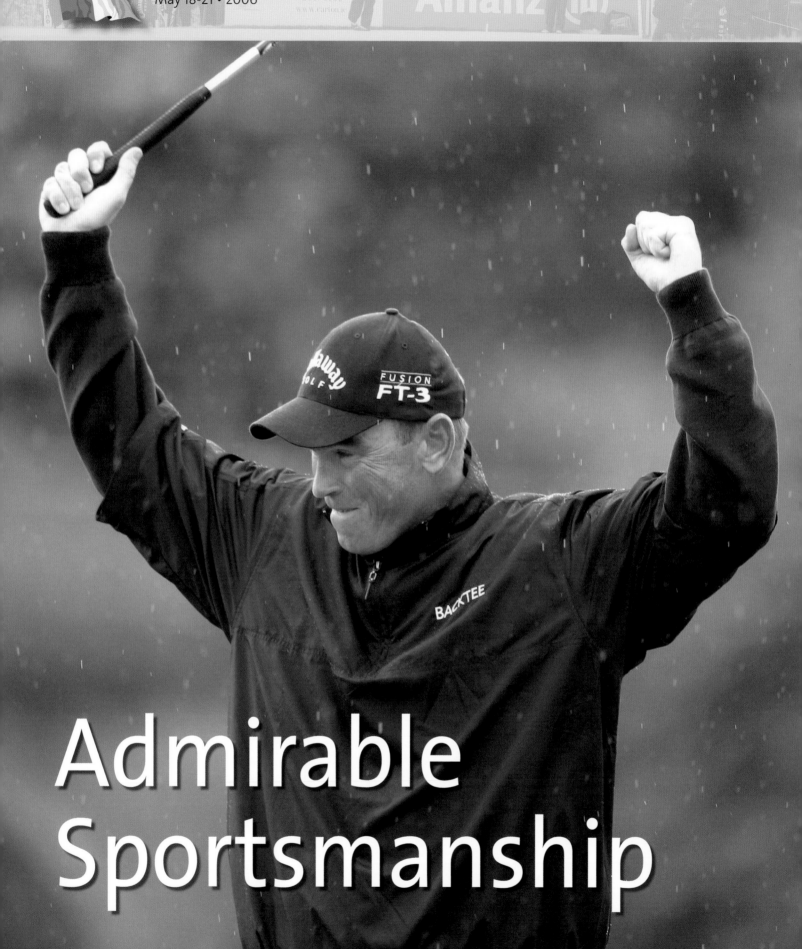

# Admirable
# Sportsmanship

Darren Clarke

**Carton House Golf Club**

| Par | Yards | Metres |
|---|---|---|
| 72 | 7301 | 6675 |

| | | | |
|---|---|---|---|
| 1 Thomas BJÖRN | 283 | -5 | |
| 2 Paul CASEY | 284 | -4 | |
| 3 Darren CLARKE | 285 | -3 | |
| 4 Peter HEDBLOM | 286 | -2 | |
| 5 Bradley DREDGE | 287 | -1 | |
| Ross FISHER | 287 | -1 | |
| Robert KARLSSON | 287 | -1 | |
| Maarten LAFEBER | 287 | -1 | |
| Robert ROCK | 287 | -1 | |
| Anthony WALL | 287 | -1 | |

S imple, Irish logic pointed in only one direction. Responsibility for the wettest Nissan Irish Open in living memory had to rest with those miserable Sassenachs and their doomsday warnings about water shortages.

That's what did it. That's what brought about the worst tournament conditions in the Emerald Isle since the British Masters of 1965 at Portmarnock, where Tony Jacklin headed off the first tee dressed in a full-length raincoat and, by his own estimation, started "something like nine, ten, jack!"

Not surprisingly, that particular round was abandoned, even though Christy O'Connor shot an astonishing 73. But through dogged determination and astute planning, every shot executed on the Montgomerie Course at Carton House Golf Club counted, even if the climactic ones had to be played on the Monday morning.

Not only did the tournament produce an admirable winner in Thomas Björn, it also gave us one of the finest examples of sportsmanship to grace the royal and ancient game. This came from Darren Clarke at the restart of play on Monday.

As the leader by two strokes, Clarke went back to the ninth hole expecting his ball to be deep in rough, where he had left it when play was suspended the previous day. But, miraculously, the lie had somehow been flattened, to the extent that where there had been no option but to pitch the ball back onto the fairway, he could now reach the green with a seven iron.

**WEATHER REPORT**

| Day One | Day Two | Day Three | Day Four | Day Five |
|---|---|---|---|---|

**EUROPEAN TOUR ORDER OF MERIT**
(After 23 tournaments)

| Pos | | € | |
|---|---|---|---|
| 1 David HOWELL | | 1,080,767.74 | |
| 2 Paul CASEY | | 875,737.89 | |
| 3 Henrik STENSON | | 818,331.76 | |
| 4 Thomas BJÖRN | | 719,956.11 | |
| 5 Retief GOOSEN | | 689,478.87 | |
| 6 Tim CLARK | | 672,293.10 | |
| 7 Johan EDFORS | | 666,230.58 | |
| 8 Nick O'HERN | | 631,002.33 | |
| 9 Paul BROADHURST | | 591,956.67 | |
| 10 Ernie ELS | | 589,759.12 | |

Anthony Wall

hole **9**
| yards | 391 |
| metres | 358 |
| par | 4 |

# Nissan Irish Open

**Maynooth, Co.Kildare, Ireland**
May 18-21 • 2006

*Maarten Lafeber*

From the outset the elements conspired to wreck the continuity of play and it was wind gusting up to 40mph, rather than rain, which caused a suspension on the opening day when balls began to move on the more exposed greens. As for Paul McGinley, however, a nagging knee problem was more of a concern.

With 13 holes played when the klaxon sounded, he decided to withdraw from the tournament and arrange a remedial operation as quickly as possible. The upshot of it was that by the time play resumed at 5.40pm, keyhole surgery on his left knee had already been performed in a Dublin hospital by orthopaedic specialist, Ray Moran, a brother of former Manchester United and Republic of Ireland centre-half, Kevin. It meant McGinley was on the mend, when he might have been completing his opening round.

According to the attending referee it could be considered a rub of the green and Clarke was entitled to play the ball as it lay. But this, in the player's view, would have given him an unfair advantage. "In all conscience, I wouldn't have felt comfortable doing it," he said afterwards. "So I hit the pitch shot I would have played the previous night." It cost him a bogey five but gained him admiration and respect from all quarters and the accolade of RBS Shot of the Month for May.

Meanwhile, Björn's golf was as unpredictable as the weather. After completing a first-round 78 on Friday morning, he had only a 50 minute break before heading out again.

“ *The golf course is in superb condition. John Plummer and his staff have done a marvellous job. The rough is tough and penal, as are the bunkers, and the greens are fantastic* ” – *Darren Clarke*

Robert Karlsson

Padraig Harrington

But sacrificing physical nourishment for the mental variety from psychologist, Jos Vanstiphout, the Dane was rewarded with a course record 66.

Still the disruption continued, with the cut having to be deferred until Saturday morning, by which stage the event was manageable, or so we thought. Just to be on the safe side, however, Tournament Director David Probyn decided on a two-tee start at 7.30am on the Sunday.

Sadly, though, by the time the leading trio of Paul Casey, Anthony Wall and Björn drove off the first tee at 9.20am with Clarke in the group in front, the rain had become merciless. "It's like working in the engine-room of the Titanic," said the beleaguered course superintendent, John Plummer.

So we had another postponement, this time with Clarke leading by two strokes over Ross Fisher, Peter Hedblom and Casey, with Björn a stroke further back. There was to be no restart this time though with everyone asked to come back on Monday morning to try again. Eventually, just after midday, it all came down to matters on the long 18th.

There, after Clarke had ended a fairytale by mis-hitting an attempted pitch and then three-putting for a bogey six, Björn won the title in style. With a beautifully judged pitch to eight feet past the pin, he sank the putt for a marvellous birdie to relegate Casey to second and become the first European Tour winner to have started with a 78 since George Burns captured the 1975 Kerrygold International Classic at Waterville.

It had been a triumph of will in circumstances where the notion of soft, Irish rain, held not the slightest semblance of romance.

**Dermot Gilleece**
*Sunday Independent*

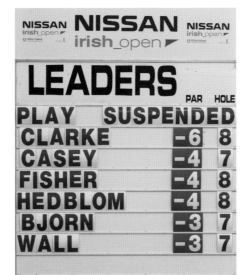

# Final Results

| Pos | Name | | Rd1 | Rd2 | Rd3 | Rd4 | Total | | € | £ |
|-----|------|---|-----|-----|-----|-----|-------|---|---|---|
| 1 | Thomas BJÖRN | DEN | 78 | 66 | 67 | 72 | 283 | -5 | 366,660.00 | 249,882.44 |
| 2 | Paul CASEY | ENG | 73 | 70 | 68 | 73 | 284 | -4 | 244,440.00 | 166,588.29 |
| 3 | Darren CLARKE | NIR | 75 | 70 | 67 | 73 | 285 | -3 | 137,720.00 | 93,857.55 |
| 4 | Peter HEDBLOM | SWE | 72 | 70 | 70 | 74 | 286 | -2 | 110,000.00 | 74,966.09 |
| 5 | Robert KARLSSON | SWE | 74 | 68 | 72 | 73 | 287 | -1 | 64,093.33 | 43,680.24 |
| | Maarten LAFEBER | NED | 71 | 74 | 71 | 71 | 287 | -1 | 64,093.33 | 43,680.24 |
| | Anthony WALL | ENG | 73 | 68 | 70 | 76 | 287 | -1 | 64,093.33 | 43,680.24 |
| | Bradley DREDGE | WAL | 71 | 73 | 72 | 71 | 287 | -1 | 64,093.33 | 43,680.24 |
| | Robert ROCK | ENG | 75 | 73 | 68 | 71 | 287 | -1 | 64,093.33 | 43,680.24 |
| | Ross FISHER | ENG | 73 | 70 | 69 | 75 | 287 | -1 | 64,093.33 | 43,680.24 |
| 11 | Padraig HARRINGTON | IRL | 71 | 74 | 69 | 74 | 288 | 0 | 40,480.00 | 27,587.52 |
| 12 | Robert-Jan DERKSEN | NED | 74 | 74 | 68 | 73 | 289 | 1 | 35,640.00 | 24,289.01 |
| | Michael CAMPBELL | NZL | 72 | 73 | 71 | 73 | 289 | 1 | 35,640.00 | 24,289.01 |
| | Jarrod LYLE | AUS | 72 | 70 | 71 | 76 | 289 | 1 | 35,640.00 | 24,289.01 |
| 15 | Christian CÉVAËR | FRA | 70 | 71 | 74 | 75 | 290 | 2 | 30,360.00 | 20,690.64 |
| | Phillip ARCHER | ENG | 75 | 69 | 70 | 76 | 290 | 2 | 30,360.00 | 20,690.64 |
| | Gregory HAVRET | FRA | 76 | 71 | 68 | 75 | 290 | 2 | 30,360.00 | 20,690.64 |
| | Stuart LITTLE | ENG | 74 | 74 | 70 | 72 | 290 | 2 | 30,360.00 | 20,690.64 |
| 19 | Richard BLAND | ENG | 76 | 72 | 69 | 74 | 291 | 3 | 24,273.33 | 16,542.52 |
| | Martin ERLANDSSON | SWE | 73 | 71 | 72 | 75 | 291 | 3 | 24,273.33 | 16,542.52 |
| | Peter LAWRIE | IRL | 75 | 68 | 75 | 73 | 291 | 3 | 24,273.33 | 16,542.52 |
| | Damien MCGRANE | IRL | 75 | 69 | 74 | 73 | 291 | 3 | 24,273.33 | 16,542.52 |
| | Niclas FASTH | SWE | 72 | 74 | 75 | 70 | 291 | 3 | 24,273.33 | 16,542.52 |
| | Colm MORIARTY | IRL | 77 | 71 | 70 | 73 | 291 | 3 | 24,273.33 | 16,542.52 |
| | Steven JEPPESEN | SWE | 72 | 71 | 72 | 76 | 291 | 3 | 24,273.33 | 16,542.52 |
| | Stephen BROWNE | IRL | 78 | 69 | 72 | 72 | 291 | 3 | 24,273.33 | 16,542.52 |
| | Nick DOUGHERTY | ENG | 75 | 72 | 72 | 72 | 291 | 3 | 24,273.33 | 16,542.52 |
| 28 | Tom WHITEHOUSE | ENG | 73 | 69 | 72 | 78 | 292 | 4 | 20,570.00 | 14,018.66 |
| | Gary ORR | SCO | 77 | 71 | 72 | 72 | 292 | 4 | 20,570.00 | 14,018.66 |
| 30 | Ignacio GARRIDO | ESP | 70 | 77 | 72 | 74 | 293 | 5 | 17,694.29 | 12,058.83 |
| | Andres ROMERO | ARG | 75 | 73 | 68 | 77 | 293 | 5 | 17,694.29 | 12,058.83 |
| | David DIXON | ENG | 74 | 70 | 74 | 75 | 293 | 5 | 17,694.29 | 12,058.83 |
| | Marc WARREN | SCO | 75 | 72 | 72 | 74 | 293 | 5 | 17,694.29 | 12,058.83 |
| | Barry LANE | ENG | 73 | 74 | 70 | 76 | 293 | 5 | 17,694.29 | 12,058.83 |
| | Ian WOOSNAM | WAL | 77 | 70 | 75 | 71 | 293 | 5 | 17,694.29 | 12,058.83 |
| | Sam LITTLE | ENG | 75 | 73 | 71 | 74 | 293 | 5 | 17,694.29 | 12,058.83 |
| 37 | Raphaël JACQUELIN | FRA | 73 | 70 | 72 | 79 | 294 | 6 | 14,300.00 | 9,745.59 |
| | Henrik STENSON | SWE | 75 | 70 | 73 | 76 | 294 | 6 | 14,300.00 | 9,745.59 |
| | Paul LAWRIE | SCO | 75 | 68 | 71 | 80 | 294 | 6 | 14,300.00 | 9,745.59 |
| | Angel CABRERA | ARG | 75 | 68 | 73 | 78 | 294 | 6 | 14,300.00 | 9,745.59 |
| | Ricardo GONZALEZ | ARG | 71 | 72 | 73 | 78 | 294 | 6 | 14,300.00 | 9,745.59 |
| | David HIGGINS | IRL | 74 | 74 | 72 | 74 | 294 | 6 | 14,300.00 | 9,745.59 |
| | François DELAMONTAGNE | FRA | 76 | 72 | 72 | 74 | 294 | 6 | 14,300.00 | 9,745.59 |
| 44 | Stephen GALLACHER | SCO | 74 | 74 | 74 | 73 | 295 | 7 | 11,660.00 | 7,946.41 |
| | Iain PYMAN | ENG | 70 | 73 | 77 | 75 | 295 | 7 | 11,660.00 | 7,946.41 |
| | Wade ORMSBY | AUS | 79 | 69 | 72 | 75 | 295 | 7 | 11,660.00 | 7,946.41 |
| | Alexandre ROCHA | BRA | 74 | 73 | 74 | 74 | 295 | 7 | 11,660.00 | 7,946.41 |
| | Gonzalo FDEZ-CASTAÑO | ESP | 71 | 76 | 72 | 76 | 295 | 7 | 11,660.00 | 7,946.41 |
| 49 | Peter GUSTAFSSON | SWE | 75 | 69 | 76 | 76 | 296 | 8 | 9,680.00 | 6,597.02 |
| | Christian L NILSSON | SWE | 74 | 71 | 73 | 78 | 296 | 8 | 9,680.00 | 6,597.02 |
| | Emanuele CANONICA | ITA | 76 | 70 | 76 | 74 | 296 | 8 | 9,680.00 | 6,597.02 |
| | Ian GARBUTT | ENG | 74 | 72 | 72 | 78 | 296 | 8 | 9,680.00 | 6,597.02 |
| 53 | Nicolas COLSAERTS | BEL | 73 | 67 | 74 | 83 | 297 | 9 | 8,140.00 | 5,547.49 |
| | Brett RUMFORD | AUS | 74 | 74 | 73 | 76 | 297 | 9 | 8,140.00 | 5,547.49 |
| | Matthew MILLAR | AUS | 75 | 72 | 72 | 78 | 297 | 9 | 8,140.00 | 5,547.49 |
| 56 | David GRIFFITHS | ENG | 77 | 70 | 72 | 79 | 298 | 10 | 6,765.00 | 4,610.41 |
| | Ariel CANETE | ARG | 76 | 68 | 75 | 79 | 298 | 10 | 6,765.00 | 4,610.41 |
| | David LYNN | ENG | 74 | 74 | 72 | 78 | 298 | 10 | 6,765.00 | 4,610.41 |
| | Francesco MOLINARI | ITA | 75 | 73 | 75 | 75 | 298 | 10 | 6,765.00 | 4,610.41 |
| 60 | Marcel SIEM | GER | 79 | 68 | 68 | 84 | 299 | 11 | 5,610.00 | 3,823.27 |
| | Johan EDFORS | SWE | 69 | 78 | 75 | 77 | 299 | 11 | 5,610.00 | 3,823.27 |
| | Carl SUNESON | ESP | 77 | 71 | 73 | 78 | 299 | 11 | 5,610.00 | 3,823.27 |
| | Ian POULTER | ENG | 71 | 70 | 73 | 85 | 299 | 11 | 5,610.00 | 3,823.27 |
| | Alastair FORSYTH | SCO | 74 | 74 | 77 | 74 | 299 | 11 | 5,610.00 | 3,823.27 |
| | Simon DYSON | ENG | 76 | 72 | 78 | 73 | 299 | 11 | 5,610.00 | 3,823.27 |
| 66 | Rafael GOMEZ | ARG | 75 | 72 | 74 | 79 | 300 | 12 | 4,620.00 | 3,148.58 |
| | Steve WEBSTER | ENG | 72 | 76 | 77 | 75 | 300 | 12 | 4,620.00 | 3,148.58 |
| | Søren HANSEN | DEN | 76 | 70 | 74 | 80 | 300 | 12 | 4,620.00 | 3,148.58 |
| 69 | Mark FOSTER | ENG | 76 | 72 | 73 | 80 | 301 | 13 | 4,180.00 | 2,848.71 |
| 70 | Richard MCEVOY | ENG | 76 | 71 | 76 | 80 | 303 | 15 | 3,660.00 | 2,494.33 |
| | Mikael LUNDBERG | SWE | 75 | 72 | 76 | 80 | 303 | 15 | 3,660.00 | 2,494.33 |
| 72 | Anders HANSEN | DEN | 70 | 75 | 77 | RETD | 222 | 6 | | |

# Total Prize Fund
€2,206,600 £1,503,817

LEADERS
PAR HOLE
PLAY SUSPENDED
CLARKE -6 8
CASEY -4 7
FISHER -4 8
HEDBLOM -4 8
BJORN -3 7
WALL -3 7

# As Good

# as It Gets

| Wentworth Club | | |
|---|---|---|
| **Par** | **Yards** | **Metres** |
| 72 | 7308 | 6682 |

| | | | | |
|---|---|---|---|---|
| 1 | **David HOWELL** | **271** | **-17** |  |
| 2 | Simon KHAN | 276 | -12 | |
| 3 | Miguel Angel JIMÉNEZ | 277 | -11 | |
| 4 | Brett RUMFORD | 279 | -9 | |
| 5 | Richard BLAND | 280 | -8 | |
| 6 | Andrew COLTART | 281 | -7 | |
| | Padraig HARRINGTON | 281 | -7 | |
| | Trevor IMMELMAN | 281 | -7 | |
| | Gary ORR | 281 | -7 | |
| | Anthony WALL | 281 | -7 | |

## WEATHER REPORT

| Round One | Round Two | Round Three | Round Four |
|---|---|---|---|

## EUROPEAN TOUR ORDER OF MERIT
(After 24 tournaments)

| Pos | | € | |
|---|---|---|---|
| 1 | **David HOWELL** | **1,789,097.74** | |
| 2 | Paul CASEY | 948,979.55 | |
| 3 | Henrik STENSON | 867,206.76 | |
| 4 | Retief GOOSEN | 738,353.87 | |
| 5 | Thomas BJÖRN | 719,956.11 | |
| 6 | Miguel Angel JIMÉNEZ | 709,258.39 | |
| 7 | Nick O'HERN | 673,289.83 | |
| 8 | Tim CLARK | 672,293.10 | |
| 9 | Johan EDFORS | 666,230.58 | |
| 10 | Ernie ELS | 638,634.12 | |

Even David Howell, king of the understatement and the most modest of golfing princes, struggled to hold back the justified hyperbole when he won the BMW Championship 2006 – The Players' Flagship, after a hugely impressive 72 hole display at Wentworth Club.

*Captain of The R&A, The Honorable Justice Thomas Gault, presents Michael Campbell of New Zealand with the trophy for Golfer of the Year for 2005 during The European Tour Annual Dinner at the BMW Championship 2006*

It may seem slightly ludicrous to suggest that, with such an outstanding victory, this outwardly reserved Englishman had at last announced his arrival amongst the most significant players in the world. After all, six months earlier, he had faced up to Tiger Woods in the last round of the HSBC Champions tournament in China and outplayed the World Number One.

Despite this, however, his victory over the West Course was not so much an endorsement of an outstanding talent, more a deserved clarion call that sounded everywhere this grand, old game matters. Do not, however, take my word for it. Take his instead.....

"This supersedes everything else I've achieved," he said. "This is as big as it comes on The European Tour and I'm absolutely delighted. I guess I never really think great things are going to happen to me but they seem to keep coming along at the moment. So, well, I'm overwhelmed."

No wonder. To overwhelm himself, Howell had to overcome the likes of defending champion Angel Cabrera, Michael Campbell, Paul Casey, Darren Clarke, Luke Donald, Ernie Els, Retief Goosen, Padraig Harrington, Miguel Angel Jiménez, Colin Montgomerie and José Maria Olazábal.

This, of course, he did wonderfully well.

Angel Cabrera

Paul Casey

Par 3
194m
212 yd

Gonzalo Fernandez-Castaño of Spain with The Sir Henry Cotton Rookie of the Year Award for 2005 during The European Tour Annual Dinner at Wentworth Club

Howell's twin strengths are his phlegmatic character and his ability at times to putt better than anyone else on the planet. With his legs planted wide enough to suggest a Mini Cooper could pass through unheeded, he might lack aesthetic appeal on the greens but his method is supremely effective.

He knows, then, that if he drives competently and his approach play is, at the very worst, reasonable, it really will be happy days all round. Well, consider this: his four rounds in a variable week of weather, were 68–65–69–69 for a total of 271. That, is 17 under par on a course that had been seriously tweaked and lengthened.

The urgent need for several old and outstanding courses to be revamped if they are to stay in the professional game is obvious. In terms of length, some can be as obsolete as a gutta-percha ball. Hazards are therefore misplaced, enabling the modern player to gun a drive over a bunker or water that was initially designed to place fear in their hearts.

Sooner or later the custodians of the world's best tracks have to bite the bullet, or at least get out the spade, the fork and several JCBs. This is the route Wentworth Club decided to take when new owner Richard Caring pressed the button for major alterations to

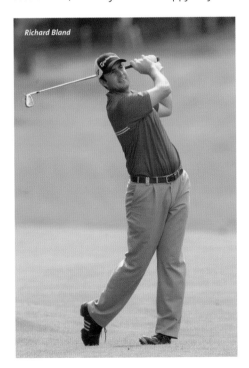

Richard Bland

Singer Ronan Keating peforms at a special concert following the Pro-Am event

Sheer driving pleasure.

BMW Golfsport

www.bmw-golfsport.com

The Ultimate Driving Machine

be carried out to the West Course that Harry Colt designed in 1927.

Tinkering with such a gem, however, was a real challenge. Caring, his Managing Director Julian Small and Golf Courses Manager Chris Kennedy, were determined to keep the Colt design obvious while, at the same time, adding length and more relevant hazards for the marquee weeks of the BMW Championship and the HSBC World Match Play Championship that so illuminate our spring and autumn each year.

This big idea required a lot of planning and even more subtlety. Enter Ernie Els. Round about the time the Wentworth team were pondering how to start this mammoth project, the club's Touring Professional was not touring anywhere. Instead, he was sitting in his Wentworth Estate home, nursing the knee injury that shredded much of his 2005 season and restlessly twiddling his thumbs.

The Big Easy was easily bored.

Andrew Coltart of Scotland (right) is presented with a magnum of Moët & Chandon champagne by Managing Director of BMW UK and President of the BMW Championship, Jim O'Donnell, following his hole in one on the tenth hole during the third round

"There's only so much sitting around and watching TV that a man can do, so when the club asked if I'd be interested in getting involved in a redesign of the West Course I jumped at the chance," said Els. "What an honour, man."

What Els did – in conjunction with the ever practical Kennedy – was to take the course

Ernie Els

Miguel Angel Jiménez

*Sir Michael Bonallack OBE presents Colin Montgomerie of Scotland with The Harry Vardon Trophy during The European Tour Annual Dinner at Wentworth Club. Montgomerie won The European Tour Order of Merit for the eighth time in 2005*

*Ryder Cup Director Richard Hills presents Ian Woosnam of Wales with an award to commemorate his 500th European Tour event during a press conference prior to the BMW Championship 2006 at Wentworth Club*

lady a kiss on both cheeks along the way. A template for the rest of golf may well have been carefully laid down in deepest Surrey.

What is for sure is that a benchmark for Wentworth golfing excellence was laid down by Howell. His opening 68 was good but it turned out to be no more than an appetiser for the entrée which was his sublime 65 on Friday that not only established a course record but also lifted him clear of his pursuers. By Sunday morning his lead over all but the doughty fighter Jiménez, was six shots.

However, Howell knew, at only three shots adrift, Jiménez was a player who would not fold like a cardboard fortress in a hurricane. Jiménez knew it, too. On Saturday evening, as he contemplated the duel to come, the Spaniard said: "David is a great golfer. But I am good, too. The competition should be fantastic but whatever happens we will be gentlemen. This is how it should be in this

from 6,998 yards to 7,308 while adding in excess of 30 bunkers. Six traps were added to the difficult fourth hole for example, while the dog-leg par five 17th was stretched to a demanding 610 yards.

All the work cleverly embraced what Colt originally produced while giving the old

great game and this is how it will be."

And they were – each player genuinely appreciative of the other's play when the occasion merited it. In the end it was Jiménez who did most of the appreciation as Howell carefully and calmly took himself to the most important title of what is proving

The Tented Village

*Simon Khan and baby daughter Ruby*

to be a seriously impressive career. Victory, when it came, was by five shots and not over Jiménez in the end, who finished third, but over another Englishman.

Simon Khan is, if anything, slightly more understated than Howell but he, too, embroidered his reputation with a final round 68 which lifted him into second place and rewarded him with the biggest cheque of his life. Afterwards he admitted he could now look at the Order of Merit without embarrassment. "It has been, delightful," he said. "Really."

Now there is a word one does not hear too often from successful young sportsmen these days – 'delightful'. It is a good word though and perfectly summed up the BMW Championship 2006 – The Players' Flagship; delight in one form or another being available to players and public alike throughout an outstanding week of top level golf.

**Bill Elliott**
*The Observer*

*European Tour Executive Director George O'Grady (fourth from right) meets Special Olympics Athletes who visited the BMW Championship 2006*

# Final Results

| Pos | Name | | Rd1 | Rd2 | Rd3 | Rd4 | Total | | € | £ |
|---|---|---|---|---|---|---|---|---|---|---|
| 1 | David HOWELL | ENG | 68 | 65 | 69 | 69 | 271 | -17 | 708,330.00 | 481,536.12 |
| 2 | Simon KHAN | ENG | 70 | 68 | 70 | 68 | 276 | -12 | 472,220.00 | 321,024.08 |
| 3 | Miguel Angel JIMÉNEZ | ESP | 71 | 69 | 65 | 72 | 277 | -11 | 266,050.00 | 180,865.82 |
| 4 | Brett RUMFORD | AUS | 72 | 73 | 69 | 65 | 279 | -9 | 212,500.00 | 144,461.52 |
| 5 | Richard BLAND | ENG | 73 | 68 | 71 | 68 | 280 | -8 | 180,200.00 | 122,503.37 |
| 6 | Trevor IMMELMAN | RSA | 70 | 73 | 73 | 65 | 281 | -7 | 112,540.00 | 76,506.82 |
| | Padraig HARRINGTON | IRL | 72 | 70 | 68 | 71 | 281 | -7 | 112,540.00 | 76,506.82 |
| | Anthony WALL | ENG | 71 | 71 | 73 | 66 | 281 | -7 | 112,540.00 | 76,506.82 |
| | Gary ORR | SCO | 71 | 70 | 73 | 67 | 281 | -7 | 112,540.00 | 76,506.82 |
| | Andrew COLTART | SCO | 71 | 72 | 69 | 69 | 281 | -7 | 112,540.00 | 76,506.82 |
| 11 | Paul CASEY | ENG | 67 | 72 | 69 | 74 | 282 | -6 | 73,241.67 | 49,791.07 |
| | Garry HOUSTON | WAL | 69 | 72 | 71 | 70 | 282 | -6 | 73,241.67 | 49,791.07 |
| | Søren HANSEN | DEN | 70 | 72 | 69 | 71 | 282 | -6 | 73,241.67 | 49,791.07 |
| 14 | Jean-François LUCQUIN | FRA | 76 | 70 | 67 | 70 | 283 | -5 | 59,925.00 | 40,738.15 |
| | Maarten LAFEBER | NED | 71 | 71 | 71 | 70 | 283 | -5 | 59,925.00 | 40,738.15 |
| | Richard GREEN | AUS | 70 | 71 | 72 | 70 | 283 | -5 | 59,925.00 | 40,738.15 |
| | José Maria OLAZÁBAL | ESP | 69 | 74 | 72 | 68 | 283 | -5 | 59,925.00 | 40,738.15 |
| | Robert KARLSSON | SWE | 69 | 68 | 74 | 72 | 283 | -5 | 59,925.00 | 40,738.15 |
| 19 | Emanuele CANONICA | ITA | 72 | 71 | 72 | 69 | 284 | -4 | 48,875.00 | 33,226.15 |
| | Ernie ELS | RSA | 69 | 74 | 69 | 72 | 284 | -4 | 48,875.00 | 33,226.15 |
| | Retief GOOSEN | RSA | 70 | 71 | 73 | 70 | 284 | -4 | 48,875.00 | 33,226.15 |
| | Raphaël JACQUELIN | FRA | 68 | 72 | 75 | 69 | 284 | -4 | 48,875.00 | 33,226.15 |
| | Steve WEBSTER | ENG | 71 | 70 | 74 | 69 | 284 | -4 | 48,875.00 | 33,226.15 |
| | Henrik STENSON | SWE | 73 | 73 | 68 | 70 | 284 | -4 | 48,875.00 | 33,226.15 |
| 25 | Peter LAWRIE | IRL | 68 | 72 | 74 | 71 | 285 | -3 | 42,287.50 | 28,747.84 |
| | Nick O'HERN | AUS | 72 | 72 | 68 | 73 | 285 | -3 | 42,287.50 | 28,747.84 |
| | Kenneth FERRIE | ENG | 69 | 73 | 73 | 70 | 285 | -3 | 42,287.50 | 28,747.84 |
| | Luke DONALD | ENG | 72 | 72 | 74 | 72 | 285 | -3 | 42,287.50 | 28,747.84 |
| 29 | François DELAMONTAGNE | FRA | 69 | 70 | 71 | 76 | 286 | -2 | 35,912.50 | 24,414.00 |
| | Miles TUNNICLIFF | ENG | 72 | 73 | 70 | 71 | 286 | -2 | 35,912.50 | 24,414.00 |
| | Niclas FASTH | SWE | 70 | 70 | 71 | 75 | 286 | -2 | 35,912.50 | 24,414.00 |
| | David PARK | WAL | 76 | 69 | 70 | 71 | 286 | -2 | 35,912.50 | 24,414.00 |
| | Angel CABRERA | ARG | 68 | 69 | 75 | 74 | 286 | -2 | 35,912.50 | 24,414.00 |
| | Andrew MCLARDY | RSA | 67 | 74 | 75 | 70 | 286 | -2 | 35,912.50 | 24,414.00 |
| 35 | Nicolas COLSAERTS | BEL | 70 | 72 | 70 | 75 | 287 | -1 | 31,450.00 | 21,380.30 |
| | Thaworn WIRATCHANT | THA | 71 | 71 | 75 | 70 | 287 | -1 | 31,450.00 | 21,380.30 |
| 37 | Paul LAWRIE | SCO | 69 | 73 | 73 | 73 | 288 | 0 | 28,900.00 | 19,646.77 |
| | Michael CAMPBELL | NZL | 72 | 73 | 73 | 70 | 288 | 0 | 28,900.00 | 19,646.77 |
| | Simon DYSON | ENG | 73 | 73 | 70 | 72 | 288 | 0 | 28,900.00 | 19,646.77 |
| | Nick DOUGHERTY | ENG | 67 | 69 | 74 | 78 | 288 | 0 | 28,900.00 | 19,646.77 |
| 41 | David CARTER | ENG | 73 | 71 | 73 | 72 | 289 | 1 | 24,650.00 | 16,757.54 |
| | Bradley DREDGE | WAL | 75 | 71 | 72 | 71 | 289 | 1 | 24,650.00 | 16,757.54 |
| | Jean VAN DE VELDE | FRA | 75 | 69 | 66 | 79 | 289 | 1 | 24,650.00 | 16,757.54 |
| | Mark FOSTER | ENG | 71 | 71 | 74 | 73 | 289 | 1 | 24,650.00 | 16,757.54 |
| | Ian WOOSNAM | WAL | 71 | 74 | 74 | 70 | 289 | 1 | 24,650.00 | 16,757.54 |
| | Ross FISHER | ENG | 71 | 72 | 75 | 71 | 289 | 1 | 24,650.00 | 16,757.54 |
| 47 | Wade ORMSBY | AUS | 74 | 69 | 69 | 78 | 290 | 2 | 19,550.00 | 13,290.46 |
| | Paul BROADHURST | ENG | 71 | 71 | 73 | 75 | 290 | 2 | 19,550.00 | 13,290.46 |
| | Ignacio GARRIDO | ESP | 76 | 70 | 70 | 74 | 290 | 2 | 19,550.00 | 13,290.46 |
| | Ian GARBUTT | ENG | 73 | 71 | 74 | 72 | 290 | 2 | 19,550.00 | 13,290.46 |
| | Alastair FORSYTH | SCO | 71 | 72 | 72 | 75 | 290 | 2 | 19,550.00 | 13,290.46 |
| | Graeme MCDOWELL | NIR | 71 | 70 | 73 | 76 | 290 | 2 | 19,550.00 | 13,290.46 |
| 53 | Phillip PRICE | WAL | 69 | 77 | 72 | 73 | 291 | 3 | 14,875.00 | 10,112.31 |
| | Jarmo SANDELIN | SWE | 77 | 69 | 75 | 70 | 291 | 3 | 14,875.00 | 10,112.31 |
| | Markus BRIER | AUT | 70 | 76 | 72 | 73 | 291 | 3 | 14,875.00 | 10,112.31 |
| | Colin MONTGOMERIE | SCO | 73 | 72 | 74 | 72 | 291 | 3 | 14,875.00 | 10,112.31 |
| | Alessandro TADINI | ITA | 77 | 68 | 69 | 77 | 291 | 3 | 14,875.00 | 10,112.31 |
| 58 | Phillip ARCHER | ENG | 72 | 73 | 79 | 68 | 292 | 4 | 12,112.50 | 8,234.31 |
| | Jyoti RANDHAWA | IND | 71 | 72 | 76 | 73 | 292 | 4 | 12,112.50 | 8,234.31 |
| | Steven JEPPESEN | SWE | 71 | 74 | 74 | 73 | 292 | 4 | 12,112.50 | 8,234.31 |
| | Peter GUSTAFSSON | SWE | 72 | 70 | 75 | 75 | 292 | 4 | 12,112.50 | 8,234.31 |
| 62 | Simon EDWARDS | WAL | 69 | 77 | 74 | 73 | 293 | 5 | 11,050.00 | 7,512.00 |
| 63 | Graeme STORM | ENG | 71 | 75 | 76 | 72 | 294 | 6 | 10,625.00 | 7,223.08 |
| 64 | Søren KJELDSEN | DEN | 70 | 75 | 72 | 79 | 296 | 8 | 10,200.00 | 6,934.15 |
| 65 | Darren PROSSER | ENG | 72 | 71 | 78 | 77 | 298 | 10 | 9,775.00 | 6,645.23 |
| 66 | John WELLS | ENG | 69 | 77 | 82 | 72 | 300 | 12 | 9,350.00 | 6,356.31 |

## Total Prize Fund
€4,216,750 £2,866,626

# The Celtic Manor Wales Open

**Newport, South Wales**
June 1-4 · 2006

# Lord of the Manor

## The Celtic Manor Resort

| Par | Yards | Metres |
|---|---|---|
| 69 | 6743 | 6165 |

| | | | | |
|---|---|---|---|---|
| 1 | **Robert KARLSSON** | **260** | **-16** | |
| 2 | Paul BROADHURST | 263 | -13 | |
| 3 | José-Filipe LIMA | 264 | -12 | |
| 4 | Colin MONTGOMERIE | 265 | -11 | |
| 5 | Phillip ARCHER | 266 | -10 | |
| | Johan SKÖLD | 266 | -10 | |
| 7 | Bradley DREDGE | 267 | -9 | |
| | Simon DYSON | 267 | -9 | |
| | Henrik NYSTROM | 267 | -9 | |
| | Gary ORR | 267 | -9 | |
| | Marcel SIEM | 267 | -9 | |
| | Lee SLATTERY | 267 | -9 | |
| | Graeme STORM | 267 | -9 | |

## WEATHER REPORT

| Round One | Round Two | Round Three | Round Four |
|---|---|---|---|

## EUROPEAN TOUR ORDER OF MERIT
(After 25 tournaments)

| Pos | | € | |
|---|---|---|---|
| 1 | **David HOWELL** | **1,789,097.74** |  |
| 2 | Paul CASEY | 948,979.55 | |
| 3 | Henrik STENSON | 867,206.76 | |
| 4 | Paul BROADHURST | 854,398.62 | |
| 5 | Retief GOOSEN | 738,353.87 | |
| 6 | Thomas BJÖRN | 719,956.11 | |
| 7 | Miguel Angel JIMÉNEZ | 709,258.39 | |
| 8 | Nick O'HERN | 673,289.83 | |
| 9 | Tim CLARK | 672,293.10 | |
| 10 | Johan EDFORS | 666,230.58 | |

# The Celtic Manor Wales Open

**Newport, South Wales**
June 1-4 • 2006

It is two more than the famous Mr Heinz had varieties, five less than The Beatles' bitter-sweet musings on advancing years, ten more than the tally of goals Bobby Charlton scored for England and two less than Beethoven's Concerto for Violin and Orchestra in D Major. It is a bit of a nondescript figure, to be honest, but in one field of human endeavour the number 59 is almost as rare as a snowflake in Hades.

Gary Orr

The number of 59s scored in a full-scale, flags-and-whistles golf tournament can be counted with some ease without recourse to the abacus. But in this week in early June there was so nearly another sighting.

Later on in The Celtic Manor Wales Open there were other matters to occupy the mind, but on the first day the paying customers almost witnessed something that they would remember not only until the end of the week, or the month, or the year, but indeed for the rest of their days.

The man who almost gave the enthusiastic spectators a present that could not be bought was one Phillip Archer, a modest chap from Warrington. At 34, Archer's previous best

rounds had all been 65s, one of which had come in the BMW Russian Open in 2004, where he went on to record one of his best European Tour finishes, a tie for sixth, before he shared third place in this year's Andalucia Open de España Valle Romano.

Now, here he was, facing a putt on the 18th for the birdie that would make him the first player to sign for a 59 on The European Tour International Schedule. If he had any reason to criticise himself, it was that he had left himself above the flag, but ten birdies offset by a solitary bogey on the par 69 Roman Road course meant that this seven footer provided no grounds for trepidation.

It did not either, he admitted it afterwards. If

*If you get on a bit of a run here, there are a lot of holes where you are just hitting wedges. So if you get the swing in the right position you are going to give yourself a lot of chances. Then it is just down to the putting* — **Phillip Archer**

anything, the confidence built on this round of his life may have been his ultimate enemy. He picked the line and got it absolutely right. He just hit it too hard, that is all, and it hit the side of the hole and spun away.

His hand, half-raised in triumph when the ball was halfway to its destination, slumped by his side. He had broken the course record by two strokes and had taken a one shot lead over Robert Karlsson, but neither of those grounds for celebration gave him much satisfaction. All he could think about was the one that had got away.

Three days later, Archer finished in a tie for fifth place, but long before that he was eclipsed by the man from whom he had led by a single shot in the first round.

It is easy to tell when Robert Karlsson is talking. The sound comes from some way above your head. He is a long fellow, all six feet five inches of him. His talent is as lofty as his altitude, too, although it had been four years since he had had the last of his

five previous victories. But this one had his name on it almost from the start and he added rounds of 63, 65 and a more modest 71 to his opening 61 to win with a 16 under par total of 260.

In 2004 Karlsson had kept his playing rights by only €13.57 (£9.39) – the amount by which he shaded Jarrod Mosely into the 116th and last place available for exempt status the next year. The handsome booty he collected in this week of glorious sunshine in the hills and valleys above Newport, gave him every reason to hope that he might, with a touch of luck and a following breeze, go close to his previous best season's finish of tenth in the Order of Merit, achieved in 1997.

José-Filipe Lima, the young Portuguese, almost emulated Archer's feats of derring-do in the second round, going to seven under with five to play but missing his chance for glory when he bogeyed the 14th. Karlsson's 63 gave him a four stroke advantage going into the weekend.

*Phillip Archer*

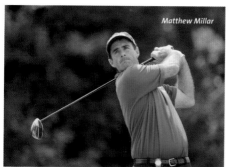

*Matthew Millar*

*Paul Broadhurst*

# First Class Golf... with extras

3 Championship Golf Courses
Golf Academy
2 Hotels
2 Spas
2 Health Clubs
4 Restaurants
5 Bars
Children's Club and Crèche
Shooting
Fishing
Walking and Mountain Biking
Retail Outlets

Call 01633 410262
or visit www.celtic-manor.com

1400 acres of breathing space

Colin Montgomerie

# Final Results

| Pos | Name | | Rd1 | Rd2 | Rd3 | Rd4 | Total | | € | £ |
|---|---|---|---|---|---|---|---|---|---|---|
| 1 | Robert KARLSSON | SWE | 61 | 63 | 65 | 71 | 260 | -16 | 364,352.49 | 250,000.00 |
| 2 | Paul BROADHURST | ENG | 64 | 64 | 67 | 68 | 263 | -13 | 242,891.95 | 166,660.00 |
| 3 | José-Filipe LIMA | POR | 69 | 61 | 70 | 64 | 264 | -12 | 136,850.80 | 93,900.00 |
| 4 | Colin MONTGOMERIE | SCO | 63 | 66 | 69 | 67 | 265 | -11 | 109,305.75 | 75,000.00 |
| 5 | Phillip ARCHER | ENG | 60 | 68 | 71 | 67 | 266 | -10 | 84,602.65 | 58,050.00 |
| | Johan SKÖLD | SWE | 65 | 66 | 67 | 68 | 266 | -10 | 84,602.65 | 58,050.00 |
| 7 | Henrik NYSTROM | SWE | 66 | 67 | 64 | 70 | 267 | -9 | 46,564.25 | 31,950.00 |
| | Graeme STORM | ENG | 65 | 67 | 68 | 67 | 267 | -9 | 46,564.25 | 31,950.00 |
| | Gary ORR | SCO | 68 | 63 | 65 | 71 | 267 | -9 | 46,564.25 | 31,950.00 |
| | Bradley DREDGE | WAL | 67 | 70 | 66 | 64 | 267 | -9 | 46,564.25 | 31,950.00 |
| | Simon DYSON | ENG | 66 | 62 | 69 | 70 | 267 | -9 | 46,564.25 | 31,950.00 |
| | Lee SLATTERY | ENG | 64 | 67 | 69 | 67 | 267 | -9 | 46,564.25 | 31,950.00 |
| | Marcel SIEM | GER | 65 | 66 | 68 | 68 | 267 | -9 | 46,564.25 | 31,950.00 |
| 14 | Jyoti RANDHAWA | IND | 67 | 70 | 66 | 65 | 268 | -8 | 32,791.72 | 22,500.00 |
| | Anthony WALL | ENG | 72 | 63 | 63 | 70 | 268 | -8 | 32,791.72 | 22,500.00 |
| 16 | Stephen DODD | WAL | 66 | 68 | 68 | 67 | 269 | -7 | 28,375.77 | 19,470.00 |
| | Graeme MCDOWELL | NIR | 68 | 67 | 64 | 70 | 269 | -7 | 28,375.77 | 19,470.00 |
| | Simon WAKEFIELD | ENG | 69 | 66 | 67 | 67 | 269 | -7 | 28,375.77 | 19,470.00 |
| | Marc WARREN | SCO | 67 | 68 | 67 | 67 | 269 | -7 | 28,375.77 | 19,470.00 |
| | Matthew MILLAR | AUS | 69 | 62 | 67 | 71 | 269 | -7 | 28,375.77 | 19,470.00 |
| 21 | Paul LAWRIE | SCO | 71 | 66 | 68 | 65 | 270 | -6 | 24,375.18 | 16,725.00 |
| | François DELAMONTAGNE | FRA | 63 | 67 | 70 | 70 | 270 | -6 | 24,375.18 | 16,725.00 |
| | Michael HOEY | NIR | 64 | 68 | 68 | 70 | 270 | -6 | 24,375.18 | 16,725.00 |
| | Jeev Milkha SINGH | IND | 68 | 69 | 69 | 64 | 270 | -6 | 24,375.18 | 16,725.00 |
| 25 | David PARK | WAL | 66 | 68 | 64 | 73 | 271 | -5 | 22,079.76 | 15,150.00 |
| | Alastair FORSYTH | SCO | 67 | 68 | 67 | 69 | 271 | -5 | 22,079.76 | 15,150.00 |
| | Wade ORMSBY | AUS | 68 | 67 | 65 | 71 | 271 | -5 | 22,079.76 | 15,150.00 |
| 28 | David HIGGINS | IRL | 68 | 66 | 71 | 67 | 272 | -4 | 19,128.51 | 13,125.00 |
| | Andrew BUTTERFIELD | ENG | 66 | 68 | 69 | 69 | 272 | -4 | 19,128.51 | 13,125.00 |
| | Brett RUMFORD | AUS | 71 | 66 | 69 | 66 | 272 | -4 | 19,128.51 | 13,125.00 |
| | Peter LAWRIE | IRL | 66 | 68 | 70 | 68 | 272 | -4 | 19,128.51 | 13,125.00 |
| | Alessandro TADINI | ITA | 68 | 65 | 70 | 69 | 272 | -4 | 19,128.51 | 13,125.00 |
| | Jean-François LUCQUIN | FRA | 71 | 66 | 69 | 66 | 272 | -4 | 19,128.51 | 13,125.00 |
| 34 | Per-Ulrik JOHANSSON | SWE | 70 | 65 | 72 | 66 | 273 | -3 | 15,302.80 | 10,500.00 |
| | Richard BLAND | ENG | 70 | 66 | 71 | 66 | 273 | -3 | 15,302.80 | 10,500.00 |
| | Robert-Jan DERKSEN | NED | 66 | 70 | 68 | 69 | 273 | -3 | 15,302.80 | 10,500.00 |
| | Mark FOSTER | ENG | 70 | 67 | 68 | 68 | 273 | -3 | 15,302.80 | 10,500.00 |
| | Andrew OLDCORN | SCO | 65 | 70 | 71 | 67 | 273 | -3 | 15,302.80 | 10,500.00 |
| | Richard STERNE | RSA | 69 | 67 | 67 | 70 | 273 | -3 | 15,302.80 | 10,500.00 |
| | Steven O'HARA | SCO | 69 | 64 | 69 | 71 | 273 | -3 | 15,302.80 | 10,500.00 |
| | Stephen GALLACHER | SCO | 68 | 65 | 72 | 68 | 273 | -3 | 15,302.80 | 10,500.00 |
| 42 | Francisco VALERA | ESP | 69 | 66 | 69 | 70 | 274 | -2 | 12,023.63 | 8,250.00 |
| | Thongchai JAIDEE | THA | 66 | 67 | 70 | 71 | 274 | -2 | 12,023.63 | 8,250.00 |
| | David GRIFFITHS | ENG | 69 | 65 | 70 | 70 | 274 | -2 | 12,023.63 | 8,250.00 |
| | Martin ERLANDSSON | SWE | 68 | 68 | 69 | 69 | 274 | -2 | 12,023.63 | 8,250.00 |
| | Garry HOUSTON | WAL | 72 | 65 | 69 | 68 | 274 | -2 | 12,023.63 | 8,250.00 |
| | Andrew MARSHALL | ENG | 67 | 70 | 71 | 66 | 274 | -2 | 12,023.63 | 8,250.00 |
| | Stuart LITTLE | ENG | 68 | 66 | 69 | 71 | 274 | -2 | 12,023.63 | 8,250.00 |
| 49 | Carl SUNESON | ESP | 66 | 70 | 71 | 68 | 275 | -1 | 8,963.07 | 6,150.00 |
| | Peter HEDBLOM | SWE | 69 | 67 | 70 | 69 | 275 | -1 | 8,963.07 | 6,150.00 |
| | Ian GARBUTT | ENG | 69 | 65 | 66 | 75 | 275 | -1 | 8,963.07 | 6,150.00 |
| | David DIXON | ENG | 67 | 69 | 72 | 67 | 275 | -1 | 8,963.07 | 6,150.00 |
| | Alexandre ROCHA | BRA | 68 | 69 | 68 | 70 | 275 | -1 | 8,963.07 | 6,150.00 |
| | Stephen SCAHILL | NZL | 64 | 71 | 70 | 70 | 275 | -1 | 8,963.07 | 6,150.00 |
| | Niclas FASTH | SWE | 68 | 67 | 72 | 68 | 275 | -1 | 8,963.07 | 6,150.00 |
| 56 | David LYNN | ENG | 69 | 66 | 73 | 69 | 277 | 1 | 6,602.07 | 4,530.00 |
| | Ignacio GARRIDO | ESP | 66 | 67 | 70 | 74 | 277 | 1 | 6,602.07 | 4,530.00 |
| | Peter O'MALLEY | AUS | 67 | 69 | 70 | 71 | 277 | 1 | 6,602.07 | 4,530.00 |
| | Miles TUNNICLIFF | ENG | 69 | 67 | 70 | 71 | 277 | 1 | 6,602.07 | 4,530.00 |
| | Barry LANE | ENG | 66 | 70 | 72 | 69 | 277 | 1 | 6,602.07 | 4,530.00 |
| 61 | Mark ROE | ENG | 70 | 66 | 71 | 71 | 278 | 2 | 5,683.90 | 3,900.00 |
| | Søren HANSEN | DEN | 68 | 69 | 70 | 71 | 278 | 2 | 5,683.90 | 3,900.00 |
| | Gary CLARK | ENG | 66 | 70 | 72 | 70 | 278 | 2 | 5,683.90 | 3,900.00 |
| 64 | Jamie DONALDSON | WAL | 67 | 67 | 73 | 73 | 280 | 4 | 4,918.76 | 3,375.00 |
| | Nicolas COLSAERTS | BEL | 71 | 65 | 66 | 78 | 280 | 4 | 4,918.76 | 3,375.00 |
| | Phillip PRICE | WAL | 69 | 66 | 75 | 70 | 280 | 4 | 4,918.76 | 3,375.00 |
| | Maarten LAFEBER | NED | 67 | 69 | 70 | 74 | 280 | 4 | 4,918.76 | 3,375.00 |
| 68 | Andrew MCLARDY | RSA | 67 | 68 | 77 | 72 | 284 | 8 | 4,372.23 | 3,000.00 |

## Total Prize Fund
€2,177,970  £1,494,410

By the end of Saturday, Karlsson had become even more of a dominant presence, his 65 setting a Tour low aggregate record of 189 for 54 holes. The previous record was held by one Tiger Woods, who had played three rounds in 192 in the World Golf Championships - NEC Invitational in 2000. Not a bad scalp to have in your locker.

He led Paul Broadhurst, the experienced Englishman enjoying a glorious late summer to his career, by six strokes. All Karlsson had to do now was remain vertical, admittedly not the easiest task in the world for this TV mast of a man if there is a wind about.

Fortunately, there was no more than the hint of a breeze in the final round and, although Karlsson was in more muted form, dropping four shots in nine holes from the third then shedding two more in the last two holes, three birdies in four holes from the 13th gave him a three stroke victory over Broadhurst.

By the end, Archer's magical stride along the Roman Road three days before had almost been forgotten. Karlsson, meanwhile, had retained his equilibrium against momentary self doubt. He had stood up and stood tall - but then, he is used to that.

**Mel Webb**

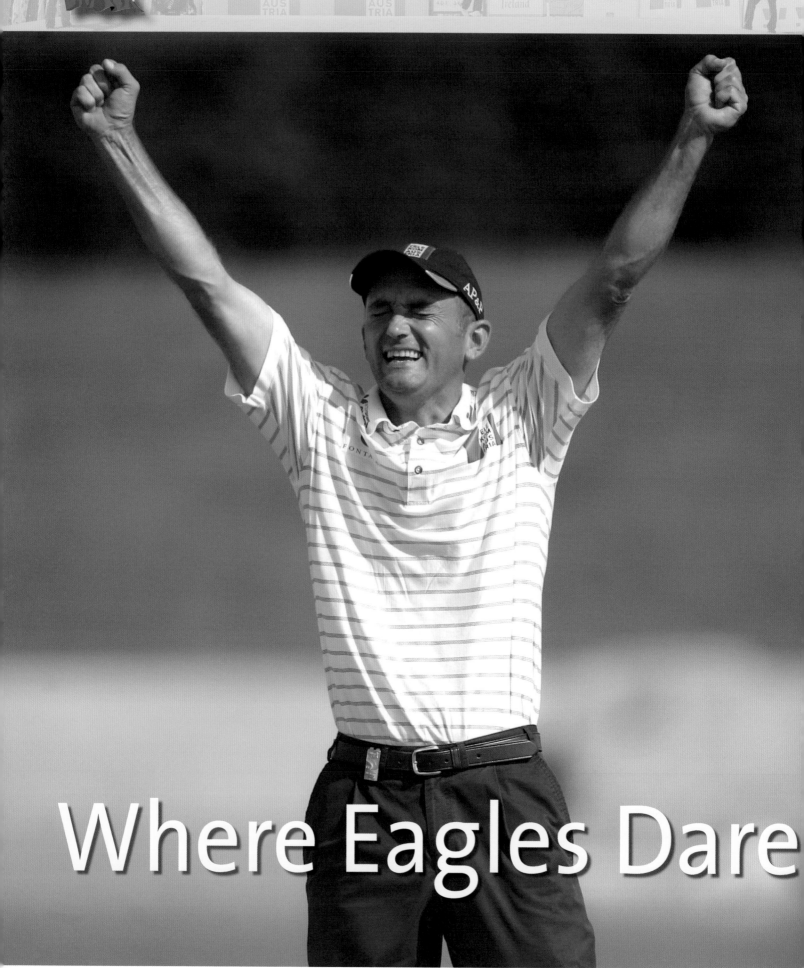

# Where Eagles Dare

Søren Hansen

Austrians are no stranger to sporting success and, indeed, for a relatively small nation in population terms, the range of triumph on the field of play is impressive. Most people are familiar with the skiing exploits of Olympic medallists Franz Klammer, Petra Kronberger and Hermann Maier, but it is sometimes overlooked that Niki Lauda was Formula 1 Motor Racing World Champion; Thomas Muster was, for a spell, the Number One tennis player in the world; and Hugo Simon won the showjumping World Cup on three separate occasions.

Golf, however, has never featured prominently on the sporting radar in this most picturesque of countries. Until, that is, the afternoon of Sunday June 11, when the stunning Fontana Golf Club in Vienna became the centre of the universe for all Austrians, from the thousands who packed the stands on the course to the millions who tuned in on television sets from Burgenland in the east to Vorarlberg in the west.

The focus of their attention was one Markus Brier who, apart from the fleeting appearances of a couple of Challenge Tour players in recent years, had flown the Austrian standard single-handedly on The European Tour International Schedule since the arrival of the new millennium.

A shrewd betting man might well have invested a few euros on Brier coming good for, if previous form was anything to go by, he was the man to watch, having won the self-same tournament at the Fontana Golf

Emanuele Canonica

**Fontana Golf Club**

| Par | Yards | Metres |
| --- | --- | --- |
| 71 | 7059 | 6455 |

| | | | | |
| --- | --- | --- | --- | --- |
| 1 | Markus BRIER | 266 | -18 | |
| 2 | Søren HANSEN | 269 | -15 | |
| 3 | Simon DYSON | 270 | -14 | |
| 4 | Richard GREEN | 271 | -13 | |
| 5 | Gary MURPHY | 274 | -10 | |
| 6 | Miguel Angel JIMÉNEZ | 275 | -9 | |
| | Jean-François LUCQUIN | 275 | -9 | |
| 8 | Emanuele CANONICA | 277 | -7 | |
| | Darren FICHARDT | 277 | -7 | |
| | Steven JEPPESEN | 277 | -7 | |

**WEATHER REPORT**

| Round One | Round Two | Round Three | Round Four |
| --- | --- | --- | --- |

**EUROPEAN TOUR ORDER OF MERIT**
(After 26 tournaments)

| Pos | | € | |
| --- | --- | --- | --- |
| 1 | David HOWELL | 1,789,097.74 | |
| 2 | Paul CASEY | 948,979.55 | |
| 3 | Henrik STENSON | 867,206.76 | |
| 4 | Paul BROADHURST | 854,398.62 | |
| 5 | Miguel Angel JIMÉNEZ | 751,508.39 | |
| 6 | Retief GOOSEN | 738,353.87 | |
| 7 | Thomas BJÖRN | 731,916.11 | |
| 8 | Nick O'HERN | 673,289.83 | |
| 9 | Tim CLARK | 672,293.10 | |
| 10 | Johan EDFORS | 666,230.58 | |

# BA-CA Golf Open, presented by Telekom Austria

**Vienna, Austria**
June 8-11 • 2006

Club in 2004 when it formed part of the European Challenge Tour.

He was also attached to the club and although that can often bring its own pressures – illustrated by the fact that Graeme McDowell is the only player previously to have won a European Tour event on his 'own' course in the 2002 Volvo Scandinavian Masters at Kungsängen – he did possess intimate knowledge of the subtleties and nuances present throughout the 7059 yards.

That was clearly evident on the opening day when a superb opening round of six under par 65 was illuminated on the 158th yard 11th hole with his second career hole in one, a perfectly struck seven iron which not only secured him a brand new Citroen Pluriel, but also pole position at the end of the day, a location he did not relinquish all week.

Alastair Forsyth

The feeling it was clearly's Brier's week was further emphasised during Saturday's third round when he holed his pitching wedge approach from 110 yards at the 13th hole for an eagle two. It helped the 37 year old end the day with his one shot lead intact, his nearest challenger and the only man who looked capable of spoiling the party, being England's Simon Dyson.

*" This is everything I've worked for and to win here is just unbelievable. Everybody who know me, knows what this course means to me and to follow my win here on the Challenge Tour by marking my first European Tour success on my home track as well, is just fantastic " – Markus Brier*

Simon Dyson

# Final Results

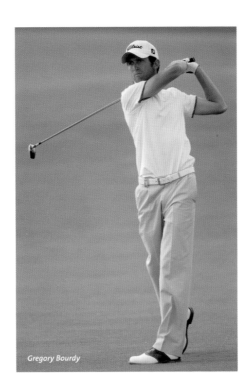

Gregory Bourdy

Both Brier's hole in one and his eagle two were greeted with thunderous cheers from the home galleries, the groundswell of support mirroring perfectly the community feeling which allowed the tournament to feature on The European Tour International Schedule for the first time since 1996 with a prize fund of €1,305,840.

Widespread backing was garnered, both from Austrian companies, and sponsors from neighbouring countries in the Danube region, such as the Czech Republic, Hungary, Slovakia, and Slovenia, all of which points towards the tournament featuring on the Schedule for the next two years at least.

All must have secretly dreamt of an Austrian winner but could not have dared to hope for the scenario which eventually unfolded on the final day as Brier brushed off the setback of a couple of early dropped shots, regrouped, and held off the challenge of Dyson, the fast finishing Dane Søren Hansen, and Scotland's Colin Montgomerie, who got to within one shot of the lead in the early stages of the final round before falling back.

"It has always been my goal to win my first European Tour event here at Fontana in front of my family and friends and to have done it at last, makes this the best day of my life after my wedding and the birth of my kids," said Brier.

"To make history as the first Austrian to win on The European Tour is fantastic. I am proud to have done it. It has taken me seven years but as I was the first Austrian to play The European Tour, it should have been me who won first!"

At the start of the year, the next big sporting event most Austrians were looking forward to was their country's joint hosting, with Switzerland, of the 2008 UEFA European Championship. Now, do not be surprised if many have pencilled in Markus Brier's title defence in the 2007 BA-CA Golf Open, presented by Telekom Austria, as a must see.

**Scott Crockett**

| Pos | Name | | Rd1 | Rd2 | Rd3 | Rd4 | Total | | € | £ |
|---|---|---|---|---|---|---|---|---|---|---|
| 1 | Markus BRIER | AUT | 65 | 67 | 66 | 68 | 266 | -18 | 216,660.00 | 148,669.14 |
| 2 | Søren HANSEN | DEN | 68 | 67 | 69 | 65 | 269 | -15 | 144,440.00 | 99,112.76 |
| 3 | Simon DYSON | ENG | 66 | 66 | 67 | 71 | 270 | -14 | 81,380.00 | 55,841.85 |
| 4 | Richard GREEN | AUS | 71 | 67 | 70 | 63 | 271 | -13 | 65,000.00 | 44,602.11 |
| 5 | Gary MURPHY | IRL | 68 | 70 | 71 | 65 | 274 | -10 | 55,120.00 | 37,822.59 |
| 6 | Jean-François LUCQUIN | FRA | 68 | 69 | 69 | 69 | 275 | -9 | 42,250.00 | 28,991.37 |
| | Miguel Angel JIMÉNEZ | ESP | 67 | 67 | 74 | 67 | 275 | -9 | 42,250.00 | 28,991.37 |
| 8 | Emanuele CANONICA | ITA | 70 | 66 | 70 | 71 | 277 | -7 | 29,206.67 | 20,041.22 |
| | Darren FICHARDT | RSA | 69 | 73 | 69 | 66 | 277 | -7 | 29,206.67 | 20,041.22 |
| | Steven JEPPESEN | SWE | 68 | 67 | 75 | 67 | 277 | -7 | 29,206.67 | 20,041.22 |
| 11 | Gregory BOURDY | FRA | 67 | 70 | 70 | 71 | 278 | -6 | 23,140.00 | 15,878.35 |
| | Gregory HAVRET | FRA | 69 | 68 | 78 | 63 | 278 | -6 | 23,140.00 | 15,878.35 |
| 13 | Colin MONTGOMERIE | SCO | 67 | 68 | 69 | 75 | 279 | -5 | 19,162.00 | 13,148.70 |
| | Gary EMERSON | ENG | 70 | 64 | 74 | 71 | 279 | -5 | 19,162.00 | 13,148.70 |
| | Mark ROE | ENG | 72 | 69 | 70 | 68 | 279 | -5 | 19,162.00 | 13,148.70 |
| | Oliver WHITELEY | ENG | 66 | 73 | 70 | 70 | 279 | -5 | 19,162.00 | 13,148.70 |
| | Steven O'HARA | SCO | 68 | 70 | 71 | 70 | 279 | -5 | 19,162.00 | 13,148.70 |
| 18 | Richard STERNE | RSA | 71 | 66 | 76 | 67 | 280 | -4 | 16,445.00 | 11,284.34 |
| | Alexandre ROCHA | BRA | 68 | 69 | 71 | 72 | 280 | -4 | 16,445.00 | 11,284.34 |
| 20 | Alastair FORSYTH | SCO | 67 | 74 | 71 | 69 | 281 | -3 | 14,516.67 | 9,961.14 |
| | Toni KARJALAINEN | FIN | 70 | 71 | 71 | 70 | 281 | -3 | 14,516.67 | 9,961.14 |
| | David HIGGINS | IRL | 67 | 68 | 72 | 74 | 281 | -3 | 14,516.67 | 9,961.14 |
| | Pedro LINHART | ESP | 70 | 71 | 73 | 67 | 281 | -3 | 14,516.67 | 9,961.14 |
| | Philip GOLDING | ENG | 71 | 68 | 71 | 71 | 281 | -3 | 14,516.67 | 9,961.14 |
| | Miguel CARBALLO | ARG | 69 | 69 | 74 | 69 | 281 | -3 | 14,516.67 | 9,961.14 |
| 26 | Thomas BJÖRN | DEN | 70 | 71 | 71 | 70 | 282 | -2 | 11,960.00 | 8,206.79 |
| | Robert COLES | ENG | 70 | 68 | 70 | 72 | 282 | -2 | 11,960.00 | 8,206.79 |
| | Simon HURD | ENG | 69 | 71 | 69 | 73 | 282 | -2 | 11,960.00 | 8,206.79 |
| | Michele REALE | ITA | 70 | 69 | 72 | 71 | 282 | -2 | 11,960.00 | 8,206.79 |
| | Titch MOORE | RSA | 72 | 67 | 74 | 69 | 282 | -2 | 11,960.00 | 8,206.79 |
| | Mikko ILONEN | FIN | 72 | 69 | 76 | 65 | 282 | -2 | 11,960.00 | 8,206.79 |
| | Tom WHITEHOUSE | ENG | 71 | 70 | 72 | 69 | 282 | -2 | 11,960.00 | 8,206.79 |
| 33 | Phil WORTHINGTON | ENG | 71 | 69 | 73 | 70 | 283 | -1 | 9,776.00 | 6,708.16 |
| | Kieran STAUNTON | ENG | 70 | 68 | 72 | 73 | 283 | -1 | 9,776.00 | 6,708.16 |
| | Lee SLATTERY | ENG | 70 | 67 | 74 | 72 | 283 | -1 | 9,776.00 | 6,708.16 |
| | David GRIFFITHS | ENG | 69 | 66 | 73 | 75 | 283 | -1 | 9,776.00 | 6,708.16 |
| | Peter SENIOR | AUS | 72 | 64 | 75 | 72 | 283 | -1 | 9,776.00 | 6,708.16 |
| 38 | Peter FOWLER | AUS | 69 | 70 | 73 | 72 | 284 | 0 | 8,450.00 | 5,798.27 |
| | José Manuel LARA | ESP | 69 | 72 | 73 | 70 | 284 | 0 | 8,450.00 | 5,798.27 |
| | Sven STRÜVER | GER | 66 | 73 | 74 | 71 | 284 | 0 | 8,450.00 | 5,798.27 |
| | Terry PILKADARIS | AUS | 71 | 70 | 73 | 70 | 284 | 0 | 8,450.00 | 5,798.27 |
| | Jorge BENEDETTI | COL | 66 | 73 | 74 | 71 | 284 | 0 | 8,450.00 | 5,798.27 |
| 43 | Nicolas MEITINGER | GER | 75 | 66 | 71 | 73 | 285 | 1 | 7,410.00 | 5,084.64 |
| | Benoit TEILLERIA | FRA | 71 | 72 | 74 | 68 | 285 | 1 | 7,410.00 | 5,084.64 |
| | Per-Ulrik JOHANSSON | SWE | 70 | 69 | 75 | 71 | 285 | 1 | 7,410.00 | 5,084.64 |
| 46 | Gary CLARK | ENG | 71 | 71 | 71 | 73 | 286 | 2 | 6,500.00 | 4,460.21 |
| | David BRANSDON | AUS | 69 | 74 | 71 | 72 | 286 | 2 | 6,500.00 | 4,460.21 |
| | Richard MCEVOY | ENG | 69 | 72 | 74 | 71 | 286 | 2 | 6,500.00 | 4,460.21 |
| | Anders SJÖSTRAND | SWE | 74 | 68 | 70 | 74 | 286 | 2 | 6,500.00 | 4,460.21 |
| 50 | Martin ERLANDSSON | SWE | 68 | 71 | 79 | 69 | 287 | 3 | 5,460.00 | 3,746.58 |
| | Scott DRUMMOND | SCO | 69 | 68 | 75 | 75 | 287 | 3 | 5,460.00 | 3,746.58 |
| | Paul MCGINLEY | IRL | 71 | 71 | 73 | 72 | 287 | 3 | 5,460.00 | 3,746.58 |
| | Marcel SIEM | GER | 71 | 70 | 74 | 72 | 287 | 3 | 5,460.00 | 3,746.58 |
| 54 | Jamie SPENCE | ENG | 69 | 73 | 72 | 74 | 288 | 4 | 4,680.00 | 3,211.35 |
| | Wilhelm SCHAUMAN | SWE | 72 | 70 | 75 | 71 | 288 | 4 | 4,680.00 | 3,211.35 |
| 56 | Benn BARHAM | ENG | 67 | 75 | 74 | 73 | 289 | 5 | 3,926.00 | 2,693.97 |
| | Ben MASON | ENG | 72 | 71 | 73 | 73 | 289 | 5 | 3,926.00 | 2,693.97 |
| | Garry HOUSTON | WAL | 69 | 70 | 78 | 72 | 289 | 5 | 3,926.00 | 2,693.97 |
| | Carl SUNESON | ESP | 71 | 70 | 72 | 76 | 289 | 5 | 3,926.00 | 2,693.97 |
| | Brad SUTTERFIELD | USA | 73 | 69 | 75 | 72 | 289 | 5 | 3,926.00 | 2,693.97 |
| 61 | Matthew MILLAR | AUS | 71 | 72 | 72 | 75 | 290 | 6 | 3,380.00 | 2,319.31 |
| | Mårten OLANDER | SWE | 70 | 71 | 78 | 71 | 290 | 6 | 3,380.00 | 2,319.31 |
| | Andrew OLDCORN | SCO | 72 | 71 | 76 | 71 | 290 | 6 | 3,380.00 | 2,319.31 |
| 64 | Stephen BROWNE | IRL | 70 | 70 | 78 | 73 | 291 | 7 | 3,055.00 | 2,096.30 |
| | David DIXON | ENG | 72 | 70 | 76 | 73 | 291 | 7 | 3,055.00 | 2,096.30 |
| 66 | Cédric MENUT | FRA | 69 | 74 | 78 | 71 | 292 | 8 | 2,730.00 | 1,873.29 |
| | Robert ROCK | ENG | 70 | 73 | 79 | 70 | 292 | 8 | 2,730.00 | 1,873.29 |
| | Marc CAYEUX | ZIM | 73 | 70 | 73 | 76 | 292 | 8 | 2,730.00 | 1,873.29 |
| 69 | Neil CHEETHAM | ENG | 71 | 71 | 77 | 74 | 293 | 9 | 2,266.67 | 1,555.36 |
| | Alvaro SALTO | ESP | 73 | 70 | 80 | 70 | 293 | 9 | 2,266.67 | 1,555.36 |
| | John BICKERTON | ENG | 70 | 72 | 79 | 72 | 293 | 9 | 2,266.67 | 1,555.36 |
| 72 | Alfredo GARCIA-HEREDIA | ESP | 70 | 72 | 80 | 73 | 295 | 11 | 1,947.00 | 1,336.00 |
| 73 | Thomas FEYRSINGER | AUT | 70 | 73 | 84 | 76 | 303 | 19 | 1,944.00 | 1,333.95 |

## Total Prize Fund
€1,305,840  £896,050

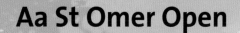

# Hail Cesar!

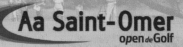

## Aa Saint-Omer
### open de Golf

They came to praise Cesar. The traditional greeting for an Argentine winner: an azure and white pennant draped across his shoulders, as his compatriots delighted in another success for their country on The European Tour International Schedule. There were no laurels to crown his head, but Cesar Monasterio felt like an emperor nonetheless.

At the age of 42, Señor Monasterio had finally tamed the hills and valleys of the Aa Saint Omer course and come through in a tournament he could have won three years earlier.

In 2003, when he equalled his career-best score in Europe with an opening round of 66 and had his best finish of tied eighth, Monasterio felt he had left a job unfinished in the Aa St Omer Open. Three years later, with a rousing final round and a brave par at the last where he was bunkered, he completed his mission in the dual ranking tournament between The European Tour and the Challenge Tour.

To do so, Monasterio had to defy the odds stacked against him. He began the final day five strokes adrift of the third round leader Henrik Nystrom of Sweden and, just like his illustrious near-namesake, Cesar had his foes even if he did not regard them as enemies.

All were seeking honour and glory, and the coveted prize of a one year exemption to The European Tour. Players like England's Paul Dwyer, who had lost out in a play-off to

Joakim Bäckström the previous year, and the South African duo of Jean Hugo and Martin Maritz, both eager to swap life on the veldt for a year or more rubbing shoulders with the big boys like compatriots Ernie and Retief. This Cesar, however, gloried in victory while the others were left with honour in defeat.

On the opening day it was not so much hail Cesar, as rain. Early morning it lashed down

Mikko Ilonen

### Aa Saint Omer Golf Club

| Par | Yards | Metres |
|-----|-------|--------|
| 71 | 6845 | 6259 |

| | | | | |
|---|---|---|---|---|
| 1 | Cesar MONASTERIO | 274 | -10 | |
| 2 | Martin MARITZ | 275 | -9 | |
| | Henrik NYSTROM | 275 | -9 | |
| 4 | Jean HUGO | 276 | -8 | |
| | Juan PARRON | 276 | -8 | |
| 6 | David DIXON | 277 | -7 | |
| | Jamie LITTLE | 277 | -7 | |
| 8 | Paul DWYER | 278 | -6 | |
| | Pedro LINHART | 278 | -6 | |
| 10 | Jesus Maria ARRUTI | 279 | -5 | |
| | Klas ERIKSSON | 279 | -5 | |
| | Mikko ILONEN | 279 | -5 | |
| | Raymond RUSSELL | 279 | -5 | |
| | Shaun P WEBSTER | 279 | -5 | |

### WEATHER REPORT

| Round One | Round Two | Round Three | Round Four |
|-----------|-----------|-------------|------------|

### EUROPEAN TOUR ORDER OF MERIT
(After 27 tournaments)

| Pos | | € | |
|-----|---|---|---|
| 1 | David HOWELL | 1,789,097.74 | |
| 2 | Paul CASEY | 948,979.55 | |
| 3 | Henrik STENSON | 867,206.76 | |
| 4 | Paul BROADHURST | 854,398.62 | |
| 5 | Miguel Angel JIMÉNEZ | 751,508.39 | |
| 6 | Retief GOOSEN | 738,353.87 | |
| 7 | Thomas BJÖRN | 731,916.11 | |
| 8 | Nick O'HERN | 673,289.83 | |
| 9 | Tim CLARK | 672,293.10 | |
| 10 | Johan EDFORS | 666,230.58 | |

Paul Casey hits out of a bunker during The Open Championship at Royal Liverpool Golf Club, Hoylake, England, July 21, 2006. 71494738, Andrew Redington

Darren Clarke, Dubai, March 2006. Andrew Redington/Getty Images for Taylor Made

Tiger Woods with the Wanamaker Trophy after winning the 2006 USPGA Championship, Medinah, Illinois, August 20, 2006. 71684390, Stuart Franklin

# Performance is passion

From St. Andrews to Shanghai.
From QSchool to the Claret Jug.
Your brand. Our imagery. One passion.

gettyimages.com/editorial

**getty**images®

# Final Results

| Pos | Name | | Rd1 | Rd2 | Rd3 | Rd4 | Total | | € | £ |
|---|---|---|---|---|---|---|---|---|---|---|
| 1 | Cesar MONASTERIO | ARG | 68 | 68 | 71 | 67 | 274 | -10 | 66,660.00 | 45,713.27 |
| 2 | Henrik NYSTROM | SWE | 69 | 65 | 68 | 73 | 275 | -9 | 34,740.00 | 23,823.57 |
| | Martin MARITZ | RSA | 71 | 67 | 66 | 71 | 275 | -9 | 34,740.00 | 23,823.57 |
| 4 | Juan PARRON | ESP | 68 | 71 | 69 | 68 | 276 | -8 | 18,480.00 | 12,672.98 |
| | Jean HUGO | RSA | 67 | 69 | 71 | 69 | 276 | -8 | 18,480.00 | 12,672.98 |
| 6 | Jamie LITTLE | ENG | 72 | 72 | 64 | 69 | 277 | -7 | 13,000.00 | 8,914.98 |
| | David DIXON | ENG | 68 | 71 | 68 | 70 | 277 | -7 | 13,000.00 | 8,914.98 |
| 8 | Pedro LINHART | ESP | 71 | 70 | 69 | 68 | 278 | -6 | 9,480.00 | 6,501.08 |
| | Paul DWYER | ENG | 70 | 66 | 73 | 69 | 278 | -6 | 9,480.00 | 6,501.08 |
| 10 | Jesus Maria ARRUTI | ESP | 70 | 69 | 71 | 69 | 279 | -5 | 6,960.00 | 4,772.94 |
| | Raymond RUSSELL | SCO | 70 | 70 | 66 | 73 | 279 | -5 | 6,960.00 | 4,772.94 |
| | Shaun P WEBSTER | ENG | 71 | 68 | 66 | 74 | 279 | -5 | 6,960.00 | 4,772.94 |
| | Klas ERIKSSON | SWE | 67 | 71 | 68 | 73 | 279 | -5 | 6,960.00 | 4,772.94 |
| | Mikko ILONEN | FIN | 72 | 68 | 66 | 73 | 279 | -5 | 6,960.00 | 4,772.94 |
| 15 | Gregory BOURDY | FRA | 73 | 71 | 70 | 66 | 280 | -4 | 5,640.00 | 3,867.73 |
| | Fredrik HENGE | SWE | 74 | 71 | 67 | 68 | 280 | -4 | 5,640.00 | 3,867.73 |
| | Christian L NILSSON | SWE | 76 | 68 | 65 | 71 | 280 | -4 | 5,640.00 | 3,867.73 |
| 18 | James HEPWORTH | ENG | 71 | 69 | 67 | 74 | 281 | -3 | 4,890.00 | 3,353.40 |
| | Nicolas VANHOOTEGEM | BEL | 69 | 69 | 70 | 73 | 281 | -3 | 4,890.00 | 3,353.40 |
| | Stephen SCAHILL | NZL | 72 | 68 | 70 | 71 | 281 | -3 | 4,890.00 | 3,353.40 |
| | Rafael ECHENIQUE | ARG | 71 | 72 | 68 | 70 | 281 | -3 | 4,890.00 | 3,353.40 |
| 22 | Lee SLATTERY | ENG | 69 | 70 | 72 | 71 | 282 | -2 | 4,340.00 | 2,976.23 |
| | Sam WALKER | ENG | 72 | 71 | 68 | 71 | 282 | -2 | 4,340.00 | 2,976.23 |
| | Gustavo ROJAS | ARG | 73 | 68 | 72 | 69 | 282 | -2 | 4,340.00 | 2,976.23 |
| | Chris GANE | ENG | 69 | 70 | 69 | 74 | 282 | -2 | 4,340.00 | 2,976.23 |
| 26 | Neil CHEETHAM | ENG | 75 | 69 | 68 | 71 | 283 | -1 | 3,680.00 | 2,523.62 |
| | Simon HURD | ENG | 69 | 76 | 66 | 72 | 283 | -1 | 3,680.00 | 2,523.62 |
| | Raphaël EYRAUD | FRA | 71 | 70 | 73 | 69 | 283 | -1 | 3,680.00 | 2,523.62 |
| | Terry PILKADARIS | AUS | 70 | 70 | 73 | 70 | 283 | -1 | 3,680.00 | 2,523.62 |
| | Felipe AGUILAR | CHI | 66 | 73 | 74 | 70 | 283 | -1 | 3,680.00 | 2,523.62 |
| | Alessio BRUSCHI | ITA | 69 | 73 | 71 | 70 | 283 | -1 | 3,680.00 | 2,523.62 |
| | Inder VAN WEERELT | NED | 71 | 73 | 71 | 68 | 283 | -1 | 3,680.00 | 2,523.62 |
| 33 | Kieran STAUNTON | ENG | 71 | 73 | 71 | 69 | 284 | 0 | 3,008.00 | 2,062.79 |
| | Ben WILLMAN | ENG | 71 | 70 | 71 | 72 | 284 | 0 | 3,008.00 | 2,062.79 |
| | Alexandre ROCHA | BRA | 71 | 73 | 70 | 70 | 284 | 0 | 3,008.00 | 2,062.79 |
| | Benoit TEILLERIA | FRA | 71 | 73 | 69 | 71 | 284 | 0 | 3,008.00 | 2,062.79 |
| | Denny LUCAS | ENG | 71 | 72 | 71 | 70 | 284 | 0 | 3,008.00 | 2,062.79 |
| 38 | Michele REALE | ITA | 69 | 73 | 73 | 70 | 285 | 1 | 2,600.00 | 1,783.00 |
| | Mark PILKINGTON | WAL | 70 | 74 | 73 | 68 | 285 | 1 | 2,600.00 | 1,783.00 |
| | Tom WHITEHOUSE | ENG | 69 | 72 | 71 | 73 | 285 | 1 | 2,600.00 | 1,783.00 |
| | Gareth PADDISON | NZL | 72 | 70 | 72 | 71 | 285 | 1 | 2,600.00 | 1,783.00 |
| | Adrien MÖRK | FRA | 68 | 71 | 72 | 74 | 285 | 1 | 2,600.00 | 1,783.00 |
| 43 | Jean-Baptiste GONNET | FRA | 70 | 73 | 67 | 76 | 286 | 2 | 2,200.00 | 1,508.69 |
| | Oskar BERGMAN | SWE | 70 | 73 | 71 | 72 | 286 | 2 | 2,200.00 | 1,508.69 |
| | Marco RUIZ | PAR | 73 | 72 | 70 | 71 | 286 | 2 | 2,200.00 | 1,508.69 |
| | Kyron SULLIVAN | WAL | 72 | 71 | 75 | 68 | 286 | 2 | 2,200.00 | 1,508.69 |
| | Malcolm MACKENZIE | ENG | 73 | 70 | 71 | 72 | 286 | 2 | 2,200.00 | 1,508.69 |
| 48 | Peter BAKER | ENG | 73 | 69 | 73 | 72 | 287 | 3 | 1,800.00 | 1,234.38 |
| | Massimo SCARPA | ITA | 73 | 71 | 71 | 72 | 287 | 3 | 1,800.00 | 1,234.38 |
| | Graham FOX | SCO | 74 | 68 | 73 | 72 | 287 | 3 | 1,800.00 | 1,234.38 |
| | James HEATH | ENG | 73 | 71 | 74 | 69 | 287 | 3 | 1,800.00 | 1,234.38 |
| | Julien FORET | FRA | 72 | 71 | 73 | 71 | 287 | 3 | 1,800.00 | 1,234.38 |
| 53 | Alvaro QUIROS | ESP | 73 | 71 | 75 | 69 | 288 | 4 | 1,366.67 | 937.22 |
| | Alexander NOREN | SWE | 73 | 72 | 71 | 72 | 288 | 4 | 1,366.67 | 937.22 |
| | Christian REIMBOLD | GER | 72 | 73 | 74 | 69 | 288 | 4 | 1,366.67 | 937.22 |
| | André BOSSERT | SUI | 70 | 72 | 71 | 75 | 288 | 4 | 1,366.67 | 937.22 |
| | Joakim BÄCKSTRÖM | SWE | 74 | 71 | 70 | 73 | 288 | 4 | 1,366.67 | 937.22 |
| | Titch MOORE | RSA | 74 | 70 | 72 | 72 | 288 | 4 | 1,366.67 | 937.22 |
| 59 | Iain STEEL | MAS | 73 | 69 | 73 | 74 | 289 | 5 | 1,160.00 | 795.49 |
| 60 | Ilya GORONESKOUL | FRA | 72 | 73 | 73 | 72 | 290 | 6 | 1,080.00 | 740.63 |
| | David DRYSDALE | SCO | 69 | 75 | 73 | 73 | 290 | 6 | 1,080.00 | 740.63 |
| | Jorge BENEDETTI | COL | 71 | 68 | 71 | 80 | 290 | 6 | 1,080.00 | 740.63 |
| 63 | Miguel CARBALLO | ARG | 73 | 72 | 73 | 73 | 291 | 7 | 940.00 | 644.62 |
| | Alvaro SALTO | ESP | 73 | 72 | 72 | 74 | 291 | 7 | 940.00 | 644.62 |
| | Anders Schmidt HANSEN | DEN | 70 | 74 | 75 | 72 | 291 | 7 | 940.00 | 644.62 |
| | Cédric MENUT | FRA | 73 | 72 | 75 | 71 | 291 | 7 | 940.00 | 644.62 |
| 67 | Roger CHAPMAN | ENG | 74 | 69 | 73 | 76 | 292 | 8 | 820.00 | 562.33 |
| | Hennie OTTO | RSA | 73 | 69 | 76 | 74 | 292 | 8 | 820.00 | 562.33 |
| 69 | Johan AXGREN | SWE | 72 | 72 | 75 | 75 | 294 | 10 | 760.00 | 521.18 |
| 70 | Phil WORTHINGTON | ENG | 73 | 69 | 79 | 75 | 296 | 12 | 740.00 | 507.47 |
| 71 | Thomas NIELSEN | DEN | 73 | 72 | 77 | 80 | 302 | 18 | 600.00 | 411.46 |

## Total Prize Fund
€400,600  £274,418

> *"The course is in very good condition and took the heavy rain of Thursday very well. It is undulating therefore it is all about placing the ball and controlling the distance with your irons. It is absolutely paramount to be in the right position on the greens"* – Peter Baker

but the course was up to it with only two hours lost for a mop-up. Then another South American took charge. Felipe Aguilar, the first Chilean businessman from his country to play The European Tour, led the way as the opening round finished just before light faded. Aguilar soared to the top but then slowly floated down to earth, giving way to Nystrom on the second day. Nystrom shot 65 and led by two from Dwyer, round in 66, Hugo and Monasterio.

Nystrom had shown promise with a share of seventh place in The Celtic Manor Wales Open and he maintained his two shot lead

Lee Slattery

on Saturday. Unfortunately, his advantage was wiped out immediately on Sunday when he began his final round with a double bogey six.

Meanwhile playing partner Maritz stepped in. The tall South African belied his lengthy absence from The European Tour fairways by moving in front. The tantalising lure of automatic playing rights, though, can apply pressure to the bravest of men. In the end, a late bogey at the 16th left him level with Nystrom, who birdied the last, and one behind Monasterio. The Argentine did not birdie the last, but he did not need to, a gritty sand save from the greenside bunker a little while before Nystrom and Maritz finished, sufficient to provide the man from Tucuman with the greatest golfing day of his life. He admitted he had thought he was getting too old to cut it with the young bloods thirsting for success.

Argentina's sports columns were, naturally, dominated by the country's exploits in the World Cup in Germany. But at the Aa Saint Omer Golf Club on June 18, as he received the accolades of his peers, Cesar could rightly say: "Veni. Vidi. Vici.".

**Norman Dabell**

# Last Man Standing

## Winged Foot Golf Club

| Par | Yards | Metres |
|-----|-------|--------|
| 70 | 7264 | 6642 |

| | | | | |
|---|---|---|---|---|
| 1 | Geoff OGILVY | 285 | +5 |  |
| 2 | Jim FURYK | 286 | +6 | |
| | Phil MICKELSON | 286 | +6 | |
| | Colin MONTGOMERIE | 286 | +6 | |
| 5 | Padraig HARRINGTON | 287 | +7 |  |
| 6 | Kenneth FERRIE | 288 | +8 | |
| | Nick O'HERN | 288 | +8 | |
| | Vijay SINGH | 288 | +8 | |
| | Jeff SLUMAN | 288 | +8 | |
| | Steve STRICKER | 288 | +8 | |
| | Mike WEIR | 288 | +8 |  |

## WEATHER REPORT

| Round One | Round Two | Round Three | Round Four |
|-----------|-----------|-------------|------------|

## EUROPEAN TOUR ORDER OF MERIT
(After 28 tournaments)

| Pos | | € | |
|-----|---|---|---|
| 1 | David HOWELL | 1,867,775.62 | |
| 2 | Paul CASEY | 1,041,362.81 | |
| 3 | Colin MONTGOMERIE | 965,605.20 | |
| 4 | Henrik STENSON | 908,629.04 | |
| 5 | Paul BROADHURST | 854,398.62 | |
| 6 | Miguel Angel JIMÉNEZ | 830,186.27 | |
| 7 | Nick O'HERN | 818,316.48 | |
| 8 | Thomas BJÖRN | 748,125.41 | |
| 9 | Retief GOOSEN | 739,936.66 | |
| 10 | Padraig HARRINGTON | 707,369.12 | |

# US Open Championship

**Mamaroneck, New York, USA**

June 15-18 • 2006

Colin Montgomerie could have, perhaps even should have, won the 2006 US Open Championship at Winged Foot Golf Club. All he needed was a little bit of luck – not buckets of it, just a smidgen.

Nick O'Hern

If, for instance, his near perfect drive to the 72nd hole had given him a solid yardage to the green, instead of being between a six and seven iron; or if his errant second shot had drawn a good lie in the rough; or if his pitch out of it had finished below instead of above the hole; then he might have been celebrating his first Major Championship victory.

None of those things happened though and Geoff Ogilvy, an affable young Australian, ended up the slightly surprising, and slightly surprised, winner. It was Ogilvy that had the luck, not Montgomerie, and the man from Adelaide, now resident in Scottsdale, Arizona, was honest enough to admit it.

"I think that I was the beneficiary of a little bit of charity," said Ogilvy. "I think I just got a bit lucky."

And so he did, although it must be said immediately that Ogilvy is certainly the calibre of golfer to win a Major Championship, having proved it in February when he won the World Golf Championships – Accenture Match Play in California, beating four previous Major winners – Michael Campbell, Tom Lehman, Davis Love III and Mike Weir – on the way. He proved it, too, with his play on the 71st and 72nd holes at Winged Foot, holing the chip of a lifetime at the former and getting up and down from below the elevated green on the latter, a good pitch

*" This is a great golf course. It has more subtleties than just about any course I've ever played – little rolls on greens, little rolls in the fairways, little fall-offs on the edges of the greens. It's a great venue – everything is spectacular " – Phil Mickelson*

*Vijay Singh and Colin Montgomerie*

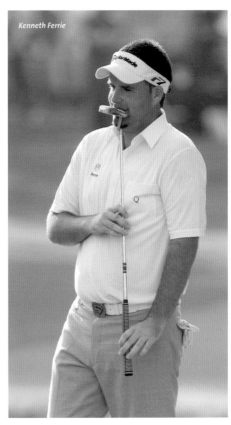

*Kenneth Ferrie*

giving him a slippery six footer that had to go in, and did.

But impressive though that was, it still needed Phil Mickelson, as Montgomerie had done some 20 minutes earlier, to implode on the final hole – and Ogilvy was able to stand in the TV booth at the back of the green to watch him do just that. As with Montgomerie, the reigning Masters Champion needed a par four to win, a bogey five for a play-off and took six. Both died of self-inflicted wounds and Ogilvy was the last man standing.

The man himself recognised it, too. "The whole thing was surreal," he said, before adding graciously, "I feel bad that no-one ever did this for Greg (Norman). He held his hand up a lot of times in the last few holes of Majors and no-one ever gave him the luck I got today."

Ogilvy could have substituted the name Montgomerie for that of Norman and been just as accurate, a fact acutely observed by the Scot himself. Looking back on a fantastic career, albeit one uninterrupted by a Major Championship, Montgomerie said: "I've played well and won ordinary tournaments and I've also had other people get bad breaks and let me win at that level. But never, ever in a Major.

"I've never had a situation like Nick Faldo had at Augusta with Scott Hoch and Ray Floyd. If it had been me, Hoch would have holed that two footer on the first play-off hole and Floyd would not have gone in the water at the second play-off hole the following year."

Ogilvy voiced precisely similar sentiments on the Greg Norman theme after his win. "If that had been Mickelson against

Ian Poulter

# Final Results

| Pos | Name | | Rd1 | Rd2 | Rd3 | Rd4 | Total | | € | £ |
|---|---|---|---|---|---|---|---|---|---|---|
| 1 | Geoff OGILVY | AUS | 71 | 70 | 72 | 72 | 285 | 5 | 969455.94 | 664821.45 |
| 2 | Colin MONTGOMERIE | SCO | 69 | 71 | 75 | 71 | 286 | 6 | 396684.75 | 272033.54 |
| | Phil MICKELSON | USA | 70 | 73 | 69 | 74 | 286 | 6 | 396684.75 | 272033.54 |
| | Jim FURYK | USA | 70 | 72 | 74 | 70 | 286 | 6 | 396684.75 | 272033.54 |
| 5 | Padraig HARRINGTON | IRL | 73 | 69 | 74 | 71 | 287 | 7 | 202313.19 | 138739.83 |
| 6 | Jeff SLUMAN | USA | 74 | 73 | 72 | 69 | 288 | 8 | 145026.65 | 99454.57 |
| | Steve STRICKER | USA | 70 | 69 | 76 | 73 | 288 | 8 | 145026.65 | 99454.57 |
| | Nick O'HERN | AUS | 75 | 70 | 74 | 69 | 288 | 8 | 145026.65 | 99454.57 |
| | Mike WEIR | CAN | 71 | 74 | 71 | 72 | 288 | 8 | 145026.65 | 99454.57 |
| | Kenneth FERRIE | ENG | 71 | 70 | 71 | 76 | 288 | 8 | 145026.65 | 99454.57 |
| | Vijay SINGH | FIJ | 71 | 74 | 70 | 73 | 288 | 8 | 145026.65 | 99454.57 |
| 12 | Ian POULTER | ENG | 74 | 71 | 70 | 74 | 289 | 9 | 104202.66 | 71458.81 |
| | Luke DONALD | ENG | 78 | 69 | 70 | 72 | 289 | 9 | 104202.66 | 71458.81 |
| | Ryuji IMADA | JPN | 76 | 73 | 69 | 71 | 289 | 9 | 104202.66 | 71458.81 |
| 15 | Paul CASEY | ENG | 77 | 72 | 72 | 69 | 290 | 10 | 92383.26 | 63353.44 |
| 16 | Robert ALLENBY | AUS | 73 | 74 | 72 | 72 | 291 | 11 | 78677.88 | 53954.74 |
| | Arron OBERHOLSER | USA | 75 | 68 | 74 | 74 | 291 | 11 | 78677.88 | 53954.74 |
| | Miguel Angel JIMÉNEZ | ESP | 72 | 75 | 74 | 72 | 291 | 11 | 78677.88 | 53954.74 |
| | David DUVAL | USA | 77 | 68 | 75 | 71 | 291 | 11 | 78677.88 | 53954.74 |
| | David HOWELL | ENG | 70 | 78 | 74 | 69 | 291 | 11 | 78677.88 | 53954.74 |
| 21 | José Maria OLAZÁBAL | ESP | 75 | 73 | 73 | 71 | 292 | 12 | 58762.48 | 40297.40 |
| | Trevor IMMELMAN | RSA | 76 | 71 | 70 | 75 | 292 | 12 | 58762.48 | 40297.40 |
| | Peter HEDBLOM | SWE | 74 | 75 | 71 | 72 | 292 | 12 | 58762.48 | 40297.40 |
| | Tom PERNICE Jnr | USA | 79 | 70 | 72 | 71 | 292 | 12 | 58762.48 | 40297.40 |
| | Adam SCOTT | AUS | 72 | 76 | 70 | 74 | 292 | 12 | 58762.48 | 40297.40 |
| 26 | Craig BARLOW | USA | 72 | 75 | 72 | 74 | 293 | 13 | 41422.28 | 28406.06 |
| | Ted PURDY | USA | 78 | 71 | 71 | 73 | 293 | 13 | 41422.28 | 28406.06 |
| | Sean O'HAIR | USA | 76 | 72 | 74 | 71 | 293 | 13 | 41422.28 | 28406.06 |
| | Ernie ELS | RSA | 74 | 73 | 74 | 72 | 293 | 13 | 41422.28 | 28406.06 |
| | Angel CABRERA | ARG | 74 | 73 | 74 | 72 | 293 | 13 | 41422.28 | 28406.06 |
| | Henrik STENSON | SWE | 75 | 71 | 73 | 74 | 293 | 13 | 41422.28 | 28406.06 |
| 32 | Woody AUSTIN | USA | 72 | 76 | 72 | 74 | 294 | 14 | 33168.85 | 22746.12 |
| | Rodney PAMPLING | AUS | 73 | 75 | 75 | 71 | 294 | 14 | 33168.85 | 22746.12 |
| | Steve JONES | USA | 74 | 74 | 71 | 75 | 294 | 14 | 33168.85 | 22746.12 |
| | Bart BRYANT | USA | 72 | 72 | 73 | 77 | 294 | 14 | 33168.85 | 22746.12 |
| | Scott HEND | AUS | 72 | 72 | 75 | 75 | 294 | 14 | 33168.85 | 22746.12 |
| 37 | Charles HOWELL III | USA | 77 | 71 | 73 | 74 | 295 | 15 | 29002.16 | 19888.74 |
| | Jay HAAS | USA | 75 | 72 | 74 | 74 | 295 | 15 | 29002.16 | 19888.74 |
| | Stewart CINK | USA | 75 | 71 | 77 | 72 | 295 | 15 | 29002.16 | 19888.74 |
| 40 | Fred FUNK | USA | 71 | 75 | 73 | 77 | 296 | 16 | 23313.63 | 15987.73 |
| | Tommy ARMOUR III | USA | 79 | 70 | 74 | 73 | 296 | 16 | 23313.63 | 15987.73 |
| | John COOK | USA | 71 | 78 | 74 | 73 | 296 | 16 | 23313.63 | 15987.73 |
| | Lee WILLIAMS | USA | 75 | 73 | 73 | 75 | 296 | 16 | 23313.63 | 15987.73 |
| | Chad COLLINS | USA | 76 | 71 | 72 | 77 | 296 | 16 | 23313.63 | 15987.73 |
| | Bo VAN PELT | USA | 72 | 75 | 73 | 76 | 296 | 16 | 23313.63 | 15987.73 |
| | Stephen GANGLUFF | CAN | 76 | 73 | 77 | 70 | 296 | 16 | 23313.63 | 15987.73 |
| | Jason DUFNER | USA | 72 | 71 | 78 | 75 | 296 | 16 | 23313.63 | 15987.73 |
| 48 | Charl SCHWARTZEL | RSA | 74 | 72 | 76 | 75 | 297 | 17 | 16209.30 | 11115.81 |
| | Charley HOFFMAN | USA | 76 | 70 | 78 | 73 | 297 | 17 | 16209.30 | 11115.81 |
| | Kent JONES | USA | 73 | 74 | 73 | 77 | 297 | 17 | 16209.30 | 11115.81 |
| | Graeme MCDOWELL | NIR | 71 | 72 | 75 | 79 | 297 | 17 | 16209.30 | 11115.81 |
| | Fred COUPLES | USA | 73 | 74 | 71 | 79 | 297 | 17 | 16209.30 | 11115.81 |
| | Thomas BJÖRN | DEN | 72 | 74 | 73 | 78 | 297 | 17 | 16209.30 | 11115.81 |
| | Phillip ARCHER | ENG | 72 | 72 | 75 | 78 | 297 | 17 | 16209.30 | 11115.81 |
| | J B HOLMES | USA | 74 | 73 | 75 | 75 | 297 | 17 | 16209.30 | 11115.81 |
| 56 | Darren CLARKE | NIR | 73 | 72 | 79 | 74 | 298 | 18 | 14269.60 | 9785.63 |
| 57 | Ben CURTIS | USA | 78 | 71 | 77 | 73 | 299 | 19 | 13939.59 | 9559.32 |
| 58 | Kenny PERRY | USA | 77 | 71 | 79 | 74 | 301 | 21 | 13676.06 | 9378.60 |
| 59 | Skip KENDALL | USA | 73 | 75 | 76 | 78 | 302 | 22 | 13197.26 | 9050.25 |
| | Jeev Milkha SINGH | IND | 73 | 76 | 77 | 76 | 302 | 22 | 13197.26 | 9050.25 |
| | Camilo VILLEGAS | COL | 74 | 72 | 79 | 77 | 302 | 22 | 13197.26 | 9050.25 |
| 62 | Ben CRANE | USA | 77 | 72 | 74 | 80 | 303 | 23 | 12761.99 | 8751.76 |
| 63 | Tim HERRON | USA | 73 | 76 | 79 | 77 | 305 | 25 | 12532.49 | 8594.38 |

Norman he would have holed out to win by a single shot."

There seems to be a belief, even among the better players, that some of their number are snake-bitten when it comes to Majors, and although Norman has the consolation of two Open Championships to his name, his talent surely demanded more like ten.

As Montgomerie said: "What I have to do is put myself in a position to win again and again and again and one of those times you are probably going to get what you deserve for your play over the years. For some people it seems as though it was written that they should win, and it hasn't been written for me.

Luke Donald

"But I'll keep going. I'm talented enough, I know that."

Montgomerie was one of 15 Europeans and 23 European Tour Members who played at the weekend. Paul Casey was one, and said: "There is a lot of talent coming through and a lot of guys keen to win a Major. The game is healthy from a European point of view."

Padraig Harrington

**David Davies**

# Total Prize Fund
€5,381,470  £3,690,437

# In Praise of
# An Old Friend

*Brett Rumford*

**The Gleneagles Hotel**

| Par | Yards | Metres |
|-----|-------|--------|
| 73 | 7260 | 6640 |

| | | | | |
|---|---|---|---|---|
| 1 | Paul CASEY | 276 | -16 |  |
| 2 | Søren HANSEN | 277 | -15 | |
| | Andrew MARSHALL | 277 | -15 | |
| 4 | Thomas BJÖRN | 278 | -14 | |
| | Colin MONTGOMERIE | 278 | -14 | |
| 6 | Alastair FORSYTH | 279 | -13 | |
| 7 | Fredrik HENGE | 280 | -12 | |
| | Brett RUMFORD | 280 | -12 | |
| 9 | Kenneth FERRIE | 281 | -11 | |
| | Robert KARLSSON | 281 | -11 | |

**WEATHER REPORT**

Round One · Round Two · Round Three · Round Four

The question was, would the 'Anybody but England' streak that was running through certain sections of Scottish society affect the Johnnie Walker Championship at Gleneagles?

After all, we were in the heart of Perthshire and football's World Cup was in full cry, with Sven's lads defying all opposition during the group stages, much to the dismay of those Scots who had combed every shop and store north of the border in the hope of picking up a Paraguay, Sweden or Trinidad and Tobago shirt.

Granted, cameraman Ian MacDonald did download an Equador flag from his laptop, printed it off, and flew it from his TV buggy on an old umbrella spoke in honour of England's last 16 opponents. It was typical of the sense of humour of the senior cameraman with The Golf Channel who tragically died two months later at his home in West Linton aged 50. A popular figure on Tour for the past 11 years, he will be sadly missed.

Apart from this spot of cross-border banter, those who turned up in record numbers merely confirmed the eclectic feel of the tournament.

The delightful girls from the 'Indulge' cafe in Auchterarder, who provided a steady supply of the sensational Tunisian orange and Moroccan walnut cakes in the media centre, reinforced the sense of internationalism pervading the heart of Scotland. They came from Poland, Bulgaria and, yes, even England.

Mind you, at the outset, it has to be said that the country was rooting for one of its own. Colin Montgomerie had just returned from his traumatic experience in the US Open Championship at Winged Foot Golf Club and, apart from the few who continue to delight in any Montgomerie misfortune, the crowds fervently hoped he would begin to ease some of the pain by becoming the first Scot to claim the Johnnie Walker Championship title.

On the first day he confessed to suffering Winged Foot flashbacks every time he stood on a fairway with an iron in his hand, but he courageously proved he was more than up to the task, and a five under

*Ian MacDonald, Senior Cameraman with The Golf Channel, sadly died in August, 2006*

**EUROPEAN TOUR ORDER OF MERIT**
(After 29 tournaments)

| Pos | | € | |
|-----|---|---|---|
| 1 | David HOWELL | 1,867,775.62 | |
| 2 | Paul CASEY | 1,383,030.27 | |
| 3 | Colin MONTGOMERIE | 1,060,316.77 | |
| 4 | Henrik STENSON | 908,629.04 | |
| 5 | Paul BROADHURST | 854,398.62 | |
| 6 | Thomas BJÖRN | 842,836.98 | |
| 7 | Miguel Angel JIMÉNEZ | 830,186.27 | |
| 8 | Nick O'HERN | 818,316.48 | |
| 9 | Retief GOOSEN | 739,936.66 | |
| 10 | Padraig HARRINGTON | 707,369.12 | |

Thomas Björn

par 68 left him only three shots behind Thomas Björn. Winning would not erase the bitter disappointment of casting away the opportunity to claim his first Major Championship, but as the sponsor's slogan put it, he intended to 'Keep Walking'.

Already, however, a representative of the Auld Enemy was looming menacingly into view. Paul Casey, one of Montgomerie's playing partners, shared second place with Argentine Andres Romero and Andrew McLardy, a South African whose father and mother, Ron and Mary, originate from the Scottish town of Helensburgh.

As Montgomerie had done, Casey raced back from Winged Foot where he had battled stoutly to finish 15th. However, unlike the eight time European Number One, he had not been involved in the mentally and physically draining final moments of an extraordinary tournament. Also significantly, of course, he is some 15 years younger than the Scot.

However, there was still enough life left in Montgomerie for him to summon a second consecutive 68 on his 43rd birthday, thus opening up a two shot lead on the field. A beautiful birthday cake, baked and iced by one of The Gleneagles Hotel's top chefs,

> **"** I wish all golf events were at Gleneagles. This course suits me because of its five par fives. It also has good memories and I always look forward to coming up here. It is a wonderful part of the world, and I get to stay in the Hotel! **"** – Paul Casey

Kenneth Ferrie and Colin Montgomerie

Andrew Marshall

| Pos | Name | | Rd1 | Rd2 | Rd3 | Rd4 | Total | | € | £ |
|---|---|---|---|---|---|---|---|---|---|---|
| 1 | Paul CASEY | ENG | 67 | 71 | 66 | 72 | 276 | -16 | 341,667.46 | 233,330.00 |
| 2 | Andrew MARSHALL | ENG | 72 | 67 | 69 | 69 | 277 | -15 | 178,052.78 | 121,595.00 |
| | Søren HANSEN | DEN | 69 | 70 | 68 | 70 | 277 | -15 | 178,052.78 | 121,595.00 |
| 4 | Colin MONTGOMERIE | SCO | 68 | 68 | 69 | 73 | 278 | -14 | 94,711.57 | 64,680.00 |
| | Thomas BJÖRN | DEN | 65 | 75 | 67 | 71 | 278 | -14 | 94,711.57 | 64,680.00 |
| 6 | Alastair FORSYTH | SCO | 72 | 69 | 67 | 71 | 279 | -13 | 71,751.19 | 49,000.00 |
| 7 | Brett RUMFORD | AUS | 69 | 71 | 67 | 73 | 280 | -12 | 56,375.94 | 38,500.00 |
| | Fredrik HENGE | SWE | 69 | 71 | 72 | 68 | 280 | -12 | 56,375.94 | 38,500.00 |
| 9 | Kenneth FERRIE | ENG | 68 | 73 | 71 | 69 | 281 | -11 | 43,460.72 | 29,680.00 |
| | Robert KARLSSON | SWE | 71 | 68 | 73 | 69 | 281 | -11 | 43,460.72 | 29,680.00 |
| 11 | Peter BAKER | ENG | 73 | 68 | 69 | 72 | 282 | -10 | 34,338.07 | 23,450.00 |
| | Simon DYSON | ENG | 72 | 72 | 69 | 69 | 282 | -10 | 34,338.07 | 23,450.00 |
| | Felipe AGUILAR | CHI | 74 | 68 | 71 | 69 | 282 | -10 | 34,338.07 | 23,450.00 |
| | Robert ROCK | ENG | 72 | 73 | 68 | 69 | 282 | -10 | 34,338.07 | 23,450.00 |
| 15 | David PARK | WAL | 74 | 72 | 71 | 66 | 283 | -9 | 28,905.48 | 19,740.00 |
| | Francis VALERA | ESP | 68 | 75 | 71 | 69 | 283 | -9 | 28,905.48 | 19,740.00 |
| | Carl SUNESON | ESP | 71 | 70 | 70 | 72 | 283 | -9 | 28,905.48 | 19,740.00 |
| 18 | Steven JEPPESEN | SWE | 70 | 74 | 72 | 68 | 284 | -8 | 26,445.44 | 18,060.00 |
| 19 | Sam TORRANCE | SCO | 69 | 74 | 69 | 73 | 285 | -7 | 24,600.41 | 16,800.00 |
| | Gary ORR | SCO | 73 | 72 | 70 | 70 | 285 | -7 | 24,600.41 | 16,800.00 |
| | Marc WARREN | SCO | 73 | 72 | 71 | 69 | 285 | -7 | 24,600.41 | 16,800.00 |
| 22 | Stephen SCAHILL | NZL | 76 | 69 | 69 | 72 | 286 | -6 | 21,627.86 | 14,770.00 |
| | Henrik NYSTROM | SWE | 69 | 75 | 71 | 71 | 286 | -6 | 21,627.86 | 14,770.00 |
| | Peter SENIOR | AUS | 74 | 69 | 75 | 68 | 286 | -6 | 21,627.86 | 14,770.00 |
| | Steve WEBSTER | ENG | 75 | 71 | 72 | 68 | 286 | -6 | 21,627.86 | 14,770.00 |
| | Paul MCGINLEY | IRL | 70 | 73 | 72 | 71 | 286 | -6 | 21,627.86 | 14,770.00 |
| | Andrew MCLARDY | RSA | 67 | 76 | 70 | 73 | 286 | -6 | 21,627.86 | 14,770.00 |
| 28 | Peter LAWRIE | IRL | 71 | 72 | 71 | 73 | 287 | -5 | 18,552.81 | 12,670.00 |
| | David LYNN | ENG | 71 | 74 | 70 | 72 | 287 | -5 | 18,552.81 | 12,670.00 |
| | José-Filipe LIMA | POR | 71 | 73 | 73 | 70 | 287 | -5 | 18,552.81 | 12,670.00 |
| | Ross FISHER | ENG | 70 | 70 | 71 | 76 | 287 | -5 | 18,552.81 | 12,670.00 |
| 32 | Matthew MILLAR | AUS | 73 | 72 | 74 | 69 | 288 | -4 | 14,821.75 | 10,122.00 |
| | Ariel CANETE | ARG | 73 | 72 | 74 | 69 | 288 | -4 | 14,821.75 | 10,122.00 |
| | Marcus FRASER | AUS | 71 | 68 | 74 | 75 | 288 | -4 | 14,821.75 | 10,122.00 |
| | Stephen BROWNE | IRL | 68 | 74 | 71 | 75 | 288 | -4 | 14,821.75 | 10,122.00 |
| | Graeme STORM | ENG | 69 | 72 | 73 | 74 | 288 | -4 | 14,821.75 | 10,122.00 |
| | David GRIFFITHS | ENG | 73 | 73 | 70 | 72 | 288 | -4 | 14,821.75 | 10,122.00 |
| | Tom WHITEHOUSE | ENG | 71 | 74 | 69 | 74 | 288 | -4 | 14,821.75 | 10,122.00 |
| | Cesar MONASTERIO | ARG | 74 | 70 | 75 | 69 | 288 | -4 | 14,821.75 | 10,122.00 |
| | Miguel Angel MARTIN | ESP | 68 | 77 | 74 | 69 | 288 | -4 | 14,821.75 | 10,122.00 |
| | Emanuele CANONICA | ITA | 70 | 73 | 69 | 76 | 288 | -4 | 14,821.75 | 10,122.00 |
| 42 | Christian CÉVAËR | FRA | 73 | 73 | 71 | 72 | 289 | -3 | 11,685.19 | 7,980.00 |
| | Peter HANSON | SWE | 74 | 68 | 70 | 77 | 289 | -3 | 11,685.19 | 7,980.00 |
| | Søren KJELDSEN | DEN | 74 | 72 | 72 | 71 | 289 | -3 | 11,685.19 | 7,980.00 |
| | Anthony WALL | ENG | 71 | 74 | 73 | 71 | 289 | -3 | 11,685.19 | 7,980.00 |
| | Jason MCCREADIE | SCO | 71 | 72 | 77 | 69 | 289 | -3 | 11,685.19 | 7,980.00 |
| 47 | David DRYSDALE | SCO | 76 | 70 | 71 | 73 | 290 | -2 | 9,635.16 | 6,580.00 |
| | David HIGGINS | IRL | 74 | 69 | 76 | 71 | 290 | -2 | 9,635.16 | 6,580.00 |
| | Jamie SPENCE | ENG | 73 | 71 | 75 | 71 | 290 | -2 | 9,635.16 | 6,580.00 |
| | Robert-Jan DERKSEN | NED | 74 | 70 | 71 | 75 | 290 | -2 | 9,635.16 | 6,580.00 |
| | Jyoti RANDHAWA | IND | 72 | 71 | 74 | 73 | 290 | -2 | 9,635.16 | 6,580.00 |
| 52 | Richard BLAND | ENG | 75 | 68 | 72 | 76 | 291 | -1 | 7,790.13 | 5,320.00 |
| | Santiago LUNA | ESP | 73 | 73 | 72 | 73 | 291 | -1 | 7,790.13 | 5,320.00 |
| | Bradley DREDGE | WAL | 69 | 75 | 75 | 72 | 291 | -1 | 7,790.13 | 5,320.00 |
| | Stuart DAVIS | ENG | 72 | 69 | 77 | 73 | 291 | -1 | 7,790.13 | 5,320.00 |
| 56 | Lee SLATTERY | ENG | 73 | 73 | 72 | 74 | 292 | 0 | 6,303.85 | 4,305.00 |
| | Sandy LYLE | SCO | 75 | 71 | 71 | 75 | 292 | 0 | 6,303.85 | 4,305.00 |
| | Sam LITTLE | ENG | 72 | 72 | 75 | 73 | 292 | 0 | 6,303.85 | 4,305.00 |
| | Wade ORMSBY | AUS | 68 | 77 | 73 | 74 | 292 | 0 | 6,303.85 | 4,305.00 |
| 60 | Miles TUNNICLIFF | ENG | 70 | 76 | 73 | 74 | 293 | 1 | 5,535.09 | 3,780.00 |
| | Andres ROMERO | ARG | 67 | 76 | 77 | 73 | 293 | 1 | 5,535.09 | 3,780.00 |
| | Raymond RUSSELL | SCO | 73 | 73 | 73 | 74 | 293 | 1 | 5,535.09 | 3,780.00 |
| 63 | Alexandre ROCHA | BRA | 70 | 72 | 76 | 76 | 294 | 2 | 4,920.08 | 3,360.00 |
| | Damien MCGRANE | IRL | 75 | 71 | 74 | 74 | 294 | 2 | 4,920.08 | 3,360.00 |
| | Shaun P WEBSTER | ENG | 72 | 73 | 72 | 77 | 294 | 2 | 4,920.08 | 3,360.00 |
| 66 | Sion E BEBB | WAL | 72 | 72 | 73 | 78 | 295 | 3 | 4,510.08 | 3,080.00 |
| 67 | Ben MASON | ENG | 72 | 77 | 73 | 74 | 296 | 4 | 4,305.07 | 2,940.00 |
| 68 | Mark LOFTUS | SCO | 69 | 75 | 77 | 76 | 297 | 5 | 3,914.59 | 2,673.33 |
| | Benoit TEILLERIA | FRA | 71 | 74 | 73 | 79 | 297 | 5 | 3,914.59 | 2,673.33 |
| | Philip GOLDING | ENG | 71 | 75 | 73 | 78 | 297 | 5 | 3,914.59 | 2,673.33 |
| 71 | Robert ARNOTT | SCO | 71 | 74 | 74 | 79 | 298 | 6 | 3,075.00 | 2,099.97 |
| 72 | Toni KARJALAINEN | FIN | 72 | 72 | 78 | 78 | 300 | 8 | 3,072.00 | 2,097.92 |
| 73 | Michele REALE | ITA | 72 | 71 | 74 | 85 | 302 | 10 | 3,069.00 | 2,095.87 |

## Total Prize Fund
€2,059,250  £1,406,293

was wheeled into the media centre, and a smiling Montgomerie duly blew out the candles and made the first cut.

Even then, however, he conveyed the feeling of a man running on air. In the newspapers that day, a Welsh health psychologist called Cliff Arnall claimed that June 23rd was statistically the happiest day of the year. Montgomerie, though, was not buying it, especially after missing a birdie putt on the last green. "Your mad professor obviously doesn't play golf and have to stand over four footers," he commented jokingly, but uneasily.

Sure enough, by Saturday evening, his lead had vanished. While the powerful Casey birdied the par five 16th and 18th holes, Montgomerie failed to pick up a shot at either. On the day England beat Equador in the World Cup, Casey powered past the Scot.

The biggest crowd to gather on any one day of the tournament swarmed over the sunlit hillsides on Sunday, still clinging to the hope that they would witness The Full Monty rather than a waning version. He tried, but Winged Foot had weakened him, and Casey, whose first win on The European Tour International Schedule was at Gleneagles in 2001, was the champion for a second time. While Montgomerie slid to joint fourth alongside Björn, another Englishman, Andrew Marshall, and Denmark's Søren Hansen shared second place.

In reality, there was not even a hint of an 'Anybody but England' feeling among the 11,500 spectators as Casey stepped up to accept the trophy and the €341,667 (£233,330) first prize. They had come to hail their hero, but left praising an old friend.

**Jock MacVicar**
*Scottish Daily Express*

# Celebration Time

Anders Hansen

It was a moment of unconfined joy. It was approaching midnight on Saturday and the streets of Versailles were filled with men, women and children celebrating France's quarter-final victory over Brazil in the World Cup. As custom demands in these parts they were also in their cars incessantly beeping their horns, something no doubt repeated all over Paris and the rest of the country.

There was already plenty to celebrate all week at the centenary Open de France ALSTOM. The only thing missing on the Sunday was a French winner to follow the successes of Jean-Francois Remesy in both 2004 and 2005. Instead, the title went back across the Channel as Englishman John Bickerton sealed the biggest victory of his 12 year European Tour career.

A cheque for €666,660 (£458,576) was obviously welcome, but the knowledge of beating such strong opponents – Padraig Harrington was runner-up while Michael Campbell, Marcus Fraser and Ian Poulter shared third place – was even better. Best of all, however, was holding up the huge trophy. Bickerton had two observations about it. "There is such a lot of history here," he said as he looked at the list of former winners, before adding: "Do I get to fill it with champagne?" Being in France, not surprisingly, the answer was a resounding 'Oui!'

Campbell, the third round leader, would have been the 19th Major Champion to have also claimed the Open de France ALSTOM title. Dating back to 1906, it is the oldest national

championship on the Continent of Europe. Arnaud Massy was the winner then and he repeated the feat 12 months later, in the same year he won The Open Championship at Royal Liverpool. He went on to win his national title again in 1911 and 1925.

Jean-François Remesy

---

### Le Golf National

| Par | Yards | Metres |
|-----|-------|--------|
| 71 | 7225 | 6607 |

| | | | | |
|---|---|---|---|---|
| 1 | John BICKERTON | 273 | -11 | |
| 2 | Padraig HARRINGTON | 274 | -10 | |
| 3 | Michael CAMPBELL | 276 | -8 | |
| | Marcus FRASER | 276 | -8 | |
| | Ian POULTER | 276 | -8 | |
| 6 | Anders HANSEN | 277 | -7 | |
| 7 | Andrew COLTART | 278 | -6 | |
| | Richard GREEN | 278 | -6 | |
| | Peter O'MALLEY | 278 | -6 | |
| 10 | Alastair FORSYTH | 279 | -5 | |
| | José Maria OLAZÁBAL | 279 | -5 | |

### WEATHER REPORT

| Round One | Round Two | Round Three | Round Four |
|-----------|-----------|-------------|------------|
| ☀ | ☀ | ☀ | ☀ |

### EUROPEAN TOUR ORDER OF MERIT
(After 30 tournaments)

| Pos | | € |
|-----|---|---|
| 1 | David HOWELL | 1,867,775.62 |
| 2 | Paul CASEY | 1,383,030.27 |
| 3 | Padraig HARRINGTON | 1,151,809.12 |
| 4 | Colin MONTGOMERIE | 1,060,316.77 |
| 5 | John BICKERTON | 1,009,045.12 |
| 6 | Henrik STENSON | 941,379.04 |
| 7 | Paul BROADHURST | 916,318.62 |
| 8 | Thomas BJÖRN | 842,836.98 |
| 9 | Miguel Angel JIMÉNEZ | 830,186.27 |
| 10 | Nick O'HERN | 818,316.48 |

# Open de France ALSTOM

Jean-François Lucquin

Seve Ballesteros, Sandy Lyle and José Maria Olazábal were amongst the Major Champions and former winners competing and all attended the sumptuous Champions Dinner on the Tuesday night. The occasion was marked by the issue of a special stamp and a Centenary Book produced by L'Equipe. There was even more to celebrate for French golf for, the previous week, Julien Guerrier won The Amateur Championship at Royal St George's. That night he was flown by helicopter from Sandwich to a celebratory dinner in Paris.

"It is great to be part of these celebrations," said Ballesteros. "So much has changed for the better since I first came to Chantilly in 1974. Look at the course. It's fantastic. It could accommodate any competition, the French Open, the World Cup or The Ryder Cup. It is a great combination of old and new – a British links with a touch of American style."

Harrington was eager to challenge for this prestigious title although, like many others, he was aware that the course and the conditions provided an ideal opportunity to hone his game for The Open Championship in addition, of course, to chasing vital Ryder Cup points.

After finishing second at the weather delayed Booz Allen Classic in America the previous week, Harrington arrived late and spent most of the week sleeping before charging into contention on Sunday. He eventually set the clubhouse target of ten under par 274 with birdies at each of the last two holes.

" *It is a great course, you really have to have your wits about you. It's a great venue as well - a really good set up with great viewing areas for the public. They could have a Ryder Cup here one day* " *– John Bickerton*

Michael Campbell

# Final Results

After a birdie at the 14th, Bickerton had a three shot lead entering the amphitheatre that is the final four holes. However, it was far from over. A poor tee shot at the 15th left the winner of the 2005 Abama Open de Canarias in the rough and on the way to a double bogey.

Campbell, however, three-putted the same hole but the 2005 US Open Champion responded magnificently with a tap-in birdie at the short 16th. Bickerton stayed one in front with a chip-and-putt par at the next but that still left the fearsome final hole, surrounded by water, to negotiate. What is more, he knew there was no room for error with a par required as Harrington was safely in the clubhouse.

Campbell, too, was still in the frame but he found the water which left Bickerton in the driving seat. He made no mistake although he confessed afterwards: "Everything was shaking. I don't think you could feel more nervous down the stretch of a Major. This means so much, I'm not sure I can take it all in yet."

So no home winner but Jean Van de Velde, defeated by Remesy in a play-off in 2005 and who finished in a share of 17th place, preferred to look at the big picture. "As an event, this is right back up there," he said. "It is a great venue and there were so many youngsters out there today. With a good date and a great purse we will get the big players. With Jean-Francois winning the last two years and a lot of French players in contention, the French people know we can win - even if not this year."

**Andy Farrell**

| Pos | Name | | Rd1 | Rd2 | Rd3 | Rd4 | Total | | € | £ |
|-----|------|----|-----|-----|-----|-----|-------|-----|---|---|
| 1 | John BICKERTON | ENG | 63 | 70 | 71 | 69 | 273 | -11 | 666,660.00 | 458,576.38 |
| 2 | Padraig HARRINGTON | IRL | 69 | 70 | 69 | 66 | 274 | -10 | 444,440.00 | 305,717.59 |
| 3 | Ian POULTER | ENG | 68 | 70 | 69 | 69 | 276 | -8 | 206,666.67 | 142,160.10 |
| | Michael CAMPBELL | NZL | 65 | 70 | 68 | 73 | 276 | -8 | 206,666.67 | 142,160.10 |
| | Marcus FRASER | AUS | 70 | 68 | 69 | 69 | 276 | -8 | 206,666.67 | 142,160.10 |
| 6 | Anders HANSEN | DEN | 70 | 68 | 68 | 71 | 277 | -7 | 140,000.00 | 96,302.00 |
| 7 | Richard GREEN | AUS | 71 | 70 | 68 | 69 | 278 | -6 | 103,200.00 | 70,988.33 |
| | Peter O'MALLEY | AUS | 71 | 68 | 71 | 68 | 278 | -6 | 103,200.00 | 70,988.33 |
| | Andrew COLTART | SCO | 68 | 73 | 70 | 67 | 278 | -6 | 103,200.00 | 70,988.33 |
| 10 | Alastair FORSYTH | SCO | 69 | 69 | 70 | 71 | 279 | -5 | 76,800.00 | 52,828.53 |
| | José Maria OLAZÁBAL | ESP | 74 | 68 | 70 | 67 | 279 | -5 | 76,800.00 | 52,828.53 |
| 12 | Søren KJELDSEN | DEN | 70 | 71 | 66 | 73 | 280 | -4 | 61,920.00 | 42,593.00 |
| | Paul BROADHURST | ENG | 68 | 70 | 75 | 67 | 280 | -4 | 61,920.00 | 42,593.00 |
| | Angel CABRERA | ARG | 73 | 67 | 74 | 66 | 280 | -4 | 61,920.00 | 42,593.00 |
| | Paul LAWRIE | SCO | 69 | 68 | 75 | 68 | 280 | -4 | 61,920.00 | 42,593.00 |
| | Simon KHAN | ENG | 74 | 67 | 71 | 68 | 280 | -4 | 61,920.00 | 42,593.00 |
| 17 | Bradley DREDGE | WAL | 69 | 66 | 71 | 75 | 281 | -3 | 50,800.00 | 34,943.87 |
| | Jean VAN DE VELDE | FRA | 69 | 70 | 70 | 72 | 281 | -3 | 50,800.00 | 34,943.87 |
| | Robert KARLSSON | SWE | 69 | 72 | 68 | 72 | 281 | -3 | 50,800.00 | 34,943.87 |
| | Darren FICHARDT | RSA | 67 | 70 | 71 | 73 | 281 | -3 | 50,800.00 | 34,943.87 |
| 21 | Mattias ELIASSON | SWE | 69 | 70 | 69 | 74 | 282 | -2 | 42,200.00 | 29,028.18 |
| | Mark FOSTER | ENG | 67 | 71 | 71 | 73 | 282 | -2 | 42,200.00 | 29,028.18 |
| | Jean-François LUCQUIN | FRA | 69 | 71 | 73 | 69 | 282 | -2 | 42,200.00 | 29,028.18 |
| | Francesco MOLINARI | ITA | 71 | 70 | 71 | 70 | 282 | -2 | 42,200.00 | 29,028.18 |
| | Jamie SPENCE | ENG | 69 | 70 | 70 | 73 | 282 | -2 | 42,200.00 | 29,028.18 |
| | Stephen DODD | WAL | 69 | 71 | 71 | 71 | 282 | -2 | 42,200.00 | 29,028.18 |
| | Graeme STORM | ENG | 74 | 69 | 67 | 72 | 282 | -2 | 42,200.00 | 29,028.18 |
| | Adrien MÖRK | FRA | 74 | 66 | 70 | 70 | 282 | -2 | 42,200.00 | 29,028.18 |
| 29 | Phillip PRICE | WAL | 70 | 68 | 70 | 75 | 283 | -1 | 32,750.00 | 22,527.79 |
| | Ricardo GONZALEZ | ARG | 75 | 67 | 71 | 70 | 283 | -1 | 32,750.00 | 22,527.79 |
| | Markus BRIER | AUT | 68 | 68 | 78 | 69 | 283 | -1 | 32,750.00 | 22,527.79 |
| | Lee WESTWOOD | ENG | 71 | 71 | 73 | 68 | 283 | -1 | 32,750.00 | 22,527.79 |
| | Henrik STENSON | SWE | 67 | 70 | 70 | 76 | 283 | -1 | 32,750.00 | 22,527.79 |
| | Eduardo ROMERO | ARG | 71 | 67 | 72 | 73 | 283 | -1 | 32,750.00 | 22,527.79 |
| | Mark ROE | ENG | 70 | 70 | 68 | 75 | 283 | -1 | 32,750.00 | 22,527.79 |
| | Phillip ARCHER | ENG | 70 | 71 | 70 | 72 | 283 | -1 | 32,750.00 | 22,527.79 |
| 37 | Joakim BÄCKSTRÖM | SWE | 66 | 69 | 78 | 71 | 284 | 0 | 27,600.00 | 18,985.26 |
| | David LYNN | ENG | 71 | 72 | 70 | 71 | 284 | 0 | 27,600.00 | 18,985.26 |
| | Robert COLES | ENG | 73 | 68 | 71 | 72 | 284 | 0 | 27,600.00 | 18,985.26 |
| 40 | Simon WAKEFIELD | ENG | 73 | 70 | 75 | 67 | 285 | 1 | 23,200.00 | 15,958.62 |
| | Charl SCHWARTZEL | RSA | 70 | 72 | 72 | 71 | 285 | 1 | 23,200.00 | 15,958.62 |
| | Jean-François REMESY | FRA | 68 | 75 | 69 | 73 | 285 | 1 | 23,200.00 | 15,958.62 |
| | Peter LAWRIE | IRL | 70 | 69 | 75 | 71 | 285 | 1 | 23,200.00 | 15,958.62 |
| | Anthony WALL | ENG | 74 | 67 | 70 | 74 | 285 | 1 | 23,200.00 | 15,958.62 |
| | Malcolm MACKENZIE | ENG | 70 | 70 | 70 | 75 | 285 | 1 | 23,200.00 | 15,958.62 |
| | José Manuel LARA | ESP | 67 | 68 | 78 | 72 | 285 | 1 | 23,200.00 | 15,958.62 |
| | Gary MURPHY | IRL | 71 | 70 | 69 | 75 | 285 | 1 | 23,200.00 | 15,958.62 |
| 48 | Kenneth FERRIE | ENG | 70 | 73 | 72 | 71 | 286 | 2 | 18,000.00 | 12,381.69 |
| | Ross FISHER | ENG | 69 | 70 | 73 | 74 | 286 | 2 | 18,000.00 | 12,381.69 |
| | Richard FINCH | ENG | 68 | 74 | 74 | 70 | 286 | 2 | 18,000.00 | 12,381.69 |
| | David PARK | WAL | 68 | 69 | 70 | 79 | 286 | 2 | 18,000.00 | 12,381.69 |
| | Andrew BUTTERFIELD | ENG | 70 | 70 | 72 | 74 | 286 | 2 | 18,000.00 | 12,381.69 |
| | Alexandre KALEKA (AM) | FRA | 74 | 69 | 73 | 70 | 286 | 2 | | |
| 54 | Niclas FASTH | SWE | 69 | 73 | 69 | 76 | 287 | 3 | 14,000.00 | 9,630.20 |
| | Gregory BOURDY | FRA | 73 | 70 | 72 | 72 | 287 | 3 | 14,000.00 | 9,630.20 |
| | Steve WEBSTER | ENG | 72 | 71 | 72 | 72 | 287 | 3 | 14,000.00 | 9,630.20 |
| | Peter HANSON | SWE | 70 | 71 | 67 | 79 | 287 | 3 | 14,000.00 | 9,630.20 |
| | Nicolas COLSAERTS | BEL | 71 | 72 | 71 | 73 | 287 | 3 | 14,000.00 | 9,630.20 |
| 59 | Gary ORR | SCO | 70 | 64 | 76 | 78 | 288 | 4 | 12,000.00 | 8,254.46 |
| 60 | David CARTER | ENG | 67 | 70 | 73 | 79 | 289 | 5 | 10,800.00 | 7,429.01 |
| | Simon DYSON | ENG | 73 | 69 | 70 | 77 | 289 | 5 | 10,800.00 | 7,429.01 |
| | Peter GUSTAFSSON | SWE | 68 | 68 | 74 | 79 | 289 | 5 | 10,800.00 | 7,429.01 |
| | Alessandro TADINI | ITA | 71 | 71 | 72 | 75 | 289 | 5 | 10,800.00 | 7,429.01 |
| | Peter FOWLER | AUS | 75 | 68 | 75 | 71 | 289 | 5 | 10,800.00 | 7,429.01 |
| 65 | James KINGSTON | RSA | 72 | 69 | 70 | 80 | 291 | 7 | 9,600.00 | 6,603.57 |
| 66 | Nicolas JOAKIMIDES | FRA | 71 | 70 | 79 | 72 | 292 | 8 | 9,000.00 | 6,190.84 |
| | Søren HANSEN | DEN | 68 | 74 | 70 | 80 | 292 | 8 | 9,000.00 | 6,190.84 |
| 68 | Paul MCGINLEY | IRL | 72 | 71 | 73 | 77 | 293 | 9 | 8,400.00 | 5,778.12 |
| 69 | Benn BARHAM | ENG | 67 | 69 | 77 | 81 | 294 | 10 | 8,000.00 | 5,502.97 |
| 70 | Michael KIRK | RSA | 75 | 68 | 79 | 76 | 298 | 14 | 7,450.00 | 5,124.64 |
| | Sandy LYLE | SCO | 71 | 70 | 76 | 81 | 298 | 14 | 7,450.00 | 5,124.64 |
| 72 | Marcel SIEM | GER | 71 | 71 | 84 | 73 | 299 | 15 | 6,000.00 | 4,127.23 |

Jean Van de Velde

# Total Prize Fund
€4,006,000 £2,755,612

# Happy Hunting Ground

Steven O'Hara

| The K Club | | |
|---|---|---|
| Par | Yards | Metres |
| 72 | 7313 | 6690 |

| | | | | |
|---|---|---|---|---|
| 1 | Stephen DODD | 279 | -9 | |
| 2 | José Manuel LARA | 281 | -7 | |
| | Anthony WALL | 281 | -7 | |
| 4 | Simon KHAN | 282 | -6 | |
| | Paul McGINLEY | 282 | -6 | |
| | Jeev Milkha SINGH | 282 | -6 | |
| | Graeme STORM | 282 | -6 | |
| | Lee WESTWOOD | 282 | -6 | |
| 9 | Bradley DREDGE | 283 | -5 | |
| | Simon DYSON | 283 | -5 | |
| | Peter HANSON | 283 | -5 | |
| | Colin MONTGOMERIE | 283 | -5 | |

**S**tephen Dodd has good reason to regard Ireland, and the county of Kildare in particular, as a happy hunting ground. For it was here, in this rich stud farm land, that the softly spoken Welshman landed the 2006 Smurfit Kappa European Open little more than a year after his victory in the 2005 Nissan Irish Open. The two venues are only a few miles apart and for Dodd they will forever remain close to his heart.

The 1989 Amateur Champion, who turned professional the following year, broke his drought on The European Tour International Schedule with victory in the 2005 Volvo China Open before following up with his success in the Nissan Irish Open. Then came his greatest, and richest, triumph in the Smurfit Kappa European Open on the Smurfit Course, across the river from the Palmer Course where The Ryder Cup would be staged.

The 2006 tournament represented the 12th anniversary of the Smurfit Kappa European Open's domicile at The K Club and was celebrated by a record prize fund featuring a winner's cheque of €578,792 (£400,000), a handsome early birthday present indeed for the Welshman who turned 40 a week later.

Dodd's might not have been the name which sprung to most people's minds when potential winners were being discussed in the run-up to the event. It was not carved in stone like some of the high profile challengers including former winners Darren Clarke and Lee Westwood, or other Ryder Cup men such as Paul Casey,

Padraig Harrington, Paul McGinley and Colin Montgomerie, all of whom he left in his slipstream in the top 25 on his way to an efficient and clinical two shot victory.

It saw him join 2005 US Open Champion Michael Campbell and former Masters Champion Bernhard Langer as the only three players to have won both blue riband tournaments on Irish soil, although Europe's next two Ryder Cup Captains, Ian Woosnam and Nick Faldo, also hold both titles in their respective golfing CVs.

It was, on the whole, an enthralling contest, greatly enhanced by Ulster Bank's novel innovation of free admission and parking for the public on the opening day which helped swell the crowd to record numbers of almost 30,000. An already demanding golf course was toughened further over the weekend by a cocktail of wind and rain on Saturday and a dry but even stronger wind on Sunday.

The conditions obviously suited Dodd more than most, as he embarked on an exhibition of ball control. His consistency

## WEATHER REPORT

Round One   Round Two   Round Three   Round Four

## EUROPEAN TOUR ORDER OF MERIT
(After 31 tournaments)

| Pos | | € | |
|---|---|---|---|
| 1 | David HOWELL | 1,867,775.62 | |
| 2 | Paul CASEY | 1,421,809.33 | |
| 3 | Padraig HARRINGTON | 1,190,588.18 | |
| 4 | Colin MONTGOMERIE | 1,128,035.43 | |
| 5 | John BICKERTON | 1,009,045.12 | |
| 6 | Henrik STENSON | 969,681.97 | |
| 7 | Paul BROADHURST | 916,318.62 | |
| 8 | Thomas BJÖRN | 842,836.98 | |
| 9 | Miguel Angel JIMÉNEZ | 830,186.27 | |
| 10 | Nick O'HERN | 818,316.48 | |

# Smurfit Kappa European Open

## Straffan, Co.Kildare, Ireland
July 6-9 • 2006

Lee Westwood

was emphasised by the fact that he was never more than two shots behind a variety of international players who hovered at or near the top of the leaderboard over the four days.

Amongst them was Bradley Dredge, Dodd's partner when Wales won the World Golf Championships - Algarve World Cup in Portugal the previous November. At one stage on Saturday the younger Welshman was five ahead of the pack but fell foul of the weather, while others to lead, singly or jointly, over the first three days included Sweden's Niclas Fasth and José Manuel Lara of Spain. Adding to Sunday's excitement was the fact that, entering the final nine holes, there were a dozen players within two shots of the lead.

*It is a very fine layout which tests all aspects of your game but it can be a little exposed on this side of the river so it is a course that needs the weather to help it. I've played it now a couple of times when the weather has not been so great and when it is like that, it is a tough test indeed* – **Padraig Harrington**

José Manuel Lara

# Final Results

| Pos | Name | | Rd1 | Rd2 | Rd3 | Rd4 | Total | | € | £ |
|---|---|---|---|---|---|---|---|---|---|---|
| 1 | Stephen DODD | WAL | 67 | 69 | 73 | 70 | 279 | -9 | 578,792.00 | 400,000.00 |
| 2 | José Manuel LARA | ESP | 72 | 68 | 67 | 74 | 281 | -7 | 301,622.98 | 208,450.00 |
| | Anthony WALL | ENG | 70 | 68 | 70 | 73 | 281 | -7 | 301,622.98 | 208,450.00 |
| 4 | Jeev Milkha SINGH | IND | 70 | 68 | 74 | 70 | 282 | -6 | 126,685.99 | 87,552.00 |
| | Paul MCGINLEY | IRL | 75 | 71 | 67 | 69 | 282 | -6 | 126,685.99 | 87,552.00 |
| | Simon KHAN | ENG | 68 | 73 | 68 | 73 | 282 | -6 | 126,685.99 | 87,552.00 |
| | Lee WESTWOOD | ENG | 70 | 75 | 67 | 70 | 282 | -6 | 126,685.99 | 87,552.00 |
| | Graeme STORM | ENG | 70 | 73 | 69 | 70 | 282 | -6 | 126,685.99 | 87,552.00 |
| 9 | Simon DYSON | ENG | 69 | 74 | 71 | 69 | 283 | -5 | 67,718.66 | 46,800.00 |
| | Bradley DREDGE | WAL | 65 | 70 | 75 | 73 | 283 | -5 | 67,718.66 | 46,800.00 |
| | Peter HANSON | SWE | 68 | 74 | 69 | 72 | 283 | -5 | 67,718.66 | 46,800.00 |
| | Colin MONTGOMERIE | SCO | 69 | 71 | 72 | 71 | 283 | -5 | 67,718.66 | 46,800.00 |
| 13 | Robert KARLSSON | SWE | 73 | 69 | 75 | 67 | 284 | -4 | 54,522.21 | 37,680.00 |
| | Steven O'HARA | SCO | 71 | 69 | 70 | 74 | 284 | -4 | 54,522.21 | 37,680.00 |
| 15 | Thongchai JAIDEE | THA | 69 | 74 | 71 | 71 | 285 | -3 | 50,007.63 | 34,560.00 |
| | Darren CLARKE | NIR | 69 | 68 | 72 | 76 | 285 | -3 | 50,007.63 | 34,560.00 |
| 17 | Angel CABRERA | ARG | 66 | 78 | 69 | 73 | 286 | -2 | 44,914.26 | 31,040.00 |
| | Jamie SPENCE | ENG | 68 | 72 | 69 | 77 | 286 | -2 | 44,914.26 | 31,040.00 |
| | Anders HANSEN | DEN | 69 | 72 | 74 | 71 | 286 | -2 | 44,914.26 | 31,040.00 |
| 20 | Maarten LAFEBER | NED | 70 | 73 | 70 | 74 | 287 | -1 | 38,779.06 | 26,800.00 |
| | Richard GREEN | AUS | 73 | 68 | 73 | 73 | 287 | -1 | 38,779.06 | 26,800.00 |
| | Padraig HARRINGTON | IRL | 70 | 75 | 69 | 73 | 287 | -1 | 38,779.06 | 26,800.00 |
| | Peter O'MALLEY | AUS | 67 | 74 | 73 | 73 | 287 | -1 | 38,779.06 | 26,800.00 |
| | Tom LEHMAN | USA | 71 | 70 | 70 | 76 | 287 | -1 | 38,779.06 | 26,800.00 |
| | Paul CASEY | ENG | 66 | 73 | 71 | 77 | 287 | -1 | 38,779.06 | 26,800.00 |
| 26 | Emanuele CANONICA | ITA | 72 | 70 | 71 | 76 | 289 | 1 | 32,991.14 | 22,800.00 |
| | Kenneth FERRIE | ENG | 73 | 72 | 70 | 74 | 289 | 1 | 32,991.14 | 22,800.00 |
| | Sam LITTLE | ENG | 72 | 70 | 74 | 73 | 289 | 1 | 32,991.14 | 22,800.00 |
| | Jean-François LUCQUIN | FRA | 71 | 73 | 73 | 72 | 289 | 1 | 32,991.14 | 22,800.00 |
| | Graeme MCDOWELL | NIR | 69 | 76 | 72 | 72 | 289 | 1 | 32,991.14 | 22,800.00 |
| 31 | Søren HANSEN | DEN | 72 | 70 | 77 | 71 | 290 | 2 | 28,302.93 | 19,560.00 |
| | Henrik STENSON | SWE | 71 | 70 | 75 | 74 | 290 | 2 | 28,302.93 | 19,560.00 |
| | Damien MCGRANE | IRL | 69 | 72 | 73 | 76 | 290 | 2 | 28,302.93 | 19,560.00 |
| | Simon WAKEFIELD | ENG | 70 | 72 | 74 | 74 | 290 | 2 | 28,302.93 | 19,560.00 |
| 35 | Niclas FASTH | SWE | 65 | 75 | 74 | 77 | 291 | 3 | 24,309.26 | 16,800.00 |
| | Markus BRIER | AUT | 73 | 71 | 72 | 75 | 291 | 3 | 24,309.26 | 16,800.00 |
| | Retief GOOSEN | RSA | 69 | 72 | 74 | 76 | 291 | 3 | 24,309.26 | 16,800.00 |
| | Stephen BROWNE | IRL | 73 | 67 | 72 | 79 | 291 | 3 | 24,309.26 | 16,800.00 |
| | Steve WEBSTER | ENG | 70 | 73 | 77 | 71 | 291 | 3 | 24,309.26 | 16,800.00 |
| | Søren KJELDSEN | DEN | 69 | 69 | 79 | 74 | 291 | 3 | 24,309.26 | 16,800.00 |
| 41 | Phillip ARCHER | ENG | 72 | 70 | 74 | 76 | 292 | 4 | 21,531.06 | 14,880.00 |
| | Louis OOSTHUIZEN | RSA | 70 | 71 | 71 | 80 | 292 | 4 | 21,531.06 | 14,880.00 |
| 43 | Andres ROMERO | ARG | 71 | 75 | 68 | 79 | 293 | 5 | 19,794.69 | 13,680.00 |
| | Nicolas COLSAERTS | BEL | 67 | 76 | 75 | 75 | 293 | 5 | 19,794.69 | 13,680.00 |
| | Marcel SIEM | GER | 71 | 72 | 72 | 78 | 293 | 5 | 19,794.69 | 13,680.00 |
| 46 | Francesco MOLINARI | ITA | 70 | 73 | 71 | 80 | 294 | 6 | 16,669.21 | 11,520.00 |
| | Alessandro TADINI | ITA | 77 | 68 | 71 | 78 | 294 | 6 | 16,669.21 | 11,520.00 |
| | Jamie DONALDSON | WAL | 70 | 73 | 75 | 76 | 294 | 6 | 16,669.21 | 11,520.00 |
| | David GRIFFITHS | ENG | 71 | 75 | 71 | 77 | 294 | 6 | 16,669.21 | 11,520.00 |
| | Christian CÉVAËR | FRA | 71 | 69 | 78 | 76 | 294 | 6 | 16,669.21 | 11,520.00 |
| | Charl SCHWARTZEL | RSA | 73 | 72 | 73 | 76 | 294 | 6 | 16,669.21 | 11,520.00 |
| 52 | David PARK | WAL | 72 | 73 | 73 | 77 | 295 | 7 | 13,196.46 | 9,120.00 |
| | Mark FOSTER | ENG | 73 | 71 | 76 | 75 | 295 | 7 | 13,196.46 | 9,120.00 |
| | Ian POULTER | ENG | 72 | 72 | 75 | 76 | 295 | 7 | 13,196.46 | 9,120.00 |
| | Peter BAKER | ENG | 70 | 74 | 71 | 80 | 295 | 7 | 13,196.46 | 9,120.00 |
| 56 | Eduardo ROMERO | ARG | 71 | 72 | 77 | 76 | 296 | 8 | 10,487.71 | 7,248.00 |
| | Peter SENIOR | AUS | 73 | 73 | 70 | 80 | 296 | 8 | 10,487.71 | 7,248.00 |
| | Andrew COLTART | SCO | 70 | 75 | 76 | 75 | 296 | 8 | 10,487.71 | 7,248.00 |
| | Tom WHITEHOUSE | ENG | 72 | 74 | 75 | 75 | 296 | 8 | 10,487.71 | 7,248.00 |
| | David HIGGINS | IRL | 74 | 72 | 73 | 77 | 296 | 8 | 10,487.71 | 7,248.00 |
| 61 | Mattias ELIASSON | SWE | 71 | 73 | 74 | 79 | 297 | 9 | 9,029.16 | 6,240.00 |
| | Andrew MARSHALL | ENG | 74 | 72 | 73 | 78 | 297 | 9 | 9,029.16 | 6,240.00 |
| | Jyoti RANDHAWA | IND | 68 | 78 | 73 | 78 | 297 | 9 | 9,029.16 | 6,240.00 |
| 64 | Leif WESTERBERG | SWE | 70 | 73 | 76 | 79 | 298 | 10 | 8,334.60 | 5,760.00 |
| 65 | Gonzalo FDEZ-CASTAÑO | ESP | 75 | 71 | 74 | 79 | 299 | 11 | 7,987.33 | 5,520.00 |
| 66 | Marcus FRASER | AUS | 72 | 73 | 79 | 76 | 300 | 12 | 7,292.78 | 5,040.00 |
| | Philip GOLDING | ENG | 71 | 74 | 75 | 80 | 300 | 12 | 7,292.78 | 5,040.00 |
| | Gary EMERSON | ENG | 70 | 71 | 77 | 82 | 300 | 12 | 7,292.78 | 5,040.00 |
| 69 | Steven JEPPESEN | SWE | 75 | 70 | 79 | 77 | 301 | 13 | 6,468.00 | 4,470.00 |
| | Peter GUSTAFSSON | SWE | 70 | 75 | 74 | 82 | 301 | 13 | 6,468.00 | 4,470.00 |
| 71 | Michael KIRK | RSA | 74 | 69 | 78 | 81 | 302 | 14 | 5,207.50 | 3,598.87 |
| | Marc CAYEUX | ZIM | 73 | 71 | 80 | 78 | 302 | 14 | 5,207.50 | 3,598.87 |
| 73 | David DIXON | ENG | 75 | 71 | 74 | 83 | 303 | 15 | 5,200.00 | 3,593.69 |
| | Miguel CARBALLO | ARG | 73 | 73 | 76 | 81 | 303 | 15 | 5,200.00 | 3,593.69 |
| | Simon THORNTON | IRL | 76 | 70 | 76 | 81 | 303 | 15 | 5,200.00 | 3,593.69 |

## Total Prize Fund
€3,498,770  £2,417,978

Dodd, however, made his move away from the pack with three birdies on the back nine; one of them at the 16th where he holed from five feet, and another at the 17th where a massive 50 foot putt dropped into the cup, to effectively end the tournament as a contest.

The unflappable Welshman is not one to make a fuss about winning but he did allow himself a smile and a wave to the gallery as he crossed the bridge to the last green to tap in his final putt for par, a round of 70 and a nine under par total of 279, two ahead of the chasing pack. England's Anthony Wall and Lara shared second place while another two Englishmen, Simon Khan and Graeme Storm, India's Jeev Milka Singh, and McGinley and Westwood finished a shot further back in a share of fourth.

Patience was the key to Dodd's success in Ireland just as perseverance has been the hallmark of his entire life as a professional golfer. "I had a pretty poor start to the year and winning here was not what I expected but golf's a funny game," he said. "You couldn't go looking for birdies out there, the wind was too tough. So I just tried to be patient all weekend and keep the ball in play."

While the Welshman ultimately triumphed, McGinley made the most remarkable recovery of the tournament. He left for Dublin Airport early on the Friday afternoon convinced he had missed the cut as he was then in 91st position.

He was sitting in the airport, his clubs and bags already loaded, when his wife phoned to tell him the weather had begun to make an about turn and suggested he do the same thing. Fortunately, his flight was delayed and he was able to get his luggage unloaded without too much inconvenience to his fellow passengers.

Having made the cut right on the two over par mark, he then proceeded to card superb rounds of 67 and 69 over the weekend to finish within three shots of the winning total.

Dodd was right. Golf is a funny game.

**Colm Smith**

Simon Khan

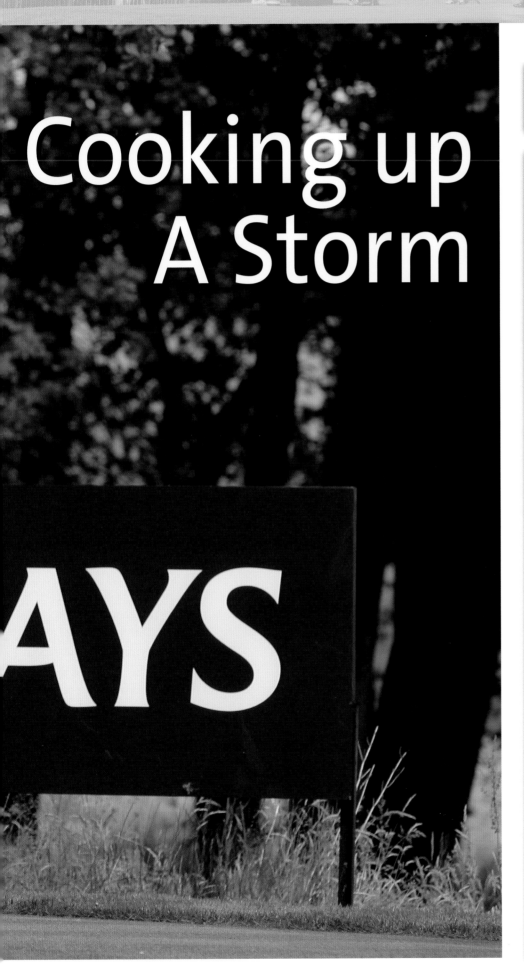

# Cooking up A Storm

| Loch Lomond | | |
| --- | --- | --- |
| Par | Yards | Metres |
| 71 | 7139 | 6524 |

| Pos | Name | Score | To Par | |
| --- | --- | --- | --- | --- |
| 1 | Johan EDFORS | 271 | -13 | |
| 2 | Luke DONALD | 273 | -11 | |
| | Andres ROMERO | 273 | -11 | |
| | Charl SCHWARTZEL | 273 | -11 | |
| 5 | Benn BARHAM | 274 | -10 | |
| | Thomas BJÖRN | 274 | -10 | |
| | Tim CLARK | 274 | -10 | |
| | Darren CLARKE | 274 | -10 | |
| 9 | Ernie ELS | 275 | -9 | |
| | Sergio GARCIA | 275 | -9 | |
| | Raphaël JACQUELIN | 275 | -9 | |

## WEATHER REPORT

Round One    Round Two    Round Three    Round Four

## EUROPEAN TOUR ORDER OF MERIT
(After 32 tournaments)

| Pos | Name | € | |
| --- | --- | --- | --- |
| 1 | David HOWELL | 1,892,725.35 | |
| 2 | Paul CASEY | 1,421,809.33 | |
| 3 | Johan EDFORS | 1,243,770.60 | |
| 4 | Padraig HARRINGTON | 1,190,588.18 | |
| 5 | Colin MONTGOMERIE | 1,162,514.57 | |
| 6 | John BICKERTON | 1,009,045.12 | |
| 7 | Henrik STENSON | 969,681.97 | |
| 8 | Thomas BJÖRN | 957,536.43 | |
| 9 | Paul BROADHURST | 931,912.20 | |
| 10 | Miguel Angel JIMÉNEZ | 830,186.27 | |

# The Barclays Scottish Open

**Glasgow, Scotland**
July 13-16 • 2006

Whether or not a sense of trepidation about eating platefuls of steaming haggis, neeps and tatties during his stay in Scotland influenced the decision of Johan Edfors to bring his own chef to the Bonnie Banks was unclear. What was not in any doubt, however, during The Barclays Scottish Open, was how Edfors cooked up a storm to claim the most significant win of his career.

Andres Romero

Crunching 300 yard drives and requiring just 24 putts on Loch Lomond's manicured greens in the final round, the 30 year old secured his third win of the 2006 season with a 13 under par total of 271. On the way, he also matched the previous lowest closing score of 63 which also earned Thomas Levet a famous victory in the 2004 tournament. Such a formidable combination of power and touch enabled the Swede to surpass his earlier successes in the TCL Classic and The Quinn Direct British Masters.

Starting 13 groups behind the third round leaders, Thomas Björn and Darren Clarke, Edfors, who first visited Scotland as an amateur 13 years earlier to compete in the Doug Sanders World Junior Tournament in Aberdeen, this time went to work each day fortified by the cordon bleu cooking of one of his compatriots.

The Swede had brought his mother and father, Karin and Bengt, his girlfriend Cecilia, his sister Kristina and brother-in-law Niclas, to Loch Lomond for a week's holiday. In order to make the week go with a swing, he also invited the head chef from a Michelin starred restaurant in Gothenburg to cook everyone in the party breakfast and dinner at their lodge in the grounds at nearby Cameron House.

Buoyed by the feast, Edfors was hungry to make up ground in the last round as he roared to the turn in 30 blows, carding six birdies and avoiding bogeys. On the back nine, other than a momentary blip on the 17th, his golf remained outstanding. Although sorry to miss out on a second Barclays Scottish Open title, Björn was gracious enough to compliment his fellow Scandinavian. "The guy played magnificently," said the Dane.

Bearing a striking resemblance to the Wimbledon champion Roger Federer, Edfors' eight under par closing effort, appropriately bore similarities, in terms of tactics, to serve and volley tennis. The Swede hit the ball hard off the tee and showed a subtle touch on the greens. "He certainly looks like Federer and if he plays golf even half as well as Federer plays tennis, then he'll be some player," observed Colin Montgomerie.

Edfors finished the week, as he had begun it, by playing golf in a thrilling fashion. On Thursday, the Swede surged into a share of the lead on 65 with Scotland's own David Drysdale, who played on a sponsor's invitation.

Having re-built his swing with the help of coaches Richard Fors and Lawrence

Sergio Garcia

BARCLAYS
SCOTTISH OPEN
**6**
625 YDS 572 m PAR 5
Long Loch Lomond

Evertsson, Edfors enjoyed the privilege of playing in the same group as the three time US Open Champion, Hale Irwin, for the first two rounds. On day one the 61 year old produced a coruscating 3-3-3-2-3 finish – five birdies in a row – to post 68. "I don't think I've ever seen anyone hit better long irons or fairway woods than Hale," admitted Edfors. "He's getting shorter off the tee, but every shot went straight at the flag. It was pretty amazing."

Edfors kept up his own good work with a 69 on day two when the spotlight switched to Clarke, whose wife Heather remained gravely ill. How Clarke could produce a 65 of such peerless quality under the circumstances astonished his playing partners – José Maria Olazábal and

*Carl Pettersson and Luke Donald*

*" Loch Lomond is one of the best golf courses I have ever played. It's well designed and I don't think there's any hole on it that could be considered weak. When you add the setting, the Loch and the mountains and everything around, it becomes an almost mystical place " – Benn Barham*

Commodities • FX • Derivatives • Equity Products • Loans • Bonds • Linkers • Emerging Markets • Fixed Income • Research • Private Equity

# Whole in one

**BARCLAYS CAPITAL**

Ian Poulter presents a cheque to Hazel Irvine of the BBC for the Sport Relief charity on behalf of The European Tour Sport Relief Challenge. The money for the 2006 edition was donated by The European Tour, sponsors BMW and Barclays, and host venues Wentworth (BMW Championship) and Loch Lomond (The Barclays Scottish Open) which took the total amount received to £110,000.00 from 2002, 2004 and 2006

Montgomerie – as much as the record crowds who swarmed to Loch Lomond.

Carding seven birdies and dropping just one shot on the 11th, Clarke was delighted to perform so well in front of the huge galleries. The Irishman had been working with Ewen Murray, the former Scottish professional who now commentates for Sky Sports, on hitting the ball harder. "If the club is in the right spot then I can do that and I'm feeling quite comfortable," he reported.

On Saturday, Clarke retained a share of the lead with 71 as Björn captured the headlines in Sunday's newspapers by following up Friday's breathtaking 64 with a fine 66. Edfors, inexplicably, dropped back into the pack with what seemed to be a costly 74 to trail the leading duo by six shots.

With players of the calibre of Angel Cabrera, defending champion Tim Clark, Luke Donald, Ernie Els, Sergio Garcia, David Howell, Tom Lehman, Colin Montgomerie, Ian Poulter, and Lee Westwood separating him from the lead, the possibility of Edfors incinerating the opposition in the fourth round could only have occured to the player himself, his family and friends.

However, in the shimmering heat of another perfect summer's day when the course and setting may have never looked more beautiful, it was Edfors who feasted with a round which did the sublime surroundings more than justice

**Mike Aitken**
*The Scotsman*

Raphaël Jacquelin

# Final Results

| Pos | Name | | Rd1 | Rd2 | Rd3 | Rd4 | Total | | € | £ |
|---|---|---|---|---|---|---|---|---|---|---|
| 1 | Johan EDFORS | SWE | 65 | 69 | 74 | 63 | 271 | -13 | 577,540.02 | 400,000.00 |
| 2 | Luke DONALD | ENG | 68 | 69 | 70 | 66 | 273 | -11 | 258,401.03 | 178,966.67 |
| | Andres ROMERO | ARG | 72 | 64 | 68 | 69 | 273 | -11 | 258,401.03 | 178,966.67 |
| | Charl SCHWARTZEL | RSA | 68 | 66 | 72 | 67 | 273 | -11 | 258,401.03 | 178,966.67 |
| 5 | Tim CLARK | RSA | 69 | 67 | 69 | 69 | 274 | -10 | 114,699.45 | 79,440.00 |
| | Darren CLARKE | NIR | 66 | 65 | 71 | 72 | 274 | -10 | 114,699.45 | 79,440.00 |
| | Thomas BJÖRN | DEN | 72 | 64 | 66 | 72 | 274 | -10 | 114,699.45 | 79,440.00 |
| | Benn BARHAM | ENG | 71 | 68 | 65 | 70 | 274 | -10 | 114,699.45 | 79,440.00 |
| 9 | Ernie ELS | RSA | 70 | 69 | 67 | 69 | 275 | -9 | 70,228.87 | 48,640.00 |
| | Sergio GARCIA | ESP | 71 | 67 | 69 | 68 | 275 | -9 | 70,228.87 | 48,640.00 |
| | Raphaël JACQUELIN | FRA | 68 | 72 | 65 | 70 | 275 | -9 | 70,228.87 | 48,640.00 |
| 12 | Kenneth FERRIE | ENG | 70 | 69 | 71 | 65 | 276 | -8 | 57,696.25 | 39,960.00 |
| | Thongchai JAIDEE | THA | 72 | 69 | 66 | 69 | 276 | -8 | 57,696.25 | 39,960.00 |
| 14 | Ian GARBUTT | ENG | 71 | 67 | 69 | 70 | 277 | -7 | 44,632.29 | 30,912.00 |
| | Angel CABRERA | ARG | 71 | 66 | 70 | 70 | 277 | -7 | 44,632.29 | 30,912.00 |
| | David LYNN | ENG | 70 | 68 | 69 | 70 | 277 | -7 | 44,632.29 | 30,912.00 |
| | Greg OWEN | ENG | 74 | 66 | 69 | 68 | 277 | -7 | 44,632.29 | 30,912.00 |
| | Retief GOOSEN | RSA | 70 | 69 | 71 | 67 | 277 | -7 | 44,632.29 | 30,912.00 |
| | Anders HANSEN | DEN | 74 | 66 | 70 | 67 | 277 | -7 | 44,632.29 | 30,912.00 |
| | Jean-François REMESY | FRA | 73 | 65 | 67 | 72 | 277 | -7 | 44,632.29 | 30,912.00 |
| | Mark FOSTER | ENG | 70 | 68 | 68 | 71 | 277 | -7 | 44,632.29 | 30,912.00 |
| | Ian POULTER | ENG | 70 | 67 | 70 | 70 | 277 | -7 | 44,632.29 | 30,912.00 |
| | Søren HANSEN | DEN | 73 | 66 | 71 | 67 | 277 | -7 | 44,632.29 | 30,912.00 |
| 24 | Colin MONTGOMERIE | SCO | 72 | 66 | 69 | 71 | 278 | -6 | 34,479.14 | 23,880.00 |
| | Damien MCGRANE | IRL | 68 | 66 | 71 | 73 | 278 | -6 | 34,479.14 | 23,880.00 |
| | Phillip ARCHER | ENG | 72 | 67 | 70 | 69 | 278 | -6 | 34,479.14 | 23,880.00 |
| | Stephen GALLACHER | SCO | 70 | 71 | 67 | 70 | 278 | -6 | 34,479.14 | 23,880.00 |
| | Paul LAWRIE | SCO | 70 | 71 | 70 | 67 | 278 | -6 | 34,479.14 | 23,880.00 |
| | Tom LEHMAN | USA | 69 | 72 | 66 | 71 | 278 | -6 | 34,479.14 | 23,880.00 |
| 30 | Lee WESTWOOD | ENG | 69 | 67 | 71 | 72 | 279 | -5 | 30,320.85 | 21,000.00 |
| | David DRYSDALE | SCO | 65 | 70 | 69 | 75 | 279 | -5 | 30,320.85 | 21,000.00 |
| 32 | Richard FINCH | ENG | 70 | 69 | 69 | 72 | 280 | -4 | 27,721.92 | 19,200.00 |
| | David BRANSDON | AUS | 67 | 71 | 73 | 69 | 280 | -4 | 27,721.92 | 19,200.00 |
| | Marcel SIEM | GER | 69 | 69 | 72 | 70 | 280 | -4 | 27,721.92 | 19,200.00 |
| 35 | David HOWELL | ENG | 70 | 68 | 71 | 72 | 281 | -3 | 24,949.73 | 17,280.00 |
| | Carl PETTERSSON | SWE | 68 | 70 | 71 | 72 | 281 | -3 | 24,949.73 | 17,280.00 |
| | Simon KHAN | ENG | 69 | 72 | 69 | 71 | 281 | -3 | 24,949.73 | 17,280.00 |
| | Oliver WILSON | ENG | 74 | 65 | 72 | 70 | 281 | -3 | 24,949.73 | 17,280.00 |
| 39 | Simon WAKEFIELD | ENG | 70 | 69 | 71 | 72 | 282 | -2 | 20,791.44 | 14,400.00 |
| | Jamie DONALDSON | WAL | 68 | 67 | 71 | 76 | 282 | -2 | 20,791.44 | 14,400.00 |
| | José-Filipe LIMA | POR | 68 | 70 | 71 | 73 | 282 | -2 | 20,791.44 | 14,400.00 |
| | Brett RUMFORD | AUS | 72 | 67 | 75 | 68 | 282 | -2 | 20,791.44 | 14,400.00 |
| | Søren KJELDSEN | DEN | 70 | 69 | 73 | 70 | 282 | -2 | 20,791.44 | 14,400.00 |
| | Maarten LAFEBER | NED | 71 | 69 | 69 | 73 | 282 | -2 | 20,791.44 | 14,400.00 |
| | Peter O'MALLEY | AUS | 69 | 69 | 74 | 70 | 282 | -2 | 20,791.44 | 14,400.00 |
| | Jean-François LUCQUIN | FRA | 71 | 70 | 68 | 73 | 282 | -2 | 20,791.44 | 14,400.00 |
| 47 | Paul MCGINLEY | IRL | 69 | 71 | 69 | 74 | 283 | -1 | 15,593.58 | 10,800.00 |
| | Paul BROADHURST | ENG | 69 | 71 | 70 | 73 | 283 | -1 | 15,593.58 | 10,800.00 |
| | José María OLAZÁBAL | ESP | 67 | 74 | 69 | 73 | 283 | -1 | 15,593.58 | 10,800.00 |
| | Gonzalo FDEZ-CASTAÑO | ESP | 69 | 68 | 71 | 75 | 283 | -1 | 15,593.58 | 10,800.00 |
| | Gary CLARK | ENG | 69 | 71 | 72 | 71 | 283 | -1 | 15,593.58 | 10,800.00 |
| | Andrew BUTTERFIELD | ENG | 67 | 73 | 73 | 70 | 283 | -1 | 15,593.58 | 10,800.00 |
| | Jarmo SANDELIN | SWE | 74 | 67 | 70 | 72 | 283 | -1 | 15,593.58 | 10,800.00 |
| 54 | Simon DYSON | ENG | 70 | 70 | 69 | 75 | 284 | 0 | 11,504.60 | 7,968.00 |
| | José Manuel LARA | ESP | 68 | 70 | 73 | 73 | 284 | 0 | 11,504.60 | 7,968.00 |
| | Steve WEBSTER | ENG | 73 | 68 | 71 | 72 | 284 | 0 | 11,504.60 | 7,968.00 |
| | Garry HOUSTON | WAL | 68 | 71 | 72 | 73 | 284 | 0 | 11,504.60 | 7,968.00 |
| | Gregory HAVRET | FRA | 69 | 67 | 73 | 75 | 284 | 0 | 11,504.60 | 7,968.00 |
| | Edoardo MOLINARI (AM) | ITA | 71 | 70 | 71 | 72 | 284 | 0 | | |
| 60 | Raymond RUSSELL | SCO | 67 | 69 | 75 | 74 | 285 | 1 | 9,875.93 | 6,840.00 |
| | Shiv KAPUR | IND | 72 | 69 | 72 | 72 | 285 | 1 | 9,875.93 | 6,840.00 |
| 62 | David GRIFFITHS | ENG | 70 | 71 | 70 | 75 | 286 | 2 | 9,182.89 | 6,360.00 |
| | Richard BLAND | ENG | 71 | 69 | 75 | 71 | 286 | 2 | 9,182.89 | 6,360.00 |
| 64 | Barry LANE | ENG | 68 | 72 | 72 | 75 | 287 | 3 | 8,489.84 | 5,880.00 |
| | Jonathan LOMAS | ENG | 69 | 71 | 74 | 73 | 287 | 3 | 8,489.84 | 5,880.00 |
| 66 | Hale IRWIN | USA | 68 | 72 | 72 | 76 | 288 | 4 | 7,970.05 | 5,520.00 |
| 67 | Nicolas COLSAERTS | BEL | 69 | 70 | 79 | 71 | 289 | 5 | 7,623.53 | 5,280.00 |
| 68 | Joakim HAEGGMAN | SWE | 72 | 69 | 72 | 80 | 293 | 9 | 7,277.00 | 5,040.00 |
| 69 | David HIGGINS | IRL | 71 | 70 | 74 | 80 | 295 | 11 | 6,930.48 | 4,800.00 |

# Total Prize Fund
€3,452,330 £2,391,060

# Tears of a Champion

**Royal Liverpool Golf Club**

| Par | Yards | Metres |
|-----|-------|--------|
| 72  | 7258  | 6637   |

| | | | | |
|--|--|--|--|--|
| 1 | **Tiger WOODS** | 270 | -18 | |
| 2 | Chris DiMARCO | 272 | -16 | |
| 3 | Ernie ELS | 275 | -13 | |
| 4 | Jim FURYK | 276 | -12 | |
| 5 | Sergio GARCIA | 277 | -11 | |
| | Hideto TANIHARA | 277 | -11 | |
| 7 | Angel CABRERA | 278 | -10 | |
| 8 | Carl PETTERSSON | 279 | -9 | |
| | Andres ROMERO | 279 | -9 | |
| | Adam SCOTT | 279 | -9 | |

**WEATHER REPORT**

| Round One | Round Two | Round Three | Round Four |
|-----------|-----------|-------------|------------|

**EUROPEAN TOUR ORDER OF MERIT**
(After 33 tournaments)

| Pos | | € | |
|-----|--|---|--|
| 1 | **David HOWELL** | 1,895,630.81 | |
| 2 | Paul CASEY | 1,435,029.17 | |
| 3 | Johan EDFORS | 1,247,039.24 | |
| 4 | Padraig HARRINGTON | 1,193,856.82 | |
| 5 | Colin MONTGOMERIE | 1,165,783.21 | |
| 6 | Ernie ELS | 1,149,786.02 | |
| 7 | John BICKERTON | 1,025,907.16 | |
| 8 | Henrik STENSON | 986,544.01 | |
| 9 | Thomas BJÖRN | 979,119.85 | |
| 10 | Paul BROADHURST | 974,186.64 | |

WHAT IF SECURITY WASN'T A CAGE?

WHAT IF INSTEAD OF KEEPING THINGS OUT,
IT LET AMAZING THINGS IN?

WHAT IF IT MADE YOU BOLDER, MORE AMBITIOUS
AND ENABLED YOU TO ACCOMPLISH MORE THAN
YOU EVER THOUGHT POSSIBLE?

WHAT IF SECURITY COULD SET YOU FREE?

Security will set you free.

## UNISYS
Secure Business Solutions. imagine it. done.

The tears, when they came, were almost as impressive as the performance had been over the previous four hours at Royal Liverpool Golf Club.

Somehow, in the supremely focused playing of this last round of The Open Championship, Tiger Woods found the conduit to relieving the grief he had been seeking over the previous ten weeks since the death of his father, guide and mentor, Earl.

As the final putt dropped to seal his 11th Major victory, drawing him level with Walter Hagen in this regard and leaving him just seven short of the record 18 wins posted so magnificently by Jack Nicklaus, Woods returned to earth from wherever he had been on this Sunday.

And everyone heard the bump. Or rather they saw the tears, great rolling waves of emotion that cascaded down the cheeks of this wonderfully gifted player as he realised this was the first big triumph his dad had not witnessed. It will, however, not be the last.

*Richard Sterne*

# The 135th Open Championship

## Hoylake, Cheshire, England
### July 20-23 • 2006

Anthony Wall

While Woods may clutch some small consolation as he considers this last thought, the rest of the field assembled on The Wirral for the first time in 39 years may do nothing but reach out to touch the edges of despair as they consider the fine detail of a Championship that was embraced by the local people more enthusiastically than anywhere outside the Home of Golf itself, St Andrews.

They all came, they all saw what lay before them and almost all of them threw in the towel in the face of a determined Woods attack. This is not to detract from the effort of the eventual Champion, but it is to suggest something is seriously wrong here.

Six years ago Sir Michael Bonallack reflected on Tiger's runaway win during the US Open Championship at Pebble Beach and said: "I

have never seen so many players collapse visibly when one man's name hit the top of the leaderboard. Quite extraordinary."

The traces of contempt that accompanied this small statement from perhaps the finest amateur combatant the British Isles ever has produced were there to see. No wonder. Golf is lucky to have Tiger Woods as its current leader but the grand, old game is sadly lacking in contemporary figures strong enough to take on the American in full and irresistible flight.

They try, certainly, but the real question is: 'Do they try hard enough?' The answer, often seems to be a resounding 'no'. This is unfortunate, not just for their ambitions but for those of us who prefer sport as a contest rather than an exhibition and who only truly savour a Championship if the eventual

*It's the people who have made it this week and it felt very much like The People's Open. The spectators have been magnificent, the course has been magnificent, Tiger was magnificent. It was magnificent for everyone. Especially golf* **– Thomas Björn**

winner comes to that last hole needing, at worst, a par to secure victory. Anything else is theatre and, like theatre, it carries all the unpredictability of a widely read script.

The hard fact is that if everyone plays as well as they can and if each then enjoys the smidgeon of good fortune any champion must enjoy, then Tiger Woods will win. The other fact is that this is a very bad thought to carry with you into an Open arena. Unless, of course, you are Tiger, in which case it is the best thought of all.

Chris DiMarco may be exempted from any of the above criticism. The New Yorker is many things, but shy and retiring are not amongst them, and you would want him on your side when the fight is at its height and your back is against a wall. His battle in the group ahead of Woods on another stiflingly hot day offered some semblance of a contest until Tiger glanced at a leaderboard over the back nine and swiftly racked up half a gear to secure the birdies that reduced his compatriot's efforts to little more than interesting.

His other rivals on this Sunday wounded themselves before he had the chance to aim a blow. Sergio Garcia showed again his reluctance to perform anywhere near the parameters of his talent during a vital fourth round, his banana yellow outfit swiftly retreating into the dusty background.

Ernie Els, having shown real signs of caressing again the game he brought to the table before freakishly injuring his left knee in the middle of 2005, felt the old doubts return, his wedge play suffering most, his campaign speared by a sudden lack of distance control.

Jim Furyk, too, never controlled himself properly while Angel Cabrera teased his supporters with his power before disappointing them with his inability to direct it properly during the hottest moments.

So, in truth, we were left with the most compelling exhibition of cold-eyed destruction many of us have ever witnessed. Woods brought with him to Lancashire his desire and his talent. He left out his driver, the one club that now causes him problems.

Hoylake's scorched acres afforded him this luxury, his ball snapping forward off fairways burned to a mixture of bronze and blond, terrain that carried all the propelling quality of the nearby motorway tarmac.

Robert Rock

Ernie Els

Like Jack Nicklaus, RBS sponsored Luke Donald knows that to be an effective performer takes more than just raw talent; success is determined by the ability to think on your feet and make adjustments mid game. This versatility is even more important when considering Luke's tough schedule, involving the totally different playing conditions of golf courses on both the European and US Tours.

At The Royal Bank of Scotland, we also believe that being responsive to market conditions is what sets us apart from our competition and enables us to consistently deliver results for our clients. It's one reason why we've grown to be one of the biggest banking groups in the world.

rbs.co.uk

## Make it happen

*Seve Ballesteros*

His game plan was simple. As ever, he blitzed the first round to place his name on the leaderboard and so strike anguish into the hearts of his main competitors and he never wavered from his core strategy of laying up short of bunkers and then relying on his accuracy and control with mid-irons to penetrate distant greens coloured the mottled shade of camouflage gear by the sun.

During the third round Els took driver off the first tee but Woods stuck with his iron. On the final day Garcia tried the same tactic and once again it was ignored. If there was an intimidatory factor at play here, and there was, then it was Woods who was passing it on.

The world's finest were either already melted or in the process of dribbling to the ground. A month earlier there was much glee at the fact that eight European Tour Members had finished in the top 16 of the US Open Championship but at Hoylake none of these ended the week in the top 30. Disappointing does not quite capture it.

Compliments, however, should be handed out to the English duo of Robert Rock and Anthony Wall. They may not have been amongst the group that arrived on The Wirral with trumpet calls echoing everywhere but on this week they each offered evidence that a man can overcome his own, and others', expectations, and play his very best golf at an Open.

Wall, let me add, had been the last man standing, or at least practising, when the Association of Golf Writers sat down in the R&A Tent at 7.30pm on Tuesday evening. While I was pouring out the first of a flock of glasses of rather pleasant white wine, he was hitting delicate chips off bare ground just a few feet away.

I raised a glass and told him through an open window that I hoped his impressive diligence worked out. "I hope so too," he said. "It's just so great to be playing in an Open." Five days later I joined in the applause as he finished his final round, recorded a 69 and ended an Open he had entered as a member of the chorus line in a tie for 11th place. Wonderful stuff.

Rock, meanwhile, carded a last day 71 to end his campaign in an unexpectedly delightful tie for 16th spot. Better yet, he did so without ever wearing a cap, withstanding the lucrative offers to cover his head on that Sunday. For this alone I commend him but there is much else for this player to enjoy from this week.

Woods, of course, wore a hat. He always does. But then if it had not been a baseball cap with the familiar swoosh, it would have been a crown. This is how good he is when the mood is on him. It is enough to make all the others start sobbing.

**Bill Elliott**

*The Observer*

# Final Results

| Pos | Name | | Rd1 | Rd2 | Rd3 | Rd4 | Total | | € | £ |
|---|---|---|---|---|---|---|---|---|---|---|
| 1 | Tiger WOODS | USA | 67 | 65 | 71 | 67 | 270 | -18 | 1,045,965.60 | 720,000.00 |
| 2 | Chris DIMARCO | USA | 70 | 65 | 69 | 68 | 272 | -16 | 624,673.90 | 430,000.00 |
| 3 | Ernie ELS | RSA | 68 | 65 | 71 | 71 | 275 | -13 | 399,500.75 | 275,000.00 |
| 4 | Jim FURYK | USA | 68 | 71 | 66 | 71 | 276 | -12 | 305,073.30 | 210,000.00 |
| 5 | Sergio GARCIA | ESP | 68 | 71 | 65 | 73 | 277 | -11 | 231,710.44 | 159,500.00 |
| | Hideto TANIHARA | JPN | 72 | 68 | 66 | 71 | 277 | -11 | 231,710.44 | 159,500.00 |
| 7 | Angel CABRERA | ARG | 71 | 68 | 66 | 73 | 278 | -10 | 185,949.44 | 128,000.00 |
| 8 | Andres ROMERO | ARG | 70 | 70 | 68 | 71 | 279 | -9 | 138,493.59 | 95,333.33 |
| | Adam SCOTT | AUS | 68 | 69 | 70 | 72 | 279 | -9 | 138,493.59 | 95,333.33 |
| | Carl PETTERSSON | SWE | 68 | 72 | 70 | 69 | 279 | -9 | 138,493.59 | 95,333.33 |
| 11 | Ben CRANE | USA | 68 | 71 | 71 | 70 | 280 | -8 | 100,722.61 | 69,333.33 |
| | S K HO | KOR | 68 | 73 | 69 | 70 | 280 | -8 | 100,722.61 | 69,333.33 |
| | Anthony WALL | ENG | 67 | 73 | 71 | 69 | 280 | -8 | 100,722.61 | 69,333.33 |
| 14 | Retief GOOSEN | RSA | 70 | 66 | 72 | 73 | 281 | -7 | 82,079.25 | 56,500.00 |
| | Sean O'HAIR | USA | 69 | 73 | 72 | 67 | 281 | -7 | 82,079.25 | 56,500.00 |
| 16 | Robert ALLENBY | AUS | 69 | 70 | 69 | 74 | 282 | -6 | 65,372.85 | 45,000.00 |
| | Mikko ILONEN | FIN | 68 | 69 | 73 | 72 | 282 | -6 | 65,372.85 | 45,000.00 |
| | Robert ROCK | ENG | 69 | 69 | 73 | 71 | 282 | -6 | 65,372.85 | 45,000.00 |
| | Brett RUMFORD | AUS | 68 | 71 | 72 | 71 | 282 | -6 | 65,372.85 | 45,000.00 |
| | Peter LONARD | AUS | 71 | 69 | 68 | 74 | 282 | -6 | 65,372.85 | 45,000.00 |
| | Geoff OGILVY | AUS | 71 | 69 | 70 | 72 | 282 | -6 | 65,372.85 | 45,000.00 |
| 22 | Charl SCHWARTZEL | RSA | 74 | 66 | 72 | 71 | 283 | -5 | 51,390.32 | 35,375.00 |
| | Phil MICKELSON | USA | 69 | 71 | 73 | 70 | 283 | -5 | 51,390.32 | 35,375.00 |
| | Greg OWEN | ENG | 67 | 73 | 68 | 75 | 283 | -5 | 51,390.32 | 35,375.00 |
| | Mark HENSBY | AUS | 68 | 72 | 74 | 69 | 283 | -5 | 51,390.32 | 35,375.00 |
| 26 | Lee SLATTERY | ENG | 69 | 72 | 71 | 72 | 284 | -4 | 42,274.44 | 29,100.00 |
| | Hunter MAHAN | USA | 73 | 70 | 68 | 73 | 284 | -4 | 42,274.44 | 29,100.00 |
| | Rory SABBATINI | RSA | 69 | 70 | 73 | 72 | 284 | -4 | 42,274.44 | 29,100.00 |
| | Paul BROADHURST | ENG | 71 | 71 | 73 | 69 | 284 | -4 | 42,274.44 | 29,100.00 |
| | Jerry KELLY | USA | 72 | 67 | 69 | 76 | 284 | -4 | 42,274.44 | 29,100.00 |
| 31 | Scott VERPLANK | USA | 70 | 73 | 67 | 75 | 285 | -3 | 35,591.89 | 24,500.00 |
| | Thaworn WIRATCHANT | THA | 71 | 68 | 74 | 72 | 285 | -3 | 35,591.89 | 24,500.00 |
| | Simon KHAN | ENG | 70 | 72 | 68 | 75 | 285 | -3 | 35,591.89 | 24,500.00 |
| | Lee WESTWOOD | ENG | 69 | 72 | 75 | 69 | 285 | -3 | 35,591.89 | 24,500.00 |
| 35 | Luke DONALD | ENG | 74 | 68 | 73 | 71 | 286 | -2 | 28,509.83 | 19,625.00 |
| | Michael CAMPBELL | NZL | 70 | 71 | 75 | 70 | 286 | -2 | 28,509.83 | 19,625.00 |
| | Marcus FRASER | AUS | 68 | 71 | 72 | 75 | 286 | -2 | 28,509.83 | 19,625.00 |
| | Robert KARLSSON | SWE | 70 | 71 | 71 | 74 | 286 | -2 | 28,509.83 | 19,625.00 |
| | Rodney PAMPLING | AUS | 69 | 71 | 74 | 72 | 286 | -2 | 28,509.83 | 19,625.00 |
| | John SENDEN | AUS | 70 | 73 | 73 | 70 | 286 | -2 | 28,509.83 | 19,625.00 |
| 41 | Søren KJELDSEN | DEN | 71 | 71 | 71 | 74 | 287 | -1 | 21,583.42 | 14,857.14 |
| | Jeff SLUMAN | USA | 71 | 72 | 68 | 76 | 287 | -1 | 21,583.42 | 14,857.14 |
| | Thomas BJÖRN | DEN | 72 | 71 | 73 | 71 | 287 | -1 | 21,583.42 | 14,857.14 |
| | Mark CALCAVECCHIA | USA | 71 | 68 | 68 | 80 | 287 | -1 | 21,583.42 | 14,857.14 |
| | Miguel Angel JIMÉNEZ | ESP | 67 | 70 | 76 | 74 | 287 | -1 | 21,583.42 | 14,857.14 |
| | Brandt JOBE | USA | 69 | 71 | 75 | 72 | 287 | -1 | 21,583.42 | 14,857.14 |
| | Stephen AMES | CAN | 72 | 71 | 72 | 74 | 287 | -1 | 21,583.42 | 14,857.14 |
| 48 | Simon WAKEFIELD | ENG | 72 | 71 | 70 | 75 | 288 | 0 | 16,862.04 | 11,607.14 |
| | John BICKERTON | ENG | 72 | 70 | 70 | 76 | 288 | 0 | 16,862.04 | 11,607.14 |
| | Simon DYSON | ENG | 74 | 69 | 70 | 75 | 288 | 0 | 16,862.04 | 11,607.14 |
| | Gonzalo FDEZ-CASTAÑO | ESP | 70 | 69 | 73 | 76 | 288 | 0 | 16,862.04 | 11,607.14 |
| | Andrew MARSHALL | ENG | 72 | 71 | 68 | 77 | 288 | 0 | 16,862.04 | 11,607.14 |
| | Tom WATSON | USA | 72 | 70 | 75 | 71 | 288 | 0 | 16,862.04 | 11,607.14 |
| | Henrik STENSON | SWE | 72 | 71 | 74 | 71 | 288 | 0 | 16,862.04 | 11,607.14 |
| | Marius THORP (AM) | NOR | 71 | 71 | 75 | 71 | 288 | 0 | | |
| 56 | José Maria OLAZÁBAL | ESP | 73 | 68 | 76 | 72 | 289 | 1 | 14,963.12 | 10,300.00 |
| | David DUVAL | USA | 70 | 70 | 78 | 71 | 289 | 1 | 14,963.12 | 10,300.00 |
| | Mike WEIR | CAN | 68 | 72 | 73 | 76 | 289 | 1 | 14,963.12 | 10,300.00 |
| | Keiichiro FUKABORI | JPN | 67 | 73 | 70 | 79 | 289 | 1 | 14,963.12 | 10,300.00 |
| | Tim CLARK | RSA | 72 | 69 | 69 | 79 | 289 | 1 | 14,963.12 | 10,300.00 |
| 61 | Graeme MCDOWELL | NIR | 68 | 73 | 72 | 79 | 290 | 2 | 14,454.66 | 9,950.00 |
| | Andrew BUCKLE | AUS | 72 | 69 | 77 | 72 | 290 | 2 | 14,454.66 | 9,950.00 |
| 63 | Marco RUIZ | PAR | 71 | 70 | 80 | 70 | 291 | 3 | 14,164.12 | 9,750.00 |
| | Mark O'MEARA | USA | 71 | 70 | 77 | 73 | 291 | 3 | 14,164.12 | 9,750.00 |
| 65 | Chad CAMPBELL | USA | 70 | 73 | 74 | 75 | 292 | 4 | 13,946.21 | 9,600.00 |
| 66 | Fred FUNK | USA | 69 | 74 | 75 | 76 | 294 | 6 | 13,728.30 | 9,450.00 |
| | Vaughn TAYLOR | USA | 72 | 71 | 77 | 74 | 294 | 6 | 13,728.30 | 9,450.00 |
| 68 | Edoardo MOLINARI (AM) | ITA | 73 | 70 | 77 | 75 | 295 | 7 | | |
| | Todd HAMILTON | USA | 72 | 71 | 74 | 78 | 295 | 7 | 13,510.39 | 9,300.00 |
| 70 | Bart BRYANT | USA | 69 | 74 | 77 | 76 | 296 | 8 | 13,365.12 | 9,200.00 |
| 71 | Paul CASEY | ENG | 72 | 70 | 79 | 77 | 298 | 10 | 13,219.84 | 9,100.00 |

# Total Prize Fund
€5,794,940  £3,989,000

# All in the Mind

## Gut Kaden

| Par | Yards | Metres |
|-----|-------|--------|
| 72  | 7290  | 6666   |

| | | | | |
|---|---|---|---|---|
| 1 | Robert KARLSSON | 263 | -25 | |
| 2 | Charl SCHWARTZEL | 267 | -21 | |
|   | Lee WESTWOOD | 267 | -21 | |
| 4 | Emanuele CANONICA | 268 | -20 | |
|   | Retief GOOSEN | 268 | -20 | |
|   | Graeme McDOWELL | 268 | -20 | |
|   | Andres ROMERO | 268 | -20 | |
| 8 | Gary ORR | 269 | -19 | |
| 9 | Sergio GARCIA | 270 | -18 | |
|   | Søren HANSEN | 270 | -18 | |

## WEATHER REPORT

| Round One | Round Two | Round Three | Round Four |
|-----------|-----------|-------------|------------|

## EUROPEAN TOUR ORDER OF MERIT
(After 34 tournaments)

| Pos | | € |
|-----|---|---|
| 1 | David HOWELL | 1,895,630.81 |
| 2 | Paul CASEY | 1,435,029.17 |
| 3 | Robert KARLSSON | 1,412,171.80 |
| 4 | Johan EDFORS | 1,265,039.24 |
| 5 | Padraig HARRINGTON | 1,225,356.82 |
| 6 | Colin MONTGOMERIE | 1,165,783.21 |
| 7 | Ernie ELS | 1,149,786.02 |
| 8 | Retief GOOSEN | 1,032,617.46 |
| 9 | John BICKERTON | 1,025,907.16 |
| 10 | Henrik STENSON | 1,024,524.01 |

# The Deutsche Bank Players' Championship of Europe

**Hamburg, Germany**
July 27-30 • 2006

A ccording to conventional wisdom, the less you think about golf the better. Take this from former Masters Tournament Champion Ben Crenshaw, for example. "I'm about five inches from being an outstanding golfer. That's the distance my left ear is from my right."

Or how about this maxim from the legendary Bobby Jones, winner of the 'Impregnable Quadrilateral' in 1930: "You swing your best when you have the fewest things to think about."

Sound advice from two of the greats of the game, but some of modern golf's finest might beg to differ judging by their results on The European Tour International Schedule in 2006. Take Denmark's Thomas Björn for example, a man who thinks so much about the game he employs not one, but two psychologists, and used them both to great effect to win the Nissan Irish Open at Carton House Golf Club.

Or how about Sweden's Robert Karlsson, stressing that golf was "only mental" after

Emanuele Canonica

his win in The Deutsche Bank Players' Championship of Europe? It would be a brave, not to mention foolish, man indeed to suggest Bobby Jones did not know what he was talking about, but it is hard to argue with Karlsson's approach either.

After spread-eagling the field to win The Celtic Manor Wales Open at the start of June, the 6ft 5in Swede was at it again at Gut Kaden to the north of Hamburg and his four shot victory would have been even more commanding but for a double bogey six on the 72nd hole.

His second win in two months was also the seventh of his career, seeing him overtake Anders Forsbrand as the most successful Swedish golfer in European Tour history.

" It is a fantastic course and I am not just saying that because I won last year and finished third the previous time. I have always liked this place. The weather is different this year which means the course is playing harder and drier but it is still the same test and it is a lovely feeling to come back " – Niclas Fasth

A notable achievement, no doubt, but how did he explain the four year gap between his previous victory in the 2002 Omega European Masters and the success in Wales? That is where the 'mental' comment came in.

The 36 year old narrowly missed out on a place in The Ryder Cup Team in 1999, finishing 11th in the qualifying table, and was subsequently overlooked for a wild card by Captain Mark James. He also came close to quitting the game after a disappointing season in 2000 when he finished a lowly 114th on the Order of Merit.

"I played very poorly and I felt very lost on the golf course," explained Karlsson. "I tried too hard. I wanted so badly to play really well and golf is only mental. If you don't feel happy and relaxed on the golf course you have no chance, no matter how good your swing is.

"I'm in a privileged position but I was not enjoying life on Tour and so in 2003 I started seeing a life coach, a Swedish woman named Ann Christine Lundstrom, and I'm a lot happier now in my relationships with everyone, from my family to my caddie.

"I would say most of the 156 players at Gut Kaden have a good chance to win when they are 'on'. But you have to be 'on' for four days in a row, and that's the big issue with the game. To be able to stay focused for four days is quite difficult. You also have three nights in between and a lot of things can happen in those hours, if you're playing bad or playing well."

Under his former psychologist, the late Dr Bengt Stern, to whom he dedicated his

*Padraig Harrington*

*Luke Donald, Sergio Garcia and Paul Broadhurst*

209

# Final Results

*Gary Orr*

*Gregory Havret*

| Pos | Name | | Rd1 | Rd2 | Rd3 | Rd4 | Total | | € | £ |
|-----|------|---|-----|-----|-----|-----|-------|---|---|---|
| 1 | Robert KARLSSON | SWE | 64 | 66 | 66 | 67 | 263 | -25 | 600,000.00 | 409,469.67 |
| 2 | Lee WESTWOOD | ENG | 63 | 68 | 67 | 69 | 267 | -21 | 312,680.00 | 213,388.29 |
| | Charl SCHWARTZEL | RSA | 68 | 64 | 68 | 67 | 267 | -21 | 312,680.00 | 213,388.29 |
| 4 | Retief GOOSEN | RSA | 64 | 68 | 69 | 67 | 268 | -20 | 141,660.00 | 96,675.79 |
| | Emanuele CANONICA | ITA | 67 | 68 | 66 | 67 | 268 | -20 | 141,660.00 | 96,675.79 |
| | Graeme MCDOWELL | NIR | 68 | 70 | 65 | 65 | 268 | -20 | 141,660.00 | 96,675.79 |
| | Andres ROMERO | ARG | 70 | 65 | 67 | 66 | 268 | -20 | 141,660.00 | 96,675.79 |
| 8 | Gary ORR | SCO | 67 | 64 | 70 | 68 | 269 | -19 | 90,000.00 | 61,420.45 |
| 9 | Søren HANSEN | DEN | 70 | 67 | 66 | 67 | 270 | -18 | 76,320.00 | 52,084.54 |
| | Sergio GARCIA | ESP | 69 | 66 | 67 | 68 | 270 | -18 | 76,320.00 | 52,084.54 |
| 11 | Ian WOOSNAM | WAL | 65 | 66 | 69 | 72 | 272 | -16 | 62,040.00 | 42,339.16 |
| | Christian L NILSSON | SWE | 67 | 66 | 73 | 66 | 272 | -16 | 62,040.00 | 42,339.16 |
| | Niclas FASTH | SWE | 68 | 66 | 70 | 68 | 272 | -16 | 62,040.00 | 42,339.16 |
| 14 | Tim CLARK | RSA | 68 | 69 | 68 | 68 | 273 | -15 | 55,080.00 | 37,589.32 |
| 15 | Luke DONALD | ENG | 67 | 66 | 71 | 70 | 274 | -14 | 50,760.00 | 34,641.13 |
| | Mikko ILONEN | FIN | 68 | 69 | 66 | 71 | 274 | -14 | 50,760.00 | 34,641.13 |
| | Angel CABRERA | ARG | 66 | 71 | 69 | 68 | 274 | -14 | 50,760.00 | 34,641.13 |
| 18 | Paul MCGINLEY | IRL | 70 | 66 | 69 | 70 | 275 | -13 | 44,010.00 | 30,034.60 |
| | Jarmo SANDELIN | SWE | 71 | 68 | 71 | 65 | 275 | -13 | 44,010.00 | 30,034.60 |
| | Daniel VANCSIK | ARG | 69 | 66 | 67 | 73 | 275 | -13 | 44,010.00 | 30,034.60 |
| | Anthony WALL | ENG | 72 | 66 | 69 | 68 | 275 | -13 | 44,010.00 | 30,034.60 |
| 22 | Garry HOUSTON | WAL | 66 | 68 | 69 | 73 | 276 | -12 | 37,980.00 | 25,919.43 |
| | Henrik STENSON | SWE | 70 | 70 | 66 | 70 | 276 | -12 | 37,980.00 | 25,919.43 |
| | Ian POULTER | ENG | 68 | 67 | 70 | 71 | 276 | -12 | 37,980.00 | 25,919.43 |
| | Jyoti RANDHAWA | IND | 68 | 69 | 67 | 72 | 276 | -12 | 37,980.00 | 25,919.43 |
| | Matthew MILLAR | AUS | 67 | 69 | 68 | 72 | 276 | -12 | 37,980.00 | 25,919.43 |
| | Shiv KAPUR | IND | 72 | 66 | 71 | 67 | 276 | -12 | 37,980.00 | 25,919.43 |
| 28 | Damien MCGRANE | IRL | 69 | 66 | 70 | 72 | 277 | -11 | 31,500.00 | 21,497.16 |
| | Padraig HARRINGTON | IRL | 68 | 65 | 72 | 72 | 277 | -11 | 31,500.00 | 21,497.16 |
| | Sven STRÜVER | GER | 68 | 70 | 70 | 69 | 277 | -11 | 31,500.00 | 21,497.16 |
| | Markus BRIER | AUT | 74 | 65 | 67 | 71 | 277 | -11 | 31,500.00 | 21,497.16 |
| | Todd HAMILTON | USA | 71 | 69 | 68 | 69 | 277 | -11 | 31,500.00 | 21,497.16 |
| | Simon KHAN | ENG | 67 | 70 | 73 | 67 | 277 | -11 | 31,500.00 | 21,497.16 |
| 34 | Stephen GALLACHER | SCO | 66 | 72 | 70 | 70 | 278 | -10 | 27,000.00 | 18,426.14 |
| | Mark FOSTER | ENG | 70 | 70 | 72 | 66 | 278 | -10 | 27,000.00 | 18,426.14 |
| | Louis OOSTHUIZEN | RSA | 69 | 67 | 72 | 70 | 278 | -10 | 27,000.00 | 18,426.14 |
| 37 | Mattias ELIASSON | SWE | 69 | 69 | 72 | 69 | 279 | -9 | 23,040.00 | 15,723.64 |
| | Søren KJELDSEN | DEN | 68 | 67 | 69 | 75 | 279 | -9 | 23,040.00 | 15,723.64 |
| | Darren FICHARDT | RSA | 71 | 68 | 69 | 71 | 279 | -9 | 23,040.00 | 15,723.64 |
| | Jean-François REMESY | FRA | 65 | 70 | 73 | 71 | 279 | -9 | 23,040.00 | 15,723.64 |
| | Gary EMERSON | ENG | 68 | 69 | 70 | 72 | 279 | -9 | 23,040.00 | 15,723.64 |
| | Thongchai JAIDEE | THA | 67 | 71 | 69 | 72 | 279 | -9 | 23,040.00 | 15,723.64 |
| | Graeme STORM | ENG | 67 | 69 | 75 | 68 | 279 | -9 | 23,040.00 | 15,723.64 |
| | Leif WESTERBERG | SWE | 70 | 69 | 70 | 70 | 279 | -9 | 23,040.00 | 15,723.64 |
| 45 | Mikael LUNDBERG | SWE | 69 | 68 | 71 | 72 | 280 | -8 | 18,000.00 | 12,284.09 |
| | Steven O'HARA | SCO | 71 | 69 | 69 | 71 | 280 | -8 | 18,000.00 | 12,284.09 |
| | Richard MCEVOY | ENG | 71 | 69 | 68 | 72 | 280 | -8 | 18,000.00 | 12,284.09 |
| | Christian CÉVAËR | FRA | 67 | 71 | 69 | 73 | 280 | -8 | 18,000.00 | 12,284.09 |
| | Johan EDFORS | SWE | 68 | 67 | 69 | 76 | 280 | -8 | 18,000.00 | 12,284.09 |
| | Anders HANSEN | DEN | 69 | 66 | 71 | 74 | 280 | -8 | 18,000.00 | 12,284.09 |
| 51 | Alessandro TADINI | ITA | 70 | 70 | 70 | 71 | 281 | -7 | 14,760.00 | 10,072.95 |
| | Phillip PRICE | WAL | 70 | 70 | 70 | 71 | 281 | -7 | 14,760.00 | 10,072.95 |
| | Tom WHITEHOUSE | ENG | 74 | 65 | 72 | 70 | 281 | -7 | 14,760.00 | 10,072.95 |
| 54 | Alastair FORSYTH | SCO | 68 | 72 | 72 | 70 | 282 | -6 | 11,952.00 | 8,156.64 |
| | Jean-François LUCQUIN | FRA | 67 | 72 | 68 | 75 | 282 | -6 | 11,952.00 | 8,156.64 |
| | Nicolas COLSAERTS | BEL | 70 | 70 | 70 | 72 | 282 | -6 | 11,952.00 | 8,156.64 |
| | Andrew MCLARDY | RSA | 68 | 69 | 73 | 72 | 282 | -6 | 11,952.00 | 8,156.64 |
| | Gregory HAVRET | FRA | 65 | 70 | 70 | 77 | 282 | -6 | 11,952.00 | 8,156.64 |
| 59 | Joakim BÄCKSTRÖM | SWE | 71 | 68 | 69 | 75 | 283 | -5 | 9,360.00 | 6,387.73 |
| | Jamie SPENCE | ENG | 72 | 68 | 70 | 73 | 283 | -5 | 9,360.00 | 6,387.73 |
| | Phillip ARCHER | ENG | 68 | 71 | 70 | 74 | 283 | -5 | 9,360.00 | 6,387.73 |
| | Bernhard LANGER | GER | 71 | 69 | 74 | 69 | 283 | -5 | 9,360.00 | 6,387.73 |
| | Peter GUSTAFSSON | SWE | 68 | 71 | 71 | 73 | 283 | -5 | 9,360.00 | 6,387.73 |
| | Michael CAMPBELL | NZL | 70 | 69 | 71 | 73 | 283 | -5 | 9,360.00 | 6,387.73 |
| | Fredrik WIDMARK | SWE | 70 | 70 | 74 | 69 | 283 | -5 | 9,360.00 | 6,387.73 |
| 66 | Tino SCHUSTER | GER | 71 | 69 | 70 | 74 | 284 | -4 | 7,740.00 | 5,282.16 |
| | José Manuel LARA | ESP | 70 | 70 | 71 | 73 | 284 | -4 | 7,740.00 | 5,282.16 |
| 68 | François DELAMONTAGNE | FRA | 72 | 68 | 74 | 71 | 285 | -3 | 7,020.00 | 4,790.80 |
| | Robert ROCK | ENG | 68 | 68 | 71 | 78 | 285 | -3 | 7,020.00 | 4,790.80 |
| 70 | Jonathan LOMAS | ENG | 68 | 72 | 72 | 74 | 286 | -2 | 6,560.00 | 4,476.87 |
| 71 | Alejandro CANIZARES | ESP | 69 | 70 | 71 | 79 | 289 | 1 | 5,400.00 | 3,685.23 |

## Total Prize Fund
€3,605,400  £2,460,503

---

victory in 2002 at Crans-sur-Sierre, that would certainly be true. Karlsson was once instructed to spend the entire night on his feet hitting ten foot putts with a friend berating him if he missed, the idea being to face a level of frustration far worse than anything he would experience in a real tournament.

Frustration was certainly at a minimum all week in Germany, only the interruptions for passing thunderstorms on Thursday and Saturday, perhaps, ruffling Karlsson's feathers.

An opening 64 was overshadowed by Lee Westwood's course record 63 as the Englishman set about attempting to win the event for the third time, while it was Ryder Cup Captain Ian Woosnam's turn to grab the headlines on Friday, a new treatment for his long-standing back injury helping the Welshman into a share of second place on 13 under par alongside Scotland's Gary Orr and Westwood.

However, low scoring is something of a Karlsson speciality and a 66 had him one shot clear of the field, an advantage he doubled with another 66 on Saturday. Westwood quickly closed the gap with a birdie on the first hole in the final round, but Karlsson was not to be denied and soon found his putting touch to edge further and further in front.

By the time he stood on the 18th tee, the towering Swede was six shots clear and no doubt composing his victory speech. Perhaps that explained the pulled drive into heavy rough and a lost ball which cost him an inglorious six, but it was a forgivable lapse with the title already secure.

Perhaps Mr Jones was right all along.

**Phil Casey**

*Press Association*

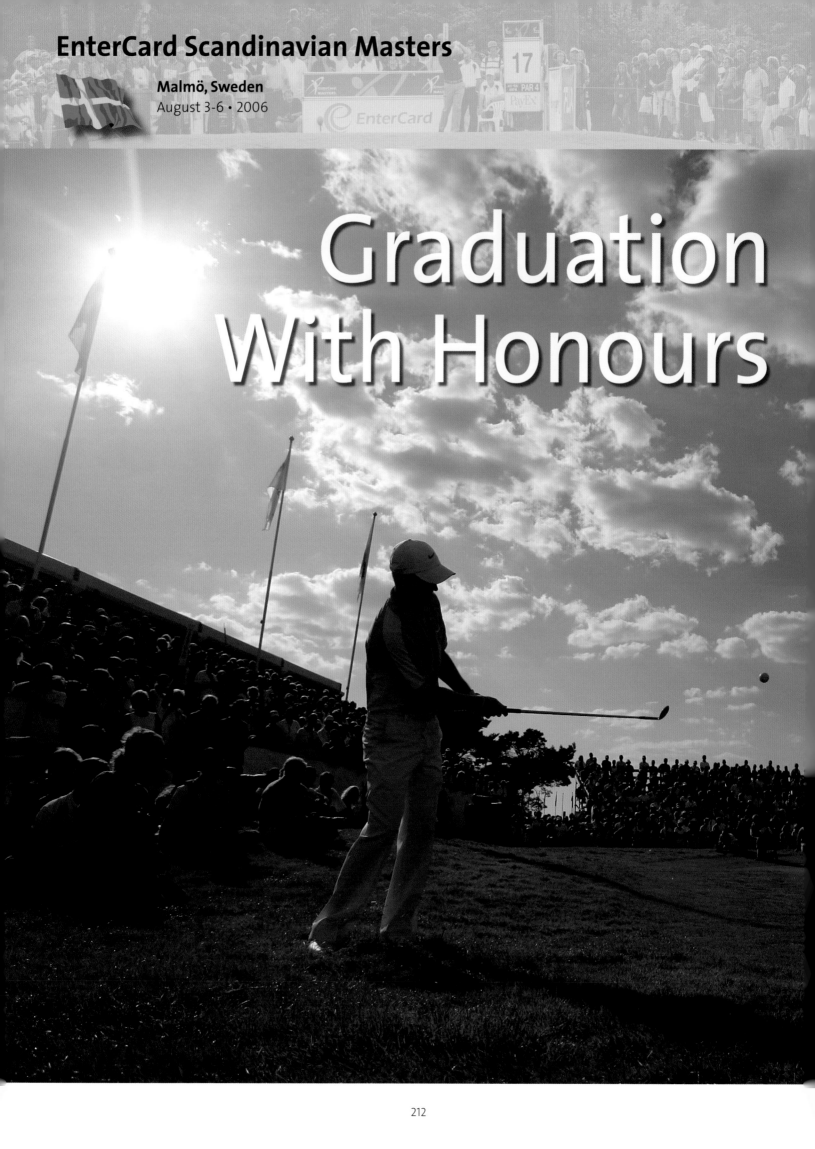

# Graduation With Honours

Marcel Siem

Luke Donald, Nick Dougherty, Graeme McDowell and the rest of his team-mates on the winning Great Britain and Ireland Walker Cup side at Sea Island, Georgia, in 2001 were not surprised in the slightest by Marc Warren's EnterCard Scandinavian Masters victory at the Barsebäck Golf & Country Club near Malmö. Nor were his rivals on the 2005 Challenge Tour where he ended the season Number One on the Rankings, and nor, to be honest, was Warren himself.

The 25 year old Scot had served his apprenticeship, graduated with honours, and knew for sure that when his chance came he possessed the experience and the temperament to grab it with both hands.

He thought like a champion and played like a champion, particularly in the final round when he came from behind to beat Swedish golf's man of the moment Robert Karlsson – winner of The Deutsche Bank Players' Championship of Europe the week before – in a sudden-death play-off.

After Karlsson packed nine birdies and an eagle into a course record 63 on the Saturday, he was odds on favourite to wrap up a third European Tour title of the summer, become the first back-to-back winner on the circuit since Ernie Els in Dubai and Qatar in 2005, and notch an eighth Swedish victory of the year.

But Warren, who coolly downed the winning putt in that 2001 Walker Cup match, was fully prepared for the challenge. "For three

months I was in contention every week on the Challenge Tour and when it came to another play-off, I was ready," he explained.

"Apart from a couple of weeks, it's been a hard and frustrating first year on the main Tour and after four missed cuts in a row I was 129th on the Order of Merit and

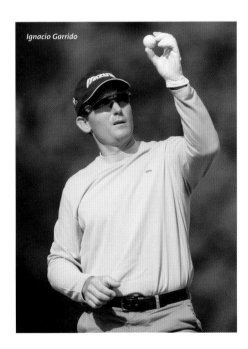

Ignacio Garrido

**Barsebäck Golf & Country Club**

| Par | Yards | Metres |
|-----|-------|--------|
| 72 | 7365 | 6735 |

| | | | | |
|---|---|---|---|---|
| 1 | Marc WARREN | 278 | -10 | |
| 2 | Robert KARLSSON | 278 | -10 | |
| 3 | Richard STERNE | 279 | -9 | |
| 4 | Marcel SIEM | 280 | -8 | |
| 5 | Peter GUSTAFSSON | 281 | -7 | |
| | Raphaël JACQUELIN | 281 | -7 | |
| 7 | Simon DYSON | 283 | -5 | |
| | Jesper PARNEVIK | 283 | -5 | |
| | Tom WHITEHOUSE | 283 | -5 | |
| 10 | Benn BARHAM | 284 | -4 | |
| | Gregory BOURDY | 284 | -4 | |
| | David CARTER | 284 | -4 | |
| | Santiago LUNA | 284 | -4 | |
| | Jarmo SANDELIN | 284 | -4 | |

**WEATHER REPORT**

| Round One | Round Two | Round Three | Round Four |

**EUROPEAN TOUR ORDER OF MERIT**
(After 35 tournaments)

| Pos | | € | |
|-----|---|---|---|
| 1 | David HOWELL | 1,895,630.81 | |
| 2 | Robert KARLSSON | 1,589,941.80 | |
| 3 | Paul CASEY | 1,435,029.17 | |
| 4 | Johan EDFORS | 1,265,039.24 | |
| 5 | Padraig HARRINGTON | 1,225,356.82 | |
| 6 | Colin MONTGOMERIE | 1,165,783.21 | |
| 7 | Ernie ELS | 1,149,786.02 | |
| 8 | Retief GOOSEN | 1,032,617.46 | |
| 9 | John BICKERTON | 1,025,907.16 | |
| 10 | Henrik STENSON | 1,024,524.01 | |

Richard Sterne

running out of tournaments to keep my card. It was in my mind that the previous Challenge Tour Number Ones – Johan Edfors, Lee Slattery and Lee James – immediately lost their European Tour cards, and I didn't want to make it four in row."

He ensured such an eventuality did not occur with a safe par four at the second time of asking on the 437 yard 18th hole after Karlsson became entangled with the trees on both sides of the fairway.

Warren emerged with €266,660 (£182,321) but also the knowledge that he had added to the kudos of the 2001 Walker Cup team, joining Donald, Dougherty and McDowell as European Tour winners.

"That team was a bit special but the Challenge Tour experience was massive too," Warren said. "It taught me how to play four day tournaments and how to cope with all the travelling. I gained so much from the high standard of competition there.

"I kept saying to myself: 'Wins on the Challenge Tour are no different to wins on

*" It is a venue which will always be on my 'must play' list – a gorgeous blend of links and parkland rarely seen anywhere in the world. It's a classic old style course, not in any way contrived, and seems to flow with the land. I love it " – Mark Roe*

Red Bull Physio Unit

# Final Results

| Pos | Name | | Rd1 | Rd2 | Rd3 | Rd4 | Total | | € | £ |
|---|---|---|---|---|---|---|---|---|---|---|
| 1 | Marc WARREN | SCO | 67 | 69 | 73 | 69 | 278 | -10 | 266,660.00 | 182,321.65 |
| 2 | Robert KARLSSON | SWE | 75 | 69 | 63 | 71 | 278 | -10 | 177,770.00 | 121,545.49 |
| 3 | Richard STERNE | RSA | 70 | 68 | 72 | 69 | 279 | -9 | 100,160.00 | 68,481.72 |
| 4 | Marcel SIEM | GER | 72 | 71 | 69 | 68 | 280 | -8 | 80,000.00 | 54,697.86 |
| 5 | Raphaël JACQUELIN | FRA | 68 | 71 | 72 | 70 | 281 | -7 | 61,920.00 | 42,336.15 |
|  | Peter GUSTAFSSON | SWE | 73 | 69 | 67 | 72 | 281 | -7 | 61,920.00 | 42,336.15 |
| 7 | Simon DYSON | ENG | 71 | 71 | 71 | 70 | 283 | -5 | 41,280.00 | 28,224.10 |
|  | Tom WHITEHOUSE | ENG | 68 | 70 | 73 | 72 | 283 | -5 | 41,280.00 | 28,224.10 |
|  | Jesper PARNEVIK | SWE | 72 | 70 | 72 | 69 | 283 | -5 | 41,280.00 | 28,224.10 |
| 10 | Santiago LUNA | ESP | 71 | 69 | 73 | 71 | 284 | -4 | 27,840.00 | 19,034.86 |
|  | Gregory BOURDY | FRA | 69 | 72 | 71 | 72 | 284 | -4 | 27,840.00 | 19,034.86 |
|  | Benn BARHAM | ENG | 67 | 73 | 74 | 70 | 284 | -4 | 27,840.00 | 19,034.86 |
|  | Jarmo SANDELIN | SWE | 69 | 73 | 66 | 76 | 284 | -4 | 27,840.00 | 19,034.86 |
|  | David CARTER | ENG | 73 | 66 | 70 | 75 | 284 | -4 | 27,840.00 | 19,034.86 |
| 15 | Niclas FASTH | SWE | 71 | 70 | 74 | 70 | 285 | -3 | 20,177.78 | 13,796.02 |
|  | Felipe AGUILAR | CHI | 72 | 69 | 74 | 70 | 285 | -3 | 20,177.78 | 13,796.02 |
|  | José-Filipe LIMA | POR | 73 | 70 | 73 | 69 | 285 | -3 | 20,177.78 | 13,796.02 |
|  | Mark ROE | ENG | 69 | 65 | 75 | 76 | 285 | -3 | 20,177.78 | 13,796.02 |
|  | José Manuel LARA | ESP | 72 | 73 | 70 | 70 | 285 | -3 | 20,177.78 | 13,796.02 |
|  | Cesar MONASTERIO | ARG | 71 | 71 | 72 | 71 | 285 | -3 | 20,177.78 | 13,796.02 |
|  | Martin ERLANDSSON | SWE | 70 | 72 | 74 | 69 | 285 | -3 | 20,177.78 | 13,796.02 |
|  | Peter LAWRIE | IRL | 70 | 72 | 72 | 71 | 285 | -3 | 20,177.78 | 13,796.02 |
|  | Wade ORMSBY | AUS | 72 | 71 | 72 | 70 | 285 | -3 | 20,177.78 | 13,796.02 |
| 24 | Mattias ELIASSON | SWE | 70 | 71 | 72 | 73 | 286 | -2 | 16,640.00 | 11,377.16 |
|  | Nicolas COLSAERTS | BEL | 67 | 67 | 73 | 79 | 286 | -2 | 16,640.00 | 11,377.16 |
|  | Ian GARBUTT | ENG | 74 | 70 | 70 | 72 | 286 | -2 | 16,640.00 | 11,377.16 |
| 27 | Maarten LAFEBER | NED | 73 | 71 | 71 | 72 | 287 | -1 | 14,720.00 | 10,064.41 |
|  | Daniel VANCSIK | ARG | 72 | 70 | 76 | 69 | 287 | -1 | 14,720.00 | 10,064.41 |
|  | Fredrik JACOBSON | SWE | 69 | 67 | 76 | 75 | 287 | -1 | 14,720.00 | 10,064.41 |
|  | David LYNN | ENG | 69 | 71 | 74 | 73 | 287 | -1 | 14,720.00 | 10,064.41 |
|  | Peter O'MALLEY | AUS | 71 | 73 | 72 | 71 | 287 | -1 | 14,720.00 | 10,064.41 |
|  | Jesper KENNEGARD (AM) | SWE | 72 | 69 | 73 | 73 | 287 | -1 |  |  |
| 33 | Oliver WHITELEY | ENG | 74 | 71 | 70 | 73 | 288 | 0 | 11,568.00 | 7,909.31 |
|  | Michael CAMPBELL | NZL | 68 | 75 | 75 | 70 | 288 | 0 | 11,568.00 | 7,909.31 |
|  | Steven O'HARA | SCO | 75 | 69 | 72 | 72 | 288 | 0 | 11,568.00 | 7,909.31 |
|  | Phillip ARCHER | ENG | 70 | 71 | 75 | 72 | 288 | 0 | 11,568.00 | 7,909.31 |
|  | Peter HANSON | SWE | 69 | 75 | 72 | 72 | 288 | 0 | 11,568.00 | 7,909.31 |
|  | Klas ERIKSSON | SWE | 70 | 71 | 70 | 77 | 288 | 0 | 11,568.00 | 7,909.31 |
|  | Joakim HAEGGMAN | SWE | 74 | 69 | 72 | 73 | 288 | 0 | 11,568.00 | 7,909.31 |
|  | Jamie SPENCE | ENG | 70 | 70 | 75 | 73 | 288 | 0 | 11,568.00 | 7,909.31 |
|  | Gregory HAVRET | FRA | 75 | 69 | 72 | 72 | 288 | 0 | 11,568.00 | 7,909.31 |
|  | Richard BLAND | ENG | 73 | 71 | 74 | 70 | 288 | 0 | 11,568.00 | 7,909.31 |
| 43 | Robert-Jan DERKSEN | NED | 72 | 72 | 75 | 70 | 289 | 1 | 8,480.00 | 5,797.97 |
|  | Andrew MCLARDY | RSA | 69 | 73 | 76 | 71 | 289 | 1 | 8,480.00 | 5,797.97 |
|  | François DELAMONTAGNE | FRA | 71 | 73 | 71 | 74 | 289 | 1 | 8,480.00 | 5,797.97 |
|  | Stephen GALLACHER | SCO | 74 | 70 | 72 | 73 | 289 | 1 | 8,480.00 | 5,797.97 |
|  | Leif WESTERBERG | SWE | 71 | 74 | 72 | 72 | 289 | 1 | 8,480.00 | 5,797.97 |
|  | Markus BRIER | AUT | 72 | 71 | 73 | 73 | 289 | 1 | 8,480.00 | 5,797.97 |
|  | James KINGSTON | RSA | 70 | 71 | 76 | 72 | 289 | 1 | 8,480.00 | 5,797.97 |
|  | Matthew MILLAR | AUS | 72 | 72 | 72 | 73 | 289 | 1 | 8,480.00 | 5,797.97 |
|  | Oliver WILSON | ENG | 72 | 73 | 71 | 73 | 289 | 1 | 8,480.00 | 5,797.97 |
| 52 | Ignacio GARRIDO | ESP | 72 | 71 | 75 | 72 | 290 | 2 | 6,080.00 | 4,157.04 |
|  | Iain PYMAN | ENG | 72 | 73 | 68 | 77 | 290 | 2 | 6,080.00 | 4,157.04 |
|  | David HIGGINS | IRL | 72 | 73 | 72 | 73 | 290 | 2 | 6,080.00 | 4,157.04 |
|  | Alexander NOREN | SWE | 73 | 71 | 72 | 74 | 290 | 2 | 6,080.00 | 4,157.04 |
|  | Sam LITTLE | ENG | 72 | 70 | 77 | 71 | 290 | 2 | 6,080.00 | 4,157.04 |
|  | Miles TUNNICLIFF | ENG | 74 | 71 | 72 | 73 | 290 | 2 | 6,080.00 | 4,157.04 |
| 58 | Adam MEDNICK | SWE | 71 | 74 | 73 | 73 | 291 | 3 | 4,720.00 | 3,227.17 |
|  | Christian L NILSSON | SWE | 73 | 72 | 73 | 73 | 291 | 3 | 4,720.00 | 3,227.17 |
|  | Magnus PERSSON | SWE | 71 | 72 | 73 | 75 | 291 | 3 | 4,720.00 | 3,227.17 |
|  | Richard FINCH | ENG | 72 | 73 | 72 | 74 | 291 | 3 | 4,720.00 | 3,227.17 |
| 62 | Fredrik WIDMARK | SWE | 76 | 68 | 74 | 74 | 292 | 4 | 4,160.00 | 2,844.29 |
|  | Peter FOWLER | AUS | 73 | 72 | 68 | 79 | 292 | 4 | 4,160.00 | 2,844.29 |
|  | David BRANSDON | AUS | 69 | 70 | 77 | 76 | 292 | 4 | 4,160.00 | 2,844.29 |
| 65 | Miguel Angel MARTIN | ESP | 72 | 71 | 74 | 76 | 293 | 5 | 3,600.00 | 2,461.40 |
|  | Michael HOEY | NIR | 73 | 72 | 70 | 78 | 293 | 5 | 3,600.00 | 2,461.40 |
|  | Alexandre ROCHA | BRA | 72 | 69 | 74 | 78 | 293 | 5 | 3,600.00 | 2,461.40 |
|  | Andrew BUTTERFIELD | ENG | 73 | 69 | 76 | 75 | 293 | 5 | 3,600.00 | 2,461.40 |
| 69 | Christian CÉVAËR | FRA | 72 | 73 | 73 | 76 | 294 | 6 | 3,120.00 | 2,133.22 |
|  | Johan AXGREN | SWE | 76 | 69 | 72 | 77 | 294 | 6 | 3,120.00 | 2,133.22 |
| 71 | Shaun P WEBSTER | ENG | 71 | 74 | 73 | 77 | 295 | 7 | 2,575.67 | 1,761.04 |
|  | Michael JONZON | SWE | 74 | 70 | 75 | 76 | 295 | 7 | 2,575.67 | 1,761.04 |
|  | Marco RUIZ | PAR | 72 | 72 | 79 | 72 | 295 | 7 | 2,575.67 | 1,761.04 |
| 74 | Ariel CANETE | ARG | 74 | 71 | 77 | 75 | 297 | 9 | 2,389.50 | 1,633.76 |
|  | Mikael LUNDBERG | SWE | 71 | 73 | 76 | 77 | 297 | 9 | 2,389.50 | 1,633.76 |
|  | Fredrik ANDERSSON HED | SWE | 68 | 71 | 81 | 77 | 297 | 9 | 2,389.50 | 1,633.76 |
|  | Pelle EDBERG | SWE | 76 | 69 | 79 | 73 | 297 | 9 | 2,389.50 | 1,633.76 |
| 78 | Francesco MOLINARI | ITA | 70 | 74 | 77 | 77 | 298 | 10 | 2,380.50 | 1,627.60 |
|  | David DRYSDALE | SCO | 74 | 70 | 77 | 77 | 298 | 10 | 2,380.50 | 1,627.60 |
| 80 | Louis OOSTHUIZEN | RSA | 72 | 70 | 80 | 81 | 303 | 15 | 2,376.00 | 1,624.53 |
| 81 | Janne MARTIKAINEN | FIN | 73 | 71 | 80 | 80 | 304 | 16 | 2,373.00 | 1,622.48 |

The European Tour no matter what calibre of player you are up against'. Going against Robert the way he was playing was tough but I know how pressure can make people make mistakes and I had my fingers crossed I would have another chance of getting my hands on the trophy after it went to a play-off."

After a couple of early mistakes in the final round, Warren birdied three of the last six holes, the best coming at the 18th where he bent a recovery shot around a tree to five feet. He said: "I was angry after three putts at the sixth and seventh but hit a great shot to a foot at the eighth for a two, which got my head back on. Then I put in a strong finish."

Warren paid tribute to his coach of 12 months, Bob Torrance, with whom he had a six hour range session before flying to Sweden, and also confessed a love of playing under pressure. He added: "I look forward to being in these type of situations. I don't really have a fear of what can go wrong. Once I get into contention I try to picture myself with the

Tom Whitehouse

trophy and think of the outcome, rather than what might happen in between.

"I have a belief when I'm under pressure, no matter what the situation, that I can conjure something up or pull off a shot when I have to. Maybe I was born with that. I enjoy playing in front of big crowds."

The 12th first time winner on The 2006 European Tour International Schedule is living proof of the value of his amateur international experience and his week-in, week-out professional competitive experience on the Challenge Tour.

**Gordon Richardson**

EnterCard

## Total Prize Fund
€1,623,865  £1,110,274

# Nostalgia
# In the Air

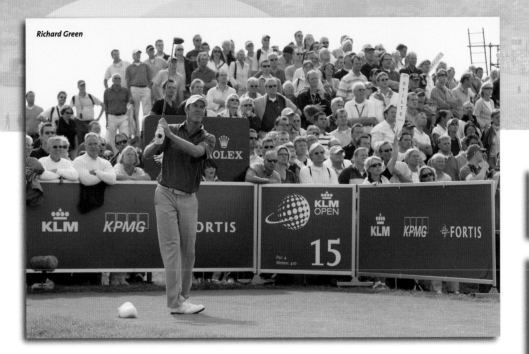

Richard Green

| | | | | |
|---|---|---|---|---|
| **Kennemer Golf & Country Club** | | | | |
| **Par** | **Yards** | | **Metres** | |
| 71 | 6862 | | 6272 | |

| | | | | |
|---|---|---|---|---|
| 1 | **Simon DYSON** | 270 | -14 |  |
| 2 | Richard GREEN | 270 | -14 | |
| 3 | Damien McGRANE | 271 | -13 | |
| 4 | Christian CÉVAËR | 272 | -12 | |
| 5 | Garry HOUSTON | 273 | -11 | |
| 6 | Peter LAWRIE | 274 | -10 | |
| 7 | Phillip ARCHER | 275 | -9 | |
| | Markus BRIER | 275 | -9 | |
| | Alejandro CANIZARES | 275 | -9 | |
| | Anders HANSEN | 275 | -9 | |
| | David LYNN | 275 | -9 | |
| | Andrew McLARDY | 275 | -9 | |

## WEATHER REPORT

| Round One | Round Two | Round Three | Round Four |
|---|---|---|---|

## EUROPEAN TOUR ORDER OF MERIT
(After 36 tournaments)

| Pos | | € | |
|---|---|---|---|
| 1 | **David HOWELL** | 1,895,630.81 | |
| 2 | Robert KARLSSON | 1,589,941.80 | |
| 3 | Paul CASEY | 1,435,029.17 | |
| 4 | Johan EDFORS | 1,265,039.24 | |
| 5 | Padraig HARRINGTON | 1,225,356.82 | |
| 6 | Colin MONTGOMERIE | 1,187,083.21 | |
| 7 | Ernie ELS | 1,149,786.02 | |
| 8 | Retief GOOSEN | 1,032,617.46 | |
| 9 | John BICKERTON | 1,025,907.16 | |
| 10 | Henrik STENSON | 1,024,524.01 | |

Y ou never leave Kennemer Golf & Country Club feeling you have not had your money's worth. When The European Tour returned to the links at Zandvoort, after a gap of 16 years, there was plenty of drama on offer once again, with another play-off to enter the Tour's record books.

This play-off, however, was in stark contrast to the one at Kennemer in 1989 when the then fully titled KLM Dutch Open Championship took an additional nine holes to decide as José Maria Olazábal moved first past Roger Chapman and then Ronan Rafferty.

The weather was so appalling – with lashing rain and high winds – that Olazábal and Rafferty had to rest after six holes as they battled the elements before the marathon play-off record for The European Tour ended after nine holes and more than two hours.

Christian Cévaër

This time, in splendid sunshine, Simon Dyson required only one hole to overcome Richard Green!

There was nostalgia in the air, too, because back in 1976, again at Kennemer, and coincidentally where his uncle, Ramon Sota, had won in 1971, Severiano Ballesteros won his first European Tour title – drawing eight shots clear of Howard Clark for a resounding success. Now he was back where he had started his glittering career and the crowds turned up in droves again to see him help launch the tournament in the curtain-raising Shoot Out. Then, the five time Major Champion retreated from the scene to let the younger men scrap for the title he had claimed 30 years previously, and again in 1980 and 1986.

When the official action did get underway, it was quickly apparent that Ballesteros, in his ceremonial role, had seen far more of the course than joint first round leader Anders Hansen. In fact, the Dane had seen nothing at all. He awoke on Wednesday morning with a severe pain in the neck and had to withdraw from the Pro-Am. Beware the injured golfer they say, and once again the old adage was given some credence as,

# The KLM Open

### Zandvoort, The Netherlands
August 10-13 • 2006

Garry Houston

playing 'blind', Hansen posted a 65 to share the lead with Frenchman Christian Cévaër.

Then came the storms. The second round was fragmented. After it eventually finished on the Saturday morning, Ignacio Garrido took the halfway lead, the Spaniard, like Hansen, looking for the past glory he had enjoyed in the PGA – now the BMW – Championship at Wentworth Club. Elsewhere, Colin Montgomerie, looking for a second win in the event after his 1993 success at neighbouring Noordwijkse, dug deep – in his pocket to be precise – to try for a double. With his putting going belly up, the Scot bought a new model from the Kennemer professional shop.

It helped Montgomerie to a third round 67 but a player who had precious little past

*" You need every shot in your repertoire here – low and high shots, lob-shots, bump-and-run shots. It is tight, too, so your driving has to be accurate, and the small greens mean you have to be on the ball with your irons "* – Simon Dyson

Peter Lawrie

# Final Results

| Pos | Name | | Rd1 | Rd2 | Rd3 | Rd4 | Total | | € | £ |
|---|---|---|---|---|---|---|---|---|---|---|
| 1 | Simon DYSON | ENG | 67 | 71 | 66 | 66 | 270 | -14 | 266,660.00 | 180,034.57 |
| 2 | Richard GREEN | AUS | 73 | 70 | 62 | 65 | 270 | -14 | 177,770.00 | 120,020.79 |
| 3 | Damien MCGRANE | IRL | 69 | 68 | 64 | 70 | 271 | -13 | 100,160.00 | 67,622.67 |
| 4 | Christian CÉVAËR | FRA | 65 | 71 | 69 | 67 | 272 | -12 | 80,000.00 | 54,011.72 |
| 5 | Garry HOUSTON | WAL | 72 | 68 | 67 | 66 | 273 | -11 | 67,840.00 | 45,801.94 |
| 6 | Peter LAWRIE | IRL | 69 | 71 | 64 | 70 | 274 | -10 | 56,000.00 | 37,808.20 |
| 7 | Andrew MCLARDY | RSA | 68 | 71 | 69 | 67 | 275 | -9 | 35,466.67 | 23,945.20 |
| | Phillip ARCHER | ENG | 68 | 68 | 70 | 69 | 275 | -9 | 35,466.67 | 23,945.20 |
| | Anders HANSEN | DEN | 65 | 72 | 71 | 67 | 275 | -9 | 35,466.67 | 23,945.20 |
| | David LYNN | ENG | 75 | 65 | 71 | 64 | 275 | -9 | 35,466.67 | 23,945.20 |
| | Markus BRIER | AUT | 66 | 73 | 68 | 68 | 275 | -9 | 35,466.67 | 23,945.20 |
| | Alejandro CANIZARES | ESP | 67 | 73 | 66 | 69 | 275 | -9 | 35,466.67 | 23,945.20 |
| 13 | David DRYSDALE | SCO | 68 | 70 | 72 | 66 | 276 | -8 | 25,760.00 | 17,391.77 |
| 14 | David CARTER | ENG | 70 | 71 | 67 | 69 | 277 | -7 | 21,300.00 | 14,380.62 |
| | Lee SLATTERY | ENG | 69 | 72 | 67 | 69 | 277 | -7 | 21,300.00 | 14,380.62 |
| | Marco RUIZ | PAR | 69 | 72 | 67 | 69 | 277 | -7 | 21,300.00 | 14,380.62 |
| | Steven O'HARA | SCO | 71 | 70 | 69 | 67 | 277 | -7 | 21,300.00 | 14,380.62 |
| | Søren KJELDSEN | DEN | 68 | 68 | 69 | 72 | 277 | -7 | 21,300.00 | 14,380.62 |
| | Gary MURPHY | IRL | 69 | 70 | 70 | 68 | 277 | -7 | 21,300.00 | 14,380.62 |
| | Jean-François REMESY | FRA | 72 | 65 | 67 | 73 | 277 | -7 | 21,300.00 | 14,380.62 |
| | Colin MONTGOMERIE | SCO | 70 | 71 | 67 | 69 | 277 | -7 | 21,300.00 | 14,380.62 |
| 22 | Jonathan LOMAS | ENG | 72 | 67 | 69 | 70 | 278 | -6 | 17,120.00 | 11,558.51 |
| | Paul MCGINLEY | IRL | 72 | 70 | 66 | 70 | 278 | -6 | 17,120.00 | 11,558.51 |
| | Alessandro TADINI | ITA | 68 | 70 | 69 | 71 | 278 | -6 | 17,120.00 | 11,558.51 |
| | Rafael GOMEZ | ARG | 68 | 73 | 67 | 70 | 278 | -6 | 17,120.00 | 11,558.51 |
| | Tom WHITEHOUSE | ENG | 70 | 73 | 65 | 70 | 278 | -6 | 17,120.00 | 11,558.51 |
| 27 | Alastair FORSYTH | SCO | 71 | 69 | 67 | 72 | 279 | -5 | 14,720.00 | 9,938.16 |
| | Klas ERIKSSON | SWE | 69 | 71 | 72 | 67 | 279 | -5 | 14,720.00 | 9,938.16 |
| | Ian WOOSNAM | WAL | 72 | 70 | 67 | 70 | 279 | -5 | 14,720.00 | 9,938.16 |
| | Ian GARBUTT | ENG | 70 | 70 | 69 | 70 | 279 | -5 | 14,720.00 | 9,938.16 |
| | Miles TUNNICLIFF | ENG | 72 | 70 | 70 | 67 | 279 | -5 | 14,720.00 | 9,938.16 |
| 32 | Neil CHEETHAM | ENG | 68 | 71 | 68 | 73 | 280 | -4 | 12,068.57 | 8,148.05 |
| | Warren ABERY | RSA | 70 | 70 | 66 | 74 | 280 | -4 | 12,068.57 | 8,148.05 |
| | Shaun P WEBSTER | ENG | 71 | 69 | 70 | 70 | 280 | -4 | 12,068.57 | 8,148.05 |
| | Andrew COLTART | SCO | 75 | 68 | 69 | 68 | 280 | -4 | 12,068.57 | 8,148.05 |
| | Raymond RUSSELL | SCO | 67 | 69 | 72 | 72 | 280 | -4 | 12,068.57 | 8,148.05 |
| | Richard MCEVOY | ENG | 71 | 68 | 68 | 73 | 280 | -4 | 12,068.57 | 8,148.05 |
| | Gregory BOURDY | FRA | 67 | 74 | 69 | 70 | 280 | -4 | 12,068.57 | 8,148.05 |
| 39 | Matthew MILLAR | AUS | 70 | 68 | 73 | 70 | 281 | -3 | 10,400.00 | 7,021.52 |
| | Adam MEDNICK | SWE | 69 | 71 | 74 | 67 | 281 | -3 | 10,400.00 | 7,021.52 |
| | Benn BARHAM | ENG | 73 | 68 | 70 | 70 | 281 | -3 | 10,400.00 | 7,021.52 |
| 42 | Ignacio GARRIDO | ESP | 68 | 67 | 73 | 74 | 282 | -2 | 9,120.00 | 6,157.34 |
| | Santiago LUNA | ESP | 71 | 72 | 68 | 71 | 282 | -2 | 9,120.00 | 6,157.34 |
| | Sam LITTLE | ENG | 72 | 71 | 71 | 68 | 282 | -2 | 9,120.00 | 6,157.34 |
| | Peter O'MALLEY | AUS | 72 | 71 | 72 | 67 | 282 | -2 | 9,120.00 | 6,157.34 |
| | Marc CAYEUX | ZIM | 72 | 71 | 69 | 70 | 282 | -2 | 9,120.00 | 6,157.34 |
| 47 | Stuart LITTLE | ENG | 73 | 69 | 70 | 71 | 283 | -1 | 7,520.00 | 5,077.10 |
| | Robert-Jan DERKSEN | NED | 69 | 71 | 70 | 73 | 283 | -1 | 7,520.00 | 5,077.10 |
| | Cesar MONASTERIO | ARG | 70 | 72 | 71 | 70 | 283 | -1 | 7,520.00 | 5,077.10 |
| | Ross FISHER | ENG | 70 | 71 | 71 | 71 | 283 | -1 | 7,520.00 | 5,077.10 |
| | Felipe AGUILAR | CHI | 73 | 69 | 71 | 70 | 283 | -1 | 7,520.00 | 5,077.10 |
| 52 | Andrew MARSHALL | ENG | 73 | 68 | 71 | 72 | 284 | 0 | 6,560.00 | 4,428.96 |
| 53 | Christian L NILSSON | SWE | 71 | 70 | 74 | 70 | 285 | 1 | 5,348.57 | 3,611.07 |
| | Gary EMERSON | ENG | 74 | 69 | 73 | 69 | 285 | 1 | 5,348.57 | 3,611.07 |
| | David BRANSDON | AUS | 68 | 71 | 71 | 75 | 285 | 1 | 5,348.57 | 3,611.07 |
| | Barry LANE | ENG | 68 | 73 | 74 | 70 | 285 | 1 | 5,348.57 | 3,611.07 |
| | Daniel VANCSIK | ARG | 73 | 69 | 67 | 76 | 285 | 1 | 5,348.57 | 3,611.07 |
| | Thongchai JAIDEE | THA | 71 | 71 | 69 | 74 | 285 | 1 | 5,348.57 | 3,611.07 |
| | David PARK | WAL | 68 | 74 | 71 | 72 | 285 | 1 | 5,348.57 | 3,611.07 |
| | Tim SLUITER (AM) | NED | 69 | 70 | 73 | 73 | 285 | 1 | | |
| 61 | Jamie DONALDSON | WAL | 69 | 71 | 72 | 74 | 286 | 2 | 4,400.00 | 2,970.64 |
| | Richard BLAND | ENG | 72 | 71 | 71 | 72 | 286 | 2 | 4,400.00 | 2,970.64 |
| 63 | Phillip PRICE | WAL | 73 | 69 | 70 | 75 | 287 | 3 | 4,000.00 | 2,700.59 |
| | Sven STRÜVER | GER | 68 | 75 | 72 | 72 | 287 | 3 | 4,000.00 | 2,700.59 |
| | Edoardo MOLINARI | ITA | 76 | 67 | 72 | 72 | 287 | 3 | 4,000.00 | 2,700.59 |
| 66 | Alexandre ROCHA | BRA | 75 | 67 | 74 | 72 | 288 | 4 | 3,600.00 | 2,430.53 |
| | Niels KRAAIJ | NED | 73 | 70 | 76 | 70 | 288 | 4 | 3,600.00 | 2,430.53 |
| 68 | Brian AKSTRUP | DEN | 73 | 69 | 73 | 74 | 289 | 5 | 3,200.00 | 2,160.47 |
| | Robert ROCK | ENG | 66 | 76 | 73 | 74 | 289 | 5 | 3,200.00 | 2,160.47 |
| | James KINGSTON | RSA | 69 | 74 | 73 | 73 | 289 | 5 | 3,200.00 | 2,160.47 |
| 71 | Leif WESTERBERG | SWE | 73 | 68 | 77 | 73 | 291 | 7 | 2,930.00 | 1,978.18 |
| 72 | Carlos RODILES | ESP | 69 | 73 | 79 | 74 | 295 | 11 | 2,400.00 | 1,620.35 |

glory, in fact not much European Tour history at all, took centre stage. Damien McGrane, who graduated from a club professional job in Ireland in 2003, led the way by three shots from Peter Lawrie, Jean-Francois Remesy and Dyson, with Cévaër and Green one shot further back.

Green had been to the nearby Zandvoort motor racing circuit during the storm delay. Later, his performance on the golf course inspired him to paint a new number on his own race car – namely 62. That represented his nine under par course record on the Saturday that saw him come zooming through the field.

If McGrane had been cruising on the penultimate afternoon, he had something

of a stall in the final round, which enabled Dyson and Green to overtake. A frustrating run of pars left the Irishman vulnerable to an attack which swiftly came. Two blistering finishes by the pair soon to become the play-off protagonists, saw Dyson and Green breast the winning line together.

Green birdied two of the last three holes; Dyson went one better by picking up three shots in the last four. McGrane had to settle for third place, a disappointment for the affable Irishman as well as for the members at Wexford, many of whom he had taught in the past, and at the Knightsbrook Hotel and Golf Resort in County Meath, his new club.

The crowd waited in anticipation. Dyson did not. After the approach shots had rained down on the green at the 388 yard 18th hole, he found he was nearer by ten feet. Green missed his birdie putt but Dyson swept his in. The Yorkshireman took his second title of the season to follow his earlier success in the Enjoy Jakarta HSBC Indonesia Open.

**Damien McGrane**

**Norman Dabell**

# Total Prize Fund
€1,602,400  £1,081,854

# Force of Nature

*Ian Garbutt*

**Le Meridien Moscow Country Club**

| Par | Yards | Metres |
|-----|-------|--------|
| 72  | 7154  | 6542   |

| | | | |
|---|---|---|---|
| 1 | Alejandro CAÑIZARES | 266 | -22 |
| 2 | David DRYSDALE | 270 | -18 |
| 3 | Mikael LUNDBERG | 271 | -17 |
|   | Gary MURPHY | 271 | -17 |
| 5 | Leif WESTERBERG | 272 | -16 |
| 6 | Alexandre ROCHA | 273 | -15 |
| 7 | Carlos RODILES | 274 | -14 |
| 8 | James HEATH | 275 | -13 |
|   | Jarrod MOSELEY | 275 | -13 |
| 10 | Jorge BENEDETTI | 276 | -12 |
|   | Seve BENSON (AM) | 276 | -12 |
|   | David DIXON | 276 | -12 |
|   | Ian GARBUTT | 276 | -12 |
|   | Fredrik HENGE | 276 | -12 |
|   | Adrien MÖRK | 276 | -12 |
|   | Massimo SCARPA | 276 | -12 |
|   | Lee SLATTERY | 276 | -12 |

**WEATHER REPORT**

| Round One | Round Two | Round Three | Round Four |
|-----------|-----------|-------------|------------|

**EUROPEAN TOUR ORDER OF MERIT**
(After 37 tournaments)

| Pos | | € | |
|-----|---|---|---|
| 1 | David HOWELL | 1,895,630.81 | |
| 2 | Robert KARLSSON | 1,589,941.80 | |
| 3 | Paul CASEY | 1,435,029.17 | |
| 4 | Johan EDFORS | 1,265,039.24 | |
| 5 | Padraig HARRINGTON | 1,225,356.82 | |
| 6 | Colin MONTGOMERIE | 1,187,083.21 | |
| 7 | Ernie ELS | 1,149,786.02 | |
| 8 | Retief GOOSEN | 1,032,617.46 | |
| 9 | John BICKERTON | 1,025,907.16 | |
| 10 | Henrik STENSON | 1,024,524.01 | |

I t was meant to be from the moment they laid eyes on each other. A match made in heaven driven together by an unstoppable force of nature; a force that inspires the most intense fulfilment and the most desperate lows; a force that no man or woman who has experienced its purest form has ever been able to fully comprehend or explain.

The young Spaniard and his new Russian love were united at a perfect moment in their lives. They met almost secretively on a Thursday morning in August, and by Sunday evening were telling the world of the thrilling, gripping four day affair that changed their lives.

His name was Alejandro Cañizares and his new found love was The 2006 Imperial Collection Russian Open.

The two were brought together by the stupefying force that is golf, and their relationship at Le Meridien Moscow Country Club will live forever in the memories of both.

Cañizares will certainly never forget the week he won for the first time as a professional, playing in only his third European Tour event, while the people of Russia, from those who helped organise and run the tournament to the spectators fascinated by a new sport, can be proud of what they achieved at the first full European Tour event to be staged in the Russian Federation.

After ten years of growth on the European Challenge Tour and, from 2003 to 2005, as a dual ranking event between The European and Challenge Tours, The Imperial Collection Russian Open finally blossomed into a full European Tour event with a unique and alluring appeal.

That appeal was characterised by the location of the tournament, hosted in a land that many of the international players, officials and media, visiting for the first time, still believed to have the characteristics of the old communist state of the USSR.

Any misconceptions, however, were quickly dispelled by the warmth and friendliness of the Russian people which added greatly to the convivial atmosphere over the week at Le Meridien Moscow Country Club.

There is no more reason to be fearful in Moscow than in any major city in the world unless, that is, you are scared of a hearty welcome and a healthy measure of the Imperial Collection's world renowned vodka.

Cañizares was one such visitor who did not know what to expect on his first trip to Russia, but, as outlined, the 23 year old quickly fell in love with the place.

Proud to be providing bespoke printed
material to The European Tour for more
than ten years.

For a competitive quote please call or email

Pin Sharp   Every Time

QUALITY

MANAGEMENT

SATISFACTION

PRECISION

# Final Results

| Pos | Name | | Rd1 | Rd2 | Rd3 | Rd4 | Total | | € | £ |
|-----|------|--|-----|-----|-----|-----|-------|--|---|---|
| 1 | Alejandro CANIZARES | ESP | 66 | 67 | 67 | 66 | 266 | -22 | 130,641.50 | 87,937.95 |
| 2 | David DRYSDALE | SCO | 62 | 70 | 69 | 69 | 270 | -18 | 87,096.94 | 58,627.06 |
| 3 | Mikael LUNDBERG | SWE | 68 | 67 | 70 | 66 | 271 | -17 | 44,132.46 | 29,706.63 |
| | Gary MURPHY | IRL | 67 | 68 | 68 | 68 | 271 | -17 | 44,132.46 | 29,706.63 |
| 5 | Leif WESTERBERG | SWE | 68 | 71 | 63 | 70 | 272 | -16 | 33,236.53 | 22,372.31 |
| 6 | Alexandre ROCHA | BRA | 69 | 68 | 69 | 67 | 273 | -15 | 27,435.81 | 18,467.71 |
| 7 | Carlos RODILES | ESP | 63 | 69 | 69 | 73 | 274 | -14 | 23,516.41 | 15,829.46 |
| 8 | Jarrod MOSELEY | AUS | 75 | 68 | 65 | 67 | 275 | -13 | 18,577.96 | 12,505.28 |
| | James HEATH | ENG | 71 | 67 | 69 | 68 | 275 | -13 | 18,577.96 | 12,505.28 |
| 10 | Adrien MÖRK | FRA | 68 | 69 | 72 | 67 | 276 | -12 | 12,967.62 | 8,728.82 |
| | David DIXON | ENG | 69 | 69 | 70 | 68 | 276 | -12 | 12,967.62 | 8,728.82 |
| | Jorge BENEDETTI | COL | 69 | 69 | 71 | 67 | 276 | -12 | 12,967.62 | 8,728.82 |
| | Seve BENSON (AM) | ENG | 71 | 70 | 69 | 66 | 276 | -12 | | |
| | Fredrik HENGE | SWE | 71 | 67 | 69 | 69 | 276 | -12 | 12,967.62 | 8,728.82 |
| | Ian GARBUTT | ENG | 71 | 70 | 68 | 67 | 276 | -12 | 12,967.62 | 8,728.82 |
| | Massimo SCARPA | ITA | 70 | 67 | 69 | 70 | 276 | -12 | 12,967.62 | 8,728.82 |
| | Lee SLATTERY | ENG | 72 | 71 | 65 | 68 | 276 | -12 | 12,967.62 | 8,728.82 |
| 18 | Marco RUIZ | PAR | 68 | 69 | 70 | 70 | 277 | -11 | 9,782.83 | 6,585.06 |
| | Fredrik ANDERSSON HED | SWE | 66 | 69 | 73 | 69 | 277 | -11 | 9,782.83 | 6,585.06 |
| | Andrew BUTTERFIELD | ENG | 68 | 67 | 71 | 71 | 277 | -11 | 9,782.83 | 6,585.06 |
| | Stephen BROWNE | IRL | 70 | 69 | 67 | 71 | 277 | -11 | 9,782.83 | 6,585.06 |
| | Felipe AGUILAR | CHI | 72 | 70 | 70 | 65 | 277 | -11 | 9,782.83 | 6,585.06 |
| 23 | Richard MCEVOY | ENG | 72 | 69 | 67 | 70 | 278 | -10 | 7,917.19 | 5,329.25 |
| | Iain PYMAN | ENG | 76 | 67 | 68 | 67 | 278 | -10 | 7,917.19 | 5,329.25 |
| | Benoit TEILLERIA | FRA | 70 | 68 | 68 | 72 | 278 | -10 | 7,917.19 | 5,329.25 |
| | Rodolfo GONZALEZ | ARG | 67 | 69 | 70 | 72 | 278 | -10 | 7,917.19 | 5,329.25 |
| | Benn BARHAM | ENG | 69 | 69 | 68 | 72 | 278 | -10 | 7,917.19 | 5,329.25 |
| | James KINGSTON | RSA | 65 | 69 | 73 | 71 | 278 | -10 | 7,917.19 | 5,329.25 |
| | Christian L NILSSON | SWE | 72 | 68 | 69 | 69 | 278 | -10 | 7,917.19 | 5,329.25 |
| | Mark MOULAND | WAL | 72 | 68 | 67 | 71 | 278 | -10 | 7,917.19 | 5,329.25 |
| | Magnus PERSSON | SWE | 69 | 70 | 68 | 71 | 278 | -10 | 7,917.19 | 5,329.25 |
| 32 | Klas ERIKSSON | SWE | 68 | 70 | 70 | 71 | 279 | -9 | 6,506.21 | 4,379.49 |
| | Toni KARJALAINEN | FIN | 69 | 70 | 68 | 72 | 279 | -9 | 6,506.21 | 4,379.49 |
| | Cédric MENUT | FRA | 66 | 72 | 68 | 73 | 279 | -9 | 6,506.21 | 4,379.49 |
| 35 | David HIGGINS | IRL | 70 | 67 | 72 | 71 | 280 | -8 | 5,722.33 | 3,851.84 |
| | Francis VALERA | ESP | 65 | 67 | 74 | 74 | 280 | -8 | 5,722.33 | 3,851.84 |
| | Robert COLES | ENG | 73 | 68 | 69 | 70 | 280 | -8 | 5,722.33 | 3,851.84 |
| | Philip GOLDING | ENG | 67 | 72 | 72 | 69 | 280 | -8 | 5,722.33 | 3,851.84 |
| | Carl SUNESON | ESP | 72 | 68 | 69 | 71 | 280 | -8 | 5,722.33 | 3,851.84 |
| 40 | Jonathan LOMAS | ENG | 68 | 72 | 72 | 69 | 281 | -7 | 4,624.89 | 3,113.13 |
| | Luis CLAVERIE | ESP | 72 | 69 | 70 | 70 | 281 | -7 | 4,624.89 | 3,113.13 |
| | Johan SKÖLD | SWE | 71 | 70 | 72 | 68 | 281 | -7 | 4,624.89 | 3,113.13 |
| | Sean WHIFFIN | ENG | 71 | 69 | 70 | 71 | 281 | -7 | 4,624.89 | 3,113.13 |
| | Henrik NYSTROM | SWE | 71 | 72 | 69 | 69 | 281 | -7 | 4,624.89 | 3,113.13 |
| | Claes NILSSON | SWE | 71 | 67 | 68 | 75 | 281 | -7 | 4,624.89 | 3,113.13 |
| | Mikko ILONEN | FIN | 68 | 73 | 74 | 66 | 281 | -7 | 4,624.89 | 3,113.13 |
| | Terry PILKADARIS | AUS | 72 | 69 | 68 | 72 | 281 | -7 | 4,624.89 | 3,113.13 |
| | Ariel CANETE | ARG | 72 | 70 | 69 | 70 | 281 | -7 | 4,624.89 | 3,113.13 |
| 49 | Roope KAKKO | FIN | 70 | 71 | 74 | 67 | 282 | -6 | 3,292.30 | 2,216.12 |
| | Gregory BOURDY | FRA | 69 | 72 | 70 | 71 | 282 | -6 | 3,292.30 | 2,216.12 |
| | Gustavo ACOSTA | ARG | 70 | 72 | 69 | 71 | 282 | -6 | 3,292.30 | 2,216.12 |
| | Jamie DONALDSON | WAL | 73 | 69 | 67 | 72 | 282 | -6 | 3,292.30 | 2,216.12 |
| | Sébastien DELAGRANGE | FRA | 73 | 66 | 71 | 72 | 282 | -6 | 3,292.30 | 2,216.12 |
| | Gary CLARK | ENG | 73 | 70 | 69 | 70 | 282 | -6 | 3,292.30 | 2,216.12 |
| | Titch MOORE | RSA | 69 | 73 | 71 | 69 | 282 | -6 | 3,292.30 | 2,216.12 |
| | Michael HOEY | NIR | 70 | 69 | 73 | 70 | 282 | -6 | 3,292.30 | 2,216.12 |
| 57 | Garry HOUSTON | WAL | 67 | 74 | 71 | 71 | 283 | -5 | 2,508.42 | 1,688.48 |
| | Pedro LINHART | ESP | 73 | 69 | 71 | 70 | 283 | -5 | 2,508.42 | 1,688.48 |
| 59 | Daniel VANCSIK | ARG | 68 | 71 | 73 | 72 | 284 | -4 | 2,273.25 | 1,530.18 |
| | Tuomas TUOVINEN | FIN | 75 | 68 | 65 | 76 | 284 | -4 | 2,273.25 | 1,530.18 |
| | Oskar HENNINGSSON | SWE | 69 | 71 | 73 | 71 | 284 | -4 | 2,273.25 | 1,530.18 |
| 62 | Sam OSBORNE | ENG | 72 | 70 | 74 | 69 | 285 | -3 | 2,077.28 | 1,398.27 |
| | Santiago LUNA | ESP | 70 | 70 | 71 | 74 | 285 | -3 | 2,077.28 | 1,398.27 |
| 64 | Pelle EDBERG | SWE | 73 | 70 | 69 | 74 | 286 | -2 | 1,842.12 | 1,239.97 |
| | Thomas SUNDSTRÖM | FIN | 71 | 71 | 72 | 72 | 286 | -2 | 1,842.12 | 1,239.97 |
| | Stephen SCAHILL | NZL | 72 | 71 | 71 | 72 | 286 | -2 | 1,842.12 | 1,239.97 |
| | Matt DEARDEN | WAL | 72 | 70 | 72 | 72 | 286 | -2 | 1,842.12 | 1,239.97 |
| 68 | Oliver WHITELEY | ENG | 71 | 70 | 73 | 73 | 287 | -1 | 1,606.95 | 1,081.68 |
| | Peter GUSTAFSSON | SWE | 75 | 68 | 73 | 71 | 287 | -1 | 1,606.95 | 1,081.68 |
| 70 | Carlos DEL MORAL | ESP | 69 | 71 | 68 | 80 | 288 | 0 | 1,489.37 | 1,002.53 |
| 71 | Marco BERNARDINI | ITA | 71 | 72 | 71 | 75 | 289 | 1 | 1,305.25 | 878.60 |
| | Kalle BRINK | SWE | 73 | 70 | 74 | 72 | 289 | 1 | 1,305.25 | 878.60 |
| 73 | Markus WESTERBERG | SWE | 72 | 71 | 74 | 73 | 290 | 2 | 1,173.00 | 789.57 |
| 74 | Robert WRAGG | ENG | 70 | 69 | 76 | 76 | 291 | 3 | 1,170.00 | 787.56 |

# Total Prize Fund
€787,400  £530,017

> " I really like this golf course, there is something about it that makes it quite special. It's very traditional and the design makes it very easy to pick out different shots. Also, when you arrive and find it in such good condition, you can't help but fall in love with it " – David Drysdale

Ten years before his Russian affair, as Englishman Carl Watts was lifting the first Russian Open title, Cañizares was a 13 year old prodigy who had dreams of following the career path of his famous father José Maria, a six time winner on The European Tour.

Just as The Imperial Collection Russian Open served its apprenticeship, so did Alejandro. The young Spanish wizard followed in the footsteps of golfing stars Paul Casey and Phil Mickelson by taking a scholarship to Arizona State University, where he won the National Collegiate All American championship (NCAA) in his freshman year.

He returned from the USA in the summer of 2006 to turn professional and make his way on The European Tour, where he found his perfect partner in Russia.

After posting rounds of 66-67-67-66, crafted in the main by his superb iron play, Cañizares set a new low scoring record of 22 under par 266 for the tournament to claim the €130,641 (£87,937) first prize, as well as a two year exemption to The European Tour.

He won by a four shot margin from Scotland's David Drysdale, with defending champion Mikael Lundberg of Sweden and Ireland's Gary Murphy finishing in a share of third place a stroke further back.

The emphatic victory, in just his third appearance, made him the fastest Affiliate Member in the history of The European Tour to win, breaking the previous record held by his fellow countryman Sergio Garcia and Northern Ireland's Graeme McDowell, who both won on their fourth outings.

"This has been an unbelievable week and means everything to me," said Cañizares. "This is the best that I have played so far in my career. To win in my third event on Tour is way beyond my expectations. I did not know much about Russia before coming here, but I have fallen in love with the place – I certainly will never forget it."

**Michael Gibbons**

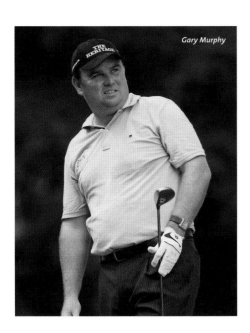

Gary Murphy

# Resplendent In Red

## Medinah Country Club

| Par | Yards | Metres |
| --- | --- | --- |
| 72 | 7561 | 6914 |

| | | | | |
| --- | --- | --- | --- | --- |
| 1 | Tiger WOODS | 270 | -18 |  |
| 2 | Shaun MICHEEL | 275 | -13 | |
| 3 | Luke DONALD | 276 | -12 | |
| | Sergio GARCIA | 276 | -12 | |
| | Adam SCOTT | 276 | -12 | |
| 6 | Mike WEIR | 277 | -11 | |
| 7 | K J CHOI | 278 | -10 | |
| | Steve STRICKER | 278 | -10 | |
| 9 | Ryan MOORE | 279 | -9 | |
| | Geoff OGILVY | 279 | -9 | |
| | Ian POULTER | 279 | -9 | |

## WEATHER REPORT

| Round One | Round Two | Round Three | Round Four |
| --- | --- | --- | --- |

## EUROPEAN TOUR ORDER OF MERIT
(After 38 tournaments)

| Pos | | € | |
| --- | --- | --- | --- |
| 1 | David HOWELL | 1,905,840.85 | |
| 2 | Robert KARLSSON | 1,622,159.28 | |
| 3 | Paul CASEY | 1,435,029.17 | |
| 4 | Johan EDFORS | 1,265,039.24 | |
| 5 | Padraig HARRINGTON | 1,225,356.82 | |
| 6 | Ernie ELS | 1,223,470.77 | |
| 7 | Colin MONTGOMERIE | 1,187,083.21 | |
| 8 | Henrik STENSON | 1,114,670.25 | |
| 9 | Retief GOOSEN | 1,059,661.33 | |
| 10 | John BICKERTON | 1,025,907.16 | |

# US PGA Championship

**Medinah, Illinois, USA**
August 17-20 • 2006

Seven years. There is an old wives' tale which states that every cell in the human body is replaced in that time and only a fool would argue with an old wife. We will put it to the test anyway.

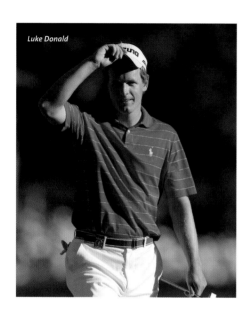

Luke Donald

In 1999, Tiger Woods won his second Major title, the US PGA Championship, at Medinah Country Club, situated in a leafy suburb to the west of Chicago. Then 23, Woods had gone into the final round five ahead yet clawed his way to a one shot victory after being harried all day by a precocious teenager named Sergio Garcia.

Seven years later, Woods won his 12th Major title, the US PGA Championship, at Medinah Country Club which, although the same course, had been stretched to 7561 yards by Rees Jones, making it the longest course in Major Championship history.

Jones also introduced 13 new tees, rebuilt and reshaped seven greens and, to borrow a word from our hosts, 'regrassed' all 18 putting surfaces. The greatest change took place at the par three 17th, where the green was moved from the crest of a steep, tree-lined hill down to the shore of Lake Kadijah, brilliantly bringing the water into play.

To the best of everyone's knowledge, Woods had not required similar reconstructive surgery in the intervening years, just a knee operation. A little more muscle, a tad less hair perhaps, but still resplendent in final round red, the 30 year old did not look much

*" I've always loved playing here. It's a straightforward golf course and I've just received Honorary Membership so it's pretty sweet! We don't play courses like these very often, classic courses which are difficult but not tricked up "* – **Tiger Woods**

different as he and England's Luke Donald went into the final round tied for the lead.

Yet the next 18 holes would reveal that Woods has indeed changed as he strolled home five strokes ahead of the field on 18 under par 270, drawing inevitable comparisons with his 15 shot US Open Championship triumph at Pebble Beach in 2000 and his eight shot Open Championship victory at St Andrews one month later that same year.

Woods said: "If you compare how I was here in 1999 to how I am now in 2006, I just have a better understanding of how to get more out of my round and how to handle the emotions better. That comes through seven more years of experience. I've been through a lot and am much better prepared to handle situations mentally than I was then."

So those old wives were right then? Smarter. Tougher. Better. Woods was invincible at Medinah Country Club and on this form, will surpass the 18 Major Championships won by Jack Nicklaus, long before his 35th birthday.

*Henrik Stenson*

*Sergio Garcia*

An unforgettable week began under the shadow of the loss of Heather Clarke, the lovely and beloved wife of Darren Clarke and mother to their young boys, Tyrone and Conor. Paul McGinley withdrew from the Championship. He, wife Ali, and their children were near neighbours and even closer friends of the Clarkes and Heather's passing rendered insignificant the Dubliner's fight for his place in Europe's Ryder Cup Team.

Clarke, however, insisted his good friends Thomas Björn and Lee Westwood and fellow countrymen Padraig Harrington and Graeme McDowell should play, while US Ryder Cup Captain Tom Lehman agreed to lead a memorial service before play began on the Thursday morning. It took place on the sun-dappled practice green behind the clubhouse and 150 people, including PGA of America President Roger Warren and many players, were moved by Lehman's heartfelt words.

Much of Medinah fell eerily silent during the first 36 holes as the majority of spectators were drawn to the grouping of Masters Tournament Champion Phil Mickelson, US Open Champion Geoff Ogilvy, and Woods.

Lucas Glover and Chris Riley led the first round with 66s but most eyes feasted on the 15 birdies served up by that illustrious trio. Seven of them were landed by Ogilvy although, ironically, all three finished that opening day all square on 69.

Americans Billy Andrade and Tim Herron, Sweden's Henrik Stenson and Donald shared the halfway lead on eight under par 136 while, in terms of 'Ryder Cup Watch', Europe lost Paul Casey, Colin Montgomerie and Harrington to the cut while America bade farewell to rookies Zach Johnson, Vaughn and Brett Wetterich, wild card Scott Verplank, and Captain Lehman himself.

Back with the marquee grouping on Friday night, Ogilvy and Woods were still tied – on seven under par 137 – after matching 68's, while Mickelson's languid slide off the pace had begun with a 71. All three had produced an array of spectacular shots but Ogilvy was the most impressive, making more birdies, hitting more fairways and greens in regulation and requiring fewest putts. As Mickelson enthused: "Man, he sure hits it pure."

OSCAR
JACOBSON
GOLF

*Join our Tee-Party!*

# Final Results

| Pos | Name | | Rd1 | Rd2 | Rd3 | Rd4 | Total | | € | £ |
|-----|------|---|-----|-----|-----|-----|-------|---|---|---|
| 1 | Tiger WOODS | USA | 69 | 68 | 65 | 68 | 270 | -18 | 959,469.52 | 645,842.13 |
| 2 | Shaun MICHEEL | USA | 69 | 70 | 67 | 69 | 275 | -13 | 575,681.71 | 387,505.27 |
| 3 | Luke DONALD | ENG | 68 | 68 | 66 | 74 | 276 | -12 | 277,180.08 | 186,576.61 |
| | Adam SCOTT | AUS | 71 | 69 | 69 | 67 | 276 | -12 | 277,180.08 | 186,576.61 |
| | Sergio GARCIA | ESP | 69 | 70 | 67 | 70 | 276 | -12 | 277,180.08 | 186,576.61 |
| 6 | Mike WEIR | CAN | 72 | 67 | 65 | 73 | 277 | -11 | 191,893.90 | 129,168.42 |
| 7 | Steve STRICKER | USA | 72 | 67 | 70 | 69 | 278 | -10 | 162,880.53 | 109,638.82 |
| | K J CHOI | KOR | 73 | 67 | 67 | 71 | 278 | -10 | 162,880.53 | 109,638.82 |
| 9 | Ian POULTER | ENG | 70 | 70 | 68 | 71 | 279 | -9 | 129,340.25 | 87,062.05 |
| | Geoff OGILVY | AUS | 69 | 68 | 68 | 74 | 279 | -9 | 129,340.25 | 87,062.05 |
| | Ryan MOORE | USA | 71 | 72 | 67 | 69 | 279 | -9 | 129,340.25 | 87,062.05 |
| 12 | Chris DIMARCO | USA | 71 | 70 | 67 | 72 | 280 | -8 | 105,431.90 | 70,968.76 |
| | Sean O'HAIR | USA | 72 | 70 | 70 | 68 | 280 | -8 | 105,431.90 | 70,968.76 |
| 14 | Henrik STENSON | SWE | 68 | 68 | 73 | 72 | 281 | -7 | 90,146.24 | 60,679.61 |
| | Tim HERRON | USA | 69 | 67 | 72 | 73 | 281 | -7 | 90,146.24 | 60,679.61 |
| 16 | Woody AUSTIN | USA | 71 | 69 | 69 | 73 | 282 | -6 | 73,684.75 | 49,598.99 |
| | Ernie ELS | RSA | 71 | 70 | 72 | 69 | 282 | -6 | 73,684.75 | 49,598.99 |
| | Phil MICKELSON | USA | 69 | 71 | 68 | 74 | 282 | -6 | 73,684.75 | 49,598.99 |
| | David TOMS | USA | 71 | 67 | 71 | 73 | 282 | -6 | 73,684.75 | 49,598.99 |
| 20 | Robert ALLENBY | AUS | 68 | 74 | 71 | 70 | 283 | -5 | 55,851.47 | 37,594.97 |
| | Harrison FRAZAR | USA | 69 | 72 | 69 | 73 | 283 | -5 | 55,851.47 | 37,594.97 |
| | Jonathan BYRD | USA | 69 | 72 | 74 | 68 | 283 | -5 | 55,851.47 | 37,594.97 |
| | Fred FUNK | USA | 69 | 69 | 74 | 71 | 283 | -5 | 55,851.47 | 37,594.97 |
| 24 | Stewart CINK | USA | 68 | 74 | 73 | 69 | 284 | -4 | 41,624.05 | 28,018.15 |
| | Anders HANSEN | DEN | 72 | 71 | 70 | 71 | 284 | -4 | 41,624.05 | 28,018.15 |
| | Steve FLESCH | USA | 72 | 71 | 69 | 72 | 284 | -4 | 41,624.05 | 28,018.15 |
| | Chad CAMPBELL | USA | 71 | 72 | 75 | 66 | 284 | -4 | 41,624.05 | 28,018.15 |
| | Tim CLARK | RSA | 70 | 69 | 75 | 70 | 284 | -4 | 41,624.05 | 28,018.15 |
| 29 | Lee WESTWOOD | ENG | 69 | 72 | 71 | 73 | 285 | -3 | 32,217.48 | 21,686.36 |
| | Heath SLOCUM | USA | 73 | 70 | 72 | 70 | 285 | -3 | 32,217.48 | 21,686.36 |
| | Jim FURYK | USA | 70 | 72 | 69 | 74 | 285 | -3 | 32,217.48 | 21,686.36 |
| | Robert KARLSSON | SWE | 71 | 73 | 69 | 72 | 285 | -3 | 32,217.48 | 21,686.36 |
| | Dean WILSON | USA | 74 | 70 | 74 | 67 | 285 | -3 | 32,217.48 | 21,686.36 |
| 34 | Davis LOVE III | USA | 68 | 69 | 73 | 76 | 286 | -2 | 27,043.87 | 18,203.88 |
| | Trevor IMMELMAN | RSA | 73 | 71 | 70 | 72 | 286 | -2 | 27,043.87 | 18,203.88 |
| | Retief GOOSEN | RSA | 70 | 73 | 68 | 75 | 286 | -2 | 27,043.87 | 18,203.88 |
| 37 | Graeme MCDOWELL | NIR | 75 | 68 | 72 | 72 | 287 | -1 | 22,928.50 | 15,433.73 |
| | Richard GREEN | AUS | 73 | 69 | 73 | 72 | 287 | -1 | 22,928.50 | 15,433.73 |
| | Billy MAYFAIR | USA | 69 | 69 | 73 | 76 | 287 | -1 | 22,928.50 | 15,433.73 |
| | J B HOLMES | USA | 71 | 70 | 68 | 78 | 287 | -1 | 22,928.50 | 15,433.73 |
| 41 | Billy ANDRADE | USA | 67 | 69 | 78 | 74 | 288 | 0 | 18,091.96 | 12,178.13 |
| | Justin ROSE | ENG | 73 | 70 | 70 | 75 | 288 | 0 | 18,091.96 | 12,178.13 |
| | J J HENRY | USA | 68 | 73 | 73 | 74 | 288 | 0 | 18,091.96 | 12,178.13 |
| | Chris RILEY | USA | 66 | 72 | 73 | 77 | 288 | 0 | 18,091.96 | 12,178.13 |
| | Daniel CHOPRA | SWE | 72 | 67 | 76 | 73 | 288 | 0 | 18,091.96 | 12,178.13 |
| 46 | Olin BROWNE | USA | 75 | 66 | 73 | 75 | 289 | 1 | 14,913.32 | 10,038.52 |
| | Lucas GLOVER | USA | 66 | 74 | 77 | 72 | 289 | 1 | 14,913.32 | 10,038.52 |
| 48 | Jerry KELLY | USA | 70 | 74 | 74 | 72 | 290 | 2 | 13,561.13 | 9,128.32 |
| 49 | Joey SINDELAR | USA | 74 | 70 | 73 | 74 | 291 | 3 | 12,176.27 | 8,196.14 |
| | Corey PAVIN | USA | 72 | 71 | 72 | 76 | 291 | 3 | 12,176.27 | 8,196.14 |
| | Nathan GREEN | AUS | 71 | 71 | 74 | 75 | 291 | 3 | 12,176.27 | 8,196.14 |
| | Ryan PALMER | USA | 70 | 73 | 72 | 76 | 291 | 3 | 12,176.27 | 8,196.14 |
| | Rich BEEM | USA | 75 | 69 | 72 | 75 | 291 | 3 | 12,176.27 | 8,196.14 |
| | Kenny PERRY | USA | 72 | 71 | 71 | 77 | 291 | 3 | 12,176.27 | 8,196.14 |
| 55 | Aaron BADDELEY | AUS | 70 | 74 | 75 | 73 | 292 | 4 | 11,225.17 | 7,555.93 |
| | Hideto TANIHARA | JPN | 73 | 71 | 78 | 70 | 292 | 4 | 11,225.17 | 7,555.93 |
| | José Maria OLAZÁBAL | ESP | 72 | 68 | 75 | 77 | 292 | 4 | 11,225.17 | 7,555.93 |
| | Stuart APPLEBY | AUS | 70 | 73 | 79 | 70 | 292 | 4 | 11,225.17 | 7,555.93 |
| | Stephen AMES | CAN | 74 | 69 | 74 | 75 | 292 | 4 | 11,225.17 | 7,555.93 |
| 60 | Steve LOWERY | USA | 70 | 72 | 76 | 75 | 293 | 5 | 10,778.35 | 7,255.17 |
| | Ben CURTIS | USA | 72 | 72 | 73 | 76 | 293 | 5 | 10,778.35 | 7,255.17 |
| 62 | Charles WARREN | USA | 73 | 70 | 77 | 75 | 295 | 7 | 10,523.59 | 7,083.69 |
| | Jeff MAGGERT | USA | 75 | 68 | 78 | 74 | 295 | 7 | 10,523.59 | 7,083.69 |
| | Jason GORE | USA | 70 | 73 | 75 | 77 | 295 | 7 | 10,523.59 | 7,083.69 |
| 65 | Miguel Angel JIMÉNEZ | ESP | 70 | 73 | 75 | 78 | 296 | 8 | 10,327.62 | 6,951.77 |
| | Bob TWAY | USA | 72 | 71 | 75 | 78 | 296 | 8 | 10,327.62 | 6,951.77 |
| 67 | David HOWELL | ENG | 71 | 71 | 73 | 82 | 297 | 9 | 10,210.04 | 6,872.63 |
| 68 | Jay HAAS | USA | 75 | 68 | 74 | 83 | 300 | 12 | 10,092.46 | 6,793.48 |
| | Don YRENE | USA | 71 | 72 | 77 | 80 | 300 | 12 | 10,092.46 | 6,793.48 |
| 70 | Jim KANE | USA | 71 | 71 | 80 | 79 | 301 | 13 | 9,974.88 | 6,714.33 |

## Total Prize Fund
€5,100,905 £3,433,543

---

Woods stamped his authority on Saturday. If Medinah had played benignly on the opening two days, its greens were softened even further by heavy overnight rain on Friday. Canada's Mike Weir leapt ahead with a course record 65, matched minutes later by Woods as he ascended to the top. Donald would join Woods on 14 under par 202 courtesy of a splendidly aggressive 66 and indeed had he rolled home a birdie putt on the 18th, he would have taken the lead into the final day.

Lee Westwood

Would that have made a difference? Who knows? We all know that Woods had previously won 11 Major titles but he had led after 54 holes in them all. Hopes that Donald might break this sequence were fuelled by the quality of the young Englishman's golf and his comfort on a course he had played many times during nine years as a Chicago resident.

Yet those hopes soon disappeared as Woods followed up a raking ten foot for birdie at the first hole of the final round with two monster putts at the sixth and eighth – he was rolling the ball beautifully after spotting a fault in his stroke as he watched television highlights the night before.

"I rehearsed it a little bit last night, came out onto the putting green this morning and just felt like 'Hey, this is back to how I putted two weeks ago at the Buick Open (which he won). It's special when you have that feeling at a tournament and even more so when it's for the entire 18 holes on Sunday at a Major."

In that zone, Woods is unstoppable. He won by 'only' five shots from fellow countryman Shaun Micheel with Adam Scott, Donald and Garcia sharing third place as well as the honour of finishing top European Tour Members for the week.

**Karl MacGinty**

*Irish Independent*

# Momentous Day

Angel Cabrera

I f August 28, 1996, was a momentous day in the life of Tiger Woods – the day he said 'hello world' on becoming a professional – then August 27, 2006, has the potential to be pretty memorable, too.

Going into the final round of the World Golf Championships - Bridgestone Invitational, the defending champion was in joint second place with Paul Casey and Davis Love III, the trio all a stroke behind Stewart Cink.

But at Firestone Country Club Woods was back on one of his happiest hunting grounds, a course where his previous seven visits had yielded a return of four wins, a second, two fourths and earnings in excess of five million dollars.

Not only was he aiming for a fifth victory at the venue, he was also trying for a fourth tournament win in a row following his triumphs at The Open Championship, the Buick Open and US PGA Championship. Plus,

it would be the 70th individual title of his ten year professional career.

The week had already been an eventful one. An opening 67 had left him four behind Adam Scott, but he then stormed into the lead with a display that playing partner Paul McGinley described as "awesome - probably the greatest golfer the game has ever seen playing at the absolute peak of his abilities."

At the end of the day, though, one shot had everybody talking - but in a way nobody could have predicted.

Needing a closing par for a 63, Woods' nine iron approach to the ninth from the right-

Ian Poulter

hand rough flew over 200 yards, over the green, over the grandstand behind, onto a cart path and, amazingly, onto the roof of the three-storey clubhouse.

It was out of sight and there was every reason for him to believe it was also out of bounds. Or lost. Or both. But neither was the case. The entire clubhouse area is in play and with the ball bouncing down in a loading bay where a chef happened to be, rules officials were able to sanction a free drop away from the grandstand which was deemed a temporary immovable obstruction.

"A huge break," agreed Woods after escaping with a bogey five. "If I'd had to re-drop and play where I played my second shot from, it would have been a tough six. I've certainly never seen or experienced anything like it - though I did once hit it into a porta-john (toilet). The gentleman in there, just happened to open the door at the wrong time!"

There had been few chinks in his armour up to that point, and there were plenty more on the Saturday. Not since 1996 had the World Number One registered four consecutive bogeys, but although he battled back for a 71 it was still the first over-par score in his last 18 rounds, leaving the respective 64s of Cink and Casey to set up a fascinating last round.

New leader Cink was trying to repeat his feat of two years earlier, namely lift the trophy six days after being given a Ryder Cup wild card. Casey was trying to become only the third European Tour Member – following Darren Clarke and Ernie Els –to capture one of the WGC individual crowns.

*❝ Firestone is right in front of you, no tricks and if it's hard and fast it can play brutally hard. Most of the modern golf courses aren't like this - they don't have trees like this or defined fairways. Every hole looks like it's an alleyway. The greens aren't that difficult, but it's more of a ball-striking course ❞ – Tiger Woods*

*Paul Casey*

# Final Results

| Pos | Name | | Rd1 | Rd2 | Rd3 | Rd4 | Total | € | £ |
|---|---|---|---|---|---|---|---|---|---|
| 1 | Tiger WOODS | USA | 67 | 64 | 71 | 68 | 270 | -10 1,014,833.58 | 691,195.24 |
| 2 | Stewart CINK | USA | 70 | 67 | 64 | 69 | 270 | -10 585,480.91 | 398,766.48 |
| 3 | Jim FURYK | USA | 69 | 65 | 69 | 68 | 271 | -9 351,288.55 | 239,259.89 |
| 4 | Davis LOVE III | USA | 67 | 65 | 70 | 71 | 273 | -7 192,232.90 | 130,928.33 |
| | Angel CABRERA | ARG | 70 | 68 | 70 | 65 | 273 | -7 192,232.90 | 130,928.33 |
| | Paul CASEY | ENG | 69 | 69 | 64 | 71 | 273 | -7 192,232.90 | 130,928.33 |
| | Lucas GLOVER | USA | 66 | 69 | 69 | 69 | 273 | -7 192,232.90 | 130,928.33 |
| 8 | David TOMS | USA | 67 | 74 | 65 | 68 | 274 | -6 119,047.79 | 81,082.52 |
| | Luke DONALD | ENG | 67 | 69 | 70 | 68 | 274 | -6 119,047.79 | 81,082.52 |
| 10 | Adam SCOTT | AUS | 63 | 71 | 71 | 70 | 275 | -5 93,676.95 | 63,802.64 |
| | J J HENRY | USA | 70 | 68 | 68 | 69 | 275 | -5 93,676.95 | 63,802.64 |
| | Arron OBERHOLSER | USA | 70 | 71 | 69 | 65 | 275 | -5 93,676.95 | 63,802.64 |
| 13 | Kevin STADLER | USA | 68 | 67 | 70 | 72 | 277 | -3 74,160.92 | 50,510.42 |
| | Ian POULTER | ENG | 71 | 71 | 67 | 68 | 277 | -3 74,160.92 | 50,510.42 |
| | Trevor IMMELMAN | RSA | 69 | 70 | 68 | 70 | 277 | -3 74,160.92 | 50,510.42 |
| 16 | Ben CRANE | USA | 73 | 67 | 70 | 68 | 278 | -2 66,354.50 | 45,193.53 |
| 17 | Michael CAMPBELL | NZL | 67 | 71 | 70 | 71 | 279 | -1 64,012.58 | 43,598.47 |
| 18 | Vaughn TAYLOR | USA | 71 | 67 | 71 | 71 | 280 | 0 60,109.37 | 40,940.02 |
| | Stephen AMES | CAN | 69 | 70 | 71 | 70 | 280 | 0 60,109.37 | 40,940.02 |
| | Robert GAMEZ | USA | 70 | 67 | 72 | 71 | 280 | 0 60,109.37 | 40,940.02 |
| | Thomas BJÖRN | DEN | 72 | 67 | 67 | 74 | 280 | 0 60,109.37 | 40,940.02 |
| 22 | Mike WEIR | CAN | 69 | 71 | 69 | 72 | 281 | 1 53,083.60 | 36,154.83 |
| | K J CHOI | KOR | 75 | 70 | 67 | 69 | 281 | 1 53,083.60 | 36,154.83 |
| | Sergio GARCIA | ESP | 69 | 73 | 68 | 71 | 281 | 1 53,083.60 | 36,154.83 |
| | José Maria OLAZÁBAL | ESP | 68 | 70 | 74 | 69 | 281 | 1 53,083.60 | 36,154.83 |
| | Robert ALLENBY | AUS | 71 | 71 | 68 | 71 | 281 | 1 53,083.60 | 36,154.83 |
| 27 | Kenny PERRY | USA | 73 | 70 | 66 | 73 | 282 | 2 47,228.79 | 32,167.16 |
| | Chris DIMARCO | USA | 68 | 72 | 71 | 71 | 282 | 2 47,228.79 | 32,167.16 |
| | Carl PETTERSSON | SWE | 70 | 72 | 68 | 72 | 282 | 2 47,228.79 | 32,167.16 |
| | Padraig HARRINGTON | IRL | 73 | 71 | 70 | 68 | 282 | 2 47,228.79 | 32,167.16 |
| 31 | Justin LEONARD | USA | 70 | 69 | 72 | 72 | 283 | 3 43,715.91 | 29,774.56 |
| | Brad FAXON | USA | 69 | 69 | 75 | 70 | 283 | 3 43,715.91 | 29,774.56 |
| | Nick O'HERN | AUS | 72 | 69 | 71 | 71 | 283 | 3 43,715.91 | 29,774.56 |
| | Henrik STENSON | SWE | 75 | 73 | 67 | 68 | 283 | 3 43,715.91 | 29,774.56 |
| | Ernie ELS | RSA | 68 | 67 | 70 | 78 | 283 | 3 43,715.91 | 29,774.56 |
| 36 | Geoff OGILVY | AUS | 69 | 76 | 70 | 69 | 284 | 4 39,422.38 | 26,850.28 |
| | Charl SCHWARTZEL | RSA | 72 | 69 | 70 | 73 | 284 | 4 39,422.38 | 26,850.28 |
| | Brett WETTERICH | USA | 72 | 73 | 71 | 68 | 284 | 4 39,422.38 | 26,850.28 |
| | Rory SABBATINI | RSA | 75 | 71 | 68 | 70 | 284 | 4 39,422.38 | 26,850.28 |
| | Zach JOHNSON | USA | 71 | 68 | 72 | 73 | 284 | 4 39,422.38 | 26,850.28 |
| | Jason GORE | USA | 65 | 76 | 73 | 70 | 284 | 4 39,422.38 | 26,850.28 |
| 42 | Tom LEHMAN | USA | 72 | 69 | 73 | 71 | 285 | 5 36,039.61 | 24,546.29 |
| | Ben CURTIS | USA | 71 | 72 | 72 | 70 | 285 | 5 36,039.61 | 24,546.29 |
| | Fred FUNK | USA | 72 | 70 | 72 | 71 | 285 | 5 36,039.61 | 24,546.29 |
| 45 | Rodney PAMPLING | AUS | 75 | 71 | 71 | 69 | 286 | 6 34,738.53 | 23,660.14 |
| | Dean WILSON | USA | 75 | 70 | 68 | 73 | 286 | 6 34,738.53 | 23,660.14 |
| | Vijay SINGH | FIJ | 70 | 74 | 73 | 69 | 286 | 6 34,738.53 | 23,660.14 |
| 48 | Corey PAVIN | USA | 74 | 73 | 68 | 72 | 287 | 7 33,762.73 | 22,995.53 |
| | Retief GOOSEN | RSA | 71 | 73 | 74 | 69 | 287 | 7 33,762.73 | 22,995.53 |
| 50 | Chad CAMPBELL | USA | 68 | 76 | 72 | 72 | 288 | 8 32,591.77 | 22,198.00 |
| | Olin BROWNE | USA | 68 | 75 | 70 | 75 | 288 | 8 32,591.77 | 22,198.00 |
| | J B HOLMES | USA | 71 | 72 | 68 | 77 | 288 | 8 32,591.77 | 22,198.00 |
| | Stephen DODD | WAL | 74 | 73 | 69 | 72 | 288 | 8 32,591.77 | 22,198.00 |
| 54 | Thomas LEVET | FRA | 77 | 69 | 69 | 74 | 289 | 9 30,835.33 | 21,001.70 |
| | Miguel Angel JIMÉNEZ | ESP | 70 | 72 | 77 | 70 | 289 | 9 30,835.33 | 21,001.70 |
| | Mark HENSBY | AUS | 74 | 76 | 68 | 71 | 289 | 9 30,835.33 | 21,001.70 |
| | Aaron BADDELEY | AUS | 73 | 74 | 69 | 73 | 289 | 9 30,835.33 | 21,001.70 |
| | Phil MICKELSON | USA | 74 | 74 | 68 | 73 | 289 | 9 30,835.33 | 21,001.70 |
| 59 | Jeff MAGGERT | USA | 75 | 70 | 75 | 71 | 291 | 11 29,274.05 | 19,938.32 |
| | Scott VERPLANK | USA | 71 | 75 | 70 | 75 | 291 | 11 29,274.05 | 19,938.32 |
| | David HOWELL | ENG | 67 | 79 | 71 | 74 | 291 | 11 29,274.05 | 19,938.32 |
| 62 | Johan EDFORS | SWE | 75 | 76 | 71 | 70 | 292 | 12 28,103.08 | 19,140.79 |
| | Robert KARLSSON | SWE | 75 | 70 | 73 | 74 | 292 | 12 28,103.08 | 19,140.79 |
| | Bart BRYANT | USA | 72 | 83 | 69 | 68 | 292 | 12 28,103.08 | 19,140.79 |
| 65 | Shiv KAPUR | IND | 72 | 75 | 72 | 74 | 293 | 13 27,322.44 | 18,609.10 |
| 66 | John BICKERTON | ENG | 74 | 75 | 70 | 75 | 294 | 14 26,736.96 | 18,210.34 |
| | Paul MCGINLEY | IRL | 77 | 75 | 70 | 72 | 294 | 14 26,736.96 | 18,210.34 |
| 68 | Mark CALCAVECCHIA | USA | 75 | 72 | 77 | 71 | 295 | 15 25,761.16 | 17,545.73 |
| | Tim HERRON | USA | 76 | 74 | 73 | 72 | 295 | 15 25,761.16 | 17,545.73 |
| | Chris COUCH | USA | 72 | 74 | 72 | 77 | 295 | 15 25,761.16 | 17,545.73 |
| 71 | Wes SHORT JR | USA | 76 | 71 | 73 | 76 | 296 | 16 24,785.36 | 16,881.11 |
| | Stuart APPLEBY | AUS | 75 | 75 | 76 | 69 | 296 | 16 24,785.36 | 16,881.11 |
| | Peter LONARD | AUS | 74 | 73 | 72 | 77 | 296 | 16 24,785.36 | 16,881.11 |
| 74 | Tim CLARK | RSA | 68 | 75 | 80 | 77 | 300 | 20 24,395.04 | 16,615.27 |
| 75 | Gonzalo FDEZ-CASTAÑO | ESP | 74 | 76 | 81 | 70 | 301 | 21 24,199.88 | 16,482.35 |
| 76 | Tatsuhiko TAKAHASHI | JPN | 81 | 73 | 75 | 75 | 304 | 24 24,004.72 | 16,349.42 |
| 77 | Lee WESTWOOD | ENG | 79 | 67 | 74 | W/D | 220 | 10 23,614.40 | 16,083.58 |
| | Fred COUPLES | USA | 73 | 71 | 71 | W/D | 215 | 5 23,614.40 | 16,083.58 |

## Total Prize Fund
€5,831,194  £3,971,581

With nine holes to play the Englishman, certain now of earning himself a second Ryder Cup cap, was out in front, but from two behind, Woods birdied the tenth, 12th and 13th while Casey bogeyed the 11th and 13th.

Suddenly there was a three stroke gap. Game over, it would have appeared to many knowing Woods' record as a front-runner. He rarely loses when leading by one with 18 holes to play, let alone by three with only three remaining.

But he is human. A poor drive down the long 16th led to a bogey six and Cink, with a birdie there and 22 foot putt on the next, drew level.

The last two winners of the title then parred the last hole to tie on ten under par 270 before going into sudden death where Cink missed three chances to win before Woods pounced. Despite the arrival of torrential rain he hit an eight iron to eight feet on the fourth extra hole and in went the birdie putt.

He had shown fallibility, but he still had not been beaten. Four wins in a row, five wins at Firestone, 13 wins in 15 play-offs. August 27, 2006, had ended just as Woods had hoped it would.

**Mark Garrod**

*Press Association*

# Tuning Up
# In Style

## Golfclub München-Nord

| Par | Yards | Metres |
|-----|-------|--------|
| 72 | 6963 | 6366 |

| | | | | |
|---|---|---|---|---|
| **1** | **Henrik STENSON** | **273** | **-15** | |
| 2 | Retief GOOSEN | 273 | -15 | |
| | Padraig HARRINGTON | 273 | -15 | |
| 4 | Martin ERLANDSSON | 274 | -14 | |
| | David HOWELL | 274 | -14 | |
| 6 | Luke DONALD | 275 | -13 | |
| | Colin MONTGOMERIE | 275 | -13 | |
| 8 | Markus BRIER | 277 | -11 | |
| | Robert-Jan DERKSEN | 277 | -11 | |
| | Peter GUSTAFSSON | 277 | -11 | |
| | Alexandre ROCHA | 277 | -11 | |
| | Simon WAKEFIELD | 277 | -11 | |

### WEATHER REPORT

| Round One | Round Two | Round Three | Round Four |

### EUROPEAN TOUR ORDER OF MERIT
(After 40 tournaments)

| Pos | | € | |
|-----|---|---|---|
| **1** | **David HOWELL** | **2,027,514.89** | |
| 2 | Paul CASEY | 1,658,309.83 | |
| 3 | Robert KARLSSON | 1,650,262.37 | |
| 4 | Henrik STENSON | 1,491,716.16 | |
| 5 | Padraig HARRINGTON | 1,447,863.37 | |
| 6 | Johan EDFORS | 1,298,526.75 | |
| 7 | Ernie ELS | 1,267,186.68 | |
| 8 | Retief GOOSEN | 1,267,134.06 | |
| 9 | Colin MONTGOMERIE | 1,253,650.97 | |
| 10 | Luke DONALD | 1,071,714.16 | |

# BMW International Open

**Eichenried, Munich, Germany**
August 31 - September 3 • 2006

With the possible exception of the new champion, Sweden's Henrik Stenson, nobody wore a happier smile in Munich on the final afternoon of the BMW International Open than European Ryder Cup Captain Ian Woosnam.

David Howell

Just three weeks before the tussle with the United States at The K Club, Woosnam looked on with deep satisfaction as Stenson recorded his second win of the season – following his success in The Commercialbank Qatar Masters in January – to top The Ryder Cup World Points List in this, the final counting event.

Not only that, but Padraig Harrington was one of those beaten in the three man sudden-death play-off (alongside Retief Goosen) while David Howell narrowly missed out on participating in the extra hole drama. With Paul Casey, Luke Donald and Colin Montgomerie also all coming home in the top 13, Woosnam's cup was almost so full as to be overflowing. "The performances of the guys in the Team have been absolutely fantastic," he said. "It's good for them, it's

good for the Team and gives us a lot of encouragement."

Ironically, the scoreboard after day one hardly suggested the composition of the eventual denouement. Playing together, Harrington and Goosen managed no better than 70 and 73 respectively while Stenson, in the group in front, split the duo with his own 71, the trio all lying comfortably back in the pack.

Goosen and Stenson crept closer to the lead with respective second rounds of 66 and 68 but it was not until the traditional 'Moving Day' of Saturday that the battle for the €333,330 (£225,356) first prize really began.

Three solid rounds in the 60s pushed Howell into pole position and, indeed, it might well have been even better for the Englishman

Peter Hedblom

*" The course has changed this year, with the rough being up and it being more of a test generally, and I think it needed to. It was a birdie fest before and I don't think that was quite right in the last tournament of a Ryder Cup campaign. This is much better " - Colin Montgomerie*

*Robert-Jan Derksen*

*Ian Woosnam*

who found the water hazard at the 18th and took six when a four was comfortably within his grasp. It left the stage set for an enthralling last day, however, as Harrington, Goosen, Montgomerie and Stenson all loomed ominously.

Few looked more composed on the final morning than Montgomerie who had travelled overnight to Hampden Park in Glasgow to show off The Ryder Cup to the fans on stage at a Robbie Williams concert. The Scot joked he was not going to sing and, ironically, his game was not really in tune on the final day either as a closing 71 saw him share sixth with Donald.

In the end, the splendid risk-reward 568 yard 18th at Golfclub München-Nord, settled the argument. Goosen set the target at 15 under par 273 when he hit a cracking approach shot to 15 feet and calmly rolled in the eagle putt to an ear-splitting roar from the delighted hordes surrounding the green. Stenson followed with a birdie to tie the lead before Harrington arrived on the tee in need of a birdie for outright victory. Unfortunately for him, a drive that had looked spot on from

the tee trickled no more than an inch into the primary rough.

It meant a par five and no better than a place in the play-off for the Irishman alongside the Swede and the South African. Good fortune was on the side of Stenson on

the trio's return to the 18th hole moments later when his five iron second shot from 210 yards, tugged slightly left, landed on a mound from where it bounced in the opposite direction and trundled down to within four feet of the cup. Goosen and Harrington made their birdies in contrasting

*George O'Grady, Executive Director of The European Tour, presents Malcolm Mackenzie of England with an engraved Ice Bucket to mark his 600th appearance in a European Tour event*

Peter Gustafsson enjoys his favourite energy drink at the BMW Championship.

Ian Woosnam The 2006 European Ryder Cup Captain

ways but that made little difference, for Stenson gleefully tapped in his four footer for an eagle three and the title.

"When you're winning you have a little bit of luck," he said. "I hadn't had a fair break at some other stages of the final round, so I felt entitled to one when it mattered most. I didn't have a great summer but I was never really worried about getting my game back and it could hardly have come at a better time with only three weeks to The Ryder Cup."

For Harrington, there was frustration borne of finishing second for the 29th time in his career. On some of those occasions, the Irishman felt he might have let himself

Martin Erlandsson

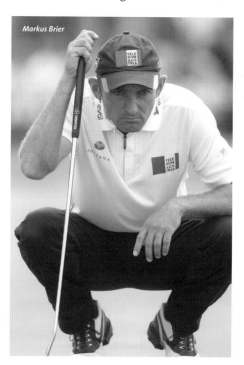

Markus Brier

down but not this time. "There was no more I could have done", he commented philosophically.

Like Stenson, he headed to The K Club in a positive frame of mind. As did Captain Woosnam.

**Charlie Mulqueen**

*Irish Examiner*

# Final Results

| Pos | Name | | Rd1 | Rd2 | Rd3 | Rd4 | Total | | € | £ |
|---|---|---|---|---|---|---|---|---|---|---|
| 1 | Henrik STENSON | SWE | 71 | 68 | 66 | 68 | 273 | -15 | 333,330.00 | 225,356.97 |
| 2 | Padraig HARRINGTON | IRL | 70 | 70 | 64 | 69 | 273 | -15 | 173,710.00 | 117,441.45 |
| | Retief GOOSEN | RSA | 73 | 66 | 67 | 67 | 273 | -15 | 173,710.00 | 117,441.45 |
| 4 | David HOWELL | ENG | 67 | 69 | 66 | 72 | 274 | -14 | 92,400.00 | 62,469.58 |
| | Martin ERLANDSSON | SWE | 67 | 68 | 69 | 70 | 274 | -14 | 92,400.00 | 62,469.58 |
| 6 | Colin MONTGOMERIE | SCO | 70 | 68 | 66 | 71 | 275 | -13 | 65,000.00 | 43,945.05 |
| | Luke DONALD | ENG | 68 | 69 | 71 | 67 | 275 | -13 | 65,000.00 | 43,945.05 |
| 8 | Peter GUSTAFSSON | SWE | 72 | 71 | 64 | 70 | 277 | -11 | 41,200.00 | 27,854.40 |
| | Alexandre ROCHA | BRA | 73 | 67 | 70 | 67 | 277 | -11 | 41,200.00 | 27,854.40 |
| | Simon WAKEFIELD | ENG | 69 | 69 | 68 | 71 | 277 | -11 | 41,200.00 | 27,854.40 |
| | Markus BRIER | AUT | 71 | 69 | 70 | 67 | 277 | -11 | 41,200.00 | 27,854.40 |
| | Robert-Jan DERKSEN | NED | 69 | 68 | 70 | 70 | 277 | -11 | 41,200.00 | 27,854.40 |
| 13 | Bernhard LANGER | GER | 70 | 69 | 71 | 68 | 278 | -10 | 29,480.00 | 19,930.77 |
| | Marcel SIEM | GER | 68 | 70 | 70 | 70 | 278 | -10 | 29,480.00 | 19,930.77 |
| | David LYNN | ENG | 69 | 70 | 67 | 72 | 278 | -10 | 29,480.00 | 19,930.77 |
| | Thomas BJÖRN | DEN | 71 | 69 | 71 | 67 | 278 | -10 | 29,480.00 | 19,930.77 |
| | Paul CASEY | ENG | 70 | 67 | 71 | 70 | 278 | -10 | 29,480.00 | 19,930.77 |
| 18 | Christian CÉVAÊR | FRA | 73 | 69 | 68 | 69 | 279 | -9 | 23,400.00 | 15,820.22 |
| | Ricardo GONZALEZ | ARG | 69 | 69 | 70 | 71 | 279 | -9 | 23,400.00 | 15,820.22 |
| | Bradley DREDGE | WAL | 68 | 70 | 69 | 72 | 279 | -9 | 23,400.00 | 15,820.22 |
| | Marc CAYEUX | ZIM | 71 | 66 | 72 | 70 | 279 | -9 | 23,400.00 | 15,820.22 |
| | Søren HANSEN | DEN | 70 | 66 | 71 | 72 | 279 | -9 | 23,400.00 | 15,820.22 |
| | Anthony WALL | ENG | 72 | 71 | 67 | 69 | 279 | -9 | 23,400.00 | 15,820.22 |
| | Garry HOUSTON | WAL | 67 | 70 | 72 | 70 | 279 | -9 | 23,400.00 | 15,820.22 |
| 25 | Søren KJELDSEN | DEN | 72 | 71 | 66 | 71 | 280 | -8 | 20,200.00 | 13,656.77 |
| | Peter HEDBLOM | SWE | 68 | 72 | 66 | 74 | 280 | -8 | 20,200.00 | 13,656.77 |
| | Alejandro CANIZARES | ESP | 71 | 65 | 71 | 73 | 280 | -8 | 20,200.00 | 13,656.77 |
| 28 | Marc WARREN | SCO | 73 | 68 | 72 | 68 | 281 | -7 | 16,666.67 | 11,267.96 |
| | Peter O'MALLEY | AUS | 71 | 68 | 67 | 75 | 281 | -7 | 16,666.67 | 11,267.96 |
| | Ian GARBUTT | ENG | 70 | 72 | 69 | 70 | 281 | -7 | 16,666.67 | 11,267.96 |
| | Lee WESTWOOD | ENG | 68 | 71 | 68 | 74 | 281 | -7 | 16,666.67 | 11,267.96 |
| | Andres ROMERO | ARG | 69 | 74 | 69 | 69 | 281 | -7 | 16,666.67 | 11,267.96 |
| | Graeme STORM | ENG | 70 | 72 | 70 | 69 | 281 | -7 | 16,666.67 | 11,267.96 |
| | Stephen GALLACHER | SCO | 72 | 68 | 69 | 72 | 281 | -7 | 16,666.67 | 11,267.96 |
| | Fredrik WIDMARK | SWE | 69 | 69 | 73 | 70 | 281 | -7 | 16,666.67 | 11,267.96 |
| | Peter HANSON | SWE | 71 | 70 | 67 | 73 | 281 | -7 | 16,666.67 | 11,267.96 |
| 37 | Sam LITTLE | ENG | 71 | 69 | 71 | 71 | 282 | -6 | 13,400.00 | 9,059.44 |
| | Jarrod MOSELEY | AUS | 71 | 71 | 69 | 71 | 282 | -6 | 13,400.00 | 9,059.44 |
| | Damien MCGRANE | IRL | 69 | 68 | 69 | 76 | 282 | -6 | 13,400.00 | 9,059.44 |
| | José-Filipe LIMA | POR | 72 | 72 | 70 | 72 | 282 | -6 | 13,400.00 | 9,059.44 |
| | David DRYSDALE | SCO | 68 | 71 | 73 | 70 | 282 | -6 | 13,400.00 | 9,059.44 |
| 42 | Niclas FASTH | SWE | 70 | 70 | 72 | 71 | 283 | -5 | 11,400.00 | 7,707.29 |
| | James KINGSTON | RSA | 70 | 71 | 71 | 71 | 283 | -5 | 11,400.00 | 7,707.29 |
| | Gary EVANS | ENG | 67 | 73 | 75 | 68 | 283 | -5 | 11,400.00 | 7,707.29 |
| | Alessandro TADINI | ITA | 70 | 70 | 68 | 75 | 283 | -5 | 11,400.00 | 7,707.29 |
| | David BRANSDON | AUS | 70 | 69 | 77 | 67 | 283 | -5 | 11,400.00 | 7,707.29 |
| 47 | Darren FICHARDT | RSA | 69 | 72 | 71 | 72 | 284 | -4 | 9,600.00 | 6,490.35 |
| | Miguel Angel JIMÉNEZ | ESP | 71 | 70 | 71 | 72 | 284 | -4 | 9,600.00 | 6,490.35 |
| | Simon KHAN | ENG | 70 | 69 | 66 | 79 | 284 | -4 | 9,600.00 | 6,490.35 |
| | David CARTER | ENG | 73 | 69 | 70 | 72 | 284 | -4 | 9,600.00 | 6,490.35 |
| 51 | Massimo SCARPA | ITA | 72 | 70 | 72 | 71 | 285 | -3 | 7,225.00 | 4,884.66 |
| | Leif WESTERBERG | SWE | 70 | 73 | 73 | 69 | 285 | -3 | 7,225.00 | 4,884.66 |
| | Gregory HAVRET | FRA | 73 | 70 | 72 | 70 | 285 | -3 | 7,225.00 | 4,884.66 |
| | Jean VAN DE VELDE | FRA | 73 | 68 | 72 | 72 | 285 | -3 | 7,225.00 | 4,884.66 |
| | Phillip ARCHER | ENG | 71 | 71 | 73 | 70 | 285 | -3 | 7,225.00 | 4,884.66 |
| | Mattias ELIASSON | SWE | 70 | 66 | 78 | 71 | 285 | -3 | 7,225.00 | 4,884.66 |
| | Marcus FRASER | AUS | 72 | 71 | 72 | 70 | 285 | -3 | 7,225.00 | 4,884.66 |
| | Steven JEPPESEN | SWE | 70 | 71 | 67 | 77 | 285 | -3 | 7,225.00 | 4,884.66 |
| 59 | Matthew MILLAR | AUS | 68 | 70 | 72 | 76 | 286 | -2 | 5,300.00 | 3,583.21 |
| | Paul BROADHURST | ENG | 72 | 71 | 67 | 76 | 286 | -2 | 5,300.00 | 3,583.21 |
| | Richard FINCH | ENG | 74 | 69 | 68 | 75 | 286 | -2 | 5,300.00 | 3,583.21 |
| | Brett RUMFORD | AUS | 72 | 68 | 76 | 70 | 286 | -2 | 5,300.00 | 3,583.21 |
| | Nicolas COLSAERTS | BEL | 70 | 68 | 75 | 73 | 286 | -2 | 5,300.00 | 3,583.21 |
| | Miles TUNNICLIFF | ENG | 70 | 70 | 70 | 76 | 286 | -2 | 5,300.00 | 3,583.21 |
| 65 | Joakim BÄCKSTRÖM | SWE | 73 | 68 | 71 | 75 | 287 | -1 | 4,500.00 | 3,042.35 |
| | Raphaël JACQUELIN | FRA | 73 | 70 | 70 | 74 | 287 | -1 | 4,500.00 | 3,042.35 |
| 67 | Andrew MARSHALL | ENG | 72 | 71 | 73 | 72 | 288 | 0 | 4,200.00 | 2,839.53 |
| 68 | Johan EDFORS | SWE | 72 | 69 | 72 | 76 | 289 | 1 | 3,816.67 | 2,580.36 |
| | Scott DRUMMOND | SCO | 74 | 69 | 74 | 72 | 289 | 1 | 3,816.67 | 2,580.36 |
| | Joakim HAEGGMAN | SWE | 70 | 71 | 73 | 75 | 289 | 1 | 3,816.67 | 2,580.36 |
| 71 | Emanuele CANONICA | ITA | 70 | 73 | 71 | 77 | 291 | 3 | 2,998.50 | 2,027.22 |
| | Wolfgang HUGET | GER | 72 | 70 | 73 | 76 | 291 | 3 | 2,998.50 | 2,027.22 |
| 73 | Daniel VANCSIK | ARG | 71 | 70 | 74 | 77 | 292 | 4 | 2,994.00 | 2,024.18 |
| 74 | Jorge BENEDETTI | COL | 71 | 72 | 70 | 82 | 295 | 7 | 2,991.00 | 2,022.15 |

# Total Prize Fund
€2,011,980  £1,360,256

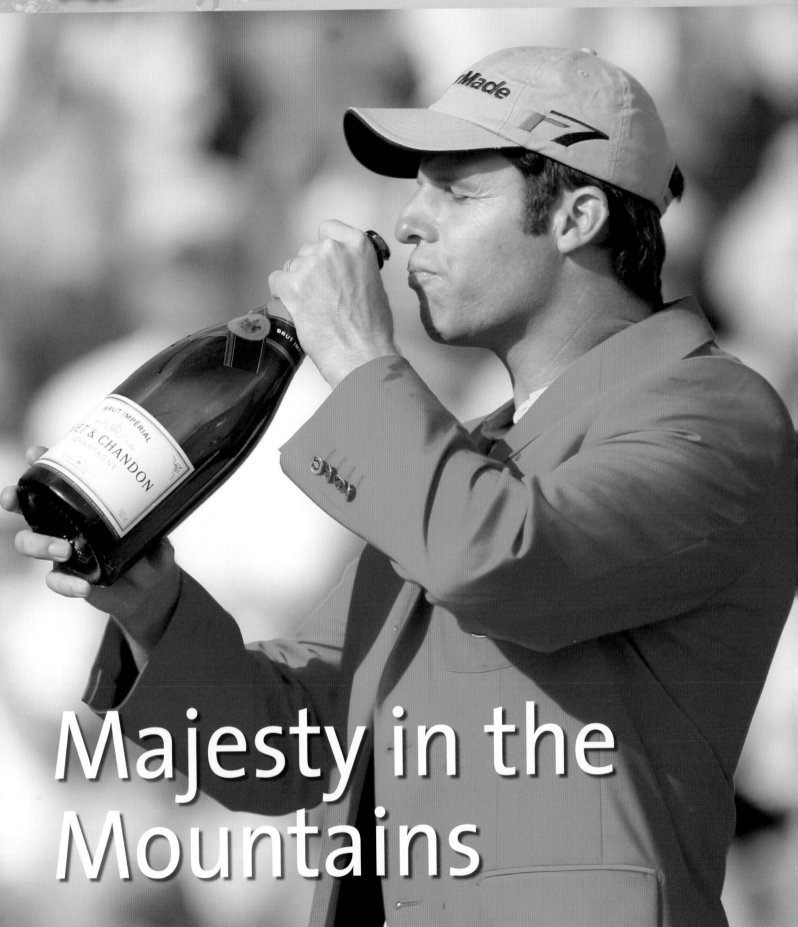

# Majesty in the Mountains

*Sergio Garcia and Michelle Wie*

Ω
## OMEGA

**Crans-sur-Sierre**

| Par | Yards | Metres |
| --- | --- | --- |
| 72 | 6857 | 6239 |

| | | | | |
| --- | --- | --- | --- | --- |
| 1 | Bradley DREDGE | 267 | -17 | |
| 2 | Francesco MOLINARI | 275 | -9 | |
| | Marcel SIEM | 275 | -9 | |
| 4 | Sergio GARCIA | 276 | -8 | |
| | Søren KJELDSEN | 276 | -8 | |
| | Marc WARREN | 276 | -8 | |
| 7 | Ariel CANETE | 277 | -7 | |
| | Martin ERLANDSSON | 277 | -7 | |
| | Mikko ILONEN | 277 | -7 | |
| | Andrew McLARDY | 277 | -7 | |
| | Cesar MONASTERIO | 277 | -7 | |

### WEATHER REPORT

| Round One | Round Two | Round Three | Round Four |
| --- | --- | --- | --- |

### EUROPEAN TOUR ORDER OF MERIT
(After 41 tournaments)

| Pos | | € | |
| --- | --- | --- | --- |
| 1 | David HOWELL | 2,027,514.89 | |
| 2 | Paul CASEY | 1,658,309.83 | |
| 3 | Robert KARLSSON | 1,650,262.37 | |
| 4 | Henrik STENSON | 1,491,716.16 | |
| 5 | Padraig HARRINGTON | 1,447,863.37 | |
| 6 | Johan EDFORS | 1,329,486.75 | |
| 7 | Ernie ELS | 1,267,186.68 | |
| 8 | Retief GOOSEN | 1,267,134.06 | |
| 9 | Colin MONTGOMERIE | 1,253,650.97 | |
| 10 | Luke DONALD | 1,071,714.16 | |

They came in their thousands to see Michelle Wie and left purring about a laconic Welshman called Bradley Dredge. As a crowd-pulling sideshow Miss Wie, a precociously talented 16 year old from Hawaii, was taking on the men in the Omega European Masters at Crans-sur-Sierre set in the picturesque Alpine town of Crans Montana.

Attendance figures were broken on the first two days as Wie, six feet tall and in a short skirt, went about her business. Her galleries were immense but not always the best behaved with the number of clicking cameras and trilling mobile phones confirming the novelty aspect of her appearance.

Sadly, the schoolgirl who had brought her homework to the mountains, found that her short game was rusty on a course that demanded accuracy. She left after rounds of 78 and 79 but impressed everyone with her demeanour and flashes of true talent.

At the same time the men were concentrating on their own games and the calculation issues caused by the altitude which makes the ball fly considerably further than normal. Aside from that, however, the weather was perfect for golf. Dry, not too hot and never more than a gentle breeze disturbing the flags. Mist meant a slight delay at the start of the second day but it soon cleared and attention turned to the top of the leaderboard.

It was a changing scene. After the opening round, David Carter, Robert Coles and

Alessandro Tadini

Francesco Molinari

Anthony Wall were locked together on five under par 66. Could they stay there? Dredge was back in a share of eighth place after a respectable 68. He was not, yet, a subject for the chattering classes, but he was soon to register his presence.

The Welshman's strategy involved attacking, firing the ball at the pins. It was something, he said, he had observed in the likes of Ernie Els, Vijay Singh and Tiger Woods. It worked for him because at the end of the second round he was tied at the top on seven under par 135 after a 67 had drawn him level with Andrew McLardy and Marcel Siem.

If Friday was good, Saturday was even better for the man who, alongside Stephen Dodd, had won the WGC – Algarve World Cup in Portugal at the end of the 2005 season.

His start was perfect as three birdies in succession set him on his way. A double-bogey at the fourth, where he went out of bounds, might have unnerved him but he regrouped and his head-to-head tussle with Siem was enthralling in its intensity.

*" This has a home feel. It is always nice coming back here. It is a wonderful place, so spectacular, so relaxed. The course itself is quite tricky. I feel like it is a nice test more than anything for your iron play and short game around the greens. You can hit a great shot and there is no guarantee it will hold the green so really tests your chipping. "* – Sergio Garcia

*Andrew McLardy*

# Final Results

| Pos | Name | | Rd1 | Rd2 | Rd3 | Rd4 | Total | | € | £ |
|-----|------|---|-----|-----|-----|-----|-------|---|---|---|
| 1 | Bradley DREDGE | WAL | 68 | 67 | 65 | 67 | 267 | -17 | 333,330.00 | 224,546.30 |
| 2 | Francesco MOLINARI | ITA | 68 | 68 | 70 | 69 | 275 | -9 | 173,710.00 | 117,018.98 |
| | Marcel SIEM | GER | 68 | 67 | 67 | 73 | 275 | -9 | 173,710.00 | 117,018.98 |
| 4 | Sergio GARCIA | ESP | 68 | 69 | 68 | 71 | 276 | -8 | 84,933.33 | 57,214.97 |
| | Søren KJELDSEN | DEN | 70 | 69 | 67 | 70 | 276 | -8 | 84,933.33 | 57,214.97 |
| | Marc WARREN | SCO | 69 | 71 | 69 | 67 | 276 | -8 | 84,933.33 | 57,214.97 |
| 7 | Ariel CANETE | ARG | 72 | 70 | 69 | 66 | 277 | -7 | 46,320.00 | 31,203.27 |
| | Mikko ILONEN | FIN | 73 | 67 | 71 | 66 | 277 | -7 | 46,320.00 | 31,203.27 |
| | Cesar MONASTERIO | ARG | 74 | 69 | 68 | 66 | 277 | -7 | 46,320.00 | 31,203.27 |
| | Martin ERLANDSSON | SWE | 70 | 68 | 70 | 69 | 277 | -7 | 46,320.00 | 31,203.27 |
| | Andrew MCLARDY | RSA | 70 | 65 | 71 | 71 | 277 | -7 | 46,320.00 | 31,203.27 |
| 12 | Johan EDFORS | SWE | 73 | 67 | 67 | 71 | 278 | -6 | 30,960.00 | 20,856.07 |
| | Miles TUNNICLIFF | ENG | 67 | 73 | 69 | 69 | 278 | -6 | 30,960.00 | 20,856.07 |
| | Phillip ARCHER | ENG | 68 | 72 | 72 | 66 | 278 | -6 | 30,960.00 | 20,856.07 |
| | Simon DYSON | ENG | 68 | 74 | 68 | 68 | 278 | -6 | 30,960.00 | 20,856.07 |
| | Simon WAKEFIELD | ENG | 68 | 75 | 65 | 70 | 278 | -6 | 30,960.00 | 20,856.07 |
| 17 | Richard MCEVOY | ENG | 70 | 72 | 71 | 66 | 279 | -5 | 24,200.00 | 16,302.22 |
| | Anthony WALL | ENG | 66 | 73 | 69 | 71 | 279 | -5 | 24,200.00 | 16,302.22 |
| | José Manuel LARA | ESP | 69 | 72 | 69 | 69 | 279 | -5 | 24,200.00 | 16,302.22 |
| | Peter HEDBLOM | SWE | 71 | 72 | 69 | 67 | 279 | -5 | 24,200.00 | 16,302.22 |
| | Sam LITTLE | ENG | 67 | 73 | 71 | 68 | 279 | -5 | 24,200.00 | 16,302.22 |
| | Christian L NILSSON | SWE | 71 | 67 | 69 | 72 | 279 | -5 | 24,200.00 | 16,302.22 |
| | Oliver WILSON | ENG | 68 | 69 | 67 | 75 | 279 | -5 | 24,200.00 | 16,302.22 |
| 24 | Miguel CARBALLO | ARG | 72 | 70 | 68 | 70 | 280 | -4 | 21,100.00 | 14,213.92 |
| | Eduardo ROMERO | ARG | 70 | 70 | 72 | 68 | 280 | -4 | 21,100.00 | 14,213.92 |
| 26 | Jean-François REMESY | FRA | 72 | 67 | 69 | 73 | 281 | -3 | 18,400.00 | 12,395.08 |
| | Darren FICHARDT | RSA | 71 | 72 | 72 | 66 | 281 | -3 | 18,400.00 | 12,395.08 |
| | Robert ROCK | ENG | 72 | 67 | 70 | 72 | 281 | -3 | 18,400.00 | 12,395.08 |
| | Rafael GOMEZ | ARG | 67 | 70 | 75 | 69 | 281 | -3 | 18,400.00 | 12,395.08 |
| | Ricardo GONZALEZ | ARG | 69 | 71 | 71 | 70 | 281 | -3 | 18,400.00 | 12,395.08 |
| | Gary ORR | SCO | 69 | 73 | 69 | 70 | 281 | -3 | 18,400.00 | 12,395.08 |
| | David CARTER | ENG | 66 | 74 | 69 | 72 | 281 | -3 | 18,400.00 | 12,395.08 |
| 33 | Wade ORMSBY | AUS | 70 | 73 | 71 | 68 | 282 | -2 | 15,250.00 | 10,273.10 |
| | Andrew MARSHALL | ENG | 68 | 72 | 71 | 71 | 282 | -2 | 15,250.00 | 10,273.10 |
| | Paul BROADHURST | ENG | 71 | 69 | 69 | 73 | 282 | -2 | 15,250.00 | 10,273.10 |
| | Joakim BÄCKSTRÖM | SWE | 72 | 66 | 69 | 75 | 282 | -2 | 15,250.00 | 10,273.10 |
| 37 | Miguel Angel JIMÉNEZ | ESP | 70 | 69 | 75 | 69 | 283 | -1 | 13,800.00 | 9,296.31 |
| | Alessandro TADINI | ITA | 69 | 71 | 71 | 72 | 283 | -1 | 13,800.00 | 9,296.31 |
| | Leif WESTERBERG | SWE | 71 | 71 | 69 | 72 | 283 | -1 | 13,800.00 | 9,296.31 |
| 40 | Carl SUNESON | ESP | 70 | 70 | 71 | 73 | 284 | 0 | 12,400.00 | 8,353.21 |
| | Jarmo SANDELIN | SWE | 71 | 67 | 71 | 75 | 284 | 0 | 12,400.00 | 8,353.21 |
| | David BRANSDON | AUS | 68 | 71 | 68 | 77 | 284 | 0 | 12,400.00 | 8,353.21 |
| | Robert-Jan DERKSEN | NED | 74 | 69 | 72 | 69 | 284 | 0 | 12,400.00 | 8,353.21 |
| 44 | Robert COLES | ENG | 66 | 72 | 73 | 74 | 285 | 1 | 10,800.00 | 7,275.37 |
| | Brett RUMFORD | AUS | 71 | 71 | 64 | 79 | 285 | 1 | 10,800.00 | 7,275.37 |
| | Graeme MCDOWELL | NIR | 71 | 71 | 69 | 74 | 285 | 1 | 10,800.00 | 7,275.37 |
| | Matthew MILLAR | AUS | 70 | 69 | 74 | 72 | 285 | 1 | 10,800.00 | 7,275.37 |
| 48 | David HIGGINS | IRL | 71 | 72 | 66 | 77 | 286 | 2 | 9,200.00 | 6,197.54 |
| | Marc FARRY | FRA | 70 | 73 | 68 | 75 | 286 | 2 | 9,200.00 | 6,197.54 |
| | Raphaël JACQUELIN | FRA | 74 | 69 | 72 | 71 | 286 | 2 | 9,200.00 | 6,197.54 |
| | Jamie SPENCE | ENG | 72 | 69 | 72 | 73 | 286 | 2 | 9,200.00 | 6,197.54 |
| 52 | Peter LAWRIE | IRL | 74 | 69 | 72 | 72 | 287 | 3 | 8,200.00 | 5,523.89 |
| 53 | Philip GOLDING | ENG | 71 | 72 | 75 | 70 | 288 | 4 | 7,400.00 | 4,984.98 |
| | Andrew BUTTERFIELD | ENG | 68 | 74 | 73 | 73 | 288 | 4 | 7,400.00 | 4,984.98 |
| | Gary CLARK | ENG | 73 | 70 | 72 | 73 | 288 | 4 | 7,400.00 | 4,984.98 |
| 56 | Ignacio GARRIDO | ESP | 71 | 68 | 75 | 75 | 289 | 5 | 6,400.00 | 4,311.33 |
| | Tom WHITEHOUSE | ENG | 71 | 70 | 72 | 76 | 289 | 5 | 6,400.00 | 4,311.33 |
| 58 | James KINGSTON | RSA | 71 | 71 | 75 | 73 | 290 | 6 | 6,000.00 | 4,041.87 |
| 59 | Gonzalo FDEZ-CASTAÑO | ESP | 70 | 70 | 76 | 75 | 291 | 7 | 5,600.00 | 3,772.42 |
| | Michael HOEY | NIR | 72 | 71 | 73 | 75 | 291 | 7 | 5,600.00 | 3,772.42 |
| | Augustin DOMINGO | ESP | 68 | 73 | 76 | 74 | 291 | 7 | 5,600.00 | 3,772.42 |
| 62 | Gregory HAVRET | FRA | 72 | 71 | 79 | 70 | 292 | 8 | 5,100.00 | 3,435.59 |
| | Anders HANSEN | DEN | 74 | 69 | 76 | 76 | 292 | 8 | 5,100.00 | 3,435.59 |
| 64 | François DELAMONTAGNE | FRA | 71 | 71 | 74 | 77 | 293 | 9 | 4,800.00 | 3,233.50 |
| 65 | David LYNN | ENG | 72 | 71 | 74 | 78 | 295 | 11 | 4,600.00 | 3,098.77 |
| 66 | Simon KHAN | ENG | 67 | 72 | DISQ | | 139 | -3 | 4,400.00 | 2,964.04 |

That Dredge had a two shot lead over the German at the end of the third round was due more than anything to his eagle three at the 519 yard 15th. His six iron second shot from 206 yards was as majestic as the mountains as it finished six feet from the hole. Siem, in turn, finished a further two shots clear of Englishman Oliver Wilson while Italian Francesco Molinari, who would feature as the tournament drew to a close, went into the final round six shots back.

Molinari ended tied second with Siem on Sunday night but the pair were mere support acts to the unerring Dredge whose final round 67 for a 17 under par total of 267 saw him win by eight strokes, at that point, the biggest winning margin of the season on The European Tour International Schedule.

*Marc Warren*

Dredge, himself, was the first to admit his win was overdue. He has been one of the most consistent players on Tour but, apart from the 2003 Madeira Island Open and the 2005 World Cup, the big prizes have eluded him. "This win is a reward for my patience," he said. "I was getting a bit frustrated but now it feels good."

Siem, added to the testimonials, saying: "Bradley played awesome golf and deserved to win. I could not think about winning as he was playing so well." Molinari, too, lined up in praise of the Welshman, adding: "Bradley's score was unbelievable as there is so much trouble out there."

Dredge had been working hard on his swing and the signs at Crans Montana were that he had eventually found the rhythm that was missing. One of the first people to congratulate him as he stepped from the home green was Eugene Cernan, the 1972 Apollo 17 Mission Commander. It was appropriate really because Dredge was, as Cernan literally had been those 34 years ago, over the moon.

**James Mossop**
*Sunday Telegraph*

# Total Prize Fund
€1,984,350  £1,356,746

# A Victory of Significance

## HSBC

### Wentworth Club

| Par | Yards | Metres |
|-----|-------|--------|
| 72  | 7308  | 6682   |

1 **Paul CASEY**

2 Shaun MICHEEL

3 Robert KARLSSON

   Colin MONTGOMERIE

5 Angel CABRERA

   Michael CAMPBELL

   Luke DONALD

   Mike WEIR

9 Tim CLARK

   Ernie ELS

   Jim FURYK

   Retief GOOSEN

   David HOWELL

   Simon KHAN

   Adam SCOTT

   Tiger WOODS

### WEATHER REPORT

| Round One | Round Two | Round Three | Round Four |
|-----------|-----------|-------------|------------|

### EUROPEAN TOUR ORDER OF MERIT
(After 42 tournaments)

| Pos | | € |
|-----|--------------------|--------------|
| 1 | **Paul CASEY**  | **2,256,193.56** |
| 2 | David HOWELL | 2,089,486.55 |
| 3 | Robert KARLSSON | 1,852,230.81 |
| 4 | Henrik STENSON | 1,491,716.16 |
| 5 | Colin MONTGOMERIE  | 1,455,619.41 |
| 6 | Padraig HARRINGTON | 1,447,863.37 |
| 7 | Johan EDFORS | 1,329,486.75 |
| 8 | Ernie ELS | 1,329,158.34 |
| 9 | Retief GOOSEN  | 1,329,105.72 |
| 10 | Luke DONALD | 1,190,455.82 |

# HSBC World Match Play Championship

**Surrey, England**
September 14-17 • 2006

As expected, a man wearing a red shirt with a Nike swoosh on the chest won the HSBC World Match Play Championship at Wentworth Club. But it was not Tiger Woods. He was 25 miles away at Stamford Bridge in London watching Chelsea play Liverpool in the Barclays Premiership.

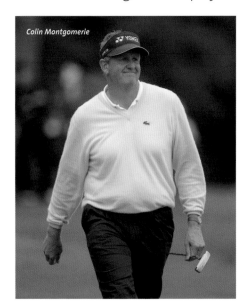

Colin Montgomerie

Instead it was England's Paul Casey who lifted the gleaming Mark McCormack trophy and pocketed the £1 million cheque after steamrollering American Shaun Micheel 10 and 8 in the 36 hole final, the biggest margin of victory in the final in the 43 year history of the illustrious event.

This latest triumph, following his win in the Volvo China Open and the Johnnie Walker Championship at Gleneagles, took Casey ahead of his good friend David Howell at the top of The European Tour Order of Merit and also into the top 20 of the Official World Golf Rankings.

Casey, who became the first rookie winner since Ernie Els in 1994, said: "It is all about believing you should be in this position - that you are capable of winning world class events. I had it. I lost it last year, and now I have it again. This is the biggest year of my career. Not just financially, but in terms of significance."

The Englishman struck the first blow in the final when he birdied the fourth in the morning. He was three up at lunch, which quickly became four with a birdie at the short second. Any hopes Micheel harboured of mounting a comeback were then crushed in

" *It has taken me a little while to get tuned into the flow of the West Course but now I have, I think the way it has been lengthened really suits my game and the greens were in absolutely magnificent condition* " – *Paul Casey*

*Angel Cabrera*

*Robert Karlsson*

a spell of sheer brilliance from his opponent. From the seventh to the tenth, Casey's laser-like iron shots set up winning birdies from four, five, seven and 20 feet.

The day before, the finalists had come through two widely contrasting semi-finals. Casey eased past a tiring Colin Montgomerie 6 and 5, the Scot never properly recovering from a poor start. He was five down after seven holes in the morning; seven down after four holes in the afternoon and was finished off on the 13th green.

"I kept on battling," said Montgomerie. "I didn't get any breaks but I suppose that's like a manager claiming four goals were offside when you lose 6-0!"

While that contest was relatively clear cut, there was never more than a cigarette paper between Micheel and the man who would go on to make his Ryder Cup debut the following week, Sweden's Robert Karlsson, in the second semi-final.

Karlsson was two up early in the morning but by lunchtime was one down to the American who closed out the match on the home green the second time round after both players found the greenside bunker. The man from Florida made the better recovery, holing from four feet for a birdie, and won by two holes.

Throughout the week, record crowds swarmed over the West Course with more than 56,000 spectators coming through the gates during the championship, comfortably beating the previous record of 52,934 set in 2004.

It was not surprising as the 16-strong field was brimming with the world's best golfers; featuring six of the top ten from the Official World Golf Ranking, including the current Numbers One and Two, Tiger Woods and Jim Furyk; seven Major Championship title winners; three former HSBC World Match Play Championship winners and the Number One and Two ranked players from The European Tour Order of Merit.

WHERE
PEOPLE
MATTER

WENTWORTHCLUB.COM
TEL +44 (0)1344 842201

The 16 competitors, fronted by defending champion Michael Campbell, gather in front of the Wentworth Clubhouse

# Final Results

**FIRST ROUND (seedings in parentheses)**

Michael Campbell (NZI) (1) beat Simon Khan (Eng) (16) 3 and 1
Colin Montgomerie (Sco) (9) beat David Howell (Eng) (8) 1 hole
Paul Casey (Eng) (12) beat Retief Goosen (RSA) (5) 6 and 4
Mike Weir (Can) (13) beat Adam Scott (Aus) (4) 3 and 2
Robert Karlsson (Swe) (14) beat Jim Furyk (USA) (3) 4 and 3
Angel Cabrera (Arg) (11) beat Ernie Els (RSA) (6) 2 and 1
Luke Donald (Eng) (7) beat Tim Clark (RSA) (10) 2 holes
Shaun Micheel (USA) (15) beat Tiger Woods (USA) (2) 4 and 3

**QUARTER - FINALS**

Montgomerie beat Campbell 1 hole
Casey beat Weir 5 and 3
Karlsson beat Cabrera 4 and 3
Micheel beat Donald 4 and 2

**SEMI - FINALS**

Casey beat Montgomerie 6 and 5
Micheel beat Karlsson 2 holes

**FINAL (36 holes)**

Casey beat Micheel 10 and 8

The crowds, however, were in for an opening day full of shocks and none more seismic that the exit of Woods. The 30 year old, who lost in the final to Mark O'Meara in 1998, was making only his second appearance at Wentworth Club and came into the Championship on the back of five successive stroke play victories, including his 12th Major title, the US PGA Championship at Medinah Country Club, in August.

Match play golf, however, is a different animal and if Woods was supposed to stride imperiously towards a sixth triumph, the largely unheralded Micheel, who had finished second to the great man at Medinah, had clearly not been handed that version of the script.

His vow not to be a "sacrificial lamb" was sensationally realised when he hunted the Tiger down 4 and 3, with Woods admitting he had been unable to find his putting pace on the Wentworth greens. To compound American misery, Karlsson then proceeded to oust Furyk by the same margin and in the process became only the third player to birdie all four of Wentworth's par threes in one round, equalling the feats of Bernhard Langer in 1985 and Seve Ballesteros in 1994.

To complete a trio of first day surprises, six time HSBC World Match Play champion Ernie Els suffered his first reverse in 11 matches when he was outgunned 2 and 1 by Angel Cabrera.

Technically, going purely on their respective seeding, it was an upset that the number 12 seed Casey beat number five seed Retief Goosen by 6 and 4 in the first round too.

What was no surprise though, the way the Englishman played for the remainder of the week, was that he emerged victorious on Sunday night.

**John Whitbread**

*Surrey Herald*

First Round Losers each received:
**€88,214 (£60,000)**
For The European Tour Order of Merit, the First Round Losers each received:
**€61,972 (£42,151)**

Losing Quarter Finalists each received:
**€117,618 (£80,000)**
For The European Tour Order of Merit, the losing Quarter Finalists each received:
**€118,742 (£80,764)**

Losing Semi Finalists each received:
**€176,428 (£120,000)**
For The European Tour Order of Merit, the losing Semi Finalists each received:
**€201,968 (£137,372)**

The Winner received:
**€1,470,230 (£1,000,000)**
For The European Tour Order of Merit, the Winner received:
**€597,884 (£406,660)**

The Runner-Up received:
**€588,092 (£400,000)**
For The European Tour Order of Merit, the Runner-Up received:
**€398,594 (£271,110)**

# Mission
# Accomplished

*Raphaël Jacquelin*

# BancoMadrid

**'G**ood morning Mr Poulter. Your mission this week, should you choose to accept it, is to win the XXXII Banco de Madrid Valle Romano Open de Madrid Golf Masters.'

The Englishman's 'Mission' might not have been 'Impossible', but such was the way he went about his business on the outskirts of Spain's capital city, one can easily picture the dapper 30 year old playing the role of Dan Briggs in the classic 1960s TV series as he was briefed on his four day assignment at La Moraleja II.

The objective was simple: Win in Madrid to re-enter the top 50 on the Official World Golf Ranking. By completing the task, Poulter also gained access to the World Golf Championships – American Express Championship to be staged at The Grove near his home town of London, as well as climbing back towards the top of The European Tour Order of Merit.

While the purpose was simple, as it always was at the beginning of any episode, Poulter's job, like Briggs', was never going to be easy as the story unfolded. Indeed, he met strong resistance in his quest with some of the game's toughest characters to overcome.

Men like Thomas Björn of Denmark, Northern Ireland's Darren Clarke, Padraig Harrington of Ireland, and the Spanish pair of Miguel Angel Jiménez and José Maria Olazábal were always going to be an obstacle to Poulter succeeding.

Björn, Jiménez and indeed Poulter himself, were desperate to show the world that they were good enough to have been considered for a place on The European Ryder Cup Team that would take on the United States at The K Club the very next week, while Clarke, Harrington and Olazábal were putting in the last minute preparations required to fine tune their games before they became part of Ian Woosnam's Team.

The tournament also took on a special significance for Clarke, who was making his first appearance on The European Tour International Schedule since the death of his wife, Heather, on August 13.

It was therefore natural that the main focus in the build-up, both from the media and the galleries at La Moraleja II, fell on the Ulsterman, which allowed Poulter the time and space to set about his objective with the kind of ruthless efficiency that would have made any member of the Mission Impossible Force of secret agents proud.

## La Moraleja II

| Par | Yards | Metres |
| --- | --- | --- |
| 72 | 7018 | 6418 |

| Pos | | Score | | |
| --- | --- | --- | --- | --- |
| 1 | Ian POULTER | 266 | -22 | |
| 2 | Ignacio GARRIDO | 271 | -17 | |
| 3 | Phillip PRICE | 272 | -16 | |
| 4 | Padraig HARRINGTON | 273 | -15 | |
| | Christian L NILSSON | 273 | -15 | |
| 6 | Ricardo GONZALEZ | 274 | -14 | |
| | Raphaël JACQUELIN | 274 | -14 | |
| 8 | David GRIFFITHS | 275 | -13 | |
| | José Maria OLAZÁBAL | 275 | -13 | |
| | Steve WEBSTER | 275 | -13 | |

### WEATHER REPORT

| Round One | Round Two | Round Three | Round Four |
| --- | --- | --- | --- |

### EUROPEAN TOUR ORDER OF MERIT
(After 43 tournaments)

| Pos | | € | |
| --- | --- | --- | --- |
| 1 | Paul CASEY | 2,256,193.56 |  |
| 2 | David HOWELL | 2,089,486.55 | |
| 3 | Robert KARLSSON | 1,852,230.81 | |
| 4 | Padraig HARRINGTON | 1,494,063.37 | |
| 5 | Henrik STENSON | 1,491,716.16 | |
| 6 | Colin MONTGOMERIE | 1,455,619.41 | |
| 7 | Johan EDFORS | 1,329,486.75 | |
| 8 | Ernie ELS | 1,329,158.34 | |
| 9 | Retief GOOSEN | 1,329,105.72 | |
| 10 | Luke DONALD | 1,190,455.82 | |

**Madrid, Spain**
September 14-17 • 2006

Christian Nilsson

His flawless opening 67 went almost unnoticed as he placed himself comfortably on the leaderboard, two strokes behind Frenchman Jean-Francois Lucquin. He then bettered his opening score by a stroke during another flawless performance on day two to remain perfectly positioned, one shot off the lead held jointly by Scotland's Gary Orr and Harrington, going into the weekend.

Having gone about his business in a stealth-like manner, Poulter let everyone know of his presence on Saturday afternoon with a third round display that proved devastating to his opponents.

❝ It is a tricky course especially early in the round. The third, fourth and fifth holes in particular are demanding. All three play over water and you have to be careful as those holes can be destructive. The course is open and not one of the longest we play but you have to be on top of your game to score well ❞
– Phillip Price

*José Maria Olazábal*

# Final Results

| Pos | Name | | Rd1 | Rd2 | Rd3 | Rd4 | Total | | € | £ |
|---|---|---|---|---|---|---|---|---|---|---|
| 1 | Ian POULTER | ENG | 67 | 66 | 64 | 69 | 266 | -22 | 166,660.00 | 113,356.41 |
| 2 | Ignacio GARRIDO | ESP | 68 | 66 | 71 | 66 | 271 | -17 | 111,110.00 | 75,573.21 |
| 3 | Phillip PRICE | WAL | 70 | 67 | 68 | 67 | 272 | -16 | 62,600.00 | 42,578.37 |
| 4 | Christian L NILSSON | SWE | 68 | 66 | 68 | 71 | 273 | -15 | 46,200.00 | 31,423.65 |
| | Padraig HARRINGTON | IRL | 67 | 65 | 72 | 69 | 273 | -15 | 46,200.00 | 31,423.65 |
| 6 | Raphaël JACQUELIN | FRA | 68 | 68 | 67 | 71 | 274 | -14 | 32,500.00 | 22,105.38 |
| | Ricardo GONZALEZ | ARG | 67 | 67 | 67 | 73 | 274 | -14 | 32,500.00 | 22,105.38 |
| 8 | José Maria OLAZÁBAL | ESP | 71 | 70 | 67 | 67 | 275 | -13 | 22,466.67 | 15,281.06 |
| | Steve WEBSTER | ENG | 71 | 68 | 67 | 69 | 275 | -13 | 22,466.67 | 15,281.06 |
| | David GRIFFITHS | ENG | 70 | 69 | 67 | 69 | 275 | -13 | 22,466.67 | 15,281.06 |
| 11 | Gary ORR | SCO | 67 | 65 | 70 | 74 | 276 | -12 | 16,340.00 | 11,113.91 |
| | Darren FICHARDT | RSA | 66 | 72 | 70 | 68 | 276 | -12 | 16,340.00 | 11,113.91 |
| | Jean-François REMESY | FRA | 72 | 65 | 70 | 69 | 276 | -12 | 16,340.00 | 11,113.91 |
| | Joakim BÄCKSTRÖM | SWE | 67 | 69 | 67 | 73 | 276 | -12 | 16,340.00 | 11,113.91 |
| | Jean-François LUCQUIN | FRA | 65 | 69 | 72 | 70 | 276 | -12 | 16,340.00 | 11,113.91 |
| 16 | Gary EVANS | ENG | 69 | 70 | 65 | 74 | 278 | -10 | 12,750.00 | 8,672.11 |
| | Miles TUNNICLIFF | ENG | 69 | 70 | 72 | 67 | 278 | -10 | 12,750.00 | 8,672.11 |
| | Jarmo SANDELIN | SWE | 69 | 70 | 72 | 67 | 278 | -10 | 12,750.00 | 8,672.11 |
| | David CARTER | ENG | 70 | 71 | 65 | 72 | 278 | -10 | 12,750.00 | 8,672.11 |
| | Alexandre ROCHA | BRA | 71 | 67 | 68 | 72 | 278 | -10 | 12,750.00 | 8,672.11 |
| | Gregory BOURDY | FRA | 70 | 70 | 69 | 70 | 278 | -10 | 12,750.00 | 8,672.11 |
| | Jose Luis GOMEZ (AM) | ESP | 69 | 70 | 68 | 71 | 278 | -10 | | |
| 23 | Niclas FASTH | SWE | 70 | 66 | 72 | 71 | 279 | -9 | 10,850.00 | 7,379.80 |
| | David HIGGINS | IRL | 70 | 68 | 73 | 68 | 279 | -9 | 10,850.00 | 7,379.80 |
| | Ian GARBUTT | ENG | 72 | 68 | 68 | 71 | 279 | -9 | 10,850.00 | 7,379.80 |
| | Damien MCGRANE | IRL | 68 | 68 | 74 | 69 | 279 | -9 | 10,850.00 | 7,379.80 |
| 27 | Mark FOSTER | ENG | 71 | 68 | 73 | 68 | 280 | -8 | 9,650.00 | 6,563.60 |
| | Sam LITTLE | ENG | 72 | 71 | 68 | 69 | 280 | -8 | 9,650.00 | 6,563.60 |
| | Simon WAKEFIELD | ENG | 74 | 67 | 69 | 70 | 280 | -8 | 9,650.00 | 6,563.60 |
| | Gonzalo FDEZ-CASTAÑO | ESP | 70 | 66 | 75 | 69 | 280 | -8 | 9,650.00 | 6,563.60 |
| 31 | Richard FINCH | ENG | 69 | 69 | 70 | 73 | 281 | -7 | 7,925.00 | 5,390.31 |
| | Ross FISHER | ENG | 70 | 70 | 72 | 69 | 281 | -7 | 7,925.00 | 5,390.31 |
| | Thomas BJÖRN | DEN | 69 | 69 | 72 | 71 | 281 | -7 | 7,925.00 | 5,390.31 |
| | Andrew BUTTERFIELD | ENG | 70 | 71 | 69 | 71 | 281 | -7 | 7,925.00 | 5,390.31 |
| | Stephen GALLACHER | SCO | 71 | 72 | 66 | 72 | 281 | -7 | 7,925.00 | 5,390.31 |
| | Warren ABERY | RSA | 72 | 69 | 68 | 72 | 281 | -7 | 7,925.00 | 5,390.31 |
| | Darren CLARKE | NIR | 68 | 72 | 69 | 72 | 281 | -7 | 7,925.00 | 5,390.31 |
| | José Manuel LARA | ESP | 73 | 69 | 72 | 67 | 281 | -7 | 7,925.00 | 5,390.31 |
| 39 | José RIVERO | ESP | 71 | 68 | 71 | 72 | 282 | -6 | 5,800.00 | 3,944.96 |
| | Phillip ARCHER | ENG | 72 | 70 | 72 | 68 | 282 | -6 | 5,800.00 | 3,944.96 |
| | Garry HOUSTON | WAL | 70 | 68 | 74 | 70 | 282 | -6 | 5,800.00 | 3,944.96 |
| | Peter LAWRIE | IRL | 74 | 69 | 69 | 70 | 282 | -6 | 5,800.00 | 3,944.96 |
| | Gary EMERSON | ENG | 69 | 68 | 76 | 69 | 282 | -6 | 5,800.00 | 3,944.96 |
| | Leif WESTERBERG | SWE | 72 | 71 | 71 | 68 | 282 | -6 | 5,800.00 | 3,944.96 |
| | Robert ROCK | ENG | 71 | 70 | 72 | 69 | 282 | -6 | 5,800.00 | 3,944.96 |
| | Gary CLARK | ENG | 70 | 71 | 72 | 69 | 282 | -6 | 5,800.00 | 3,944.96 |
| | Johan SKÖLD | SWE | 71 | 71 | 69 | 71 | 282 | -6 | 5,800.00 | 3,944.96 |
| | Peter GUSTAFSSON | SWE | 72 | 71 | 64 | 75 | 282 | -6 | 5,800.00 | 3,944.96 |
| | José-Filipe LIMA | POR | 71 | 69 | 69 | 73 | 282 | -6 | 5,800.00 | 3,944.96 |
| | Anders SJÖSTRAND | SWE | 69 | 69 | 72 | 72 | 282 | -6 | 5,800.00 | 3,944.96 |
| 51 | Felipe AGUILAR | CHI | 73 | 67 | 72 | 71 | 283 | -5 | 4,200.00 | 2,856.70 |
| | Benn BARHAM | ENG | 70 | 71 | 70 | 72 | 283 | -5 | 4,200.00 | 2,856.70 |
| | Peter HEDBLOM | SWE | 71 | 70 | 71 | 71 | 283 | -5 | 4,200.00 | 2,856.70 |
| | Maarten LAFEBER | NED | 73 | 68 | 70 | 72 | 283 | -5 | 4,200.00 | 2,856.70 |
| 55 | Philip GOLDING | ENG | 71 | 72 | 71 | 70 | 284 | -4 | 3,700.00 | 2,516.61 |
| 56 | Andrew MCLARDY | RSA | 74 | 69 | 73 | 69 | 285 | -3 | 2,933.33 | 1,995.15 |
| | Søren HANSEN | DEN | 71 | 69 | 74 | 71 | 285 | -3 | 2,933.33 | 1,995.15 |
| | Mattias ELIASSON | SWE | 69 | 72 | 75 | 69 | 285 | -3 | 2,933.33 | 1,995.15 |
| | Mikko ILONEN | FIN | 71 | 70 | 68 | 76 | 285 | -3 | 2,933.33 | 1,995.15 |
| | Iain PYMAN | ENG | 68 | 73 | 75 | 69 | 285 | -3 | 2,933.33 | 1,995.15 |
| | John BICKERTON | ENG | 72 | 67 | 72 | 74 | 285 | -3 | 2,933.33 | 1,995.15 |
| | Stephen BROWNE | IRL | 71 | 72 | 71 | 71 | 285 | -3 | 2,933.33 | 1,995.15 |
| | Alfredo GARCIA-HEREDIA | ESP | 71 | 73 | 70 | 72 | 285 | -3 | 2,933.33 | 1,995.15 |
| | Steven O'HARA | SCO | 71 | 71 | 70 | 73 | 285 | -3 | 2,933.33 | 1,995.15 |
| 65 | Gabriel CANIZARES | ESP | 70 | 69 | 71 | 76 | 286 | -2 | 2,250.00 | 1,530.37 |
| | Francis VALERA | ESP | 71 | 72 | 74 | 69 | 286 | -2 | 2,250.00 | 1,530.37 |
| | Cesar MONASTERIO | ARG | 73 | 69 | 75 | 69 | 286 | -2 | 2,250.00 | 1,530.37 |
| | Neil CHEETHAM | ENG | 72 | 70 | 73 | 71 | 286 | -2 | 2,250.00 | 1,530.37 |
| 69 | Peter FOWLER | AUS | 70 | 69 | 76 | 72 | 287 | -1 | 2,000.00 | 1,360.33 |
| 70 | Alessandro TADINI | ITA | 70 | 72 | 72 | 74 | 288 | 0 | 1,865.00 | 1,268.51 |
| | Carlos DE CORRAL | ESP | 74 | 68 | 74 | 72 | 288 | 0 | 1,865.00 | 1,268.51 |
| 72 | Benoit TEILLERIA | FRA | 73 | 70 | 74 | 72 | 289 | 1 | 1,495.50 | 1,017.19 |
| | Edoardo MOLINARI | ITA | 69 | 73 | 74 | 73 | 289 | 1 | 1,495.50 | 1,017.19 |
| | Miguel Angel MARTIN | ESP | 66 | 74 | 77 | 72 | 289 | 1 | 1,495.50 | 1,017.19 |
| | Jamie SPENCE | ENG | 69 | 72 | 73 | 75 | 289 | 1 | 1,495.50 | 1,017.19 |
| 76 | David BRANSDON | AUS | 69 | 74 | 77 | 70 | 290 | 2 | 1,488.00 | 1,012.09 |
| 77 | Oliver WILSON | ENG | 69 | 70 | 76 | 77 | 292 | 4 | 1,485.00 | 1,010.05 |

The winner of six previous titles on The European Tour International Schedule hit top gear to surge clear of the field with a clinical display that saw him post the best round of the tournament, a flawless eight under par 64, to move four clear of Argentina's Ricardo Gonzalez with just 18 holes to play.

Poulter's dedication to his task, and his refusal to be beaten, made the fourth and final round a virtual procession as he carded a three under par 69 to post an outstanding 22 under par aggregate of 266 and win by five strokes from Spain's Ignacio Garrido, and by six from Phillip Price of Wales, to collect the €166,660 (£113,356) top prize.

"I had a job to do this week and I did it," he said. "I played great and I have finished the job. End of story."

He had indeed finished the job. Mission accomplished. In Dan Briggs' world, the tape then used to disappear in a plume of smoke. Thankfully for Ian Poulter, there was no danger of him pressing the self-destruct button.

**Michael Gibbons**

*Ricardo Gonzalez*

VALLE ROMANO

estepona COSTA DEL SOL

# Total Prize Fund
## €1,008,950  £686,356

# Discipline
# Of
# Choice

**The Grove**

| Par | Yards | Metres |
|-----|-------|--------|
| 71 | 7125 | 6512 |

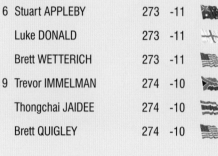

| | | | | |
|---|---|---|---|---|
| 1 | **Tiger WOODS** | **261** | **-23** | |
| 2 | Ian POULTER | 269 | -15 | |
| | Adam SCOTT | 269 | -15 | |
| 4 | Jim FURYK | 270 | -14 | |
| 5 | Ernie ELS | 271 | -13 | |
| 6 | Stuart APPLEBY | 273 | -11 | |
| | Luke DONALD | 273 | -11 | |
| | Brett WETTERICH | 273 | -11 | |
| 9 | Trevor IMMELMAN | 274 | -10 | |
| | Thongchai JAIDEE | 274 | -10 | |
| | Brett QUIGLEY | 274 | -10 | |

**WEATHER REPORT**

| Round One | Round Two | Round Three | Round Four |
|-----------|-----------|-------------|------------|

**EUROPEAN TOUR ORDER OF MERIT**
(After 44 tournaments)

| Pos | | € | |
|-----|---|---|---|
| 1 | **Paul CASEY** | **2,286,281.16** | |
| 2 | David HOWELL | 2,166,366.21 | |
| 3 | Robert KARLSSON | 1,914,750.48 | |
| 4 | Henrik STENSON | 1,568,595.82 | |
| 5 | Padraig HARRINGTON | 1,560,490.52 | |
| 6 | Ernie ELS | 1,555,792.14 | |
| 7 | Colin MONTGOMERIE | 1,496,647.95 | |
| 8 | Ian POULTER | 1,480,469.42 | |
| 9 | Johan EDFORS | 1,388,098.94 | |
| 10 | Retief GOOSEN | 1,367,399.02 | |

$A$fter the shenanigans and the deeds of European derring-do of the previous week on the furthest outskirts of Dublin, this might, on the face of it, have seemed likely to turn into something of an anti-climax. You know, Cirque de Soleil being followed by a clown and a couple of fire-eaters. In the event, it became a very special parade of its own.

It was by no means a multi-faceted pageant. Far from it. It was, rather, a one-man show. But it was none the less glorious for that.

It is rare that one individual commands total hegemony of his discipline of choice. Bill Gates and Microsoft have always been given a run for their money by Apple, albeit a vain one. Luciano Pavarotti was never ahead of Placido Domingo or Jose Carreras by enough to make it a total wipe-out.

But Tiger Woods? He is so far ahead of the other stars of world golf as to be in a far away, and not-to-be countenanced, galaxy.

Now, there are those who might contend that Woods, like Jack Nicklaus before him, loses more tournaments that he wins. Well, to some extent that is true, but the immutable fact is that when Woods, like The Golden Bear before him in the days of yore, really, really needs to win, more often than not, he does.

Woods has a remarkable talent that gives him the ability to produce enough from the core that resides in him, bone-deep, when it is becomes necessary. Actually, it was not that mandatory for him to delve so deeply this time. But he did, anyway.

Maybe he did it for the sheer, simple hell of it. He had had a good enough Ryder Cup, after all. He was as good as, and better than, practically all of his team-mates.

But now he was here, in the verdant pastures of a golf course close to London. And now he was playing for himself. Somehow, it was different. Somehow, it certainly was.

The simple fact was that Woods won the tournament by eight strokes. What lay behind it was a whole lot more significant.

Apart from Phil Mickelson, who had hung up his sticks for a few months after being a relatively insignificant factor in The Ryder Cup, and Tom Lehman, who left to attend the funeral of Byron Nelson, Woods faced the best of his peers in one of the elite events in world golf. And he smashed them. He wiped them out. He slaughtered them. He laid them to waste. He was utterly, totally, dominant.

# World Golf Championships – American Express Championship

**Chandlers Cross, Hertfordshire, England**
September 28-October 1 • 2006

*Jyoti Randhawa*

It might be that nobody, in the fullness of time, will ever be able accurately to summarise just how good Woods is, or was. All that could be said for now is that in the autumn of 2006, as in the previous - what, decade? - he was playing golf as well as anybody ever had.

For those who wallow in plain facts, Woods led the tournament by one stroke after the first round, by five after the second, by six after the third and by an-almost obscene eight by the fourth and last.

It was not so much a no-contest as a never-contest-to-begin-with. In the aftermath of another humbling reverse for him and his American comrades, Woods had

*" The golf course is wide off the tee but if you miss the fairways, you have a hard time getting to the green. The greens are undulating but they're really smooth. And with them being smooth, it was no surprise the guys made some putts "* – **Tiger Woods**

*David Howell*

# Final Results

| Pos | Name | | Rd1 | Rd2 | Rd3 | Rd4 | Total | | € | £ |
|---|---|---|---|---|---|---|---|---|---|---|
| 1 | Tiger WOODS | USA | 63 | 64 | 67 | 67 | 261 | -23 | 1,015,944.64 | 683,778.65 |
| 2 | Ian POULTER | ENG | 64 | 71 | 68 | 66 | 269 | -15 | 476,712.48 | 320,849.98 |
| | Adam SCOTT | AUS | 67 | 68 | 65 | 69 | 269 | -15 | 476,712.48 | 320,849.98 |
| 4 | Jim FURYK | USA | 67 | 65 | 69 | 69 | 270 | -14 | 269,616.08 | 181,464.33 |
| 5 | Ernie ELS | RSA | 65 | 70 | 69 | 67 | 271 | -13 | 226,633.80 | 152,535.23 |
| 6 | Stuart APPLEBY | AUS | 71 | 66 | 70 | 66 | 273 | -11 | 169,324.11 | 113,963.11 |
| | Luke DONALD | ENG | 68 | 70 | 67 | 68 | 273 | -11 | 169,324.11 | 113,963.11 |
| | Brett WETTERICH | USA | 70 | 66 | 69 | 68 | 273 | -11 | 169,324.11 | 113,963.11 |
| 9 | Brett QUIGLEY | USA | 70 | 64 | 67 | 73 | 274 | -10 | 117,224.38 | 78,897.54 |
| | Thongchai JAIDEE | THA | 71 | 67 | 71 | 65 | 274 | -10 | 117,224.38 | 78,897.54 |
| | Trevor IMMELMAN | RSA | 68 | 68 | 68 | 70 | 274 | -10 | 117,224.38 | 78,897.54 |
| 12 | Arron OBERHOLSER | USA | 69 | 72 | 66 | 68 | 275 | -9 | 93,779.51 | 63,118.03 |
| 13 | Lucas GLOVER | USA | 69 | 68 | 68 | 71 | 276 | -8 | 76,879.66 | 51,743.64 |
| | Henrik STENSON | SWE | 68 | 67 | 68 | 73 | 276 | -8 | 76,879.66 | 51,743.64 |
| | David HOWELL | ENG | 66 | 66 | 71 | 73 | 276 | -8 | 76,879.66 | 51,743.64 |
| | Stewart CINK | USA | 65 | 67 | 70 | 74 | 276 | -8 | 76,879.66 | 51,743.64 |
| 17 | José Maria OLAZÁBAL | ESP | 70 | 67 | 71 | 69 | 277 | -7 | 66,427.15 | 44,708.60 |
| | Padraig HARRINGTON | IRL | 64 | 69 | 71 | 73 | 277 | -7 | 66,427.15 | 44,708.60 |
| | Jyoti RANDHAWA | IND | 66 | 71 | 71 | 69 | 277 | -7 | 66,427.15 | 44,708.60 |
| | Carl PETTERSSON | SWE | 69 | 70 | 67 | 71 | 277 | -7 | 66,427.15 | 44,708.60 |
| 21 | Robert KARLSSON | SWE | 67 | 76 | 72 | 64 | 279 | -5 | 62,519.67 | 42,078.69 |
| 22 | Chris DIMARCO | USA | 69 | 70 | 70 | 71 | 280 | -4 | 58,612.19 | 39,448.77 |
| | Michael CAMPBELL | NZL | 69 | 71 | 69 | 71 | 280 | -4 | 58,612.19 | 39,448.77 |
| | Dean WILSON | USA | 71 | 70 | 70 | 69 | 280 | -4 | 58,612.19 | 39,448.77 |
| | Johan EDFORS | SWE | 70 | 68 | 71 | 71 | 280 | -4 | 58,612.19 | 39,448.77 |
| 26 | Nick O'HERN | AUS | 67 | 69 | 75 | 70 | 281 | -3 | 52,099.73 | 35,065.57 |
| | Darren CLARKE | NIR | 68 | 71 | 72 | 70 | 281 | -3 | 52,099.73 | 35,065.57 |
| | Angel CABRERA | ARG | 71 | 70 | 67 | 73 | 281 | -3 | 52,099.73 | 35,065.57 |
| | Robert ALLENBY | AUS | 69 | 73 | 69 | 70 | 281 | -3 | 52,099.73 | 35,065.57 |
| | Tim CLARK | RSA | 68 | 70 | 73 | 70 | 281 | -3 | 52,099.73 | 35,065.57 |
| | Bart BRYANT | USA | 70 | 74 | 67 | 70 | 281 | -3 | 52,099.73 | 35,065.57 |
| 32 | Louis OOSTHUIZEN | RSA | 71 | 70 | 72 | 69 | 282 | -2 | 47,671.25 | 32,085.00 |
| | Lee WESTWOOD | ENG | 71 | 66 | 73 | 72 | 282 | -2 | 47,671.25 | 32,085.00 |
| | Chad CAMPBELL | USA | 67 | 70 | 73 | 72 | 282 | -2 | 47,671.25 | 32,085.00 |
| | Sergio GARCIA | ESP | 69 | 73 | 71 | 69 | 282 | -2 | 47,671.25 | 32,085.00 |
| | K J CHOI | KOR | 72 | 66 | 73 | 71 | 282 | -2 | 47,671.25 | 32,085.00 |
| 37 | J J HENRY | USA | 70 | 70 | 70 | 73 | 283 | -1 | 45,326.76 | 30,507.05 |
| 38 | Simon DYSON | ENG | 67 | 69 | 75 | 73 | 284 | 0 | 43,763.77 | 29,455.08 |
| | Rodney PAMPLING | AUS | 70 | 69 | 72 | 73 | 284 | 0 | 43,763.77 | 29,455.08 |
| | Scott VERPLANK | USA | 70 | 68 | 73 | 73 | 284 | 0 | 43,763.77 | 29,455.08 |
| 41 | Colin MONTGOMERIE | SCO | 72 | 67 | 69 | 77 | 285 | 1 | 41,028.53 | 27,614.14 |
| | Thomas BJÖRN | DEN | 70 | 71 | 73 | 71 | 285 | 1 | 41,028.53 | 27,614.14 |
| | Charl SCHWARTZEL | RSA | 73 | 69 | 70 | 73 | 285 | 1 | 41,028.53 | 27,614.14 |
| | Rory SABBATINI | RSA | 73 | 67 | 73 | 72 | 285 | 1 | 41,028.53 | 27,614.14 |
| 45 | Zach JOHNSON | USA | 70 | 71 | 73 | 73 | 287 | 3 | 38,293.30 | 25,773.20 |
| | John BICKERTON | ENG | 72 | 73 | 75 | 67 | 287 | 3 | 38,293.30 | 25,773.20 |
| | Retief GOOSEN | RSA | 71 | 70 | 75 | 71 | 287 | 3 | 38,293.30 | 25,773.20 |
| 48 | Tom PERNICE Jnr | USA | 69 | 70 | 71 | 78 | 288 | 4 | 36,339.56 | 24,458.24 |
| | Tim HERRON | USA | 73 | 69 | 71 | 75 | 288 | 4 | 36,339.56 | 24,458.24 |
| 50 | Paul BROADHURST | ENG | 74 | 72 | 70 | 73 | 289 | 5 | 34,385.82 | 23,143.28 |
| | Anthony WALL | ENG | 71 | 76 | 68 | 74 | 289 | 5 | 34,385.82 | 23,143.28 |
| | Tetsuji HIRATSUKA | JPN | 73 | 69 | 71 | 76 | 289 | 5 | 34,385.82 | 23,143.28 |
| 53 | David TOMS | USA | 73 | 75 | 69 | 73 | 290 | 6 | 32,822.83 | 22,091.31 |
| 54 | Sean O'HAIR | USA | 70 | 75 | 71 | 75 | 291 | 7 | 31,650.58 | 21,302.33 |
| | Thaworn WIRATCHANT | THA | 71 | 71 | 75 | 74 | 291 | 7 | 31,650.58 | 21,302.33 |
| 56 | Vijay SINGH | FIJ | 73 | 75 | 72 | 72 | 292 | 8 | 30,087.59 | 20,250.37 |
| | Paul CASEY | ENG | 74 | 75 | 72 | 71 | 292 | 8 | 30,087.59 | 20,250.37 |
| 58 | Craig PARRY | AUS | 74 | 74 | 70 | 75 | 293 | 9 | 28,915.35 | 19,461.39 |
| 59 | Toru TANIGUCHI | JPN | 73 | 73 | 76 | 75 | 297 | 13 | 27,743.10 | 18,672.42 |
| | Gregory BOURDY | FRA | 74 | 77 | 71 | 75 | 297 | 13 | 27,743.10 | 18,672.42 |
| 61 | Ben CRANE | USA | 74 | W/D | | | 74 | 3 | 26,180.11 | 17,620.45 |
| | Stephen AMES | CAN | 73 | W/D | | | 73 | 2 | 26,180.11 | 17,620.45 |
| 63 | Tom LEHMAN | USA | W/D | | | | | | | |

something to be proved, even if he did not really need to prove it for himself.

Why should he, indeed? He is, at least, a becomingly modest individual, well versed in the modern sciences of the word-bite and knowing, always, that he will say the right things at the right times.

So it was that here he did not take anything for granted. He never claimed victory before it was achieved. He never, once, denigrated the best of the rest. But he knew, all right, he knew with utter certainty that he was just too good for them.

Just as he and his fellow Americans had been brought to their knees the week before by the pride of Europe, he knew now that when it came to one-on-however-many, mano a mano, he had the beating of them.

People such as Tiger Woods do not come by once in a generation. They are much rarer than that and pass much less frequently. Once more, here, in the green, leafy fields of Hertfordshire, he proved it once again. As though it needed proving in the first place.

**Mel Webb**

# Total Prize Fund
€5,764,700 £3,879,917

# Alfred Dunhill Links Championship

**Scotland**
October 5-8 · 2006

# Déjà Vu....
# All Over Again

## ALFRED DUNHILL
### LINKS CHAMPIONSHIP

**Old Course, St Andrews**

| Par | Yards | Metres |
|-----|-------|--------|
| 72  | 7279  | 6655   |

**Carnoustie**

| Par | Yards | Metres |
|-----|-------|--------|
| 71  | 7316  | 6690   |

**Kingsbarns**

| Par | Yards | Metres |
|-----|-------|--------|
| 72  | 7099  | 6492   |

| | | | | |
|---|---|---|---|---|
| 1 | **Padraig HARRINGTON** | **271** | **-16** | |
| 2 | Bradley DREDGE | 276 | -11 | |
| | Edward LOAR | 276 | -11 | |
| | Anthony WALL | 276 | -11 | |
| 5 | Ernie ELS | 277 | -10 | |
| 6 | Paul CASEY | 278 | -9 | |
| | Peter HANSON | 278 | -9 | |
| 8 | Paul BROADHURST | 279 | -8 | |
| | Simon DYSON | 279 | -8 | |
| | Johan EDFORS | 279 | -8 | |
| | James KINGSTON | 279 | -8 | |
| | Søren KJELDSEN | 279 | -8 | |
| | Henrik STENSON | 279 | -8 | |
| | Lee WESTWOOD | 279 | -8 | |

**WEATHER REPORT**

| Round One | Round Two | Round Three | Round Four |
|-----------|-----------|-------------|------------|
|  | |  |  |

**EUROPEAN TOUR ORDER OF MERIT**
(After 45 tournaments)

| Pos | | € | |
|-----|---|---|---|
| 1 | **Paul CASEY** | **2,409,241.60** |  |
| 2 | Padraig HARRINGTON | 2,191,056.88 | |
| 3 | David HOWELL | 2,166,366.21 | |
| 4 | Robert KARLSSON | 1,964,042.75 | |
| 5 | Ernie ELS | 1,716,208.22 | |
| 6 | Henrik STENSON | 1,641,237.06 | |
| 7 | Ian POULTER | 1,520,951.78 | |
| 8 | Colin MONTGOMERIE | 1,496,647.95 | |
| 9 | Johan EDFORS | 1,460,740.18 | |
| 10 | Retief GOOSEN | 1,367,399.02 | |

# Alfred Dunhill Links Championship

**Scotland**
October 5-8 • 2006

Had he viewed events, Yogi Berra, the legendary New York Yankees baseball player might have been tempted to reiterate his immortal quote: 'It's like déjà vu all over again,' and, frankly, not even the self-appointed custodian of the English language, Lynn Truss, would have taken umbrage with another flagrant betrayal of the mother tongue.

Peter Hanson

There was, indeed, a distinct sense of having been there before as Padraig Harrington, professional golfer, and his Pro-Am partner, JP McManus, professional entrepreneur, carried off a second Alfred Dunhill Links Championship. In fact, the similarities to 2002 were uncanny.

Four years earlier, just a matter of days after Europe's Ryder Cup victory over the United States at The De Vere Belfry, Harrington and McManus tackled St Andrews, Carnoustie and Kingsbarns with considerable style and vigour.

The duo struck up an instantly harmonious partnership in the second edition of this glorious celebration of links golf. Thanks to Harrington's sudden-death victory over Eduardo Romero, the professional prize went to The Ryder Cup player; the Team award was also secured by the indomitable Irish duo.

This time around, another Ryder Cup was in Europe's safekeeping after a momentous 18½ - 9½ triumph at The K Club. It was a portent of things to come as Harrington and the fearless Irish tycoon, playing off a distinctly useful 16, tore through the field to pull off an unprecedented double.

St Andrews

" The three golf courses were all fantastic and I like the fact that they are all different. Carnoustie is, without doubt, an extraordinarily difficult test, Kingsbarns is fun and an absolutely fantastic new design, and St Andrews you just can't beat. It throws everything at you " – Padraig Harrington

The beaming smile which lit up JP's face after crossing the bridge over the historic Swilcan Burn and walking the walk down the 18th at the Old Course was reminiscent of the days when his Champion Hurdle hero, Istabraq, pulverised all pretenders up the notorious hill at Cheltenham.

For Harrington, winning by five strokes with a 16 under par total of 271, enabled him to savour the moment, unlike that previous success which was earned the hard way at the second extra hole. Other than that, it really was a case of déjà vu. Even the golf cart ride back to the bridge for the official photographs and the obligatory visit to the Media Centre mirrored the post-tournament responsibilities of the winning pair.

"There is no more special place than this," observed Harrington, with the cheque for €630,566 (£427,441) safely lodged in his pocket. "To come down the last in an amphitheatre like the Old Course with a four shot lead...well, there's nothing quite like it. You don't win many tournaments being able to walk down the 18th knowing the job's done. When you do it in front of the St Andrews galleries, it is all the more special."

All of which begs the question: Why does the Pro-Am format sit so comfortably with the Irishman? Many professionals find the five and a half hour rounds in the company of an amateur over four days a complete anathema. Not so Harrington.

Let him explain. "The format suits me, without a doubt. I find it relaxing to have another outlet on the golf course, somebody to talk to, somebody living the experience with you, whether you are making birdies or bogeys. Also, somebody to encourage you.

"JP is a man of few words, but the words he comes up with are very wise and he does tend to say the right thing at the right time on the golf course. It does help having somebody out there and it also motivates me. Rather than brood over a missed putt, I find it therapeutic to go over and get involved with, say, a ten footer that JP might have for birdie."

*Paul Casey*

*Hugh Grant*

*Michael Douglas*

# Team Results

| Team | Rd1 | Rd2 | Rd3 | Rd4 | Total | € | £ |
|---|---|---|---|---|---|---|---|
| 1  Padraig Harrington and JP McManus | 63 | 62 | 65 | 62 | 252 (-35) | 39,410.40 | 26,715.11 |
| 2  Angel Cabrera and Federico Cabrera | 64 | 62 | 69 | 62 | 257 (-30) | 23,646.24 | 16,029.07 |
| 3  Robert Karlsson and Dermot Desmond | 62 | 64 | 68 | 65 | 259 (-28) | 13,793.64 | 9,350.29 |
|    Johan Edfors and Mats Andersson | 63 | 62 | 68 | 66 | 259 (-28) | 13,793.64 | 9,350.29 |
| 5  Alejandro Canizares and Barry Sundelson | 66 | 64 | 67 | 64 | 261 (-26) | 7,882.08 | 5,343.02 |
| 6  Richard Sterne and Phillip Behr | 67 | 66 | 67 | 62 | 262 (-25) | 3,941.04 | 2,671.51 |
| 7  Bradley Dredge and William Dewsall | 62 | 64 | 69 | 68 | 263 (-24) | 3,941.04 | 2,671.51 |
| 8  Henrik Stenson and Rurik Gobel | 63 | 69 | 68 | 64 | 264 (-23) | 3,941.04 | 2,671.51 |
|    David Park and Jim Crane | 64 | 66 | 68 | 66 | 264 (-23) | 3,941.04 | 2,671.51 |
|    Phillip Price and Alex Martin | 68 | 64 | 67 | 65 | 264 (-23) | 3,941.04 | 2,671.51 |
| 11  David Lynn and Ruud Gullit | 67 | 63 | 66 | 69 | 265 (-22) | 3,941.04 | 2,671.51 |
|    José Manuel Lara and Brand de Villiers | 66 | 65 | 67 | 67 | 265 (-22) | 3,941.04 | 2,671.51 |
|    Paul Casey and Eric J. Gleacher | 63 | 66 | 70 | 66 | 265 (-22) | 3,941.04 | 2,671.51 |
| 14  Gregory Havret and Grant Andrews | 65 | 65 | 70 | 67 | 267 (-20) | 3,941.04 | 2,671.51 |
|    Gary Evans and Robert Hissom | 63 | 67 | 70 | 67 | 267 (-20) | 3,941.04 | 2,671.51 |
| 16  Ignacio Garrido and Tico Torres | 65 | 66 | 68 | 69 | 268 (-19) | 3,941.04 | 2,671.51 |
|    Hennie Otto and Peter Dawson | 64 | 66 | 69 | 69 | 268 (-19) | 3,941.04 | 2,671.51 |
| 18  Scott Drummond and Klaus Gobel | 64 | 65 | 69 | 71 | 269 (-18) | 3,941.04 | 2,671.51 |
| 19  Paul Lawrie and Martin Gilbert | 67 | 62 | 71 | 71 | 271 (-16) | 3,941.04 | 2,671.51 |
|    Mikko Ilonen and Chad Morse | 66 | 66 | 68 | 71 | 271 (-16) | 3,941.04 | 2,671.51 |

# silk touch
## BY PROQUIP

## The next step in performance weatherv

The lightest, softest, quietest, most stretchable waterproof ever from ProC

**ProQuip is proud to supply**

**www.proquipgolf.com**

*Bradley Dredge*

**5**
568 yds 519 mtrs
Par 5
OLD COURSE

ALFRED DUNHILL
LINKS CHAMPIONSHIP

ALFRED DUNHILL
LINKS CHAMPIONSHIP

# Final Results

| Pos | Name | | Rd1 | Rd2 | Rd3 | Rd4 | Total | | € | £ |
|-----|------|---|-----|-----|-----|-----|-------|---|---|---|
| 1 | Padraig HARRINGTON | IRL | 66 | 69 | 68 | 68 | 271 | -16 | 630,566.36 | 427,441.76 |
| 2 | Anthony WALL | ENG | 70 | 70 | 69 | 67 | 276 | -11 | 282,128.53 | 191,246.35 |
| | Bradley DREDGE | WAL | 64 | 67 | 71 | 74 | 276 | -11 | 282,128.53 | 191,246.35 |
| | Edward LOAR | USA | 70 | 66 | 70 | 70 | 276 | -11 | 282,128.53 | 191,246.35 |
| 5 | Ernie ELS | RSA | 69 | 67 | 71 | 70 | 277 | -10 | 160,416.08 | 108,741.18 |
| 6 | Paul CASEY | ENG | 63 | 74 | 73 | 68 | 278 | -9 | 122,960.44 | 83,351.14 |
| | Peter HANSON | SWE | 68 | 68 | 75 | 67 | 278 | -9 | 122,960.44 | 83,351.14 |
| 8 | Søren KJELDSEN | DEN | 69 | 68 | 73 | 69 | 279 | -8 | 72,641.24 | 49,241.29 |
| | Henrik STENSON | SWE | 68 | 70 | 71 | 70 | 279 | -8 | 72,641.24 | 49,241.29 |
| | Paul BROADHURST | ENG | 70 | 69 | 72 | 68 | 279 | -8 | 72,641.24 | 49,241.29 |
| | Johan EDFORS | SWE | 64 | 70 | 76 | 69 | 279 | -8 | 72,641.24 | 49,241.29 |
| | Simon DYSON | ENG | 66 | 68 | 75 | 70 | 279 | -8 | 72,641.24 | 49,241.29 |
| | Lee WESTWOOD | ENG | 68 | 75 | 71 | 65 | 279 | -8 | 72,641.24 | 49,241.29 |
| | James KINGSTON | RSA | 71 | 65 | 74 | 69 | 279 | -8 | 72,641.24 | 49,241.29 |
| 15 | Richard STERNE | RSA | 68 | 71 | 74 | 67 | 280 | -7 | 49,292.27 | 33,413.73 |
| | Robert KARLSSON | SWE | 68 | 69 | 71 | 72 | 280 | -7 | 49,292.27 | 33,413.73 |
| | Simon KHAN | ENG | 68 | 70 | 71 | 71 | 280 | -7 | 49,292.27 | 33,413.73 |
| | Paul LAWRIE | SCO | 71 | 65 | 72 | 72 | 280 | -7 | 49,292.27 | 33,413.73 |
| | Joakim BÄCKSTRÖM | SWE | 71 | 70 | 67 | 72 | 280 | -7 | 49,292.27 | 33,413.73 |
| | Damien MCGRANE | IRL | 70 | 67 | 74 | 69 | 280 | -7 | 49,292.27 | 33,413.73 |
| | Mark ROE | ENG | 67 | 70 | 76 | 67 | 280 | -7 | 49,292.27 | 33,413.73 |
| 22 | Raphaël JACQUELIN | FRA | 67 | 70 | 74 | 70 | 281 | -6 | 40,482.36 | 27,441.76 |
| | Phillip ARCHER | ENG | 72 | 69 | 72 | 68 | 281 | -6 | 40,482.36 | 27,441.76 |
| | Ian POULTER | ENG | 75 | 65 | 74 | 67 | 281 | -6 | 40,482.36 | 27,441.76 |
| | Vijay SINGH | FIJ | 65 | 70 | 72 | 74 | 281 | -6 | 40,482.36 | 27,441.76 |
| | Charl SCHWARTZEL | RSA | 67 | 67 | 77 | 70 | 281 | -6 | 40,482.36 | 27,441.76 |
| 27 | Hennie OTTO | RSA | 69 | 69 | 71 | 73 | 282 | -5 | 34,807.26 | 23,594.78 |
| | David PARK | WAL | 68 | 71 | 72 | 71 | 282 | -5 | 34,807.26 | 23,594.78 |
| | Thomas BJÖRN | DEN | 70 | 71 | 71 | 70 | 282 | -5 | 34,807.26 | 23,594.78 |
| | Gary EVANS | ENG | 65 | 71 | 76 | 70 | 282 | -5 | 34,807.26 | 23,594.78 |
| | Nick DOUGHERTY | ENG | 66 | 72 | 71 | 73 | 282 | -5 | 34,807.26 | 23,594.78 |
| 32 | Graeme STORM | ENG | 72 | 69 | 72 | 70 | 283 | -4 | 28,943.00 | 19,619.58 |
| | Niclas FASTH | SWE | 69 | 75 | 70 | 69 | 283 | -4 | 28,943.00 | 19,619.58 |
| | Ignacio GARRIDO | ESP | 68 | 70 | 76 | 69 | 283 | -4 | 28,943.00 | 19,619.58 |
| | Joakim HAEGGMAN | SWE | 73 | 67 | 72 | 71 | 283 | -4 | 28,943.00 | 19,619.58 |
| | Peter BAKER | ENG | 70 | 71 | 70 | 72 | 283 | -4 | 28,943.00 | 19,619.58 |
| | Oliver WILSON | ENG | 72 | 72 | 69 | 70 | 283 | -4 | 28,943.00 | 19,619.58 |
| 38 | Alejandro CANIZARES | ESP | 69 | 69 | 76 | 70 | 284 | -3 | 24,213.75 | 16,413.76 |
| | Miguel Angel JIMÉNEZ | ESP | 67 | 69 | 75 | 73 | 284 | -3 | 24,213.75 | 16,413.76 |
| | José Manuel LARA | ESP | 69 | 73 | 71 | 71 | 284 | -3 | 24,213.75 | 16,413.76 |
| | Ricardo GONZALEZ | ARG | 70 | 69 | 75 | 70 | 284 | -3 | 24,213.75 | 16,413.76 |
| | Angel CABRERA | ARG | 72 | 68 | 73 | 71 | 284 | -3 | 24,213.75 | 16,413.76 |
| | Thongchai JAIDEE | THA | 71 | 70 | 72 | 71 | 284 | -3 | 24,213.75 | 16,413.76 |
| 44 | Mikko ILONEN | FIN | 66 | 69 | 76 | 74 | 285 | -2 | 19,295.33 | 13,079.72 |
| | Robert COLES | ENG | 71 | 67 | 76 | 71 | 285 | -2 | 19,295.33 | 13,079.72 |
| | Phillip PRICE | WAL | 71 | 71 | 70 | 73 | 285 | -2 | 19,295.33 | 13,079.72 |
| | Barry LANE | ENG | 68 | 71 | 73 | 73 | 285 | -2 | 19,295.33 | 13,079.72 |
| | Anders HANSEN | DEN | 65 | 72 | 74 | 74 | 285 | -2 | 19,295.33 | 13,079.72 |
| | José Maria OLAZÁBAL | ESP | 70 | 68 | 75 | 72 | 285 | -2 | 19,295.33 | 13,079.72 |
| | Maarten LAFEBER | NED | 71 | 71 | 71 | 72 | 285 | -2 | 19,295.33 | 13,079.72 |
| 51 | Gregory HAVRET | FRA | 72 | 69 | 73 | 72 | 286 | -1 | 15,133.59 | 10,258.60 |
| | Jonathan LOMAS | ENG | 69 | 76 | 68 | 73 | 286 | -1 | 15,133.59 | 10,258.60 |
| | David LYNN | ENG | 71 | 71 | 76 | 72 | 286 | -1 | 15,133.59 | 10,258.60 |
| | David CARTER | ENG | 71 | 70 | 72 | 73 | 286 | -1 | 15,133.59 | 10,258.60 |
| 55 | Scott DRUMMOND | SCO | 66 | 69 | 76 | 76 | 287 | 0 | 12,863.55 | 8,719.81 |
| | Marcus BOTH | AUS | 73 | 70 | 71 | 73 | 287 | 0 | 12,863.55 | 8,719.81 |
| 57 | Anton HAIG | RSA | 71 | 70 | 73 | 74 | 288 | 1 | 11,539.36 | 7,822.10 |
| | Mattias ELIASSON | SWE | 70 | 70 | 74 | 74 | 288 | 1 | 11,539.36 | 7,822.10 |
| 59 | Tjaart VAN DER WALT | RSA | 70 | 69 | 72 | 78 | 289 | 2 | 10,971.85 | 7,437.48 |
| | Mikael LUNDBERG | SWE | 71 | 72 | 71 | 75 | 289 | 2 | 10,971.85 | 7,437.48 |
| 61 | Henrik NYSTROM | SWE | 73 | 71 | 71 | | 215 | 1 | 5,325.83 | 3,610.22 |
| | Brett RUMFORD | AUS | 71 | 73 | 71 | | 215 | 1 | 5,325.83 | 3,610.22 |
| | Steven O'HARA | SCO | 69 | 71 | 75 | | 215 | 1 | 5,325.83 | 3,610.22 |
| | Gonzalo FDEZ-CASTAÑO | ESP | 68 | 73 | 74 | | 215 | 1 | 5,325.83 | 3,610.22 |
| | Paul MCGINLEY | IRL | 71 | 72 | 72 | | 215 | 1 | 5,325.83 | 3,610.22 |
| | Ian GARBUTT | ENG | 73 | 68 | 74 | | 215 | 1 | 5,325.83 | 3,610.22 |
| | Gary EMERSON | ENG | 73 | 73 | 69 | | 215 | 1 | 5,325.83 | 3,610.22 |
| | Søren HANSEN | DEN | 72 | 70 | 73 | | 215 | 1 | 5,325.83 | 3,610.22 |
| | Sam LITTLE | ENG | 72 | 70 | 73 | | 215 | 1 | 5,325.83 | 3,610.22 |
| | Nicolas COLSAERTS | BEL | 76 | 69 | 70 | | 215 | 1 | 5,325.83 | 3,610.22 |
| | Martin ERLANDSSON | SWE | 74 | 67 | 74 | | 215 | 1 | 5,325.83 | 3,610.22 |
| | Sam TORRANCE | SCO | 67 | 72 | 76 | | 215 | 1 | 5,325.83 | 3,610.22 |
| | Costantino ROCCA | ITA | 76 | 69 | 70 | | 215 | 1 | 5,325.83 | 3,610.22 |
| | Scott BARR | AUS | 72 | 72 | 71 | | 215 | 1 | 5,325.83 | 3,610.22 |
| | Ross FISHER | ENG | 70 | 70 | 75 | | 215 | 1 | 5,325.83 | 3,610.22 |
| | Wade ORMSBY | AUS | 70 | 70 | 75 | | 215 | 1 | 5,325.83 | 3,610.22 |

Difficult to imagine similar words emanating from the lips of, say, Tiger Woods, a magician of the game but clearly so cocooned in his own bubble of concentration that any distraction, no matter how small, might disturb the earth from its axis.

Before the tournament, the Chairman of the Championship Committee, Johan Rupert, had urged the amateurs to 'pick up and keep up' if they had no part to play in each hole. His wise words helped play to move along more effortlessly and, not surprisingly, the amateurs were universally uplifted by the experienced.

It was left to the voluble Hollywood actor Michael Douglas – who sadly missed the final day action as did his professional partner, the defending champion Colin Montgomerie – to encapsulate a week where celebrity and sport were happy bed-fellows.

Without even referring to a script, Douglas spoke from the heart when he said: "God bless the handicap system. It's the only sport where you are allowed to play on the same playing field as the greatest players in the world. It's a joy that we are allowed to do it and they can put up with us!"

Back to the winners, and one element which was not repeated was the decision last time to return home to Ireland with the booty before the champagne had even been cracked open. McManus, in his typical understated way, observed: "The last time we went straight home and we've regretted the fact that we didn't stay and celebrate properly. Tonight we will!"

**Gordon Simpson**

*Joakim Bäckström*

## Total Prize Fund
€3,783,400  £2,564,650

# Sound of a
# Champion

David Carter

D etermination to succeed can take many forms. For some, such as renowned sailor Sir Robin Knox-Johnston, circumnavigating the globe single-handedly once is not enough, hence the 67 year old's desire to repeat his 1969 feat once again in 2006; for others more modest achievements such as the completion of the morning crossword is reason enough for quiet satisfaction.

It is the same within the world of golf. Success can mean different things to different players and nowhere was that better illustrated than in the Mallorca Classic at Pula Golf Club. For most, it represented the penultimate event on The 2006 European Tour International Schedule but, for some, it took on the guise of The Last Chance Saloon. But more of that later.

Nowhere near that establishment, however, was Niclas Fasth. One of the more deliberate players around, as a result, the 34 year old is gently chided by his peers with the tongue-in-cheek middle name of 'NotSo'. As with most of life on Tour, it is good natured and received in such a fashion, for those same peers also recognise the Swede's undoubted talent for the game.

It was that ability which brought him his maiden European Tour title in Madeira in 2000, a runners-up place in the 2001 Open Championship at Royal Lytham & St Annes, his Ryder Cup debut at The De Vere Belfry in 2002 and victories in both New Zealand and Germany on The European Tour last season.

Another title was pocketed in April in the Andalucia Open de España Valle Romano at the San Roque Club before Fasth completed his own Spanish double in 2006 with a comprehensive three shot victory in Majorca.

Having held at least a share of the lead since his opening 66, Fasth became the fifth wire-to-wire winner on The 2006 European Tour thanks to subsequent rounds of 71, 70 and 68, the latter more than sufficient to hold off the challenge of the crowd favourite Sergio Garcia, who was attempting to bag the title for himself for the second time in three years.

He also became, alongside Per-Ulrik Johansson and Jesper Parnevik, the third most successful Swedish golfer in European Tour history with five wins, the trio one success behind six time winner Anders Forsbrand and two adrift of seven time champion Robert Karlsson.

So what does success mean for Fasth? Listen to his summation for the answer. "To be

**Pula Golf Club**

| Par | Yards | Metres |
|-----|-------|--------|
| 70  | 6850  | 6263   |

| | | | | |
|---|---|---|---|---|
| 1 | Niclas FASTH | 275 | -5 | |
| 2 | Sergio GARCIA | 278 | -2 | |
| 3 | José Manuel LARA | 279 | -1 | |
| | Marc WARREN | 279 | -1 | |
| 5 | Peter O'MALLEY | 280 | 0 | |
| 6 | Søren KJELDSEN | 281 | +1 | |
| | Paul MCGINLEY | 281 | +1 | |
| 8 | Benn BARHAM | 282 | +2 | |
| | Robert-Jan DERKSEN | 282 | +2 | |
| | Ricardo GONZALEZ | 282 | +2 | |
| | Gregory HAVRET | 282 | +2 | |
| | Robert KARLSSON | 282 | +2 | |

**WEATHER REPORT**

| Round One | Round Two | Round Three | Round Four |
|-----------|-----------|-------------|------------|

**EUROPEAN TOUR ORDER OF MERIT**
(After 46 tournaments)

| Pos | | € | |
|-----|---|---|---|
| 1 | Paul CASEY | 2,409,241.60 |  |
| 2 | Padraig HARRINGTON | 2,191,056.88 | |
| 3 | David HOWELL | 2,166,366.21 | |
| 4 | Robert KARLSSON | 2,000,092.75 | |
| 5 | Ernie ELS | 1,716,208.22 | |
| 6 | Henrik STENSON | 1,641,237.06 | |
| 7 | Ian POULTER | 1,520,951.78 | |
| 8 | Colin MONTGOMERIE | 1,496,647.95 |  |
| 9 | Johan EDFORS | 1,460,740.18 | |
| 10 | Retief GOOSEN | 1,367,399.02 |  |

Paul McGinley

for the bulk of the tournament before, understandably as the adrenalin ebbed, he dropped back to 13th place at the close. With his 2007 future assured, try convincing the genial Irishman that 13 is traditionally thought of an unlucky number.

Then there was Carter. The 34 year old, who came through potentially fatal brain surgery in Dubai in 1997, knows better than most what it takes to battle the odds and succeed and he did just that once again in Majorca.

Having started the week in 120th place on the Order of Merit, the man who won the World Cup of Golf for England in tandem with Nick Faldo in 1998, knew he had to finish 37th or better to grab one of the precious cards, no mean feat for a player who had only achieved such a goal in five of his 25 starts this season.

called a champion again has a lovely sound to it," he said. "I feel great."

However, as hinted earlier, there are many definitions of success as two players, seated within The Last Chance Saloon in Majorca, can testify. From a purely statistical standpoint, tying for 13th place and 27th place respectively should not signal great cause for celebration. But, try telling Gary Murphy and David Carter that.

At the start of the tournament, Murphy occupied 118th place on the Order of Merit, a significant position as it represented the last place where players would, by right, retain their playing privileges for the 2007 season. Having delighted at the birth of his first child in the summer, to not have a European Tour card for the first time since 2002 was not the news he wanted to take home to wife Elaine and little Hollie.

And it wasn't. A performance packed with ability and guts saw him match Fasth

*" There have been some excellent improvements to the course over the last few years which have made Pula Golf Club a very demanding and unforgiving layout. It requires total concentration over every shot as trouble is never very far away " – Niclas Fasth*

*Gary Murphy*

| Pos | Name | | Rd1 | Rd2 | Rd3 | Rd4 | Total | | € | £ |
|---|---|---|---|---|---|---|---|---|---|---|
| 1 | Niclas FASTH | SWE | 66 | 71 | 70 | 68 | 275 | -5 | 291,660.00 | 196,557.58 |
| 2 | Sergio GARCIA | ESP | 70 | 70 | 70 | 68 | 278 | -2 | 194,440.00 | 131,038.39 |
| 3 | José Manuel LARA | ESP | 69 | 72 | 71 | 67 | 279 | -1 | 98,525.00 | 66,398.67 |
|  | Marc WARREN | SCO | 70 | 68 | 71 | 70 | 279 | -1 | 98,525.00 | 66,398.67 |
| 5 | Peter O'MALLEY | AUS | 70 | 70 | 68 | 72 | 280 | 0 | 74,200.00 | 50,005.39 |
| 6 | Paul MCGINLEY | IRL | 75 | 70 | 69 | 67 | 281 | 1 | 56,875.00 | 38,329.60 |
|  | Søren KJELDSEN | DEN | 72 | 68 | 71 | 70 | 281 | 1 | 56,875.00 | 38,329.60 |
| 8 | Robert-Jan DERKSEN | NED | 76 | 69 | 67 | 70 | 282 | 2 | 36,050.00 | 24,295.07 |
|  | Ricardo GONZALEZ | ARG | 68 | 74 | 72 | 68 | 282 | 2 | 36,050.00 | 24,295.07 |
|  | Robert KARLSSON | SWE | 71 | 71 | 70 | 70 | 282 | 2 | 36,050.00 | 24,295.07 |
|  | Gregory HAVRET | FRA | 75 | 70 | 66 | 71 | 282 | 2 | 36,050.00 | 24,295.07 |
|  | Benn BARHAM | ENG | 70 | 71 | 72 | 69 | 282 | 2 | 36,050.00 | 24,295.07 |
| 13 | Jeev Milkha SINGH | IND | 71 | 75 | 69 | 68 | 283 | 3 | 26,337.50 | 17,749.56 |
|  | Gary MURPHY | IRL | 66 | 71 | 70 | 76 | 283 | 3 | 26,337.50 | 17,749.56 |
|  | Phillip ARCHER | ENG | 68 | 75 | 68 | 72 | 283 | 3 | 26,337.50 | 17,749.56 |
|  | Peter HANSON | SWE | 71 | 70 | 68 | 74 | 283 | 3 | 26,337.50 | 17,749.56 |
| 17 | Jamie SPENCE | ENG | 78 | 69 | 66 | 71 | 284 | 4 | 22,225.00 | 14,978.03 |
|  | Carlos RODILES | ESP | 75 | 73 | 64 | 72 | 284 | 4 | 22,225.00 | 14,978.03 |
|  | Peter FOWLER | AUS | 69 | 78 | 67 | 70 | 284 | 4 | 22,225.00 | 14,978.03 |
|  | Steven JEPPESEN | SWE | 72 | 69 | 69 | 74 | 284 | 4 | 22,225.00 | 14,978.03 |
| 21 | Maarten LAFEBER | NED | 72 | 76 | 68 | 69 | 285 | 5 | 18,987.50 | 12,796.19 |
|  | Alessandro TADINI | ITA | 74 | 70 | 70 | 71 | 285 | 5 | 18,987.50 | 12,796.19 |
|  | Andrew MCLARDY | RSA | 66 | 76 | 73 | 70 | 285 | 5 | 18,987.50 | 12,796.19 |
|  | Miles TUNNICLIFF | ENG | 73 | 71 | 75 | 66 | 285 | 5 | 18,987.50 | 12,796.19 |
|  | Emanuele CANONICA | ITA | 71 | 73 | 72 | 69 | 285 | 5 | 18,987.50 | 12,796.19 |
|  | Carl SUNESON | ESP | 74 | 73 | 70 | 68 | 285 | 5 | 18,987.50 | 12,796.19 |
| 27 | Joakim BÄCKSTRÖM | SWE | 74 | 70 | 69 | 73 | 286 | 6 | 16,100.00 | 10,850.23 |
|  | Martin ERLANDSSON | SWE | 73 | 73 | 72 | 68 | 286 | 6 | 16,100.00 | 10,850.23 |
|  | David PARK | WAL | 69 | 76 | 70 | 71 | 286 | 6 | 16,100.00 | 10,850.23 |
|  | David CARTER | ENG | 71 | 73 | 69 | 73 | 286 | 6 | 16,100.00 | 10,850.23 |
|  | Markus BRIER | AUT | 75 | 70 | 69 | 72 | 286 | 6 | 16,100.00 | 10,850.23 |
| 32 | Francis VALERA | ESP | 72 | 75 | 71 | 69 | 287 | 7 | 13,387.50 | 9,022.20 |
|  | Andrew MARSHALL | ENG | 70 | 70 | 72 | 75 | 287 | 7 | 13,387.50 | 9,022.20 |
|  | Francesco MOLINARI | ITA | 73 | 73 | 68 | 73 | 287 | 7 | 13,387.50 | 9,022.20 |
|  | Diego BORREGO | ESP | 71 | 68 | 75 | 73 | 287 | 7 | 13,387.50 | 9,022.20 |
|  | Gary EVANS | ENG | 70 | 76 | 69 | 72 | 287 | 7 | 13,387.50 | 9,022.20 |
|  | Simon KHAN | ENG | 70 | 74 | 69 | 74 | 287 | 7 | 13,387.50 | 9,022.20 |
| 38 | Robert COLES | ENG | 75 | 69 | 73 | 71 | 288 | 8 | 11,025.00 | 7,430.05 |
|  | Gary ORR | SCO | 71 | 72 | 72 | 73 | 288 | 8 | 11,025.00 | 7,430.05 |
|  | Sam LITTLE | ENG | 72 | 73 | 70 | 73 | 288 | 8 | 11,025.00 | 7,430.05 |
|  | Jonathan LOMAS | ENG | 68 | 73 | 74 | 73 | 288 | 8 | 11,025.00 | 7,430.05 |
|  | Alastair FORSYTH | SCO | 73 | 73 | 70 | 72 | 288 | 8 | 11,025.00 | 7,430.05 |
|  | Brett RUMFORD | AUS | 73 | 74 | 71 | 70 | 288 | 8 | 11,025.00 | 7,430.05 |
|  | Matthew MILLAR | AUS | 73 | 75 | 68 | 72 | 288 | 8 | 11,025.00 | 7,430.05 |
| 45 | Jarmo SANDELIN | SWE | 70 | 74 | 73 | 72 | 289 | 9 | 9,100.00 | 6,132.74 |
|  | Marc CAYEUX | ZIM | 75 | 70 | 70 | 74 | 289 | 9 | 9,100.00 | 6,132.74 |
|  | Richard BLAND | ENG | 73 | 73 | 68 | 75 | 289 | 9 | 9,100.00 | 6,132.74 |
|  | David BRANSDON | AUS | 79 | 68 | 70 | 72 | 289 | 9 | 9,100.00 | 6,132.74 |
| 49 | Christian L NILSSON | SWE | 69 | 75 | 71 | 75 | 290 | 10 | 7,525.00 | 5,071.30 |
|  | Jean VAN DE VELDE | FRA | 75 | 73 | 72 | 70 | 290 | 10 | 7,525.00 | 5,071.30 |
|  | Stephen GALLACHER | SCO | 71 | 74 | 72 | 73 | 290 | 10 | 7,525.00 | 5,071.30 |
|  | Oliver WILSON | ENG | 74 | 71 | 74 | 71 | 290 | 10 | 7,525.00 | 5,071.30 |
|  | Alfredo GARCIA-HEREDIA | ESP | 72 | 68 | 77 | 73 | 290 | 10 | 7,525.00 | 5,071.30 |
| 54 | Wade ORMSBY | AUS | 75 | 73 | 71 | 72 | 291 | 11 | 5,366.67 | 3,616.74 |
|  | Terry PRICE | AUS | 71 | 76 | 70 | 74 | 291 | 11 | 5,366.67 | 3,616.74 |
|  | Benoit TEILLERIA | FRA | 76 | 72 | 73 | 70 | 291 | 11 | 5,366.67 | 3,616.74 |
|  | Henrik NYSTROM | SWE | 74 | 74 | 71 | 72 | 291 | 11 | 5,366.67 | 3,616.74 |
|  | Tom WHITEHOUSE | ENG | 68 | 78 | 71 | 74 | 291 | 11 | 5,366.67 | 3,616.74 |
|  | José-Filipe LIMA | POR | 75 | 71 | 73 | 72 | 291 | 11 | 5,366.67 | 3,616.74 |
|  | Mark FOSTER | ENG | 71 | 71 | 73 | 76 | 291 | 11 | 5,366.67 | 3,616.74 |
|  | Thomas BJÖRN | DEN | 73 | 73 | 69 | 76 | 291 | 11 | 5,366.67 | 3,616.74 |
|  | Andrew BUTTERFIELD | ENG | 70 | 73 | 69 | 79 | 291 | 11 | 5,366.67 | 3,616.74 |
| 63 | Michael HOEY | NIR | 71 | 74 | 72 | 75 | 292 | 12 | 4,375.00 | 2,948.43 |
| 64 | Ian GARBUTT | ENG | 77 | 71 | 74 | 71 | 293 | 13 | 4,112.50 | 2,771.53 |
|  | Andrew OLDCORN | SCO | 73 | 75 | 70 | 75 | 293 | 13 | 4,112.50 | 2,771.53 |
| 66 | Tomas Jesus MUÑOZ | ESP | 71 | 76 | 79 | 68 | 294 | 14 | 3,675.00 | 2,476.68 |
|  | Jamie DONALDSON | WAL | 72 | 74 | 72 | 76 | 294 | 14 | 3,675.00 | 2,476.68 |
|  | Edoardo MOLINARI | ITA | 72 | 75 | 71 | 76 | 294 | 14 | 3,675.00 | 2,476.68 |
| 69 | Carlos DE CORRAL | ESP | 74 | 73 | 74 | 74 | 295 | 15 | 3,050.00 | 2,055.48 |
|  | Jean-François LUCQUIN | FRA | 76 | 72 | 74 | 73 | 295 | 15 | 3,050.00 | 2,055.48 |
|  | Barry LANE | ENG | 72 | 70 | 78 | 75 | 295 | 15 | 3,050.00 | 2,055.48 |
| 72 | Carlos DEL MORAL | ESP | 75 | 73 | 73 | 75 | 296 | 16 | 2,620.50 | 1,766.03 |
|  | Graeme STORM | ENG | 71 | 73 | 75 | 77 | 296 | 16 | 2,620.50 | 1,766.03 |
| 74 | Richard FINCH | ENG | 72 | 76 | 75 | 79 | 302 | 22 | 2,614.50 | 1,761.98 |
|  | David DIXON | ENG | 75 | 73 | 73 | 81 | 302 | 22 | 2,614.50 | 1,761.98 |
| 76 | Richard GREEN | AUS | 71 | 71 | WD | | | | | |

But, with the experience of veteran caddie Pete Coleman on his bag to help him, Carter held his nerve magnificently. He was tied 23rd at the halfway stage, joint 17th after 54 holes, and finished in a share of 27th place after a closing 73 for a six over par total of 286. He made a crucial birdie putt from ten feet at the 16th which gave him breathing space and allowed him to three putt the last for a bogey four and still be safe, his cheque for €16,100 (£10,850) elevating him to 117th place.

Unfortunately, professional sport decrees that where there is joy there will be, simultaneously, disappointment and the man who had to step down from the top 118

as Carter stepped up, was Scotland's David Drysdale, who finished just €1189 short.

Drysdale, however, will be as determined as Fasth to return to the fray, and he can take comfort from the Swede's own rehabilitation. For in 1996, Fasth lost his card by one place, and a small matter of €1120, and, well, the rest is history.

**Scott Crockett**

*Peter O'Malley*

## Total Prize Fund
€1,763,100  £1,188,197

# Indian Summer

## Club de Golf Valderrama

| Par | Yards | Metres |
|---|---|---|
| 71 | 6952 | 6356 |

| | | | | |
|---|---|---|---|---|
| **1** | **Jeev Milkha SINGH** | **282** | **-2** | |
| 2 | Luke DONALD | 283 | -1 | |
| | Sergio GARCIA | 283 | -1 | |
| | Padraig HARRINGTON | 283 | -1 | |
| 5 | Niclas FASTH | 284 | 0 | |
| | David HOWELL | 284 | 0 | |
| 7 | José Maria OLAZÁBAL | 285 | +1 | |
| | Lee WESTWOOD | 285 | +1 | |
| 9 | Phillip ARCHER | 286 | +2 | |
| | Raphaël JACQUELIN | 286 | +2 | |
| | José Manuel LARA | 286 | +2 | |
| | David LYNN | 286 | +2 | |
| | Peter O'MALLEY | 286 | +2 | |
| | Gary ORR | 286 | +2 | |
| | Ian POULTER | 286 | +2 | |
| | Marcel SIEM | 286 | +2 | |
| | Henrik STENSON | 286 | +2 | |

## WEATHER REPORT

| Round One | Round Two | Round Three | Round Four |
|---|---|---|---|

## EUROPEAN TOUR ORDER OF MERIT
(Final after 47 tournaments)

| Pos | | € | |
|---|---|---|---|
| **1** | **Padraig HARRINGTON** | **2,489,336.88** |  |
| 2 | Paul CASEY | 2,454,084.45 | |
| 3 | David HOWELL | 2,321,166.21 | |
| 4 | Robert KARLSSON | 2,044,935.61 | |
| 5 | Ernie ELS | 1,716,208.22 | |
| 6 | Henrik STENSON | 1,709,359.28 | |
| 7 | Luke DONALD | 1,658,059.93 | |
| 8 | Ian POULTER | 1,589,074.00 | |
| 9 | Colin MONTGOMERIE | 1,534,747.95 | |
| 10 | Johan EDFORS | 1,505,583.03 | |

# Volvo Masters

## Sotogrande, Spain
### October 26-29 • 2006

The ever-growing multiplicity of The European Tour International Schedule was reflected by the fact that, of the 54 players who gathered at Club de Golf Valderrama for the season-ending Volvo Masters, no fewer than 17 different nationalities, from the northern and southern hemispheres and with a diversity of cultures, were represented. All had one thing in common, however, they were chasing a dream.

David Howell

For four players, that dream had as much to do with winning the Harry Vardon Trophy, the prestigious award presented annually to the leading player on The European Tour Order of Merit, as it did with claiming the €666,660 (£446,598) first prize on offer for the Volvo Masters itself.

Of course, the fact that victory in the tournament would seal the initial deal made the event itself an even more important stop-off point on the globetrotting itineraries of Paul Casey, Padraig Harrington, David Howell and Robert Karlsson, the quartet of players – team-mates the previous month in Europe's record win in The Ryder Cup at The K Club – who arrived in southern Spain with a chance to claim that Order of Merit title.

Of the other 50 players who assembled, eight were having their first look at Valderrama, including India's Jeev Milkha Singh, who had won the Volvo China Open at the Honghua International Golf Club in Beijing in April and was, therefore, seeking a unique Volvo double.

On arrival, Singh, who had played collegiate golf in the United States before becoming the first Indian golfer to become a Member of The European Tour, immediately liked the test presented by the course. He liked how it demanded accuracy off the tee, and how it challenged a player to manufacture approach shots to greens where the putter became the most important club in the bag. In short, he liked his chances of becoming the first debutant, since Alex Cejka in 1995, to win.

*I think Valderrama is an excellent golf course that suits my game. I played just one practice round but I've watched it so many times on the television, during the Volvo Masters and, of course, The Ryder Cup in 1997, that I felt very comfortable here* – Jeev Milkha Singh

The subplot of who would win the Order of Merit offered its own intrigue

Padraig Harrington and Paul Casey

but, as the week progressed, the two became increasingly intertwined as the Volvo Masters worked its way towards a thrilling conclusion.

At the start of the week, Casey, who had grabbed pole position in the Order of Merit after winning the HSBC World Match Play Championship at Wentworth in September, had a lead of €218,185 (£147,041) over Harrington, his nearest pursuer. The two main protagonists were paired together for the first round, and Harrington got to view at first hand the distressing physical state of Casey, who had consumed a meal of melon, ham and pasta the previous night. Something disagreed with him, though, for the Englishman spent much of the first round – where he battled bravely to a 76 - in considerable distress.

His caddie, Craig Connelly, brought some medication, but Casey's condition had deteriorated to such an extent by the 11th that he called for an injection from a doctor.

"I've never felt so bad on a golf course in my life and I was close to being sick out there a couple of times," he said. "My whole body was aching."

If Harrington found the situation to be a distraction, he refused to blame it for a two over par round of 73. In truth, it was on the greens where his discord lay, requiring 33 putts as Spain's José Manual Lara took the first round lead with a 66. Singh, meanwhile, barely earned a second look when he signed for an opening 71.

Henrik Stenson, who holed the winning putt for Europe in The Ryder Cup, appeared immune from the hardship inflicted on the majority of the field in the second round as he assumed the halfway lead. The Swede produced an extraordinary run of five successive birdies from the 13th hole to sign for a 68 and a four under par total of 138.

Stenson's endeavours in strong winds and heavy rain often defied belief, as he chipped

in twice and required only three putts in those five holes. Meanwhile, four shots behind after his second consecutive 71, was the stealthy Singh.

As far as the ongoing race for the Vardon Trophy was concerned, Harrington, who started the day amongst a group of players in 30th position, finished it sharing ninth place after a second round 69 that moved him alongside Singh. The mathematicians had calculated that a top two finish was required by the Irishman to leapfrog Casey. As his fellow Dubliner Paul McGinley observed, "Padraig's doing everything he needs to do,

Robert Karlsson

Birdie num-num

## Turn a bogey into a birdie with Nokia N93

**With Nokia N93 you can do much more than call to improve relationships – with Pro Session Golf you can improve your handicap.**

Pro Session Golf is a great help in golf teaching and for personal game improvement. You can record swings and analyze them with drawing tools, frame by frame playback or by comparing them side by side. Share swings with teaching pros, friends, golf communities or download golf content. With Nokia N93 and Pro Session Golf you get a cutting-edge multimedia computer and an easy way to stay on top of the game.

Nokia Nseries
See new. Hear new. Feel new.

Carl Zeiss Optics

EUROPEAN TOUR
OFFICIAL SPONSOR

NOKIA
Connecting People

*Jaime Ortiz-Patiño, Past President of Valderrama, with Sergio Garcia*

## Final Results

| Pos | Name | | Rd1 | Rd2 | Rd3 | Rd4 | Total | | € | £ |
|---|---|---|---|---|---|---|---|---|---|---|
| 1 | Jeev Milkha SINGH | IND | 71 | 71 | 68 | 72 | 282 | -2 | 666,660.00 | 446,598.56 |
| 2 | Padraig HARRINGTON | IRL | 73 | 69 | 72 | 69 | 283 | -1 | 298,280.00 | 199,819.13 |
| | Sergio GARCIA | ESP | 71 | 70 | 70 | 72 | 283 | -1 | 298,280.00 | 199,819.13 |
| | Luke DONALD | ENG | 69 | 71 | 74 | 69 | 283 | -1 | 298,280.00 | 199,819.13 |
| 5 | Niclas FASTH | SWE | 67 | 75 | 71 | 71 | 284 | 0 | 154,800.00 | 103,701.22 |
| | David HOWELL | ENG | 70 | 73 | 70 | 71 | 284 | 0 | 154,800.00 | 103,701.22 |
| 7 | José Maria OLAZÁBAL | ESP | 74 | 71 | 71 | 69 | 285 | 1 | 110,000.00 | 73,689.50 |
| | Lee WESTWOOD | ENG | 69 | 70 | 72 | 74 | 285 | 1 | 110,000.00 | 73,689.50 |
| 9 | Raphaël JACQUELIN | FRA | 71 | 73 | 69 | 73 | 286 | 2 | 68,122.22 | 45,635.39 |
| | José Manuel LARA | ESP | 66 | 76 | 77 | 67 | 286 | 2 | 68,122.22 | 45,635.39 |
| | Phillip ARCHER | ENG | 69 | 71 | 77 | 69 | 286 | 2 | 68,122.22 | 45,635.39 |
| | Henrik STENSON | SWE | 70 | 68 | 73 | 75 | 286 | 2 | 68,122.22 | 45,635.39 |
| | Ian POULTER | ENG | 70 | 75 | 70 | 71 | 286 | 2 | 68,122.22 | 45,635.39 |
| | Marcel SIEM | GER | 69 | 72 | 72 | 73 | 286 | 2 | 68,122.22 | 45,635.39 |
| | Peter O'MALLEY | AUS | 70 | 78 | 66 | 72 | 286 | 2 | 68,122.22 | 45,635.39 |
| | Gary ORR | SCO | 72 | 74 | 72 | 68 | 286 | 2 | 68,122.22 | 45,635.39 |
| | David LYNN | ENG | 69 | 71 | 72 | 74 | 286 | 2 | 68,122.22 | 45,635.39 |
| 18 | Paul MCGINLEY | IRL | 73 | 72 | 70 | 72 | 287 | 3 | 51,533.33 | 34,522.41 |
| | Anders HANSEN | DEN | 72 | 72 | 72 | 71 | 287 | 3 | 51,533.33 | 34,522.41 |
| | Søren KJELDSEN | DEN | 73 | 75 | 68 | 71 | 287 | 3 | 51,533.33 | 34,522.41 |
| 21 | Johan EDFORS | SWE | 68 | 74 | 69 | 77 | 288 | 4 | 44,842.86 | 30,040.43 |
| | Robert KARLSSON | SWE | 69 | 74 | 70 | 75 | 288 | 4 | 44,842.86 | 30,040.43 |
| | Miguel Angel JIMÉNEZ | ESP | 68 | 74 | 72 | 74 | 288 | 4 | 44,842.86 | 30,040.43 |
| | Søren HANSEN | DEN | 71 | 72 | 73 | 72 | 288 | 4 | 44,842.86 | 30,040.43 |
| | John BICKERTON | ENG | 71 | 71 | 70 | 76 | 288 | 4 | 44,842.86 | 30,040.43 |
| | Paul CASEY | ENG | 76 | 72 | 71 | 69 | 288 | 4 | 44,842.86 | 30,040.43 |
| | Gonzalo FDEZ-CASTAÑO | ESP | 75 | 75 | 69 | 69 | 288 | 4 | 44,842.86 | 30,040.43 |
| 28 | Angel CABRERA | ARG | 71 | 71 | 72 | 75 | 289 | 5 | 38,100.00 | 25,523.36 |
| | Richard GREEN | AUS | 67 | 73 | 74 | 75 | 289 | 5 | 38,100.00 | 25,523.36 |
| | Paul BROADHURST | ENG | 73 | 74 | 71 | 71 | 289 | 5 | 38,100.00 | 25,523.36 |
| | Colin MONTGOMERIE | SCO | 77 | 73 | 69 | 70 | 289 | 5 | 38,100.00 | 25,523.36 |
| 32 | Graeme MCDOWELL | NIR | 67 | 78 | 74 | 71 | 290 | 6 | 34,500.00 | 23,111.71 |
| | Jarmo SANDELIN | SWE | 70 | 73 | 72 | 75 | 290 | 6 | 34,500.00 | 23,111.71 |
| | Thongchai JAIDEE | THA | 79 | 71 | 71 | 69 | 290 | 6 | 34,500.00 | 23,111.71 |
| 35 | Simon DYSON | ENG | 73 | 69 | 74 | 75 | 291 | 7 | 31,800.00 | 21,302.96 |
| | Anthony WALL | ENG | 71 | 77 | 69 | 74 | 291 | 7 | 31,800.00 | 21,302.96 |
| | Kenneth FERRIE | ENG | 77 | 69 | 73 | 72 | 291 | 7 | 31,800.00 | 21,302.96 |
| 38 | Simon KHAN | ENG | 74 | 70 | 72 | 76 | 292 | 8 | 29,100.00 | 19,494.22 |
| | Simon WAKEFIELD | ENG | 69 | 76 | 75 | 72 | 292 | 8 | 29,100.00 | 19,494.22 |
| | Thomas BJÖRN | DEN | 78 | 72 | 72 | 70 | 292 | 8 | 29,100.00 | 19,494.22 |
| 41 | Marc WARREN | SCO | 74 | 74 | 71 | 75 | 294 | 10 | 26,850.00 | 17,986.94 |
| | Charl SCHWARTZEL | RSA | 74 | 73 | 75 | 72 | 294 | 10 | 26,850.00 | 17,986.94 |
| 43 | Ricardo GONZALEZ | ARG | 71 | 78 | 74 | 72 | 295 | 11 | 25,050.00 | 16,781.11 |
| | Peter HANSON | SWE | 74 | 75 | 72 | 74 | 295 | 11 | 25,050.00 | 16,781.11 |
| 45 | Markus BRIER | AUT | 73 | 74 | 73 | 76 | 296 | 12 | 22,800.00 | 15,273.82 |
| | Nick DOUGHERTY | ENG | 77 | 76 | 71 | 72 | 296 | 12 | 22,800.00 | 15,273.82 |
| | Graeme STORM | ENG | 72 | 79 | 76 | 69 | 296 | 12 | 22,800.00 | 15,273.82 |
| 48 | Damien MCGRANE | IRL | 76 | 76 | 74 | 71 | 297 | 13 | 21,000.00 | 14,068.00 |
| 49 | Francesco MOLINARI | ITA | 81 | 70 | 73 | 74 | 298 | 14 | 20,100.00 | 13,465.08 |
| 50 | Stephen DODD | WAL | 80 | 76 | 70 | 73 | 299 | 15 | 18,750.00 | 12,560.71 |
| | Bradley DREDGE | WAL | 77 | 75 | 73 | 74 | 299 | 15 | 18,750.00 | 12,560.71 |
| 52 | Emanuele CANONICA | ITA | 76 | 75 | 78 | 71 | 300 | 16 | 17,500.00 | 11,723.33 |
| 53 | Brett RUMFORD | AUS | 73 | 79 | 75 | 75 | 302 | 18 | 16,800.00 | 11,254.40 |
| 54 | Andres ROMERO | ARG | 78 | 79 | 78 | 74 | 309 | 25 | 16,300.00 | 10,919.44 |

he's keeping himself in contention. Maybe this is the year for him."

Ironically, Saturday's third round brought contrasting fortunes for Singh, who carded a 68 to secure the 54 hole lead, and Harrington, who had three bogeys in his final five holes for a 72 to fall four behind. So it was, they went into Sunday's final round, with Singh chasing the dream of the biggest win of his career and Harrington needing some assistance from the golfing gods if he was to realise his own ambition.

Singh, with a closing round of 72 for a two under par total of 282, did indeed claim the title. When the dust had settled, the Indian player had one stroke to spare over a trio of players: Luke Donald, Sergio Garcia......and Harrington.

The Irishman's closing 69 included two long birdie putts on the 14th and 16th and courageous pars on the 17th – where he put his approach shot in the lake – and the 18th – where he pulled his tee shot into trees.

Each time, however, with play he described as "vintage Harrington," he managed to salvage par.

With Casey having finished in a tie for 21st place, even then, Harrington's fate depended on Garcia bogeying the 72nd hole, which moved the Spaniard from second place on his own down to a share of second with himself and Donald. Harrington did not see Garcia's missed par putt on the 18th. He had been watching the action on television in the Players' Lounge but, at the crucial time, slipped under a table to play Power Rangers with his three year old son, Patrick.

Garcia's missed 30 footer for par meant the Irishman had beaten Casey by the margin of €35,252 (£23,616) in the race to be Order of Merit champion. It was safe to come out from under the table again.

**Philip Reid**

*Irish Times*

## Total Prize Fund
### €3,912,700 £2,621,135

# WGC – Barbados World Cup

**The Sandy Lane Resort, St James, Barbados**
December 7-10 • 2006

*Stephen Dodd and Bradley Dredge*

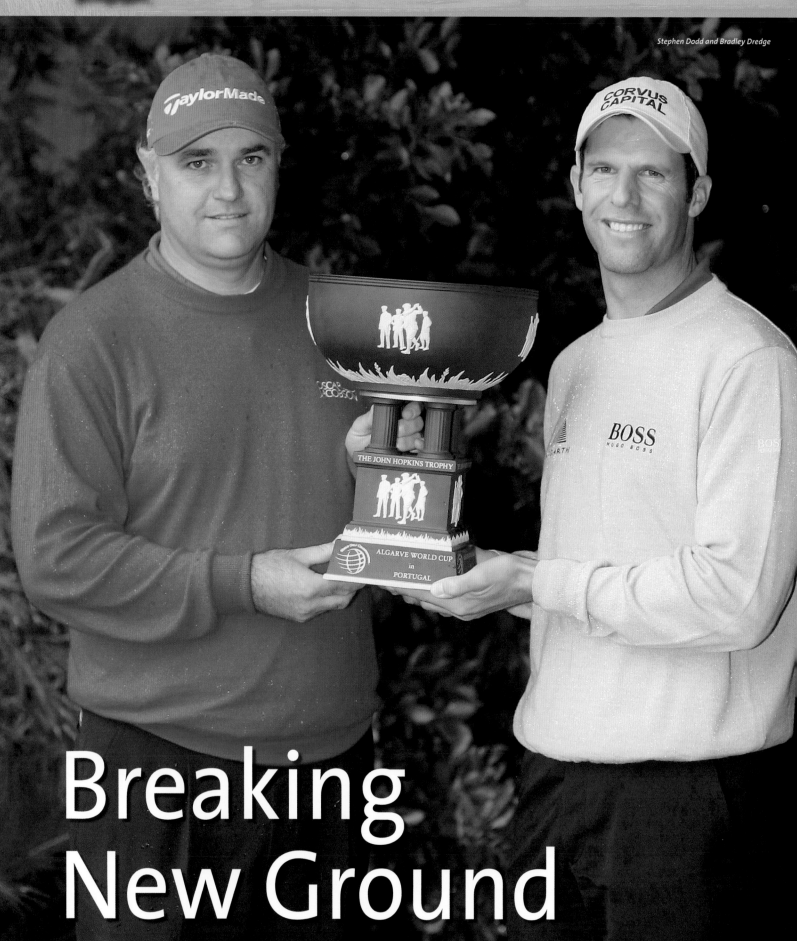

# Breaking New Ground

The Sandy Lane Resort

Luke Donald and Paul Casey (2004)

Another exhilarating chapter in the history of the World Golf Championships – World Cup unfolded when the 52nd edition of this prestigious event was played at The Sandy Lane Resort, St James, Barbados.

For the 2006 World Golf Championships – Barbados World Cup marked the 25th time that the event had been hosted by a different nation.

The World Cup, first played as the Canada Cup in 1953, has a tradition of visiting many of the world's great golf venues in exotic locations. Indeed over the years the event has been played in Argentina, Australia, Canada, China, Columbia, England, France, Greece, Indonesia, Ireland, Italy, Japan, Malaysia, Mexico, New Zealand, Philippines, Portugal, Puerto Rico, Singapore, South Africa, Spain, Thailand, the United States and Venezuela.

In fact the World Cup had been played in Puerto Rico on two occasions – in 1961 and 1994 – so when the 24 nations competed on The Country Club Course at The Sandy Lane Resort, it marked the third time that the event had been played in the Caribbean.

The Honourable Noel Lynch, M.P., Minister of Tourism and International Transport for Barbados, commented prior to the event: "Barbados is a world-class destination. The hosting of the Barbados World Cup followed by the World Cup Cricket in 2007 will enable us to globally showcase our beautiful island and firmly establish Barbados as the Caribbean's leading country for sports, activity and lifestyle tourism."

The WGC – World Cup also broke new ground in 2005 when it was played in Portugal at the Victoria Clube de Golf at Vilamoura. The event was won by Wales, who also captured the title in Hawaii in 1987, with Stephen Dodd and Bradley Dredge finishing two strokes ahead of England's Luke Donald and David Howell and Sweden's Niclas Fasth and Henrik Stenson. Raphaël Jacquelin and Thomas Levet of France finished fourth. The victory by Wales followed that by England at the Real Club de Golf de Sevilla in Spain in 2004 when Paul Casey and Donald linked superbly together.

The World Cup of Golf became the fourth event of the World Cup Championships in 2000 when the International Federation of PGA Tours entered into an agreement with the International Golf Association, the organisation which operated the World Cup from the beginning. In 2007 and 2008 it will be played at the Mission Hills Golf Club in China.

**Mitchell Platts**

Niclas Fasth and Henrik Stenson, joint 2005 runners-up

275

## Road To Glory

*England's Tom Whitehouse is presented with the trophy for winning The 2005 European Tour Qualifying School - Final Stage by George O'Grady, Executive Director of The European Tour*

W hen Sweden's Johan Edfors won the TCL Classic and The Quinn Direct British Masters within two months on The 2006 European Tour International Schedule, it significantly emphasised the power of The European Tour Qualifying School for nurturing new champions.

Edfors had returned to the Qualifying School at the end of 2005, when a record 876 players sought the card to put them on the Road to Glory, after the frustration of losing his playing privileges, earned in 2003 by finishing Number One on the European Challenge Tour.

This time the 30 year old from Varberg grasped the nettle in stunning style with the early season victories in Hainan Island, China, and at The De Vere Belfry, England, transforming his career. What is more, he became the first

player since José Maria Olazábal in 1986 to achieve multiple victories on The European Tour the season after graduating from the Qualifying School. Furthermore, he produced an electrifying final round of 63 to win The Barclays Scottish Open at Loch Lomond in July on the way to finishing tenth on The European Tour Order of Merit with winnings of €1,505,583 (£1,008,956).

Edfors said: "It was important to get my card back and the Qualifying School provided that

opportunity. It also made me realise that I had to improve my overall game to compete against the best and the outcome has been fantastic."

More evidence of the quality of competitors produced by the Qualifying School came from Spain's Gonzalo Fernandez-Castaño, a graduate from 2004. He not only won The KLM Open in 2005 but firmly established himself by capturing the BMW Asian Open in 2006. His subsequent progress in the Official World Golf Ranking and challenge for Ryder

*Paul McGinley*

*José Maria Olazábal*

EUROPEAN TOUR

# Final Results (2005)

| Pos | Name | Country | Rd1 | Rd2 | Rd3 | Rd4 | Rd5 | Rd6 | Agg | € |
|-----|------|---------|-----|-----|-----|-----|-----|-----|-----|---|
| 1 | Tom WHITEHOUSE | (Eng) | 70 | 66 | 72 | 71 | 72 | 68 | 419 | 22205 |
| 2 | Robert ROCK | (Eng) | 69 | 69 | 72 | 71 | 69 | 71 | 421 | 16284 |
| 3 | David GRIFFITHS | (Eng) | 71 | 68 | 70 | 72 | 68 | 76 | 425 | 12583 |
| 4 | Mattias ELIASSON | (Swe) | 72 | 71 | 73 | 74 | 71 | 66 | 427 | 8615 |
| 5 | Louis OOSTHUIZEN | (^A) | 71 | 68 | 73 | 77 | 71 | 67 | 427 | 8615 |
| 6 | Shaun P WEBSTER | (Eng) | 72 | 73 | 69 | 72 | 73 | 68 | 427 | 8615 |
| 7 | David DIXON | (Eng) | 76 | 71 | 69 | 73 | 71 | 69 | 429 | 6987 |
| 8 | Iain PYMAN | (Eng) | 71 | 71 | 73 | 73 | 74 | 69 | 431 | 6543 |
| 9 | Leif WESTERBERG | (Swe) | 79 | 74 | 70 | 72 | 74 | 63 | 432 | 5539 |
| 10 | Jarmo SANDELIN | (Swe) | 69 | 72 | 72 | 76 | 74 | 69 | 432 | 5539 |
| 11 | Alexandre ROCHA | (Bra) | 72 | 73 | 73 | 70 | 74 | 70 | 432 | 5539 |
| 12 | Michele REALE | (It) | 75 | 69 | 73 | 68 | 76 | 71 | 432 | 5539 |
| 13 | Johan EDFORS | (Swe) | 71 | 75 | 68 | 71 | 75 | 72 | 432 | 5539 |
| 14 | Ross FISHER | (Eng) | 76 | 71 | 75 | 71 | 72 | 68 | 433 | 4431 |
| 15 | Francisco VALERA | (Sp) | 71 | 73 | 71 | 74 | 73 | 71 | 433 | 4431 |
| 16 | Oliver WHITELEY | (Eng) | 73 | 72 | 68 | 73 | 73 | 74 | 433 | 4431 |
| 17 | Miguel CARBALLO | (Arg) | 74 | 73 | 75 | 73 | 70 | 69 | 434 | 3863 |
| 18 | Felipe AGUILAR | (Chl) | 76 | 70 | 70 | 77 | 72 | 69 | 434 | 3863 |
| 19 | Darren FICHARDT | (SA) | 73 | 72 | 73 | 73 | 75 | 68 | 435 | 3316 |
| 20 | David BRANSDON | (Aus) | 72 | 72 | 69 | 79 | 73 | 70 | 435 | 3316 |
| 21 | Matthew MILLAR | (Aus) | 71 | 72 | 74 | 75 | 72 | 71 | 435 | 3316 |
| 22 | Christian L NILSSON | (Swe) | 73 | 70 | 78 | 73 | 69 | 72 | 435 | 3316 |
| 23 | Wilhelm SCHAUMAN | (Swe) | 76 | 72 | 72 | 76 | 72 | 68 | 436 | 2599 |
| 24 | Gary CLARK | (Eng) | 73 | 71 | 78 | 75 | 69 | 70 | 436 | 2599 |
| 25 | Henrik NYSTROM | (Swe) | 74 | 71 | 70 | 75 | 76 | 70 | 436 | 2599 |
| 26 | Warren ABERY | (SA) | 76 | 75 | 67 | 75 | 72 | 71 | 436 | 2599 |
| 27 | Santiago LUNA | (Sp) | 71 | 74 | 71 | 75 | 74 | 71 | 436 | 2599 |
| 28 | Benoit TEILLERIA | (Fr) | 71 | 68 | 74 | 77 | 75 | 71 | 436 | 2599 |
| 29 | Kieran STAUNTON | (Eng) | 76 | 69 | 73 | 76 | 70 | 72 | 436 | 2599 |
| 30 | Stephen SCAHILL | (NZ) | 74 | 69 | 77 | 70 | 74 | 72 | 436 | 2599 |
| 31 | Anders SJÖSTRAND | (Swe) | 66 | 74 | 76 | 75 | 72 | 73 | 436 | 2599 |
| 32 | Tuomas TUOVINEN | (Fin) | 77 | 70 | 67 | 76 | 70 | 76 | 436 | 2599 |
| 33 | Malcolm MACKENZIE | (Eng) | 72 | 76 | 73 | 76 | 72 | 68 | 437 | 1036 |
| 34 | Magnus P ATLEVI | (Swe) | 76 | 70 | 73 | 73 | 75 | 68 | 437 | 1036 |
| 35 | Marcus BOTH | (Aus) | 77 | 78 | 67 | 71 | 76 | 68 | 437 | 1036 |
| 36 | David DRYSDALE | (Scot) | 71 | 73 | 74 | 79 | 71 | 69 | 437 | 1036 |
| 37 | Jamie LITTLE | (Eng) | 72 | 73 | 76 | 70 | 74 | 72 | 437 | 1036 |
| 38 | Cedric MENUT | (Fr) | 69 | 76 | 74 | 72 | 72 | 74 | 437 | 1036 |
| 39 | Ariel CANETE | (Arg) | 72 | 72 | 75 | 72 | 69 | 77 | 437 | 1036 |
| 40 | David PATRICK | (Scot) | 72 | 75 | 72 | 77 | 74 | 68 | 438 | 1036 |
| 41 | Alfredo GARCIA | (Sp) | 70 | 76 | 76 | 74 | 72 | 70 | 438 | 1036 |
| 42 | Brian AKSTRUP | (Den) | 78 | 70 | 70 | 75 | 75 | 70 | 438 | 1036 |
| 43 | Keith HORNE | (SA) | 71 | 74 | 72 | 75 | 75 | 71 | 438 | 1036 |
| 44 | Patrik SJÖLAND | (Swe) | 72 | 71 | 78 | 74 | 71 | 72 | 438 | 1036 |
| 45 | Phil WORTHINGTON | (Eng) | 73 | 76 | 74 | 69 | 72 | 74 | 438 | 1036 |
| 46 | Alexander NOREN | (Swe) | 68 | 73 | 75 | 74 | 71 | 77 | 438 | 1036 |
| 47 | Simon HURD | (Eng) | 71 | 71 | 73 | 77 | 76 | 71 | 439 | 1036 |
| 48 | F ANDERSSON HED | (Swe) | 70 | 73 | 75 | 75 | 74 | 72 | 439 | 1036 |
| 49 | Ivo GINER | (Sp) | 69 | 78 | 68 | 74 | 77 | 73 | 439 | 1036 |
| 50 | Massimo SCARPA | (It) | 73 | 70 | 77 | 78 | 73 | 70 | 440 | 1036 |
| 51 | Inder VAN WEERELT | (NL) | 73 | 72 | 75 | 74 | 76 | 70 | 440 | 1036 |
| 52 | Johan AXGREN | (Swe) | 76 | 73 | 74 | 70 | 75 | 72 | 440 | 1036 |
| 53 | Julien QUESNE | (Fr) | 77 | 67 | 74 | 76 | 73 | 73 | 440 | 1036 |
| 54 | Paul NILBRINK | (Nor) | 74 | 67 | 73 | 73 | 78 | 75 | 440 | 1036 |
| 55 | Jorge BERENDT | (Arg) | 77 | 71 | 75 | 73 | 76 | 69 | 441 | 1036 |
| 56 | Sergio ACEVEDO | (Arg) | 77 | 73 | 75 | 71 | 74 | 71 | 441 | 1036 |
| 57 | André BOSSERT | (Swi) | 75 | 74 | 70 | 77 | 73 | 72 | 441 | 1036 |
| 58 | R CABRERA BELLO(AM) | (Sp) | 68 | 74 | 75 | 78 | 74 | 72 | 441 | |
| 59 | Fredrik HENGE | (Swe) | 72 | 76 | 70 | 76 | 73 | 74 | 441 | 1036 |
| 60 | Denny LUCAS | (Eng) | 75 | 70 | 72 | 80 | 69 | 75 | 441 | 1036 |
| 61 | Jorge BENEDETTI | (It) | 72 | 74 | 75 | 76 | 75 | 70 | 442 | 1036 |
| 62 | Diego BORREGO | (Sp) | 71 | 74 | 75 | 77 | 72 | 73 | 442 | 1036 |
| 63 | Gareth WRIGHT | (Wal) | 78 | 73 | 73 | 71 | 72 | 75 | 442 | 1036 |
| 64 | Stuart MANLEY | (Wal) | 76 | 71 | 72 | 73 | 74 | 76 | 442 | 1036 |
| 65 | Jarrod LYLE | (Aus) | 76 | 71 | 73 | 72 | 72 | 78 | 442 | 1036 |
| 66 | Pedro LINHART | (Sp) | 75 | 73 | 69 | 80 | 72 | 74 | 443 | 1036 |
| 67 | Anders S HANSEN | (Den) | 73 | 71 | 74 | 77 | 73 | 75 | 443 | 1036 |
| 68 | Gary LOCKERBIE | (Eng) | 76 | 73 | 72 | 72 | 74 | 76 | 443 | 1036 |
| 69 | Graham FOX | (Scot) | 75 | 76 | 77 | 69 | 73 | 74 | 444 | 1036 |
| 70 | Raymond RUSSELL | (Scot) | 77 | 71 | 71 | 75 | 74 | 76 | 444 | 1036 |
| 71 | Carlos RODILES | (Sp) | 75 | 69 | 70 | 77 | 73 | 77 | 444 | 1036 |
| 72 | Ralph MILLER | (NL) | 76 | 72 | 75 | 74 | 73 | 75 | 445 | 1036 |
| 73 | Juan PARRON | (Sp) | 74 | 78 | 70 | 75 | 77 | 72 | 446 | 1036 |
| 74 | Marcus HIGLEY | (Eng) | 75 | 73 | 73 | 76 | 77 | 72 | 446 | 1036 |
| 75 | Erol SIMSEK | (Ger) | 79 | 74 | 75 | 69 | 77 | 73 | 447 | 1036 |
| 76 | Ben WILLMAN | (Eng) | 74 | 76 | 70 | 77 | 70 | 80 | 447 | 1036 |
| 77 | Kariem BARAKA | (Ger) | 74 | 76 | 72 | 70 | 74 | 81 | 447 | 1036 |
| 78 | Michael JONZON | (Swe) | 71 | 73 | 74 | 75 | 78 | 77 | 448 | 1036 |
| 79 | Jean HUGO | (SA) | 71 | 72 | 73 | 74 | 79 | 80 | 449 | 1036 |
| 80 | Johan SKÖLD | (Swe) | 70 | 70 | 76 | 77 | 79 | 77 | 449 | 1036 |
| 81 | Nicolas MEITINGER | (Ger) | 74 | 71 | 74 | 78 | 74 | 78 | 449 | 1036 |
| 82 | Manuel QUIROS | (Sp) | 72 | 78 | 70 | 76 | 80 | 75 | 451 | 1036 |
| 83 | Andrew MCARTHUR | (Scot) | 77 | 73 | 69 | 77 | 74 | 82 | 452 | 1036 |

*The first 32 players became eligible for
Category 11 Membership on The 2006
European Tour International Schedule*

Cup honours, alongside Edfors, highlighted the opportunities at hand for those who qualify from the School.

Ireland's Paul McGinley and Olazábal are perhaps the finest illustrations of players starting out on the Road to Glory at the Qualifying School. McGinley played in the 1991 Walker Cup – helping Liam White beat Phil Mickelson and Bob May – then gained his card at his first visit to the Qualifying School that year. The rest, as they say, is history. McGinley holed the winning putt in The 2002 Ryder Cup and with his win in the 2005 Volvo Masters took his earnings to approaching ten million euros. He has also represented Ireland in 12 World Cups, winning with Padraig Harrington in 1997, not to mention playing in seven Alfred Dunhill Cups, two Seve Trophys and, of course, three Ryder Cups. Olazábal, after his electrifying start in 1986, has won no fewer than 30 tournaments worldwide and in 2006 he teed-up in his seventh Ryder Cup.

No fewer than 24 players have moved on from the School to win the very next year on The European Tour – Gordon Brand Jnr, Paul Way, Greg Turner, José Maria Olazábal, Vijay Singh, Paul Broadhurst, Mike McLean, Per-Ulrik Johansson, Ian Palmer, Andrew Oldcorn, Padraig Harrington, Niclas Fasth, Roger Chapman, Ian Poulter, Gregory Havret, Jorge Berendt, Arjun Atwal, Adam Mednick, Philip Golding, Robert-Jan Derksen, Christopher Hanell, Joakim Bäckström, Fernandez-Castaño and Edfors.

Others have returned to the School, such as Jarmo Sandelin in 2005, to resurrect their careers. Sandelin, who won five times on The

European Tour between 1995 and 2002 and played in The 1999 Ryder Cup, successfully regained his card then set about reclaiming past glories. He did so in good style, finishing runner-up in the Telecom Italia Open, on his way to 44th on the Order of Merit, and said: "If you don't wake up when you lose your card, you're never going to wake up. I was delighted to get my card back at the School. It was a new start for me. All good things have to start somewhere."

Few events can rival the drama and the tension of The European Tour Qualifying School. The pressure, with the ultimate dream of Membership of The European Tour at stake, warmed-up in 2006 at the First Stage, held at six venues across England, France, Italy and Sweden, and the Second Stage, held at Costa Ballena Club de Golf, Cadiz; Sherry Golf, Jerez; Emporda Golf; and PGA Golf de Catalunya, Girona, in Spain with 156 players eventually contesting the Final Stage at the San Roque Club, Cadiz, Spain, where, in 2005, Tom Whitehouse, who finished ahead of Robert Rock and David Griffiths, led an England 1-2-3. The original entry for 2005 came from 44 nations with England providing the highest number (226) of competitors.

Uniquely, the Qualifying School is one tournament where the goal is not necessarily to triumph but simply to finish in the upper echelons. The higher you finish can maximise playing opportunities but, in reality, anyone finishing the six rounds with a card unlocks the way to that Road to Glory.

**Mitchell Platts**

# A Bountiful
# Harvest

*Trevor Immelman*

T he European Tour is rightly proud of many aspects, from its cultural diversity and variety of locations to the wonderful array of golf courses where its tournaments are staged. However, one of the most gratifying aspects is the international flavour of its Membership.

As well as competing on The European Tour International Schedule itself, these players exhibit their golfing skills in many countries around the world with a considerable degree of success and this season proved no exception as European Tour Members continued to amass silverware across the globe.

During the course of 2005-2006, players from no fewer than 12 different countries picked up a total of 26 titles across Europe, America, Africa and Asia – a truly bountiful harvest – and taking the honour of providing the most number of international victories was South Africa where seven Members won eight tournaments in total.

Headlining that impressive group was Trevor Immelman who achieved something not many people did in 2006, namely holding off a charging Tiger Woods to win his first tournament on the US PGA Tour, the Cialis Western Open at the Cog Hill Golf & Country Club in Illinois in July.

Immelman, a three time winner on The European Tour, had come close before in the EDS Byron Nelson Championship and the Wachovia Championship, but this time he came up trumps, holing a 30 foot breaking putt for birdie on the 72nd hole to complete a round of 67 and a total of 13 under par 271, beating Australian Matthew Goggin and Woods by two shots.

The World Number One immediately paid tribute to Immelman, saying: "He has an inordinate amount of talent and has come so close to victory before. So good for Trev."

Of course, it was also the perfect way for Immelman and wife Carminita to herald the birth of their first child, a son Jacob, who came into the world a little more than two weeks later.

Another South African to achieve a first in 2006 was Retief Goosen who delivered a first successful title defence of his career when he retained the Volkswagen Masters – China title at the Yalong Bay Golf Club in October.

The 2001 and 2002 European Tour Number One finished the week with an impressive 21 under par total of 267 to win by three shots from his fellow European Tour Member Michael Campbell of New Zealand.

"This is a great feeling," said Goosen. "I've won back to back titles as an amateur but never as a professional so it will be wonderful to come back next year and see if I can go one better with a hat-trick."

The other six victories all came from South African golfers on their home turf on the Sunshine Tour, Tim Clark leading the way at the end of 2005 with victory, in partnership with Vincent Tshabalala, in the Nelson Mandela Invitational tournament at the Arabella Estate.

Immediately after his victory Clark – another three time winner on The European Tour – showed the true caring side of golf when it was revealed he had taken the opportunity to give a little girl a better chance of life.

Siobhan, a pupil at the Carel du Toit School for the Hearing Impaired in Cape Town, so touched Clark when he met her on a visit that he donated all of his winner's cheque to help with her development.

"Apparently it costs R150,000 for the cochlear implant she needs and therefore I wanted all

Tim Clark with Vincent Tshabalala

Retief Goosen

Warren Abery

*Luke Donald*

*Charl Schwartzel*

*Adam Scott*

of my winnings to go towards helping her with that," he said. "She was my inspiration for the weekend."

In February 2006 it was the turn of Warren Abery and Charl Schwartzel to succeed, Abery's 15 under par total of 265 good enough for a two shot victory in the Nashua Masters at the Wild Coast Country Club before, three weeks later, Schwartzel triumphed in the Vodacom Tour Championship.

Schwartzel birdied the final hole of the Pretoria Country Club for a closing 67 and a 14 under par total of 270 to take the title by four shots from Darren Fichardt. There was double reason to celebrate for the 21 year old for the victory also saw him secure the Sunshine Tour Order of Merit for the second consecutive year.

Completing the South African Roll Call of Honour on the Sunshine Tour's Winter Tour in April and May were Challenge Tour Member Jean Hugo and European Tour Affiliate Member Thomas Aiken.

Hugo's back-to-back successes came in the Vodacom Origins of Golf event at the Arabella Country Estate in the Western Cape and in the South African Airways Pro-Am Invitational at the Paarl Golf Club in Cape Town before, the following week, Aiken won the Samsung Royal Swazi Sun Open at the Royal Swazi Sun Country Club near Mbabane.

The next most prolific nations in terms of providing winners were England and Australia with three apiece, England's successes coming via Ryder Cup man Luke Donald, who won twice, and two-time European Tour winner Miles Tunnicliff, while Australia's triumphs came via the respective talents of Adam Scott and European Tour Affiliate Member Scott Strange.

Both Donald's successes came in the United States and began at the end of 2005 when

he emerged victorious from the elite 16-man field to win the Tiger Woods-presented Target World Challenge at the Sherwood Country Club in California.

The 28 year old started the final round six shots adrift of leader Darren Clarke but matched the record for the best closing round by a winner in the seven year history of the event, a closing 64 giving him a 16 under par total of 272 and a two shot victory.

"I played great today but fortunately for me, the guys in the top two groups didn't play their best and let me have this one a little bit. This year has been a lot of nearlys for me so luckily I got the last one," he said.

If, in December, Donald had had to rely on a little help, three months later in March it was all his own doing when he claimed his second US PGA Tour title in the Honda Classic at Palm Beach Gardens in Florida, holding off Australian Geoff Ogilvy with a closing 69 for a 12 under par total of 276 to win by two shots.

"Any time you can win is a huge boost of confidence," he said. "I'm very steady and that is the main reason why I think, if I keep playing the way I am then there is no reason that I cannot contend in Major Championships and strive to be the best player in the world."

Completing the triumvirate of English successes was Tunnicliff who, at the same time as Donald was winning the Target World Challenge in California, was retaining his Mauritius Open title at the Belle Mare Plage Legend course, an eight under par total of 207 in the three round event good enough for a one shot victory over José-Filipe Lima of Portugal and Christian Cévaër of France.

Strange set Australia's ball rolling in Asia in May when he romped to an emphatic five shot triumph in the Philippine Open at

the Wack Wack Golf and Country Club. He closed with a two under par 70 to complete a wire-to-wire victory on eight under par 280 and claim his second career title on the Asian Tour.

Three months later, at the beginning of September, it was the turn of his compatriot Scott to get his hands on silverware in Asia, the five time winner on The European Tour retaining the Barclays Singapore Open title after beating former European Tour Order of Merit winner Ernie Els in a three hole play-off.

The duo were joint third round leaders on eight under par 205 but the fourth round was cancelled due to adverse weather. Into the play-off, both Els and Scott parred the first two holes before the Australian provided the killer blow at the par five 18th, Scott holing from five feet for a birdie four as Els three putted for a bogey six.

"This is the first time I have successfully defended a title and it's a great feeling and something that I will cherish," said Scott. "It has been a long time coming this win, since last year, and hopefully I can keep going from here."

The 26 year old certainly achieved that ambition in fine style when he captured the season-ending Tour Championship on the US PGA Tour at the East Lake Golf Club in Atlanta. Scott, three ahead going into the final round, maintained that advantage at the end with a closing 66 for an 11 under par total of 269 to relegate Jim Furyk into second place.

Three other nations provided multiple victories in 2006; Argentina, India and the United States, the Argentine triumphs coming from Eduardo Romero and Andres Romero, the Indian victories provided by Shiv Kapur and Jyoti Randhawa, while the Stars and Stripes was raised thanks to the sterling efforts of Kevin Stadler.

The elder Romero, Eduardo, won his first Senior Major Championship, the JELD-WEN Tradition at the Reserve Vineyards and Golf Club in Oregon.

Only a month before, Romero had been bitterly disappointed to miss out in a play-off to American Loren Roberts in The Senior British Open Championship, presented by Aberdeen Asset Management, at the Westin Turnberry Resort in Scotland. But the familiar smile was back on his face after he closed with the best round of the championship, a seven under par 65, for a 13 under par total of 275 to tie American Lonnie Nielsen before, this time, emerging victorious from a play-off with a birdie at the first hole.

The younger Romero, Andres, followed up a fine rookie year on The European Tour when he claimed a wire-to-wire 54 hole victory in his native country's Torneo de Maestros at the Olivos Golf Club after the final round was cancelled due to thunderstorms. The tournament was, therefore, decided over three rounds with Romero winning with a nine under par total of 204, three shots clear of Angel Cabrera and four ahead of Daniel Vancsik.

In his native Asia, Kapur won the Volvo Masters of Asia at the Thai Country Club in Bangkok with a tournament record total of 20 under par 268, while compatriot Randhawa lifted the Hero Honda Indian Open at the Delhi Golf Club, for the second time in his career, returning on Monday morning to beat fellow countrymen S.S.P. Chowrasia and Vijay Kumar in a sudden-death play-off after all three had finished on 18 under par 270.

Back on home soil in the United States, Stadler had an excellent end to the 2006 season on the Nationwide Tour after having had a brilliant start with victory on The European Tour in the Johnnie Walker Classic at The Vines Resort and Country Club in Perth.

Kevin Stadler

Stephen Ames

Carl Pettersson

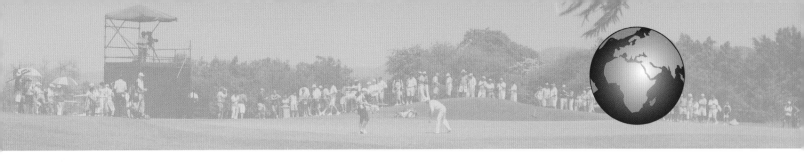

The son of the 1982 Masters Tournament Champion, Craig, set the ball rolling in August when he won the Xerox Classic at the Irondequoit Country Club in Rochester, New York, and followed that up with victory in the Albertsons Boise Open, presented by First Health, at the Hillcrest Country Club in Idaho in September.

As well as the tournaments above, the United States continued to prove a fertile hunting ground for other European Tour Members with four victories going to a wide variety of players.

By far the most prestigious success was claimed by Canada's Stephen Ames when he stayed cool in the pressure-cooker atmosphere generated around the Stadium Course at the TPC at Sawgrass in March to win The Players Championship. Ames closed with a five under par 67 for a 14 under par total of 274 to relegate fellow European Tour Member Retief Goosen to second place, six shots adrift.

"This is big," he said. "I beat the top players in the world here this week. I think I put myself in another gear that I've probably only felt a couple of times before in my career, but not for all four days like I did this week."

Three months later in June, European Tour Members Carl Pettersson and Vijay Singh dominated the US PGA Tour for two weeks running, the Swede mounting the winners' platform first after victory in the Memorial Tournament while, seven days later, the Fijian repeated the feat in the Barclays Classic.

Pettersson's success, on June 4, completed a memorable day for Swedish golf as his winning 12 under par total of 276 at Muirfield Village in Ohio came only a few hours after his compatriot Robert Karlsson had romped to victory on The European Tour in The Celtic Manor Wales Open.

A week later it was Singh who was in charge

as he lifted his first title in almost ten months at the Westchester Country Club in New York State, where he had won twice before. The Fijian began the final day one shot off the lead but posted a final round 68 for a ten under par total of 274 to relegate Adam Scott to second place by two shots.

"This is the biggest win I've had for a long time," he said. "It gives me a lot of confidence and gives me the feeling that if I get into contention I can finish it off. It makes people think that once they see my name up there, that I'm back."

Back in Asia, the turn of the year also saw Thailand's Thaworn Wiratchant win the Carlsberg Masters Vietnam at the Chi Linh Star Golf and Country Club in Hanoi with a seven under par total of 281.

Finally, France and Scotland ensured their respective places in the 2006 record books thanks to the efforts of Gregory Bourdy and Dean Robertson.

In South Africa in February, Bourdy followed three consecutive 66s with a 69 to complete a wire-to-wire victory in the Telkom PGA Championship at the Country Club in Johannesburg, while in Scotland in September, Dean Robertson returned home in triumph to win the Gleneagles Scottish PGA Championship on the Tartan Tour, the 35 year old beating Stirling-based professional Craig Lee at the second hole of a play-off after the pair had finished together on 17 under par 275.

It was heartening to see Robertson – who lost two years of his career to clinical depression – back with a broad smile on his face, an emotion shared by all the winners across the world in another memorable season.

**Scott Crockett**

Vijay Singh

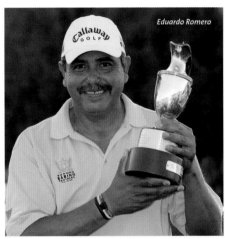

Eduardo Romero

Gregory Bourdy

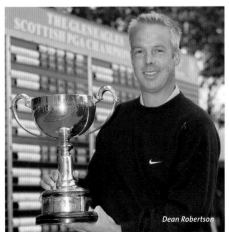

Dean Robertson

Sam Torrance

# Striving for The Future

José Rivero

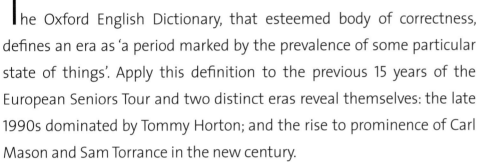

Nick Job

Bobby Lincoln

The Oxford English Dictionary, that esteemed body of correctness, defines an era as 'a period marked by the prevalence of some particular state of things'. Apply this definition to the previous 15 years of the European Seniors Tour and two distinct eras reveal themselves: the late 1990s dominated by Tommy Horton; and the rise to prominence of Carl Mason and Sam Torrance in the new century.

Mason topped the Order of Merit in 2003 and 2004 and has finished runner-up in both the following years. The reason he has not been able to close on Horton's record haul of five Order of Merit wins is simple: the form of one Samuel Robert Torrance OBE.

In the space of 36 events spanning three and a half years on the European Seniors Tour, the 2002 winning Ryder Cup Captain has collected eight tournament victories and has finished inside the top ten a further 19 times.

Three of the wins came in 2005 when Torrance collected his first John Jacobs Trophy, courtesy of finishing €20,307 (£13,717) ahead of Mason. In 2006, he won four times and was confirmed as the 2006 Number One with record earnings of €347,525 (£232,250) - €79,072 (£52,843) clear of Mason.

"Winning back-to-back Order of Merits is a tremendous achievement and something Carl knows all about. It is something I strived for all year. I played in nearly every event and showed how much I wanted this," said Torrance.

"Tommy's record of five is something else to strive for and I would love to do it. It will be a challenge to win it again, especially as we have a number of good players reaching 50, but I think I will be up for it. My swing will last forever and I still have a strong will to win, so it's a question of my body holding up."

Three of European golf's greatest players – Spain's Seve Ballesteros, England's Nick Faldo and Germany's Bernhard Langer, who between them have won a total of 13 Major Championships – all celebrate their 50th birthdays in 2007 and become eligible to play on the European Seniors Tour, while Torrance is also aware of the emerging challenge from within the current ranks, evidenced by the number of first-time winners this year.

Gordon J Brand of England, Guillermo Encina of Chile, Juan Quiros of Spain, American Loren Roberts, José Rivero of Spain and Japan's Katsuyoshi Tomori – six men who also underline the international nature of the Tour - all experienced the joy of securing their maiden titles in 2006.

In fact it was Rivero, a member of Europe's Ryder Cup-winning Teams in 1985 and 1987,

Kevin Spurgeon

# COPTHORNE
# TARA HOTEL
### LONDON KENSINGTON

The Copthorne Tara Hotel London Kensington is situated in the heart of fashionable Kensington just a short hop from Notting Hill. It is an area of enormous historic interest complimented by some of London's finest bars and restaurants.

During your stay why not enjoy the benefits of our Club Lounge, offering a relaxing meeting space, complimentary broadband internet access and beverages throughout the day. You are welcome to use these facilities after a hard day working or shopping!

Club rates include all of the above and Continental Breakfast.

We look forward to welcoming you to London's friendliest 4 * Hotel in the near future

Copthorne Tara Hotel London Kensington
Scarsdale Place
Kensington
London
W8 5SR

Tel: [44] (0)20 7937 7211
Fax: [44] (0)20 7937 7100

Email: sales.tara@mill-cop.com

## www.millenniumhotels.com

**Christchurch    London    New York    Paris    Singapore**

Carl Mason and Sam Torrance

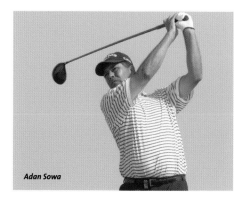

Adan Sowa

Jim Rhodes

Delroy Cambridge

Guillermo Encina

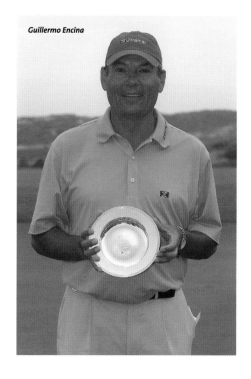

who got the season off to an enthralling start by defeating England's David J Russell at the fourth hole of a sudden-death play-off to capture the DGM Barbados Open at Royal Westmoreland Golf Club, Barbados, after both men had finished the 54 holes locked at nine under par 207.

Torrance also got into the winning act early on, closing with a faultless five under par 67 to capture the Sharp Italian Seniors Open by four strokes from Eamonn Darcy, who was runner-up for a second successive year.

Beaten in a play-off by Frenchman Gery Watine at Circolo Golf Venezia in 2005, this time around the Irishman faded in regulation play and a final round 71 left him four adrift of Torrance's winning aggregate of 11 under par 205.

The following week saw 25 members of the European Seniors Tour cross the Atlantic for the 67th US Senior PGA Championship, played in difficult windy conditions at Oak Tree Golf Club, Edmond, Oklahoma, USA.

Rivero, Tomori and Torrance all featured prominently and, indeed, Tomori finished in seventh place after an impressive final round 67, before Jay Haas went on to defeat fellow American Brad Bryant in a play-off to secure the first prize.

Torrance transported his form straight back across the Atlantic Ocean to capture the AIB Irish Seniors Open, in association with Greenstar and Fáilte Ireland, following a four-man play-off at the Sheraton Fota Island Golf Resort and Spa in Cork.

Having won the Irish Open on The European Tour in 1981 and 1995, the Scot claimed the Seniors version in some style by hitting his 150 yard approach to within 14 feet of the flag on the second extra hole and converting the eagle putt to defeat American Jerry Bruner, who could only manage a birdie four.

Earlier, Australia's Stewart Ginn and Encina had dropped out on the first extra hole after failing to match the birdies carded by the other two. The four had all finished the tournament locked at six under par 207.

# The European Seniors Tour

Giuseppe Cali

Gery Watine

Simon Owen

Martin Poxon

Bertus Smit

Bruce Heuchan

Encina quickly made amends by producing a brilliant final round of six under par 66 to seal his maiden Seniors title at the Irvine Whitlock Seniors Classic. The smooth-swinging South American compiled a seven under par total of 209 to finish three clear of New Zealand's Simon Owen and Americans Rex Caldwell and Alan Tapie at La Moye Golf Club, Jersey.

The Tour then moved to Wales for the lucrative FIRSTPLUS Wales Seniors Open at the Vale Hotel, Golf and Spa Resort near Cardiff and ultimately it was Rivero who coped best with the tricky, sun-baked Wales National Course. The Spaniard started the final round six shots back but a birdie at the 54th hole saw him finish on four under par 212 and snatch a dramatic one shot victory over Quiros, Russell, Torrance and Watine.

However, the best come-from-behind victory of the season came from Giuseppe Cali, who made up a seven stroke deficit in the final round of the Bendinat London Seniors Masters at The London Golf Club, Kent, England.

The Italian carded a five under par 67 to tie Delroy Cambridge on six under par 210, before defeating the Jamaican at the fifth play-off hole on the Jack Nicklaus-designed Heritage Course.

England's Mark James produced three successive under par rounds at the tough Prairie Dunes Country Club in Hutchinson,

Kansas, USA, the following week to go into the final round of the US Senior Open with a chance of victory. However, The 1999 Ryder Cup Captain could only manage a 75 on Sunday to finish in 14th place, as Allen Doyle of the United States retained the title with a four round total of eight under 272.

Next up was the Tour's biggest event of the season and another Major Championship, The Senior British Open Championship, presented by Aberdeen Asset Management.

The spectacular Westin Turnberry Resort in Scotland hosted the world's best senior golfers and after four days of memorable competition - during which the legendary Gary Player beat his age with a first round 69 and Eduardo Romero, one of four Argentine members of the European Seniors Tour, reeled off a scintillating seven under par 63 - Loren Roberts captured the €231,225 (£157,799) first prize and the replica Claret Jug after defeating Romero at the first play-off hole.

Roberts and Romero had finished the four rounds tied at six under par 274, one ahead

Martin Gray

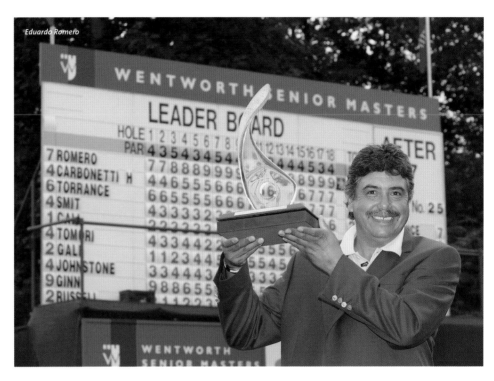

Eduardo Romero

of American Dick Mast with his fellow countryman Craig Stadler, the 1982 Masters Tournament Champion, in fourth place.

The runners-up finish boosted Romero's confidence and the following week he hit top spot with a successful defence of the Wentworth Senior Masters at Wentworth Club, Surrey, England, where he closed with a round of 70 for a winning nine under par total of 207, two better than Horacio Carbonetti of Argentina and Torrance in second place.

From England the players flew to Switzerland for the ever popular Bad Ragaz PGA Seniors Open at Golf Club Bad Ragaz, where Quiros registered his maiden victory in only his seventh start on the European Seniors Tour. The Spaniard, aided by the altitude of the Alps, produced the lowest 18 hole score of the year with a nine under par second round 61 en route to a 14 under par total 196 and a two stroke win over Mason.

The following week, Tomori joined the club of first-time winners with victory at Helsingör

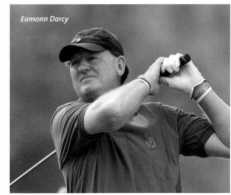

Eamonn Darcy

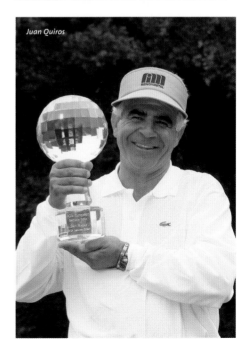

Juan Quiros

David J Russell

# From the front nine to the backyard, you can count on us.

With over 90 years of experience, Toro is the most trusted supplier of turf equipment and irrigation systems to golf courses, parks and individual lawns around the world. Our commitment to providing innovative, high quality products and systems to help grow and maintain turf is legendary. We care about preserving the tradition of golf and we also care about providing the right solution to you. Make Toro the preferred name at your home today.

**TORO. Count on it.**

Golf Club, Denmark, in the Scandinavian Senior Open, following in the footsteps of Seiji Ebihara, Noboru Sugai and Dragon Taki by becoming the fourth Japanese winner in the history of the European Seniors Tour.

Tomori closed with a brilliant 66 to complete a winning 54 hole total of 14 under par 199, two clear of Rivero and Darcy, the latter registering his seventh runners-up finish as his search for that elusive first win continued.

Back-to-back triumphs then followed for Torrance in the PGA Seniors Championship at The Stoke By Nayland Golf Club, Suffolk, England, where he finished three ahead of Argentine Luis Carbonetti on 20 under par 268, and the Charles Church Scottish Seniors Open at the Marriott Dalmahoy Hotel & Country Club, Midlothian, Scotland, where his three under par total of 213 beat fellow Scot Bill Longmuir by a shot.

Torrance made up seven shots in 36 holes on Dalmahoy's revamped East Course to capture his fourth title of the season and the 40th of his professional career: yet another landmark in a truly memorable season for the man from Largs.

The rest of the year was defined by the performances of Carl Mason, who turned around an indifferent season by winning the

Katsuyoshi Tomori

Luis Carbonetti

Bob Cameron

Bill Longmuir

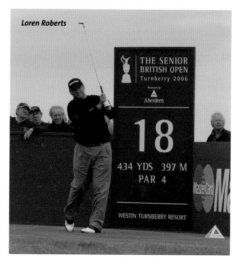
Loren Roberts

Jerry Bruner

# The European Seniors Tour

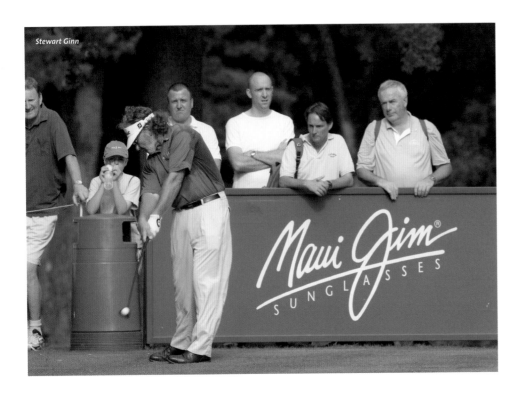

Stewart Ginn

John Bland

European Senior Masters on the Duke's Course, Woburn Golf Club, Bedfordshire, England, The Midas Group English Seniors Open at St Mellion International, Saltash, Cornwall, England, and the Estoril Senior Open of Portugal at Quinta da Marinha Oitavos Golfe, Portugal.

"The victory in the European Senior Masters changed my year and I became much more confident," said the 53 year old, whose three round total of seven under 209 was two better than Horacio Carbonetti in second place. "Throughout my career I have always wanted to win at one of the great courses like Woburn."

At St Mellion, Mason carded a battling final round 71 to hold off a charging Ginn, the Australian closing with a 67 to finish one adrift of the Englishman's four under par total of 212. Mason's win completed a unique hat-trick in the event following his triumphs at Hillside Golf Club in 2003 and Formby Hall Golf Club in 2004. It also thrust Mason into contention for the Order of Merit, a position he improved the following week with a runner-up finish behind Brand in the OKI Castellón Open de España Senior at Sergio Garcia's

Terry Gale

Gordon J Brand

Carl Mason and Tony Johnstone

## The European Seniors Tour Order of Merit 2006

| Pos | Name | Country | Played | € | £ |
|---|---|---|---|---|---|
| 1 | Sam TORRANCE | (SCO) | (15) | 347,525.10 | 232,250.09 |
| 2 | Carl MASON | (ENG) | (17) | 268,453.00 | 179,406.42 |
| 3 | José RIVERO | (ESP) | (16) | 233,373.82 | 155,963.10 |
| 4 | Gordon J BRAND | (ENG) | (18) | 196,002.48 | 130,987.93 |
| 5 | Stewart GINN | (AUS) | (14) | 178,260.39 | 119,130.94 |
| 6 | Juan QUIROS | (ESP) | (12) | 159,071.13 | 106,306.81 |
| 7 | Horacio CARBONETTI | (ARG) | (14) | 147,655.45 | 98,677.74 |
| 8 | David J RUSSELL | (ENG) | (18) | 140,783.98 | 94,085.55 |
| 9 | Giuseppe CALI | (ITA) | (18) | 138,241.68 | 92,386.55 |
| 10 | Luis CARBONETTI | (ARG) | (16) | 136,375.28 | 91,139.24 |
| 11 | Guillermo ENCINA | (CHI) | (17) | 126,615.90 | 84,617.06 |
| 12 | Nick JOB | (ENG) | (18) | 120,017.25 | 80,207.21 |
| 13 | Tony JOHNSTONE | (ZIM) | (15) | 115,928.71 | 77,474.85 |
| 14 | Eamonn DARCY | (IRL) | (12) | 112,502.80 | 75,185.32 |
| 15 | Gery WATINE | (FRA) | (15) | 104,676.24 | 69,954.85 |
| 16 | Bertus SMIT | (RSA) | (16) | 101,748.25 | 67,998.08 |
| 17 | Simon OWEN | (NZL) | (16) | 95,402.24 | 63,757.06 |
| 18 | Bobby LINCOLN | (RSA) | (16) | 86,868.98 | 58,054.30 |
| 19 | Bill LONGMUIR | (SCO) | (12) | 83,039.52 | 55,495.09 |
| 20 | Bob CAMERON | (ENG) | (18) | 80,840.06 | 54,025.20 |
| 21 | Delroy CAMBRIDGE | (JAM) | (16) | 75,948.82 | 50,756.39 |
| 22 | Adan SOWA | (ARG) | (14) | 74,426.72 | 49,739.18 |
| 23 | Bruce HEUCHAN | (CAN) | (16) | 70,862.21 | 47,357.02 |
| 24 | Martin POXON | (ENG) | (17) | 67,537.22 | 45,134.94 |
| 25 | Martin GRAY | (SCO) | (18) | 66,466.87 | 44,419.63 |
| 26 | Jim RHODES | (ENG) | (17) | 64,237.57 | 42,929.79 |
| 27 | Terry GALE | (AUS) | (18) | 60,298.33 | 40,297.21 |
| 28 | John BLAND | (RSA) | (7) | 60,150.50 | 40,198.42 |
| 29 | Kevin SPURGEON | (ENG) | (17) | 58,833.91 | 39,318.55 |
| 30 | Jerry BRUNER | (USA) | (17) | 57,885.90 | 38,684.99 |
| 31 | John CHILLAS | (SCO) | (16) | 57,852.22 | 38,662.48 |
| 32 | Gavan LEVENSON | (RSA) | (17) | 57,093.06 | 38,155.14 |
| 33 | Pete OAKLEY | (USA) | (17) | 53,308.29 | 35,625.78 |
| 34 | Jimmy HEGGARTY | (NIR) | (14) | 53,145.12 | 35,516.74 |
| 35 | Des SMYTH | (IRL) | (6) | 50,261.23 | 33,589.44 |
| 36 | Glenn RALPH | (ENG) | (11) | 49,897.77 | 33,346.54 |
| 37 | Doug JOHNSON | (USA) | (11) | 44,459.71 | 29,712.31 |
| 38 | Denis O'SULLIVAN | (IRL) | (13) | 43,520.38 | 29,084.55 |
| 39 | Mike MILLER | (SCO) | (17) | 42,002.81 | 28,070.36 |
| 40 | David GOOD | (AUS) | (16) | 41,397.26 | 27,665.68 |
| 41 | Angel FERNANDEZ | (CHI) | (16) | 40,527.26 | 27,084.26 |
| 42 | Bob LARRATT | (ENG) | (15) | 40,149.51 | 26,831.81 |
| 43 | Alan TAPIE | (USA) | (11) | 38,324.55 | 25,612.20 |
| 44 | Tony ALLEN | (ENG) | (10) | 32,066.92 | 21,430.24 |
| 45 | Emilio RODRIGUEZ | (ESP) | (13) | 31,991.25 | 21,379.66 |
| 46 | Seiji EBIHARA | (JPN) | (6) | 31,654.57 | 21,154.66 |
| 47 | Manuel PIÑERO | (ESP) | (13) | 31,170.30 | 20,831.03 |
| 48 | John MASHEGO | (RSA) | (14) | 30,360.64 | 20,289.94 |
| 49 | Ian MOSEY | (ENG) | (16) | 26,640.28 | 17,803.63 |
| 50 | Rex CALDWELL | (USA) | (10) | 26,426.17 | 17,660.54 |
| 51 | Peter TERAVAINEN | (USA) | (11) | 26,032.62 | 17,397.53 |
| 52 | Bob LENDZION | (USA) | (14) | 25,826.29 | 17,259.64 |
| 53 | Martin FOSTER | (ENG) | (11) | 24,120.19 | 16,119.46 |
| 54 | Jean Pierre SALLAT | (FRA) | (14) | 23,576.18 | 15,755.90 |
| 55 | Noel RATCLIFFE | (AUS) | (13) | 23,549.84 | 15,738.29 |
| 56 | Mike FERGUSON | (AUS) | (14) | 22,861.12 | 15,278.03 |
| 57 | Tony CHARNLEY | (ENG) | (16) | 22,317.64 | 14,914.82 |
| 58 | Bill HARDWICK | (CAN) | (13) | 20,948.02 | 13,999.51 |
| 59 | John BENDA | (USA) | (9) | 20,553.19 | 13,735.64 |
| 60 | Maurice BEMBRIDGE | (ENG) | (16) | 20,468.70 | 13,679.18 |
| 61 | Ray CARRASCO | (USA) | (13) | 16,723.36 | 11,176.18 |
| 62 | Hank WOODROME | (USA) | (11) | 15,960.88 | 10,666.61 |
| 63 | Jeff HAWKES | (RSA) | (7) | 15,711.17 | 10,499.73 |
| 64 | David CREAMER | (ENG) | (14) | 15,624.78 | 10,442.00 |
| 65 | Malcolm GREGSON | (ENG) | (11) | 15,198.72 | 10,157.26 |
| 66 | Denis DURNIAN | (ENG) | (11) | 15,121.78 | 10,105.85 |
| 67 | Gordon TOWNHILL | (ENG) | (12) | 14,180.68 | 9,476.91 |
| 68 | Alan MEW | (TRI) | (8) | 13,558.37 | 9,061.02 |
| 69 | Craig MALTMAN | (SCO) | (13) | 12,756.08 | 8,524.86 |
| 70 | Eddie POLLAND | (NIR) | (13) | 10,386.71 | 6,941.41 |
| 71 | Robin MANN | (ENG) | (12) | 9,025.25 | 6,031.55 |
| 72 | Victor GARCIA | (ESP) | (12) | 8,931.33 | 5,968.78 |
| 73 | Antonio GARRIDO | (ESP) | (14) | 8,354.23 | 5,583.11 |
| 74 | Neil COLES | (ENG) | (6) | 7,635.44 | 5,102.74 |
| 75 | Liam HIGGINS | (IRL) | (10) | 7,600.45 | 5,079.36 |
| 76 | Bill MALLEY | (USA) | (9) | 7,384.71 | 4,935.18 |
| 77 | Craig DEFOY | (WAL) | (12) | 7,060.72 | 4,718.66 |
| 78 | Stephen CHADWICK | (ENG) | (7) | 5,350.86 | 3,575.96 |
| 79 | Paul LEONARD | (NIR) | (10) | 4,853.91 | 3,243.85 |
| 80 | Philippe DUGENY | (FRA) | (2) | 4,037.63 | 2,698.34 |
| 81 | Kurt COX | (USA) | (11) | 3,974.10 | 2,655.88 |
| 82 | Donald STIRLING | (AUT) | (3) | 3,798.65 | 2,538.62 |
| 83 | Steve WILD | (ENG) | (6) | 3,548.77 | 2,371.63 |
| 84 | Rigoberto VELASQUEZ | (COL) | (4) | 3,272.71 | 2,187.15 |
| 85 | Bill MCCOLL | (SCO) | (1) | 2,430.00 | 1,623.96 |
| 86 | Bob SHEARER | (AUS) | (5) | 2,199.34 | 1,469.81 |
| 87 | Mike GALLAGHER | (ENG) | (4) | 2,143.83 | 1,432.72 |
| 88 | Alberto CROCE | (ITA) | (5) | 1,975.23 | 1,320.04 |
| 89 | John CURTIS | (IRL) | (7) | 1,942.57 | 1,298.21 |
| 90 | Mike WILLIAMS | (ZIM) | (3) | 1,828.52 | 1,221.99 |
| 91 | Peter BARBER | (ENG) | (1) | 1,742.22 | 1,164.32 |
| 92 | Greg HOPKINS | (USA) | (4) | 1,725.71 | 1,153.29 |
| 93 | Anders JOHNSSON | (SWE) | (6) | 1,110.36 | 742.05 |
| 94 | TR JONES | (USA) | (2) | 805.92 | 538.59 |
| 95 | Scott DAVIDSON | (ENG) | (3) | 374.91 | 250.55 |
| 96 | Gary WINTZ | (USA) | (3) | 237.07 | 158.43 |

home course of Club de Campo del Mediterráneo, Spain.

Brand closed with a level par 72 to hold off a star-studded field, which included two-time Open Champion Greg Norman, to secure his maiden Seniors title with a winning total of 13 under par 203.

The in-form Mason was back on top in the Estoril Seniors Open of Portugal the following week, where he collected his third title in four events thanks to a brilliant final day display in atrocious weather conditions.

After entering the back nine trailing by a stroke, Mason produced three birdies in torrential rain to win by four from Torrance and Ginn, the latter achieving his eighth top ten of the year. Mason finished with a level par 71 for a winning aggregate of nine under par 204 and his 14th title in less than four years on the European Seniors Tour.

Then it was off to Riffa Views in Bahrain for the traditional climax, the Arcapita Seniors Tour Championship, open to the leading 42 players on the Order of Merit. Des Smyth flew over from America to defend the title, but Gordon J Brand came through the field with a superb six under par last round 66 then beat Adan Sowa, the overnight leader, at the third extra hole. Brand's win lifted him to fourth place in The European Seniors Tour Order of Merit with €196,002 which meant that the final top four - Torrance, Mason, Rivero and Brand - had between them earned €1,045,353.

**Steven Franklin**

Horacio Carbonetti

*Andy Stubbs, Managing Director of The European Seniors Tour, presents The John Jacobs Trophy to Sam Torrance on finishing Number One on The European Seniors Tour Order of Merit 2006*

# Vintage Year

With the richest stand alone tournament in its 18 year history, the first score of 59 recorded, and the emergence of one of the most exciting European golfing talents in many years, 2006 was a vintage year for the European Challenge Tour.

The €300,000 Kazakhstan Open at the Nurtau Golf Club, Almaty, Kazakhstan, was the event in question and, as a result of its €48,000 first prize, was always going to play a significant role in identifying the player of the year.

The fact that Mark Pilkington won, cements that observation. His victory in the third last event of the season moved him to second place on the Rankings and provided the impetus required to finish the year on a high in the Apulia San Domenico Grand Final at San Domenico Golf, Savalletri, Italy. There he tied for second place behind Englishman James Hepworth, to finish Number One in the Rankings with season's earnings of €119,151.

While Hepworth finished fifth on the Rankings, Pilkington became the first Welshman to finish top of the Challenge Tour Rankings and, in a year where Ian Woosnam led Europe to a record third consecutive Ryder

Johan Axgren

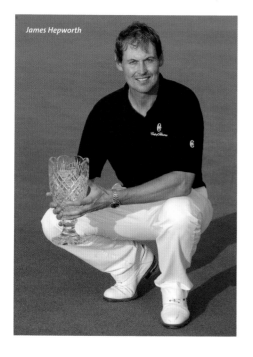

James Hepworth

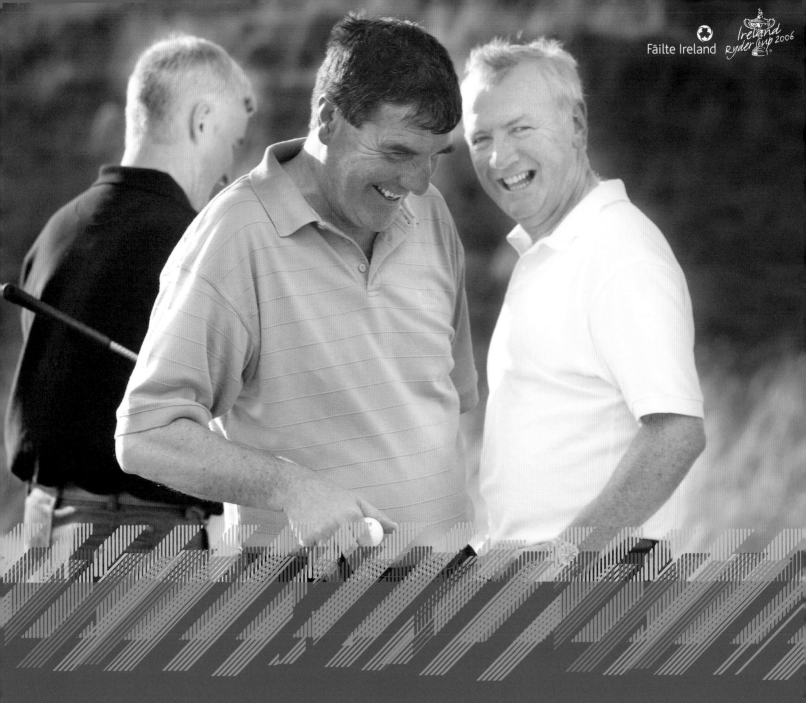

# After three hours of hard competition, the stress was starting to take its toll.

You used to work hard and play hard. Now you just work hard. So isn't it time you gave yourself a break doing what you enjoy best. Like golfing some of the best courses anywhere, and enjoying the banter with a few old friends. Laughter is the best medicine. *So come on. Let's play.*

 **ireland.ie**

# Ireland 2006 *Let's play.*

Discover more at **www.ireland.ie**

Alexander Noren

Rafael Echenique

Kyron Sullivan

Gareth Davies

Cup victory, further enhanced a marvellous season for the Principality.

The man he pushed into second place was Sweden's Johan Axgren, who had led the way for the bulk of the season but who fell just short, by €13,453, at the denouement. Axgren won twice in the space of four weeks at the beginning the year – at the Kai Fieberg Costa Rica Open 2006 at the Cariari Country Club, San Jose, Costa Rica, and the Tusker Kenya Open at the Karen Golf Club, Nairobi, Kenya – to soar to the top, a position he held until Pilkington leapfrogged him.

While Axgren and Pilkington were leading from the front, the next generation of European golfing talent was emerging from behind as the Challenge Tour players exhibited their skills in 31 tournaments across 22 countries spread throughout Africa, Asia, Central and South America and, of course, Europe,

# The European Challenge Tour

Martin Kaymer

Mads Vibe-Hastrup

The single most outstanding performance of the year came during the second round of the Tikida Hotels Agadir Moroccan Classic at Golf du Soleil in Agadir, Morocco, as Frenchman Adrien Mörk recorded the first 59 in the history of The European, Challenge and Seniors Tours. Given his scorecard contained a double bogey at the second, Mörk produced a miraculous performance for 17 holes, putting together an eagle, 13 birdies and just three pars to rewrite the history books.

Having opened the tournament with an eight under par 63, Mörk's 36 hole total of 20 under par 122 saw him enter the Tour's record books as the holder of lowest opening 36 hole score on any of the three

Tours. The Frenchman went on to win a second Challenge Tour title at the OKI Mahou Challenge de España at the Centro Nacional de Golf, Madrid, Spain, and he finished the season in 20th place on the Rankings to take the last available European Tour card.

In total, the 2006 Challenge Tour crowned 28 champions but, such is the high standard required to succeed nowadays, 13 of those tournament winners came tantalisingly close to finishing within the top 20 and securing a card, but were left ultimately disappointed.

In fact Antonio Maldonado of Mexico claimed the first event of the 2006 season, the 48th Abierto Mexicano Corona at Club

Juan Parron

de Golf de Hacienda, Mexico City, Mexico. He was followed onto the winners' rostrum a week later by Kevin Stadler after the American's excellent win in the Abierto Visa de la Republica, presented by Bridgestone, at the Jockey Club in Buenos Aires, Argentina. Stadler, of course, had no concerns in terms of a card for, two months later, he won the Johnnie Walker Classic on The European Tour itself, to guarantee his playing privileges until the end of 2008.

Following Stadler's win in Argentina, the following week, the South American country's own Miguel Carballo won the Abierto Movistar Guatemala Open 2006 at the Hacienda Neuva Country Club, Guatemala City, Guatemala.

In Europe, Scotland's David Drysdale took the Peugeot Challenge R.C.G. El Prat at the Real Club de Golf El Prat, Barcelona, Spain; the French duo of Julien Foret and Anthony Snobeck won the Golf Open International de Toulouse at Golf de Toulouse-Seilh, Seilh, France and the Tessali-Metaponto Open di Puglia e Basilicata at Riva dei Tessali and Metaponto Golf Club in southern Italy respectively; Sweden's Kalle Brink secured

the Lexus Open at the Larvik Golf Club, Larvik, Norway, Toni Karjalainen of Finland took the Telenet Trophy at Limburg Golf and Country Club, Houthalen, Belgium; England's Sam Walker won the Scottish Challenge at Murcar Links Golf Club, Aberdeen, Scotland; Welshman Sion Bebb triumphed at home in the Ryder Cup Wales Challenge at Nefyn

Golf Club, Wales; while the following week Australian John Wade won the Ireland Ryder Cup Challenge at Mahony's Point, Killarney Golf and Fishing Club, Ireland. Finally, the Spanish trio of Francisco Cea, Carlos Del Moral and Alvaro Salto had respective victories at the Credit Suisse Challenge at Wylihof Golf, Luterbach, Switzerland; the

Adrien Mörk

# San Domenico Golf

HOME OF THE
APULIA GRAND FINAL

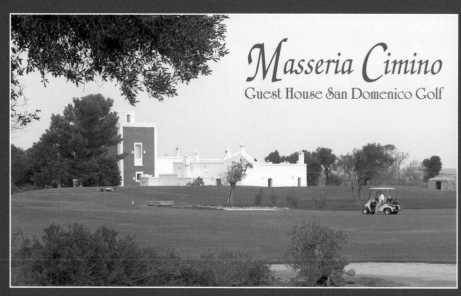

## Masseria Cimino
### Guest House San Domenico Golf

72010 Savelletri di Fasano (Brindisi) - ITALY
Tel. +39 (0)80 4829200 - Fax +39 (0)80 4827944
e-mail: info@sandomenicogolf.com
www.sandomenicogolf.com

MEMBER OF

INTERNATIONAL ASSOCIATION OF GOLF TOUR OPERATORS

Jean-Baptiste Gonnet

Texbond Open over Gardagolf, Brescia, Italy, and the Parco di Monza Challenge at the Golf Club Milano in Monza, Italy.

The Challenge Tour has often seen the first glimpse of many of The European Tour's biggest stars. Included in that number is Thomas Björn, who has financially supported his own Challenge Tour event for the past two seasons – the Thomas Björn Open – won in 2006 by Marcus Higley at the Horsens Golf Club in Denmark, the Englishman going on to finish tenth on the Rankings.

Of the 20 men who graduated from the 2006 Challenge Tour, Martin Kaymer stood out for many as a player to watch after a truly astonishing run of results in the second half of the season.

The German, who carded a 59 on the Satellite EPD Tour before joining the Challenge Tour in August, played only eight events on the 2006 Schedule but made a stunning impact, winning twice – on his Challenge Tour debut in the Vodafone Challenge at Golf Club Elfrather Mühle, Dusseldorf, Germany, and then in the Open des Volcans - Challenge de France at Golf des Volcans, Clermont Ferrand, France – and registering a further four top five finishes en route to taking fourth place on the final Rankings.

It was not just Kaymer's results that were impressive. His golf swing, attitude and level of performance over the closing stages of the Challenge Tour season were awesome, and it will be no surprise to anyone who came across the hugely impressive 22 year old if

James Heath

# The European Challenge Tour

The European Challenge Tour's 2006 graduates who won places on The 2007 European Tour International Schedule via the top 20 on the Rankings (from left to right): James Heath, Gary Lockerbie, Johan Axgren, Mads Vibe-Hastrup, Gareth Davies, Lee S James, Marcus Higley, Sam Walker, Mark Pilkington, James Hepworth, Adrien Mörk, Rafael Echenique, Shaun P Webster, Jean-Baptiste Gonnet, Rafael Cabrera Bello, Kyron Sullivan, Martin Kaymer, Alvaro Quiros, Alexander Noren, Juan Parron

*Shaun P Webster*

he follows 2005 Challenge Tour Number One Marc Warren as The Sir Henry Cotton Rookie of the Year on The 2007 European Tour.

Of the 20 Challenge Tour graduates, Kaymer and Mörk will be two of 13 Rookies on The 2007 European Tour. The other 11 players who will play a full European Tour season for the first time in their careers all have the ability to establish themselves at the top level for years to come if they can continue to progress and improve.

Sweden's Alexander Noren finished one place ahead of Kaymer on the Rankings after winning the Rolex Trophy at the Golf Club de Genève, Genèva, Switzerland, and looks capable of going all the way on The European Tour. Likewise, Kyron Sullivan of Wales, who took the sixth card assisted by his win in the Estoril Challenge at Penha Longa, Estoril, Portugal, and Argentina's Rafael Echenique,

winner of the Telia Challenge Waxholm at the Waxholm Golf Club, Stockholm, Sweden, on his way to seventh place.

In Rafael Cabrera Bello, Alvaro Quiros and Juan Parron, the Challenge Tour also produced a trio of Spanish graduates who have the pedigree to add to the 22 Spanish players who have tasted success on The European Tour International Schedule since 1972.

Cabrera Bello, who took 13th place, won the MAN NÖ Open at Golfclub Adamstal, Ramsau, Austria; Quiros triumphed in the Morson International Pro-Am Challenge at Marriott Worsley Park Hotel and Country Club, Manchester, England, en route to finishing the year in 18th place, while Parron took first place in the Open Mahou de Madrid at Club de Golf La Herreria, Spain, as well as a notable share of fourth place in the dual ranking Aa St Omer Open at the

*Sam Walker*

# The European Challenge Tour
# Rankings 2006

| Pos | Name | Country | Played | € |
|---|---|---|---|---|
| 1 | Mark PILKINGTON | (WAL) | (22) | 119151.68 |
| 2 | Johan AXGREN | (SWE) | (23) | 105698.83 |
| 3 | Alexander NOREN | (SWE) | (22) | 99631.14 |
| 4 | Martin KAYMER | (GER) | (8) | 93320.58 |
| 5 | James HEPWORTH | (ENG) | (20) | 84236.11 |
| 6 | Kyron SULLIVAN | (WAL) | (25) | 83364.13 |
| 7 | Rafael ECHENIQUE | (ARG) | (26) | 82737.24 |
| 8 | Juan PARRON | (ESP) | (18) | 71089.47 |
| 9 | Sam WALKER | (ENG) | (19) | 69853.39 |
| 10 | Marcus HIGLEY | (ENG) | (26) | 67851.15 |
| 11 | Shaun P WEBSTER | (ENG) | (8) | 65535.60 |
| 12 | Gary LOCKERBIE | (ENG) | (23) | 64072.72 |
| 13 | Rafael CABRERA BELLO | (ESP) | (27) | 62849.06 |
| 14 | James HEATH | (ENG) | (23) | 60346.32 |
| 15 | Gareth DAVIES | (ENG) | (24) | 60189.22 |
| 16 | Lee S JAMES | (ENG) | (24) | 59704.22 |
| 17 | Jean-Baptiste GONNET | (FRA) | (27) | 59342.95 |
| 18 | Alvaro QUIROS | (ESP) | (19) | 57278.08 |
| 19 | Mads VIBE-HASTRUP | (DEN) | (25) | 52484.88 |
| 20 | Adrien MÖRK | (FRA) | (20) | 52136.50 |
| 21 | Hernan REY | (ARG) | (25) | 50570.13 |
| 22 | Nicolas VANHOOTEGEM | (BEL) | (19) | 48983.49 |
| 23 | Anthony SNOBECK | (FRA) | (26) | 48066.50 |
| 24 | Martin MARITZ | (RSA) | (14) | 47840.80 |
| 25 | Antonio MALDONADO | (MEX) | (10) | 45971.08 |
| 26 | Jean HUGO | (RSA) | (13) | 45778.02 |
| 27 | Andrew MCARTHUR | (SCO) | (26) | 45731.81 |
| 28 | Alvaro SALTO | (ESP) | (18) | 44928.60 |
| 29 | Jan-Are LARSEN | (NOR) | (26) | 44020.51 |
| 30 | Jesus Maria ARRUTI | (ESP) | (16) | 43987.89 |
| 31 | Sebastian FERNANDEZ | (ARG) | (23) | 43657.64 |
| 32 | Chris GANE | (ENG) | (25) | 43421.83 |
| 33 | Oskar BERGMAN | (SWE) | (20) | 43331.82 |
| 34 | Tim MILFORD | (ENG) | (26) | 42633.67 |
| 35 | Ivo GINER | (ESP) | (22) | 42366.60 |
| 36 | Sion E BEBB | (WAL) | (13) | 39495.80 |
| 37 | Felipe AGUILAR | (CHI) | (11) | 39441.12 |
| 38 | Denny LUCAS | (ENG) | (26) | 37665.57 |
| 39 | Anders Schmidt HANSEN | (DEN) | (27) | 36878.46 |
| 40 | Gareth WRIGHT | (WAL) | (20) | 36744.57 |
| 41 | David DRYSDALE | (SCO) | (8) | 35966.00 |
| 42 | Rafael GOMEZ | (ARG) | (10) | 35055.56 |
| 43 | Johan SKÖLD | (SWE) | (13) | 33566.53 |
| 44 | Gustavo ROJAS | (ARG) | (20) | 33309.37 |
| 45 | Julien FORET | (FRA) | (13) | 32621.91 |
| 46 | Miguel CARBALLO | (ARG) | (10) | 30613.73 |
| 47 | Alvaro VELASCO | (ESP) | (18) | 29066.64 |
| 48 | Kalle BRINK | (SWE) | (19) | 29060.69 |
| 49 | Roope KAKKO | (FIN) | (24) | 27853.67 |
| 50 | Magnus A CARLSSON | (SWE) | (19) | 27579.55 |
| 51 | Carlos DEL MORAL | (ESP) | (15) | 27342.96 |
| 52 | Francisco CEA | (ESP) | (17) | 26463.00 |
| 53 | Jamie LITTLE | (ENG) | (22) | 26371.84 |
| 54 | Mickael DIEU | (FRA) | (21) | 26090.93 |
| 55 | Gareth PADDISON | (NZL) | (18) | 26042.50 |
| 56 | Rodolfo GONZALEZ | (ARG) | (17) | 26039.24 |
| 57 | Stuart MANLEY | (WAL) | (22) | 25675.83 |
| 58 | Peter KAENSCHE | (NOR) | (22) | 25598.30 |
| 59 | Toni KARJALAINEN | (FIN) | (10) | 25459.59 |
| 60 | Kariem BARAKA | (GER) | (22) | 24781.25 |
| 61 | John WADE | (AUS) | (10) | 24033.00 |
| 62 | Chris DOAK | (SCO) | (11) | 23521.36 |
| 63 | Luis CLAVERIE | (ESP) | (10) | 21707.93 |
| 64 | Ben MASON | (ENG) | (19) | 21074.80 |
| 65 | Klas ERIKSSON | (SWE) | (13) | 20892.03 |
| 66 | Alessio BRUSCHI | (ITA) | (22) | 20403.73 |
| 67 | Pedro LINHART | (ESP) | (10) | 19680.00 |
| 68 | Julien VAN HAUWE | (FRA) | (26) | 19581.10 |
| 69 | Niki ZITNY | (AUT) | (17) | 19324.98 |
| 70 | Stuart DAVIS | (ENG) | (22) | 19135.78 |
| 71 | Peter WHITEFORD | (SCO) | (25) | 18651.90 |
| 72 | Julio ZAPATA | (ARG) | (11) | 18400.60 |
| 73 | Mikko KORHONEN | (FIN) | (15) | 17768.72 |
| 74 | Cédric MENUT | (FRA) | (17) | 17632.57 |
| 75 | Olivier DAVID | (FRA) | (19) | 17529.99 |
| 76 | Edward RUSH | (ENG) | (22) | 16895.08 |
| 77 | Magnus PERSSON | (SWE) | (15) | 16889.42 |
| 78 | Neil CHEETHAM | (ENG) | (13) | 16805.67 |
| 79 | Fredrik ANDERSSON HED | (SWE) | (19) | 16751.15 |
| 80 | Inder VAN WEERELT | (NED) | (24) | 16577.24 |
| 81 | Carlos DE CORRAL | (ESP) | (16) | 16400.08 |
| 82 | Matthew KING | (ENG) | (22) | 16310.39 |
| 83 | Miguel RODRIGUEZ | (ARG) | (22) | 16222.48 |
| 84 | Jerome THEUNIS | (BEL) | (13) | 16216.57 |
| 85 | Jorge BENEDETTI | (COL) | (22) | 15865.03 |
| 86 | Gustavo ACOSTA | (ARG) | (14) | 15713.52 |
| 87 | Mikko ILONEN | (FIN) | (9) | 15308.06 |
| 88 | Birgir HAFTHORSSON | (ISL) | (17) | 15253.07 |
| 89 | José Manuel CARRILES | (ESP) | (10) | 15051.86 |
| 90 | Thomas NORRET | (DEN) | (2) | 14764.00 |
| 91 | Michael McGEADY | (IRL) | (9) | 14678.00 |
| 92 | Michiel BOTHMA | (RSA) | (15) | 14355.67 |
| 93 | Michael LORENZO-VERA | (FRA) | (4) | 14305.00 |
| 94 | Wilhelm SCHAUMAN | (SWE) | (13) | 14288.53 |
| 95 | Zane SCOTLAND | (ENG) | (11) | 13954.35 |
| 96 | Ben WILLMAN | (ENG) | (20) | 13876.65 |
| 97 | Gabriel CANIZARES | (ESP) | (16) | 13791.20 |
| 98 | Peter JESPERSEN | (DEN) | (20) | 13493.05 |
| 99 | Alfredo GARCIA-HEREDIA | (ESP) | (16) | 13434.53 |
| 100 | Van PHILLIPS | (ENG) | (26) | 13175.95 |

*Exempt Status for 2007 European Tour International Schedule*
**10a** - The top 10 from the 2006 Challenge Tour Rankings
**11** - 11 - 15 from the 2006 Challenge Tour Rankings
**11b** - The top 30 and ties from The 2006 European Tour Qualifying School
**11c** - 16 - 20 from the 2006 Challenge Tour Rankings

Aa Saint Omer Golf Club in Lumbres, France - won by Argentina's Cesar Monasterio - on his way to eighth place on the Rankings.

Of the eight Englishmen to win a place among the top 20, Gareth Davies, James Heath, Marcus Higley and Gary Lockerbie will be Rookies on The 2007 European Tour.

Heath realised the potential he had shown throughout a victory-laden amateur career with his maiden professional success in the ECCO Tour Championship at Odense Golf Club, Denmark.

Davies and Lockerbie may not have won in 2006, but their level of consistency was remarkable, Davies returning nine top 25 finishes from his 24 starts while Lockerbie missed just five cuts from his 23 events. Such consistency can also bring lucrative rewards on The European Tour.

Jean-Baptiste Gonnet of France was another player who did not win an event in 2006 but can look back on his season with tremendous satisfaction as he took 17th place on the Rankings on the back of six top ten finishes to secure his place on The European Tour for the first time in his career.

For the 13 rookies a voyage of self discovery lies ahead and for those setting sail again on The European Tour another exciting opportunity exists to grasp all that can be seen on the horizon.

**Michael Gibbons**

# The European Tour Golfer of the Month Awards 2006

The European Tour Golfer of the Month Awards are presented throughout the year followed by an Annual Award

## ANNUAL WINNERS

| Year | Winner | |
|------|--------|---|
| 2005 | Michael Campbell | |
| 2004 | Vijay Singh | |
| 2003 | Ernie Els | |
| 2002 | Ernie Els | |
| 2001 | Retief Goosen | |
| 2000 | Lee Westwood | |
| 1999 | Colin Montgomerie | |
| 1998 | Lee Westwood | |
| 1997 | Colin Montgomerie | |
| 1996 | Colin Montgomerie | |
| 1995 | Colin Montgomerie | |
| 1994 | Ernie Els | |
| 1993 | Bernhard Langer | |
| 1992 | Nick Faldo | |
| 1991 | Severiano Ballesteros | |
| 1990 | Nick Faldo | |
| 1989 | Nick Faldo | |
| 1988 | Severiano Ballesteros | |
| 1987 | Ian Woosnam | |
| 1986 | Severiano Ballesteros | |
| 1985 | Bernhard Langer | |

GONZALO FERNANDEZ-CASTAÑO - April

HENRIK STENSON - January

CHARL SCHWARTZEL - February

JEAN VAN DE VELDE - March

DAVID HOWELL - May

JOHN BICKERTON - June

ROBERT KARLSSON - July

ALEJANDRO CAÑIZARES - August

PAUL CASEY - September

PADRAIG HARRINGTON - October

# The RBS Shot of the Month Awards 2006

**RBS**

PAUL CASEY *receives his RBS Shot of the Month Award for September from Alex Rodger, Managing Director, RBS International Corporate Banking*

The RBS Shot of the Month
Awards are presented
throughout the year followed
by an Annual Award

**ANNUAL WINNERS**

2005   Paul McGinley

2004   David Howell

2003   Fredrik Jacobson

**HENRIK STENSON - January**

**KEVIN STADLER - February**

**PAUL BROADHURST - March**

**JOSÉ MARIA OLAZÁBAL - April**

**DARREN CLARKE - May**

**COLIN MONTGOMERIE - June**

**ERNIE ELS - July**

**MARC WARREN - August**

## Stroke Average

| Pos | Name | Stroke Average | Total Strokes | Total Rounds |
|---|---|---|---|---|
| 1 | Ernie ELS | 70.02 | 3641 | 52 |
| 2 | Sergio GARCIA | 70.04 | 3222 | 46 |
| 3 | Luke DONALD | 70.09 | 3084 | 44 |
| 4 | Mikko ILONEN | 70.29 | 2390 | 34 |
| 5 | Robert KARLSSON | 70.48 | 7471 | 106 |
|  | Padraig HARRINGTON | 70.48 | 4863 | 69 |
| 7 | Paul CASEY | 70.50 | 6063 | 86 |
| 8 | Thongchai JAIDEE | 70.52 | 5712 | 81 |
| 9 | Pedro LINHART | 70.54 | 1693 | 24 |
| 10 | Ian POULTER | 70.56 | 5504 | 78 |
| 11 | Retief GOOSEN | 70.60 | 3671 | 52 |
| 12 | Nick O'HERN | 70.65 | 2826 | 40 |
| 13 | Henrik STENSON | 70.68 | 5796 | 82 |
| 14 | Anders HANSEN | 70.71 | 6010 | 85 |
| 15 | Simon DYSON | 70.75 | 7570 | 107 |
| 16 | Richard GREEN | 70.76 | 4741 | 67 |
| 17 | Søren KJELDSEN | 70.77 | 7289 | 103 |
|  | Alejandro CANIZARES | 70.77 | 1840 | 26 |
| 19 | Colin MONTGOMERIE | 70.78 | 5733 | 81 |
|  | Bradley DREDGE | 70.78 | 5238 | 74 |
| 21 | Anthony WALL | 70.79 | 6513 | 92 |
| 22 | Lee WESTWOOD | 70.81 | 4178 | 59 |
| 23 | Niclas FASTH | 70.84 | 6092 | 86 |
|  | David HOWELL | 70.84 | 4746 | 67 |
| 25 | Angel CABRERA | 70.92 | 4397 | 62 |
| 26 | Phillip ARCHER | 70.94 | 7591 | 107 |
| 27 | Charl SCHWARTZEL | 70.97 | 6103 | 86 |
| 28 | Ricardo GONZALEZ | 71.00 | 4828 | 68 |
|  | José Manuel LARA | 71.00 | 6816 | 96 |
| 30 | Søren HANSEN | 71.01 | 6462 | 91 |
| 31 | Paul BROADHURST | 71.04 | 5967 | 84 |
|  | Thaworn WIRATCHANT | 71.04 | 3907 | 55 |
|  | Raphaël JACQUELIN | 71.04 | 5754 | 81 |
| 34 | Thomas BJÖRN | 71.05 | 6679 | 94 |
| 35 | Klas ERIKSSON | 71.08 | 1706 | 24 |
| 36 | Jeev Milkha SINGH | 71.09 | 3839 | 54 |
| 37 | José Maria OLAZÁBAL | 71.10 | 3555 | 50 |
| 38 | Vijay SINGH | 71.14 | 2561 | 36 |
|  | Gary ORR | 71.14 | 5478 | 77 |
| 40 | Lee SLATTERY | 71.15 | 4625 | 65 |
| 41 | Magnus PERSSON | 71.19 | 1851 | 26 |
| 42 | Peter O'MALLEY | 71.23 | 5200 | 73 |
| 43 | Peter LAWRIE | 71.25 | 6626 | 93 |
|  | Gregory BOURDY | 71.25 | 4489 | 63 |
| 45 | Paul LAWRIE | 71.27 | 4490 | 63 |
| 46 | Miguel Angel JIMÉNEZ | 71.29 | 6345 | 89 |
|  | Michael CAMPBELL | 71.29 | 3707 | 52 |
| 48 | David GRIFFITHS | 71.30 | 4991 | 70 |
| 49 | David LYNN | 71.31 | 6703 | 94 |
| 50 | Jyoti RANDHAWA | 71.33 | 5350 | 75 |

| Pos | Name | Stroke Average | Total Strokes | Total Rounds |
|---|---|---|---|---|
| 51 | Johan EDFORS | 71.34 | 5921 | 83 |
| 52 | Fredrik HENGE | 71.35 | 2640 | 37 |
|  | Jarrod LYLE | 71.35 | 1855 | 26 |
| 54 | Lian-Wei ZHANG | 71.36 | 1998 | 28 |
| 55 | Steve WEBSTER | 71.39 | 4783 | 67 |
|  | Christian L NILSSON | 71.39 | 4997 | 70 |
| 57 | Alexandre ROCHA | 71.40 | 5498 | 77 |
| 58 | Darren CLARKE | 71.43 | 3357 | 47 |
| 59 | Maarten LAFEBER | 71.48 | 5718 | 80 |
|  | Darren FICHARDT | 71.48 | 4146 | 58 |
|  | Paul MCGINLEY | 71.48 | 4789 | 67 |
|  | Jarmo SANDELIN | 71.48 | 6219 | 87 |
| 63 | Carl PETTERSSON | 71.50 | 2002 | 28 |
|  | Scott STRANGE | 71.50 | 3003 | 42 |
| 65 | Mattias ELIASSON | 71.51 | 4934 | 69 |
|  | Terry PILKADARIS | 71.51 | 3933 | 55 |
| 67 | Nick DOUGHERTY | 71.52 | 6008 | 84 |
| 68 | Miles TUNNICLIFF | 71.53 | 6366 | 89 |
| 69 | Alastair FORSYTH | 71.54 | 5437 | 76 |
|  | Mark FOSTER | 71.54 | 5795 | 81 |
| 71 | Simon KHAN | 71.56 | 5725 | 80 |
| 72 | Gregory HAVRET | 71.57 | 6155 | 86 |
| 73 | Johan SKÖLD | 71.59 | 2649 | 37 |
| 74 | Graeme MCDOWELL | 71.60 | 3938 | 55 |
|  | Sven STRÜVER | 71.60 | 2148 | 30 |
| 76 | Simon WAKEFIELD | 71.63 | 7163 | 100 |
|  | José-Filipe LIMA | 71.63 | 5229 | 73 |
| 78 | Damien MCGRANE | 71.64 | 7236 | 101 |
|  | Stephen GALLACHER | 71.64 | 5373 | 75 |
|  | Robert-Jan DERKSEN | 71.64 | 6304 | 88 |
| 81 | Shiv KAPUR | 71.66 | 4873 | 68 |
| 82 | Peter HANSON | 71.67 | 5805 | 81 |
|  | David PARK | 71.67 | 5375 | 75 |
| 84 | Ross FISHER | 71.70 | 6596 | 92 |
| 85 | Andrew MCLARDY | 71.71 | 5163 | 72 |
|  | Ian GARBUTT | 71.71 | 6526 | 91 |
|  | David CARTER | 71.71 | 5665 | 79 |
| 88 | Jean VAN DE VELDE | 71.72 | 4949 | 69 |
| 89 | Oliver WILSON | 71.73 | 5810 | 81 |
| 90 | Christian CÉVAËR | 71.76 | 5884 | 82 |
|  | David DRYSDALE | 71.76 | 4234 | 59 |
| 92 | Peter GUSTAFSSON | 71.77 | 6244 | 87 |
| 93 | Emanuele CANONICA | 71.78 | 5527 | 77 |
|  | Matthew MILLAR | 71.78 | 5742 | 80 |
| 95 | Francesco MOLINARI | 71.79 | 5743 | 80 |
|  | Ignacio GARRIDO | 71.79 | 5528 | 77 |
|  | Leif WESTERBERG | 71.79 | 5528 | 77 |
| 98 | Peter BAKER | 71.81 | 2585 | 36 |
| 99 | John BICKERTON | 71.82 | 6392 | 89 |
|  | Graeme STORM | 71.82 | 6392 | 89 |

| Pos | Name | Stroke Average | Total Strokes | Total Rounds |
|---|---|---|---|---|
| 101 | Andrew BUTTERFIELD | 71.83 | 6896 | 96 |
|  | Steven O'HARA | 71.83 | 6177 | 86 |
| 103 | David BRANSDON | 71.84 | 5819 | 81 |
| 104 | Marco RUIZ | 71.85 | 3952 | 55 |
| 105 | Peter HEDBLOM | 71.86 | 5102 | 71 |
|  | Santiago LUNA | 71.86 | 3162 | 44 |
| 107 | Garry HOUSTON | 71.87 | 6971 | 97 |
|  | Andrew MARSHALL | 71.87 | 5534 | 77 |
|  | Tom WHITEHOUSE | 71.87 | 5534 | 77 |
| 110 | Markus BRIER | 71.88 | 5535 | 77 |
|  | Mahal PEARCE | 71.88 | 1797 | 25 |
| 112 | Felipe AGUILAR | 71.89 | 4026 | 56 |
| 113 | Richard STERNE | 71.90 | 4817 | 67 |
| 114 | Marcus FRASER | 71.91 | 5609 | 78 |
| 115 | Chris RODGERS | 71.92 | 1726 | 24 |
|  | Brett RUMFORD | 71.92 | 5466 | 76 |
| 117 | Christopher HANELL | 71.93 | 2086 | 29 |
|  | Mark ROE | 71.93 | 4100 | 57 |
| 119 | Sam LITTLE | 71.95 | 6260 | 87 |
|  | Andres ROMERO | 71.95 | 4389 | 61 |
| 121 | Titch MOORE | 71.96 | 3382 | 47 |
| 122 | Alessandro TADINI | 71.97 | 6261 | 87 |
|  | Gary MURPHY | 71.97 | 5614 | 78 |
| 124 | Cesar MONASTERIO | 71.98 | 2951 | 41 |
| 125 | Stephen SCAHILL | 72.00 | 3744 | 52 |
| 126 | Benn BARHAM | 72.01 | 5905 | 82 |
| 127 | Hennie OTTO | 72.03 | 2449 | 34 |
| 128 | Richard BLAND | 72.04 | 5691 | 79 |
|  | Keith HORNE | 72.04 | 3458 | 48 |
|  | Daniel VANCSIK | 72.04 | 4971 | 69 |
|  | Wade ORMSBY | 72.04 | 5259 | 73 |
| 132 | Henrik NYSTROM | 72.06 | 3747 | 52 |
| 133 | Rahil GANGJEE | 72.07 | 2090 | 29 |
| 134 | Phillip PRICE | 72.10 | 4398 | 61 |
| 135 | Stephen DODD | 72.11 | 5480 | 76 |
| 136 | Marc WARREN | 72.12 | 5625 | 78 |
| 137 | Ariel CANETE | 72.16 | 4185 | 58 |
|  | Steven JEPPESEN | 72.16 | 6567 | 91 |
| 139 | David HIGGINS | 72.17 | 6062 | 84 |
| 140 | Rafael GOMEZ | 72.18 | 3681 | 51 |
| 141 | Joakim BÄCKSTRÖM | 72.19 | 6064 | 84 |
|  | James KINGSTON | 72.19 | 5198 | 72 |
| 143 | Marcel SIEM | 72.20 | 6137 | 85 |
|  | Carl SUNESON | 72.20 | 5343 | 74 |
| 145 | Ian WOOSNAM | 72.21 | 3466 | 48 |
| 146 | Scott BARR | 72.22 | 1950 | 27 |
| 147 | Raymond RUSSELL | 72.24 | 3323 | 46 |
| 148 | Joakim HAEGGMAN | 72.28 | 5927 | 82 |
|  | Robert ROCK | 72.28 | 4626 | 64 |
| 150 | Jamie SPENCE | 72.29 | 5060 | 70 |

## Driving Distance (yds)

| Pos | Name | Average Yards | Stats Rounds |
|---|---|---|---|
| 1 | Christian L NILSSON | 314.1 | 62 |
| 2 | Titch MOORE | 312.2 | 36 |
| 3 | Tuomas TUOVINEN | 306.8 | 26 |
| 4 | Angel CABRERA | 305.1 | 36 |
| 5 | Johan EDFORS | 304.5 | 67 |
| 6 | Joakim BÄCKSTRÖM | 304.3 | 76 |
| 7 | Emanuele CANONICA | 303.2 | 73 |
| 8 | Daniel VANCSIK | 303.1 | 62 |
| 9 | Marcel SIEM | 302.0 | 81 |
| 10 | Anders SJÖSTRAND | 300.9 | 31 |
| 11 | Sergio GARCIA | 300.8 | 24 |
| 12 | Ross FISHER | 300.7 | 86 |
| 13 | Ricardo GONZALEZ | 300.6 | 64 |
| 14 | Louis OOSTHUIZEN | 299.8 | 56 |
| 15 | Nicolas COLSAERTS | 299.3 | 79 |
| 16 | Robert KARLSSON | 299.2 | 86 |
| 17 | Andres ROMERO | 299.1 | 52 |
| 18 | José-Filipe LIMA | 298.9 | 70 |
| 19 | Carl SUNESON | 298.7 | 64 |
| 20 | Francis VALERA | 298.4 | 52 |
| 21 | Paul CASEY | 298.2 | 64 |
| 22 | David BRANSDON | 297.7 | 78 |
| 23 | Stephen BROWNE | 296.6 | 46 |
| 24 | Mattias ELIASSON | 296.3 | 65 |
| 25 | Henrik STENSON | 296.1 | 55 |
| 25 | Stephen GALLACHER | 296.1 | 72 |

## Driving Accuracy (%)

| Pos | Name | % | Stats Rounds |
|---|---|---|---|
| 1 | Oliver WHITELEY | 77.7 | 44 |
| 2 | Peter O'MALLEY | 75.6 | 70 |
| 3 | Felipe AGUILAR | 72.6 | 48 |
| 4 | Alexandre ROCHA | 71.3 | 68 |
| 5 | Raymond RUSSELL | 70.8 | 41 |
| 6 | John BICKERTON | 70.2 | 72 |
| 7 | Richard GREEN | 70.1 | 54 |
| 8 | Colin MONTGOMERIE | 69.8 | 64 |
| 9 | Jean-François REMESY | 69.7 | 64 |
| 10 | David HIGGINS | 69.1 | 79 |
| 11 | Costantino ROCCA | 68.7 | 38 |
| 12 | Philip GOLDING | 68.4 | 68 |
| 13 | Garry HOUSTON | 68.3 | 90 |
| 14 | Scott DRUMMOND | 67.8 | 62 |
| 15 | Peter LAWRIE | 67.6 | 89 |
| 16 | Leif WESTERBERG | 67.5 | 73 |
| 17 | Paul MCGINLEY | 67.2 | 54 |
| 18 | Maarten LAFEBER | 67.1 | 74 |
| 19 | Søren KJELDSEN | 67.0 | 95 |
| 20 | Francesco MOLINARI | 66.9 | 77 |
| 20 | Henrik NYSTROM | 66.9 | 41 |
| 22 | Robert-Jan DERKSEN | 66.6 | 85 |
| 23 | Darren CLARKE | 66.5 | 30 |
| 24 | David DRYSDALE | 66.4 | 46 |
| 25 | Paul CASEY | 66.1 | 64 |

## Average Putts Per Round

| Pos | Name | Putts per Round | Stats Rounds |
|---|---|---|---|
| 1 | Thaworn WIRATCHANT | 28.0 | 46 |
| 2 | Paul BROADHURST | 28.2 | 70 |
| 2 | Matthew MILLAR | 28.2 | 78 |
| 4 | Christian CÉVAËR | 28.3 | 79 |
| 4 | David HOWELL | 28.3 | 42 |
| 6 | Peter BAKER | 28.4 | 25 |
| 6 | Padraig HARRINGTON | 28.4 | 45 |
| 8 | Darren CLARKE | 28.5 | 30 |
| 8 | David LYNN | 28.5 | 90 |
| 8 | Simon DYSON | 28.5 | 94 |
| 11 | Jarmo SANDELIN | 28.6 | 81 |
| 12 | Cesar MONASTERIO | 28.7 | 30 |
| 12 | Henrik STENSON | 28.7 | 55 |
| 12 | Simon WAKEFIELD | 28.7 | 92 |
| 12 | David HIGGINS | 28.7 | 79 |
| 12 | Jeev Milkha SINGH | 28.7 | 26 |
| 17 | Damien MCGRANE | 28.8 | 95 |
| 17 | Søren KJELDSEN | 28.8 | 95 |
| 17 | Stephen DODD | 28.8 | 65 |
| 17 | Peter GUSTAFSSON | 28.8 | 80 |
| 21 | Richard GREEN | 28.9 | 54 |
| 21 | Darren FICHARDT | 28.9 | 58 |
| 21 | Jamie SPENCE | 28.9 | 67 |
| 21 | Warren ABERY | 28.9 | 52 |
| 21 | Robert KARLSSON | 28.9 | 86 |
| 21 | Benn BARHAM | 28.9 | 75 |
| 21 | David DRYSDALE | 28.9 | 46 |
| 21 | Andres ROMERO | 28.9 | 52 |
| 21 | Marc WARREN | 28.9 | 75 |
| 21 | Scott STRANGE | 28.9 | 38 |
| 21 | Peter FOWLER | 28.9 | 62 |
| 32 | Colin MONTGOMERIE | 29.0 | 64 |
| 32 | Ricardo GONZALEZ | 29.0 | 64 |
| 32 | Thongchai JAIDEE | 29.0 | 71 |
| 35 | Anders HANSEN | 29.1 | 76 |
| 35 | Martin ERLANDSSON | 29.1 | 75 |
| 35 | Ian POULTER | 29.1 | 55 |
| 35 | Richard BLAND | 29.1 | 75 |
| 35 | Johan SKÖLD | 29.1 | 30 |
| 35 | Mark ROE | 29.1 | 54 |

## Greens In Regulation (%)

| Pos | Name | % | Stats Rounds |
|---|---|---|---|
| 1 | Titch MOORE | 75.6 | 36 |
| 2 | Angel CABRERA | 75.2 | 36 |
| 3 | Peter O'MALLEY | 74.6 | 70 |
| 3 | Paul CASEY | 74.6 | 64 |
| 5 | Steven O'HARA | 74.1 | 83 |
| 6 | Peter HANSON | 73.8 | 77 |
| 7 | Retief GOOSEN | 73.7 | 30 |
| 8 | Oliver WHITELEY | 73.4 | 44 |
| 9 | Miguel Angel MARTIN | 72.2 | 56 |
| 10 | Jean-François LUCQUIN | 72.1 | 75 |
| 10 | Ian WOOSNAM | 72.1 | 43 |
| 12 | Jean VAN DE VELDE | 72.0 | 66 |
| 12 | Sergio GARCIA | 72.0 | 24 |
| 14 | Tom WHITEHOUSE | 70.7 | 70 |
| 14 | José Manuel LARA | 70.7 | 92 |
| 16 | David HOWELL | 70.5 | 42 |
| 17 | Johan EDFORS | 70.3 | 67 |
| 17 | Stephen GALLACHER | 70.3 | 72 |
| 19 | Maarten LAFEBER | 70.1 | 74 |
| 20 | Mattias ELIASSON | 70.0 | 65 |
| 20 | Miguel Angel JIMÉNEZ | 70.0 | 65 |
| 22 | Ian POULTER | 69.9 | 55 |
| 22 | Bradley DREDGE | 69.9 | 66 |
| 24 | Steve WEBSTER | 69.8 | 65 |
| 24 | Jyoti RANDHAWA | 69.8 | 66 |

## Sand Saves (%)

| Pos | Name | % | Stats Rounds |
|---|---|---|---|
| 1 | Emanuele CANONICA | 75.9 | 73 |
| 2 | David HOWELL | 71.1 | 42 |
| 3 | Mark ROE | 70.9 | 54 |
| 4 | Gordon BRAND JNR | 69.0 | 26 |
| 5 | Titch MOORE | 68.9 | 36 |
| 6 | Paul LAWRIE | 68.4 | 57 |
| 6 | David CARTER | 68.4 | 73 |
| 8 | Benoit TEILLERIA | 67.3 | 42 |
| 9 | Christian CÉVAËR | 65.8 | 79 |
| 10 | Andres ROMERO | 64.7 | 52 |
| 11 | Stuart LITTLE | 63.9 | 75 |
| 12 | Robert KARLSSON | 63.8 | 86 |
| 13 | Carl SUNESON | 63.5 | 64 |
| 14 | Martin ERLANDSSON | 63.3 | 75 |
| 14 | Matthew MILLAR | 63.3 | 78 |
| 16 | Lee WESTWOOD | 63.2 | 38 |
| 16 | Jean-François REMESY | 63.2 | 64 |
| 18 | Fredrik HENGE | 63.0 | 29 |
| 19 | Marc WARREN | 62.9 | 75 |
| 20 | Gary ORR | 62.5 | 73 |
| 21 | Thomas BJÖRN | 62.2 | 68 |
| 22 | Thongchai JAIDEE | 62.1 | 71 |
| 23 | Robert-Jan DERKSEN | 61.7 | 85 |
| 23 | Sergio GARCIA | 61.7 | 24 |
| 25 | Miguel Angel JIMÉNEZ | 61.5 | 65 |

## Putts Per Green In Regulation

| Pos | Name | Putts per GIR | Stats Rounds |
|---|---|---|---|
| 1 | Thaworn WIRATCHANT | 1.718 | 46 |
| 2 | David HOWELL | 1.724 | 42 |
| 3 | Darren CLARKE | 1.727 | 30 |
| 4 | Robert KARLSSON | 1.736 | 86 |
| 4 | David HIGGINS | 1.736 | 79 |
| 6 | Paul BROADHURST | 1.737 | 70 |
| 6 | Toni KARJALAINEN | 1.737 | 32 |
| 8 | Padraig HARRINGTON | 1.738 | 45 |
| 9 | Henrik STENSON | 1.740 | 55 |
| 9 | Matthew MILLAR | 1.740 | 78 |
| 11 | Phillip ARCHER | 1.741 | 99 |
| 12 | Ian POULTER | 1.744 | 55 |
| 13 | Christian CÉVAËR | 1.746 | 79 |
| 14 | Bradley DREDGE | 1.751 | 66 |
| 14 | Retief GOOSEN | 1.751 | 30 |
| 16 | Cesar MONASTERIO | 1.754 | 30 |
| 16 | Anthony WALL | 1.754 | 78 |
| 16 | Stephen DODD | 1.754 | 65 |
| 19 | Garry HOUSTON | 1.755 | 90 |
| 19 | Darren FICHARDT | 1.755 | 58 |
| 19 | David LYNN | 1.755 | 90 |
| 19 | Jarmo SANDELIN | 1.755 | 81 |
| 23 | Ricardo GONZALEZ | 1.758 | 64 |
| 23 | Thongchai JAIDEE | 1.758 | 71 |
| 25 | Richard GREEN | 1.759 | 54 |
| 25 | David DRYSDALE | 1.759 | 46 |
| 25 | Niclas FASTH | 1.759 | 76 |
| 25 | Charl SCHWARTZEL | 1.759 | 63 |
| 29 | Warren ABERY | 1.760 | 52 |
| 29 | Alastair FORSYTH | 1.760 | 70 |
| 29 | Nick DOUGHERTY | 1.760 | 74 |
| 32 | Colin MONTGOMERIE | 1.762 | 64 |
| 32 | David CARTER | 1.762 | 73 |
| 34 | Peter BAKER | 1.763 | 25 |
| 34 | Richard BLAND | 1.763 | 75 |
| 34 | Simon DYSON | 1.763 | 94 |
| 37 | Thomas BJÖRN | 1.764 | 68 |
| 38 | Anders HANSEN | 1.765 | 76 |
| 38 | Sergio GARCIA | 1.765 | 24 |
| 40 | Lee WESTWOOD | 1.767 | 38 |
| 40 | David GRIFFITHS | 1.767 | 70 |

## Scrambles

| Pos | Name | % | AVE SPR | AVE Missed GPR | Total Missed GIR | Total Scrambles | Stats Rounds |
|---|---|---|---|---|---|---|---|
| 1 | Sergio GARCIA | 66.1 | 3.3 | 5 | 121 | 80 | 24 |
| 2 | Simon DYSON | 65.3 | 4.1 | 6 | 588 | 384 | 94 |
| 3 | David HOWELL | 64.6 | 3.4 | 5 | 223 | 144 | 42 |
| 4 | Thongchai JAIDEE | 64.1 | 3.7 | 6 | 407 | 261 | 71 |
| 5 | Richard GREEN | 63.7 | 3.5 | 5 | 295 | 188 | 54 |
| 6 | Padraig HARRINGTON | 63.4 | 3.8 | 6 | 268 | 170 | 45 |
| 7 | Søren KJELDSEN | 63.3 | 3.9 | 6 | 581 | 368 | 95 |
| 8 | Peter BAKER | 62.6 | 4.3 | 7 | 171 | 107 | 25 |
| 9 | Christian CÉVAËR | 62.4 | 4.5 | 7 | 566 | 353 | 79 |
| 10 | Henrik STENSON | 62.3 | 3.5 | 6 | 310 | 193 | 55 |
| 11 | Thaworn WIRATCHANT | 62.1 | 4.2 | 7 | 311 | 193 | 46 |
| 11 | Simon WAKEFIELD | 62.1 | 4.1 | 7 | 614 | 381 | 92 |
| 13 | Paul BROADHURST | 61.5 | 4.1 | 7 | 468 | 288 | 70 |
| 14 | Andrew MARSHALL | 61.4 | 3.9 | 6 | 448 | 275 | 70 |
| 15 | Colin MONTGOMERIE | 61.3 | 3.4 | 6 | 357 | 219 | 64 |
| 16 | Søren HANSEN | 61.0 | 3.4 | 6 | 497 | 303 | 88 |
| 17 | Anders HANSEN | 60.9 | 3.4 | 6 | 425 | 259 | 76 |
| 18 | Scott STRANGE | 60.8 | 3.8 | 6 | 240 | 146 | 38 |
| 19 | Damien MCGRANE | 60.7 | 4.1 | 7 | 634 | 385 | 95 |
| 19 | Paul LAWRIE | 60.7 | 3.4 | 6 | 318 | 193 | 57 |
| 21 | David LYNN | 60.5 | 4.0 | 7 | 597 | 361 | 90 |
| 22 | Graeme MCDOWELL | 60.1 | 4.0 | 7 | 263 | 158 | 40 |
| 23 | Jeev Milkha SINGH | 60.0 | 4.3 | 7 | 185 | 111 | 26 |
| 24 | Darren CLARKE | 59.9 | 3.5 | 6 | 177 | 106 | 30 |
| 25 | Johan SKÖLD | 59.3 | 3.8 | 6 | 194 | 115 | 30 |

# The European Tour Order of Merit 2006

Flag (A-I)

| Argentina |
| Australia |
| Austria |
| Belgium |
| Brazil |
| Canada |
| Chile |
| China |
| Denmark |
| Dubai |
| England |
| Fiji |
| Finland |
| France |
| Germany |
| Hong Kong |
| India |
| Indonesia |
| Ireland |

| Pos | Name | Country | Played | € | £ |
|---|---|---|---|---|---|
| 1 | Padraig HARRINGTON | (IRL) | (20) | 2489336.88 | 1667618.07 |
| 2 | Paul CASEY | (ENG) | (25) | 2454084.45 | 1644002.31 |
| 3 | David HOWELL | (ENG) | (21) | 2321166.21 | 1554959.78 |
| 4 | Robert KARLSSON | (SWE) | (30) | 2044935.60 | 1369911.64 |
| 5 | Ernie ELS | (RSA) | (15) | 1716208.21 | 1149695.67 |
| 6 | Henrik STENSON | (SWE) | (23) | 1709359.28 | 1145107.54 |
| 7 | Luke DONALD | (ENG) | (13) | 1658059.92 | 1110741.86 |
| 8 | Ian POULTER | (ENG) | (22) | 1589074.00 | 1064527.88 |
| 9 | Colin MONTGOMERIE | (SCO) | (26) | 1534747.94 | 1028134.61 |
| 10 | Johan EDFORS | (SWE) | (25) | 1505583.03 | 1008596.90 |
| 11 | Sergio GARCIA | (ESP) | (12) | 1456752.32 | 975884.99 |
| 12 | Retief GOOSEN | (RSA) | (16) | 1367399.01 | 916026.80 |
| 13 | Anthony WALL | (ENG) | (27) | 1303230.68 | 873040.15 |
| 14 | Thomas BJÖRN | (DEN) | (26) | 1188504.44 | 796184.51 |
| 15 | Niclas FASTH | (SWE) | (25) | 1180140.02 | 790581.15 |
| 16 | Jeev Milkha SINGH | (IND) | (17) | 1173177.42 | 785916.88 |
| 17 | Angel CABRERA | (ARG) | (19) | 1166917.68 | 781723.45 |
| 18 | Charl SCHWARTZEL | (RSA) | (23) | 1148275.41 | 769234.91 |
| 19 | Paul BROADHURST | (ENG) | (28) | 1141431.46 | 764650.11 |
| 20 | John BICKERTON | (ENG) | (28) | 1140281.37 | 763879.66 |
| 21 | Simon DYSON | (ENG) | (31) | 1092156.40 | 731640.53 |
| 22 | Bradley DREDGE | (WAL) | (21) | 1075590.71 | 720543.10 |
| 23 | Miguel Angel JIMÉNEZ | (ESP) | (26) | 985389.24 | 660116.72 |
| 24 | Lee WESTWOOD | (ENG) | (18) | 960303.97 | 643311.98 |
| 25 | Simon KHAN | (ENG) | (27) | 960122.38 | 643190.34 |
| 26 | Nick O'HERN | (AUS) | (12) | 919331.70 | 615864.48 |
| 27 | Richard GREEN | (AUS) | (21) | 865668.76 | 579915.43 |
| 28 | José Maria OLAZÁBAL | (ESP) | (14) | 840005.54 | 562723.52 |
| 29 | Stephen DODD | (WAL) | (25) | 795145.71 | 532671.72 |
| 30 | José Manuel LARA | (ESP) | (29) | 784986.97 | 525866.33 |
| 31 | Michael CAMPBELL | (NZL) | (18) | 784914.53 | 525817.81 |
| 32 | Vijay SINGH | (FIJ) | (11) | 752403.14 | 504038.28 |
| 33 | Anders HANSEN | (DEN) | (23) | 731040.62 | 489727.43 |
| 34 | Søren HANSEN | (DEN) | (27) | 712648.90 | 477406.73 |
| 35 | Andres ROMERO | (ARG) | (21) | 694363.11 | 465157.00 |
| 36 | Søren KJELDSEN | (DEN) | (29) | 692035.60 | 463597.78 |
| 37 | Thongchai JAIDEE | (THA) | (24) | 669225.75 | 448317.36 |
| 38 | Francesco MOLINARI | (ITA) | (27) | 657143.30 | 440223.27 |
| 39 | Nick DOUGHERTY | (ENG) | (27) | 653080.44 | 437501.55 |
| 40 | Gonzalo FDEZ-CASTAÑO | (ESP) | (24) | 649354.14 | 435005.28 |
| 41 | Phillip ARCHER | (ENG) | (30) | 636490.79 | 426388.07 |
| 42 | Marc WARREN | (SCO) | (29) | 610885.24 | 409234.79 |
| 43 | Darren CLARKE | (NIR) | (14) | 583348.07 | 390787.52 |
| 44 | Jarmo SANDELIN | (SWE) | (28) | 568046.12 | 380536.67 |
| 45 | Raphaël JACQUELIN | (FRA) | (26) | 551745.49 | 369616.81 |
| 46 | David LYNN | (ENG) | (26) | 543466.90 | 364070.94 |
| 47 | Peter O'MALLEY | (AUS) | (23) | 530327.06 | 355268.50 |
| 48 | Gary ORR | (SCO) | (22) | 524371.58 | 351278.90 |
| 49 | Markus BRIER | (AUT) | (25) | 506359.25 | 339212.36 |
| 50 | Marcel SIEM | (GER) | (28) | 493956.39 | 330903.63 |
| 51 | Brett RUMFORD | (AUS) | (24) | 491907.01 | 329530.73 |
| 52 | Paul MCGINLEY | (IRL) | (22) | 478244.29 | 320378.02 |
| 53 | Graeme STORM | (ENG) | (29) | 474651.35 | 317971.09 |
| 54 | Kenneth FERRIE | (ENG) | (25) | 471775.23 | 316044.37 |
| 55 | Ricardo GONZALEZ | (ARG) | (20) | 451204.38 | 302263.86 |
| 56 | Damien MCGRANE | (IRL) | (32) | 447415.22 | 299725.49 |
| 57 | Peter HANSON | (SWE) | (24) | 440564.09 | 295135.88 |
| 58 | Graeme MCDOWELL | (NIR) | (17) | 437801.82 | 293285.42 |
| 59 | Emanuele CANONICA | (ITA) | (26) | 437672.22 | 293198.60 |
| 60 | Simon WAKEFIELD | (ENG) | (30) | 430785.87 | 288585.41 |
| 61 | Paul LAWRIE | (SCO) | (21) | 394034.12 | 263965.24 |
| 62 | Carl PETTERSSON | (SWE) | (10) | 392584.81 | 262994.34 |
| 63 | José-Filipe LIMA | (POR) | (26) | 381222.34 | 255382.57 |
| 64 | Stephen GALLACHER | (SCO) | (25) | 376571.46 | 252266.93 |
| 65 | Marcus FRASER | (AUS) | (25) | 375626.01 | 251633.56 |
| 66 | Ross FISHER | (ENG) | (30) | 370275.11 | 248048.98 |
| 67 | Peter LAWRIE | (IRL) | (29) | 360888.56 | 241760.88 |
| 68 | Jyoti RANDHAWA | (IND) | (23) | 351468.49 | 235450.33 |
| 69 | Darren FICHARDT | (RSA) | (19) | 343411.54 | 230052.95 |
| 70 | Maarten LAFEBER | (NED) | (26) | 340704.62 | 228239.57 |
| 71 | Oliver WILSON | (ENG) | (27) | 331706.14 | 222211.44 |
| 72 | Richard BLAND | (ENG) | (27) | 319391.43 | 213961.76 |
| 73 | Andrew MARSHALL | (ENG) | (24) | 318002.19 | 213031.11 |
| 74 | Garry HOUSTON | (WAL) | (34) | 315751.18 | 211523.15 |
| 75 | Mattias ELIASSON | (SWE) | (22) | 314018.13 | 210362.17 |
| 76 | Gary EMERSON | (ENG) | (32) | 312329.94 | 209231.25 |
| 77 | Jean VAN DE VELDE | (FRA) | (20) | 308781.95 | 206854.43 |
| 78 | Richard STERNE | (RSA) | (22) | 306472.86 | 205307.56 |
| 79 | Mark FOSTER | (ENG) | (26) | 302659.60 | 202753.04 |
| 80 | Thaworn WIRATCHANT | (THA) | (15) | 296692.97 | 198755.97 |
| 81 | Steve WEBSTER | (ENG) | (23) | 286273.41 | 191775.85 |
| 82 | Alastair FORSYTH | (SCO) | (26) | 285494.41 | 191254.00 |
| 83 | Andrew COLTART | (SCO) | (28) | 285309.18 | 191129.91 |
| 84 | Jean-François LUCQUIN | (FRA) | (27) | 285045.11 | 190953.01 |
| 85 | Stephen AMES | (CAN) | (7) | 282708.17 | 189387.48 |
| 86 | Robert-Jan DERKSEN | (NED) | (27) | 278976.75 | 186887.79 |
| 87 | Ignacio GARRIDO | (ESP) | (26) | 277058.14 | 185602.50 |
| 88 | Jean-François REMESY | (FRA) | (25) | 274817.91 | 184101.76 |
| 89 | Peter HEDBLOM | (SWE) | (24) | 270494.51 | 181205.50 |
| 90 | Christian CÉVAËR | (FRA) | (28) | 261544.95 | 175210.15 |
| 91 | Lee SLATTERY | (ENG) | (20) | 260548.96 | 174542.93 |
| 92 | Gregory HAVRET | (FRA) | (28) | 258835.59 | 173395.13 |
| 93 | Louis OOSTHUIZEN | (RSA) | (21) | 256466.12 | 171807.81 |
| 94 | Martin ERLANDSSON | (SWE) | (28) | 254660.63 | 170598.31 |
| 95 | Tom WHITEHOUSE | (ENG) | (25) | 250951.85 | 168113.78 |
| 96 | Andrew MCLARDY | (RSA) | (26) | 245718.53 | 164607.96 |
| 97 | Benn BARHAM | (ENG) | (30) | 245310.42 | 164334.56 |
| 98 | Miles TUNNICLIFF | (ENG) | (27) | 241538.25 | 161807.57 |
| 99 | David PARK | (WAL) | (25) | 235094.25 | 157490.70 |
| 100 | Peter GUSTAFSSON | (SWE) | (29) | 230760.98 | 154587.83 |

| Pos | Name | Country | Played | € | £ |
|-----|------|---------|--------|---|---|
| 101 | Christian L NILSSON | (SWE) | (21) | 226788.76 | 151926.82 |
| 102 | Gregory BOURDY | (FRA) | (20) | 224684.67 | 150517.28 |
| 103 | Steven JEPPESEN | (SWE) | (32) | 223795.73 | 149921.77 |
| 104 | Gary MURPHY | (IRL) | (29) | 220781.53 | 147902.55 |
| 105 | Barry LANE | (ENG) | (28) | 220351.46 | 147614.44 |
| 106 | James KINGSTON | (RSA) | (26) | 217646.26 | 145802.21 |
| 107 | David GRIFFITHS | (ENG) | (22) | 217166.09 | 145480.55 |
| 108 | Joakim BÄCKSTRÖM | (SWE) | (29) | 217070.07 | 145416.22 |
| 109 | Alejandro CANIZARES | (ESP) | (9) | 216793.55 | 145230.98 |
| 110 | Alessandro TADINI | (ITA) | (28) | 215570.94 | 144411.95 |
| 111 | Steven O'HARA | (SCO) | (30) | 210127.82 | 140765.58 |
| 112 | Mikko ILONEN | (FIN) | (9) | 209315.95 | 140221.70 |
| 113 | Richard FINCH | (ENG) | (26) | 208815.23 | 139886.27 |
| 114 | Robert ROCK | (ENG) | (21) | 208636.90 | 139766.80 |
| 115 | Matthew MILLAR | (AUS) | (26) | 207385.78 | 138928.67 |
| 116 | Shiv KAPUR | (IND) | (20) | 207041.70 | 138698.17 |
| 117 | David CARTER | (ENG) | (26) | 204365.79 | 136905.57 |
| 118 | Ian GARBUTT | (ENG) | (31) | 201580.68 | 135039.81 |
| 119 | David DRYSDALE | (SCO) | (20) | 200391.80 | 134243.37 |
| 120 | Jonathan LOMAS | (ENG) | (34) | 197033.09 | 131993.36 |
| 121 | Phillip PRICE | (WAL) | (21) | 193382.00 | 129547.48 |
| 122 | Sam LITTLE | (ENG) | (30) | 193345.42 | 129522.98 |
| 123 | Jamie SPENCE | (ENG) | (23) | 193215.17 | 129435.72 |
| 124 | David BRANSDON | (AUS) | (27) | 185267.97 | 124111.85 |
| 125 | Alexandre ROCHA | (BRA) | (25) | 179877.77 | 120500.93 |
| 126 | François DELAMONTAGNE | (FRA) | (27) | 173485.93 | 116219.01 |
| 127 | David HIGGINS | (IRL) | (28) | 169638.23 | 113641.42 |
| 128 | Nicolas COLSAERTS | (BEL) | (28) | 168948.44 | 113179.33 |
| 129 | Andrew BUTTERFIELD | (ENG) | (31) | 168157.73 | 112649.62 |
| 130 | Mark ROE | (ENG) | (23) | 165523.44 | 110884.90 |
| 131 | Leif WESTERBERG | (SWE) | (24) | 165150.16 | 110634.84 |
| 132 | Cesar MONASTERIO | (ARG) | (14) | 157749.52 | 105677.12 |
| 133 | Wade ORMSBY | (AUS) | (26) | 157173.41 | 105291.18 |
| 134 | Ian WOOSNAM | (WAL) | (18) | 154975.17 | 103818.57 |
| 135 | Carl SUNESON | (ESP) | (27) | 147013.10 | 98484.74 |
| 136 | Joakim HAEGGMAN | (SWE) | (28) | 144619.06 | 96880.97 |
| 137 | Jarrod LYLE | (AUS) | (8) | 140864.22 | 94365.58 |
| 138 | Mardan MAMAT | (SIN) | (16) | 138560.42 | 92822.25 |
| 139 | Peter FOWLER | (AUS) | (29) | 136158.44 | 91213.16 |
| 140 | Henrik NYSTROM | (SWE) | (19) | 131394.95 | 88022.07 |
| 141 | Terry PILKADARIS | (AUS) | (15) | 127942.14 | 85709.02 |
| 142 | Peter LONARD | (AUS) | (6) | 125241.86 | 83900.09 |
| 143 | Ariel CANETE | (ARG) | (20) | 122346.06 | 81960.18 |
| 144 | Daniel VANCSIK | (ARG) | (25) | 120812.27 | 80932.69 |
| 145 | Keith HORNE | (RSA) | (16) | 116734.55 | 78201.01 |
| 146 | Marc CAYEUX | (ZIM) | (29) | 113888.71 | 76294.56 |
| 147 | Johan SKÖLD | (SWE) | (15) | 109788.78 | 73548.01 |
| 148 | Fredrik WIDMARK | (SWE) | (27) | 103913.64 | 69612.22 |
| 149 | Scott STRANGE | (AUS) | (13) | 103499.83 | 69335.01 |
| 150 | Stuart LITTLE | (ENG) | (29) | 102950.99 | 68967.34 |
| 151 | David DIXON | (ENG) | (26) | 101142.09 | 67755.54 |
| 152 | Richard MCEVOY | (ENG) | (29) | 97978.60 | 65636.31 |
| 153 | Stephen BROWNE | (IRL) | (22) | 97820.49 | 65530.39 |
| 154 | Greg OWEN | (ENG) | (3) | 97590.37 | 65376.23 |
| 155 | Robert COLES | (ENG) | (30) | 97174.50 | 65097.64 |
| 156 | Mikael LUNDBERG | (SWE) | (23) | 96955.33 | 64950.81 |
| 157 | Lian-Wei ZHANG | (CHN) | (10) | 95984.55 | 64300.48 |
| 158 | Felipe AGUILAR | (CHI) | (19) | 95818.81 | 64189.45 |
| 159 | Titch MOORE | (RSA) | (16) | 94333.43 | 63194.39 |
| 160 | Peter BAKER | (ENG) | (13) | 93840.03 | 62863.86 |
| 161 | Jamie DONALDSON | (WAL) | (25) | 91400.04 | 61229.30 |
| 162 | Fredrik HENGE | (SWE) | (13) | 90476.06 | 60610.32 |
| 163 | Benoit TEILLERIA | (FRA) | (21) | 88471.94 | 59267.75 |
| 164 | Francis VALERA | (ESP) | (20) | 88366.08 | 59196.84 |
| 165 | Warren ABERY | (RSA) | (21) | 87244.21 | 58445.29 |
| 166 | Miguel CARBALLO | (ARG) | (21) | 86151.84 | 57713.50 |
| 167 | Gary EVANS | (ENG) | (22) | 83162.30 | 55710.80 |
| 168 | John DALY | (USA) | (6) | 80711.13 | 54068.75 |
| 169 | Santiago LUNA | (ESP) | (17) | 77652.41 | 52019.70 |
| 170 | Gary CLARK | (ENG) | (22) | 76133.28 | 51002.03 |
| 171 | Pedro LINHART | (ESP) | (7) | 74532.58 | 49929.71 |
| 172 | Mahal PEARCE | (NZL) | (9) | 74037.06 | 49597.76 |
| 173 | Rafael GOMEZ | (ARG) | (19) | 71875.55 | 48149.76 |
| 174 | Marco RUIZ | (PAR) | (22) | 66713.52 | 44691.69 |
| 175 | Carlos RODILES | (ESP) | (17) | 62871.49 | 42117.89 |
| 176 | Hennie OTTO | (RSA) | (11) | 61003.67 | 40866.64 |
| 177 | Peter SENIOR | (AUS) | (8) | 60953.08 | 40832.74 |
| 178 | Thomas AIKEN | (RSA) | (9) | 60813.93 | 40739.52 |
| 179 | Sven STRÜVER | (GER) | (11) | 60553.82 | 40565.27 |
| 180 | Scott DRUMMOND | (SCO) | (27) | 58422.25 | 39137.33 |
| 181 | Adrien MÖRK | (FRA) | (5) | 57767.62 | 38698.79 |
| 182 | Christopher HANELL | (SWE) | (10) | 54227.27 | 36327.09 |
| 183 | Raymond RUSSELL | (SCO) | (15) | 53319.84 | 35719.20 |
| 184 | Thomas LEVET | (FRA) | (7) | 53131.54 | 35593.06 |
| 185 | Philip GOLDING | (ENG) | (29) | 51300.65 | 34366.53 |
| 186 | Oliver WHITELEY | (ENG) | (21) | 50523.62 | 33846.01 |
| 187 | Michael HOEY | (NIR) | (27) | 50414.23 | 33772.72 |
| 188 | Stephen SCAHILL | (NZL) | (20) | 50257.59 | 33667.79 |
| 189 | Martin MARITZ | (RSA) | (4) | 48013.30 | 32164.32 |
| 190 | Juan PARRON | (ESP) | (2) | 46915.00 | 31428.57 |
| 191 | Jarrod MOSELEY | (AUS) | (4) | 43891.40 | 29403.05 |
| 192 | Jesper PARNEVIK | (SWE) | (4) | 42847.76 | 28703.90 |
| 193 | Klas ERIKSSON | (SWE) | (7) | 42406.54 | 28408.33 |
| 194 | Shaun P WEBSTER | (ENG) | (20) | 41938.65 | 28094.89 |
| 195 | Magnus PERSSON | (SWE) | (8) | 41129.19 | 27552.63 |
| 196 | Brad KENNEDY | (AUS) | (5) | 39490.20 | 26454.66 |
| 197 | Iain PYMAN | (ENG) | (20) | 39361.69 | 26368.57 |
| 198 | Andrew OLDCORN | (SCO) | (24) | 37935.45 | 25413.13 |
| 199 | Marcus BOTH | (AUS) | (14) | 37187.34 | 24911.97 |
| 200 | Miguel Angel MARTIN | (ESP) | (23) | 37087.84 | 24845.31 |

# Flag (I-Z)

Italy

Korea

Malaysia

The Netherlands

New Zealand

N. Ireland

Paraguay

Portugal

Russia

Scotland

Singapore

South Africa

Spain

Sweden

Switzerland

Thailand

USA

Wales

Zimbabwe

# The European Tour International Schedule 2006

## First Time Winners

**CHRIS DiMARCO**

**KEVIN STADLER**

**CHARLIE WI**

**GEOFF OGILVY**

**SIMON DYSON**

**MARDAN MAMAT**

**JOHAN EDFORS**

| Date | | Tournament | Venue |
|------|------|------------|-------|
| Nov | 10 - 13 | HSBC Champions tournament | Sheshan International GC, Shanghai, China |
| | 24-27 | Volvo China Open | Shenzhen GC, China |
| Dec | 1 - 4 | UBS Hong Kong Open | Hong Kong GC, Fanling, Hong Kong |
| | 8 - 11 | dunhill championship | Leopard Creek, Mpumalanga, South Africa |
| | 15-18 | South African Airways Open | Fancourt GC, George, South Africa |
| Jan | 7-8 | The Royal Trophy* | Amata Spring CC, Bangkok, Thailand |
| | 19-22 | Abu Dhabi Golf Championship | Abu Dhabi Golf Club, Abu Dhabi |
| | 26-29 | The Commercialbank Qatar Masters | Doha GC, Qatar |
| Feb | 2-5 | Dubai Desert Classic | Emirates GC, Dubai |
| | 9-12 | Johnnie Walker Classic | The Vines Resort & CC, Perth, Australia |
| | 16-19 | Maybank Malaysian Open | Kuala Lumpur G&CC, Malaysia |
| | **22-26** | **WGC - Accenture Match Play** | **La Costa Resort & Spa, Carlsbad, California, USA** |
| Mar | 2-5 | Enjoy Jakarta HSBC Indonesia Open | Emeralda G&CC, Indonesia |
| | 9-12 | OSIM Singapore Masters | Laguna National G & CC, Singapore |
| | 16-19 | TCL Classic | Yalong Bay GC, Sanya, Hainan Island, China |
| | 23-26 | Madeira Island Open Caixa Geral de Depositos | Santo da Serra, Madeira, Portugal |
| | 30-2 | Algarve Open de Portugal Caixa Geral de Depositos | Le Meridien Penina Golf & Resort, Portugal |
| **Apr** | **6-9** | **MASTERS TOURNAMENT** | **Augusta National, Georgia, USA** |
| | 13-16 | Volvo China Open | Honghua International GC, Beijing, China |
| | 20-23 | BMW Asian Open | Tomson Shanghai Pudong GC, Shanghai, China |
| | 27-30 | Andalucia Open de España Valle Romano | San Roque Club, Cadiz, Spain |
| May | 4-7 | Telecom Italia Open | Castello di Tolcinasco G&CC, Milan, Italy |
| | 11-14 | The Quinn Direct British Masters | The De Vere Belfry, Sutton Coldfield, Warwickshire, England |
| | 18-21 | Nissan Irish Open | Carton House GC, Maynooth, Co.Kildare, Ireland |
| | **25-28** | **BMW CHAMPIONSHIP - THE PLAYERS' FLAGSHIP** | **Wentworth Club, Surrey, England** |
| Jun | 1-4 | The Celtic Manor Wales Open | The Celtic Manor Resort, Newport, South Wales |
| | 8-11 | BA-CA Golf Open, presented by Telekom Austria | Fontana GC, Vienna, Austria |
| | **15-18** | **US OPEN CHAMPIONSHIP** | **Winged Foot GC, Mamaroneck, New York, USA** |
| | 15-18 | Aa St Omer Open | Aa Saint Omer GC, Lumbres, France |
| | 22-25 | Johnnie Walker Championship at Gleneagles | The Gleneagles Hotel, Perthshire, Scotland |
| | 29-2 | Open de France ALSTOM | Le Golf National, Paris, France |
| Jul | 6-9 | Smurfit Kappa European Open | The K Club, Straffan, Co. Kildare, Ireland |
| | 13-16 | The Barclays Scottish Open | Loch Lomond, Glasgow, Scotland |
| | **20-23** | **135th OPEN CHAMPIONSHIP** | **Royal Liverpool GC, Hoylake, Cheshire, England** |
| | 27-30 | The Deutsche Bank Players' Championship of Europe | Gut Kaden, Hamburg, Germany |
| Aug | 3-6 | EnterCard Scandinavian Masters | Barsebäck G&CC, Malmö, Sweden |
| | 10-13 | The KLM Open | Kennemer G&CC, Zandvoort, The Netherlands |
| | **17-20** | **US PGA CHAMPIONSHIP** | **Medinah CC, Medinah, Illinois, USA** |
| | 17-20 | The Imperial Collection Russian Open | Le Meridien Moscow CC, Moscow, Russia |
| | **24-27** | **WGC - Bridgestone Invitational** | **Firestone CC, Akron, Ohio, USA** |
| | 31-3 | BMW International Open | Golfclub München-Nord, Eichenried, Munich, Germany |
| Sep | 7-10 | Omega European Masters | Crans-sur-Sierre, Crans Montana, Switzerland |
| | 14-17 | XXXII Banco Madrid Valle Romano Open de Madrid Golf Masters | La Moraleja II, Madrid, Spain |
| | 14-17 | HSBC World Match Play Championship | Wentworth Club, Surrey, England |
| | **22-24** | **THE 2006 RYDER CUP** | **The K Club, Straffan, Co.Kildare, Ireland** |
| | **28-1** | **WGC - American Express Championship** | **The Grove, Chandlers Cross, Hertfordshire, England** |
| Oct | 5-8 | Alfred Dunhill Links Championship | Old Course, St Andrews, Carnoustie and Kingsbarns, Scotland |
| | 19-22 | Mallorca Classic | Pula GC, Majorca, Spain |
| | **26-29** | **Volvo Masters** | **Club de Golf Valderrama, Sotogrande, Spain** |

^ Reduced to 54 holes due to inclement weather

\* Denotes Approved Special Event        \*\* Denotes play-off victory

| Winner | Score | First Prize<br>€ | Total Prize Fund<br>€ |
|---|---|---|---|
| David Howell, ENG | 65-67-68-68=268 (-20) | 704,516 | 4,227,270 |
| Paul Casey, ENG** | 71-69-70-65=275 (-13) | 184,533 | 1,100,890 |
| Colin Montgomerie, SCO | 69-66-66-70=271 (-9) | 170,590 | 1,021,680 |
| Ernie Els, RSA | 71-67-68-68=274 (-14) | 158,579 | 1,002,790 |
| Retief Goosen, RSA | 73-70-69-70=282 (-10) | 158,579 | 1,007,000 |
| Europe beat Asia | 9-7 | Winners each received 105,556 | 1,266,670 |
| Chris DiMarco, USA | 71-67-63-67=268 (-20) | 275,411 | 1,652,450 |
| Henrik Stenson, SWE | 66-68-71-68=273 (-15) | 275,546 | 1,636,190 |
| Tiger Woods, USA** | 67-66-67-69=269 (-19) | 329,760 | 1,996,320 |
| Kevin Stadler, USA | 64-69-66-69=268 (-20) | 305,468 | 1,837,240 |
| Charlie Wi, KOR | 66-68-63=197 (-19) ^ | 174,773 | 1,051,800 |
| **Geoff Ogilvy, AUS** | **def Davis Love III 3&2** | **1,091,886** | **6,299,350** |
| Simon Dyson, ENG | 66-68-67-67=268 (-20) | 140,261 | 850,000 |
| Mardan Mamat, SIN | 65-70-70-71=276 (-12) | 138,560 | 841,290 |
| Johan Edfors, SWE | 66-66-63-68=263 (-25) | 140,215 | 839,790 |
| Jean Van de Velde, FRA | 69-65-71-68=273 (-15) | 116,660 | 695,980 |
| Paul Broadhurst, ENG | 64-69-71-67=271 (-17) | 208,330 | 1,261,210 |
| **Phil Mickelson, USA** | **70-72-70-69=281 (-7)** | **1,037,976** | **5,624,350** |
| Jeev Milkha Singh, IND | 72-69-67-70=278 (-10) | 247,748 | 1,483,780 |
| Gonzalo Fdez-Castaño, ESP** | 71-71-69-70=281 (-7) | 247,810 | 1,493,550 |
| Niclas Fasth, SWE** | 67-68-66-69=270 (-18) | 275,000 | 1,657,420 |
| Francesco Molinari, ITA | 68-65-67-65=265 (-23) | 233,330 | 1,385,960 |
| Johan Edfors, SWE | 68-69-70-70=277 (-11) | 437,949 | 2,622,910 |
| Thomas Björn, DEN | 78-66-67-72=283 (-5) | 366,660 | 2,206,600 |
| **David Howell, ENG** | **68-65-69-69=271 (-17)** | **708,330** | **4,216,750** |
| Robert Karlsson, SWE | 61-63-65-71=260 (-16) | 364,352 | 2,177,970 |
| Markus Brier, AUT | 65-67-66-68=266 (-18) | 216,660 | 1,305,840 |
| **Geoff Ogilvy, AUS** | **71-70-72-72=285 (+5)** | **969,455** | **5,381,470** |
| Cesar Monasterio, ARG | 68-68-71-67=274 (-10) | 66,660 | 400,600 |
| Paul Casey, ENG | 67-71-66-72=276 (-16) | 341,667 | 2,059,250 |
| John Bickerton, ENG | 63-70-71-69=273 (-11) | 666,660 | 4,006,000 |
| Stephen Dodd, WAL | 67-69-73-70=279 (-9) | 578,792 | 3,498,770 |
| Johan Edfors, SWE | 65-69-74-63=271 (-13) | 577,540 | 3,452,330 |
| **Tiger Woods, USA** | **67-65-71-67=270 (-18)** | **1,045,965** | **5,794,940** |
| Robert Karlsson, SWE | 64-66-66-67=263 (-25) | 600,000 | 3,605,400 |
| Marc Warren, SCO ** | 67-69-73-69=278 (-10) | 266,660 | 1,623,870 |
| Simon Dyson ENG ** | 67-71-66-66=270 (-14) | 266,660 | 1,602,400 |
| **Tiger Woods, USA** | **69-68-65-68=270 (-18)** | **959,469** | **5,100,905** |
| Alejandro Cañizares, ESP | 66-67-67-66=266 (-22) | 130,641 | 787,400 |
| **Tiger Woods, USA**** | **67-64-71-68=270 (-10)** | **1,014,833** | **5,831,190** |
| Henrik Stenson, SWE** | 71-68-66-68=273 (-15) | 333,330 | 2,011,980 |
| Bradley Dredge, WAL | 68-67-65-67=267 (-17) | 333,330 | 1,984,350 |
| Ian Poulter, ENG | 67-66-64-69=266 (-22) | 166,660 | 1,005,950 |
| Paul Casey, ENG | def Shaun Micheel 10 & 8 | 1,470,230 | 3,587,360 |
| **Europe** | **18 ½ - 9 ½** | | |
| **Tiger Woods, USA** | **63-64-67-67=261 (-23)** | **1,015,940** | **5,764,700** |
| Padraig Harrington, IRE | 66-69-68-68=271 (-16) | 630,560 | 3,783,400 |
| Niclas Fasth, SWE | 66-71-70-68=275 (-5) | 291,660 | 1,763,095 |
| **Jeev Milkha Singh, IND** | **71-71-68-72=282 (-2)** | **666,660** | **3,912,700** |

## First Time Winners

*JEEV MILKHA SINGH*

*FRANCESCO MOLINARI*

*MARKUS BRIER*

*CESAR MONASTERIO*

*MARC WARREN*

*ALEJANDRO CAÑIZARES*

**The European Tour supports The Golf Foundation**

GOLF FOUNDATION
*Developing Junior Golf*

# The European Tour

## DIRECTORS

N. C. Coles, MBE, *Chairman*
A. Gallardo, *Vice Chairman*
R. Chapman
P. Eales
T. A. Horton, MBE
D. Jones
R. Lee
J. E. O'Leary
D. J. Russell
O. Sellberg
J. Spence
J. Van de Velde

Sir M. F. Bonallack, OBE
(*Non Executive Tour Group Director*)
P. A. T. Davidson
(*Non Executive Tour Group Director, Finance*)
B. Nordberg
(*Non Executive Tour Group Director*)
K. S. Owen
(*Non Executive Tour Group Director, Broadcasting*)

## TOURNAMENT COMMITTEE

J. Spence, *Chairman* (Eng)
T. Björn (Den)
R. Chapman (Eng)
D. Clarke (N. Ire)
J. Haeggman (Swe)
R. Jacquelin (Fra)
M. A. Jiménez (Esp)
B. Lane (Eng)
B. Langer (Ger)
P. McGinley (Ire)
C. Montgomerie, OBE (Sco)
M. Roe (Eng)
H. Stenson (Swe)

EXECUTIVE DIRECTOR .................................................. G. C. O'Grady
DIRECTOR OF INTERNATIONAL POLICY .................................. K. Waters
RYDER CUP DIRECTOR AND HEAD OF PLAYER RELATIONS .............. R. G. Hills
FINANCIAL DIRECTOR ........................................................ J. Orr
GROUP MARKETING DIRECTOR ........................................ S. F. Kelly
DIRECTOR OF CORPORATE AFFAIRS AND PUBLIC RELATIONS ...... M. S. Platts
DIRECTOR OF TOUR OPERATIONS .................................... D. W. Garland

MANAGING DIRECTOR, EUROPEAN SENIORS TOUR ............... K. A. Stubbs
DIRECTOR OF CHALLENGE TOUR .............................. A. de Soultrait
CHIEF REFEREE ........................................................ J. N. Paramor
ASSISTANT DIRECTOR OF TOUR OPERATIONS .................. D. A. Probyn
SENIOR REFEREE ...................................................... A. N. McFee
SENIOR TOURNAMENT DIRECTOR AND QUALIFYING SCHOOL DIRECTOR ... M. R. Stewart
CHAMPIONSHIP DIRECTOR, WORLD GOLF CHAMPIONSHIPS ........... P. Adams
DIRECTOR OF TOURNAMENT DEVELOPMENT ...................... J. Birkmyre
DIRECTOR OF TOURNAMENT SERVICES .............................. E. Kitson
DIRECTOR OF IT & NEW MEDIA .............................. M. Lichtenhein
DIRECTOR, SPECIAL PROJECTS ............................... M. MacDiarmid
SALES DIRECTOR ........................................................ T. Shaw
DIRECTOR OF COMMUNICATIONS ................................. G. Simpson

## Photographers

**Photography by** gettyimages

**Main Contributors:**
Andrew Redington, David Cannon, Ross Kinnaird, Warren Little, Stuart Franklin, Richard Heathcote, Ian Walton, Scott Halleran, Harry How

**Additional Contributors:**
Phil Inglis
Touchline Photo
Andy Forman
Qamber Mohamed
Art Browne